A HISTORY OF BAPTISTS IN ARKANSAS
1818-1978

E. Glenn Hinson

Little Rock, Arkansas
Arkansas Baptist State Convention
1979

The History Committee of the Executive Board of the Arkansas Baptist State Convention was appointed in 1977. The express purpose of the Executive Board was for the Committee to initiate and oversee the writing of a comprehensive history of Baptists in Arkansas. The amount of money allocated for the project was suggested to be in the area of $25,000. The five-member Committee began by reading various state convention histories and formulated what we believed to be the best model for Arkansas. Thirty-two areas were designated and assigned to people both in our state and outside our state to write essays on their assigned subject.

Next we sought to employ a writer to do research and assimilate the various areas being researched. E. Glenn Hinson, a noted historian and author, was selected by the Committee to write and interpret events in Arkansas Baptist history.

The Committee believed that facts apart from interpretation would be meaningless. We believe that the history of Arkansas Baptists has not taken place in a vacuum but rather has been hammered out in the arena of real life.

There can be no doubt in the mind of even the casual reader of this book that Arkansas Baptists have been a people dedicated to the propagation of the Gospel at any cost.

Jerry Wilcox, Chairman
History Committee

EDWARD GLENN HINSON

David T. Porter Professor of Church History
The Southern Baptist Theological Seminary
Louisville, Kentucky

EXPERIENCE

Associate Pastor, First Baptist Church, Affton, Missouri, 1955-56.
Pastor, First Baptist Church, Eminence, Indiana, 1957-59.
Instructor in New Testament, Southern Baptist Theological Seminary, 1959-60.
Assistant Professor of Church History, Southern Baptist Seminary, 1962-66.
Associate Professor of Church History, Southern Baptist Seminary, 1966-73.
Professor of Church History, Southern Baptist Seminary, 1973-   .

WRITINGS

The Church: Design for Survival, Broadman Press, 1967.
Glossolalia, with Stagg and Oates, Abingdon Press, 1967.
Seekers After Mature Faith, Word Books, 1968.
I and II Timothy, Titus, "Broadman Bible Commentary," Vol. XI, Broadman Press, 1971.
A Serious Call to a Contemplative Lifestyle, Westminster Press, 1974.
Soul Liberty, Convention Press, 1975.
Jesus Christ, Vol. I in *The Church of Our Fathers,* Consortium, 1977.
The Integrity of the Church, Broadman, 1978.
Doubleday Devotional Classics, Protestant Series, 3 Vols., Doubleday, 1978.

TABLE OF CONTENTS

LIST OF TABLES

LIST OF MAPS

LIST OF CHARTS

LIST OF DIAGRAMS

Preface

There have been several histories of the Arkansas Baptist State Convention, but insofar as I can discover, only one of these, J.S. Rogers', was published. The first history, from which Rogers copied extensively, was J.B. Searcy's. This one, however, may never have gotten farther than note form. In 1912 the State Convention was informed that it was "almost ready" and that publication would cost about $1,500.[1] A year later, however, the Convention named a special committee "to suggest means **for putting in permanent form the data gathered by** Dr. J.B. Searcy for a history of Arkansas Baptists."[2] At the next annual Convention this committee concluded that Searcy himself was "better fitted" than anyone to see to the history's publication, hinting thereby that the work was incomplete. They asked the Convention to instruct the Executive Board to publish it "as soon as possible" in view of Searcy's advanced age. Although Searcy lived until September 14, 1920, he seems never to have arranged his notes in a publishable form.[3]

In 1935 the Convention tried a second time to obtain a history. It authorized the Executive Board to arrange for E.J.A. McKinney to finish a **History of Arkansas Baptists** he had begun.[4] The Board engaged him to do so in February, 1936, but ill health intervened. He died July 5, 1936.

A third try proved successful. In 1944 the Executive Board arranged for J.S. Rogers to compose a history which, they hoped, would appear in 1945.[5] The size of the undertaking, however, delayed publication until 1948. In the form originally presented to the publisher, the book would have been 800 to 900 pages.[6]

The present work will be the first "history" of Baptists in Arkansas in the proper sense of the term. Although J.S. Rogers collected much useful data for the composition of a history, he did not put them together in a manner which would help Arkansas Baptists understand how they developed. If Rogers dealt here and there with development, a historian's major concern, the structure and the content of his **History of Arkansas Baptists** place it somewhere between an encyclopedia and a chronicle. Major divisions are devoted to churches, biographies, associations, the State Convention, and institutions, not to chronology. Except for the sections dealing with the Convention, Dr. Rogers made little effort to explain or to interpret why events turned out as they did.

Two other histories devoted to segments of Arkansas Baptist

history, both doctoral theses, have followed on the trail blazed by Rogers. Frank F. Norfleet, covering the period from the beginning to 1900, organized his study on the same pattern as Rogers. Garland H. Allen, limiting his study to "A History of the Arkansas Baptist State Convention, 1900-1950," wrote chiefly institutional history. Although he assembled much useful information about the growth of institutions, he left untold the larger story of Arkansas Baptist development within their society.

Historians emphasize various factors in their effort to explain why things turn out as they do. In popular understanding it is common to single out "the great man" as the key to history. In line with that, Dr. Rogers focused on "churches, church life and pastors" as his "major theme."[7] Although I have tried to give a proper amount of credit to persons, conscious that some matter a great deal, I have sought to explain development with multiple factors in view: sociological, psychological, economic, geographical, and spiritual, as well as personal. If forced to describe my approach in one phrase, I would call it "socio-institutional history." The title, **A History of Baptists in Arkansas,** contains a hint of this approach. It is not intended to suggest that I have dealt with **all** Baptist groups in the state. Where possible, I have brought the history of others, especially black Baptists, into the narrative, but precise data on other groups are very limited.

It will be readily apparent to the reader that I am convinced that churches, associations, conventions, schools, orphans' homes, hospitals, and other institutions or programs develop within and are strongly influenced by their social and cultural context. In Arkansas, for instance, as in the rest of the South, the business model which gradually dominated the society also came to prevail in the churches. In and of itself there is no problem with this; it has something to do with the incarnation of the Word of God in particular times and circumstances. The churches' effectiveness depends upon the embodiment of the Word in the social and cultural forms of the day. But, as the history of Arkansas Baptists will make crystal clear, there are dangers inherent in it, too. Contemporary social and cultural forms may dominate to such an extent that they obscure or annul the effectiveness of the Word of God itself. The churches face a constant challenge to keep that from happening, and they are tempted to avoid the challenge by not adapting. To do so, however, as the Landmark faction in Arkansas did, is to limit the prospects for genuine incarnation.

The broad pattern of this work is chronological and does not require comment. Within each chapter, however, I have discussed not only numerical and institutional growth but also the interior and exterior character of Arkansas Baptists church life. By "interior" I mean such things as edifices, worship, discipline, and personal piety; by "external" I mean political, economic, and social involvement in Arkansas society. All of these are integral parts of Arkansas Baptist history. I have introduced personalities usually in an illustrative rather than definitive way. Although some may be disappointed that I failed to mention certain persons, I believe I have told the **Baptist** story as a whole. Biographies belong to encyclopedias rather than histories. Many biographical sketches can be found in the **Encyclopedia of Southern Baptists.**

Initially the Historical Committee of the State Convention employed me as "editor" of a history of Arkansas Baptists. They engaged numerous other persons to do research articles on selected topics. As the work proceeded, however, it became clear to me that I would have to do much more than assemble materials supplied by others. The approach which I have described above required extensive additional research. Besides doing research myself, I employed four graduate students in church history at Southern Seminary—Fred Grissom, Randall Payne, Gerald Rudolph, and Robin Smith—to supplement my research. Among various research articles done by others I incorporated only one directly. Composed by O.W. Taylor, it will be found in the section on "Baptists and Slavery" in Chapter II. All research articles are listed in Appendix K, "Contributors of Research Articles."

I express heartfelt thanks to the History Committee of the Arkansas Baptist State Convention: Dr. Charles H. Ashcraft, Mrs. Ladd S. Davies, Dr. Burton A. Miley, Dr. Bernes Selph, Mrs. Billie Ruth Wright, and the Reverend Jerry Wilcox, Chairman. They did everything possible to assist me in seeing this project through to its completion. It was the kind of project which I found entrancing, and I regret that research of a lifetime had to be compressed into a two-year span with all of the flaws such haste invites. My hope is that, whatever the faults of this work, it will supply Arkansas Baptists with an accurate enough picture of their historical development that they will understand a mite why they are what they are now.

Louisville, Kentucky
August 4, 1979

[1] Proceedings, ABSC, 1912, pp. 29f.
[2] Proceedings, ABSC, 1913, p. 29; my italics.
[3] Proceedings, ABSC, 1914, p. 59.
[4] Proceedings, ABSC, 1935, p. 8.
[5] Annual, ABSC, 1944, pp. 41f.
[6] Annual, ABSC, 1947, p. 40.
[7] History of Arkansas Baptists (Little Rock: Arkansas Baptist State Convention, 1948), p. 16.

Chapter I

BAPTISTS IN ARKANSAS TERRITORY

1818-1835

Baptists got off to a modest start in the period before Arkansas entered the Union as the twenty-fifth state in 1836. Pushing westward across the Mississippi River with other immigrants in the early 1800s, they left few traces of their presence until 1818, when Benjamin Clark and Jesse James organized the first Baptist church in what was still Missouri Territory on Fourche-a-Thomas River in northeast Arkansas. By 1836 Baptists broadcast their seed across much of Arkansas Territory, planting about forty churches and beginning three or four associaitons.

Early Pioneers

Arkansas itself, of course, had not become a possession of the United States until the famous Louisiana Purchase of 1803. Once this occurred, however, four events hastened the settlement of the area. (1) A treaty concluded with the Osage Indians, November 10, 1808, opened new lands to whites. (2) Congress bestowed equal amounts of land on hapless settlers who lost their possessions in the New Madrid Earthquake in southeast Missouri in 1811. (3) In 1814 Congress made generous grants of land, two million acres in Arkansas Territory, to soldiers who had served in the War of 1812. (4) Settlement of the Spanish land grants generated a massive rush to gain title to land. Between 1810 and 1819, when President James Monroe signed an act declaring "Arkansas" a territory, the population of the territory, excluding Indians, increased from 1,062 to 14,255. By 1835 it had mushroomed to 51,809; by 1840 to 97,574.

Baptists, many freshly converted and filled with evangelistic zeal in the "Second Great Awakening" of the early 1800s, accompanied this stream of immigrants. They came from Kentucky, where the religious revival burned brightest, Tennessee, Georgia, Mississippi, Missouri, and other states. We know few names. The first Baptist preacher to pass through what became Arkansas Territory was probably John Clark, who, according to J.B. Searcy and John Mason Peck, traveled on foot about 1810 from the extreme frontiers of Missouri to Florida. Major Jacob Wolf, appointed Indian agent to the Arkansas Cherokee Nation by President Thomas

1

Jefferson about 1808, was a Baptist preacher in later years, but we do not know his religious affiliation at the time of his appointment or the date of his ordination.[2]

We have more precise information about George Gill, a Baptist preacher who moved into northeast Arkansas in 1814 and settled on White River at a place called Mount Olive, where he preached his first sermon on Christmas day. Gill migrated from Virginia to South Carolina and then to Missouri before coming to Arkansas, where he spent the remainder of his life. After residing at Mount Olive six years he was forced across the river by Indian raiding parties. He not only preached and organized churches in this area, but he also wrote for David Benedict's **Baptist Almanac,** thus recording much about his own work as well as that of other early Baptists within the state.

About 1815 a group of Kentuckians settled on the Fourche-a-Thomas River. One of the families in this group, the Lindseys, became prominent among Baptists in the state. Caleb Lindsey, the father, was a surveyor and farmer who died in Little Rock in 1826. He helped establish the settlement later named Lindsville.[3]

In 1816 he conducted a school in a cave near his home on Fourche-a-Thomas, the first tuition-free school in the area. John Young Lindsey, a son, moved with his family and others from Kentucky to the center of the state, settling a few miles northwest of the present city of Benton in the community which bears the name Kentucky. About 1836 John Young, a deacon when he entered the territory, began preaching and served as pastor of the Kentucky church for twenty-eight years. He played a large part in Baptist affairs during this time.

Early Churches

Baptists planted churches first in the north, northeastern part of the state, then southwards through the central and southern part, and gradually fanned out over the remaining parts. The rationale for this pattern is easy to see. The Southwestern Trail running from St. Louis southwest to Mexico entered the northeastern corner of Arkansas and ran generally toward the southwestern corner. By 1817 settlers had advanced down this trail to Davidsonville in Lawrence country. By 1820 they had extended through Batesville to Cadron on the Arkansas River. By 1821 they had moved on through Clark and Hempstead counties to the Red River. A "trace" extending from Natchitoches, Louisiana to Hot Springs and connecting with a road to Little Rock was little more than an obscure path. Branches ran from the Trail East and West, but they were little more than foot paths. The Trail skirted the lowlands lying to the East and the hills and mountains lying to the West. The eastern part of the state, laced by rivers and marshes, was largely shunned because of floods and unhealthy climate, a fact which helps to explain why Arkansas Post failed to develop and why Little Rock was selected as the site of the capitol in 1820. Although the Ozarks and Ouachitas made travel more difficult, many sought them because of their healthier climate.

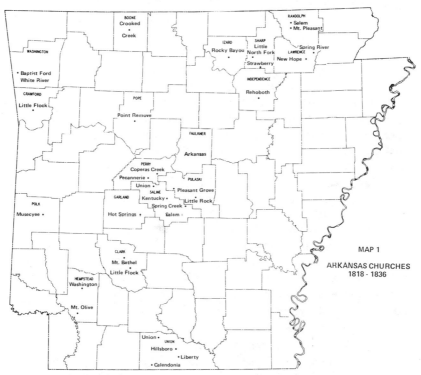

MAP 1

ARKANSAS CHURCHES
1818 - 1836

The earliest churches were founded through varied means—associations sponsoring mission work, individual missionaries and preachers, and lay initiative. The fact that Baptists did not require a trained and officially recognized ministry assisted their spread, for wherever a few persons resided in a community they could unite to form a church. Churches frequently began with as few as five or six members. Since most settlers coming to Arkansas had been touched by the frontier revival of the early 1800s, they brought with them a powerful missionary spirit, one that made them eager for worship and to win others. Consequently, as Arkansas' population multiplied, Baptist churches multiplied.

The first Baptist church in what became Arkansas Territory was founded through the efforts of missionaries dispatched by the Bethel

Association in Missouri. In 1817 this one-year-old Association appointed James Phillip Edwards to preach and to organize churches in the lower part of the Missouri Territory which, when President James Monroe gave official recognition, in 1819, became Arkansas Territory. During his first year Edwards traveled more than a thousand miles visiting the widely scattered pioneer settlements. In 1818 he, along with Benjamin Clark and Jesse James, organized Salem church at Fourche-a-Thomas which, according to John Mason Peck, was "the first church ever gathered in that region."[4] Salem had two ministers, Clark and James, and twelve members. It was located on the east side of Fourche-a-Thomas in Lawrence County, which then covered more than half the present state of Arkansas as well as a strip of southern Missouri. It later changed its name from Salem to Columbia as the little town of Columbia grew up around it. Both church and town gradually declined and disappeared, however, after the town of Pocahontas was founded in 1835.

In 1822 the Bethel Association also sponsored the organization of the Union and the Little Flock churches in Lawrence county by the Elders Clark, Edwards, and William Street. Jesse James evidently had died in the interim. These churches joined Bethel Association the next year.

Other churches came into being through the tireless efforts of missionaries such as David Orr. Born in Bourbon County, Kentucky in 1798, Orr was converted and baptized by Jeremiah Vardaman, a celebrated Kentucky revival preacher. In 1823 he migrated from Cincinnati, Ohio, to Missouri. Orr himself recorded in his memoirs how he came to work in northeast Arkansas:

> In the spring of 1828 some two or three pious and cross bearing old sisters who had never seen my face but had heard that I devoted my time principally to travelling and preaching Christ and him crucified to the destitute of Missouri forwarded me a letter which came to hand in due time. Their wants were made known and their solicitations were too pressing to be passed with indifference. I immediately laid the letter before one of the churches which I then had charge of. Some of the church objected to my going, stating at the same time that my health was bad and that the numerous calls in my own vicinity were more than sufficient to fill up all my time and to grace the whole they insisted that if the people of Arkansas are worthy God will sent them a preacher. But all the sympathies of my soul appeared to be roused in favor of the destitute in Arkansas and all their remonstrances were ineffectual. In a few days I started for the

4

territory with the intention of staying five or six weeks.

As it turned out, however, Orr returned to Missouri only to move his possessions and stayed the rest of his life preaching and planting churches in Arkansas, held there by the need he perceived. In his memoirs just cited he continued:

> *Arriving there I was not a little surprised at finding the whole country destitute of Baptist preaching. Not a solitary Baptist preacher lived north and northeast of the Arkansas River with the exception of two old brethren Flourry and James. Neither of these then were able to advance the cause by reason of age and mental ability and what was more heart rendering if possible was the scattered and distressed state of the lambs of Christ's flock. Some years before a missionary had been sent to visit the territory who had organized one or two churches but preaching not being kept up the flock had scattered, but some retained amidst the conflicting scenes a great veneration for the Shepherd and Bishop of their souls. This spirit of engagedness and solemn devotion appeared in the congregation when I preached. Sinners were awakened and mourners were brought to a knowledge of their sins forgiven.*[5]

David Orr had a fabulous career in Arkansas Territory. In 1828 he assisted in the organization of the Spring River, Richland, and New Hope churches. The next year, he led in the establishment of the Rehobeth and the Little Fork churches in Lawrence County and in the forming of the Spring River Association, composed of the five churches he helped organize. Orr was elected moderator of the new Association. By 1831 the Association had grown to ten churches, nine of which Orr himself had helped found. In 1832 Orr, George Gill, Benjamin Hawkins, and Thomas Mercer (all employed by the newly formed American Baptist Home Mission Society) organized the Rocky Bayou church in White County. In addition to his leadership in this area, however, Orr traveled throughout the northern part of Arkansas Territory preaching revivals, assisting in the ordination of ministers, and doing whatever he could to promote the spread of Baptist work. He also served in the Arkansas Territorial Legislature, where he obtained the sobriquet of "David, the High Priest."[6]

Up to 1832 the Baptist Foreign Mission Board of Massachusetts furnished a salary for David Orr and other missionaries working in Arkansas. Each received from fifty to a hundred dollars a year. In 1831 the Spring River Association began to supplement

Orr's salary. In 1832, however, Baptists in America formed a general society specially charged with responsibility for aiding in "the spreading of the kingdom of Christ in North America," called the American Baptist Home Mission Society. The Home Mission Society sponsored a number of missionaries in Arkansas besides Orr: John B. Graham, W.B. Karr, John McCarthy, Henry McElmurry, G.W. Baines, Benjamin Hawkins, Benjamin Clark, William W. Settle, John Woodrome, Thomas Mercer, and William Kellet. Most of these served one or two years, but Benjamin Hawkins served three and David Orr five and a half years. Some were picked up by the Society after they came to the state without sponsorship. W.B. Karr, an earnest and successful misssionary, joined the Baptist cause by way of immersion into the Cumberland Presbyterian Church. Some churches manifested early signs of "Landmarkism" by refusing to accept him into their fellowship. Ignoring such slights, Karr worked closely with Orr, an intimate friend, and probably ranks just under him in the prodigiousness of his efforts.

Another distinguished contributor to Baptist work in Arkansas during this period was Silas Toncray. A Baptist preacher by profession and a silversmith and jeweler by trade, he came to Little Rock in 1824 to join his brother-in-law, Isaac Watkins. Ordained in July, 1821 at Brashears Creek in Shelby County, Kentucky, Toncray had served two years as clerk of the Long Run Association and was held in high esteem by his fellow Baptists as "a young preacher of excellent attainments." Shortly after his arrival in Little Rock, he placed an announcement in the **Arkansas Gazette** advertising the formation of a Baptist Church. The announcement reveals much about the purpose and procedure of Baptists in founding churches and merits quotation:

> For the promotion of morality and the prosperity of the Redeemer's Kingdom in this part of the world, I desire to constitute a regular church of Jesus Christ, on the fourth Saturday of July (instant) at the state house in this town; but if any public business should interfere, the constitution will take place at the house of Mr. Isaac Watkins, at 11 o'clock a.m.
>
> Those persons who have been regularly dismissed from regular Baptist churches, are notified to attend, and are invited to engage in the work, if they wish to do so.
>
> The great design of regularly organized churches is to help Christians forward in their progress to Zion, and to operate as a check upon vice and immorality, and thus become as the salt of the earth, or as a light in the midst of a dark and benighted land, to guide the footsteps of

weary travellers to the mansions of eternal glory, and in order to carry into operation the will of heaven, it is necessary to become a regularly constituted church of Jesus Christ, in order to carry on the public worship of God, maintain the ordinances of the gospel, etc., etc., together with a great many other solemn duties imposed on us by the great head of the church, for our comfort and consolation, that we may wait upon God without distraction, and serve him in the beauty of holiness. Signed: Silas T. Toncray, a minister of the regular Baptist church, Little Rock, July 5, 1824.[7]

With Silas Toncray presiding and Major Isaac Watkins acting as clerk, the church was organized in the Watkins home in Little Rock on July 24. In November of the same year Toncray led in the organization of the Little Rock Association of Regular Baptists, the first formed in the Territory. He was elected moderator and Isaac Watkins clerk. During the five years he lived in Little Rock. Toncray assisted in the founding of two other churches, served as president of the Little Rock Baptist Bible Society, recognized as an auxiliary of the American Bible Society, and took an active part in civic and political affairs. Among other things, he sought to raise funds to become postmaster and **Gazette** agent at Conway courthouse in Conway County. Due to the death of a brother, however, he was called to Memphis, Tennessee, shortly afterwards and never returned to Little Rock. The Little Rock Baptist Church never had another pastor after he left. It was disrupted and taken over by the Disciples of Christ three years later.

Most Baptist Churches in Arkansas probably resulted from active mission efforts like those described above. Even though Baptists have considered theirs a lay movement, they have depended on an educated and dedicated ministry to take the lead in their work. They have benefited too from effective and well organized cooperative efforts by which they could support missionaries and pastors. Some churches, nonetheless, came into existence in more spontaneous ways, which are often difficult to trace. We know, for example, that two churches were organized in Arkansas Territory in 1819. One of these was founded by James P. Edwards of Missouri while on a missionary tour, but we do not know its name or location. The other, the Pecannerie church, located on the Arkansas River near the present site of Morrilton, is of uncertain origin. Traveling preachers called "strollers" often organized churches, and one may have led in this at Pecannerie. In those days, however, laypersons did not wait for preachers. They held services, organized churches, and worshiped in their homes until they could erect suitable buildings and secure capable leaders.

Traveling preachers and missionaries experienced many hardships. Like the settlers themselves, of course, they made their way on foot, on horseback, or by wagon. As early as 1820, however, steamboats began to paddle their way up and down the Arkansas River and later other streams. In 1826 stagecoaches initiated operations between Little Rock and Arkansas Post, in 1831 between Little Rock and Memphis, and in 1835 from Little Rock to Hot Springs and to northeast Missouri.

Harbingers of the gospel depended upon the settlers for hospitality. The latter could offer few conveniences, only crude accomodations, limited space, and meager fare; but it was rare for a traveler to be denied the comforts of a night's lodging and the best that the host could provide.

The Churches Inside Out

The Baptists who migrated to Arkansas from other states were a mixed lot. Generally speaking, they reflected a stern and practical piety shaped by the rugged frontier. Isaac Watkins' story, while not altogether typical, opens a small window into the larger Baptist story in the Territory.

The son of Thomas and Sallie Walton Watkins, he was born in Virginia, April 10, 1777. His uncle, George Walton, was a signer of the Declaration of Independence and served as governor of Georgia. His father migrated to Kentucky but died at an early age, leaving a small estate and a large family. Isaac, growing up at Shelbyville, Kentucky, became a man of influence and wealth. He obtained a good education and acquired a blameless reputation. He was commissioned a major in the Kentucky militia. In 1820, however, he signed a friend's note and, when the latter defaulted, lost much of his wealth paying off the indebtedness. To recuperate his fortune he moved to Arkansas in 1824.

When Watkins and his family arrived in Little Rock, the only house available was a log cabin near the intersection of Fourth and Scott Streets, then on the extreme outskirts of the town. Here they lived until they could construct a frame house into which they moved the following year. Watkins used this home as a hotel, naming it the "Little Rock Tavern." He also established a mill operated by horse power in which he could "grind six bushels of grain per hour by pushing the horses a little." Mrs. Watkins found only one other woman in Little Rock when she arrived, Eliza Cunningham, the wife of Dr. Matthew Cunningham, who had settled there two or three months before the Watkins' arrival.

In 1825 Watkins ran for the territorial legislature, but he lost. According to Josiah Shinn, the loss was due to the fact that he was "too good a Baptist to be a good politician."[8] Baptists, like some other Protestants, looked with disfavor on church members running for office, and being a good church member did not assist one in a political career.

Watkins' untimely death in 1827 illustrates the ruggedness of the times and the challenges faced by these early Baptists. Watkins owned a large tract of land on the north side of the Arkansas River about three miles south of Little Rock. While visiting his plantation on December 12, he found some livestock missing. He traced it to the cabin of a certain John Smith, where he found a dead carcass of one of his hogs. He accused Smith of thievery. At the time the latter did not appear to be disturbed. The next day, however, he walked into McLane's General store with a rifle on his shoulder. For a while he engaged the proprietor in conversation. Suddenly he wheeled around, hoisted the rifle to his shoulder, and fired into the body of Major Watkins, who sat less than ten feet away. Watkins died within an hour. In the confusion that ensued Smith escaped. A posse was formed and $575 offered as a reward for his capture, but he made good his escape. Watkins left a wife and two children.

We have a number of descriptions of early Baptist "meeting houses" erected as soon as congregations grew large enough to move out of private homes. They were usually built of hand hewn logs cut in the vicinity. The dimensions of the first Mount Pleasant Church in Randolph County, for instance, were thirty by forty-five feet.[9] Sometimes such buildings doubled as school houses or for other public functions, since Baptists attached no special significance to buildings.[10] Floors were usually dirt or puncheon, that is, split logs or slabs with the flat surface turned up. The buildings were heated by huge log and brick fireplaces. Windows were shuttered. Pews were made of split logs held up by large pegs. Home-made candles hung on the walls furnished light for nighttime meetings. Wooden shutters protected the windows.

The early "meetings" consisted chiefly of preaching, but the Lord's Supper and even footwashings were thrown in for good measure. J.H. Rhea, who moved to northwest Arkansas in 1829, when he was two years old, recorded his memories of these early worship services.

> *Our first recollection of hearing preaching was in our cabin by an old Revolutionary soldier, Uncle Johnnie Smith. He was a lean, stooped old man of the hard shell Baptist persuasion, the same as my father and mother. On these occasions the neighbors for ten or twelve miles around would gather into our cabin, and with few rustic benches brought in, such as father had*

9

made for his trial days, as he was justice of the peace, the company would be seated, and the venerable old man would begin in a deliberate, measured tone to talk to the people upon the all important subject of religion. Pretty soon his zeal would warm and his feelings begin to rise, till at length, in a nasal whine and twang, he would become furious, pacing to and fro, and spitting, he would cease to reason to talk, but simply rant in the heavenly tone, till mother, good soul, and others would begin to shout. I felt that such and such only was really preaching.

Not all of the early Baptists would have shared the views of the Hard Shell Baptists, but the latter exerted a strong influence in northern Arkansas. Rhea added a note on their observance of foot washing.

They practised feet washing and close communion. On the occasions of washing feet I was always much interested. Uncle Bill Paxton, a venerable preacher of the 'Whang-doodle' tone, preached generally all day. Soon after he began to preach he would roll up his sleeves, open his collar, push back his long hair, strongly mixed with white, and open at a furious rate, pacing to and fro rapidly, spitting and foaming as if by a madman.

Neither preaching nor ordinances, however, mattered more than fellowship. Isolated as these early settlers were, they made their meetings social occasions. The host provided food and refreshments, including alcoholic ones.

At these meetings the whole company would be fed at our hospitable board, mother being a good cook, as all mothers are, always serving the choicest delicacies at her command, making such gatherings very interesting to the children on account of the good things to eat. It must not be omitted that the inevitable jug or demi-john of good corn whiskey was freely drawn upon at such times. Our venerable minister found the labor of such occasions to be exceedingly exhausting and hence demanded much exhilirating and recuperative influence of the distilled beverage; so much so indeed in some instances that the gravest hearers feared that he had taken even more than Baptist propriety could allow.[11]

The spirit of hospitality, friendliness, and mutual concern reflected in the preceding quotation extended outward to the community and helps to explain the spread of Baptist churches. If a

10

member of a settler's family became ill, neighbors were soon at the bedside, solicitous and attentive to that person's needs. Since there were no hospitals or trained nurses and few doctors, home remedies had to suffice. These, of course, frequently failed, and, when death came, the bereaved and their comforters gently prepared the dead for burial. Those with carpenter's skills fashioned coffins. Others dug graves. Usually the community formed a procession to bear the deceased to the cemetary and expressed heartfelt and sincere condolences. Such occasions afforded opportunities for directing people's thoughts to spiritual matters, and preachers usually took advantage of them to do so.

Baptist Interdependence

In Arkansas a spirit of interdependency led to the formation of associations which overshadowed anti-organizational sentiment, although the latter has surfaced many times since and done serious damage to Baptist fellowship and service. The first association of Baptist churches in Arkansas, the Little Rock Association, was organized in 1824, the same year Silas Toncray led in establishing the First Baptist Church in Little Rock. Several churches founded prior to this, one will remember, belonged to the Bethel Association in Missouri Territory, which was instrumental in their founding. The Little Rock Association was composed of three churches: Little Rock, Salem in Clark County, and Arkansas in Pecannerie settlement. Reports made in the first meeting, held on the fourth Friday of November in the State House, Little Rock, indicated a total membership of twenty-five persons in the three churches—ten in Little Rock, twelve in Salem, three in Arkansas. Silas Toncray delivered the introductory sermon, using Nehemiah 13:3 as his text: "Now it came to pass, when they heard the law, that they separated from Israel all the mixed multitude."

The Spring River Association was organized in 1829 under the leadership of David Orr, who had moved to Arkansas the same year. It consisted of four churches which had belonged originally to the Bethel Association in Missouri—Richland, Spring River, New Hope, and Little North Fork—plus one other, Rehobeth. Bethel lent assistance in its organization, at the request of the four churches asking for dismissal. It appointed five elders—J. Williams, J. Frost, J. Wilburn, M. Bailey, and William Street—to meet with messengers from the churches wishing to organize.

In January, 1831, the St. Francis Association was organized at Franklin, county seat of St. Francis County, located north of the present site of Forrest City. The Association elected Reverend

Mark W. Izard, who owned a farm where Forrest City now stands, its first moderator and Philander Littell its first clerk.

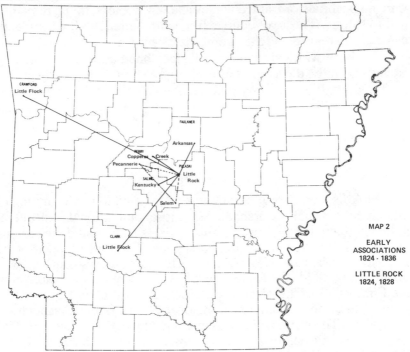

MAP 2

EARLY
ASSOCIATIONS
1824 - 1836

LITTLE ROCK
1824, 1828

The Rocky Bayou Association may have been organized as early as 1833, but this date has been contested. In a history compiled in 1901, W.M. Duren, W.K. Estes, J.C. Melton, and J.P. Lovelace contended that the Rocky Bayou church was organized with eight members in 1832 as the first Baptist church in Izard County and that the Association was constituted a year later. Against this view, however, stands that of Dr. P.S.G. Watson, who migrated to Arkansas from Kentucky in 1843 along with his father-in-law, William Oldham, and ten other Baptists and settled on Reed's Creek. Watson held that the Rocky Bayou Association met first in 1840 when the Spring River Association disbanded.

Early Baptist associations such as these served several purposes. First of all, annual meetings offered an occasion for fellowship. In this period the paucity of members in individual churches heightened the need for fellowship. Closely related to this, secondly, they supplied inspiration and edification through prayer, singing, and preaching. Thirdly, they helped establish Baptist identity among member churches. Before the first meeting of the Little Rock Association adjourned, for example, the messengers adopted a confession of faith, the Articles of Faith of the Little Rock

Church, and drafted a letter to be circulated to members. The Articles contained a statement about the long controverted issues of "close communion" and the resurrection of the just and unjust.

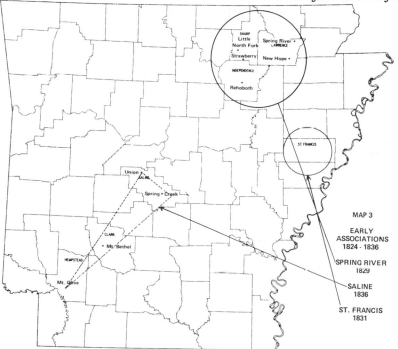

MAP 3

EARLY ASSOCIATIONS 1824 - 1836

SPRING RIVER 1829

SALINE 1836

ST. FRANCIS 1831

Finally and most importantly, associations assisted one another in evangelism and missions. The first churches in Arkansas, one will recall, got started through sponsorship of the Bethel Association in Missouri. The Spring River Association, moreover, caught the spirit of its founder, David Orr. By 1831 it had grown to ten churches with 292 members. Its ten churches contributed $3.62 ½ to its work, a sum not so meager as it sounds today. David Orr was appointed a missionary within the bounds of the Association and charged with the responsibility of circulating from church to church until the next annual session. The Association named one person to solicit and disburse monies for Orr, thus supplementing his salary from the American Baptist Home Mission Society. The same year, it conducted a revival meeting on camp grounds owned by the Methodists.

These, then, were the associations formed while Arkansas was still a territory. Unfortunately all soon fell on hard times. The Little Rock Association disbanded in 1829 when Silas Toncray moved to Memphis. The Spring River Association continued until 1840, but internal strife of a largely personal nature led to its dissolution. The

13

St. Francis Association did effective mission work for a time, but antimissionism dried up its spirit and activities.

Opposition to Organization and Missions

Baptists had hardly gotten their seed planted in Arkansas Territory before they were disrupted by controversy over organization and the use of "means" for missions. The three chief leaders of the "anti-mission" movement were John Taylor, Daniel Parker, and Alexander Campbell. All three have fostered many children in Arkansas.

In a treatise entitled **Thought on Missions,** published in 1819, Taylor, a Kentucky Baptist preacher, vehemently attacked Luther Rice and the entire mission program of Baptists. His views created suspicion and doubt about missionary organization in the minds of frontier folk which they imported to the southwest.

The same year, Daniel Parker launched an attack on the efforts of John Mason Peck in Illinois. According to Peck, he did his best "to induce the churches within his range to declare non-fellowship with all Baptists who united with any missionary or other benevolent (or as he called them, 'new fangled') societies."[12] Although lacking formal education, Parker mesmerized "the lower and less educated class of frontier people," who had a natural suspicion of organization anyway. In 1820 he published a book attacking the Baptist Board of Foreign Missions (the so-called Triennial Convention), objecting to the fact that it was not created nor directly controlled by the churches. He persuaded his own congregation to break fellowship with a neighboring church because its members contributed to such a society. This move disrupted fellowship in the association and spread eventually to other associations.[13]

Alexander Campbell thought of himself as a reformer. The son of Thomas Campbell, pastor of a Seceder Presbyterian Church in Ireland until he migrated to the United States in 1807, Alexander served first as pastor of a Seceder church in Washington County, Pennsylvania. Eventually, however, he withdrew from the Anit-Burgher Synod to which this church belonged and, in 1809, established "The Christian Association of Washington" with a view to effecting a more ecumenical church union based on the Bible rather than creeds. Refused merger with the Presbyterian Synod of Pittsburgh in 1810, the Christian Association organized a regular church at Brush Run in May, 1811. Convinced that the scriptures taught believer's baptism when faced with the baptism of his first child, he, his wife, his father and the latter's family, received immersion at the hands of a Baptist preacher. In the fall 1813 the

Campbells applied for and received admission of the Brush Run church to the Redstone Baptist Association.

Early in the 1820s Alexander Campbell began to debate the subject of baptism with Presbyterian opponents. In the course of these debates it became clear that he taught baptismal regeneration. To sustain as much support as possible he transferred his membership from the Redstone Association to the Mahoning Association in the Western Reserve. In August, 1823 he began publishing the **Christian Baptist,** in which, among other things, he caricatured missionary societies, salaried clergy, Bible societies, and church associations. In 1829 he changed the name to the **Millenial Harbinger.**

Touring the western states, Campbell gained increasing influence among Baptists, but ministers split over the soundness of his teachings. The net result of the latter was the reduction of minister's salaries, discouragement of educational institutions, and shrinking of missionary societies. Several associations disbanded and reorganized as yearly meetings for counsel and fellowship. Numerous "Reformed Baptist churches" withdrew from their associations or were excluded.

While Campbell's influence was most notable in Kentucky, it reached also to Arkansas Territory, where it was most visible in the conversion of the Baptist Church in Little Rock to Campbell's "reform" in 1832. In that year an evangelist named Benjamin Hall, a "reformer," came to Little Rock from Kentucky and held a revival meeting in the Baptist church house. He so entranced the small congregation, which had been without a pastor since Silas Toncray left in 1829, that, on July 4, all or part of them met "for the purpose of renouncing their creed, rules of decorum, their name and every other appendage of human invention, taking only Jesus as their King and Lawgiver." Subsequently, seven women and two men adopted resolutions naming themselves "Christians" and their church the "Christian Church." Although some members may have dissented, they evidently did not contest their rights in the organization or ownership of the property.[14] Ironically the building retained the same Baptist, for, when the Arkansas Legislature met to pass on statehood in 1836, the **Arkansas Gazette** reported that they "met in the Baptist Church."

The influence of these opponents of mission societies and paid missionaries was to make itself strongly felt in Arkansas. Already in 1841 one association, Salem, adopted an anti-mission line. It claimed support of ten churches and 140 members.[15] Two years later, anti-missioners claimed three associations with 27 churches and 517 members.[16] Simultaneously they boasted nationwide 147

15

associations, 1,907 churches, 865 ordained ministers, and 69,663 constituents.[17] Fortunately their strength soon ebbed away, evidently sapped by the religious revival sweeping Arkansas. By 1848 or 1849 anti-missioners in Arkansas reported only two associations, 26 churches, and 480 constituents.[18] Although the **American Baptist Almanac** stopped reporting on the anti-mission churches after 1850, anti-mission forces continued active with varying degrees of effectiveness. Unfortunately, they got a strong boost from the anti-Campbell movement.

The reaction of Arkansas Baptists to Alexander Campbell's "reform" was defensive, as one would expect. With churches and associations debating and dividing over the movement many eagerly seized the coattails of the Landmark movement initiated by J.R. Graves in Tennessee in the 1840s. Unhappily for the later history of Arkansas Baptists, the Landmarkers, fighting fire with fire, fostered suspicions of organization for effecting the church's mission similar to those fostered by Parker, Taylor, and Campbell. Blended with the rigid anti-missionism already thoroughly engrained in the consciousness of many Arkansans, it eventually produced a tragic split among Arkansas Baptist churches and the formation of competing denominations.

John Mason Peck recorded three major reasons for opposition to mission organizations: (1) Some refused to allow any organization, for example, societies or associations, not expressly laid down in scriptures. (2) Some opposed the use of any means to effect conversions, even the sending of missionaries. This type of thinking would have derived from the Hyper-Calvinist conviction (represented by Parker) that, if God wants people converted, he will do it without human help. (3) Some acted out of "sheer selfishness."[19] The word "jealousy" would have been more apt. Uneducated frontier preachers feared embarrassment from missionaries such as Peck and David Orr and avoided it by attacking their activities.

Baptists and Arkansas Society

Baptists have often experienced severe criticism for the individualistic character of their piety and their lack of involvement in social and political matters. To some extent this criticism would be applicable to Baptists in Arkansas Territory, but it does not tell the full story. Some, to be sure, were suspicious of "politics" and "politicians." Occasional misadventures reinforced their suspicions. One of these, involving the exchange of public lands for property on which a new state house would be located in Little Rock, raised a scandal around the tireless missionary David Orr. The ten

16

sections of public lands authorized for sale by President Andrew Jackson were worth far more than the residence of Robert Crittenden in Little Rock for which they were to be exchanged. A bitter fight took place in the Territorial Legislature. Supporters of the transaction were charged with bribery, being accused of offering Kentucky hams and alcoholic beverages in exchange for votes. David Orr was named a participant and attacked in the public newspaper. Whether he was innocent or guilty, the incident made many Baptists skeptical of their ministers getting into politics.

Such suspicions notwithstanding, many Baptists did participate actively in public affairs, recognizing the importance of Christian moral influence in this unsettled and difficult formative period. The essentially lay character of the Baptist ministry tended to blur the lines so that ministers frequently played political roles. Mark Izard, for instance, who migrated to St. Francis County from Alabama in 1825, served six sessions in the Arkansas Legislature and twice as president of the Senate. Later, 1855-1857, he became governor of Nebraska. Major Jacob Wolf—a farmer, blacksmith, and Baptist preacher—moved to Arkansas in 1809 as an appointee of President Thomas Jefferson to be agent of the Cherokee Indians located in Arkansas. The house he built on the White River near the mouth of North Fork served multiple purposes: as a stopping place between Batesville and Springfield, Missouri; as an Indian agency headquarters; as the Izard County courthouse; and as a post office, inn, trading post, steamboat landing, and ferry house; as well as a home. Major Wolf held a seat in the Territorial Council five times and represented Izard County when Arkansas became a state in 1835.[20]

Through their churches, Baptists exerted a certain amount of moral suasion which gradually registered as Arkansas took shape as a society. They envisioned their task in the Territory partly in terms of "the promotion of morality," as Silas Toncray's advertisement regarding the formation of the Little Rock church confirms. No one, of course, can measure accurately how well they accomplished this goal, but they undoubtedly left their imprint.

Early on, visitors to Arkansas Territory left ample observations of a society plagued by violence, gambling, rudeness of speech and manners, drunkenness, and petty to serious crime. A regulation passed by the newly elected trustees of Little Rock on February 4, 1826 prohibiting shooting on the streets on Sabbath days offers a pointed commentary on the situation. George W. Featherstonbough, an English geologist who traveled through the Territory in 1834-1835 painted a similar dark and gruesome picture of life in Little Rock.

> *At (William Woodruff's) store we used to call to hear the news of the day: which were various and exciting enough; for with some honorable exceptions, perhaps there never was such another population assembled . . . broken tradesmen, refugees from justice, traveling gamblers, and some young bucks and bloods, who, never having had the advantage of good examples for imitation, had set up a standard of manners consisting of everything that was extravagantly and outrageously bad. Quarreling seemed to be their principal occupation, and these puppies, without family, education, or refinement of any kind, were continually resorting to what they called the "Law of Honor," a part of the code which, in Little Rock, is to administer justice with your own hand at the first convenient opportunity. A common practice with these fellows was to fire at each other with a rifle across the street, and then dodge behind a door; every day groups were to be seen gathered round these wordly bullies, who were holding knives in their hands, and daring each other to strike, but cherishing the secret hope that the spectators would interfere. At one time they were so numerous and overbearing that they would probably have overcrowded the town, but for the catastrophe which befell one of their leaders, and checked the rest for a while.*
>
> *One of the most respectable inhabitants told me, that he did not suppose there were twelve inhabitants in the place who ever went into the streets without . . . for some motive or another . . . being armed with pistols or large hunting knives about a foot long and an inch and half broad, originally intended to skin and cut up animals, but which were made and ornamented with great care and kept exceedingly sharp for the purpose of slashing and sticking human beings.*[21]

A few years later, we find reports lauding these new settlers for honesty, industry, integrity, and other virtues, which Baptists presumably helped to inculcate. Friedrich Gerstaecker, a German novelist who spent much of the six years he was in the United States (1837-1843) traveling in Arkansas, observed that Arkansas had both good and bad characters. Having crossed the state in every direction, he declared that alongside the disreputable, he had also "met with as honest and upright people as are to be found in any part of the union."[22] Similarly, in 1841, Senator William S. Fulton, with obvious reason for bias, paid tribute to the early settlers when he spoke in behalf of a homesteading bill pending before Congress.

For generosity, capacity to endure hardship and noble daring, no people are equal to the preemptioners of the South and West. They go there with their wives and children, poor and penniless, and in a year are found in a snug cabin surrounded by a cultivated field, with an abundance of everything necessary to support life. From this humble beginning, by the exercise of industry and perseverance, they soon become independent, and in time become the best and worthiest of the inhabitants.[23]

Baptists were also making a cultural contribution to their society. In 1816 Caleb Lindsey, one of the earliest Baptist settlers in what became Arkansas Territory, conducted a school in a cave near his home on the Fourche-a-Thomas River. Silas Toncray served as a member of a committee investigating the merits of a privately sponsored school in Little Rock. About 1827 Ezra M. Owen, who united subsequently with the Baptist Church at Benton, and some neighbors laid off a townsite on the Military road about fifteen miles southwest of Little Rock, naming the proposed site Collegeville, with the intention of starting a school which Owen hoped would become a university. Although the plan fell through, it indicates the positive attitude which some Baptists had toward education.

The relationship between Baptist churches and Arkansas society was often a reciprocal one in this era. The **Arkansas Gazette,** established by William Woodruff in 1819, as the voice of the capitol, used its pages to inform its readers of Baptist undertakings. The editor himself frequently sounded the Baptist perspective on social, moral, and political issues. Baptist meeting houses doubled as community gathering places.

Baptists and Indians

Among those who paid the highest price for the westward migration of whites, the Indians ranked at the top. In November, 1808 the Osage Indians ceded their lands in Arkansas to the United States government. Between 1808 and 1840 broken treaties and usurpation of property by fights created a state of continuous conflict between whites and the Indians remaining in Arkansas: the Osage in the northwestern part of the Territory, the Quapaws in the central and eastern, the Choctaw in the west and west-central, and the Caddoes in the south and southwest. Many Indians learned to hate not only the white man, but also the white man's religion, for they suffered much from the white man's greed and his whiskey.

There is little evidence to indicate that Baptists entertained different attitudes toward Indians than other early settlers. Like others, they undoubtedly welcomed the bounties of land opened up by forced migrations of the various tribes. In one respect, however, they mitigated their worst prejudices, that is, by continued efforts to win Indian converts. The American Baptist Home Mission Society inaugurated its work among the Creek Indians in Arkansas in 1832. Isaac McCoy, the most eminent of the Society's missionaries to the Indians, was present at the organization of the Muscogee church on October 9 in what was then the western part of Arkansas Territory (now part of Oklahoma). He described the preparation made by predecessors:

> I enjoyed a blessed season in Arkansas with our excellent missionaries Davis and Lewis. Lewis was in a land of strangers and penniless, without knowing when I would arrive for relief. Nevertheless, he went to work with Mr. Davis. They preached to the Creeks and visited from house to house; and before I had reached them, they had fixed a day for the constitution of a Baptist Church.[24]

The membership included Lewis and his wife, missionaries from New York, John Davis, a Creek Indian, and three black men, slaves of the Creeks. The Indian mission never won many converts.

Retrospect and Prospect

By the time Arkansas attained statehood Baptists had barely begun their work. The future, however, looked bright, for many of the eager pilgrims flocking to this new state had Baptist roots. Baptists, therefore, could be assured of rapid growth. Whether they could consolidate their gains organizationally, however, depended on an ability to overcome the powerful anti-organization and anti-mission sentiment which had reared its head in opposition to fledgling associations and mission activities. The early experience would now prove crucial.

TABLE I
EARLIEST CHURCHES AND ASSOCIATIONS

DATE	CHURCH	ASSOCIATION
1818	Fourche-a-Thomas	
1819	Unnamed Church Founded by J.P. Edwards of Mo.	
	Pecannerie (near Morrilton)	
1822	Union (Lawrence Co.)	
	Little Flock (Lawrence Co.)	
	Kentucky (near Benton)	
	Salem (Alum fork of Saline River)	
1824	Little Rock	Little Rock
1825	Little Flock (Clark Co.)	
	Arkansas (Faulkner Co.)	
	Mt. Pleasant (Randolph Co.)	
	Little Flock (Crawford Co.)	
1828	Spring River	
	Richland	
	New Hope	
	Copperas (Perry Co.)	
	Saline (Saline Co.)	
1829	Rehobeth	Spring River
	Little North Fork (Lawrence Co.)	
1830	Union (Saline Co.)	
	Baptist Ford (Washington Co.)	
	Washington (Hempstead Co.)	
	White River (Washington Co.)	
	Pleasant Grove (now Ferndale, West of Little Rock)	
1831	Strawberry (Strawberry River)	St. Francis
1832	Rocky Bayou (White Co.)	
	Muscogee (NW Ark.; now Ok.)	
1833	Caledonia (Union Co.)	Rocky Bayou (possibly 1840)
	Hillsboro (Union Co.)	
	Mt. Olive (Hempstead Co.)	
	Reed's	
	White River	
	Liberty	
	Point Remove	
1834	Union (Union Co.)	
	Crooked Creek (near Harrison)	
1836	Mt. Bethel (Clark Co.)	Saline
	Unnamed Church on Big Fork of White River	
	First, Hot Springs	
	Little Red River (Lafayette Co.)	
	Spring Creek (now First), Benton	

NOTES

[1] J.B. Searcy, "Reminiscenses," **Arkansas Baptist Advance,** November 2, 1911, p. 3.

[2] "Wolf House," **Arkansas Gazette Sunday Magazine,** May 15, 1977, p. 1.

[3] J.S. Rogers, **History of Arkansas Baptists** (Little Rock: Arkansas Baptist State Convention, 1948), p. 103.

[4] **Memoir of John Mason Peck,** ed. Rufus Badcock (Philadelphia: American Baptist Publication Society, 1864), p. 107.

[5] Ibid.

[6] Rogers, op. cit., p. 184.

[7] **Arkansas Gazette,** July 4, 1824.

[8] Josiah Shinn, **Pioneers and Makers of Arkansas** (Baltimore: Genealogical Publishing Co., 1967), p. 232.

[9] Rogers, op. cit., pp. 121f.

[10] So Mt. Zion Baptist Church in Green County. See R.C. Medaris, **Historical Sketch of the Mt. Zion Baptist Church, Green County, Arkansas** (Jonesboro: n.p., 1927).

[11] Cited by Boyd Johnson, **The Arkansas Frontier** (Little Rock: The Perdue Printing Co., 1957), pp. 91-92.

[12] Rev. Rufus Badcock, Jr., and John Mason Peck, **Brief View of the Baptist Interest in Each of the United States** (Old State House, Little Rock: Arkansas Historical Commission; Quarterly Register, 1841-42), p. 118.

[13] Ibid., pp. 118-119.

[14] Report of E.J.A. McKinney in Rogers, op. cit., p. 120.

[15] **American Baptist Almanac, 1844,** p. 28.

[16] Ibid., **1846,** p. 26.

[17] Ibid., p. **1845,** p. 31.

[18] Ibid., p. **1850,** p. 26.

[19] Peck, op. cit., pp. 109-110.

[20] "Wolf House," **Arkansas Gazette Sunday Magazine,** loc. cit.

[21] In Johnson, op. cit., pp. 126-127.

[22] Ibid., p. 130.

[23] In Dallas T. Herndon, **Centennial History of Arkansas** (Chicago & Little Rock: S.J. Clark Publishing Co., 1922), I: 214.

[24] In Rogers, op. cit., pp. 26-27.

Chapter II

BOOM TIME IN CHURCH AND SOCIETY

1836-1860

Arkansas' early statehood years, until the Civil War, ushered in a time of prosperity in both society and church. The population mushroomed from 51,809 in 1835 to 325,000, including over 110,000 slaves, in 1860.

White colonization, of course, signified the final expulsion of Indians. Most of the latter had migrated to Oklahoma by the time Arkansas obtained statehood. In 1838, however, armies of Cherokee Indians, about 15,000 strong, made an arduous trek through Nashville into Kentucky via Ohio and Illinois and the Mississippi at Cape Girardeau to plunge through Northwestern Arkansas into Indian territory. About 4,000 lost their lives en route and the rest did not complete the "Trail of tears" until March of 1839. The heart-rending character of this retreat was recorded by Friedrich Gerstaecher, a German hunter who lived in Arkansas at this time.

> *Numerous square holes cut in the fallen trees showed where the squaws had pounded the maize to make bread. More melancholy traces were visible in the bones of human beings and animals which were strewn about. Many a warrior and squaw died on the road from exhaustion and the malady engendered by their treatment; and their relations and friends could do nothing more for them than fold them in their blankets, and cover them with boughs and bushes, to keep off the vultures, which followed their route by thousands, and soared over their heads; for the drivers would not give them time to dig a grave and bury their dead. The wolves, which also followed at no great distance, soon tore away so frail a covering and scattered the bones in all directions.*
>
> *The government had contracted with individuals for a certain sum which was quite sufficient to convey the poor Indians comfortably; but they were obliged to part with all they had for bread; and while they died of hunger and disease, the contractors made a fortune.[1]*

Meantime, with vast reserves of free land, white Arkansas prospered. The capital city, Little Rock, founded less than twenty years before, experienced a boom in fine houses, a theater, two or three churches, a hotel, and the state capitol building, designed by Gideon Shryock. Stage coaches ran regularly to Arkansas Post and Hot Springs. Work was begun in 1854 on a railroad connecting Little Rock and Memphis, but, due to the Civil War, was not completed until 1871.

An otherwise happy economic story was marred by a recession in 1837. In 1839 a panic closed the State Bank and the Real Estate Bank in the shaky new capital. The economy did not fully right itself for a decade. In the next decade, 1849-1859, however, Arkansas experienced prosperity never known before.

The new state, as one would expect, produced contrasting types of economies. The lowlands, benefiting from a cotton boom, depended heavily upon slaves, and it is easy to see why the slave population skyrocketed there as Arkansas became a state. Except for the cotton gin and the steamboat, the economy was a manual one. The Ozarks differed sharply from the lowlands. Its population was made up of independent dirt farmers who had little to do either with cotton or slavery. They worked hard and stayed clear of politics. Nearly all farmers raised sheep. None fought in the Civil War until Missouri jayhawkers and bushwhackers struck in 1862. They scarcely thought of themselves as southerners until the Reconstruction Militia ravaged the state in 1868-1869.

Baptist Expansion

During this period, Baptists expanded more rapidly than the population as a whole. Although statistics are largely a matter of guessing at this stage, we can see a sharp upward trajectory. From a few hundred in 1835 and only 810 reported in 1840 they grew to 11,341 in 1860. Figured on an annual percentage basis, while the population was growing approximately 16.5 percent a year, Baptists averaged almost 29 percent. Churches and associations also multiplied. In 1840 Arkansas Baptists reported only four associations and thirty-seven churches. In 1860 they reported sixteen associations and 321 churches.

A look at the table of Baptist growth in this period (Table II) reveals two major spurts. The first, 1840-1848, followed a revival which broke out after the recession of 1837. On this occasion (See Map 4) the expansion represented a push outwards from the areas Baptists had previously occupied, chiefly down the northeast-southwest trail along which the first churches sprouted. The second, 1848-1860, followed the organization of the Arkansas Baptist State Convention.

24

MAP 4

NEW
ARKANSAS CHURCHES
1837 - 1848

The growth pattern indicates that Baptist success in this era can be explained only in part by the escalation of population by imigration. Equally important were the aggressive missionary spirit which the new immigrants brought with them, ministers and missionaries who served selflessly in preaching and establishing churches, and, above all, the organizing of effort in associations and, after 1848, in the State Convention, despite anti-organizational efforts of "hardshell" and "landmark" Baptists.

The founding of churches and associations continued along lines very similar to those described in the preceding chapter. Despite a burgeoning population to draw from, churches began modestly. Spring Creek (now First Baptist), Benton, in Saline County, for instance, was organized on April 2, 1836 with six members in the home of David Dodd. New Hope near Smithville began in 1844 with three members in the home of Corney S. Sturgham.

Such churches depended for their survival upon cooperation with others and quickly joined existent associations or proposed the formation of new ones. The Spring Creek church was fairly typical.

TABLE II
BAPTIST GROWTH, 1840-1860

Year	Association	Churches	Baptisms	Membership
1840	3	25	2	372
1841	6	43	105	798
1842	6	46	8	860
1843	7	56	244	1,782
1844	5	51	227	1,621
1845	6	58	150	1,771
1846	6	67	75	2,015
1847	5	58	75	1,600
1848	6	73	307	2,355
1849	6	79	310	2,509
1850	6	79	310	2,509
1851	9	120	443	3,752
1852	..... Data not available			
1853	9	129	537	4,483
1854	12	144	644	5,155
1855	15	166	888	5,859
1856	15	179	945	6,479
1857	16	213	972	7,158
1858	16	255	971	8,704
1859	16	269	838	9,491
1860	16	301	1,204	10,974

N.B. Statistics given in the **American Baptist Almanac** represent sometimes the previous year and sometimes two years previously. They cannot be taken as exact or complete. However, they will give a general picture of development.

At its second meeting a deacon, Jesse Bland, suggested that an invitation be sent to surrounding churches to meet and organize an association. In October six churches, consisting of seventy-three members, met at Benton and organized Saline Baptist Association. It was this body which, in 1847, called for a general meeting of Arkansas Baptists to form a state convention. In 1859 Spring Creek moved from the Military Road east of Benton into the town and changed its name to Benton Baptist Church.

Baptist expansion in Arkansas also benefited from active and organized mission efforts on the part of the American Baptist Home Mission Society. Founded in 1832, just before Arkansas became a state, this Society from the first displayed vital concern and interest in this area. In its report for 1836 it noted the challenge of the westward migration and recorded that the Western Association of Ladies of the First Baptist Society in Providence, Rhode Island, had sent $150.00 "for the support of their missionary in Arkansas."[2] During the period 1833-1848, the Society authorized forty commissions for work in Arkansas. Altogether, the missionaries—David Orr, William Kellett, W.B. Karr, Benjamin Clark, John Woodrome, G.W. Baines, William Suttle, Thomas Mercer, Benjamin Hawkins, John McCarthy, and H. McElmurry—reported 1,316 weeks of labor and 285 baptisms. The Society appropriated $4,125 for their work.[3]

A remarkable wave of conversions and new church plantings occurred in the wake of the recession which struck in 1838. The **Baptist Banner and Western Pioneer** of Kentucky reported eighty professions of faith in revivals in northern Arkansas in 1840. Elder George Gill, pastor of Rehobeth Baptist Church and a veteran missionary, baptized twenty-one persons, some of whom joined Strawberry Church. In this same year Baptists organized nine new churches.

Such growth continued through the 1840s, reaching a peak in 1848, the year Arkansas Baptists organized a statewide convention, when twenty or more new churches were started. Since the main thrust of this revivalistic outburst began in 1843, when six new churches were begun, one wonders if there may have been some connection with the prediction of William Miller, founder of the Seventh Day Adventist movement but a Baptist at one time, that Christ would return to set up his millenial kingdom on October 24, 1844. Millerism did make some inroads in Arkansas. The continuance of the revival after the failure of this prediction to be fulfilled, however, suggests that other factors also played a role in what happened.

Among these, war clouds hovering on the horizon doubtless created a kind of apocalyptic atmosphere. In 1845 and 1846 Arkansas would have felt the effects of the Mexican War rather keenly, for United States troops regularly made their way down the Southwestern Trail to Texas. Like their neighbors, they looked with favor on the annexation of Texas. In October, 1835 Sam Houston had led American settlers in driving Mexican forces out of the Rio Grande area. November 12, 1835 Davy Crockett, already a legend, appeared in Little Rock and fired Arkansans to fight a renewed

invasion led by General Santa Anna. In April, 1836 Houston
defeated Santa Anna and the great rush for the land of the Lone Star
Republic began, bringing new hordes into and through Arkansas.

TABLE III
CHURCHES, 1837-1848

DATE	CHURCH	ASSOCIATION
1837	Old Liberty (Lee County now Marianna)	Washington County
1838	Mount Gilead (Montgomery Co.)	
	Rock Creek (near Batesville)	
1839	Ruddel Hill (near Batesville)	
1840	Mt. Zion (Greene Co.)	White River
	Loftus Creek (Poinsett Co.)	
	Big Creek (Poinsett Co.)	
	Friendship (Fulton Co.)	
	Mt. Pleasant (Izard Co.)	
	Unnamed Church in Athens	
	Mine Creek (Howard Co.) (now First, Nashville)	
	Brush Creek (Carroll Co.)	
	Manchester (Dallas Co.)	
1841	Macedonia (Craighead Co.)	Arkansas, Union
1842	Salem (Clay Co.)	
	First, Camden (?)	
1843	Sugar Creek (later Twelve Corners) (Benton Co.)	
	Hydrick (Cross Co.)	
	Lebanon (Cross Co.)	
	Shady Grove (Bradley Co.)	
	Gilgal (Union Co.)	
	Rocky Springs (near Batesville)	
1844	Enon (Cross Co.)	
	Bethel (Cross Co.)?	
	Providence (on Reed's Creek)	
	Harmony (near Reed's Creek)	
	Mt. Zion (Hempstead Co.)	
	New Hope (near Walnut Ridge)	
	New Hope (Lawrence Co.)	
	Clear Creek (Drew Co.)	
	Yellville (Marion Co.)	
	Independence (near Batesville)	

28

	North Fork (?)	
	Antioch (Independence Co.) Stone?	
1845	Brownsville (later Tulip)	Liberty
	Manchester (Dallas Co.)	
	Princeton (Dallas Co.) (?)	
	Mountain Springs (Dallas Co.) (?)	
	First, El Dorado (Union Co.)	
	Hopewell (near El Dorado)	
	Flat Creek (Ashley Co.)	
	Bluff Springs (Saline Co.)	
1846	New Hope (White River Assoc.)	
	(St. Francis Co.)	
	Pleasant Grove (Fulton Co.)	
	Rocky Springs (Lawrence Co.)	
	Bethel (Independence Co.)	
	Fellowship (Ashley Co.)	
	New Hope (Clay Co.)	
1847	Mt. Zion (Washington Co.)	
	Antioch (Independence Co.) Stone	
	Union (Jefferson Co.)	
	Pleasant Hill (Carroll Co.)	
	Ozan (Hempstead Co.)	
	Philadelphia (Marion Co.)	
	Shady Grove (Bradley Co.)	
	Bethesda (Calhoun Co.)	
	Batesville (Independence Co.)	
1848	Mt. Olivet (Washington Co.)	Red River
	Smithville (Lawrence Co.)	Salem (Batesville)
	Liberty (Phillips Co.)	New Salem
	New Hope (Phillips Co.)	
	New Hope (St. Francis)	
	Liberty (Monroe Co.)	
	Egypt (Ashley Co.)	
	Pleasant Hill (Clark Co.)	
	Pleasant Hill (Columbia Co.)	
	Caddo Valley (Saline Assoc.)	
	Cedar Grove (Independence Co.)	
	Bethel (Caddo River Co.)	
	LaGrance (near Marianna)	
	Spring Hill (Jefferson Co.)	
	Philadelphia (Marion Co.)	
	Pleasant Grove (Anneville)	
	Friendship (Washington Co.)	
	El Paso (White Co.)	
	Shiloh (Saline Co.)	
	Princeton (Dallas Co.)	
	Brush Creek (Hot Springs Co.)	

As tensions mounted over slavery, Arkansas would have had further reason for testing their religious moorings. Baptists shared in a general escalation of religious fervor preceding the Civil War.

Camp meetings served prominently as an instrument for church growth. In this early phase of Arkansas history such meetings, attended by persons of all denominations, were necessitated by the sparsity of the early settlements. P.S.G. Watson, a noted missionary, and later editor of the **Arkansas Baptist,** described the role of camp meetings when he moved to Reed's Creek in Lawrence County in 1844. At the time Reed's Creek Baptist Church maintained a camp ground and buildings adjoining the church. Other denominations each had their own: the Cumberland Presbyterians three miles down the creek, the Disciples of Christ three miles up, and the Methodists twenty miles away on Flat Creek. By mutual agreement all four denominations staggered the times for holding their annual meetings. Baptists began their two-week effort in July. Presbyterians, Methodists, and finally the "Reformers" followed in turn with two-week meetings. Persons attending lived in cabins usually called "tents," built of long, slim logs covered with boards. Food was stored in a common storehouse and by Watson's description, "every table was as free as the flowing water." One cabin in every camp, called "The Preachers' Tent," was reserved for the preachers. A committee appointed by the host church before the meeting managed the two week affair.

Preachers belonging to the various denominations were expected to attend at least four sessions. The committee managing the operation, however, selected preachers for each session and admonished them not to preach "anything these four denominations cannot indorse," that is, "only Christ and Him crucified." Selection depended upon who, in the committee's mind, could do the most effective job. Only the host church, however, could receive members during a particular revival, the others waiting until their meeting to add to their rolls.

Watson confessed that he found the ecumenical aspect of this arrangement highly unsatisfactory and eventually stopped attending the meetings. Ministers frequently complained, "If I had controlled the meeting, I feel satisfied that more good would have been accomplished!" Even though he had ample opportunity to preach, Watson thought the stipulation too restrictive. "Let a minister preach only what can be indorsed by the Baptists, the Methodists, the

Cumberland Presbyterians, and the Reformers," he declared, "and he will find very little that he can preach."[4]

Revivals also took place in various churches. Protracted meetings were held once a year during the summer in most churches. Often a brush arbor was erected near the church to accomodate the crowds. These meetings gave the people of the community a unique opportunity to get together and see one another and exchange news and gossip. The meetings always lasted two full weeks and often longer. The entire community was expected to attend. It was customary for two or more preachers to speak at such meetings. One preacher would deliver an hour-and-a-half sermon and then call on a second preacher to "exhort" the congregation. Some preachers were known as "exhorters." The exhortation would usually go on for at least fifteen minutes. Shouting was common. Often there would be as many as fifteen or twenty shouting at the same time. The mourners' bench was also a part of the protracted meeting. This was always located at the front and usually at right angles to the other seats. Those "under conviction" would go down to the mourners bench to pray and be prayed for and counseled by believers in the congregation.[5]

Finally, Baptists owed much of their expansion to the efforts of individual missionaries such as George Gill, Sherrod Winningham, William Nutt, and P.S.G. Watson. On coming to Arkansas from Kentucky in 1814, Gill settled near Batesville. A slave owning farmer, he may first have belonged to a Methodist church, though this is disputed. He was baptized in the Rehobeth Church by David Orr. Soon after this, he was ordained a Baptist minister and played an active role in Baptist life. He served as pastor of several churches in Independence and Izard Counties, including Rehobeth, and more times as moderator of the White River Association.[6]

Arkansas Baptist State Convention

The fledgling work of Baptists in Arkansas got a tremendous boost in 1848 through the organization of a state convention devoted chiefly to mission work. The decision to establish a state convention pumped added life into an already vigorous missionary effort of churches and associations throughout Arkansas. Between 1848 and

1860 nine or ten new associations, restricted now to smaller areas, were formed. Churches multiplied even more rapidly. The **American Baptist Register** for 1852 listed nine associations and 124 churches, thirty-nine organized between 1848 and 1850. By 1860 these numbers puffed out to sixteen associations and 321 churches. According to the **Baptist Almanac,** pioneer preachers baptized nearly 5,000 persons between 1854 and 1860. One association, Red River, organized in 1848, leaped from six churches to nineteen by 1852 and to thirty-two by 1860.

The Arkansas Baptist State Convention was organized on September 21, 1848 at Brownsville, now Tulip, in response to a request made a year earlier by the Saline Associaiton. In issuing such a request, leaders in this Association properly sensed that the time for a statewide organization had arrived. Among other things, the rapid growth of their own association would have given some assurance of success. Several other factors, however, prepared for its successful organization, "hardshell" opposition notwithstanding, at this particular time.

1. **The example of Baptists in other southern states.** Organization of benevolent and mission effort on a statewide basis was a prevalent pattern in the South. The first state convention, South Carolina's, came into existence in 1821. Close on its heels were Georgia's in 1822, Virginia's and Alabama's in 1823, North Carolina's in 1830, Missouri's in 1834, Maryland's and Mississippi's in 1836, and Kentucky's in 1837. The Louisiana and Texas conventions were organized the same year as Arkansas', Florida's in 1854.

2. **The formation of the Southern Baptist Convention in 1845.** The formation of a southwide convention undoubtedly boosted the convention model among the states, as organization of the Louisiana, Texas, and Arkansas conventions just three years later would indicate. By this time Baptists in the South were developing a southern consciousness as a result of growing tensions over slavery. Had there been no antipathy toward the North to crystalize this sentiment, it is doubtful they would have acted in such a concerted pattern. Although Arkansans did not identify fully with the South at this early date, they leaned in that direction.

3. **The heritage of associationalism in Arkansas itself.** By 1848 Baptists in Arkansas had already formed at least fourteen associations: Little Rock (1824-1832), Spring River (1829-1840),

St. Francis (1831-1850?), Saline (1836-present), Washington County (1837-?), Salem in northwest Arkansas (1840-?), White River (1840-present), Rocky Bayou (1840-present), Arkansas in north central Arkansas (1841-?), Union (1841-?), Liberty (1845-present), Red River (1848-present), Salem near Batesville (1847-1848), and New Salem (1848-1852). Even though several of these soon lapsed, the associational principle made an impact. The major reason some early associations folded was the opposition of "hard-shells" to organization and mission effort beyond the local congregation. However, Baptist interconnectionalism and cooperation were strong enough to assure the widening of contacts.

4. **Commitment to missions and education.** The newly formed Convention stated expressly in its Constitution that its "primary objects" were:

> *to supply the destitute regions within its bounds, with the unadulterated word of Life, and a living ministry, and to aid, by appropriate and scriptural means, all destitute and feeble churches, and also supply the community with such books as may be approved by this body, and as may be thought best calculated to communicate information as to the distinctive doctrines and ordinances of the Gospel of Christ, as received by our denomination.*

To this statement it added that "The Convention may whenever consistent with the conditions of the treasury adopt means for the advancement of education and also the cause of Foreign Missions."[7]

5. **The controversy with Campbellism.** Embedded in the allusion to communication of "the **distinctive** doctrines and ordinances of the Gospel of Christ, as received by our denomination" in the statement of purpose cited above is evidence of the storm which was brewing over the movement begun by Alexander Campbell. It is significant that, five years later, several associations unreservedly endorsed the Landmark doctrines of J.R. Graves, as will be indicated later.

In its composition the newly formed Arkansas Baptist State Convention paralleled the societies which Baptists, along with other denominations, had developed to do mission or benevolent work. According to the Constitution, it was to be "composed of delegates from Baptist Associations, churches, and individual contributors, who are members of the Baptist Church, in good standing" (Art. 2).

33

Associations were entitled to five, churches to three delegates (Art. 3). The Landmark controversy of 1901 caused a restriction of representation to churches and substitution of the word "messenger" for "delegate," as in other states.

The Convention conceived itself as an assisting organization, neither holding ecclesiastical jurisdiction nor even acting as "an advisory council" nor interfering in any way with churches or associations (Art. 4). Local associations, as the battle with Campbellism will show, did function in an advisory capacity and even disciplined churches. Thus care was being taken to avoid any semblance of centralization and as much overlapping of functions as possible. It was not long, however, before some problems arose regarding this cooperative arrangement and the purposes of the Convention. Indicative of the crisis, in 1854 the Saline Association, which originally called for the Convention, and the Red River Association passed resolutions calling for suspension of its operations "for the present." In 1858 the Convention itself passed a resolution restricting its efforts to "Ministerial Education and Denominational Schools."[8]

It is quite clear that, initially, in forming the Convention, delegates placed missions, especially the evangelization of Arkansas, before the advancement of education, as both the structure and the early efforts of the Convention prove. Early minutes (1850 on) referred to the annual meetings of the Convention as "for missionary purposes." The Constitution provided for an Executive Committee composed of a president, a recording secretary, two vice-presidents, a corresponding secretary, a treasurer, and ten or more "managers." They were expected to "transact all business during the recess of the Convention and disburse funds," "fill all vacancies of its own body," and submit an annual report. In 1850 the Convention placed its business in the hands of several committees appointed by the president. While some of these had to do with housekeeping chores, most focused on the mission effort. Working committees included: Agencies, Destitution, Foreign Missions, Ministerial Education, Sunday Schools, the Colored Population, Bible Cause, and Circulation of Books. The importance of most of these committees is self-evident from their names. In three or four instances, however, the function of some committees may not be clear because we now use other designations. The Committee on Agencies had to do with the employment of agents to collect funds for support of mission work, that on Destitution with the needs of the state for ministerial help, and that on Bible Cause with supplying people throughout the state with Bibles.

Much more substantive in demonstrating the essentially missionary aims of the Convention is the fact that each of the major committees conceived and articulated its work in terms of evangelization. The Committee on Sunday Schools justified its efforts by insisting, "In no way can christians more effectively promote the cause of religion, and give permanency to our free institutions, than by engaging **heartily and prayerfully** in Sunday Schools."[9] The Committee on Ministerial Education used a similar rationale, contending that "high intellectual culture and moral discipline, but the better prepares its possessors to proclaim the great truths of the Gospel to a dying world; . . ."[10]

The intensity of early missionary concern, therefore, is quite clear. An educational emphasis was present, but it was subordinated to broader concerns. Why, then, did Arkansas Baptists shift their focus after 1855? Several factors undoubtedly played a role. One was the widespread movement among Baptists in this day to train their ministers better, as we will note later, in recognition of the challenge posed by a more sophisticated American public. A second may have been the growing sensitivity of some types of mission effort, notably among the slaves. It is significant, I think, that what started as a report on mission effort among the "Colored Population" became in 1854 a report "On Duties to Servants." A third was probably the nationwide panic of 1857, which frightened many church leaders. In response to it they called for a retrenchment.

A fourth factor, of greater importance than either of these, was apprehension concerning spheres of responsibility. Up to the formation of the State Convention, of course associations and churches had borne the main responsibility for the evangelization of the state. The Convention, though seeing its work chiefly as an auxiliary extended its efforts as far as it could, given limitation of resources. It may have threatened the associations. That, at any rate, is the clear implication of the resolution adopted at the 1858 annual Convention:

Inasmuch as the several associations within the bounds of this Convention have taken up the subjects of Home Missions, Temperance, Colored Population, Foreign Missions, Circulation of Books, therefore be it resolved that we drop for the present these objects from our minutes; and as we have adopted a measure on Ministerial Education Agencies, Resolved that we devote all our time to that object, viz., Ministerial Education and Denominational Schools.[11]

Closely related to this factor was a fifth, that is, pre-occupation of associations with internal conflicts, especially those generated by the followers of Alexander Campbell and vis-a-vis slavery. It is surely striking that the very association which proposed a state-wide convention should call for its dissolution because "They were failing to secure cooperation."[12] Internal strife seems to have sapped the missionary spirit, and concentration on education offered a way to conserve cooperation and to avert the destruction of the Convention itself.

Whatever may have been the complex causes of the shift, the Convention increasingly concentrated all of its attention upon education. Significantly, in 1857, it replaced its agent collecting funds for mission work with an agent, Professor W.R. Trawick, who would solicit them for a college. Until the Civil War intervened, the latter met with considerable success.

Despite these threats to its existence, the Arkansas Baptist State Convention survived. In 1859 it applied to the General Assembly of the state and was incorporated by it on February 12, 1859.[13] Its domicile was listed as Princeton. Unfortunately the Civil War brought its operation to a premature halt.

Other Large Conventions

Close on the heels of the formation of the Arkansas Baptist State Convention came the organization of two others: the White River Arkansas Baptist Convention and the General Association of Eastern Arkansas. "The Board of Managers of the White River Baptist Missionary Society North of Arkansas River; constituted and organized by the friends of Missions in the Baptist Denomination," as the White River State Convention was named formally, held its organizational meeting in Batesville, Independence County, September 14, 1850. The Society elected P.S.G. Watson, Henry McElmurry, and J.C. Brickey its first officers. From 1850 to 1857 it conducted an extensive program of mission work in northern Arkansas.

The General Association of Eastern Arkansas, whose exact

date of organization is unknown, was composed in part of churches formerly belonging to the White River Arkansas Baptist Convention. It delineated its territory as follows: "Commencing at the mouth of Arkansas River—thence to Little Rock City—thence to Jacksonport by the way of Searcy—then up Black River to the Missouri line—thence to the Mississippi River."[14]

In view of the fact that the Arkansas Baptist State Convention had already come into existence, we may be a bit surprised to see two other conventions formed so soon. Why? There are perhaps several reasons, none of which was negative. The chief factor was geographical. A glance at Map 6 will show quickly that the headquarters of the newly formed State Convention was located in the center of the southern half of the state, that is, below the Arkansas River. Its first constituency came exclusively from the south. Given the difficulties of travel at this time, it is not surprising that churches north of the Arkansas River did not send delegates and, instead, formed separate conventions.

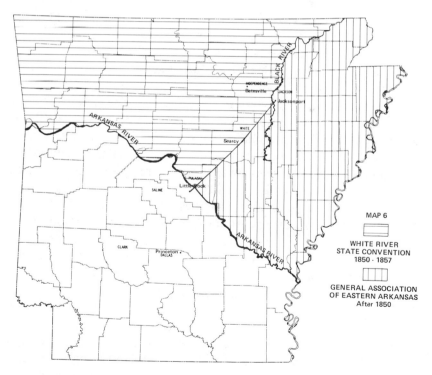

MAP 6

WHITE RIVER
STATE CONVENTION
1850 - 1857

GENERAL ASSOCIATION
OF EASTERN ARKANSAS
After 1850

This judgement coincides with the White River Arkansas Baptist Convention's purpose.

Whereas, the Law of Christ requires, not only of his ministers, but of all his Disciples, to be a part in the great work of evangelizing the world, and as all may, according to their various circumstances, promote this great end and aim of true discipleship. It was therefore thought advisable by the friends of Zion, that a Convention, composed by the Baptists, should be organized in the Northern part of the State of Arkansas, for the purpose of carrying the Gospel into all the destitution of this part of God's moral vineyard.[15]

One might also ask: Why two and not just one? A glance at Map 4, I think, will show the reason for this. By about 1850 churches north of the Arkansas River formed two large clusters. One, centered around Batesville, became the nucleus of the White River State Convention in 1850. The other, which ran down the eastern edge of Arkansas to the Arkansas River, became the General Association of Eastern Arkansas. At first, the White River Arkansas Baptist Convention seems to have claimed both areas, but the extent of the territory simply made it infeasible for the eastern churches to rely on White River. Hence, they formed their own Convention.

The choice of names for the two auxiliary conventions indicates that Baptists in northern Arkansas, the Ozarks, entertained stronger reservations about organizations than their southern counterparts. The source of such reservations would have been "hardshell" sentiment, always more intense among backwoods farmers. In addition, by 1852 the White River Arkansas Baptist Convention was struggling with the reform of Alexander Campbell and invoking the position of J.R. Graves in opposition to it.

Neither of these struggles thwarted the White River Arkansas Baptist Convention, and presumably the General Association of Eastern Arkansas also, from zealously pursuing their stated missionary objectives for a time. In its initial session the White River Convention employed A.W. Elledge and Henry McElmurry as missionaries. Shortly, thereafter, it added P.S.G. Watson, who was the first president of the Convention, and applied to the Southern Baptist Domestic Mission Board at Marion, Alabama, for a supplement of $300 to assist in paying its missionaries. The next year, it added John Wolf, an industrious and successful missionary. In 1854 there were four missionaries: C.H. Boatright, George W. Kennard, James M. Snead, and John W. Miller. In subsequent years it employed numerous others, seven in 1856. In 1854 the Convention also expressed an interest in establishing a Baptist school in Batesville.

The panic of 1857, followed by the Civil War, evidently sapped the resources and the spirit of both the White River Arkansas Baptist Convention and the General Association of Eastern Arkansas. After the War neither of them reorganized. By that time transportation had improved sufficiently to allow one Convention to serve the entire state.

The Churches Inside Out

Baptist church life continued very much as it had appeared in the earlier period. Small bands of believers still gathered in homes to share worship and fellowship. Where special buildings were erected, they were still of log construction, having few windows, floored with puncheon floors, and furnished with split-log benches. One supposes that, in the more affluent lowlands, a few churches were frame or brick, but Arkansas remained largely frontier until the Civil War. Significant of the times, a church built at Hot Springs in 1842 had only three apertures—a front door, a side opening or window about two-and-a-half feet square, and another opening about two feet square behind the pulpit which would allow the slaves on the outside to hear.[16] Such buildings still served multiple purposes. Bethany Baptist Church, the first church to be organized in what is now Jonesboro, for instance, erected a log building in 1854 which doubled as the community school house.[17]

Most churches had only part-time services, quarter-time or half-time at most. At quarter-time churches, the preacher usually arrived on Saturday and conducted services on Saturday morning or night and then preached again on Sunday morning. Some churches also had Sunday night services.

Services consisted chiefly of preaching, singing, and praying. Baptist preachers, typically uneducated farmers with prejudice against educated and paid ministers, relied heavily upon experience. In their sermons and exhortations they issued dire warnings about death and the judgement to come. Among these converts of the frontier awakening exhortations probably figured more prominently than exposition.

Singing of some kind was an integral part of worship among Baptists during this period. At this early date churches did not possess song books. Consequently, someone lined out the songs, two lines at a time, and the congregation simply joined in—at least those who could sing, and often those who couldn't.[18] Some churches had instrumental music, but others could not afford it and some, true to their Puritan heritage, had reservations about musical accompaniment.

Prayers, like sermons, were simple, direct, and pointed. The following prayer for rain by a hard-shell Baptist preacher does not come from Arkansas, but it would not be unlike those sometimes heard in Arkansas religious gatherings:

Almighty God, thou knowest the wants of us, and we need not be telling you. We have come to this ground to show Thee our penitence and how badly whipped we feel and how willing we are to thank Thee for past blessings and prepare ourselves to thank Thee for the blessings Thou art going to give us in the future. Now, Almighty God, Thou knowest how we are suffering down here, and we want you to come to our relief. We want you to come with no little sprinkle or Pentecostal shower, but, Oh God in Heaven, send us an old-time, old-fashioned gully washer and root-soaker, and be quick about it. Amen[19]

Churches usually baptized once a year in a nearby river, stream, or pond at the close of the summer revival. Baptistries did not begin to appear until after the Civil War. Although Baptists participated in revivals with other churches, the strife raised by the Disciples' movement caused them early to be cautious about recognizing so-called "alien immersions," that is, baptisms by churches other than Baptist. Opposition to such acknowledgements was reinforced during this period through the influence of J.R. Graves, scion of what is known as Landmarkism, an influence which we will examine in detail in a later section.

Churches usually observed the Lord's Supper on a quarterly basis. At this early date, associations also observed it. As the debate with the "Reformers" heated up, however, a more restrictive policy developed and, under Landmark influence, gradually predominated in Arkansas churches. Two differing customs appeared: One restricted communion to members of a particular congregation. Anyone who wished to participate would have to become a member of this church. Evangelists often carried church letters with them in order to join the churches where they preached just for the sake of participating in the Lord's Supper. The other custom restricted communion to persons "of like faith and order," that is, other Baptists.

Strong Landmark perceptions in Arkansas resulted in the eruption of a major controversy in 1965, when the State Convention withdrew fellowship from the First Baptist Church of Russellville and, subsequently, three other churches for accepting "alien immersions" and holding "open communion." Ironically, J.R. Graves' own views, which had so dominant an influence, grew more and more restrictive as he attempted to counter the Disciples' movement. Early on, he presided over a communion service for an association. In his last years he took the view that persons moving from one local congregation to another had to be rebaptized!

A number of Arkansas Baptist churches still practiced footwashing. Most of them probably did not consider it a church ordinance equivalent to baptism or the Lord's Supper, but a few did. The washing was sometimes done by one person, sometimes by pairs. At Macedonia Baptist Church, for instance, the wife of a deacon, Mrs. Thomas White, donned a long apron, took towels and water basin, and single-handedly washed the feet of all persons present.[20] At other churches those present paired off and washed one another's feet.

The churches educated their constituency chiefly through preaching. Although the Sunday School movement, initiated in England by Robert Raikes during the late eighteenth century, began to make some headway in America in the 1830s and 1840s, it did not get a friendly reception on the frontier. The rugged folk who moved into Arkansas looked with considerable suspicion upon education in general and religious education in particular. Education, they feared, would interfere with the Spirit's instruction. When churches did begin to tolerate Sunday schools for children, they often would not allow them to be conducted in church buildings. Instead, classes met in homes, under trees, and in schoolhouses. The earliest State Conventions strongly endorsed "Sabbath" schools, but as late as 1881, Arkansas Baptists reported only 150.

These early churches, small and intimate fellowships, kept a watchful eye on their members. Usually this resulted in expressions of concern and ministry in times of illness, tragedy, death, and bereavement. But it also resulted in discipline of errant members for drunkenness or immorality. Church minutes of the period indicate dismissal and restoration of members for various infractions of the Christian code.

41

Although individual wealth increased after the depression of 1837, Arkansas Baptists did little thinking about stewardship. Many of them opposed paying a pastor. There were several reasons for this: One was the fact that Baptists always thought of theirs as an essentially lay movement. As a result, they thought they did not require a trained ministry. On the frontier, moreover, small and scattered congregations simply could not pay salaries required for a minister and his family. Many Arkansas Baptists, moreover, did not feel as strong a need for well-trained ministers as their counterparts in more populous areas did. Finally, whatever reservations they had about an educated and paid ministry, these were raised to a pitch by the "hardshell" views inherited from Daniel Parker.

Responsible stewardship, therefore, developed slowly and against strong opposition. Consciousness of the obligation sprouted and grew chiefly in conjunction with the missionary endeavors of associations. By the time the Arkansas Baptist State Convention was organized in 1848, this stewardship consciousness had reached sufficient heights to encourage cash and pledges of nearly $1,700. Even then, reports reveal strong footdragging. Henry McElmurry, a missionary commissioned by the American Baptist Home Mission Society, reported that he collected $4.00 in 1850 and $9.20 in 1851 among the churches of the White River Arkansas Baptist Convention.[21] The latter Convention, active, as we saw earlier, from 1850-1857, tried to deal with this problem by requiring every church affiliated with it to prove its faith by sending an offering when it joined, but this proved only partially successful.

During the early days of the Arkansas Baptist State Convention, agents were employed chiefly to raise funds. In 1850 the Convention approved a recommendation that "our missionaries be constituted sub-agents" and "authorized to take up collections and obtain subscriptions for the support of the convention."[22] Subsequently, fund-raising was focused increasingly on the funding of a college, but the Civil War sidetracked this effort also.

Campbellism and Landmarkism

We have referred several times already, both in the previous chapter and in this one, to the effect of anti-organization and anti-mission sentiment imported into Arkansas by the new settlers. The effect of these in the schism of 1901 will be examined later. At this point, however, it will be worth our while to examine in greater detail the early contest between Campbellism and Landmarkism, for this struggle left an indelible mark on Arkansas Baptists in the form of extreme Landmarkism. This is another of the many instances in Christian history whereby an overreaction produced an opposite which was a near facsimile of the thing rejected. For reaction to the anti-mission sentiment of Campbell resulted in an equally rigid anti-mission sentiment of Graves and the loss of about half the churches of the Arkansas Baptist State Convention.

It will not be necessary or possible to delineate the shifts of individuals, churches, or associations to the "Reformers." The case of the Baptist church in Little Rock, mentioned in Chapter I, was not exceptional or unusual. At this early stage most persons would have viewed these as shifts from one **Baptist** perspective to another. Within a few years, however, the differences sharpened to the extent that some Baptist leaders perceived the "Reformation" of Campbell as more than a difference of opinion about Baptist views. It represented a divisive force which threatened the strong Baptist missionary drive itself. For a majority of Arkansas Baptists J.R. Graves appeared as "the man of the hour," and his solution to the problem, namely, hard-headed resistance, the most logical one. Arkansas, more than any other state, opted wholeheartedly for the Landmark solution.

Graves, born in Vermont in 1820, separated from the Congregational Church and united with the North Springfield Baptist Church at the age of fifteen. Moving with his family to Ohio in 1839, he taught school. Meantime, during his two years there, he was ordained and entered the lists, along with his pastor, against Campbellism. After spending four years in Kentucky where he studied hard to make up for a lack of formal education and taught school, he move in 1845 to Nashville, Tennessee, to teach. In November, 1846 he became assistant editor of **The Baptist** (after 1847 called **The Tennessee Baptist**), founded in 1839 by R.B.C. Howell, pastor of the First Baptist Church, Nashville. In June, 1848 Graves succeeded Howell as editor. From the time he became Howell's assistant the paper became more aggressive in its attacks on churches which practiced infant baptism and in its articulation and defense of Baptist principles. By 1860 **The Tennessee Baptist** claimed about 12,000 subscribers and was the most influential Baptist paper in the southwest. Graves frequently visited the southern states and, in 1851, assisted in the founding of the First Baptist Church of Helena, Arkansas.

It is clear from references to Graves and his paper in associational minutes and annuals of the Arkansas Baptist State Convention that most Baptists in Arkansas considered Graves their leader in the battle with the Disciples. In its first session, in 1848, the Convention passed a resolution recommending **The Tennessee Baptist** "to the denomination throughout the state" along with the **Southern Baptist Missionary Journal,** published at Richmond, and the **South Western Baptist Chronicle,** published at New Orleans.[23]

Local associations, many just coming into being, struggled even more vigorously than the Convention with the identity crisis created by Campbell. In its organizational meeting in September, 1853, the Mount Vernon Baptist Association reflected this struggle. By this time Baptists distinguished themselves from Campbell's followers in both faith and practice. The associational By-laws tried to steer a careful course between local autonomy and associational authority:

The Association shall regard the churches as independent bodies in all their internal affairs, and exercise no ecclesiastical jurisdiction or claim any legal or judicial prerogative over them; nevertheless, the Association may exercise authority over its own members, the representatives of the churches, and power to withdraw from, and disown all churches which may depart from the Gospel as understood and held by this body, by becoming heterodox in faith, or disorderly in practice; and should regard all the churches united in the Association with a vigilant eye for good; and may give, at its own discretion, and in its own way, advice or information when sought, to any church connected with it.

Baptist Churches not before united in the Association or those dismissed from other associations, may be admitted as members into this Union, on application by a written petition or letter, presented by one or more messengers duly appointed by such church or churches; provided they give satisfactory evidence that they are orthodox in faith and correct in the practice of the Gospel ordinances.[24]

In response to the crisis of identity created by the reformist movement of Campbell, some associations endorsed Graves explicitly and directly. In 1854 the Red River Baptist Association, on its sixth anniversary, passed a resolution stating that its members "heartily approve of the course of Elder J.R. Graves, Editor of the **Tennessee Baptist,** in relation to, and the exposition (i.e. expulsion) of Campbellism."[25] In the same year the White River Arkansas Baptist Convention, denouncing Campbell's claim that "many Baptist ministers, in the South and West, are in feeling and sympathy with him, in his vile Dogmas of water Salvation," took similar action in backing Graves and his repudiation of Campbell.[26] A year later, at its fifteenth session, the Rocky Bayou Association recommended that its constituent churches procure a Landmark library: G.H. Orchard's **A Concise History of Foreign Baptists,** published that very year with an introductory essay by J.R. Graves, Graves's **Great Iron Wheel,** J.B. Jeter's **Exposition of Campbellism, The Parlor Visitor, The Southern Baptist Review and Eclectic,** and *The Tennessee Baptist.*[27]

In these Arkansas Baptists would find all the major tenets of Graves's extreme Baptist "high churchism": (1) the theory that Baptists go back directly to the apostolic age by way of a *succession of churches* independent of the Catholic Church; (2) the local church as the visible expression of the Kingdom of God; (3) rejection of "alien immersions"; (4) "closed communion," viz. its restriction to members of these local churches; (5) rejection of "pulpit affiliation," viz. allowing non-Baptist ministers to preach in Baptist pulpits; and (6) recognition of Baptist ordinations only. The lynch pin was, of course, baptism. Scriptural baptism, Graves and his supporters insisted, required (a) the right mode (immersion), (b) the right administrator, (c) the right subject, and (d) the right meaning. Since other denominations failed to meet these tests, they were in effect disenfranchised. Even Campbell, who claimed to be a Baptist, failed on one of these four criteria, that is, interpretation of the meaning of baptism, for he taught "baptismal regeneration." Thus only Baptist churches, Graves and his followers contended, are true "gospel churches." Ministers ordained in other churches do not qualify as gospel ministers; they cannot properly perform gospel ordinances. Baptist successionism was not actually necessary to undergird the theory, but it added an extra validation. Where other denominations claimed apostolic or episcopal succession, Baptists claimed church succession. They were not a recent and novel sect, but heirs of the true successors of the teaching of Jesus and the apostles.

Controversy with the "Reformers" reached a fever pitch on the eve of the Civil War. During the War, as attention was diverted elsewhere, it subsided. It resumed, however, in the post-war era.

45

Although it means looking beyond the period we are considering now, the sequel to the present story ought to be mentioned here.

A few years after the war closed, Arkansas Baptists again displayed their anxiety about this vigorous reformist movement which, despite Campbell's death in 1864, continued to claim church members and churches. A "Special Report" to the Saline Baptist Association in 1868 recommended adoption of a thoroughly Landmark platform framed at Mayfield, Kentucky and published in **The Baptist** July 18, 1868. This platform articulated the main Landmark tenets:

> *We believe that Christ organized a visible Church while upon the earth, and that he has seen fit to perpetuate churches similar to that in organization, in faith, and in ordinances, through all ages since his ascension, and will perpetuate such churches until he comes again. We hold and teach that the inseparable characteristics of the Church of Christ are:*
>
> *1. A membership professing regeneration of heart by the operation of the Holy Spirit, not in connection with baptism, or any other churchly rite.*
>
> *2. The immersion of a professedly regenerated person in water into the name of the Trinity by a duly qualified administrator, with the scriptural design, as a prerequisite to membership.*
>
> *3. We believe the Lord's Supper is a church ordinance to which no one is entitled who is not a member of the Church holding the faith and walking in the order of the gospel.*
>
> *We hold that no organization that does not possess these characteristics is entitled to be called or regarded as a Scriptural Church. . . .*
>
> *Finally. While we have no fellowship for Romaism, Protestantism, Methodism or Campbellism, as such, yet we extend our Christian fellowship to all persons in all denominations who give evidence of scriptural regeneration by manifesting the spirit of Christ in their godly lives and conversation; and while we are compelled to regard them as walking disorderly, it is not for us to judge their demerit, but love them and by all means seek to convert them from the error of their way.*[28]

J.R. Graves remained something of a hero among Arkansas Baptists until he died in 1893. He preached the Convention sermon at the annual convention in 1869.[29] The annual for that year carried a full-page advertisement of **The Baptist,** characterizing it as the "Journal of Arkansas Baptists." In 1870 he again addressed the Convention, this time in the interest of the Southern Baptist Publication Society. In 1872 he preached the Sunday morning sermon at the Convention. Following his death in 1893 the **Annual** lamented his death. "In his death our loss is irreparable," it noted. "We have all felt his power and influence. He was truly a great man; he wrought well in his work. We can but rejoice in the very precious example of the child-like faith and implicit confidence of our brother to the last."[30]

A few years hence, Arkansans were to learn that Graves's contribution to them in stemming the tide of Campbellism would cost them dearly. It is not difficult to understand, however, why, in earlier days, many saw Landmarkist ecclesiology as the main hope of establishing Baptist identity over against the teachings of Alexander Campbell. It in unfortunate that both sides went to extremes.

Baptists and Arkansas Society

As Arkansas Baptists increased, they exerted an ever greater impact on the young society through their stern piety and moral teachings. Overcoming both lower class reservations about participation in politics and some unfortunate early experiences, some Baptists continued to contribute to the construction of a political framework for the new state. One such contributor was George Washington Baines, great grandfather of Lyndon Baines Johnson. A native of North Carolina, he moved first to Georgia and then settled on a farm near Tuscaloosa, Alabama, staying long enough to work his way through the University of Alabama. In 1837 he moved to Arkansas, where he homesteaded 160 acres on Crooked Creek in Carroll County. An ordained Baptist minister like his father and grandfather before him, he served as a missionary for the American Baptist Home Mission Society and founded three churches in the Ozarks, baptizing 150 persons. In 1842 he was elected to the Arkansas legislature. For two years he served diligently and showed special interest in public education. In 1844, however, he pulled up stakes again and moved to Louisiana and then, in 1850, to Texas.[31]

As a frontier people, Arkansas Baptists moved more hesitantly than Baptists in some of the older southern states in recognizing what their new status demanded. In time, however, they discovered that continued growth depended on the development of institutions of learning which could prepare ministers and lay persons who would effectively carry the Baptist message to the people of Arkansas.

The period with which we are dealing was one in which Arkansas Baptists, particularly in the lowlands, began to give evidence of strong interest in education both at the elementary and secondary levels. In 1852 the State Convention noted that Baptists operated four "Literary Institutions" in southern Arkansas. One of these, Mine Creek Male and Female School opened in February, 1851 under the direction of the Reverend Allen M. Scott and his daughters. Mine Creek is now known as Nashville, Arkansas. This School evidently folded after a few years. A second and third were Arkadelphia Institute and Arkadelphia Female Institute, opened in July, 1851, as precursors of Ouachita College. Arkadelphia Institute offered free tuition to young men wishing to prepare for the ministry "provided they have the approbation of their respective churches or give good evidence that they posses qualifications essential to the Gospel ministry." In their initial advertisement its founders, the Reverend Samuel Stevenson and James Hilton Gilkey, denied sectarian influence but emphasized "due respect and reverence for all things sacred." They pledged a strong effort "to develop and strengthen the intellectual, moral, and physical abilities of those committed to their care."[32] The fourth was the Camden Female Institute, also founded in 1851 by Jesse B. Hartwell, pastor of Camden Baptist Church from 1848 to 1857. The Civil War closed its doors. It is understandable that the more affluent cotton belt would foster this type of education more quickly than the uplands. The "good life" in the South required education for both men and women.

It was natural that Arkansas Baptists would expand their interest in education to embrace a concern for higher education as they took part in their state's cultural boom. In this they followed in the footsteps of their Baptist forebears elsewhere.

After a slow start in the eighteenth century, founding their first college (Rhode Island College, now Brown University) in 1765, Baptists in America realized the growing necessity of an educated ministry to keep pace with the demands of a better educated and more sophisticated American populace. In 1821, primarily through the efforts of Luther Rice, they established Columbian College (now

48

George Washington University) to serve all Baptists in the United States. As interest in and support for this college dwindled, various states started making plans for state Baptist colleges. Within a few years most southern states witnessed the founding of Baptist colleges to train and educate ministers—Furman (South Carolina) in 1826, Georgetown (Kentucky) in 1829, Richmond (Virginia) in 1832, Mercer (Georgia) in 1833, Wake Forest (North Carolina) in 1834, Union (Tennessee) in 1834, Baylor (Texas) in 1846, William Jewell (Missouri) in 1849, and Carson-Newman (Tennessee) in 1851. In time the purpose of these colleges expanded to prepare Christian teachers and others equipped for the shaping of society.

In the South in general and in Arkansas in particular, however, developments in higher education lagged. The lag was due to several factors: too few Baptists with sufficient money to support colleges, too few Baptist scholars to build competent faculties, and too little interest on the part of an anti-intellectual agrarian constituency. In some instances the establishment of state-supported land-grant colleges throughout the South also delayed the movement.

Despite such obstacles, Baptists in Arkansas soon registered strong support for a state Baptist college and, as indicated earlier, within a few years concentrated most of their energies on that goal. In the initial meeting of the Arkansas Baptist State Convention Samuel Stevenson, chairman of the Education Committee of the Convention, presented a rationale for Baptist colleges:

> *The present being an age peculiarly distinguished for intellectual and scientific improvement, we deem it of the utmost importance for the universal spread of the glorious Gospel against all error, that we have as far as possible, an educated ministry.*[33]

A year later, the Education Committee reiterated the concern of the previous year that young ministers "avail themselves of every laudable means in their power, to gain information both literary and theological."[34] In 1850 a Committee on Ministerial Education recommended that the Convention take steps to finance a "Seminary for the education of her Ministry."[35] In 1853 the Convention, confessing its lack of funding, displayed further interest in higher education by cooperation with the Baptist State Convention in Louisiana in the creation of Mt. Lebanon University, particularly in the formation of a "Theological Department," and pledged to "cheerfully contribute to its endowment as far as we are able to do so."[36]

From 1855 on, as we have observed earlier, the Convention turned up the burner on its educational goals as it turned one down on other mission endeavors. In 1856 it appointed three agents to solicit money for ministerial education and to establish "a Denominational Male School of High Character."[37] The Reverend W.R. Trawick, Financial Secretary of Education, headed the campaign to raise funds for a college. By 1861 he had raised $75,000 toward its establishment. Unfortunately the Civil War interrupted these early efforts and wiped out the funds accumulated for the proposed school. As a result, Arkansas Baptists waited nearly three more decades before they obtained their own college.

The Arkansas Baptist

The ascension of Arkansas Baptists up the numerical and social ladder gradually generated a need for a special news organ to promote Baptist causes. For a time they managed to get along with the help of secular papers such as the **Arkansas Gazette** for promoting local concerns. As they formed a statewide convention, however, they needed an instrument which might voice broader concerns. For several years **The Tennessee Baptist,** founded in 1835 by R.B.C. Howell and edited from 1848 by J.R. Graves, served this purpose. As indicated in an earlier section, many associations and also the Arkansas Baptist State Convention officially sanctioned use of this paper by Arkansas Baptists. The extent of its influence is reflected in the fact that, for a number of years, it carried an Arkansas page, edited as late as 1880 by J.B. Searcy.

In 1858 the Arkansas Baptist State Convention voted to establish its own paper, called **The Arkansas Baptist,** edited by P.S.G. Watson and J.F. Hooton. The first issue, priced at two dollars a year, appeared in January, 1859. For four months it boasted 1,600 and in its second year 2,200 subscribers. Had the Civil War not intervened, it would have grown further, but the War caused its collapse after two years and five months. The owners—Watson, J.F. Hooten, and E.N. Chenault—lost $3,000.00

The instant success of the paper was a result of several factors. The strongly "Landmark" tendencies of **The Tennessee Baptist** doubtless limited its acceptability among Arkansas Baptists to some extent. J.R. Graves, however, stood so high in the estimation of most

Arkansans, that this factor would not have weighed heavily against his paper. It would be more accurate to see a convergence of state identity in the face of an impending crisis with the push of Baptists to accomplish their missionary and educational goals. A state paper was needed to articulate the goals and to unite Baptists throughout the state in an effort to implement them. Watson, a popular missionary in the North, pushed the right buttons for success.

Baptists and Slavery

Before concluding this chapter, we need to examine at length Baptist involvement in the institution which was the prime motive for the War Between the States. In general, it can be said that Baptists differed little from their Arkansas neighbors either in their attitudes toward slavery or in their treatment of slaves they themselves owned. Many Baptists, however, especially in the uplands, did not own slaves, and Baptist policy, emphasizing the local congregation, allowed considerable room for diversity of opinion.

Arkansas had few slaves before the Louisiana Purchase of 1803. Thereafter, the numbers multiplied steadily—to 300 in 1810, to 1,617 in 1820, the year after Arkansas was separated from Missouri Territory, and to 4,576 in 1830. After Arkansas achieved statehood in 1836 the numbers grew still more rapidly—to 19,935 in 1840, to 47,100 in 1850, and to 111,115 in 1860. The rate of growth from 1820 to 1850 exceeded that of any other territory or state; from 1850 to 1860 it was exceeded only by that of Texas.

During territorial days a majority of Arkansas slaves lived in the more easily-settled uplands north and west of the "highland line" bisecting Arkansas diagonally from northwest to southwest. But as plantations were developed rapidly in the lowlands after 1836, the slave population became increasingly concentrated in the southeast—three quarters of the total by 1860. In that year there were slaves in every county, but with wide variations in density, from less than one percent of the population in Newton County in the northwest to eighty-one percent in Chicot County in the extreme southeast. In 1860 half of the slaves were concentrated in ten of the fifty-six counties, all but one—Hempstead—wholly in the southeastern lowlands or low hills. Slaves outnumbered whites in six of the ten—Phillips, Chicot, Union, Arkansas, Lafayette, and Desha. Slavery in Arkansas was overwhelmingly a rural institution, with less than four percent of the slaves in 1860 living in the small cities and towns, the largest of which, Little Rock, had a total population of

51

only 3,727.

In keeping with the frontier character of the state, a smaller percentage of the white people of Arkansas in 1860 owned slaves than in the South at large. Yet about eighteen percent were owners or members of their immediate families, with about forty-three percent of the total population—including the slaves—thus directly involved in slavery. When the many non-slaveowners—overseers, merchants, artisans, and others—who were indirectly involved in slavery are added, it is apparent that a majority of the people of the state benefited from the institution. Significantly, the slaveholding class controlled the state politically and economically, thus insuring perpetuation of slavery as long as possible.

Arkansas slaves were held in subjection by a legal code governing all aspects of their lives. Those who violated the code were punished, but neither rigid control nor severe punishment could break their spirit, and most managed to maintain individualistic personal lives when free of direct scrutiny of masters or overseers. Slave protests against restrictions and mistreatment included passive resistance and violence against masters and overseers. Some slaves ran away, an action made simpler by the proximity of the frontier. Most run-aways never succeeded in getting out of the state, but some escaped to free states and to Indian tribes to the West. A few fled as far away as Mexico and Canada. But the majority of Arkansas slaves had neither opportunity nor resources for a break for freedom and could only endure their lives in bondage until the Emancipation Proclamation and the Union Army set them free.

Prior to the Civil War Baptists had a larger constituency in Arkansas than any religious group other than the Methodists and thus, presumably, were second only to the Methodists in the extent of their work with the slaves. Statistics on Baptist churches in this period, however, are notoriously unreliable, as we have noted earlier. Just how many of the 15,000 or so Baptists we could estimate in Arkansas in 1860 were slaves is impossible to determine. If it is assumed that slaves comprised the same proportion of the membership of Baptist churches as they did of the population of the state as a whole (25 percent in 1860), the number of slave Baptists would be approximately 3,750. But this figure may be too high, since it is likely that a smaller percentage of slaves than whites were formally affiliated with churches. In addition, white Baptists ranked fairly low on the social and economic scale of the state at that time, and thus were less likely to own slaves than the average Arkansan. Thus 3,000 slave Baptists is a reasonable estimate.[38]

It is evident, then, that the long-held idea that most slaves were Baptists is largely fictional. The statistics also give little support to the old stereotype of Negro slaves as devoutly religious people who bore their burdens with Christian long-suffering. The number of slaves formally affiliated with all denominations in Arkansas probably did not exceed fifteen or twenty percent of the total slave population at any given time. The primary function of the slave was to work, and only the particularly religious and considerate master paid much attention to the religious lives of his slaves. Life on many farms and plantations must have been like that later described by Columbus Williams, who had been a slave in Union County:

> *We didn't have no church nor nothing. No Sunday Schools, no nothin'. Worked from Monday morning till Saturday night. On Sunday we didn't do nothin' but set right down there on that big plantation. Couldn't go nowhere.*[39]

It must be remembered, however, that slaves who were members of churches comprised only a portion of the larger "church community." The Baptist church community, including young children as well as adults who were not actual members of a church, could have totaled as many as 7,500 slaves. In addition, slaves frequently worshipped in secret meetings unrelated to organized churches. One ex-slave in Arkansas described such secret meetings as follows:

> *My father (a slave preacher) would have church in dwelling houses and they had to whisper. My mother was dead and I would go with him. Sometimes they would have church at his house. That would be when they would want a real meeting with some real preachin'. It would have to be durin' the week nights. You couldn't tell the difference between Baptists and Methodists then. They was all Christians. . . . They used to sing their songs in a whisper and pray in a whisper. (There) was a prayer meeting from house to house. . . . once or twice a week.*[40]

The organized Baptist bodies in Arkansas—associations, the state convention, and churches—were fully conscious of the generally low state of religion among the slaves, and continually worked to improve it. Concern for the spiritual welfare of the slaves was regularly expressed at the annual meetings of the associations in the reports of committees entitled "Committee on the State of the Colored Population" or something similar. At the 1854 meeting of the Red River Regular Baptist Association, for instance, such a committee expressed its concern that Arkansas slaves stood "in a more remote relation to the institutions of the **"Gospel"** than was true in other southern states. It proceeded to make several suggestions for rectifying the situation: (1) that various churches in the Association expand their buildings to accomodate blacks in their area; (2) that they assure slaveholders that slaves who attend will be properly supervised; (3) that they insist that both ministers and laypersons adopt "a general system of personal invitation of the colored people to attend the Gospel"; and (4) that they try to schedule meetings on the "Sabbath" when slaves could attend.[41] Since the language of such reports is very similar, it is possible that they were more statements of general concern than calls to immediate and direct action. At the least, however, they served to remind the churches periodically of the religious needs of the slaves.

The Arkansas Baptist State Convention articulated a similar concern. At the organization of the Convention in 1848 the "Committee on Instruction of the Colored Population" recommended that owners make provisions for (1) family instruction by heads of families or by qualified persons and require attendance at family worship; (2) that churches prepare a special "apartment" for slaves to hear the preaching of the Gospel, ministers preaching to them as often as possible; and (3) that each church having slave members appoint a committee of instruction who, one day each month, would read scriptures to the slaves.[42] At this same meeting evangelistic services were held for slaves who had accompanied their masters. Samuel Stevenson, pastor of Mount Bethel Church near Arkadelphia, sent an enthusiastic report to the **American Baptist Register.** "The master and the servant, the child and parent, the self-righteous moralist and the profane sceptic bowed at the same altar of prayer," he exulted, "and ere the meeting closed more than 40 hopeful converts were added to the militant kingdom of Christ."[43]

The mission program of the Convention included work among the slaves. In August, 1849 the Executive Board of the Convention appointed Elder B.L. Wright as "missionary to the Blacks on Red River" in southwestern Arkansas, paying him $45.00 for his services from August until October.[44] At the annual meeting that year the

"Committee on the Condition on the Colored Population" commended his efforts and recommended the continued employment of a missionary to the blacks.[45] Wright was reappointed, and at the 1850 meeting he received a commendation from both the "Committee on the Condition of the Colored Population" and the Executive Committee, the latter noting that "he has baptized over thirty willing converts; and but for his illness would probably have baptized many more."[46]

The original burst of enthusiasm in the Convention was fading, however, for, given the factors discussed earlier, it was becoming increasingly difficult to raise money for mission work. Consequently, Wright was not reappointed, and Convention reports of 1851, 1852, and 1853 contain no references to mission work among slaves. That it had been abandoned to the churches and associations, along with other mission activity, is evident from the report of the "Committee on Duties to Servants" at the Convention in 1854: "We very much regret that, with the limited resources of the Convention, no satisfactory provision can be made for supplying this much neglected portion of our population."[47]

Although the State Convention focused all its efforts on education after 1855, associations did continue to promote and carry on mission work among the slaves. Red River Association carried on one of the most extensive programs of mission work among slaves, supporting four missionaries within its area in a single year.[48] The Association apparently assumed responsibility for the work the State Convention had begun. The fact that B.L. Wright served as chairman of the Association's "Committee on the State of the Colored Population" may indicate that he was one of the missionaries, simply shifting from the Convention to the Association.[49]

As useful as their work with slaves was, the State Convention and the associations were nevertheless primarily promotional and coordinating agencies, and it was the local Baptist congregations which had the most direct and sustained contacts with the slaves.[50] Slaves were frequently among the charter members of churches. In the preceding chapter mention was made of the fact that three Negro men, slaves of the Creek Indians, became charter members of Muscogee Baptist Church in 1832 along with two white missionaries and one Creek Indian, a missionary preacher. Two years later, thirteen slaves and six Indians joined the church during a revival. One slave was among the charter members of Liberty Church, Union County, organized in 1832, and also of Bethesda Church, organized near present-day Alleene, Little River County, in 1857.[51]

Although slaves usually comprised only a small minority of the membership of Baptist churches, sometimes the number was substantial. When the First Baptist Church of Pine Bluff was constituted on October 6, 1853, a free Negro woman but no slaves were among the ten members. Within little more than a year, however, the rapidly-growing membership of 138 included 57 blacks, almost all slaves. A number of the slaves belonged to Mrs. Nancy Hardwick, a member of the church noted for the religious influence she had upon her slaves.[52] Slaves comprised more than 20 percent of the 81 members of Flat Creek Church, Ashley County, in 1860; that year the 10 churches of Bartholomew Baptist Association, of which Flat Creek Church was a member, reported 53 blacks, or less than 6 percent, in the total membership of 946.[53]

Most Baptist slaves belonged to the same church as their masters. Services for the slaves were held at various times, even in a single church. The variety of times is well-illustrated in the minutes of the First Baptist Church of Arkadelphia. Samuel Stevenson, the pastor, after preaching to the white members of the church on the morning of May 10, 1853, preached to the slave members in the afternoon and "opened a door for the reception of members—when Lucy and Harry Servants of S. Dickinson was received by Experience and the ordinance of Baptism was administered the same evening."[54] At times services were held for the white members Saturday evening and for the slaves Sunday morning. At other times slaves attended the Sunday morning services and joined the church along with white people. On Sunday, September 13, 1851, for instance, "three servants belonging to the estate of W. Heard Ether Jane and David was received by letter."[55] Finally, the church also held Saturday evening services for slaves.

Some Baptist churches, particularly smaller ones holding services only one weekend a month, permitted slaves to participate in all the services regardless of when they were conducted. Shady Grove Baptist Church in Bradley County, for example, accepted slave members at each of four services it held in October, 1851.

Joint worship services for whites and blacks were common, but some white leaders felt that they were ineffective. In the 1854 report to the Mt. Vernon Association referred to above, P.S.G. Watson argued that their ineffectiveness was proved "by the very small number of (blacks) that are professors of religion." Alternatively, he suggested that "competent white ministers" should preach regularly to black congregations.[56]

Despite the inherently unbridgeable chasm between races in that period, even in church, relationships between white and slave members in Baptist churches seem to have been more informal than in those of other denominations. White members were paternalistic toward black members, to be sure, but in at least some Baptist churches an idealistic equality before God was more nearly achieved. Baptist churches, for instance, sometimes ordained slaves as preachers just as they did whites. This was possible because each congregation was independent and could ordain preachers without authorization from any central policy-making body. A slave, James Staryan, was the first minister ordained by the First Baptist Church of Pine Bluff. He had been authorized to preach in 1854, a year after the church was founded.[57]

Usually black ministers preached only to blacks, but sometimes they also preached to whites, as did Tom Clements, for many years an active member of Mount Zion Baptist Church in Green County. Tom came to Arkansas before 1850 with his master, the Reverend M.E. Clements, a farmer-preacher who was pastor of Mount Zion Church for several years. Many years later the Reverend M.C. Medaris, who had known Tom well before and after the Civil War, said of him:

He was an outstanding soldier of the Cross. He was always present at every meeting of the church. He was always ready for every good work. He could lead in singing; he could conduct a prayer service; he could bury the dead. He could pray with more spirit and fervor than any one I ever heard, white or colored. He was true to every trust committed to him. . . He was a good obedient slave until he was made free, and after that remained with the Clements family until his death. . . It is said that he officiated at the funerals of over one hundred white people in the faith.[58]

The "official" attitude which white Baptists in Arkansas manifested toward the institution of Negro slavery contrasted somewhat with the solicitous, paternalistic attitude toward the slave as an individual which has been described above. That "official" attitude was one of full, unqualified, unapologetic, and unchanging support of the institution of slavery. Nevertheless, it should be emphasized that Arkansas Baptists could not really

57

establish an "official" position on any matter, including slavery, due to their emphasis on the independence of the local congregation, then as now. And the white members of Arkansas Baptist churches appear to have accepted the institution of slavery so unquestioningly that they seldom felt any need to comment on it, much less defend it. Consequently, while most of the minutes of local churches mentioned slaves in connection with routine matters such as admission, discipline, and dismissal, research for this history turned up only one reference to the **institution** of slavery. In 1860 the Charleston Baptist Church issued a strong defense of slavery on the grounds that it was scriptural and of positive benefit to the slaves. The document, published in the **Arkansas Baptist,** was composed in response to reception of "incendiary documents" sent by "Northern Abolition fanatics" with a request that the pastor read them to the congregation. It emphasized the standard southern belief that the lower classes of the North fared much less well than slaves in the South. Professing great offense, it insisted that:

> *Our church is southern to the core, and supports and endorses Southern institutions. We regard slavery as scriptural and moral in its tendency and by far the best situation in which the African can be placed. We request these silly disturbers of the peace to keep their papers at home; and would advise them to spend their money for bread to feed the starving poor in their midst, instead of spending it in publishing and sending out murderous and diabolical documents, where they are neither asked for nor desired.*[59]

Preachers in Baptist churches did, of course, preach slavery, but only fragmentary references to such sermons have survived. These are admonitions to slaves in the congregation to be good and obedient servants. A former slave recorded the following reminiscence of such preaching:

> *Uncle Jasper . . . recalls that on the Pomprey plantation near the trading post of Benton (Saline County), Arkansas, in the old days the preacher made one sermon do for both races. A big long shed served as meeting house. Into it the white people went to hear the preacher in his powerful exhortations to right living. "Us servan's stayed outside, an' set down on de logs close by. When de preacher get all warm up, an' had de white folks*

58

inside de shed thinkin' on de way to glory, he stick his haid out de window now and den ter exhort us servan's: 'You cullud people out dar—lissen at me! Der way to make good slaves, is ter obey you' Massa an' Missis! Obey 'em constant—' Den he stick his haid back in, and preach til he had some mo' words fo' us-all."[60]

There is no indication of denomination in this quotation, but it cannot be doubted that such sermons were common in Arkansas Baptist churches. Lucretia Alexander remembered that preachers would ". . . just say, 'Serve your masters. Don't steal your master's turkey. Don't steal your master's hawgs. Don't steal your master's meat. Do whatever your master tells you to do.' Same old thing all the time."[61] Mollie Finley, born near Forrest City, remembered that the white preacher in her community "would say, 'you may get to the kitchen of heaven if you obey your master, if you don't steal, if you tell no stories, etc.'"[62] Frank Larkin of Pine Bluff gave a very succinct slaves-eye view of Baptist religious life: "We went to church, sat in de back seat of the white folks church. It was a Baptist. Baptized in pool. White preacher said: 'Obey your master.'"[63]

Although unofficial, then, statements on slavery by organizations or institutions beyond the local congregation reflected prevailing attitudes. The most common statements of this type were reports of committees in the annual minutes of the associations. Most of these, as indicated earlier, were very much of a type and were devoted primarily to calls for intensified ministry to the slaves. Occasionally, however, they expressed the current religious rationale for the institution of slavery. In a report presented at the 1859 session of the Judson Baptist Association, held at Princeton, Dallas County, W.M. Lea combined a thorough exposition of the scriptural justification for slavery with a plea for evangelization of the slaves.

This race of mankind was appointed to bondage by the Lord. Noah had three sons born unto him, Sham (sic), Ham and Japeth—Gen. 9:18. Ham is the father of Canaan, and for an impropriety of his towards his father, Noah, a curse was put on him by his father, (see 25th verse same chapter). Cursed by Canaan, a servant of servants shall he be unto his brethren. In the days of Joshua the Canaanites were subdued by Israel—Josh. 9th chap. and 23 verse. Now, therefore, ye are Cursed, and there shall none of ye be freed from being bondmen

*and hewers of wood and drawers of water, for the House
of my God. The apostle Paul understood them to occupy
the same relative position to the gospel dispensation as
they did in the law, hence he said to Titus, (2nd chap. and
19th verse,) "Exhort servants to be obedient unto their
own masters," &c. Again in Ephesians 6th chap. and 5th
verse, "Servants be obedient to them that are your
masters according to the flesh," &c., and in the 9th verse:
"Masters forbear threatening, knowing that your master
also is in Heaven." The great anxiety manifested by this
race of mankind for the gospel, calls aloud to us to supply
them with the Word of Life. No doubt but that the Lord
has placed them under our charge for a wise purpose, and
how fearful the consequences if we withhold the means of
salvation from them. . . .*[64]

At no time did the Arkansas Baptist State Convention make any
statement which could be construed as expressing a policy toward
the institution of slavery. During its earliest years, as we have seen,
the Convention appointed and received reports from committees on
the colored population, but the reports were, like most of those to the
associations, admonitions to more active ministry to the slaves or
reports on mission work. In the absence of evidence to the contrary,
however, the Convention, like the churches and the associations,
gave tacit approval to the institution of slavery.

State Baptist newspapers in the antebellum period, as now, were
considered to be unofficial voices of the denomination. Since the
Arkansas Baptist existed so briefly and made few references to
slavery, it has not been quoted in three contemporary studies dealing
partially with the attitudes of Southern Baptist state newspaper
editors toward slavery. But given the general uniformity of Baptist
opinion in the South, it may be assumed that the attitudes of editors in
the older states were equally applicable to Arkansas. In his general
history of Southern Baptist papers, Claude Sumerlin concluded that
"Some of the editors chose almost to ignore (slavery), some took a
middle-of-the-road attitude, while most openly defended it as an
institution ordained by God . . ." and that, as the case in Arkansas,
"Most Southern Baptist editors had trouble enough finding adequate
financial support . . . without opposing the powerful vested interests
of the slaveholders."[65]

In its brief life, the **Arkansas Baptist** published only two statements on the institution of slavery, both indirect but strongly defending it. One was the letter from the Charleston Baptist Church cited above. The other, published in the issue of May 13, 1859, in in Chapter VII of a serial entitled "Dogwood Grove and Its Inmates," written by Elder William H. Barksdale of Helena, regularly listed in the paper as a "special correspondent" and in the April 29, 1859 issue as a member of the Board of Managers of the Southern Baptist Sabbath School Union. Chapter VII is a masterful piece of pro-slavery propaganda, praising the treatment slaves received, condemning the abolitionists, justifying the institution on biblical grounds—and shrewdly putting the whole argument into the mouths of slaves themselves, who are protrayed as not only reconciled to their lot, but thankful for it!

But the great majority of Baptists in Arkansas never would have resorted to such an elaborate defense of slavery. As Orville W. Taylor said in his excellent work on slavery in Arkansas, ". . .most of them merely accepted it as a part of the pattern of life."[66]

The Lull Before the Storm

To all appearances the future of Arkansas Baptists looked bright in 1860. From meager beginnings they had grown rapidly during the early years of Arkansas statehood. In numbers only Methodists surpassed them. Among their constituents they could count on an increasing band of well born, educated, and cultured folk in the southeast alongside the poor, uneducated, and uncultured people in the Ozarks. More important, they were beginning to work together on a statewide basis in the evangelization of the state and in efforts to provide education for their ministers and gaining a sense of their stewardship obligations. Even the Cambellite controversy, disruptive as it was, proved not too disastrous, for, while Baptists lost members and churches to the "Reformers," they intensified their own evangelistic efforts to recoup their losses. And for the first time perhaps, they began to acquire a more distinct if less charitable sense of identity over against other denominations which would aid them in future efforts.

The tides of history, however, often shift, and, as they do, they change the face of things and alter the lives of persons and the institutions or movements of which they are a part. For the Baptist people of this young state, as of the nation as a whole, the Civil War proved cataclysmic and catastropic. It wiped away with a swish those dreams and plans which they had dreamed and wrought in the preceding years. Seldom would so many pay so much for so long. As in Pharoah's dream, lean years followed fat ones. Arkansas Baptists, with their compatriots, were entering a time of tears and travail unmatched either before or since.

NOTES

[1]In Josiah Shinn, **Pioneers and Makers of Arkansas** (Baltimore: Genealogical Publishing Co., 1967), p. 132.

[2]**A.B.H.M.S. Report for 1836,** p. 11.

[3]**A.B.H.M.S. Report for 1872,** pp. 57, 69.

[4]In J.S. Rogers, **History of Arkansas Baptists** (Little Rock: Arkansas Baptist State Convention, 1948), pp. 153-5.

[5]See John Quincy Wolf, **Life in the Leatherwoods** (Memphis, Tennessee: Memphis State University, 1974), p. 111.

[6]Report by John Q. Wolf in Rogers, op. cit., pp. 185f.

[7]Constitution, Art. 5; **Proceedings, ABSC,** 1848, p. 5.

[8]J.B. Searcy in Rogers, op. cit., p. 476; **Minutes, Red River Regular Baptist Association, Saline Regular Baptist Association, and ABSC, 1854,** p. 2.

[9]**Proceedings, ABSC, 1950,** p. 7.

[10]Ibid., p. 8.

[11]J.B. Searcy, in Rogers, op. cit., p. 476.

[12]**Minutes, Red River Regular Baptist Association. . .,** 1854, p. 2.

[13]See Appendix B.

[14]**Constitution of the General Association of Eastern Arkansas,** Microfilm, Southern Baptist Theological Seminary.

[15]**Minutes, Organization of the White River Arkansas Baptist Convention,** Microfilm, Southern Baptist Theological Seminary.

[16]**Arkansas: A Guide to the State** (New York: Hastings House, 1941), p. 85.

[17]Harry L. Williams, **History of Craighead County, Arkansas** (Little Rock: Parke-Harper Co., 1930), p. 224.

[18]Wolf, loc. cit.

[19]**A Treasury of Southern Folklore,** ed. B.A. Botkin (New York: Crown Publishers, 1949), p. 97.

[20]Rogers, op. cit., p. 136.

[21]Ibid., pp. 325-326.

[22]**Proceedings, ABSC, 1850,** p. 7.

[23]**Proceedings, ABSC, 1848,** p. 3.

[24]Minutes, Mt. Vernon Baptist Association, 1853, p. 6.

[25]Minutes, Red River Baptist Association, 1854, p. 3.

[26]Minutes, White River Arkansas Baptist Convention, 1854, p. 7.

[27]Minutes, Rocky Bayou Baptist Association, 1855, p. 4.

[28]Minutes, Saline Baptist Association of Arkansas, 1868, pp. 3-4.

[29]Proceedings, ABSC, 1869, pp. 6-7.

[30]Proceedings, ABSC, 1893, p. 30.

[31]See Harry S. Ashmore, Arkansas: A History (New York: W.W. Norton & Co., Inc., 1978), p. 50.

[32]Proceedings, ABSC, 1850, back page.

[33]Proceedings, ABSC, 1848, p. 9.

[34]Proceedings, ABSC, 1849, p. 9.

[35]Proceedings, ABSC, 1850, p. 8.

[36]Proceedings, ABSC, 1853, p. 8.

[37]Proceedings, ABSC, p. 4.

[38]Orville W. Taylor, Negro Slavery in Arkansas (Durham, N.C.: Duke University Press, 1958), p. 176, estimated the number at 6,000. The figure 3,000 is a revised estimate, given in the article prepared for inclusion in this volume.

[39]Federal Writers Project Slave Narratives (1936-1938), published in The American Slave: A Composite Autobiography, ed. George P. Rawick (19 vols.; Westport, Conn.: Greenwood Publishing Co., 1972), Vol. 11, Arkansas Narratives, Pt. 7, p. 155.

[40]Ibid., Pt. 1, p. 35.

[41]Minutes, Red River Association, 1854, p. 4.

[42]Proceedings, ABSC, 1848, p. 7.

[43]Cited in Rogers, op. cit., p. 448.

[44]Proceedings, ABSC, 1849, pp. 16, 17.

[45]Ibid., pp. 14-15.

[46]Proceedings, ABSC, 1850, p. 13.

[47]Proceedings, ABSC, 1854, p. 22.

[48]Rogers, op. cit., p. 491.

[49]Minutes, Red River Association, 1854, p. 4.

[50]See Taylor, op. cit., pp. 176-181.

[51]Rogers, op. cit., pp. 127, 130, 169.

[52]Minutes of the First Baptist Church of Pine Bluff, 1853-; Edwin Ryland and Anna F. Bassett, History of the First Baptist Church, Pine Bluff, Arkansas (Pine Bluff, 1936, n.p.).

[53]E.H. Acuff, Bartholomew Baptist Association of Arkansas, 1850-1950 (n.p., 1950), n.p.; Rogers, op. cit., pp. 339-

40, 144.

[54]Minutes of the First Baptist Church, Arkadelphia, Arkansas, 1851-.

[55]Ibid.

[56]Minutes, Mt. Vernon Association, 1854, p. 7.

[57]Minutes of the First Baptist Church of Pine Bluff, 1853-.

[58]R.C. Medaris, Historical Sketch of the Mt. Zion Baptist Church, Greene County, Arkansas, also a Short Historical Sketch of Mt. Zion Baptist Association (Jonesboro, Arkansas, 1927), p. 20; Rogers, op. cit., pp. 135-136.

[59]Arkansas Baptist, August 8, 1860.

[60]Lay My Burden Down: A Folk History of Slavery, ed. Benjamin A. Botkin (Chicago: University of Chicago Press, 1945), p. 223.

[61]Arkansas Narratives, Pt. 1, p. 35.

[62]Ibid., Pt. 2, p. 294.

[63]Ibid., Pt. 4, p. 235.

[64]Minutes, Judson Association, 1859, pp. 12-13.

[65]Claude W. Sumerlin, "A History of Southern Baptist State Newspapers," (Unpublished Ph.D. dissertation, University of Missouri, 1968), p. 53.

[66]Taylor, op. cit., p. 37, n. 21.

Chapter III

THE VALLEY OF DRY BONES

1861-1880

Baptists had little time to savor the triumphs they had chalked up in the first four decades of their history in Arkansas. The Civil War, erupting in April of 1861, blasted their work to pieces at all levels at which they had chosen to carry it on—in local congregations, in district associations, and then in the Arkansas Baptist State Convention.

Some churches, it is true, managed to continue their efforts throughout the war years. But many others, left leaderless by the general mobilization of the population, closed their doors and did not reopen them until after the conflict. All suffered from loss of members, funds, property, and heart.

A few associations also met throughout the War, but most could not, and none could carry on missionary, educational, and benevolent activities as before. More typical was the White River Association, organized in 1840, which made no reports from 1860 to 1868 and only irregular and incomplete ones from 1869 to 1875. Some associations did not resume work after the War.

After a dreary and sparsely attended meeting at Fort Smith in 1861, the Arkansas Baptist State Convention did not meet again to resume its work until 1867. Meantime the **Arkansas Baptist,** which began with a flourish, succumbed; funds collected for a college vanished; able-bodied men, both lay and clerical, entered either the Confederate or, in fewer cases, the Union Army, and energies which would have gone into missions and evangelism were diverted to the war effort.

The story may not be as bleak as these data make it sound, for numerous conversions and rededications, especially among the troops, have been claimed and would be expected, though without accurate documentation. "Foxhole" conversions are not infrequent.[1] It does not require much digging, however, to discover that **organized** Baptist work suffered severely. At best Baptists barely recouped their losses from the War between 1865 and 1870, and they did only slightly better, despite sacrificial efforts, in the decade which followed, the turbulent Reconstruction era. Late in the latter decade, however, after about 1875, circumstances in which they pursued their work improved markedly, insuring a brighter future. Among other things, large numbers of immigrants again began pouring into the state around 1875. Whereas the 1870 population (484,471) topped that of 1860 (435,450) by less than 50,000, the 1880 population (806,525) nearly doubled that of 1870. By this time, too, the Baptist constituency was beginning to mature as Arkansas matured and advanced beyond frontier status. Alongside rough, "hardshell," backwoods Baptists, there were college graduates, people of refinement and education who could assume places of prominence in Arkansas society and change the Baptist image. Such persons appreciated the importance of organized effort, education, and a properly paid clergy in ways which their forebears could not. The next phase of Arkansas Baptist history, 1881-1901, therefore, would prove more fortuitous in many ways. But it would also reveal a deep cleft between the "new breed" which these persons represented and the "old breed" who still predominated in many Arkansas churches.

Baptists in the Civil War

Baptist Involvement in the War

Arkansas Baptists evidently differed little from the majority of their compatriots in their attitudes toward the Civil War and in their involvement in it. As we have seen already, Arkansans were divided in their sentiments, even if geographically and economically they faced toward the South. Uplanders owned few slaves, and they could not have made a hearty defense of the institution. As residents of a frontier state, moreover, Arkansans were preoccupied, as John Fletcher Gould[2] has remarked, with such practical matters as raising log cabins, discovering the best kind of religion, and curing the milk sickness. They looked West rather than East, and the West did not care about the war. Thus, although the Confederacy began February 22, 1861 with the election of Jefferson Davis as provisional president, Arkansans did not act until President Lincoln issued a call for 75,000 volunteers after confederates fired on Fort Sumter, South Carolina, April 12. On April 22 Governor Rector wrote Lincoln that Arkansas would send no troops but rather would defend "honor, lives, and property against Northern mendacity and usurpation."[3] After once turning down secession, at a Convention assembled on May 6, 65 delegates voted in favor of, 5 against secession. One of the latter group, Isaac Murphy, an Ozarker from near the Missouri border, refused subsequently to change his vote even when the other four nay-sayers did so as a token of unanimity. After Union troops occupied the capital in 1863, he was appointed provisional governor of Arkansas.

Arkansas suffered less from the ravages of the War than other southerners, because, for them, the War did not last long. Ill-prepared to fight, the confederates lost a bitter battle at Pea Ridge in Missouri on March 7 and 8, 1862. Thereafter, Ozarkers tended to withdraw. This was not their war. Non-slaveholders viewed the exemption of those holding twenty slaves or more as another proof that this was "a rich man's war but a poor man's fight." Arkansas confederates put up their last serious effort in December, 1862 at Prairie Grove, near Fayetteville. Subsequently 25,000 of them fought at Chickamauga. Federal troops occupied Little Rock in early September, two months after Vicksburg fell. After this, Arkansas put up a little last-ditch resistance throughout 1864 around Arkadelphia and Camden. The remnant of an army finally surrendered May 26, 1865. Many of the last leaders fled across Texas to Mexico.

The meager and scattered records we now possess do not allow us to ascertain the number of Baptists who served in the Confederate or Union armies. Most of the able-bodied men in Arkansas, about 60,000, wore the Confederate uniform, but another 8,789, largely from the northwest, volunteered for Union service. In addition, more than 5,000 blacks served in the Arkansas Volunteers of African Descent organized by the Federal forces after they occupied the state in 1863. Since Baptists at this time composed about three percent of the total population, we can probably guess proportionately about military service.

Baptists served throughout the ranks, doubtlessly enhancing the Baptist image in the process. One or two examples will illustrate the general pattern. W.A. Forbes, who was born in Mississippi in 1844 but was reared by an uncle at Lewisville, Arkansas, served in the ranks throughout the War. After the War he found employment in Tennessee, where he began preaching. He graduated from Bethel College in Kentucky in 1871 and returned to Arkansas, serving as pastor of several churches. In 1886 he became editor of the **Arkansas Baptist Evangel.**

James P. Eagle, governor of Arkansas from 1888 to 1893, enlisted in the confederate army as a private, but he was promoted through the ranks to Lieutenant Colonel, surrendering to General

John Johnson in North Carolina at the end of the war and returning to his farm in Pulaski (now Lonoke) County. He did not receive baptism until 1867, however. Subsequently he took an active part in Baptist affairs. Ordained in 1869, he worked tirelessly as a missionary. His immense leadership gifts led to his election as President of the Arkansas Baptist State Convention 21 times (1880-1904) and President of the Southern Baptist Convention thrice (1901-1904).

Instances such as these will not occasion great surprise today, for Baptists have seldom expressed serious reservations about military service. Somewhat more surprising, however, may be the fact that many Baptist **ministers** served, not only as chaplains but also in the ranks during the Civil War. In taking note of such cases, however, we must remember that, in these early years, Baptists made little distinction between laity and clergy. Most ministers were farmer-preachers, even if they differed markedly in their educational preparation. It was not until the 1880s and after that college or seminary-trained ministers began to appear in some numbers in Arkansas.

Many poignant stories illustrate involvement of Baptist ministers in the conflict. The Elder Samuel Halliburton, who migrated to Arkansas in 1853 from Mississippi, died in a federal prison in St. Louis, Missouri, during the war. The Reverend John Wolf, chaplain in the Confederate army, got sick while on duty in Cross County and died on Crowley's Ridge in 1863. He had done extensive mission work throughout Arkansas. The Elder E.L. Compere became pastor of the newly formed Fort Smith Church in 1860, devoting half his time to work among the Cherokees in Indian Territory. During the War, he served as a chaplain under Stand Watie. Not until March, 1866 was he able to return to resume his pastoral role in Fort Smith, where he served four more years.[4]

The Effects of the War

The Civil War had few immediate good effects upon Baptist life. In the long run, however, it altered the course of Arkansas Baptist history in some respects which, in retrospect, could be given a positive interpretation. Most important of these would have been the strengthening of determination which such crises often engender, thus preparing the way for Baptist advance. In addition, women began of necessity to assume more important roles. By the 1880s strong women's organizations supported the Baptist mission effort. Of more ambiguous character was the development of a strong southern identity which could have encouraged more determined effort. By the end of the Reconstruction era, at any rate, Baptists in the South had taken the bit in their teeth and moved on apace with less regard for the activities of their northern counterparts.

In the short run the Civil War proved disastrous. No further mention need be made of the fact that the Arkansas Baptist State Convention and numerous associations halted their efforts altogether during the war years. The full cost of the War made itself felt particularly in local congregations, which Baptists have consistently identified as the hub of their corporate expression of faith.

It was to be expected, of course, that the War would put the brakes on the thriving effort at planting churches during the preceding decade. Bethesda in Sevier and Little Rock Counties was founded August 20, 1863. Long Ridge in what is now the Black River Association, Pleasant Grove in what is now Trinity Association, and Point De Luce, nine miles from DeWitt, Arkansas County, were also founded in 1863. Mount Olive in the Little Red River Association dates its origins from 1864. They were, so far as I can determine, the exceptions to the general rule. The resumption of the mission effort had to await the cessation of hostilities between North and South.

Church after church closed their doors during the War, being without pastors or male leadership. In most instances, presumably, for we have few explicit records to show what actually happened, little bands of Baptists continued to gather in homes or other locations for Bible reading, prayer, and instruction, in many cases under the leadership of women, an event which prepared the way for women to assume larger roles in Baptist life after the War. Even here, churches ran into difficulties. The First Baptist Church of Fayetteville, founded in 1857, for instance, held services in homes. In 1863, however, the War stopped even these and scattered members and records. It was not until 1866 that nine persons resumed worship in a building in Fayetteville under the leadership of the Reverend W.Z. Mayes. They continued to meet in the Masonic Hall until 1879, when they erected a small frame building.

Buildings as well as congregations experienced the destructiveness of the bitter War. Dardanelle Church, founded in the 1840s, owned a "very good house" in 1860. Late in the War, northern soldiers camped in it but, before vacating the area in 1865, burned it to the ground. Years later, the United States government granted an indemnity of $1,650 for a new structure, which stood until 1909.[5]

Sugar Creek, founded in 1843, the oldest church in Benton County, stood just to the south of the Pea Ridge battlefield. During the War, bushwhackers killed the church clerk and burned his house together with all old records. Services were not resumed until December of 1865, when nineteen members met and reorganized. Erecting a log structure with twelve corners, they renamed the church Twelve Corners, after one located at Murfreesboro, Tennessee. This unusual building remained until destroyed by fire in 1896, being replaced by a frame building.[6]

The War exacted its price in other ways, too. It generated ambivalence about the cause which produced it and about the conduct of persons involved on different sides. This must have been especially acute along the northern border separating Missouri and Arkansas, which produced a number of volunteers for the Union Army. White Walnut Church, located in Mount Zion Association in the extreme northeast, for instance, did not meet during the War. When it attempted to reorganize after the War, according to J.H. Kitchens, "two factions developed in the Church on account of the conduct of some of the members during the War, . . ."[7] Tensions among church members remained for many years and impeded the recovery of many churches.

In the southeastern part off the state an increasing number of Baptists belonged to the affluent and aristocratic class whose interests the War sought to conserve. Some Baptists were wealthy enough to employ their own chaplains! An opulent farmer named Peter Siler, for instance, supplied funds for building Redfield Church and employed the Reverend R.J. Coleman for $100 a year to preach once a month. Siler, his wife, and two other men and their wives formed the original nucleus. Several others were added by baptism. In 1869 Coleman held another meeting there and baptized eight.[8]

Gathering Up the Fragments

The Civil War, therefore, left a shambles, jumbled fragments of churches and disorganized efforts at evangelism, missions, education, and benevolent work. To a people weary of war and economically depressed, the task of gathering up the remains and restoring them to life must have seemed overwhelming. It is little short of miraculous that not only did congregations abandoned during the War regroup and resume their efforts but that, almost immediately, new ones appeared. True, few of these flourished before about 1880, but withered plants did revive and begin to show some of their old life. Simultaneously, these same churches revived their associations and created new ones and resumed their statewide work through the Arkansas Baptist State Convention.

What will account for this "valley of dry bones" coming to life again? One important factor was the strong evangelistic and missionary impulse so deeply embedded in the consciousness of Arkansas Baptists. The War obviously thwarted efforts to exercise this concern through normal patterns of church life, but it did not squelch it completely. Vigorous evangelistic efforts went on within the military ranks and spilled over into civilian life afterwards. The Reverend Jacob King, for instance, a native of North Carolina, held revivals in the Confederate Army. After four years of service he surrendered his sword to General Ulysses S. Grant. In 1866 he moved to Arkansas, residing at Mountain View. His son, T.J.D. King, also became a Baptist minister.

Another was the efforts of particular persons, especially preachers and missionaries, to revive old churches and to plant new ones. The War scattered many ministers and their flocks, but it did not destroy them. In some instances ministers were able to resume the pastoral functions they abandoned on account of the War. E.L. Compere, for instance, picked up the reins again at Fort Smith in 1866. At first both whites and blacks worshipped in the same building, which they owned jointly. Later in the year whites moved to a new building. In most instances other persons stepped in to pick up the work. At Camden, for example, J.B. Searcy led in the reorganization of the church formerly served by Jesse B. Hartwell which had closed during the War. At Lewisburg the Reverend M. Bledsoe directed about twenty members in the resurrection of a congregation which had had no pastor at all from the time of its founding in 1860 and almost became defunct. In 1878 this congregation moved to Morrilton, becoming the First Baptist Church there.

A third factor was organized mission efforts of the Home Mission Board of the Southern Baptist Convention, associations, and the Arkansas Baptist State Convention. In 1858 P.S.G. Watson and E.N. Chenault and their wives had led in the founding of a second Baptist church in Little Rock. The next year this congregation entertained the State Convention. Although it reported 38 members in 1860, we hear nothing further of it until 1866. At this time it had reorganized and was meeting in the home of Deacon Benjamin Brantly. In April 1866 Brantly asked the Reverend R.J.

Coleman to baptize four new members on the fifth Sunday. Thereafter Coleman preached every fifth Sunday for some time. Then the Home Mission Board of the Southern Baptist Convention allocated funds for support of the church's first post-war pastor, the Reverend W.H. Roberts. Similar support lent by associations and the State Convention will be noted in a subsequent section.

Another significant factor in Baptist expansion during this period is probably to be found in **the spirit of the times.** A religious revival frequently follows wars. The war experience itself tends to encourage search for the ultimate meaning of life, for some kind of bedrock upon which people may build. For those who survive, if they do not become cynical, religion may take on new and increased importance. It is not surprising, then, that Baptist statistics shot up rapidly following the Civil War. We lack exact statistics, for reports from Arkansas sent to the **American Baptist Yearbook** were incomplete during this period and indiscriminately included both white and black Baptists. Those given in the following chart, however, will reflect at least the general trajectory of growth.

TABLE IV
BAPTIST GROWTH, 1861-1880

Year	Churches	Church Membership	Baptisms
1861	321	11,341	1,272
1867	331	12,637	578
1868	424	15,160	1,169
1869	499	28,911	904
1870	539	30,009	1,030
1871	648	36,040	2,481
1872	763	38,666	......
1873	830	39,444	217
1874	907	44,901	748
1875	949	46,460	1,273
1876	................No report available...............		
1877	993	44,619	407
1878	1,101	48,005	2,304
1879	1,110	47,398	1,552
1880	1,118	52,798	2,144

If these figures represent accurately the general drift of things, Baptists in Arkansas quadrupled numerically between 1867 and 1880. They also more than tripled the number of churches. Several things need to be observed in assessing these figures, however. (1) Many associations failed to report regularly, so that the figures will represent little more than educated guesses. The dates of reports also lagged at different times. (2)The doubling of membership between 1867 and 1869 probably is to be accounted for, in part, by an ingathering of returning veterans, many of whom had made decisions in the army. Note, for instance, that the number of baptisms was in no way commensurate with this multiplication of members in the churches. (3) The vast increase in number of churches was connected with growth, but it was due in great part to shifting population as returnees got resettled and new immigrants flooded the state of Arkansas, where millions of acres lay open to them. (4) We need also to keep in mind that the freed slaves now had to organize their own congregations, for they could no longer worship comfortably with former owners. Not many could continue to worship in white churches in the way Uncle Tom Clements did. Some black congregations did try to maintain cordial relations with white ones, as at Fort Smith in northwest Arkansas, but the tense atmosphere of the Reconstruction era soon foreclosed on this possibility. (5) Churches were small, as in the earliest period of Arkansas history, tiny seeds beginning to sprout and grow. Many would not survive.

New Life for Associations

The reconstruction era witnessed a boom in associations just as it did in churches. The **American Baptist Yearbook** for these years recorded an increase in these by two-and-a-half times between 1867 and 1880. A major increase evidently occurred in 1867, the first year associations began to regroup after the War, when at least seven and quite possibly as many as 17 new associations came to life. (The **Yearbook** editors, of course, merely guessed that a dozen or so did not report at this time.) It is not at all implausible that the regrouping of scattered bands led to a doubling of the number of associations which existed before the War. A second surge of associationalism occurred in 1874 and 1878, chiefly by addition of black Baptist associations. In the interim the number of associations mounted steadily, as Table V shows.

TABLE V
GROWTH OF ASSOCIATIONS, 1860-1880

| Year | Associations Reporting | | | Associations Estimated |
	White	Black	Total	
1860	16		16	
1867	6		6	18
1868	23		23	35
1869	27		27	
1870	27		27	
1871	27		27	
1872	26	3	29	
1873	27	4	31	
1874	32	4	36	
1875	32	4	36	
1876	. . .	. . .	. . .	
1877	32	4	36	
1878	34	8	42	
1879	35	9	44	
1880	38	9	47	

How do we explain the sudden and rapid growth in the number of associations? It may be ascribed in part to the Baptist principle of interconnectionalism. which even frontier individualism and independence could not thwart. In addition, it was, after the War as before it, a child of necessity. Small, struggling congregations needed the encouragement, fellowship, and support which their fellow Baptists could offer. They could not survive alone. In the last analysis, however, it was a natural response to the mission challenge faced by the churches. The bleak situation which Baptists shared with other citizens of Arkansas during Reconstruction—poverty, devastation of homes and lives, military rule from 1867 to 1874, lack of education, racial tensions—necessitated cooperation on the broadest scale. Small handfuls of people could not achieve the aims which most Arkansas Baptists conceived for the church— evangelism, missions, education of ministers, and training of a growing constituency in biblical faith and practice. United in associations, they could accomplish far more.

In this depressed era the work of the associations did not proceed smoothly or easily. The number of churches participating in them fluctuated up and down year by year, as Table VI, drawn from information recorded by the **American Baptist Yearbook,** readily confirms. Although we cannot rely on particular figures in this Table, they do reflect the vicissitudes of the various associations, both white and black. Several disruptive factors stand out: the effort of blacks to find a place for themselves, continued strife over involvement in the Civil War, anti-organization sentiment, Campbellism, and the generally unsettled condition of the times.

It is not surprising, of course, that blacks would organize their own churches rather soon after the War along the lines laid down by their white counterparts, but it would be difficult to estimate how much this affected white churches or associations. Blacks seem to have developed district associations very similar to those formed by whites in the earliest phases of their history. Their first association, the First Missionary Baptist Association, presumbly organized in 1867 or 1868, claimed 225 churches and nearly 10,000 members in 1877. Other associations, however, soon challenged it and reduced its size. By 1879 there were nine black Baptist associations.

The resurrection of anti-organization, anti-mission sentiment was not surprising either. The vestige of Daniel Parker's and John Taylor's teaching did much damage in several associations. The Ouachita Association, for instance, blossomed briefly between 1868 and 1871 and then went into eclipse when the anti-missioners formed a separate association and claimed many of its churches.

All factors considered, it is remarkable that the associations held together and functioned as well as they did. In 1867 and 1868, a time of dire poverty, nine associations raised $3,000 in cash for support of ten missionaries. Reports of successful missionary or educational work, however, are rather scattered and thin; individual churches were doing the lion's share of the work. Many associations maintained missionaries as they had before the war, but the general effort staggered under a load of difficulties. In 1871, for example, the huge Dardanelle Association, composed of 52 churches, contributed only $30.75 to missions. In its annual meeting it added ten churches and dismissed twelve others to form a new association. It passed a motion recommending that its member churches not accept members baptized by "pedo-baptists, Campbellites, and Freewill Baptists." On the brighter side, it endorsed a proposal for a "male high school and female institute," passed a motion noting the need of churches at Fort Smith and Dardanelle for assistance and asking the Domestic and Indian Mission Board of the Southern Baptist Convention to help them support a competent pastor, and urged its churches to support their pastors by systematic giving as well as prayer.[9]

TABLE VI
CHURCHES AND MEMBERS IN ASSOCIATIONS, 1867-1880

Association	1867	1868	1869	1870	1871	1872	1873	1874	1875+	1877	1878	1879	1880
1. Antioch District	7	31	18				12	12	12	14	19	19	19
	1,068	878	1,566				375	375	375	601	601	601	601
2. Ark. R. Union			25	25	25								
			1,975	1,975	1,975								
3. Baptist				13	13	13	13	13	13	34	34	34	34
				453	453	453	453	453	453	1,640	1,640	1,640	1,640
4. Bartholomew			18	18	18	18	18	37	37	38	37	42	39
			838	920	920	920	920	1,473	1,473	1,571	1,600	1,650	1,600
5. Bentonville			37	37	37	30	30	30	30	30	30	30	30
			1,764	1,764	1,764	1,543	1,543	1,543	1,543	1,543	1,543	1,543	1,543
6. Bethel			314	314	314								
7. Bethlehem											24	17	17
											722	620	620
8. Blue Mountain											17	17	17
											547	547	547
9. Bradley*			....	....	....	....	....	....	....	....	....	....	....
10. Caddo River							5	6	6	6	6	6	6
							170	185	185	185	185	185	185
11. Cadron		7	7	7	7	7	7	7	7	7			
		328	328	328	328	328	328	328	328	328			
12. Cane Creek			22	22	22	22	22	22					
			430	430	430	430	430	430					
13. Clear Creek								8	8	8	8	8	8
								....	....	....	708	708	708

Association												
14. Caroline	····	····	21/1,293	21/1,293	30/1,666	30/1,666	30/1,666	34/1,923	34/1,923	34/1,671	36/1,904	36/1,904
15. Central District												28/1,597
16. Columbia	1,312	1,312	1,312									
17. Concord					36/1,689	36/1,689	36/1,689	36/1,689	36/1,689	36/1,011	36/1,011	36/1,011
18. Concord*								36/1,530	45/1,614	47/1,646	50/1,997	20/700
19. Crooked Creek	····	····	····	····	····	····	····	····	····	····	····	····
20. Dardanelle							11/250	14/319	14/319	14/319	14/319	14/319
21. East Arkansas			29/600	63/600	63/600	63/600	25/942	25/942	38/1,335	41/1,384	42/1,181	41/1,535
22. Fayetteville												29/4,054
23. First Missionary*			106/8,227	106/8,227	106/8,227	46/5,671	46/5,671	19/719	19/719	19/719	19/719	19/719
24. Friendship								77/5,000	225/9,719	190/9,719	77/5,000	39/3,850
25. Grand Prairie							24/1,099	27/1,127	22/1,042	22/1,042	22/1,042	22/1,042
26. Gum Springs	····	····	····	····	····	····	····	····	····	····	····	····
27. Independence		17/820	17/1,023	17/1,023	32/1,565	32/1,565	32/1,565	32/1,565	32/1,565	629	20/666	15/656

No.	Association													
28.	Judson		21 / 664	29 / 664	29 / 664	20 / 807	20 / 1,000	20 / 1,000	20 / 1,000	19 / 895	19 / 770	18 / 811	21 / 764	21 / 911
29.	Liberty	26 / 1,136	25 / 1,285	25 / 1,285	25 / 1,285	25 / 1,285	23 / 1,160	20 / 1,046	20 / 1,046	20 / 1,046	20 / 1,050	20 / 973	24 /	24 / ....
30.	Little Red River	....	.... / 555	.... / 545	.... / 545	.... / 545	.... / 545	.... / 545	.... / 554	17 / 577	50 / 4,220	.... / 973	20 / 661	20 / 661
31.	Missionary Baptist*									50 / 4,220		103 / 5,690	109 / 7,117	
32.	Mount Vernon	21 / 617	21 /	25 / 903	25 / 903	25 / 1,394	25 / 1,394	25 / 1,394	25 / 1,394	25 / 1,394	29 / 1,394	29 / 934	29 / 934	29 / 934
33.	Mount Zion	.... / 182	.... / 643	.... / 643	22 / 643	22 / 1,019	....	....	....	17 / 567	17 / 567	16 / 664	25 / 800	
34.	Ouachita*	....	....	22 / 1,019	22 / 1,019	22 / 1,019	22 / 1,019	22 / 1,019	22 / 1,019	22 / 1,665	22 / 1,665	22 / 1,665	22 / 1,665	
35.	Ouachita	6 / 726	6 / 726	6 / 726	....									
36.	Ouachita Anti-Mis.	....	....	....	....	....	....							
37.	Pine Bluff	18 / 1,106	21 / 982	21 / 982	21 / 982	26 / 1,052	26 / 1,052	26 / 1,052	26 / 1,052	26 / 1,052	26 / 1,052	26 / 916	26 / 916	26 / 916
38.	Red River	27 / 1,210	25 / 1,255	25 / 1,255	25 / 1,394	28 / 1,394	34 / 1,563	30 / 2,000	30 / 2,000	32 / 1,877	32 / 1,877	32 / 1,943	40 / 1,776	39 / 1,829
39.	Rocky Bayou	....	....	....	....	....	....	....	....	17 / 718	17 / 741	17 / 718	22 /	22 / 690
40.	Sabine	20 / 868	20 /	20 / 1,191	1,191	1,191	1,191	1,191	1,191	741	718	....	690	
41.	Saline	....	.... / 868	20 / 868	20 / 868	34 / 1,279	41 / 1,293	41 / 1,360	41 / 1,360	41 / 1,275	41 / 1,097	41 / 1,097	41 / 1,097	
42.	Shoal Creek	....	....	....	....	....	....	....	....					
43.	Sixth Missionary*	....	....	24	24	24	24	24	24	24	24	24	24	24

78

No.	Association											
44.	Spring River	....	....	....	1,678	1,678	1,678	1,678	1,678	1,678	1,678	1,678
									22	22	22	22
									779	779	779	779
45.	Springfield	420	420	420	420	....	....	....	....	....	....	....
46.	Springtown							....	....	....	....	....
47.	State Corner							....	....	....	....	....
48.	Union	....	....	....	19	15	19	19	19	19	19	19
					893	716	800	737	737	737	737	737
49.	Union Baptist								30	30	35	
									1,498	1,498	2,290	
50.	United					25	25	25	25	25	25	
					1,118	1,118		1,047	1,047	1,047		
51.	West Arkansas										22	
52.	White County									199	199	638
											6	6
53.	White River							17	568	568	568	8
								15	15	17	257	
54.	White R. Valley							619	591	702	702	522
										14	10	

*Indicates Black Association
+1876 omitted.

79

The Red River Association, though faced with similar problems, fared somewhat better. Recovering more quickly than many other associations from the ravages of the War, in 1870 it employed four missionaries to work among former slaves—H.H. Coleman and J.O. Browning in Clark County, J.B. Robins in Hempstead County, and David DeLaughter in Ouachita County.[10] In 1876 it founded Arkadelphia High School, a forerunner for Ouachita College ten years later.

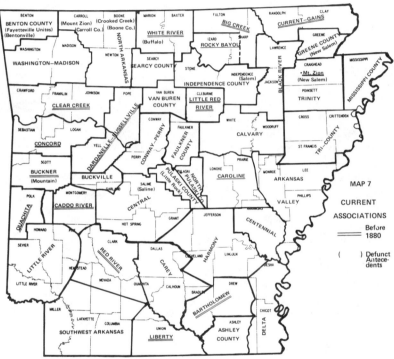

MAP 7

CURRENT
ASSOCIATIONS

═══ Before
1880

( ) Defunct
Antece-
dents

Several associations shared in the steady expansion of the Baptist constituency during this period. Bartholomew Association in the southeast, Caroline in the south central, Dardanelle in the northwest central, and Red River in the southwest central section enjoyed a steady upward trend in number of churches and members, and it is not difficult to see why these have continued to the present day. Other associations, however, barely held their own, waiting for better times. Several succumbed to internal strife and the inevitable change which the reconstruction era necessitated. Map 7 shows how many of the associations refounded during this time survived to supply a nucleus for the current associational organization of the state.

The Arkansas Baptist State Convention

New Beginnings

Like the churches and the associations, the Arkansas Baptist State Convention struggled to its feet again slowly and with considerable pain. Only a few churches and associations rallied to the initial meeting to reorganize in 1867. Through the next thirteen years the Convention wrestled with numerous tensions carried over from the War and from its own pre-war days.

The resuscitation of the Convention was, in many respects, a surprising development. In its brief history up to the war this organization had experienced considerable ambivalence and strife as to its major purpose. In addition, largely for geographical reasons, it had failed to gain the support of Baptists north of the Arkansas River, the latter forming regional conventions of their own in an effort better to achieve their own missionary goals. Finally, the Convention had barely scrambled up on its wobbly legs before the Civil War sent it crashing down again.

The revitalization of the Convention, therefore, required a powerful motive, and can be explained only by looking at several factors which worked in its favor. One of these, of course, was the simultaneous recovery and development of associational life, an activity which added impetus to the Convention movement. The fact is, most of the struggling associations needed all of the outside assistance they could find. Even if they occupied themselves chiefly with missionary or educational concerns in their own bailiwicks, they usually had a larger field of vision which persistent "hardshell" tendencies could not obscure.

A second factor in the resuscitation of the Convention was one which brought the statewide organization into existence in the first place, that is, the recognition that effecting the aims of Arkansas Baptists, zealous as most were for missions, necessitated cooperation on a broad scale. The revival of the Convention proved again that Arkansas Baptists, at least their leaders, were conscious of being heirs of the connectionalism of their forebears in England and early America.

Perhaps the most important factor was the small core of leaders committed to the revival of the Convention. We do not know how many attended the Convention in Little Rock on November 8, 1867. The meeting appears to have been informally arranged with a view to seeing whether Arkansas Baptists could pick up the pieces "that remained of the State Convention—after the lapse of several years of the effects of the 'cruel war.'"[11] Indicative of the seriousness of those who met, however, the Convention appointed a new State Mission Board and elected the Elder William M. Lea as General Missionary Agent for the state in cooperation with the American Baptist Home Mission Society. A year later, twenty persons gathered again in Little Rock and elected Lea their president as well as state missionary. Subsequently the number of those attending and the representation of churches and associations grew steadily. The Convention faltered, but it did not fail.

The State Mission Board elected in 1868 probably represents the nucleus of persons who deserve credit for the Convention's resuscitation. Among others, it included W.M. Lea; W.H. Roberts, also Secretary of the Convention; Samuel Stevenson, founder of Arkadelphia Institute; N.P. Moore, pastor in the Pine Bluff Association; E.L. Compere, at the time pastor at Fort Smith and missionary among the Creek Indians; Moses Green, founder and pastor of a church in Austin; R.J. Coleman, Recording Secretary of the Convention in 1856 and 1857; and W.D. Mayfield, pastor in Helena, elected convention president the next year. Subsequently, J.B. Searcy (1830-1920) played a major role, as General Missionary Agent for one year (1872-1873), Recording Secretary ten years, Vice-President several times, editor of the Arkansas page in J. R. Graves's **The Baptist,** and at various times pastor of numerous churches.[12]

The work of the resuscitated State Convention proceeded hesitantly and haltingly until the 1880s. The Convention lacked funds and, in a depressed financial era, it could scarcely expect to raise an adequate amount to support its programs. It had to wrestle with internal tensions and ambivalence: Campbellism, "hardshellism," and indecision about its purpose.

I alluded in the previous chapter to the struggle to define Baptist identity in the face of the "Reform" of Alexander Campbell. The War merely interrupted this process and, not surprisingly, the struggle proceeded in the same direction, by endorsing J.R. Graves's "Landmarkism." By the end of the century Arkansas Baptists were to pay a high price for this decision, but, at the time, it appeared to the majority to be the proper course to take.

The opposition of "Hardshell" Baptists to the use of means, or, more precisely, the development of institutions and programs, to carry out mission work tended to coalesce and eventually to blend into Landmarkism. A large number of persons of "Hardshell" persuasion, of course, had dropped out along the way and formed their own churches and associations. Enough remained, however, to generate waves for the revival of the State Convention as well as the associations. They made fund-raising especially difficult, and one is not surprised to note much vacillation in the reports.

Defining Goals

All of these factors, taken together, increased the difficulty of defining the objectives of the Convention. For the period 1867 to 1880 four chief concerns shine through: (1) the evangelization of the state, (2) foreign missions in cooperation with the Southern Baptist Convention, (3) education and support of ministers, and (4) training of church members through Sunday schools. But partly for economic and partly for other reasons, the emphasis on the four was variable and uneven.

The vacillation in defining objectives is most evident in the case of what is probably to be regarded as the overriding concern of Arkansas Baptists, viz. the evangelization of the state. The newly revived State Convention, reversing its pre-War decision to concentrate on education, started with a single-minded commitment to this aim, allowed the work virtually to lapse about 1874, and then, through encouragement and assistance from the Domestic and Indian (now Home) Mission Board of the Southern Baptist Convention, revived its efforts.

At its first meeting after the War, the State Convention appointed a Mission Board and elected W.M. Lea as its General Missionary Agent. During the next year, essentially, Lea supplemented mission work done by ten missionaries employed by nine of the sixteen associations then in existence. At the annual Convention in 1869 a panel composed of J.K. Murphy, B.F. Thomas, W.M. Lea, J.B. Scarcy, J.T. Craig, and J.R. Graves debated "What is the Mission of Baptists in Arkansas?" and concluded that "it is the mission of Baptists in Arkansas to let every community in Arkansas know what Baptists believe."[13] In 1871 the State Mission Board gave a depressing report about lack of funds and personnel. During the year, it had received a total of only $64.25 in cash and pledges and thus had had to appoint the Reverend J.M. Brundridge as missionary in the White River Association on a self-sustaining basis. In 1872 the situation improved slightly. The Board was able to employ six missionaries and pay them $885.45; it received $538.05

in cash and pledges.

In 1873, however, the mission effort took a bad turn. J.B. Searcy resigned after one exhausting year as General Missionary of the State. As Secretary of the State Mission Board, he reported to the Convention that, due to the economic straits of the Convention (in a depression year), the Board had appointed no missionary agents. During the year, it had received only $125.50 except for $12 more given at the preceding Convention. Of this amount it paid T.A. Reid, pastor at Pine Bluff, $32.45 and J.B. Searcy, as General Missionary Agent, $94.05. One other missionary, the Elder H.E. Hempstead, was working under the Board's appointment as a self-sustaining missionary in "a very destitute place on the southeastern border of the state."[14] The financially distressed Convention disbanded the State Mission Board and turned its work over to two General Missionary-Secretaries, J.D. Rasberry for the territory south and T.P. Boone for that north of Little Rock. This could have eased the difficulties of travel, especially crossing the Arkansas River. Probably for financial reasons, however, neither of these men had undertaken to fulfill the work entrusted to them when the Convention met in 1875. For the time being, missions came to a standstill.

The mission pump did not remain dormant long, however. In 1877 it was primed through the reestablishment of ties with the Domestic and Indian Mission Board of the Southern Baptist Convention. A Committee on Domestic Missions—composed of Samuel Stevenson, M.D. Early, A.M. Russell, W.N. Chadoin, J.B. Searcy, W.H. Passley, and J.M. Hart—took note of "considerable destitution in parts of the State that ought to be supplied" and the offer of help from the SBC and recommended the appointment of one or more missionaries to work in destitute areas under the direction of the Executive Board of the Convention. Noting areas of special need (Pine Bluff, Helena, Batesville, Jacksonport, Camden, and "many other smaller towns"), they urged a collection by the Convention, which netted $276.25.[15] The next year, W.A. Clark, who had been employed as General Missionary Agent, beginning January 1, reported visits to 42 churches, 82 baptisms, 53 professions not by baptism, travels of 4,164 miles, and a collection of $481.55. In 1878 the Committee on Domestic Missions gave its most encouraging report since the Civil War. Noting "progress," they concluded that "The advancement made, we think for the last few years, is to be attributed largely to the state missionaries who have been sent by the Board of this convention, and whose visits to the various parts of our

State have been highly appreciated by the people and in many instances they were much blessed of God."[16] They proceeded to encourage enlarged effort and sacrificies and recommended that attention of state missionaries be focused on "well known localities of much importance, . . ."[17]

It is not hard to see why the work often languished until the 1880s. Travel throughout the state was prohibitive, and the Convention simply did not have the funds to employ an adequate number of personnel. Small wonder that a dedicated missionary tendered his resignation after a single year! In 1873, for example, J.B. Searcy reported that he had traveled 5,000 miles, preached 154 sermons, baptized 104 persons, and ordained two deacons. He had assisted churches in Camden, Magnolia, Batesville, Pine Bluff, and Little Rock secure sites for buildings, obtain financing, find pastors, and do myriad other tasks to put Baptist work on a solid footing. A few years later (1882), the completion of a railway network throughout Arkansas would ease the job, but in this era only the strong and dedicated could survive.

The State Convention did not do a somersault concerning its priorities as it had before the War. It did, however, manifest strong interest in the other three areas of concern. Alongside its concern for the evangelization of Arkansas, it displayed a striking interest in foreign missions, particularly a mission which the Southern Baptist Convention initiated in Italy in 1870. In 1871 the Convention appointed a standing Committee on Foreign Missions (J.B. Searcy, T.B. Espy, and R.M. Thrasher) and collected $65, stipulating that $25 should go to Rome, a remarkable amount considering that cash and pledges for home missions that year totaled a meager $64.25! Reports of contributions of Arkansas Baptists to Foreign and Home Missions between 1873 and 1880 reveal the level of interest in each. Some states reversed the pattern.

Year	Foreign Missions	Home Missions
1873	$145.55	$ 45.96
1874	53.03	18.25
1875	124.80	31.00
1876	192.00	25.10
1877	462.75	4.65
1878	265.82	25.80
1879	119.31	1,032.90
1880	248.85	34.00

J.B. Searcy later served several terms as Vice-President of the Foreign Mission Board of the Southern Baptist Convention.

Concern for education of ministers, an all-consuming interest just prior to the War, heated up again gradually as the Convention resumed its work. In 1869 the Convention organized a Board of Ministerial Education and instructed it "to adopt the most energetic means to raise as soon as possible the sum of $10,000" for education of ministers and to open an annual "Ministerial Institute" of five or six days for lectures on relevant issues. In 1870 a committee appointed to draft a revised plan recommended an annual stipend of $150 for education of young ministers approved by their churches. Meantime, the Board of Ministerial Education employed W.M. Lea and E.L. Compere as agents to solicit money for ministerial education. The first year, they obtained $850.95 in cash and $2,000 in pledges, plus donations of land, for this purpose. In 1871 and again in 1872 the Board reported cash and pledges totaling almost $2,500 and support of numerous young ministers in various schools, including Mississippi College, adopted in 1870 as the official school of Arkansas Baptists. The fund for ministerial education suffered a drastic drop in 1873 and 1874, however, due to the panic and a drought which followed. Meantime, sentiment in favor of a state college mounted, peaking in 1877. In that year the Committee on Education, citing education as a key to "the evangelization of the world," insisted that the time had come for the establishment of a college.

The Convention also gave increasing attention to the establishment of Sunday schools throughout the state. In 1869 the Committee on Sunday Schools posited it as the second duty of every Baptist church, just behind procuring a pastor and meeting his needs, "to organize and sustain a Baptist Sunday School" and to use literature published by the Sunday School Board of the Southern Baptist Convention, especially **Kind Words**.[18] In 1871 the Convention appointed a committee of five "to gather statistics, and to advise in reference to the Sunday school work" and present these for discussion the next year.[19] Unfortunately the state of the work and the ardors of travel forbade any accurate assessment. In 1874 the committee reported that a State Sunday School Convention had been organized a few months before and recommended the appointment of a Sunday School Agent, a suggestion followed up by the Convention, which appointed O.M. Lucas. When the work of the Sunday School Convention failed to justify its continuance, the

Sunday School committee recommended that the Arkansas Baptist State Convention undertake promotion of Sunday schools and

> *adopt such policy as will be calculated to revive this interest in every part of the State and hasten the time when every church shall have its Sunday-school, or rather, when the Sunday-school will be all the members of the church engaged on the Lord's day in teaching the Gospel to all under its influence, both old and young;. . .* [20]

They also called for the appointment of a State Sunday School Secretary, R.M. Thrasher, to gather statistics, establish ties with the Domestic and Indian Mission Board of the Southern Baptist Convention, Marion Alabama, and work with Sunday schools throughout the state.

The statistics on Sunday schools carried by the **American Baptist Yearbook** cannot be trusted to give a true picture of the work in Arkansas. They suggest, however, a depressed condition and strong resistance to Sunday schools until about 1880. Compared to the number and size of Sunday schools remained infinitesimal, as Table VII shows.

TABLE VII
SUNDAY SCHOOLS, 1871-1880

Year	Churches	Sunday Schools	Enrollment Churches	S.S.	Benevolent Contributions
1871	648	100	36,040	5,000	$5,452.71
1872	763	100	38,666	5,000	5,452.71
1873	830	75	39,444	3,000	779.45
1874	907	75	44,901	3,000	5,572.00
1875	949	75	46,460	3,000	2,220.55
1876	. . . . Report Not Available				
1877	993	75	44,619	3,000	176.90
1878	1,101	75	48,005	3,000	1,565.00
1879	1,110	80	47,398	4,000	2,756.67
1880	1,118	100	52,798	5,000	5,207.80

The slow response of Arkansas Baptists to the Sunday School movement can be attributed to several factors: (1) the lack of definite promotion of Sunday school work by the State Convention; (2) the emphasis pastors gave to preaching, "soul winning," and doing mission work to the exclusion of teaching and training of church members; (3) opposition to Sunday schools as unscriptural; (4) the fact that, initially, Sunday schools were designed for children only, not for all persons; (5) the absence of strong leadership, especially in the predominately rural churches of the state; (6) the isolation of many churches combined with poor transportation, making it difficult to maintain regular schools; and (7) until 1891, the lack of a southwide Sunday School Board to promote Sunday school work. After 1891 Sunday school work improved markedly.

Looking back over the preceding discussion, it becomes evident at a glance that Arkansas Baptists placed the evangelization of the state on the top rung of their ladder. They realized increasingly, however, that they could not accomplish this aim without education of ministers at the college and seminary levels and of the Baptist constituency through Sunday schools. These two concerns caused them to focus their attention on the establishment of academies, high schools, and a state college and to push for vastly improved Sunday school programs. In both of these they rode the tide along with Baptists throughout the South, but they responded also to their particular times and needs. Because of the times, they could scarcely do more than lay a foundation. But they at least began to lay one on which they could build in the 'eighties and 'nineties.

Two Other General Associations

It should probably come as no surprise that two other general associations came into existence during this period, not so much to compete with the Arkansas Baptist State Convention as to supplement its work in certain regions, for travel was still exceptionally difficult in some parts of the state and one general organization hardly sufficed to meet needs everywhere.

The Baptist General Association of Western Arkansas and Indian Territory held its first session November 24-25, 1876 at Charleston in Franklin County. Like the Arkansas Baptist State Convention, it opened the door for participation of churches, associations and individuals. The Association articulated four objectives: (1) promotion of "missionary operations, and especially home missions"; (2) "dissemination of Religious and Denominational Literature"; (3) promotion of Sunday schools; and (4) establishing and maintaining "a literary institution of high order in our territory."[21] At this first session the Association appointed a Board of Trustees to discharge the fourth task, which appears to have been the primary one. The result was the immediate opening of Buckner College at Witcherville.

In the 1880s some friction arose between the State Convention and the Association, evidently regarding the college, but the Association appointed a delegation composed of E.L. Compere and six other ministers to visit the State Convention. As a result, the tension subsided.

The work of the General Association of Western and Indian Territory paralleled that of the State Convention. It employed E.L. Compere as General Missionary Agent with special responsibiltiy for evangelizing the Creek Indians, a neglected aspect of Arkansas Baptist work. Subsequently its missionaries included some Indians, for instance, W.J. Crowder, a Choctaw, and John Jumper, a Seminole. In 1898, the year before the Association disbanded at Shawnee, Oklahoma, its Mission Board listed for the preceding year, among other items, 63 missionaries, 530 baptisms, the organization of 19 churches and 56 Sunday Schools, the ordination of 20 ministers, the building and repairing of 14 church houses, travels of 30,019 miles by missionaries, collection of $2,319.75 on the field for missions, and donation of $3,644 worth of clothing by Women's Mission Societies. It also received $2,175 from the Home Mission Board of the Southern Baptist Convention toward pay of missionaries.

In the interest of preserving harmony vis-a-vis the Buckner and Ouachita Associations and the Arkansas Baptist State Convention the Association discontinued its work in September, 1899. The decision had an important bearing on continuance of mission work in Oklahoma.

The other regional organization which supplemented the State Convention's work for a time was the Baptist General Association of Southeast Arkansas. This Association, organized in October, 1875 at New Edinburgh, was formed, like the Baptist General Associaiton of Western Arkansas and Indian Territory, to achieve educational and evangelistic aims. It immediately laid plans for founding Centennial Baptist Institute and hired two ministers to do mission work. Testimony of the fact that this Association did not mean to compete with the State Convention is the fact that J.B. Searcy was one of its leaders. To avert conflict, however, in 1879 the State Convention dispatched a special committee to visit both associations and express fraternal regard for them and interest in their work. The General Association of Southeast Arkansas continued both educational and mission work until about 1882 when fire destroyed Centennial; thereafter, it ceased operation.[21a]

The Churches Inside Out

Baptist church life did not change a great deal during this period. The average congregation struggled to kindle new life from the skeleton left by the War. During his year as General Missionary Agent for the Arkansas Baptist State Convention (1872-1873), J.B. Searcy compiled graphic descriptions of the state of affairs in Camden, Magnolia, Batesville, Pine Bluff, and Little Rock. His description of the situation in Camden is revealing and merits lengthy quotation.

> ...*Here I found a noble little band of brethren and sisters last winter without house or pastor. Having long been neglected, they were very much discouraged. Yet they have a rented hall and a good Sunday School. However, it seemed to them like idle tales of getting a house of worship and a pastor. With earnest zeal, and I believe God's blessings we went to work. Received some valuable accessions by letter and baptism. A committee to build or buy a church house was appointed. Your Missionary was made a member of that committee. After much earnest labor and prayer an unfinished brick building formerly owned by this church, but which passed out of their hands during the war was purchased at the reduced price of $2,000 to be paid in three equal installments. The prime cost of putting up the house having been about $13,000. The money was raised and paid for the first installment and the deed procured. The completion of the house to the extent that it would do for a place of worship and a Sabbath School purposes were put under contract. This work has been done in a very satisfactory manner, on very reasonable terms, and nearly all paid for. The house is now used for preaching and Sabbath School purposes. They have recently called Brother L.W. Coleman as pastor and agree on their part to pay him $200, together with his board and lodging for the next year, and they expect us to supplement his salary with enough to keep*

90

him there. The place is already one of vast commercial importance and bids fair to greatly increase when the Ouachita Valley Railroad reaches there, which will place them in direct connection with St. Louis.[22]

Dr. Searcy's account alludes to several facets of Baptist church life which must have been common in the post-war era. Congregations frequently met for several years in temporary quarter. Many, as in territorial days, met in the homes of members. Others, such as Board Camp in Ouachita Association and Mount Zion in Phillips County, met in school houses until they could erect their own buildings. The First Baptist Church of Fayetteville, as noted earlier, resumed worship after the war in an unnamed building and then met in the Masonic Hall until 1879 when they could erect a small frame edifice.

Most church houses were probably still rectangular buildings of log construction. When the Baptist congregation in Searcy erected a new structure about 1870, for example, they built one long room, thirty-five by forty feet, with two smaller rooms on each side of the pulpit. The building cost $4,000.[23] The unusual Twelve Corners Church mentioned earlier was also made of logs but arranged in the form of a cross. Three of the four sections were approximately eighteen feet square while that in which the rostrum and pulpit stood was shallower. The building, even though log, thus accommodated a large congregation, all of whom could readily see and hear the preacher.[24]

Even before the Civil War, as noted in the preceding chapter, a few buildings of frame or brick construction began to appear. They would not have been common, for lumber and bricks would have been extremely expensive until improved transportation made them available at lower cost. The fact that the Camden congregation had erected such a building before the War shows the affluence of Baptists in some of the southern counties.

Extensive discussion and numerous exhortations in records of the State Convention and associations indicate that churches throughout Arkansas provided poorly for pastors and their families. Judging by the discussions, few churches had awakened to the necessity of systematic giving and paying stated salaries. In fact, many "hardshells" objected strenuously to either custom. It was not until the next period of their history that most churches raised the level of their support enough to secure properly trained ministers who could devote most of their time to their evangelistic and pastoral roles. In this period, as in the preceding one, the number of churches still nearly doubled the number of pastors, a fact which necessitated infrequent and irregular services.

TABLE VIII
CHURCHES AND MINISTERS, 1867-1880

Year	Churches	Ordained Ministers
1867	331	149
1868	424	181
1869	499	312
1870	539	284
1871	648	408
1872	763	497
1873	830	432
1874	907	490
1875	949	510
1876	.... Report Not Available	
1877	993	467
1878	1,101	552
1879	1,110	535
1880	1,118	616

Worship services continued with little alteration. The "usual services" consisted chiefly of preaching, singing, and praying. John Q. Wolf, a citizen of Batesville, described services during his boyhood in the Ozarks in the 1870s. For several years there were no church houses in his neighborhood, so that preaching normally took place once a month in a member's home. When two church houses were built, the monthly services remained the norm. Wolf recalled that the sermons were long and tedious.[25] Singing played an increasingly large role in Baptist worship. Ray Granade, in a history of the First Baptist Church of Arkadelphia, has observed that choirs led worship of that church probably as early as the 1870s and certainly by the early 1880s.[26] Many Baptist churches, however, still had no instrumental music.

Churches still usually baptized out-of-doors at the end of a summer revival. Only a few had baptistries constructed in their buildings. About 1870 the Baptist Church in Searcy constructed a baptistry under the pulpit. For baptisms pulpit and podium were scooted aside and the floor opened back on hinges revealing the baptistry.[27]

If the statistics cited earlier are accurate, ten or fifteen percent of the churches conducted Sunday schools. Most of these were small and irregular. When J.D.J. Faulkner came to Greene County in 1874, for instance, the seven Baptist churches in the County had a little Sunday school only during the months of good weather. No meetings were held in the winter months because of bad roads and unheated buildings.[28]

Discipline in Baptist churches seems to have grown stricter during the post-War era as problems mounted. Social turmoil—marauders and bandits, the Ku Klux Klan, the Brooks-Baxter War, general lawlessness—probably equalled or surpassed that of territorial era. The notorious James boys—Jesse and Frank—even made one foray into Arkansas on January 15, 1874. Curiously both were "good" Baptists. Jesse always carried a Bible, prayed fervently, and treated his mother well. The Jameses ended their bank-robbing career on September 7, 1876 after barely escaping a foiled plot to rob a Minnesota bank. Both lived respectable lives until Jesse was killed six years later by a former associate. Frank gave himself up and received a pardon.

Indicative of the ruggedness of the times, President Grant appointed Judge Isaac Parker to preside over the Federal Court at Fort Smith, which had jurisdiction only in Indian Territory. Parker earned the dubious title of "the hanging judge." During his tenure, the Court tried nearly 10,000 persons. Parker sentenced 168 to be hanged, building a gallows which would execute twelve persons at once.

Against this background one can understand readily why Baptist churches tended to apply rigorous discipline. The statistics reported to the **American Baptist Yearbook,** as seen in Table IX, reflect an unusually high number of exclusions compared to restorations.

Exclusions resulted from several infractions: non-attendance, drunkenness, or breaches of fellowship. Bethesda near Alleene in Little River County, for instance, a church formed in 1863, excluded members absent from three consecutive services without a good excuse.[29] During and after the Civil War, alcoholism became one of the chief social ills, especially on the frontier. Although Baptists were not teetotalers at first, they became that as alcoholism increased. Consequently, they took a strong stand against public drunkenness and quickly excluded offenders. The figures for these

TABLE IX
DISCIPLINE, 1867-1880

Year	Exclusions	Restorations
1867	93	25
1868	148	42
1869	202	59
1870	130	75
1871	264	135
1872	315	68
1873	36	9
1874	164	59
1875	296	112
1876	.... Report Not Available	
1877	151	50
1878	713	428
1879	340	167
1880	460	298

years, however, were inflated further by exclusions over breaches of fellowship or doctrine.

An interesting illustration of doctrinal discipline is the case of Samuel Kelley. Born of an illustrious family in Clark County, Louisiana Territory, now Pike County, Arkansas, in May of 1817, Kelley moved to Illinois in 1838, married, and was ordained a Baptist minister. In 1849 he returned to Arkansas and became a farmer, a mill operator, and a member of the state legislature. When his term in the legislature expired, he became pastor of the Friendship Baptist Church in the Red River Association. In this capacity he was invited to preach the candle-light sermon in the annual meeting of the Caddo River Baptist Association in 1856. In his sermon he vividly endorsed the doctrine of final apostasy, an anathema among Baptists of Calvinistic background. The next morning, the Association passed the following resolutions:

> *Resolved, that we will not receive or hold in our fellowship a member that has never been baptized by a Baptist.*
>
> *Resolved, that the Friendship Church is illegally constituted from the fact that Elder Samuel Kelley assisted in her constitution, who has never been baptized by a Baptist, and also the said Kelley preaches the final apostacy of those who have been regenerated.*
>
> *Resolved, that we drop correspondence with the Red River Association because she holds churches in her fellowship, that hold members in their fellowship who have never been baptized by a Baptist.*[30]

The two associations later settled their differences and restored fellowship with one another. Between 1869 and 1870, however, the Philippi Church of the Caddo River Baptist Association began to practice open communion as a result of Kelley's influence. The church also began to call itself Philippi Church of Christ (no relation to the body or churches known as the Churches of Christ). The Association thereupon withdrew fellowship from the Philippi Church. Kelley, however, had enough of a following in other churches that these too joined his movement. Today five such churches still exist in Hot Springs and Clark Counties, relating to each other in the Council of the Church of Christ.[31]

Baptists in Arkansas Society

Baptist stock rose markedly during the Civil War as a result of the contribution of Baptists to the war effort. In the post-War years it continued to rise as the number of Baptists, churches, and associations increased. The conservation of such gains, however, depended, as numerous leaders recognized, on the education of the Baptist constituency at a level commensurate with that of the society at large. A primary concern, as Baptists elsewhere also discerned, was, for obvious reasons, the training of ministers who could take the lead in the evangelization of the state, and, as we have seen, Arkansas Baptists pursued that concern with fervor. But ministerial education could not remain the sole concern. If Baptists were to make a real impact they had to educate their whole constituency at a level commensurate with that of the populace as a whole. Accordingly, in 1871 the Board of Ministerial Education, headed by W.D. Mayfield, clearly articulated the importance of educating the entire

Baptist constituency.

> *Our sons and daughters must be educated, if we would keep pace with this enlightened civilization. Every Baptist who fails in this matter neglects one of his highest duties to posterity. Our ministers, our children, all the people, must be educated. This is a part of our glorious mission to which our hearts and hands should be given. . . Our hope for the future is lodged in the question of education. We hope Baptists appreciate this fact, and will do what they can to push forward the good work.*[32]

Perceptions of this fact added to the incentive of Arkansas Baptists to found academies, high schools, and a college which could educate both men and women.

We have noted already that, prior to the Civil War, Baptists, either privately or together, opened a number of schools for both males and females. On the very eve of the War in 1860, as a matter of fact, the Caroline Association endeavored to establish "Caroline Female Institute." The War, however, wiped out all of these institutions; after it, Baptists had to begin with a clean slate.

The post-War educational revival began at the associational level. Judson Baptist "University" opened at Judsonia in 1871 under the leadership of R.M. Forey, who served as President until 1874. Not a university in the proper sense, it aspired to become the Baptist state college. From 1870 on, however, ministerial students from Arkansas had been given stipends to attend Mississippi College, at the invitation of the Mississippi Baptist State Convention. The effort of Judson to obtain statewide sanction led to a showdown at the State Convention in Searcy in 1876. No split occurred over the matter, but the Convention continued to favor Mississippi College until Ouachita was founded ten years later.[33]

Shiloh Baptist Institute, endorsed by the Fayetteville, Dardanelle, and State Corner Associations in Arkansas and the Shoal Creek Association in Missouri, was founded at Springdale in Washington County in 1872 under the leadership of the Reverend Lewis Barnes. A special committee appointed by the State Convention in 1872, noting that the Shiloh Institute was "the first Denominational School established in the State,"[34] followed up a request of messengers from the Springfield Association in recommending adoption of the school by the State Convention. It, too, functioned only a few years before closing. This evidently occurred in 1878, for, while it was mentioned in the list of schools meriting Baptist patronage in the report of a Committee on Education in 1878, it was not mentioned in 1879.

Centennial Baptist Institute, sponsored by "The Baptist General Association of Southeast Arkansas" under the leadership of J.B. Searcy, M.S. Kennard, and other leaders in the southeast, opened at Warren in January, 1876, with Professor Kennard as president. It prospered for several years. In 1880 it enrolled 100 students. As noted earlier, it closed a few years later after fire consumed its building.

Red River Baptist Academy and Arkadelphia Baptist High School were founded in 1876 by the Red River Association and located on property purchased from the state which had once housed the State Institute for the Blind. In 1880 the High School enrolled 175 students. In 1886 Ouachita College located its campus on the same grounds.

Forrest City Baptist High School opened in 1876 after five years of debate in the Mount Vernon Association. This school, headed first by the Reverend Joseph Shackelford, lasted only five years, experiencing difficulties throughout its history.

Buckner College at Witcherville was evidently operating under the presidency of E.L. Compere when the Arkansas Baptist State Convention met at Monticello in 1876, for the Committee on Education recommended it for Baptist patronage as one of "the schools already established." As noted earlier, it was organized, owned, and operated by the General Association of Western Arkansas and Indian Territory. In 1883 the Trustees reported that the school had almost completed a building and enrolled "a good number of students."[35] Casting a wary eye toward Arkadelphia at the opening of the new college sponsored by the State Convention, the Education Committee, denying that Buckner would compete with Ouachita, urged support for it. They emphasized the time and money already expended and the need of Baptists of the West for "an institution of learning to cherish and love." For about three years, 1887-1890, the college came under Episcopal control after Episcopalians assumed a mortgage on the property, but it returned to Baptist hands in 1891. In 1904 the property was transferred to the General (Landmark) Association, but this group, though continuing to hold title to the property, did not maintain a school on the same grounds.

In each session of the Arkansas Baptist State Convention from

1877 on sentiment mounted in favor of withdrawing support from schools outside the state, such as Mississippi College, and investing it in Arkansas schools. Because Arkansas lacked comparable schools and numerous ministers had received their training at Mississippi College, leaders voiced this sentiment cautiously. In 1878, nonetheless, a Committee on Education chaired by W.E. Paxton, President of Centennial Institute, cited the six schools named above as evidence that "the Baptists of Arkansas are not content to yield the palm to others in this work," claiming that "In these institutions we afford the very best facilities for academic training."[36] A year later, a Committee on Education composed of W.A. Forbes, W.A. Clark and W.F. Mack cited growth of these institutions as "an index of the real prosperity of our denomination" and insisted that "it is necessary to our future success that, all things being equal, Arkansas Baptists should patronize home institutions." This Committee recommended hearty support of schools endorsed by "Associations, General or Local," citing five of the six schools named above, omitting Shiloh Institute, which had evidently closed.[37]

In this same period pressures mounted also in favor of the establishment of a genuine college supported by the State Convention. In 1877 a Committee on Education chaired by Joseph Shackleford, President of Forrest City High School, pressed the argument, anticipating objections.

> We fully endorse the sentiment that religious bodies ought to exercise a fostering care over institutions of learning, and not only this, but they should establish such institutions when it is in their power to do so. Religion and learning are by no means antagonistic. Together they exert a most salutary influence and triumph most signally when most closely allied. Since the era of the Reformation, the ministers and votaries of religion have been the most devoted and successful students, instructors and authors in all the various departments of learning. And in the future progress of her effort for the evangelization of the world Christianity is destined to confer on learning the highest honor in employing it as her chief auxiliary.[38]

The Committee named a College Committee of thirteen to proceed with the reviving of the "Arkansas Baptist College" project. In 1878 the Committee on Education responded further to what, by this time, were open objections to a college in language designed to convince a largely agrarian constituency.

The first great want of the people is primary education, but to stop with this is to arrest the progress of civilization in its infancy. As well might the husbandman content himself with the primitive implements of husbandry, discarding these wonderful inventions of modern times for saving labor and increasing productiveness. Higher education bears the same relation to elementary, that the reaping and threshing machines do to the ancient sickle and flail. This is a happy element in our mental and moral constitution that we aspire to better and higher things. But for this principle, ignorance and barbarism would become crystalized and human progress would be arrested. It is a hopeful sign that our people are waking up to high appreciation of advanced education, and it is greatly to the credit of our denomination that we have won the distinction of being the leading educator of this land.[39]

The appeal was strongly put, but it did not effect its aim immediately. Most Arkansas Baptists, having limited educational backgrounds themselves, could not appreciate higher education. In addition, most had limited funds themselves and could not be expected to contribute to something they could not support with enthusiasm. Arkansas, like other southern states, was far from recovering its economic equilibrium; that would take many more years. Further, the financial problem was exacerbated by the fact that potential support for a state college was being siphoned off in support for several other schools. As a public educational system developed, this problem would be alleviated. At the moment it was severe. Before Ouachita opened, most of the other schools closed— Shiloh in 1878, Forrest City in 1881, and Judson in 1883. Only Buckner College, too far toward the northwestern corner of the state to offer serious competition, and Arkadelphia Baptist High School remained when Ouachita was founded in 1886. It is significant of the financial situation that Ouachita was located on the property owned by the latter.

Women in Arkansas Baptist History

To this point, we have not taken special note of the contributions of women to the work of Arkansas Baptists, citing only instances here and there in which they played a role in organizing churches or in fostering missions. The reason for this omission is not that women contributed little or nothing in the first two periods of Arkansas Baptist history. Quite the contrary, earlier discussion shows that women accompanied the first settlers and that many of them, such as the wives of John Young Lindsey and Isaac Watkins, supported and assisted their spouses in founding churches. Women also accompanied their husbands as missionaries. Moreover, it was the request of "two or three pious and cross bearing old sisters" which brought David Orr to Arkansas Territory in 1828. Finally, the names of numerous women appear in the annals of early churches, if not specifically stating at least implying that they played leading roles.

In the pioneer setting of early Arkansas it was to be expected that women would sometimes assume unusual leadership positions by virtue of the absence of males. An outstanding illustration of this is the case of Sarah Gardner Hale, who moved to the Hot Springs area in 1831 from the mountains of Tennessee with her husband, John C. Hale, and several small children. Although John Hale was a devout Baptist, Mrs. Hale evidently took the lead in the family's exercise of faith. In 1835 the Hales acquired from a John Percival the title to property upon which the whole of Hot Springs is now located. The next year, they deeded a plot of ground for a church and paid for the erection of the first log church building there, completed in 1843.[40]

Mrs. Hale has been described as "leader, director, backbone, financial supporter, and advisor" of this church.[41] In fact, she sustained it for years and was consulted in all aspects of its management. It has been reported that, during her active years, she made sure that the church doors opened every Sunday morning, rain or shine. If no preacher was available, as often happened, she took her Bible, selected a portion of the scriptures, read and commented on it, and conducted her own worship services. A "close communionist," when the Lord's Supper was observed, she saw to it that non-members were invited to leave; no one except members of the local congregation were allowed to remain. When the original log structure and its furnishings burned in 1860, or possibly the latter part of 1859, "Grandma" Hale, as she came to be called, contracted

100

with Sam T. Henderson to build a frame house on the grounds known as the "Mud Hole." The Masons, who had lost their building by fire a few years before, requested Mrs. Hale's permission to build a hall above the church, a request which she granted with the proviso that the lodge make satisfactory arrangements with Mr. Henderson, a member. When in late years Mrs. Hale could no longer attend worship services, the deacons still consulted her about church affairs.[42]

Another woman who, in this early period, figured prominently in Arkansas Baptist history was George Ann Bledsoe. A resident of Tulip and possessed of considerable wealth, she played a substantial role in the forumulation of the Arkansas Baptist State Convention. She, her pastor, the Reverend W.H. Bayliss, and Colonel Nathaniel G. Smith laid plans for the organizational meeting of the Convention in Tulip in 1848. Unfortunately, Mrs. Bledsoe died before this meeting took place. An ardent supporter of missions, however, before she died she willed her large square piano, a priceless possession at the time, to be sold and the proceeds applied to the missionary cause.

Other names could be mentioned. Of more immediate interest here, however, is the woman's movement which resulted from the social changes wrought by the Civil War. During the War, as one would expect, women were compelled by the circumstances to perform many functions they did not usually perform. Besides keeping their homes together as their companions marched off to fight, the affluent superintended the planting and gathering of crops and the poor planted, cultivated, and harvested the crops themselves. Women of all stations spun thread, wove cloth, and cut and made uniforms for soldiers as well as their own families. They nursed the sick and wounded. Observing that women were "as active as men, or more so, in missionary and every other good work" during this time, J.B. Searcy recorded a personal reminiscence of the direct involvement of women in the battle situation:

> On Saturday, April 30, 1864, the battle of Jenkins Ferry, on Saline River in Arkansas, Dr. B.A. Jowdon, a prominent Baptist and personal friend of mine, asked me to go take charge of a field hospital. He said he would furnish me all the nurses I wanted. I entered upon the work with good help. Next day was the Sabbath. We had no appetizing food for the wounded men, but, perhaps by

10 o'clock, that day women began to pour in from the surrounding country with a great variety of appetizing dishes, all of which they put in my charge. I served to the nurses and the nurses to the wounded men. We all rejoiced that the Lord had given us such good friends as these dear women. Doubtless this was true at divers other hospitals.[43]

Similar incidents were indeed happening in other places. Relief societies were formed by districts throughout the South and, when wounded soldiers were brought to any city, they received immediate help from patriotic women.

Women also assumed new roles in schools and churches as a result of the War. Before the War women ordinarily did not teach except in connection with service as governesses on large plantations. In the absence of able-bodied men and adequate funds, few schools were able to remain open during the War. We know, however, that, in a number of instances, women on plantations gathered children (and sometimes slaves, though their education was a debatable practice) and taught them the fundamentals, chiefly through study of the Bible. In some uplands areas they may occasionally have kept schools going in their homes.

Some Baptists maintained a concern for the education of women both before and after the War, though we cannot assume uniformity of attitudes. In 1858, in the midst of its powerful education drive, the Arkansas Baptist State Convention unanimously adopted a resolution sustaining the importance of education for women as for men.

We feel the great importance of Female Education to the rising generation, both socially and religiously. Therefore, be it resolved that we earnestly entreat our brethren throughout the State to consider well this is an important subject, and, whatever they do, not to neglect the education of their daughters.[44]

The Committee added its endorsement of the Fayetteville Institute, the Camden Female Institute, and the Arkadelphia Female Institute. Associations in the more affluent southern part of the state also supported the education of women and, as we have seen, operated schools for that purpose.

Although it was not customary for women to teach prior to the War, some women's schools did employ women. In 1854 the faculty of the Camden Female Institute included Miss H.M.R. Southwick, instructor of English and drawing; Miss E. Maddox, instructor of English; and Miss M. H. Hartwell, daughter of the Reverend Jessie Hartwell, proprietor and principal of the school, instructor of music and embroidery. Similar arrangements were made following the Civil War as new schools appeared.

We do not know the exact roles which women played in the Sunday school movement which began to make a weak start during the period under discussion. Sabbath or Sunday schools unquestionably aimed at religious education for both boys and girls, but it did not include adults at this time, as a report of the Committee on Sunday Schools to the Arkansas Baptist State Convention in 1874 suggests. This report urged adoption of a policy calculated to "hasten the time. . . when Sunday-school will be all the members of the church engaged on the Lord's day in teaching the Gospel to all under its influence, both old and young."[45] We have no way to determine how many women led or taught Sunday Schools, but it is likely that the number was significant and had much to do with the growth of a women's movement in Arkansas as elsewhere.

The principal outlet for the energies and efforts of women in Baptist life, however, was in the mission movement. The enlargement of the role of women in Arkansas, of course, coincided with the world missionary movement, which was reaching a peak about the time the Civil War erupted. Shortly after the turn of the nineteenth century women, more than men, got caught up in the movement to form societies in support of the world mission effort. In the South tensions over slavery and then the Civil War itself interrupted a vast organizing effort in support of missions. Just after the War, however, in 1867, Baptist women organized the Baptist Female Missionary Prayer Meeting in Baltimore to collect funds for the Canton Baptist Mission in its effort to reach Chinese women. This group soon focused their prayer efforts on the appointment of unmarried women missionaries by the Foreign Mission Board of the Southern Baptist Convention. The concern was aroused by reports coming out of China that women alone could reach the isolated and carefully secluded women of oriental homes. The efforts of women in Baltimore led gradually to the formation of women's missionary societies throughout the South and, before the end of 1872, to the appointment of two unmarried women missionaries: Edmonia Moon of Virginia to North Carolina and Lula Whilden of South Carolina to the South China Mission.

As might be expected in view of the frontier situation of the state, Arkansas lagged behind other southern states in organizing women's missionary societies. Actually a statewide organization called the Central Committee, was not formed until 1883. Prior to that time, however, a number of churches responded to the recommendation of the Woman's Work Committee of the Southern Baptist Convention in 1876 that every Baptist church establish a female missionary society "which all the ladies should be invited to join."[46] One can understand the hesitation here, for the Southern Baptist Convention itself moved timorously in recognizing the growing contribution of women and even more timorously in encouraging organization of women's work. A strong approval for the organization of Central Committees in states did not come from the Southern Baptist Convention until 1878.

The organizing of women's missionary effort was a big step for Arkansas Baptists, not taken until the next period of their history. It was made possible, as elsewhere, by recognition of women's contributions and achievements. Mary Brantley (afterwards Mr. C.B. Davidson) perhaps symbolized the evolution of attitudes taking place. When a new Baptist church was organized in the home of her parents in Little Rock following the War, two earlier ones having succumbed (one to the Reformer's movement, the other to War), Mary, then a young girl and a charter member of the church, went about the village announcing the impending services at the church to each Baptist home. Because of her faithful service, she earned the nickname of "the Baptist Bell" of Little Rock. Years later, she served as the Corresponding Secretary of the state Women's Missionary Union.

White and Black

The Civil War left Arkansas impoverished. The state treasury stood empty in 1865. Poverty was rife. From June, 1865 to September, 1866 the government issued 1,705,000 food rations in Arkansas and Missouri. Ex-jayhawkers and ex-bushwackers turned bandits marauded and terrorized the northern and western parts of the state. The sharecropper system developed. Blacks returned to plantations for housing, food, and a twenty acre plot of land. Later the system was extended to whites also.

Over President Andrew Johnson's veto in 1867 the "Reconstruction Act" divided the South into five military districts—Arkansas and Mississippi comprising the fourth. June 20, 1867

Congress voted Arkansas back into the Union as the basis of its adoption of a "Reconstruction Constitution." Powell Clayton, a "carpetbagger" (a northerner working toward "reconstruction" in the South), succeeded Isaac Murphy as governor.

As one would expect, Reconstruction policies, intended to restore the seceding states to the Union and to obtain complete civil rights for blacks as mandated by the Fourteenth Amendment, ratified July 28, 1868, caused further deterioration of the tense situation. The Ku Klux Klan, formed in Pulaski, Tennessee in 1866, worked covertly to stir the brewing pot—terrifying blacks, warning carpetbaggers, and killing a few persons. Governor Clayton had to put the state under martial law when real violence erupted during the election of 1868.

The tense situation exploded in the "Brooks-Baxter War" of 1874. On April 15, 1874 Joseph Brooks forcibly ousted Elisha Baxter, a Republican, as governor. President Ulysses S. Grant refused to send federal troops to restore Baxter. Brooks had the support of former Governor Powell Clayton, Baxter the support of H. King White and a large black contingent. President Grant finally ordered the dispute settled by the state legislature, which quelled the revolt in Baxter's favor. Until Winthrop Rockefeller was elected governor, Baxter was the last Republican to hold the governor's office in Arkansas.

There are few data to show how Baptists were responding to this confused situation. Presumably they divided, much as other citizens, in their attitudes toward freed blacks competing with them for a place in Arkansas society. We have no evidence of serious efforts of churches, associations, or the State Convention to assist former slaves and their families to obtain land, homes, and the necessities. They did respond, as we will see in a moment, to the appeals of blacks for help.

The dizzying whirl of events surrounding the War and Reconstruction led inevitably to a rift between the races which a century and considerable human effort still have failed to heal. After the War it is clear that blacks quickly formed their own churches. Some black churches, of course, antedated the War, but there is no way to document how many. Following the War, the number of these multiplied rapidly. Although white Baptists have often exaggerated the "naturalness" with which blacks gravitated toward the Baptist tradition with its freedom and spontaneity, the statistics show that Baptists claimed a fair share of black adherents. Only Methodists competed seriously for their allegiance. In 1869 the **American Baptist Yearbook** reported one association, First Missionary, claiming 46 churches and 5,671 members. In 1871 this Association reported 106 churches and 8,227 members; in 1877 225 churches and 9,719 members. By 1880 the number of black Baptist associations had expanded to nine. Only six of these associations reported their statistics, but they alone claimed 248 churches and 17,201 members. The total was probably much larger. By 1882 black Baptists had formed a statewide convention claiming to represent 230 churches and 32,000 communicants. A report which the new state convention made to the Arkansas Baptist State Convention judged, in addition, that about 12,000 black Baptists in the state had no connection with their convention.

The letter from this Regular Missionary Baptist State Convention, meeting in Marianna, Arkansas, August 26, 1882, to the Arkansas Baptist State Convention reflects an effort of blacks to imitate their white counterparts in missions, education, publication, and other matters. Some of their comments could be interpreted as self-serving, that is, to obtain financial assistance of whites for education of black ministers. Taken as a whole, however, the letter betrays a fairly solid fraternal relationship.

> *The Regular Missionary Baptist State Convention (colored), of Arkansas, To the Missionary Baptist State Convention (white), of Arkansas, sendeth Christian greeting.*
>
> *The Lord has blessed his cause among the colored Baptists of this State with an increase that make glad our hearts. Our statistics are as follows:*
>
> *Number of churches represented in the Convention, 230; number of communicants, 32,000. There are in our judgment about 12,000 Baptist communicants in this State who are not connected with the Convention, making all total about 44,000 Baptists in Arkansas.*
>
> *We are glad to say that the leading brethren of this denomination are united, and we feel safe in saying that much good has been accomplished during the past year.*
>
> *We have arranged to commence the publication of a paper for the benefit of our denomination, also we have done much towards educating our young ministers by supporting them in the Nashville Institute, and toward*

*erecting a University at Helena for the benefit of the
colored youths.*

*We are unable at this writing to give a correct
statement of how many churches have been built by the
colored Baptists during the past year, but much has been
done in that direction.*

*It is the earnest desire of our brethren to start a
school for our denomination, but find ourselves unable at
present to put the school in operation and pay teachers,
and we would most respectfully ask the assistance of
educating our ministers.*

*We send as Corresponding Messengers, to sit with
you in your deliberations, our beloved brethren: Rev.
H.H. Hoke, of Augusta; Rev. E. Neely, of Searcy; Rev.
J.T. White, of Helena; Rev. E.C. Morris, of Helena.
Trusting that they may be received by you, we are yours in
the cause of religion, The Regular (colored) Baptist State
Convention, of Arkansas. E.C. Morris, President, Willis
A. Holmes, Cor. Sec'y.*[47]

As we have seen earlier, the War interrupted the evangelistic
and educational efforts of associations and the State Convention
which were predicated on recognition that joint worship was "very
defective and inefficient" in producing black communicants.[48] The
plan devised to rectify the situation was to employ white ministers to
work among the slaves. Following the War, the State Convention did
not appoint a "Committee on the Colored Race" until 1878, their
relationships evidently being too confused to allow such a step. The
first report of this Committee reflected the hesitancy with which
whites sought to reestablish ties and to aid their black counterparts.
The tone was, not surprisingly, paternalistic and condescending, and
the letter shows that, even then, objections were anticipated. As a
whole, however, it also indicates that some leaders were trying to
take a big stride across the chasm which separated the races.

*Your Committee on the Colored Race beg per-
mission to report as follows:*

*The colored people deserve our attention, and
should be helped by us in establishing churches and
instructing their preachers. They are quite zealous, but
uninformed, and, as a general thing, welcome information from us.*

We are apt to let our prejudice lead us from duty, but we should look to what these people are to be, and not what they have been.

They are building up in the towns strong congregations, and where they have informed and converted men to lead them, they are doing well. We recommend to every preacher to visit, when convenient, their churches, and instruct and preach for them, and that our State Missionary make this a part of his duty. They are naturally included to the Baptists; we should therefore, given them every chance to be intelligent Baptists. Let us who raised them, nursed them in sickness, and to whom we are naturally attached, not leave them to wander down to death without an effort on our part to save them. They turn to us, their former owners, and now their warmest friends, for that Gospel which makes us free indeed. Let them not call on us in vain.[49]

Some associations, as noted in an earlier section, also continued efforts to assist black Baptists. Fraternal assistance was to be the chief mode of their relationship, however, for, by 1880, separation was an accomplished fact. We cannot document the amount of help whites gave blacks; it was undoubtedly meager. In the future the rift would grow rather than diminish until radical changes in social patterns created conditions for a drive to effect a harmony between races.

New Day Dawning

There were few bright spots and little to be romanticized about the era we have just examined. It was, for the most part, a depressing period in both society and church.

The Civil War itself blasted away the foundations of work done previously by churches, associations, and the State Convention. It also left in its wake economic, social, and political problems which would hamper the recovery of the churches' efforts for two decades or more. It halted the flow of immigrants which brought potential new members for the churches. It aroused animosities and hostilities both outside and inside the churches. It hindered the effort to develop institutions which could effect the aims of the churches. It sapped them of leadership.

Given the circumstances, the resuscitation of Baptist church life in Arkansas was in many ways remarkable. A "valley of dry bones" came to life, first feebly and then, by the end of this era, confidently. To explain this, we have called attention to numerous factors: social, economic, personal. In the midst of all of these it is important to note a certain dynamism in the Baptist movement which even the War and the era of Reconstruction could not suppress. A powerful missionary urge propelled enough Baptists to put their shoulders to the wheel that eventually they got it turning again. As a result of their efforts, a new day began to dawn for Baptists in Arkansas. For them the sun would shine much brighter in the next period of their history. A night of pain and distress had helped to prepare for a new day.

NOTES

[1]**Southern Baptist Handbook, 1945,** ed. E.P. Alldredge (Nashville: Sunday School Board, 1946), p. 57, claimed 150,000 "conversions" up to 1865. The rapid recovery of churches following the War would sustain this judgment to some degree, but the figure is much too high.

[2]**Arkansas** (Chapel Hill, N.C.: University of North Carolina Press, 1947), p. 145.

[3]Cited by ibid., p. 147.

[4]Amy Compere Hickerson, "Compere, Ebenezer Lee," **Encyclopedia of Southern Baptists,** III, 304.

[5]J.S. Rogers, **History of Arkansas Baptists** (Little Rock: Arkansas Baptist Convention, 1948), p. 127.

[6]Ibid., p. 137.

[7]In ibid., p. 163.

[8]Ibid., p. 168.

[9]Ibid., pp. 363f.

[10]**Minutes, Red River Baptist Association, 1870,** p. 8.

[11]J.B. Searcy, in Rogers, op. cit., p. 509.

[12]See details in L.C. Tedford, "Searcy, James Bryant," **Encyclopedia of Southern Baptists,** II, 1188.

[13]**Proceedings, ABSC,** 1869, pp. 3, 11.

[14]**Proceedings, ABSC,** 1874, p. 8.

[15]J.B. Searcy, in Rogers, op. cit., p. 544.

[16]T.B. Espy and E.S. Lindsey, in Rogers, op. cit., pp. 549f. Rogers has given 1879, but this date is in error. Since I had no copy of the **Proceedings** for 1878, I have had to conjecture that this was the year intended.

[17]Ibid., p. 550.

[18]Proceedings, ABSC, 1869, p. 8.

[19]Proceedings, ABSC, 1871, p. 15.

[20]Proceedings, ABSC, 1874, p. 9.

[21]Minutes, Baptist General Association of Western Arkansas and Indian Territory, 1876, p. 67.

[21a]J.B. Searcy, "The General Association of Southeastern Arkansas," Baptist Advance, November 12, 1903, p. 2. Searcy says the Association and school last "three fourths of a decade."

[22]In Rogers, op. cit., p. 534

[23]Raymond Muncy, Searcy Arkansas: A Frontier Town Grows Up With America (Searcy: Harding Press, 1976), p. 105.

[24]L.C. Tedford, in Rogers, op. cit., p. 137.

[25]John Quincy Wolf, Life in the Leatherwoods (Memphis: Memphis State University, 1974), p. 111.

[26]Ray Granade, A Covenanted People: History of the First Baptist Church, Arkadelphia, Arkansas 1851-1976, p. 113.

[27]Muncy, op. cit., p. 105.

[28]Vivian Hansbrough, History of Greene County, Arkansas (Little Rock: Democrat Printing and Lithographic Co., 1946), p. 93.

[29]The ruling appears on p. 1 of the Minutes but is dated October, 1893. I am unclear why this is so, since the original entries which follow began with 1863, then skipped to 1890. The handwriting and ink, however, are the same as those recording the original minutes. I suspect this was a copy made in 1893, after the rule was adopted regarding attendance.

[30]Cited by Willard D. Hughes, "A Study of the Kelleyites," unpublished master's thesis, Missionary Baptist Seminary, Little Rock, 1976, pp. 17-18.

[31]Details can be found in ibid.

[32]Proceedings, ABSC, 1871, p. 10.

[33]J.B. Searcy, in Rogers, op. cit., p. 542. Judson Closed in 1883.

[34]Proceedings, ABSC, 1872, p. 13.

[35]Minutes, Baptist General Association of Western Arkansa and Indian Territory, 1883, p. 11.

[36]In Rogers, op. cit., p. 547.

[37]In ibid., p. 550.

[38]In ibid., p. 545.

[39]Proceedings, ABSC, 1878, p. 5.

[40]C.V. Hickerson, in Rogers, op. cit., p. 133.

[41]Lila W. Pye, The Yield of the Golden Years, A History of the Baptist Woman's Missionary Union of Arkansas (Little Rock: Author, 1938), p. 22.

[42] Annie Guinn Massey, **At the King's Command** (Little Rock: H.G. Pugh & Co., 1929).

[43] Cited by Annie Guinn Massey, **History of the Woman's Missionary Union, Auxiliary to the Arkansas Baptist State Convention** (Little Rock: Executive Board of the W.M.U., 1913) pp. 16-17.

[44] **Proceedings, ABSC, 1858,** pp. 7-8.

[45] **Proceedings, ABSC, 1874,** p. 9.

[46] **Minutes, SBC, 1876,** p. 16.

[47] **Proceedings, ABSC, 1882,** p. 12.

[48] **Proceedings, ABSC, 1850,** p. 5.

[49] **Proceedings, ABSC, 1878,** p. 12.

Chapter IV

"ON EAGLES' WINGS"

1881-1900

The title of this chapter intentionally plays on the names of the stellar leaders of the Arkansas Baptist State Convention during this era—James P. and Mary K. Eagle. For all except three of these twenty years James P. Eagle served as president of the Convention. Contemporaneously his wife, Mary, sparked the increasingly significant complementary work of the Baptist women of the state. Together they typified the "new breed" of wealthier, better educated, more urbane Baptists which Baptist churches were themselves attracting and producing and who were in turn changing the face of Baptist churches and institutions.

The rapid evolution of Baptists ended in a severe trauma as this era ended. Many Baptists of modest means, poorly educated, and of rural background and outlook were ill-prepared to understand and to accept the changes necessarily taking place as Baptists expanded and institutionalized their efforts. From the first they had shown an affinity for anti-organizational movements fostered by such persons as Alexander Campbell, Daniel Parker, and John Taylor. In an effort to find a Baptist identity over against the "reform" of Alexander Campbell, moreover, they readily fell under the spell of J.R. Graves and his Baptist high churchism. Although not strongly anti-organizational at the outset, the Landmark movement veered more and more in that direction as its leaders sought to answer critics. The net result was a rending of the Arkansas Baptist State Convention and its associations and churches to form a competing Baptist denomination.

The tensions which led to this split should not be seen as a purely internal affair, as they often are. Actually they paralleled tensions which characterized the state as a whole. More than anything, they were a result of growing pains.

The era we are discussing in this chapter proved crucial in the development of the state of Arkansas. The population mounted steadily between 1880 and 1900. From 802,525 in 1880 the census rose to 1,128,211 by 1890 and then leveled off to 1,211,465 by 1900. Most of the increase, of course, resulted from immigration. The continuation of this flow, many saw, depended to a considerable degree upon industrialization. Despite its rich resources, so long as Arkansas remained predominantly agrarian, it had only limited hopes for attracting immigrants. The exploitation of resources required a system of transportation which the railroads quickly moved to supply during this period.

It was in control of railroad companies that the ambivalence of Arkansas surfaced most visibly, but it had much deeper and more far reaching roots than that. The majority of Arkansas' people were rugged farmers and woodspeople. With their limited education and highly individualistic spirit they could not have been expected to understand the socio-economic and political changes their state was experiencing. They feared radical changes which industrialization brought to their way of life.

In the 1880s and 1890s progressive Arkansas governors and legislators pushed forward in the industrialization process. These included James P. Eagle, governor from 1889-1893, the prime leader of the Arkansas Baptist State Convention. Among other things, he recommended measures to encourage immigration, favored a state-supported system of roads, urged liberal support of education, and proposed a revamping of the state prison system. But politicians such as Eagle had to act with caution, for a strong populist spirit constantly challenged their plans. Farmers feared that Eagle would not show enough sensitivity to their plight and listened too much to "big business." In 1891 the formation of a Populist Party split the Democratic Party's vote, encouraging Eagle to retire after two terms. Although Populist candidates never polled many votes, they did succeed in keeping the issue of the "little man" alive. And by 1898 the populist spirit overtook the Democratic Party as Jeff Davis, self-professed champion of the common people and "hardshell" Baptist, was elected first attorney-general, then governor for three terms, and finally a United States Senator. Davis pitted himself and the powers of his office against the press, big business, and lobbies.

In James P. Eagle and Jeff Davis the two faces of Arkansas and of Arkansas Baptists are starkly portrayed. Eagle represented the educated, progressive, genteel element who grasped the importance of institutional development if both state and church were to make progress. Davis, an Ozarker, represented the poorly educated, reactionary, backwoods element who, for reasons they could not fully understand, set themselves vigorously against the structures and ideas which threatened their individuality and independence. In both state and church the two types existed alongside one another, but in time they were bound to go their separate ways.

Baptist Expansion

Within this twenty-year span Arkansas Baptists doubled their membership almost exactly, increasingly from 35,597 in 1880 to 71,419 in 1900. The number of churches increased about one and one-half times, from 879 in 1880 to 1,321 in 1900. The number of associations, however, remained relatively stable, the state being more or less fully organized by at least 1885.

Table X shows a relatively steady upward progression between 1880 and 1900 with no dramatic leaps upward either in number of churches or in membership. Although the figures are somewhat incomplete and unreliable, they will at least establish a trajectory. As previously, Baptists were aided in their expansion by a continuous influx of immigrants, many of whom would have been Baptists. Statistically, however, Baptists grew more rapidly than the population. While the latter was increasing by fifty percent or an average of 2.5 per cent per year over these twenty years, Baptists were increasing by a hundred percent or an annual average of 5.0 percent. Consequently we must look for other factors besides immigration to explain the growth.

Steady growth as reflected in Table X points to the organized effort of Arkansas Baptists as the chief reason for their growth: churches, Sunday schools, associations, state missionaries, and schools. It is quite evident that the State Convention played an increasingly prominent role in inspiring and assisting work going on at the congregational and associational levels, a fact which aroused suspicion among anti-organizationalists and eventually precipitated the rift of 1901.

The starting and organizing of Baptist mission work throughout the state was assisted immensely by improvement of travel. In 1882 the railway companies completed a north-south trunk line and began an east-west line. They took advantage of the eagerness of the churches to benefit from their services in the evangelization of the state. They issued free passes for state missionaries to travel from one end of the state to another and gave special rates to Baptists attending meetings of the State Convention. In 1894 the American Baptist Publication Society seized upon the evangelistic opportunities offered by an expanding railroad network by lending a chapel car named "Evangel" to the State Mission Board and funding a

TABLE X
BAPTIST GROWTH, 1881-1901

Year	Churches	Associations	Membership	Baptisms
1880	870	38	35,997	1,662
1881	782	35	37,111	191
1882	830	35	37,116	265
1883	863	36	39,151	2,028
1884	937	40	43,500	2,335
1885	927	40	40,486	2,446
1886	976	41	45,338	3,399
1887	1,028	39	47,604	4,308
1888	1,053	41	49,793	4,248
1889	1,092	43	52,402	5,349
1890	1,125	42	55,497	4,725
1891	1,176	47	49,345	5,375
1892	1,255	48	64,912	4,859
1893	1,240	49	63,758	4,870
1894	1,302	50	67,805	6,086
1895	1,345	50	71,171	5,145
1896	1,372	49	72,560	6,534
1897	1,396	48	74,360	5,262
1898	1,354	47	71,223	2,559
1899	1,341	48	70,955	3,896
1900	1,321	47	71,419	4,241

missionary, J.S. Thomas, to manage it. The car was moved about by rail, parked for a few months on a siding in one of the little towns springing up everywhere as new immigrants pushed out from the main arteries, and then relocated. This approach proved sufficiently successful that, in 1895, the Convention requested and received an extension of the ABPS's loan.

Putting Missions First

As we have seen in earlier periods, Arkansas Baptists shared with other Baptists in the South a consummmate concern for missions and, in this era, continued to organize their efforts with that end in view. The centrality of this concern was reflected not merely in the maintenance of special committees and boards for mission work—state, Domestic (Home), and Foreign—but also in the interpretation of work of other committees, boards, or institutions.

Education

Education, whether of ministers or of the Baptist constituency in general, was promoted as a necessary aid to the mission effort. Ministerial training, of course, served this purpose quite directly and explicitly. Arkansas Baptist leaders at least realized that, opposition notwithstanding, ministers had to be educated at a level commensurate with the culture of Arkansas as a whole. In 1889 the Committee on Ministerial Education of the State Convention argued that ministerial education was essential

> *To prepare men for standing alongside of other educated men in the ministry; to prepare them for standing in the face of opposers of the truth; to prepare them to wield the pen of ready writers; to furnish the Mission field with suitable men; and last, but most important, to prepare men to preach more powerfully the Word of God—the unsearchable riches of Christ—. . .* [1]

Many other reports sought to "impress upon our young ministers the great importance of the best possible theological and pastoral training," in Baptist seminaries as well as in college. [2]

An evangelistic twist, however, was not confined to the education of ministers. It turned up also in definitions of the purpose of Baptist schools, as Baptists became more and more self-conscious of their aims. In 1885, for instance, the Committee on Education of the State Convention, looking ahead to the opening of Ouachita College a year later, urged the establishment of "distinctively Christian schools." Such schools, the Committee argued, "are absolutely essential to the purity and perpetuity of the Church, of Christian churches, and to the highest well-being of the State." [3] Subsequent reports viewed with increasing concern the secularity of public

116

educational institutions on elementary, secondary, and higher education levels. Though we must make allowances for considerable ministerial "rhetoric" in the promotion of existing Baptist institutions, some Baptists came to favor a parochial education. In 1889, for instance, the Committee on Education urged it as the "individual duty" of every Baptist "to place his children for education where the teachings of home and parents will not be antagonized or neutralized" and to support Baptist schools in the state.[4] Two years later, the Committee on Education confessed that it was "almost impossible to religiously impress" and "to reach with the influence peculiar to Baptists" youth who attended state colleges.[5] The next year, the Committee called for "more good district, common and high schools, taught by Christian men and women only. . ." along with "more Christian home teaching."[6] A more or less spontaneous push to establish a network of Baptist schools throughout the state scarcely got off the ground because it lacked financial support, but the existence of such a drive illustrates the close connection of missions and education in the minds of many Baptists. The schools themselves, moreover, regularly justified their existence by reporting on conversions, the spiritual climate, and the number of ministerial students attending. Their supporters posited a direct apologetic mission to the colleges. Among other things, the Committee on Education in 1899 argued that "they are designed to develop character, test all science in the crucible of Christ before teaching it to pupils, and to give us a broader manhood and a nobler womanhood. . . to shelter and protect the truth" against the "thunder bolts" of unbelief, agnosticism, and atheism.[7]

Sunday Schools

Sunday schools came to be promoted with a similar urgency as instruments for effecting the missionary purposes of the denomination. In 1880 the Convention elected O.M. Lucas as its "Sunday-school Missionary." As we will discover later, the promotion of Sunday schools got rather dismal responses in many churches. As late as 1896, the Committee on Sunday Schools lamented to the State Convention that only a fourth of the churches (293) reported schools, and less than a sixth of the people were attending. Furthermore, the Sunday school continued to be viewed throughout the period as a children's school. Church leaders, however, soon recognized and began to exploit the Sunday school's value not only in increasing knowledge of the Bible but in winning and nurturing converts. This type of thinking received a strong boost when the

Southern Baptist Convention formed a Sunday School Board in 1891. In 1899 the Sunday School and Colportage Board put together the strongest possible plea for Sunday schools in every church. They contributed, the argument ran, to the formation of character early in life, supplied many of the converts or additions to the churches who came forward in protracted meetings, and accounted for seven-eighths of the money given to the churches. "To open and maintain Sunday-schools is to thin out the inmates of our poor houses, decrease the rate of taxation and deplete the population of our penitentiaries," this document continued. If every church were to establish a Sunday school, "you will have solved every problem connected with our denominational work in the State and the beginning of the end will be in sight."[8] The next year, the Board called the Sunday school "the largest and most fruitful field for the evangelization of the churches."[9]

A State Paper

Publications, including the state paper, which was revived in 1881 as the **Arkansas Evangel,** were tied also to the missionary endeavor. In 1882 the Committee on Publications commended the **Evangel,** along with the Bible, as "an indespensible (sic) necessity to the growth and prosperity of our denomination in the State."[10] A year later, the Committee again urged widespread support of the fledgling paper on the grounds that "Missions, churches, the convention, everything in the State would suffer without the paper."[11] The next year, the Committee envisioned the **Evangel's** purpose in terms of propagating "a pure and individual spirituality, a sound theology and a distinctive denominationalism publicly, intelligently and faithfully."[12] In 1895 the Committee lamented "a deplorable decline of interest in religious literature" and a corresponding increase of interest in secular literature, urging pastors to labor to overturn this state of affairs.[13] The next year, it candidly noted that the state paper, now called the **Arkansas Baptist,** "does not fully meet the demands of our great and important work," alluding to the anti-organizational editorial work of W.A. Clark, the disaffected former state superintendent of missions. Although a resolution later smoothed over the editor's injured feelings, this statement shows that Arkansas Baptist leaders expected the paper to promote the missionary aims of the Convention.[14]

Women's and Children's Organization

The **Woman's Central Committee,** newly organized in 1883, promoted the missionary aims of the Convention still more directly. In the annual Convention at Fayetteville a Committee on Woman's Work urged pastors to organize societies in their churches with the promise that "a new impetus will be given to the cause of missions, and instead of the meager sum now reported, hundreds, and even thousands of dollars will flow into the treasury of the Lord."[15] Although the movement to organize the efforts of women required much special pleading, by the end of the era we are dealing with the women's societies were contributing a major portion of the funds which went to state, home, and foreign mission causes, as well as college and ministerial aid. When, in 1889, the Baptist Woman's Mission and Aid Societies held their first annual meeting in conjunction with the State Convention, they gave an impressive report of six years' work.

Comparison of Woman's Missionary Union contributions (Table XV) with other funds raised by the Convention (Table XI) readily reveals the significance of this organization in the mission enterprise. Although they began modestly, collecting 6 percent of the total missions budget in 1883, after 1888 they regularly collected more than half of it.

Children's Missionary Societies, spin offs from the women's societies, also illustrate the intense missionary spirit which fired Arkansas Baptists. There is a graphic example of children's fervor for missions in the minutes of the State Convention in 1881. Eleven year old Laura Longley, president of the Children's Missionary Society of the Calvary Baptist Church of Little Rock, in which the Convention was meeting, had been circulating among persons present and quietly asking for money. W.D. Mayfield, pastor of the church, took note of this and requested the Convention to fill her hands with money for the mission cause. "In a few seconds," the minutes record, "they ran over, and she went to the Bible, on the platform, and held her hands over that, and it was covered. We could see no tearless eyes in the congregation while it was announced she hoped to go the heathen herself." The collection incidentally, amounted to $24.50.[16]

North or South?

Before looking at the way in which Arkansas Baptists sought to discharge their intense missionary vocation, it will be useful to examine their struggle to decide whether to face north or south in their Baptist affiliation. Early on, they had chosen to identify with the Southern Baptist Convention which had been organized at Augusta, Georgia, in 1845, and dispatched delegates to the annual meeting. After the Civil War, however, Southern Baptists had still not decided to what extent they would travel a path independent of their northern counterparts. To a degree, of course, they asserted their independence, especially in developing separate organizations for both foreign and home mission work. It was not until 1891, however, that they entered the publishing field with the establishment of the Sunday School Board. Up to this time, many Baptists of both North and South expected and hoped for an eventual reconciliation; thereafter, it became highly unlikely.

In the meantime, Baptists in impoverished states like Arkansas turned in every direction looking for help in pursuit of their mission work. Through much of the period under discussion they received Bibles and literature from the American Baptist Publication Society as well as from the Sunday School Board of the Southern Baptist Convention. Similarly they obtained massive aid from the Home Mission Society as well as the Domestic and Indian (Home) Mission Board of the SBC. It was not until nearly the turn of the century that the boards of the Southern Baptist Convention assumed almost complete support and received in turn almost complete allegiance from Arkansas Baptists.

In part, we may ascribe this ambivalence to the peculiar complex of factors in Arkansas which left its citizens uncertain about affiliation with either North or South before, during, and after the Civil War. The state was as much western as southern. Its citizens were divided culturally—uplanders being backwoods types, lowlanders being gentlemen farmers. But there was also a practical reason for walking a line between northern and southern Baptists. So long as both groups competed for the affiliation of Arkansas Baptists, the churches of Arkansas could exploit the generosity of both. Such an arrangement, however, generated problems as time went on, for despite efforts to cooperate, neither northern nor southern Baptists felt comfortable in a competitive relationship.

Literature and Sunday Schools

In the publications area the tensions did not become noticeable until after the Sunday School Board was created in 1891. Previously, some privately sponsored publishing companies tried to supply a "Southern Baptist" literature, but these did not receive the

120

official sanction of the Southern Baptist Convention. The most widely circulated items, such as **Kind Words,** rather, were published and distributed by the Home Mission Board. Even these did not detract seriously from the much better established publications of the American Baptist Publication Society which Arkansas Baptists regularly used. The Society supplied Bibles, funded Sunday school missionaries, and, as we saw earlier, even loaned the Chapel Car "Evangel." The Committee on Publications or other committees of the State Convention regularly recommended both **Kind Words** and publications of the ABPS. Although questions about the latter were sometimes voiced, Arkansas Baptists consistently reaffirmed their ties with the Society. In 1882, for instance, the Committee on Sunday Schools stated its belief "that the continuance of the relation between our Convention and the Publication Society can but be productive of increasing benefits to our cause in Arkansas." It also recommended Sunday School literature published by the Southern Baptist Convention.[17]

These warm connections with the Publication Society began to cool about 1885 as a recession in the north limited the ability of northern Baptists to assist those in the South. For the first time in 1886 the Committee on Sunday Schools stated openly a preference for literature published by the Home Mission Board of the Southern Baptist Convention as "equal to those published elsewhere in point of cheapness, neatness and soundness in the faith, . . ."[18] Subsequently, committees on publication dropped their endorsements of the Society's publications and did not resume them until much later. For several years Arkansas Baptists looked to the South for assistance in this area. Thus, in 1891, the year the Sunday School Board came into existence, the Committee on Sunday Schools of the Arkansas Baptist State Convention proposed asking the Sunday School Board and, **"only if that failed"** turning to the American Baptist Publication Society for literature, cash, and colportage. The same year, the Committee on Publications "specially" recommended to the Baptists of Arkansas the publications of the Sunday School Board.

As Arkansas Baptists organized their Sunday School drive, they looked for help in paying the salary of Sunday School "missionaries," "evangelists," or "general secretaries." In 1893 they immediately received a pledge of $500 per year from the Sunday School Board. At the time, however, the financially strapped Publication Society could offer no support beyond the employment of J.S. Thomas, a Sunday school "missionary" already working for them as manager of the "Evangel." This disappointment notwithstanding, Arkansas Baptists continued to cooperate with both the Board and the Society and to receive help from both. In 1896 the Committee on Sunday Schools referred the issue of cooperation with the Publication Society to the State Sunday School Board. The next year, the latter reported to the Convention that both the Publication Society and the Sunday School Board had "responded nobly to our appeals" and recommended that the **churches** "make a choice between the two boards, . . ."[19] In subsequent years the state Board expressed gratitude to both in similar ways.

State Missions

The position of Arkansas Baptists **vis-a-vis** missionary efforts by northern and southern Baptists was somewhat more complicated. For one thing, some considered missions the exclusive purview of churches and associations and resisted any organized effort beyond that level. The impoverished state of the churches, associations, and even the State Convention, however, forced most of them to reach for help in various directions. At first the Convention turned to the American Baptist Home Mission Society to obtain support for a "general missionary" or a "superintendent of missions." As envisioned by a special committee appointed to deal with this problem, this person would "be regarded as the joint representative of the Society and the (State) Convention," report to both regarding his work, and receive half his salary from each.[20]

This arrangement immediately posed some problems about church affiliation. Consequently, the next year M.F. Locke introduced a resolution which authorized the State Board to accept aid from either the Home Mission Society or the Home Mission Board. Which of these two would be approached for help was to rest with an individual church or missionary. Should either the Society or the Board refuse help on condition that Arkansas Baptists decline help from the other, it was proposed that "we decline to co-operate with the Board so refusing."[21] For a number of years Arkansas Baptists pursued their mission work with this dual arrangement. Normally they paid half the salary of missionaries and the Society or the Board paid the other half. As early as 1883, however, the balance seems to have swung in the direction of the Home Mission Board. In that year the Arkansas Home Mission Board took special note of the fact that the New York Home Mission Society had to withdraw support of several missionaries due to "liabilities," while the Home Mission

Board of the Southern Baptist Convention paid each of those it had agreed to help support. This situation, chiefly the result of the recession in the North, eroded the confidence of Arkansas Baptists in the Society, even though they continued to talk about cooperation with both the Society and the Board. In 1884 the State Board omitted any mention of assistance from the Society and instead lauded the Home Mission Board. The latter, it noted, "has proven a friend indeed in this our time of need. What little we have been able to do, has been greatly stimulated by that Board."[22] Understandably, the Home Mission Board of the Southern Baptist Convention, led by I.T. Tichenor, seized upon this opportunity to expand its own efforts, and we can ascribe some credit for the advance of mission organization in Arkansas, despite strenuous resistance, to this Board. Even the latter, however, sometimes floundered in its efforts to help. In 1892, for instance, it had to notify the Executive Board of the Arkansas Baptist State Convention that it could not offer financial help due to a depression. Later, finding some resources, it agreed to pay one dollar for every two Arkansas Baptists appropriated for mission work, and found a $500 supplement. Still, many missionaries had to continue their work on a voluntary basis. The year 1892 seems to have been especially bleak. This depressed state of affairs lasted only a short while, however, and, with Home Mission Board support, mission work again blossomed during the last years of the nineteenth century. In 1896, for instance, the Home Mission Board of the Southern Baptist Convention appropriated $1,000 for the salary of the state corresponding secretary and field evangelists with the stipulation that Arkansas raise at least $1,600 for the same work and $750 for the Home Mission Board's work elsewhere. Unfortunately, before the turn of the century, anti-organizational sentiment threatened to sever such ties even as these. A disastrous split saved them for a part of Arkansas Baptists.

Arkansas Baptists' Missionary Vision

During the period we are reviewing, Arkansas Baptists kept their gaze fixed primarily on the evangelization of the state and gave secondary attention to foreign and home missions pursued outside the state. As regards the latter concerns they exhibited a higher level of interest in foreign than in home missions, certainly if we measure interest by financial contributions (Table XI).

Foreign Missions

At the outset interest in home missions was greater than that in foreign missions. The latter was stimulated by the Foreign Mission Board of the Southern Baptist Convention, through occasional appearances of missionaries at the annual conventions, through publications such as **The Foreign Mission Journal,** and through the efforts of mission-minded leaders in Arkansas itself. It took considerable effort, however, to stir a provincial and isolated people who had little contact with the outside world. Early on, committees on foreign missions repeatedly remonstrated with pastors for not calling missions to their peoples' attention. They felt constrained to remind their constituency that foreign missions is "as much a part of the system of missions and grows as legitimately out of the Savior's last command as does Home Missions."[23] From about 1884 on, the financial picture brightened, but the contributions of Arkansans still remained small throughout this period, the largest part of them being raised by women's missionary societies. In 1889 the Committee on Foreign missions reported contributions of $2,028.44, the largest to date, and set a goal of $2,500 for the next year. Riding an economic wave, in 1891 they set their sights on $5,000, but a depression shattered that goal and they collected only a fourth of that in 1892. It was not until 1894 that the economy righted itself and allowed a resumption of the earlier support.

The economy, however, was not the only problem. In 1895 the Committee on Foreign Missions lamented that "While there has been some progress in the interest our people have in Foreign Missions, there is still deplorable ignorance and indifference among the masses of our people and among many of our pastors."[24] A year later, this Committee recommended "a thorough course on education on missions, on the part of each pastor, both for himself and the flock under his care."[25] In addition to lack of funds and ignorance, "Hardshell" and "Landmark" influences were undermining support for foreign missions. In 1897 the Committee on Foreign Missions alluded directly to "Hardshell" opposition to organized mission effort beyond the local church level. They asked, "Why are we increasing, while our hardshell brethren are decreasing?" The answer was, "We, in a measure, obey the great commission of our Lord and Saviour Jesus Christ, while they ignore it."[26] Combined "Hardshell" and "Landmark" opposition brought the issue directly to a head in 1901 in the division of the churches. Their impact, however, was felt earlier upon contributions to foreign missions.

Despite fairly substantial growth and immense efforts to raise mission consciousness, contributions still remained at a low level. In 1900 the Committee on Foreign Missions delivered an optimistic report to the State Convention, but the figures they cited (even more, those they omitted) scarcely warranted the optimism.

TABLE XI
MISSION CONTRIBUTIONS, 1880-1900

Year	Foreign Missions	Home Missions	State Missions
1880	248.85	34.00	
1881	374.45	23.45	
1882	388.72	12.50	
1883	1,080.79	1,697.59	4,971.13
1884	957.24	175.80	2,707.96
1885	984.32	51.20	3,800.00
1886	1,500.00	7,156.00	
1887	1,800.00	1,750.00	
1888	2,000.00	482.65	2,770.48
1889	2,002.27	483.48	2,679.30
1890	2,500.76	511.30	304.25
1891	1,629.10	838.80	2,018.41
1892	1,711.16	538.16	3,751.84
1893	1,435.70	649.57	1,400.00
1894	1,892.76	1,411.52	2,659.61
1895	1,248.34	1,656.00	1,607.87
1896	1,827.96	1,193.79	2,119.23
1897	2,114.10	2,418.47	691.36
1898	1,714.44	854.03	2,242.48
1899	2,321.22	1,718.36	2,798.07
1900	2,890.62	1,534.65	4,094.68

Home Missions

Arkansas Baptist enthusiasm and support for Home Mission work outside of Arkansas ran at a still lower level. At first glance this might occasion some surprise in view of the close connection which exists between state mission work and that of the Home Mission Board or Home Mission Society. Here again, however, we can see the effect of provincialism and limited resources which restricted the vision of Arkansas Baptists in other ways as well. Arkansas was itself a mission field and not capable of doing much beyond its borders. Annual contributions to home missions were negligible at best, and the Home Mission Board finally had to stipulate that it would give money to buttress state mission work only if Arkansas Baptists matched this with contributions to the Home Mission Board. Leaders prodded and pulled, but with limited effect.

State Missions

The chief focus of attention, as we noted above, was the evangelization of the state, but several things hampered clear articulation and pursuit even of this task. One hindrance was the ever-present resistance to organized effort beyond the congregational or associational level. Prior to the split of 1901, this resistance made itself felt time and again in reluctance to support, either financially or practically, the various offices needed to pull together the missionary or evangelistic work of the state. Assistance from the American Baptist Home Mission Society and the Home Mission Board of the Southern Baptist Convention was required to get a functional organization. Such opposition was often registered openly. In 1881, for instance, the Superintendent of Missions, B.W. Harmon, reported "a feeling that the churches were imposed upon when called to contribute for any **general** work." Harmon went on to explain that "they thought they should give only to their own Associations." He recommended a change of name on the grounds that "some regard it as indicating undue authority over ministers and churches." At the same time he urged the appointment of additional personnel and the division of the state into districts with one person responsible for each district. Despite his awareness of reservations, moreover, he commented: "The **people** are anxious for **unification** of the work by cooperating with the State Convention."[27]

The sensitive issue of jurisdiction in mission work was never resolved during this period, but it was defused somewhat by avoiding certain titles and by strong efforts of the State Mission Board to pursue its work **in cooperation with** the churches and the associations. The problem of naming the office was, of course, a superficial one, reflecting a much deeper concern. The State Convention toyed with a number of alternate titles: Superintendent of Missions, General Missionary, Corresponding Secretary, and State Evangelist. Eventually it settled on a title which sounded least authoritarian, that of Corresponding Secretary.

The fear which underlay all of this was that control over mission work might be exercised from above. In this reaction, of course, Arkansas Baptists aligned themselves with their heritage both as Baptists and as frontier Americans. State Convention leaders tried to

126

assuage anxieties by making careful cooperative arrangements, but they never succeeded fully, for the fears grew strong enough to lead to the division of the Convention. Some doubtless underestimated the strength of resistance to the burgeoning business model on which they operated. Most, however, took due note of the problem and thus proceeded with caution to reassure the churches and associations that they wanted to assist and not to dominate. In 1882, for instance, the Committee on State Misssions recommended a three point plan for the pursuit of the missionary task: (1) the securing of a "General Missionary, who shall both evangelize and instruct in Christian giving"; (2) cooperation between the State Board and associational boards in supporting a missionary pastor or an associational missionary in each association; and (3) systematic giving in the churches.[28]

Subsequently the Convention tried to steer its mission work down the track of cooperation, but derailment of the whole program constantly threatened. Convention leaders were torn between waiting for the churches or associations and getting on with the business of winning the state. In 1884, for instance, the State Mission Board urged the employment of "one or more Evangelists. . . to travel over as much of the state as possible, preach the Gospel, collect funds for the Board, seek to induce the preachers, churches and associations, throughout the entire state, to co-operate with the convention in its work—and to be under the direction of the Board."[29] Presumably the last clause referred to the evangelists and not churches or associations. Though taking explicit note of "some difference of opinion among our people as to the best plan of conducting this work," a year later the Board went ahead with an earlier decision of the Convention which had directed the State Board to "procure at the earliest praticable day, some efficient corresponding Secretary, to vigorously prosecute this work in accordance with the plan above suggested."[30] Continuing widespread suspicion induced the Committee on State Missions in 1889 to recommend election of as associational "representative" in each association "whose duty shall be to represent the interests of his Association before the Board and also represent the Board in his Association."[31]

After barely surviving the rugged recession of 1891 and 1892 missionary spirits soared. In 1894 James P. Eagle, Financial Secretary of the Board, gave a highly optimistic report about the

127

cooperation which existed. "The missionary spirit is growing," he exulted. "Our people are willing contributors to our mission work in its various departments. They are in full sympathy with our state work and ready to co-operate with your board in its efforts to give the pure gospel of peace to the people of our own state."[32] Eagle either spoke "ministerially" or misjudged the situation entirely, for a year later a special Committee on Plans and Recommendations proposed several items which betrayed that the situation was not well at all as Eagle had supposed. Two of the eight resolutions give off especially self-evident clues. One proposed "That the State Board be urged to co-operate with each association in their method of mission work as far as practicable, and that the State Board endeavor, through each of its associational members, to keep in touch with the pastors and churches of each association, and in this way keep constant and systematic work in progress." The other proposed "That, if practicable, the board organize a system of evangelistic work by the pastors of the State."[33] The Committee on State Missions alluded to the same burning issue still more explicitly. "We feel that the cooperative system has not been carried into, and with, the rural churches as it deserves to be, but are compelled to relegate this and similar questions,. . ., to the State Board."[34] In 1896 and again in 1897 the Committee on Plans and Recommendations reiterated the above recommendations almost verbatim. When in 1897 O.L. Hailey offered a resolution encouraging the fostering of Baptist Young People's Union work in the state, he did so with the proviso that the Convention "express our earnest solicitude that any organization in connection with the churches be in the closest relation and under the direct control of the church."[35]

By 1899 anxieties over the development of organizations to promote mission work throughout the state had reached a fever pitch. The state Executive Board took care to report that the Corresponding Secretary, W.E. Atkinson, had "gone to no field except upon invitation of those in charge of the work. . .visited no church except at the instance or with the consent of the pastor. . .gone to no association except upon consultation and with the consent of its representatives." They proceeded to reassure their constituency that "Every effort at building the work has been to accomplish the same along natural lines, through the churches and their pastors, and through the associations and their regular representatives." Further, in visits to churches, etc., Atkinson had "taken part as was agreeable to those in charge," so as to avoid friction or disagreement.[36] The

Board also conceded rather candidly that the work of W.A. Clark in Spring River and adjacent associations in northern Arkansas turned out rather badly because "this section was not in a condition to receive his work, . . ."[37] Nevertheless, all was not negative. The Board also reported that many associations which had previously refused cooperation and even openly opposed the State Convention now "have declared in their recent meetings their sympathy with the work, their willingness to contribute and their prayerful anxiety for its prosperity."[38]

At this point Arkansas Baptists could not have perceived what was happening to them in a subtle way. The business or corporation model which was becoming so much a dominating factor in American society and culture was subtly imposing itself on the churches and the way they carried on their work. Occasionally the extent of this influence surfaced. It stood out in the names used for various agencies, for example, that of "Executive Board." It was reflected now and then in reports at the State Convention. In 1900, for instance, the Executive Board appended this note to its financial statement: "We have tried to be governed by the business principle universally recognized and regarded in all secular business matters by all successful business men, namely, that wise outgo for income is the best kind of economy."[39] The business model, however, was far more pervasive than this. It was creating a radically different model by which the churches carried on their work and, in doing so, was generating an explosive situation for Arkansas Baptists.

The Churches Inside Out

We will return to these matters in the next chapter as we examine the division of the State Convention. Presently we will look at the life of Arkansas Baptists in the context of local congregations. With the information available, of course, we cannot put together a precise picture, but we can give some representative sketches.

The people and the churches were overwhelmingly rural still. A majority of the churches still operated on a quarter or half-time schedule, for, as late as 1916, three-fourths of all Southern Baptist churches were still quarter-time.[40] The Corning Baptist Church would have been fairly typical.

Founded in Corning on April 30, 1887, this little flock secured the services of A.S. Hall, pastor of the Baptist Church at Paragould. to conduct services the fourth weekend of each month. According to church minutes, he arrived on Thursday to perform various pastoral duties. He held worship services at 7:00 p.m. on Saturday, then at 11:00 a.m. and 7:00 p.m. on Sunday. In the absence of a regular pastor the church conducted a Union Sunday School each Sunday afternoon in the Methodist Episcopal Church, which preceded the Baptist Church in Corning. Subsequently the Sunday School met in the County Court House. The Corning Baptist Church did not complete their own building, a simple rectangular frame house with the pulpit at the same end as the main entrance, until November 1891. Shortly after this they began half-time services under the leadership of F.C. Neely, who divided his time with the Reyno Church. In 1901 the Corning Church reported that they had painted the exterior of the building at a cost of $90 and estimated that the white frame building was worth about $1,250. They conducted a sparsely attended prayer meeting on Wednesday evenings throughout the year and a Sunday School whose average attendance was 45 and average collection $.55. Their present membership, "known and unknown within and without the bound of the church," was 134. From the fourth Sunday in September 1900 through the month of March 1901 they paid their pastor $72. They collected also $22.00 for Sunday literature and helps, $5.30 for needy widows, $3.81 for Home Missions, and $2.98 for Sunday School missions. The total budget was $201.00.[41]

Revival meetings still played an important role in the growth of Arkansas churches. The Corning **Courier** reported a spectacular one in March of 1895. First came the announcement in the local paper:

> *Eld. Bearden announced he will commence a revival Monday with Eld. W.A. Gibony of Helena, one of the ablest revivalists in the state, doing the preaching. A quartette of singers will assist him. . .*

Subsequently the **Courier** noted that "nearly everybody in town now attends services night and day while the revival continues at the Baptist church. . . A.L. Barnett shut down his mill and closed his store Wednesday in order that his employees might attend." At the close of the revival the local editor summed up the remarkable outcome: "Never was such interest taken in a revival in Corning as in the one just closed. There were about 70 conversions and many Christians awakened from their lethargy."[42]

130

Revivals such as this filled a social as well as a religious need. They also supplied fellowship and entertainment. The article just cited, for instance, added an announcement about post-revival happenings. "Elder Gibony has one of the finest magic lantern outfits and will give an exhibition at the Baptist church next week. The lantern will reflect pictures 13 feet in diameter."

Baptisms were also important social occasions, but for many they turned out to be painful pieces of physical experience. Although, as we saw in the preceding chapter, some churches now possessed indoor baptistries, most still baptized in creeks, rivers, and lakes. The Corning Church, for instance, baptized in a lake south of the town. At the end of one protracted meeting, February 16, 1900, there was ice along the edge of the lake. That may explain why nearly every person in the little town of 600 turned out to witness the baptizings![43]

Some churches fared better than the Corning Baptist Church. The First Baptist Church of Fort Smith, for example, founded in 1857, was able to hold full-time services throughout the period we are discussing. After struggling mightily through the Civil War and Reconstruction eras in 1885 they borrowed $1,000 and erected a substantial building to house both their sanctuary and the Sunday school. Unfortunately this structure was leveled to the ground by a fierce cyclone which struck the city of 20,000 on January 10, 1898. After the cyclone the members constructed a much larger and finer building out of limestone costing between $14,200 and $16,000. They held their first services in it in October, 1899.

Arkansas Baptists still suffered from an inadequate supply of trained ministers. As Table XII shows, there were only about half as many ordained ministers as there were churches, which partially explains and is explained by the fact that most churches were part-time. We cannot put together an accurate estimate of the number who had received college or seminary training, but the figure would have been exceedingly low. Churches in the larger towns or cities alone would have had well-educated pastors.

The pay of ministers fluctuated up and down with the financial fortunes of the members. Without supplements from the Arkansas State Mission Board few churches could have employed pastors on a full-time basis. Most ministers depended still on other means of support such as farming unless, like James P. Eagle, they had independent wealth. A handful of churches, however, especially those in larger towns, rose above the average level to provide fair

TABLE XII
ORDAINED MINISTERS, 1880-1900

Year	Churches		Ministers	
	White	Black	White	Black
1880	1,110		525	
1881	1,118		616	
1882	1,143		655	
1883	1,192		697	
1884	1,233		700	
1885	1,225		714	
1886	1,442		802	
1887	1,225		700	
1888	1,463		890	
1889	1,452		897	
1890	1,536		1,073	
1891	1,176	457	712	373
1892	1,586		1,035	
1893	1,214	558	746	431
1894	1,235	785	812	467
1895	1,281	810	720	173
1896	2,172		1,200	
1897	1,372	817	818	141
1898	1,379	873	816	536
1899	1,306	848	859	534
1900	1,370	868	896	593

sustenance for their pastors. The Fort Smith Church, for instance, with supplements from the State Board, raised their pastors' salaries from $720 in 1882 to $1,000 in 1885 to $1,600 in 1892. After the recession that year they dropped back to $1,400. We can readily see here the importance of the State Mission Board.

Worship services continued in most churches along lines similar to those of the previous period. Preaching still held pride of place. Other elements, such as prayer and singing, however, also made important contributions. In many churches the quality of music improved as hymnals and choristers became more common. At this early date, of course, the State Convention made no organized effort to promote music programs as it did to promote Sunday schools. But for several years the Committee on Publications did plug a song book entitled **Harvest Bells,** compiled by W.E. Penn, an outstanding evangelistic singer in the southwest at the time.[44] If the hymns contained in this hymnal were typical of those popular in Arkansas Baptist churches, as is likely, Arkansas Baptists liked gospel songs with a strong evangelistic flavor. The theme hymn, "Harvest Bells," shows the paramountcy of evangelism.

> *Christian reapers, lift your eyes,*
> *See the fields already white*
> *For the harvest of the skies,*
> *'Tis a grand and glorious sight.*
> *Souls are waiting—seek and find,*
> *Bring them to the Lord and say:*
> *Lo: my Master, thus we bind*
> *Heavenly sheaves for Thee today.*
> *Think as idly here we stand,*
> *Should the Lord of harvest come*
> *Finding us with empty hand,*
> *Would we not for shame be dumb?*
> *Hasten ere the Lord has come,*
> *When he calls, may we be found*
> *Ready for His harvest home;*
> *Work all done, and sheaves all bound.*

Some churches began to develop choirs, but worship, like other things, was subordinated in most churches to the passionate concern for evangelism.

Discipline in Arkansas Baptist churches still remained strict, judging by the figures reported in the **American Baptist Yearbook.** Although the latter are notoriously inexact, we can at least discern in Table XIII the persistence of Baptist concern for a disciplined fellowship as they added significantly to their numbers. A striking feature of these figures is the sharp increase of exclusions from the year 1888 on through the 1890s. Such a sudden and dramatic jump could be ascribed in part to more accurate reporting, especially by blacks. A more likely explanation, however, would be the mushrooming of alcoholism and a corresponding crackdown on its use

TABLE XIII
DISCIPLINE IN BAPTIST CHURCHES, 1880-1900

Year	Exclusions		Restorations	
	White	Black	White	Black
1880	713		428	
1881	460		298	
1882	195		94	
1883	520		252	
1884	280		117	
1885	649		225	
1886	561		331	
1887	652		203	
1888	970		445	
1889	921		307	
1891	1,160	280	596	179
1892		1,076	519	
1893	1,118	293	673	142
1894	1,327	511	462	304
1895	1,501	288	720	173
1896		1,655	681	
1897	1,654	333	818	141
1898	680	1,043	426	711
1899	1,795	1,176	787	773
1900	1,776	1,531	777	1,002

among church members. In church minutes of this date drunkenness frequently appears as the number one reason for exclusions. Here is a typical entry from the minutes of the Bethesda Baptist Church, located in Sevier and Little Rock Counties, dated Saturday before the second Sunday in January, 1891: "Bro. Claude Rogers made his acknowledgement and ask (sic) the Church to forgive him of drinkin (sic), which the Church did so and received him in full fellowship."[45]

Dancing and other matters of "conduct" also accounted for exclusions and restorations. The same Bethesda minutes, for example, reported that, in May 1891, the church appointed a delegation "to see sister Mattie Walker in regard to dancin (sic)."[46] As a result, she was excluded at the business meeting on Saturday before the second Sunday in June. In January, 1892, the church appointed a delegation to see "Bro. B. Walker and Sister Walker" regarding unspecified "conduct." In March Walker was excluded, his wife "retained." The "conduct" must have had something to do with a family quarrel, but it was not explained.[47]

Careful observation of the preceding entries will give some general impressions of the character of the Baptist constituency. Fortunately these impressions may be filled out more fully with additional biographical data on both lay persons and pastors. At a later point we will look more closely at the "new breed" of better educated and more affluent people like James P. and Mary K. Eagle. Here we may cite a couple of the more representative Baptists in Arkansas' small and struggling churches.

Sylvanus Bishop and his wife, Mary Elizabeth, pillars of the Corning Baptist Church, can serve as lay representatives. Born in Erie, Pennsylvania, March 1, 1842, Sylvanus grew up in Pine, Indiana, near Logansport, to which his family moved about 1850. Early on, he made a profession of faith, was baptized, and became a member of a Baptist Church in that community. During the Civil War, he served as a Union Soldier. Attaining the rank of sergeant, he suffered a severe arm fracture in the battle of Shiloh and also contracted smallpox. After the war, on January 31, 1866, he married Mary Elizabeth Benedict near the present town of Denver, Indiana. He learned the wagonmakers' trade. Ten years later, he traded his property near Logansport for a tract of land a mile west of Corning. In February, 1877 he and his family moved to their new home. Finding the land practically untillable, he resumed his trade as a wagonmaker.

Sylvanus Bishop became a charter member of the Corning Church, carrying his letter from Logansport with him. Elected clerk of the church presbytery, a position he held until failing health compelled him to relinquish it, he led the members in building their first church house, donating land and contributing $300 in cash. He also donated his services for completing and furbishing the building. Possessed of an excellent bass voice, he took pleasure in singing with the choir. He died December 7, 1904 and was buried in a family plot at Logansport.

Mary Elizabeth Benedict was born March 8, 1843, near Pen Yan, New York. About 1850 her parents moved to Miami County, Indiana, near Denver. She made a profession of faith, was baptized, and became a member of a Baptist Church at age seventeen.

135

Subsequent to her marriage to Sylvanus Bishop, she transferred her membership to the Baptist Church in Logansport to which her husband belonged. When the family moved to Corning in 1877, she too came with letter in hand to become a charter member. She led in the organization of the "Ladies' Aid Society" of the Church, serving as its first president. She was remembered for her practical and unselfish ministries to others. Totally blind the last ten years of her life, she died October 27, 1919, and was buried in the family plot at Logansport.[48]

Training the Flock

The education of the Baptist constituency moved ahead at a very slow pace as state leaders pushed Sunday schools and, before the end of the period, Baptist Young people's Unions. Though associated closely with the evangelistic work of the churches, the instituting of Sunday schools required an uphill struggle throughout this period. In 1881 Arkansas churches reported only 150 schools. Five years later, O.M. Lucas, Sunday School Missionary, lamented the fact that his work was at a standstill.[49] In 1888 the Committee on Sunday Schools complained about an evident lack of interest in Sunday schools, "not more than one third of our churches reporting schools and half of these live only in summer."[50] Though the Sunday school movement took an upward turn thereafter, due to vigorous promotional efforts, in 1896 the Committee on Sunday Schools reported only 293 schools, which meant schools in one-fourth of the churches, enrolling 12,694 pupils, less than one-sixth of persons attending the church services.[51] Moreover, the situation improved little over the next decade or two.

There were numerous reasons for the slow progress. A powerful one was the widespread lack of general education and even suspicion of it among these early Arkansas Baptists. Undergirding this was a strong impression that religion was caught and not taught, and that chiefly by preaching. Early on, Sunday schools were designed to educate children, not merely in Christian faith but in elementary knowledge, and many doubted their place in the churches, as we have seen earlier. Another reason for slow progress was the lack of trained leaders who could help to promote Sunday schools. By the end of the period we are discussing, of course, that situation began to change but not radically. In the towns the churches often had a few persons who could serve as Sunday school superintendents, but in rural areas they frequently had no one. A third reason was that the State Convention moved somewhat more slowly in its promotion of Sunday schools than it had in organizing churches. This is understandable, for after the Civil War the Convention had to fight a battle for survival before it could do anything. Once it won that battle, it needed to concentrate on the evangelization of the State. Education thus entered the picture in a tangential way. A fourth reason was ambivalence over allegiance—whether to the American Baptist Publication Society, which had been at work in the South before the War, or to the Sunday School Board of the Southern Baptist Convention, organized in 1891—as we discussed earlier.

Arkansas Baptists sought to solve the Sunday school issue in much the same way they handled that of state missions. They employed an executive—variously called "Secretary of Sunday Schools," "Superintendent of Missions," "Sunday-school Missionary," "General Secretary," "General Manager," and "Corresponding Secretary." From time to time, they added "Sunday-school evangelists" to assist him. Both in paying salaries and in effecting other parts of their program they relied on help from the Publication Society and Sunday School Board.

The strategy for promoting Sunday school work varied from time to time, depending on the genius of the "Secretary." In 1899 J.G. Doyle, Corresponding Secretary for the Sunday School and Colportage Board, gathered together a number of earlier programs under one plan: (1) organize new Sunday schools, (2) strengthen and assist existing ones, (3) sell or give Bibles, Testaments, or other religious books, (4) organize and assist Sunday school conventions and hold or assist Sunday school institutes, and (5) carry on Sunday school and colportage work in needy associations.[52] Conventions and institutes, conducted in various associations, were especially crucial for training and maintaining a corps of leaders. Unfortunately, Doyle complained, "in many places, especially in the rural districts, the preachers and Sunday-school workers, do not take interest in our Sunday-school conventions and Sunday-school institutes that we believe their importance demands."[53] He believed that pastors would be a key. If a pastor became concerned, no church would go without a Sunday school for long.

Although the preceding discussion has highlighted the bleak features of the picture, there were some brighter ones. Quite early, the Committee on Sunday Schools pointed out in 1882, many churches recognized that Sunday schools were a key to increased

Bible study, Christian activity, development of a missionary spirit, and, in rural areas, the shift from part-time to full-time. Contrariwise, when they forfeited this opportunity, their children often ended up attending Methodist or Presbyterian Sunday schools and becoming Methodists or Presbyterians.[54]

During the era we are considering, a youth movement also caught up with Arkansas Baptists. The first Baptist Young People's Union in Arkansas was organized in the Second Baptist Church of Little Rock. In 1889 a group of young people realized they needed Bible study and training in Christian service. Three young men presented a plan for a young people's society to their pastor, A.B. Miller, and the deacons. The society was organized on a Sunday afternoon in June, 1889; in 1891, when the national organization called the Baptist Young People's Union of America came into existence, the young people in Second Baptist changed their name accordingly.

The B.Y.P.U. got the same mixed reception in Arkansas Baptist churches as the Sunday school had. Some churches quickly seized the opportunity to educate their constituency, but, predictably, others dragged their feet. When in 1894 B.Y.P.U. representatives petitioned the State Convention to be recognized, the matter was deferred. The Southern Baptist Convention, of course, did not recognize the B.Y.P.U. as an auxiliary until 1895, so that Arkansas Baptists had no precedent to go by. When the Arkansas committee charged with bringing a recommendation on this matter finally did so three years later, therefore, they cautiously commended the work "to the thoughtful and prayerful consideration of the churches" with the stipulation that the organization be "in the closest relation and under the direct control of the church."[55]

Associations

Little need be said here about associations. This is not to say that they did not continue to do important work. It recognizes, rather, an important shift taking place in the work of Arkansas Baptists. In cooperation with the churches and the Arkansas Baptist State Convention associations sponsored missionaries, Sunday school institutes and conventions, and even academies, high schools, and colleges, as they had before. Out of concern for more effective work in these areas, however, responsibility tended to devolve upward toward a more centralized organization. The net result, as we have already seen in looking at mission and Sunday school work by the State Convention, was the creation of frictions as the State Convention subsumed certain roles formerly assumed by churches or associations. Most associations, however, succeeded in keeping the lid on these frictions until the explosion of 1901.

The chief focus of associational work, like that of the State Convention, was missions. Few associations, however, had the resources to hire the personnel needed and thus turned to the State Mission Board, the Home Mission Board of the Southern Baptist Convention, the American Baptist Home Mission Society, or the American Baptist Publication Society. The stringency of an associational budget is reflected in the report of the Executive Board of the eight-year old Current River Baptist Association in 1889:

> *About two months ago we employed Bro. (F.C.) Neely at $75 per month with the understanding that he should call upon assistance when needed, the American Baptist Publication Society paying one half of the salary and this Association one half. Knowing that $75 we pledged at the last meeting our missionary went to work. We must collect and pay up our part.*[56]

The report of Neely and another missionary, W.P. Kime, reflects a valiant effort to fan a few coals into a flame in this fledgling association, founded in 1881 with six quarter-time churches boasting 212 members.

> *We your missionaries make report of work done in your Association beginning July 9, 1889. Our first effort was with Liberty Church which was in a very cold state. God blessed us in giving us a glorious meeting which lasted two weeks. Seven professed conversion—13 additions to the church. The church is much encouraged to call pastor. . . . We next visited Hazeldell. . .Continued seven days of earnest, hard work amid much coldness. . . . The next place we visited was Hopewell. The brethren had already commenced the meeting with good interest. Meeting continued six days after we arrived. Seven professed conversion and several were added to the church. Bro. Kime was not able to be with me. . . The next visited was Mt. Pleasant East. Found the church in a very cold state. There was a great deal of sickness and other hinderances. Result, one conversion and no*

*additions. Bro. Kime was with me two days. A summary
of our work is as follows: No. days 65, miles traveled 556,
confessions 15, additions 22, amount collected on field
$18.40. Books, Bibles, etc., distributed 75, Sunday
schools organized 1, religious visits 110.*

F.C. Neely, W.P. Kime[57]

Associations like this one show why State Convention leaders
moved aggressively to encourage missions, education, and other
programs. The Current River Association heard their first reports on
state missions, foreign missions, and education in 1888 when J.N.
Hall, editor of the **Arkansas Baptist,** and J.W. Conger, President of
Ouachita College, paid them a visit. In addition, they got exposed to
literature other than that of Landmark Baptists. Whereas they had
recommended previously each year the **American Baptist Flag,**
published in St. Louis by D.B. Ray, his **Textbook on Campbellism
and Baptist Succession,** and J.R. Graves's **Tennessee Baptist,** this
year the Committee on Publications urged use of **The Arkansas
Baptist** and Sunday school literature published by the Baptist Book
House in Little Rock. It should probably come as no surprise to learn
that, when the split occurred in 1901, almost all churches and
preachers in this association joined the Landmark side!

Not all associations, to be sure, were as backward as the
Current River Association. Older and better established ones, such
as Caroline and Red River, carried stronger and more self-sustaining
mission programs. That even these, however, were not capable of
maintaining all of the programs Arkansas Baptists needed at the time
is reflected in the story of academies, high schools, and colleges.
Associations initiated most of these schools, but they could not
sustain them without a broader base of support than they had in a
single association or even several associations. Inevitably, therefore,
they turned to surrounding associations and the State Convention for
help.

One illustration of the struggle which went on in an association
to maintain such schools is Mountain Home College. In 1889 a
Committee on Christian Education urged the White River Association to "take active steps at an early day to establish a denominational school under the control of the White River Baptist
Association" and named a Board of Trustees. The Trustees immediately organized, made plans to locate the college at Mountain
Home, and proceeded with the raising of a subscription. Before the

building got underway, however, tragedy struck. Articles of incorporation and a petition for a certificate of incorporation were destroyed when the Baxter County courthouse burned to the ground and crop failure forestalled payment on subscriptions. As a result, it was not until 1891 that an agent employed by the Trustees resecured old pledges and obtained new ones. After completion of the first building the College opened in September 1893, burdened with a bank mortgage for $5,000. In 1894 the Trustees confessed that "Owing to the illness of the field agent and the cry of 'Hard Times' nothing was paid on the indebtedness on the college building. . ."[58] Despite its financial woes, Mountain Home got off to a fairly favorable start, reporting 11 faculty and 166 students the first session. Almost from the outset, however, it had to appeal to the Arkansas Baptist State Convention for help. The Trustees reported that the Association had subscribed $4,200 to pay off a $6,000 indebtedness on the building with the proviso that the Arkansas Baptist State Convention would pledge the remaining $1,800. In its previous annual meeting the Association had voted to turn the College over to the Convention.[59] Unfortunately, the financial distress of Mountain Home did not cease there. In 1897 the Trustees reported "very short crops in the territory contiguous to the college" and failure of many persons to make good on pledges to pay off $2,000 indebtedness due to "the exceedingly hard times."[60] The next year, the College had to close for several months when its second president, M.S. Kennard, resigned. After two years under a new president, J.F. Howell, it closed again for a year (1901-1902). When it reopened in 1902, it operated as an academy in the Ouachita-Central System and then as a mountain school jointly sponsored by the State Convention and the Home Mission Board of the Southern Baptist Convention.

We will examine further the negative side of the State Convention's willingness to stretch its own helping hands too far when we discuss the division of 1901 in the next chapter. It suffices here to point out that as the State Convention increased, the associations decreased in importance. The heyday of associations was passing as Baptists in Arkansas united forces on a larger and larger scale.

It is true that a number of new associations came into existence during this period. Most of these, however, were created by black Baptists, who were striving to organize their efforts along lines similar to those employed by whites. Among both groups one notices some fluctuation up and down. Annual reports, especially by black

141

churches, were often so fragmentary that it would not be wise to infer much from minor changes. As regards the white Baptist associations,

TABLE XIV
ASSOCIATIONS, 1880-1900

Year	Number of Associations		Year	Number of Associations	
	White	Black		White	Black
1880	38	9	1891	48	25
1881	38	9	1892	42(?)	25
1882	39	11	1893	47	18(?)
1883	39	13	1894	48	30
1884	39	14	1895	49	31
1885	40	15	1896	49	31
1886	41	19	1897	50	31
1887	44	13(?)	1898	48	30
1888	42	19	1899	50	29
1889	39(?)	25	1900	50	30
1890	43	25			

it suffices to point out that they increased only by twelve during this twenty year period. For the most part the increase involved no more than one or two additions per year except in 1891 when five new ones appeared. We have already seen that 1891 was a bright year for State Convention activities. The next year, however, a depression struck and undercut many of these gains.[61]

Baptists and Their Peers

In earlier chapters we have alluded to the Baptist search for identity in relation to other denominations, especially the "Reform" movement of Alexander Campbell. In the period now under study we can discern a growing competitiveness among various Protestant groups combined with substantial cooperation. By the end of this era, as Baptists escalated their mission thrust, they often let the former override the latter.

There are, to be sure, ample signs of cooperation among the denominations. As in the earlier periods, Baptists, Methodists, Presbyterians, and Disciples (Christians) participated in one another's revivals. On occasion they shared church buildings. After the cyclone of 1898 demolished the buildings of the First Baptist Church of Fort Smith, the church immediately received invitations from the First Presbyterian, Cumberland Presbyterian, First

Christian, and Lutheran churches and also the Jewish synagogue(!) to make use of their buildings until Baptists could rebuild. For a few weeks the Baptists took advantage of this kindness and then rented a hall owned by the Turners athletic club.

Other denominations also manifested an ecumenical spirit **vis-a-vis** the activities of the State Convention. Throughout the period we are considering local congregations extended invitations to leaders attending annual conventions to preach to them on Sundays. The number of invitations naturally depended on the number of churches in a local area, but there seems to have been a surprising openness here, which Baptists reciprocated when they had opportunity. At Hope, for instance, in 1885, Baptist leaders preached in Presbyterian, Cumberland Presbyterian, Disciples, Methodist, and black Baptist, as well as other white Baptist churches. Quite often, moreover, persons of other denominations contributed to Baptist fund drives as Baptists presumably did to theirs. At Fayetteville in 1883, for example, Methodists contributed more to the Baptist collection for state and foreign missions than Baptists. The figures are worth citing, for they show a genuine spirit of mutual concern for missions:

Baptists	$10.00
Presbyterians	3.60
Methodists	11.40
Cumberland Presbyterians	3.25
Disciples	4.25

A major exception to the cooperativeness shown here was the general attitude of Baptists, as well as other Protestants, toward Roman Catholics. In this early period, of course, Arkansas had few Catholic immigrants; when the latter came to the United States, they usually stayed in the northeast. The impressions of Catholicism, therefore, were second hand and tended to be strongly biased, often shaped under the influence of radical groups like the Ku Klux Klan. Occasionally some local or national issue touched off the grossest suspicions.

We see an example of this in a resolution passed by the Arkansas Baptist State Convention in 1894 in response to Roman Catholic efforts to obtain federal monies to support parochial schools. The resolution illustrates not only the Baptist fears of Roman Catholicism but the ties which they felt bound them to other Protestants in withstanding the Catholic influence. It demonstrates

143

too, in an incidental way, the willingness of Baptists to use political means to effect some of their own objectives.

Resolved, That we, the representatives of seventy thousand Baptists, view with uneasiness bordering on alarm, the growing power of the Roman Catholic church over the Congress of the United States, and the different departments of the Federal government. We desire to utter anew, and in no uncertain tone, the time honored truth ever held by Baptists, and for which they have in all ages sacrificed their lives, that there shall be no inter dependency whatever between church and state, and we denounce all legislation which provides that the revenues of the Federal govenment shall be expended in sustaining wholly, or in part, any Roman Catholic or sectarian school, in the territories of the United States or elsewhere.

We further call on all Protestants by whatever name known, unite with us in stemming the current of legislation which is being directed by Romanists to the maintenance of their churches and schools, at the expense of the tax-papers (sic) of the nation. We heartily endorse and approve the following as an amendment to the Constitution of the United States:

No state shall pass any law respecting an establishment of religion, or prohibiting the free exercise thereof, or use its property or credit, or any money raised by taxation, or authorize either to be used, for the purpose of founding, maintaining or aiding, by appropriation, payment for services, expenses or otherwise, any church, religious denomination, or religious society, or any institution, society or undertaking, which is wholly, or in part, under sectarian or ecclesiastical control.

Further that a copy of these resolutions be forwarded by the Secretary of the Convention to each of our Representatives and Senators in Congress.[62]

Even with other Protestant denominations the cooperative spirit often give way to competition and even invective, especially in the late 1890s. Competition, of course, was often wholesome and good natured—Baptists kidding others or being kidded about their views and practices. Sometimes, however, it went well beyond the point of challenge and resulted in some bitter attacks from both sides. The Baptist "high churchism" of J.R. Graves and J.M.Pendleton fueled the flames of hostility from the Baptist side, but it was matched by similar doctrinaire thought from the side of Presbyterians, Methodists, and Disciples.

Illustrations of the tensions abound for all levels of Baptist life. In 1886 the White River Baptist Association adopted a resolution discouraging patronage of secular newspapers which referred to the followers of Alexander Campbell as the Christian Church. The resolution predicated its appeal on the argument that "they un-christianize us by calling the Campbellite society the Christian church, thus excluding all others."[63]

By about 1895 Baptist exclusivism was reaching a high level. We must always make some allowance for the rhetoric of such statements, but the report of a Committee on Foreign Missions to the State Convention in 1895 probably reflected the actual sentiment of many. "We, as Baptists," the Committee urged, "are especially called to this work, for we alone teach the truth and the whole truth."[64] They may not have seen any anomaly in the fact that they responded cordially the same week to invitations to preach in churches of other denominations! On the contrary, the Greenbriar Association recorded with obvious satisfaction the "conversion" and baptism of a Methodist preacher and the promise of asso-ciational missionary C.B. Parsons that "Others will follow."[65]

The Whitsitt Controversy in Arkansas

The triumphalist note in the preceding statements was under-girded by Baptist successionism, the theory that Baptist churches could trace their history from John's baptism of Jesus at the Jordan River through a succession of churches not connected with the Catholic Church. As we have seen, this theory entered Arkansas territory early in 1855, with the publication of G.H. Orchard's **Concise History of Foreign Baptists.** Had it not been for the struggle with Alexander Campbell's "Reform," the theory might not have caught on as strongly as it did. In a period of crisis in identity,

145

however, it served nicely to validate the Baptist claim. Then, as Baptists revved up their mission efforts, it provided continuous inspiration. Any threat to this theory was seen as a threat to the entire Baptist cause, any support for it a support for that cause.

The demolition job which William H. Whitsitt did on the succession theory in his **Question in Baptist History: Whether the Anabaptists in England Practiced Immersion before the Year 1641?**, published in 1896, drew intense fire from Baptists all over Arkansas. In the same year a Committee on Resolutions of the State Convention composed of A.H. Autry, O.L. Hailey, J.W. Conger, P.C. Barton, T.C. Swofford, and J.G. Doyle, citing Whitsitt's publication, expressed outrage about Whitsitt's "method" and "teaching" and appealed to the Board of Trustees of Southern Seminary in Louisville "to remove the existing difficulties or secure Dr. Whitsitt's resignation or removal."[66] The next year numerous associations followed the State Convention's lead in reiterating the demand for Whitsitt's resignation. At the State Convention A.H. Autry based the demand on the fact that Whitsitt had "written things at variance with the teachings of the denomination" which "serve to alienate brethren and threaten the disruption of our Baptist Zion."[67] Later in the convention A.G. McManaway tried to put teeth into the Arkansas position by offering a resolution instructing Arkansas delegates to the Southern Baptist Convention "to use all proper means and to vote as a unit towards securing the immediate retirement of Dr. W.H. Whitsitt from all connections with the Southern Baptist Theological Seminary."[68] Whitsitt, as is well known, satisfied his opponents by resigning in 1898. That fall, Arkansas Baptists proceeded to reaffirm "support of the Seminary, both moral and financial, as a convention, whenever all obstacles thereto shall have been removed."[69] Though trained Church historians would support Whitsitt, the succession theory was destined to survive Whitsitt's criticisms and to hold on tenaciously in the minds of many Baptists.

Baptists in Arkansas Society

Up to now, we have been looking chiefly at the life and work of Arkansas Baptists from the inside. We turn now to examine their involvement in Arkansas society. Here, as I have observed before, we must pay careful attention to the two faces of Arkansas Baptists. On one side, a minority of well-educated and cultured people took an active role in Arkansas society and pressed Baptist churches, associations, and the State Convention to follow suit. On the other side, a majority of poorly educated and unrefined people understood religion almost wholly in individual terms and resisted involvement. Being poor farmers and woodsmen, they lacked both the understanding and the resources to contribute much beyond the level of individual honesty and integrity in their dealings with others.

Baptists and Politics

As we have seen in preceding chapters, Arkansas Baptists often manifested a keen interest in social and political matters and used their influence effectively at both local and state levels. During the present period, we can see this especially in their campaign on behalf of temperance, which we will examine more closely in a moment. Baptist concerns, however, extended beyond the sale and use of alcoholic beverages. We have noted, for instance, the strongly worded resolution opposing federal aid to parochial schools. Baptists operated their own schools, moreover, with a concern for the creation of a Christian citizenry and, in their most eloquent moments, promoted them as a benefit not only to the churches but to the state and even human civilization.[70] Occasionally, too, they articulated directly their support of political decisions and activities which had far-reaching moral inplications. In 1895, for instance, the State Convention issued a formal resolution lauding Governor James P. Clarke and Judges Duffey and Martin for "exercising the whole power of the commonwealth in the suppression of the carnival of crime so recently imminent in Hot Springs, . . ." They went on to express the opinion that the action would "mark an epoch in our State's history in anticipating and preventing organized resistance to law, aided by criminal official indifference or connivance,. . ." and urged every Christian to "pray and labor for its realization."[71]

Although Baptists normally left political decisions to individuals, we can see in the preceding instances a type of corporate political action which had an important bearing on the development of the state. In this, of course, Baptists acted very much as other Protestants. More revealing still of their general perspective on politics, however, was the involvement of some, including ministers, in political office. It may occasion some surprise today to note that in 1891 one-fifth of all representatives in the state legislature were ordained ministers. But we must remember that, at the time, ministers made up a sizeable part of the educated minority of the

147

Arkansas populace. An outstanding example of the minister-politician of this day was James P. Eagle, twenty-one times president of the State Convention and thrice president of the Southern Baptist Convention.

After several terms in the Arkansas House of Representatives, in 1885 Eagle was elected its Speaker. During his tenure in that position, the legislature passed a number of bills reflecting a Baptist slant. One prohibited Sunday baseball. Numerous bills supported the temperance movement. A resolution submitted in 1886 favored a constitutional amendment prohibiting the manufacture or the sale of alcoholic beverages. The House passed 18 measures to restrict the sale of "ardent spirits" within as many localities. Another measure prohibited saloon keepers from allowing minors to play cards or other games in their establishments. Another placed a $50 state tax and a $100 county tax on every wholesale dealer in malt liquors. A "blue law" forbade stores or saloons to open on Sunday and persons observing another day to disturb a religious congregation meeting on Sunday. A bill allowing butcher or bake shops to open until 10:00 a.m. on Sundays passed both houses but was vetoed by the governor; though it again passed the Senate, it failed in the House.

Although many of these bills coincided with Baptist views, we should not conclude that they passed by Baptist effort alone; other church groups held similar views. Nor should we suppose that James P. Eagle steered them through the House singlehandedly; he had plenty of support. When elected governor in 1888, moreover, he proved that he was no mere Baptist partisan. Basing his campaign on his war and peace record and honesty and efficiency in government, he tried to represent the entire constituency of the state in the best way he could. He advocated the creation of an equilization board, urged liberal support of education, recommended measures to encourage immigration, favored pure elections, called for legislation to establish a commission to regulate the railroads, favored a state-supported road system, and proposed a revamping of the state prison system. Interestingly he gained substantial support from blacks in his first campaign. During his second term, however, the legislature passed a bill requiring separate railroad cars for blacks and whites. Two incidents—the murder of John M. Clayton, brother of former governor, Powell Clayton, and shortages in the state treasury—greatly embarrassed him. A Populist Party arose, splitting the vote. As a result, Eagle retired in 1893 after only two terms. He left his party sufficiently strong, however, that another Democrat, William

Fishback, handily defeated Republican and Populist candidates.

But populism was gaining strength in Arkansas. Jeff Davis, representative of the more backwoodsy type Baptist, ran for attorney general in 1898. Two years later, he moved into the governor's mansion, presaging a period of defeat for the forces typified by Eagle in both state and church.[72]

Baptists and Temperance

The issue which preoccupied Baptists more than any other during this era, judging by the amount of attention it received in associations or conventions, was temperance. Early on, as we have seen in previous chapters, not all Baptists were teetotalers. Abuses connected with the use of alcohol escalated so much and so rapidly during the post-Civil War era, however, that Baptists rode the public tide pushing along toward absolute prohibition.

We can find evidence of this growing concern manifested in the churches, in associational meetings, and at the annual State Convention. We need not repeat what was said earlier concerning disciplinary action taken regarding the use of alcohol in individual congregations. Associations followed suit. At its second session, in 1872, for instance, the Concord Baptist Association recommended teetotalism.[73] Similarly the Baptist General Association of Western Arkansas and Indian Territory, which continued active until 1897, repeatedly urged teetotalism, acknowledging the evils liquor produced in that part of the state.[74]

The issue got even fuller airing in the State Convention. In 1880 a Special Committee on Temperance recommended that the Convention approve "all proper efforts to procure the enactment of a rigorous prohibitory liquor law in the State of Arkansas."[75] Subsequently, as the temperance campaign gathered steam, the Committee on Temperance became a standing committee of the Convention, and, symbolic of the narrowing thrust of temperance, one year (1896) was called the Committee on Total Abstinence and Prohibition.[76] In 1885, encouraged by legislation going through the state legislature, the Committee called for total abstinence as "the only safe rule for individual practice" and "the absolute prohibition of the manufacture and sale of intoxicating drinks, . . ."[77] It is evident that Baptists hesitated a bit to use political clout to obtain prohibition, but, becoming ever more sensitive about the matter, eventually laid aside this inhibition. In 1888, for instance, they put themselves on record "against even the moderate use of alcoholic stimulants and tobacco in all forms" but did not think temperance should be a political issue; instead, they urged the election of "dry" candidates.[78] Seven years later, they had forgotten such reservations. The Committee on Temperance boldly urged Arkansas Baptists to "exert our influence to both **check** and **stop** the use of alcoholic beverages," cooperating with such legislation and avoiding touching, tasting, or handling. They also challenged the churches to make the issue "a test of church fellowship."[79] Similarly, in 1898, the Committee on Temperance proposed "unceasing warfare" against alcohol and cooperation with civil authorities in banning it.[80] Even more explicitly, in 1900, the Committee offered a resolution "That the Arkansas Baptist Convention. . .would respectfully ask our legislature in its coming session to memorialize Congress to pass such laws as will prohibit the granting of licenses in prohibition districts."[81]

The use of tobacco did not receive as much attention from Arkansas Baptists as the use of alcohol. Late in this period, however, it became an issue frequently coupled with temperance. In 1888, for instance, the Convention went on record against the use of "tobacco in all forms," and subsequent conventions reiterated this stand. By 1895 tobacco had evidently become more controversial, for a special resolution adopted that year recommended "That it be the sense of this Convention that the use of tobacco be discouraged among **all** Baptists."[82] It is clear from the wording of this statement that Baptists were far from the kind of consensus they had achieved in their opposition to the manufacture, sale, and use of alcoholic beverages.

Arkansas Baptist Orphans' Home

The social consciousness of Arkansas Baptists also manifested itself in other ways during this period. One of these was in the founding of a home for orphans at Monticello.

Inspiration for an orphans' home came from Miss Hannah Hyatt, who in 1894 offered her home and eighty acres of land to the State Convention for this purpose. On a recommendation brought by R.C. Medaris the Convention appointed a committee to "see about the legality and tender of the property."[83] Within a year it had secured the deed, adopted Articles of Incorporation, and contracted for the construction of a building to accomodate orphans.[84] Persons attending the convention in 1894 pledged $600 and encouraged churches, Sunday schools, and other organizations to take at least one collection for the home the following year.

The home opened in 1896 with four "inmates," as they were

then called. The number of occupants mounted steadily upward: 18 in 1897, one of whom died; 21 in 1898, of whom one died and another was placed in a private home; 25 in 1899; and 37 in 1900. Already in 1898 this expansion necessitated more facilities and the hiring of an agent, W.W. Gardner, to raise money.

The home fared better financially than many other projects entered into by the Arkansas Baptist State Convention. Contributions were large enough at the outset to pay for construction of the first building. Subsequently they enabled the Board of Directors to begin paying Hannah Hyatt Gardner a modest stipend in 1899; previously, after donating the property for the home, she had devoted her services as matron free of charge.

Baptists and Education

An important part of the Baptist contribution to the shaping of Arkansas society in this period, as in earlier ones, came from its educational institutions. These, as we have seen previously, were usually begun by associations; indeed, from an early date, a major part of the **raison d'être** of associations was educational. The period we are dealing with, however, demonstrated the inability of associations to carry on an adequate program of education. They simply did not have the resources to do so. As a result, responsibility for education spiraled gradually upward to become a concern of the State Convention.

We need not report on the numerous academies, high schools, and colleges which associations initiated or sought to maintain during this period. When the period opened, Baptists of Arkansas were supporting a Baptist High School in Arkadelphia, Judson University, and Centennial Institute at Warren. They were awaiting too the opening of Buckner College, an event which finally took place in 1882. Meantime, pressures were building up to establish a Baptist College sponsored by all Baptists of the State, which might supplant the impotent and struggling schools then in existence.

We have seen dreams and plans for such a school dating back to the pre-Civil War era revived in the 1870s. In 1882 the Convention took the first big step in agreeing to consolidate the many small associational schools into one. In 1883, concluding that "The Baptists of Arkansas cannot afford to lag behind the tide of (en)lightenment," it appointed a five-man Educational Commission to "consider the advisability of establishing a Baptist State College,

151

and if thought advisable, to take steps at once to found and fully organize such an institution of learning."[85]

This Commission did not register immediate success, but by 1885, backed by Caroline, Friendship, Red River, Bartholomew, Union, Liberty, Judson, Columbia, Dardanelle, Southwestern, and Mount Vernon Associations, it was able to take the momentous step of proposing a Board of Trustees, which would be self-perpetuating and have absolute control of the College, and initiate plans to build. The Board of Trustees met in Little Rock on April 8, 1886, to consider bids from eight towns for location of the school. After considerable debate, discussion, and dissension, they settled on Arkadelphia on the seventy-second ballot.[86]

The Red River Association agreed to transfer thirteen acres and the building used for the Baptist Academy and High School to the Board of Trustees of the newly established college. Citizens of Arkadelphia pledged $10,000 of an estimated $50,000 required to erect a new building on the campus. On June 22 the Board elected J.W. Conger, a pastor in Prescott, the first president of the school, officially named Ouachita Baptist College. The college opened in one building with three departments—primary, preparatory, and collegiate—with music, art, and bookkeeping also in the curriculum. Indicative of the demand, enrollment in the coeducational school leaped from 166 students in the fall of 1886 to 235 in the spring of 1887. During President Conger's administration (1886-1907), Ouachita added several buildings, increased its faculty to twenty-six and its enrollment to 476. The number of graduates however, fluctuated up and down, as the following table shows, as the economy rose and fell.

Year	Graduates	Year	Graduates
1888	3	1895	15
1889	13	1896	13
1890	10	1897	18
1891	10	1898	12
1892	6	1899	16
1893	8	1900	22
1894	11	1901	23

The sharp drop of graduates in 1892 and 1893 reflects the impact of the recession noted several times before.

Responding to pressures from a sizeable part of its constituency, the State Convention opened a women's college at Conway, after surmounting initial difficulties in September, 1893. The decision was a sensitive one, for Ouachita was coed and had erected a special boarding house for women. To lessen tensions over the matter, B.G. Maynard proposed a resolution assuring full support to Ouachita and that the move to establish a female college "does not in the least lessen confidence and interest in the original conception of this institution as to the co-education of its sexes."[87] Central Female College opened with 56 students. The second year it enrolled more than a hundred, the third year 106. Subsequently, however, enrollment rose and fell as the college floundered financially. In 1896, for example, the Trustees of Central complained about a lack of Baptist patronage and pled for $600 to save $2,000 worth of furniture. Although they obtained $660 in pledges, many contributors failed to pay their subscriptions, and the College continued a marginal existence.

It is not necessary to dwell on the oppressive financial burden under which all of the Arkansas Baptist colleges labored—Ouachita, Central, Mountain Home, and Buckner. Reports of the trustees of these institutions belabored that point often enough. We should note, however, a growing concern during the 1890s about the relation of the colleges to the State Convention. Some leaders pressed for closer ties between the Convention and the colleges. In 1892, for example, G.W. Reeves moved that the Convention ask the trustees of Ouachita to "examine anew the provisions of the charter of the school, and see whether or not any alterations are needed in it, in order to bring it into closer organic connection with this Convention."[88] Exactly what lay behind this motion is not clear, but the same concern surfaced again in 1897, when the Convention named a special committee of seven to investigate the connection and propose a plan to relieve their financial distress and to create and conserve "a close organic connection."[89] Later in the same convention, a more strongly worded resolution was adopted to the effect that the colleges had to be brought "under the absolute legal control of this convention."[90]

The question of control which we are pointing to here seems to have combined with mounting financial pressures in an era when Baptists felt increasing need for parochial education to evoke a proposal for a statewide Baptist educational system. In 1900 the Committee on Education, rejoicing in the growth of Baptist colleges and in the interest associations were manifesting in academies and high schools, recommended the appointment of a committee to study "the advisability of affiliating and systematizing all our Baptist schools in the State, so that there will be no misdirected or averted energy or funds."[91] This recommendation was backed up by the Board of Trustees of Ouachita College, who, decrying low salaries and consequent loss of faculty, urged a three-pronged approach: (1) a fund drive to liquidate debts, (2) fostering of ties between colleges and other schools, and (3) raising endowment.[92] The next year, the Convention took a further step in this direction with the establishment of the Ouachita-Central System.

Before closing this statement on education, we need to add a word about its shifting challenge and focus. Early on, Baptists, along with other Christian groups, established and sustained the only schools there were, for public education had not yet taken hold on the frontier. This situation changed radically during and after the Civil War, when in 1862 the Morrill Act set in motion a program of higher education through land grant colleges. By the period now under discussion Arkansas Baptists began to get a taste of "secular" education, that is, education not under direct Christian influence. What they experienced, they did not like and instead reacted with some alarm to this challenge.

For one thing they discovered that Baptists, whose constituency were chiefly in the lower socio-economic bracket, were not fairly represented on the faculties of secular schools and petitioned for greater consideration. In 1880, for instance, the State Convention directly requested the trustees of the Arkansas Industrial University to consider "the propriety of having the Baptist denomination represented in the Faculty of the State Institution."[93] Smarting over the fact that the trustees chose to ignore this resolution, the next year the Convention repeated its petition and, remonstrating over "sectarianism" in the University, urged Baptists throughout the state to "give attention to this matter, and by all proper methods, make themselves felt in this as in all the public interests of Arkansas."[94] Such rebuffs as this did much to accelerate the pace at which Baptists developed their own schools.

Baptist leaders correctly saw that, to compete with such schools as the University of Arkansas, opened at Fayetteville in 1872, they had to foster quality education. In 1883, therefore, as they built up momentum for a state college, the Committee on Education urged the Convention to "take steps toward the means and best plans of endowing a first class institution of learning in this state."[95] In time

154

the competition between public and denominational schools grew more fierce, and, as it did, Arkansas Baptists not only promoted their schools but criticized their competitors, both secular and religious. In 1889, for instance, the Education Committee gave their report a particularly strident tone:

> *The great question for our people is to determine whether our children shall be committed to the tuition of those who have sought to exterminate us with the sword and at the stake, and to their descendants; to those who despise the cardinal doctrines in all true culture—the cross of our Lord Jesus Christ; or shall we commit them to the training and care of those who realize that to Him belongs 'the kingdom, the power and glory,' and reverently kneel at the cross and teach that 'obedience is better than sacrifice.' Your committee recommend that every Baptist in Arkansas be urged that it is an individual duty to place his children for education where the teachings of home and parents will not be antagonized or neutralized, and that those institutions built and fostered by Baptists, especially those within the bounds of our State, be supported.*[96]

In 1891 the Education Committee specifically argued against education at the University of Arkansas with the comment that youths in state schools were "almost impossible to religiously impress" and "to reach, with the influence peculiar to Baptists."[97] In 1894 the Committee on General Education of the State Convention published a still stronger statement. Chaired by J.W. Conger, President of Ouachita, they cited another source which maintained that "secular education is always narrow. Christian education is broad." They proceeded to insist that "the only justification we can urge for maintaining our colleges is that they are 'outspokenly Christian, aggressively evangelistic, and frankly denominational.'"[98] Other reports continually remonstrated with Baptists for failing to send their children to Baptist colleges.

The antipathy which we see here carried over into elementary and secondary education, leading to a strong push to found Baptist academies and high schools. In 1892 the Committee on Education of the State Convention called for "more good district, common and high schools, taught by Christian men and women only."[99] The next year, the Committee sounded a bit more realistic when it urged "a few good high schools, wisely located and managed to prepare pupils for the College."[100]

Women in Arkansas Baptist Churches

The importance of women in the life of Arkansas Baptist churches continued to rise during this period. They did not gain recognition easily, however, and we must not assume that all Arkansas Baptists looked with favor upon the growing involvement and leadership of women in the work of Arkansas Baptist churches. Women first wrung from their peers a begruding consent to organize a women's effort on behalf of missions. Only gradually did even that role win general acceptance and enthusiastic applause.

Women and Missions

As in previous periods, women continued in this one to play important roles in local churches. In 1886, for instance, James P. Eagle, President of the Arkansas Baptist State Convention, called attention to the efforts of one woman to erect a church building in Bentonville. "Here that noble, Godly woman, Sister A.N. Hobbs, has for years been praying and struggling to build a house for God. When completed, the house will be one of the most beautiful in the State."[101] Women also led in special projects such as the establishment of the home for orphans at Monticello which we discussed earlier. Their most spectacular contribution, however, had to do with the mission work of Arkansas Baptists, both foreign and home.

Ironically the first proposal for a woman's organization which would support the Baptist mission effort in Arkansas came not from a woman but from a man, M.D. Early, a pastor in Morrilton and Vice-president for Arkansas of the Home Mission Board of the Southern Baptist Convention. In 1883 he urged the women of Arkansas to follow the lead of women in other states in forming a Central Committee whose purposes would be to organize new societies, to stimulate interest in missions, and to collect reports for publication. Responding to Early's suggestion, a small group of women convened at Russellville in September, 1883, electing Mary K. Eagle, wife of James P. Eagle, their president, and Mrs. M.D. Early their secretary.

It was not an easy task to organize the women of Arkansas in support of missions. Having grown up in a society and in churches where men normally took command of things and sharing the suspicion of organization characteristic of Arkansans, they dragged their feet even in such matters as reporting the work of their local

156

societies. Nevertheless, under the forceful leadership of Mary K. Eagle, they inched forward, doing a remarkable job of fund raising if nothing else. In 1888, following the lead of the Woman's Missionary Union Auxiliary to the Southern Baptist Convention, they organized a state Woman's Missionary Union. This body held its first annual meeting in Little Rock in 1889.

The Constitution of the Woman's Baptist Missionary Union of Arkansas envisioned a dual purpose for the organization:

> *1. To distribute missionary information and stimulate effort, through the State Central Committee, and to encourage the organization of Woman's Missionary Societies and Children's Mission Bands.*
>
> *2. To secure the earnest, systematic co-operation of women and children in collecting and raising money for missions.*[102]

The Arkansas Woman's Missionary Union, as Table XV shows, experienced ups and downs in meeting both objectives. They evidently were more successful at raising funds than at getting accurate reports on organizations, for Mrs. Eagle continually

TABLE XV
THE WOMAN'S MISSIONARY UNION OF ARKANSAS, 1883-1900

Year	Societies Reporting	Contributions
1883	20	$ 457.43
1884	21	541.50
1885	16	830.45
1886	32	2,573.45
1887	50	4,278.70
1888	28	3,535.06
1889	38	5,730.19
1890	47	7,685.66
1891	no report	3,592.57
1892	no report	2,601.79
1893	33	4,041.09(4,456.86)
1894	44	8,270.75
1895	44	7,977.17(4,977.17)
1896	no report	no report
1897	50	7,968.03
1898	61	4,102.74
1899	40	5,630.49
1900	40	4,120.44

complained about the inadequate information she was receiving. The problem ran deeper than the reporting of statistics, however. Once again, as in the organizing of the Arkansas Baptist mission effort in general, it was a matter of widespread unreadiness of the people of Arkansas for a change in their way of doing things. Mrs. Eagle, like her husband, saw the necessity of organized effort to achieve the goals of both state and church, but most of her constituency did not. She also discerned the strength of opposition to organization. Not surprisingly, her last address as President of the Arkansas W.M.U., delivered at Paragould in 1901, a year and a half before she died, was a defense of organization.

Organization, she argued, had been "a blessing to women in general." She admitted that women might give too much time to a certain organization, but that could not happen in the service of God. The women's organization of the Southern Baptist Convention, she insisted, "is most beautiful to contemplate." The field, Arkansas, is "white unto harvest." Arkansas women have not yet caught up with women in other states in keeping records and working together. They could do far more if they entered "the fields made available to them by the perfect co-operation and sympathy of all forces now in operation." They should be embarrassed that they have done so little. Organized, they could do what they should.[103]

In addition to outright opposition to organization, a number of other factors retarded the development of women's societies in local churches. Many pastors failed to encourage them and often opposed them directly. In most instances, they probably did so on the grounds that women should not take active roles in church life. Sometimes they may have found other reasons. In 1889, for instance, a report presented at the Woman's Missionary Union Convention noted that the success of women in raising money tended to decrease the concern of men about it. Some women, moreover, encountered criticism for sponsoring church suppers to raise money on the charge of gambling! They responded, "We would suggest to our brother pastors that they put a limit on our way of working for the church and save us the humiliation of being called gamblers."[104]

Women, too, however, held back. In 1886 D.A. (Mrs. M.D.) Early gave a pessimistic appraisal of the chances the Woman's Central Committee had in involving all the women of Arkansas in their work. "They have been educated to have the husband, the father, the brother make all the contributions of the family—not fully realizing that religion, with all of its duties, is a personal matter, and it is the imperative duty of each woman who is adopted into God's family to make contributions of her time and money for the advancement of His kingdom."[105] With limited education many Arkansas Baptist women were ill equipped to do many of the things Mary Eagle and D.A. Early proposed.

Nevertheless, not all was negative. Women did receive some support, encouragement, and praise for their work. The State Convention established a Committee on Woman's Work in 1883, the year the Central Committee was formed. Composed of leaders such as M.D. Early, this Committee lauded the work of women and campaigned for expansion of it. The first Committee, for instance, urging pastors to organize women's societies in their churches, promised that "glorious results will follow, a new impetus will be given to the cause of missions, and instead of the meager sum now reported, hundreds, and even thousands of dollars will flow into the treasury of the Lord."[106] In time the fund raising success of women undercut much of the suspicion and hostility to their work.

Women's Leadership

We cannot suppose, however, that many Arkansas Baptists were ready to recognize the leadership of women in their churches, associations, or State Convention. Most, even women, held firmly to women's subordination in churches as elsewhere, and many pastors feared that the organization of women for mission causes might lead to a usurping of their authority. Sensitive to this issue, in 1887 the Committee on Woman's Work of the State Convention reassured them that "our sisters have no thought of separate and distinct effort,. . ."[107]

Even persons who favored the development of women's mission organizations considered women subordinate and dependent upon men in the church. As in marriage, so in the Church, women were "helpmeets" but clearly subject to their husbands. In 1891, for instance, the Committee on Woman's Work of the State Convention prefaced their report with a reminder that the gospel has taken woman from a condition of servitude and placed her "where the Creator placed her, by the side of man in the home, in the community, and in the church as his true and faithful help meet,. . ." They went on, however, to remind that she does not "ask or seek divorcement from her Divinely appointed position, only desiring, as her loving and clinging nature prompts, to be unto man a true and faithful companion, sympathizing with him and helping him in all the trials and duties of life, and rejoicing with him in the liberty where the gospel makes both men and women free."[108] In 1893 the Committee replied to critics of the Woman's Missionary Union who cited 1 Corinthians 14:34-35 in opposition to women taking leadership roles. Noting that Paul allowed Priscilla as well as Aquila to teach "in a private manner," they contended that the Apostle's injunction against women speaking in the churches did not imply that they could "take no active part in the work of our Master's Kingdom." But the Committee did not envision "active" in terms of leadership, for they added: "Although it does not appear that they are fitted by nature or Divine call for the ministry, still there are broad fields in which they should labor."[109]

These attitudes notwithstanding, some women were ready for and did exercise leading roles. They not only organized a women's effort but also a children's effort in missions. Miss Mayme Gardiner organized the first Sunbeam Band at Monticello in June of 1891. Two women were among the twenty-five agents appointed in 1888 by the Liberty Association to raise money in its churches for Ouachita College.[110] Mary K. Eagle presented reports at the Arkansas Baptist State Convention.

Among many women assuming increasingly significant roles Mary Kavanaugh Oldham Eagle stands out. Like her husband, she represented the "new Breed" of wealthier, better educated, more refined, sophisticated, and socially conscious Baptists Arkansas was producing. And she had both the training and the desire to advance the cause of women. Born in Madison County, Kentucky, February 4, 1854, she was educated at Science Hill, an elite girls' academy in Shelbyville. She joined a Baptist church at age twenty. On January 3, 1882 she married James P. Eagle. They resided on their plantation at Lonoke until 1889. After the election of Eagle as governor, they moved to Little Rock, ramaining there until her death on February 15, 1903.

During her years in Arkansas, Mrs. Eagle was highly active in both public and religious affairs. Although slow to give her consent for Eagle to run for governor, she campaigned vigorously in his behalf. According to the governor's own account, "During my two terms of office, she had full control of the social side of the administration, exercising her own judgment and good taste in receiving and entertaining friends and visitors in our home. What she wanted to do, she did, and did it well."[111] Eagle was prepared to entrust to her even the affairs of state. When he fell ill as he was preparing his final message to be delivered to the General Assembly, he called on his wife to complete the message, read the proof, see that it was printed, and have it ready for the meeting as required by law.[112]

At the Columbian Exposition in 1893 Mrs. Eagle was a member of the Board of Lady Managers and served on the Executive, the Historical and the Woman's Congresses committees. As chairperson of the last, she presided over meetings, engaged speakers and lecturers, and edited for publication the papers read in the congress. Meantime, she participated in numerous local clubs and organizations in Little Rock and was one of the founders of the Woman's Co-operative Association.

Against the background of these involvements we should not be surprised that she took the lead in the women's movement in Arkansas Baptist churches. Very soon after her arrival in Arkansas, she led in the organization of the Woman's Central Committee. From 1888 until her death she served as president of the Woman's Missionary Union of Arkansas, injecting into it much of the vigor it had. She also served several years as a Vice-President of the Woman's Missionary Union of the Southern Baptist Convention. A tireless traveler, she participated actively in meetings of associations, the State Convention, and the Southern Baptist Convention. She was the only woman in this era to address the State Convention publicly. She raised funds for schools and colleges and the Baptist orphans' home at Monticello. She organized missionary societies in churches throughout the state.

In women's roles, as in other matters, the Eagles were a generation or more ahead of the majority of Arkansas Baptists. They moved too quickly, and, in this area as in others, the payoff was misunderstanding and resentment which culminated in the split of 1901.

Women's Education

A spin off from the women's movement of the post-Civil War period was a heightening of concern for their education. Prior to the Civil War, of course, as we have seen earlier, Arkansas Baptists sought educational opportunities for their daughters as well as their sons. After the War, various associations followed up on this concern in their academies and high schools. The vast expansion of mission effort to include single women, however, made the education of women still more imperative and resulted in pressure to establish women's academies, high schools, and colleges. For Southern Baptists the appointment of Lottie Moon for mission service in China in 1872 gave a special push in this direction.

When Ouachita College opened in 1886, it was coeducational, but only a small percentage of the students were women. As a result of pressures within the Convention, a special committee was appointed in 1890 to look into the feasibility of establishing a "female college."[113] Finding support for this adequate, in 1891 the Committee recommended appointment of a Board of Trustees which would receive bids from various localities desiring such an institution.[114] In 1892 the Ouachita Trustees sought to discourage the move, reminding the Convention that the coed system of Ouachita had "proven satisfactory" and reporting that ther school had twelve female as well as five male teachers and an elegantly furnished young ladies home. But the die was cast already, and Central Female College opened at Conway in 1893.

White and Black

The period we are considering here saw the growth of tensions between blacks and whites in Arkansas. In 1881 and 1882 much of the state experienced both floods and drought which resulted in much suffering and discontent among the poor in the ten counties along the Mississippi River in lower Arkansas. There was a near race riot in Howard County related to an assault on a black by a white man named Wyatt. When fifty blacks approached Wyatt in his field, he opened fire and killed one; he was riddled with bullets as he tried to flee. The countryside was inflamed. When local authorities proved unable to quell the strife, Governor Berry acted promptly. Forty blacks were indicted. Thirty pleaded guilty of second degree murder. Three cases were dropped. Three men were sentenced to hang and the rest sent to the penitentiary. Two of those sentenced to be hanged later managed to get new trials. Governor Berry pardoned five of those sent to prison.[115]

This story illustrates the tenuous situation of blacks in the post-Reconstruction era. So far as can be ascertained, white Baptists probably did little to alleviate the lot of their fellow citizens. They did not protest the law passed in 1891 requiring separate railroad cars for blacks or other acts limiting black citizenship. To their credit, however, they did maintain fraternal ties with blacks and blacks with them. Moreover, they offered modest help in the development of black educational institutions.

TABLE XVI
BLACK CHURCH GROWTH, 1880-1900

Year	Associations	Churches	Membership	Baptisms
1880	9			
1881	9		17,194	
1882	9		17,825	
1883	10		18,000	
1884	11	244	22,413	
				434
1885	13	417	28,196	628
1886	14	450	30,829	349
1887	19	403	29,597	559
1888	25	450	32,699	684
1889	25	466	32,493	858
1890	25	468	32,493	
1891	25	457	30,793	570
1892	25	.... no report....................		
1893	18	558	37,405	965
1894	30	785	50,268	1,261
1895	31	810	51,695	435
1896	.... no report....................			
1897	31	817	53,161	619
1898	30	873	54,673	2,040
1899	29	848	55,128	2,112
1900	30	868	59,033	2,599

Blacks, of course, continued on the separate course they had been forced to chart for themselves in the preceding period. We do not have accurate statistics on the growth of their churches and associations, for, until 1881, the **American Baptist Yearbook** did not give separate statistics for blacks and whites. It is possible, however, using both Southern Baptist Convention **Annuals** and the **Yearbook,** to get a general impression of that growth. Table XVI shows that organization among black Baptists developed along lines similar to those which white Baptists experienced. Until 1886 the number of district associations remained rather small, and the associations which did exist covered large areas. The formation of the American National Baptist Convention in St. Louis in that year, however, encouraged the multiplication of associations and the restriction of their jurisdictions. In 1893 black Baptists organized another convention, the Baptist National Educational Convention, at Washington, D.C., but it probably had little effect on Baptists in

Arkansas. In 1895 these groups merged to form the National Baptist Convention of America. These national conventions probably helped to inspire more accurate reporting, as reflected in statistics after 1894, as well as actual church growth.

Black and white Baptists did not work closely together after the Civil War, but they did maintain cooperative and fraternal ties. Whites regularly preached in black churches when the State Convention met. Blacks often sent fraternal messengers and messages. In 1894, for instance, the Northeastern District Association of Colored Baptists assembled at Hazen, Arkansas, sent eight "corresponding messengers" to "sit in" the Arkansas Baptist State Convention convened at Lonoke.[116] Whites invited a messenger to speak.

Late in the period we are discussing, the concern of whites for blacks took a sharp turn upward. The State Convention appointed a Committee on Work among the Negroes. In 1900 this Committee, eyeing the formation of the National Baptist Convention, urged Arkansas Baptists to pick up the challenge which they had let slip after the Civil War. They sounded optimistic:

> *The negroes are beginning to realize again that Southern Christians are their friends, and that southern people, with whom they have lived all their lives, understand them better than any others can. They are now turning to us for help as never before since the war. Neither can we any longer excuse ourselves from helping on the plea of poverty. We earnestly beg the Convention to take up this problem and, if possible, to formulate some plan for solving it. The existence of nearly ten millions of negroes in our very midst—over one-third of our entire population—and in the condition in which the negroes are, is not a problem that a Convention like ours can afford longer to practically ignore, or to remand so largely to our brethren who can hardly claim to really know and understand the negro. Our co-operative work with the Home Mission Society in behalf of the negroes needs to be supplemented in some way by Southern Baptists.*[117]

The most significant contacts between blacks and whites were in the area of education. Both blacks and whites, of course, recognized the critical need here. Long neglected and deprived of educational opportunities, blacks were ill-prepared to do anything besides farming.

The American Baptist Home Mission Society took the first step in this direction. In 1882 they proposed a school for freedmen at least partially supported by the Society and the Arkansas Baptist State Convention.[118] In pursuit of this objective the Home Mission Society of New York dispatched H. Woodsmall to work with black Baptists in the state.[119] Arkansas Baptists welcomed such efforts and added their own modest effort to it.

Although Arkansas Baptists concentrated their support of education chiefly upon the education of ministers, they sometimes articulated a broader concern. The most far reaching statement appeared in a resolution proposed by D.D. Swindall in 1888:

> *Whereas, The colored people of our State have become citizens among us; and, whereas the good of our civil government, as these people have been enfranchised, depends to a great extent upon their mental culture; and, whereas also their qualifications for citizenship depend upon their moral and religious culture; and, whereas these colored people are dependent upon the white christians; therefore,*
>
> *Resolved, That we, the members of this Convention, advise our ministering brethren to endeavor to help the colored people, especially their ministers, by aiding them all we can in this direction.*[120]

As one might expect, knowing the modest circumstances of Arkansas in this period, whites offered more in the way of prayers and encouragement than in substantive contributions. Nonetheless, they did contribute more than promises. In 1882 the report of the Education Committee of the State Convention was amended to include a plea for a Baptist college for blacks and a pledge that "as a Convention, we will do all we can to encourage our colored Breteren (sic) in this noble enterprise."[121] Subsequent reports regularly lamented the inadequacy of white efforts to assist blacks, especially in training their clergy. From 1889 on whites responded annually to appeals from J.A. Booker, President of Arkansas (Colored) Baptist College, for aid in constructing the school in Little Rock. Their assistance came in the form both of private and public subscriptions. We do not have complete figures on this, but Convention minutes report modest responses on several occasions: $40.05 in 1889, $100.80 in 1890, $60.35 in 1891, $118.65 in 1893, $35.15 in 1895, and $80.00 in 1899. They rallied to the college's side when a fire destroyed the first buildings in 1893.

Although the most significant help came in the form of support for Arkansas Baptist College, founded in 1883, Arkansas Baptists also looked for other ways to assist in the training of ministers. In 1886, on recommendation of the Committee on State Missions, the Convention adopted a plan to engage a white minister to hold ministers' institutes, "with the view of instructing their preacher (sic) in the way of the Lord more perfectly,..."[121] In 1893 the Convention adopted a rather far-reaching program outlined in a resolution offered by J.G.B. Simms, which called for support of Arkansas Baptist College, ministers' institutes, and even the dispatching of missionaries "empowered and directed to take any action in the premises which their judgment shall dictate."[122] This plan seems never to have been effectively implemented, but not all of its import was lost. In 1896 a resolution called for "closer co-operation between our convention and the work of the Negro Baptists of Arkansas, especially with reference to ministerial education among them."[123] A year later, the Convention hired Benjamin Cox, a white minister, to offer a theological course for ministerial students in Arkansas Baptist College. At the Convention in 1898 the Committee on Education reported "increased sympathy and co-operation between the white and colored Baptists of the State in the matter of education." They recommended continuation of this plan and suggested appointment of a committee "to visit the college in behalf of the convention" and the extension of "such moral and financial support as may be deemed expedient and wise."[124] The visitation committee, composed of Cox, F. Bozeman, and H.C. Roseman, returned with a glowing report about "a heroic effort" to complete a dormitory and the soundness of President J. A. Booker's administration. They recommended "that our people help them in every way they can" and that the State Board continue the theological lectureship by Cox.[125] Subsequent conventions reiterated these recommendations. In 1901 the Committee on Work among the Negroes suggested that the State Convention support this educational effort from its mission fund and encouraged the Convention and all Baptists in Arkansas to rally behind President Booker.[126]

Clouds on the Horizon

For the most part, the two decades we have described in this chapter were filled with sunshine for Baptists in Arkansas. The effects of Reconstruction has worn off, and, with the development of railroads and industry, the economy blossomed. The churches experienced steady if not spectular growth and attracted numbers of better educated and more affluent members. Associations continued steadily in their evangelistic and educational efforts. The State Convention, overcoming opposition from "Hardshells" and "Landmarkers," developed sufficient organization to carry out its missionary and educational aims in conjunction with the Southern Baptist Convention as well as the American Baptist Home Mission Society. Except for a couple of "recession" years, contributions for all causes increased significantly. Baptists played a larger and larger role in their society.

But there were ominous clouds on the horizon. Small and insignificant at first, they passed almost unnoticed by Convention leaders until the 1890s. By then, they were growing dark enough to block out some of the rays of sun. Soon they would send thunderbolts crashing in upon the churches, the associations, and the State Convention, ripping and tearing all of them to pieces. The next decade of Arkansas Baptist history was going to match that produced by the Civil War. Only, this time its causes would be internal rather than external.

NOTES

[1] Proceedings, ABSC, 1889, p. 24.
[2] Proceedings, ABSC, 1898, p. 39.
[3] Proceedings, ABSC, 1885, p. 20.
[4] Proceedings of the Arkansas Baptist State Sunday-School Convention, State Convention, Woman's Mission Societies, 1889, p. 32.
[5] Proceedings, ABSC, 1891, p. 26.
[6] Proceedings, ABSC, 1892, p. 49.
[7] Proceedings, ABSC, 1899, p. 41.
[8] Proceedings, ABSC, 1899, p. 37.
[9] Proceedings, ABSC, 1900, p. 41.
[10] Proceedings, ABSC, 1882, p. 15.
[11] Proceedings, ABSC, 1883, p. 16.
[12] Proceedings, ABSC, 1884, p. 7.

[130] Proceedings, ABSC, 1895, p. 15.
[14] Proceedings, ABSC, 1896, pp. 17, 34.
[15] Proceedings, ABSC, 1883, p. 18.
[16] Proceedings, ABSC, 1881, p. 22.
[17] Proceedings, ABSC, 1882, p. 17.
[18] Proceedings, ABSC, 1886, p. 14.
[19] Proceedings, ABSC, 1897, p. 10.
[20] Proceedings, ABSC, 1881, p. 20.
[21] Proceedings, ABSC, 1882, p. 7.
[22] Proceedings, ABSC, 1884, p. 25.
[23] Proceedings, ABSC, 1882, p. 14.
[24] Proceedings, ABSC, 1895, p. 38.
[25] Proceedings, ABSC, 1896, pp. 18f.
[26] Proceedings, ABSC, 1897, p. 28.
[27] Proceedings, ABSC, 1881, p. 11.
[28] Proceedings, ABSC, 1882, p. 18.
[29] Proceedings, ABSC, 1884, p. 25.
[30] Proceedings, ABSC, 1885, p. 19.
[31] Proceedings, ABSC, 1889, p. 28.
[32] Proceedings, ABSC, 1894, p. 37.
[33] Proceedings, ABSC, 1895, pp. 16-17.
[34] Ibid., p. 24.
[35] Proceedings, ABSC, 1897, p. 31.
[36] Proceedings, ABSC, 1899, pp. 19-20.
[37] Ibid., p. 21.
[38] Ibid., p. 23.
[39] Proceedings, ABSC, 1900, p. 17.
[40] Victor I. Masters, Country Church in the South (Atlanta: Home Mission Board, SBC, 1916), pp. 17, 111.
[41] Reported by Leroy Carson Tedford, A History of the Corning Baptist Church (Popular Bluff, Mo.: The Author, 1947), p. 10.
[42] Cited by ibid., p. 20.
[43] Ibid., pp. 20-21.
[44] See especially the resolution of 1892; Proceedings, ABSC, 1892, p. 53.
[45] Unpublished Minutes, p. 7; original in Ouachita College Archives.
[46] Ibid., p. 19.
[48] Materials taken from Tedford, op. cit., pp. 31-33.
[49] Proceedings, ABSC, 1886, p. 14.
[50] Proceedings, ABSC, 1888, p. 18.

[51] Proceedings, ABSC, 1896, p. 16.

[52] Proceedings, ABSC, 1899, p. 36.

[53] Ibid., p. 36.

[54] Proceedings, ABSC, 1882, p. 16.

[55] Proceedings, ABSC, 1897, pp. 30-31.

[56] Cited by Leroy Carson Tedford, A History of the Current River Baptist Association (Popular Bluff, Mo.: The Author, 1948), p. 10.

[57] In ibid., pp. 9-10.

[58] Cited by H.D. Morton, A History of the White River Baptist Association (Salem, Ark.: The Author, 1954), p. 94.

[59] Proceedings, ABSC, 1895, pp. 29-30.

[60] Proceedings, ABSC, 1897, p. 25.

[61] The above statistics were taken from the American Baptist Yearbook; they differ at times from these found in the SBC Annuals, but the latter included no details on black churches.

[62] Proceedings, ABSC, 1894, pp. 3-4.

[63] Cited by Morton, op. cit., p. 23.

[64] Proceedings, ABSC, 1895, p. 39.

[65] Cited by Alex McPherson, A History of Greenbrier Baptist Association (Conway, Ark.: The Author, ca. 1926), p. 17.

[66] Proceedings, ABSC, 1896, p. 14.

[67] Proceedings, ABSC, 1897, p. 17.

[68] Ibid., p. 36.

[69] Proceedings, ABSC, 1898, p. 17.

[70] See Proceedings, ABSC, 1885, p. 20.

[71] Proceedings, ABSC, 1895, p. 10.

[72] Full data may be found in Arkansas and Its People, ed. David Y. Thomas (New York: American Historical Society, 1930), I: 215-216.

[73] Minutes, Concord Baptist Association, 1872, p. 7.

[74] Cf. Minutes, Baptist General Association of Western Arkansas and Indian Territory, 1884, p. 3.

[75] Proceedings, ABSC, 1880, p. 15.

[76] Proceedings, ABSC, 1896, p. 17.

[77] Proceedings, ABSC, 1885, p. 9.

[78] Proceedings, ABSC, 1888, p. 24.

[79] Proceedings, ABSC, 1895, p. 26; italics in the original text.

[80] Proceedings, ABSC, 1898, pp. 33-34.

[81] Proceedings, ABSC, 1900, p. 52.

[82] Proceedings, ABSC, 1895, p. 37; italics in the original text.

[83] Proceedings, ABSC, 1894, p. 31.

[84] Proceedings, ABSC, 1895, pp. 32-33.

[85] Proceedings, ABSC, 1883, p. 20.

[86] Arkansas Gazette, April 9, 1886.

[87] Proceedings, ABSC, 1891, p. 47.

[88] Proceedings, ABSC, 1892, p. 33.

[89] Proceedings, ABSC, 1897, p. 9.

[90] Ibid., p. 37.

[91] Proceedings, ABSC, 1900, p. 31.

[92] Ibid., pp. 32-36.

[93] Proceedings, ABSC, 1880, p. 9.

[94] Proceedings, ABSC, 1881, p. 24.

[95] Proceedings, ABSC, 1883, p. 19f.

[96] Proceedings, ABSC, 1889, p. 32.

[97] Proceedings, ABSC, 1891, p. 26.

[98] Proceedings, ABSC, 1894, pp. 32-33.

[99] Proceedings, ABSC, 1892, p. 49.

[100] Proceedings, ABSC, 1893, p. 29.

[101] Proceedings, ABSC, 1886, p. 9.

[102] Art. II; in Annie Guinn Massey, History of the Woman's Missionary Union Auxiliary to the Arkansas Baptist State Convention (Little Rock: Executive Board of the W.M.U., 1913), p. 28.

[103] Cited by Massey, op. cit., pp. 49-54.

[104] Proceedings, ABSC, 1898, p. 37.

[105] Proceedings, ABSC, 1886, p. 28.

[106] Proceedings, ABSC, 1883, p. 18.

[107] Proceedings, ABSC, 1887, p. 20.

[108] Proceedings, ABSC, 1891, p. 34.

[109] Proceedings, ABSC, 1893, p. 24.

[110] Minutes, Liberty Association, 1888, pp. 7, 9.

[111] Preface to a memorial volume by James P. Eagle, cited by Massey, op. cit., p. 34.

[112] Ibid., p. 35.

[113] Proceedings, ABSC, 1890, pp. 39f.

[114] Proceedings, ABSC, 1891, p. 36.

[115] Full data may be found in Arkansas and Its People, ed. David Y. Thomas, I: 193.

[116] Proceedings, ABSC, 1894, p. 35.

[117] Proceedings, ABSC, 1900, p. 48.

[118] Proceedings, ABSC, 1882, p. 13.

[119] Proceedings, ABSC, 1885, p. 34.

[120] Proceedings, ABSC, 1888, p. 27.

[121] Proceedings, ABSC, 1886, p. 17.
[122] Proceedings, ABSC, 1893, p. 28.
[123] Proceedings, ABSC, 1897, p. 17.
[124] Proceedings, ABSC, 1898, p. 39.
[125] Ibid., p. 42.
[126] Proceedings, ABSC, 1901, pp. 65-66.

Chapter V

PAIN AND PROMISE

1901-1926

Arkansas Baptists faced the incoming century with cautious optimism. The painful division which had been in the making all along finally came to pass in 1901. The Arkansas Baptist State Convention eventually lost about a third or more of its churches and its members to the Landmark faction. The situation was so confused until 1921, however, that they continued to report the Landmark churches, associations, and constituency in their annual report without distinction from the Convention's. In addition, many continued to hope for complete reconciliation.

The split aside, the story of these years was not entirely tragic. When Arkansas Baptists finally took a count of their own constituency independent of the Landmark faction, in 1921, they found that they had increased from 74,117 at the time of the break in 1901 to 98,376. By 1927 they had increased by over 10,000 more to 108,961. This increase of about 32 percent was slightly better than that of the population in general. The latter rose about 30 percent—from 1,311,561 in 1900 to 1,854,482 in 1930. After 1910, in fact, the rate of population increase declined. Whereas between 1900 and 1910 it increased 20 percent (to 1,574,449), between 1910 and 1920 it increased only 11.3 percent (to 1,752,204), and between 1920 and 1930 only 5.8 percent. At worst Arkansas Baptists were more than holding their own.

As these figures indicate, the times were not favorable for the state of Arkansas. The cotton area prospered as it had earlier. However, the Ozarks remained impoverished, and Ozarkers held fast to their characteristic suspicion of city folks and city ways. Agrarian discontent ran high. The Grange failed, but it was succeeded by the Agricultural Wheel, which gained powerful influence.

The backwoods people of Arkansas, still a majority of the population, found a champion in Jeff Davis, a self-styled "sort of hardshelled Baptist." As Attorney General (1898-1900), he waged a fierce battle for "the little man" against the "trusts." His campaign oratory had a strong religious cast. "I believe in foot-washing, I believe in baptism by immersion, and I believe in using the straight edge," he boasted in a speech delivered at Crown Point, February 12, 1900, during his race for the governor's office. "What is the straight edge? The law. I sued them all." On a strong populist platform Davis won a convincing gubernatorial victory in 1900, carrying every county in the state except one. In 1902 he gained the majority in all except five of the seventy-five counties. In 1904 he overcame an investigation into his conduct to win a third term. Then, in 1906 he was elected to the United States Senate, where his campaign to stop trusts and railroads floundered. He died suddenly January 3, 1913.

The impoverished state struggled throughout this era to bolster its economy. More than eighty percent agricultural, it looked for ways to strengthen the farming enterprise. New crops such as rice were introduced to diversify the economy. The legislature established four agricultural high schools in 1909; subsequently, these became colleges. Despite such efforts, however, severe money problems plagued Arkansas, especially after 1914. Sharecroppers, who made up half of the farm populace, had the toughest time. Governor Charles H. Brough, also a Baptist, improved the situation considerably during his two terms, 1917-1921. As late as 1940, however, the average per capita income in Arkansas was only $200 per year.

Arkansas Baptists Split

All of these developments had a significant impact on Baptists in Arkansas to which we will return later. Of more immediate significance to an understanding of what happened in the period being discussed is the grievous split which occurred in 1901.

We have seen earlier that this division was in the making long before it actually occurred. It was deeply rooted in the natural divisions of Arkansas society—uplanders and lowlanders, backwoodsmen and planters, impoverished and wealthy, uneducated and cultured. It also had some roots in "hardshellism" which immigrants brought with them from Kentucky and other states. Unfortunately all of these elements were pulled together by Landmarkism, which developed initially as a way of defining Baptist identity over against the "reform" movement of Alexander Campbell. In Arkansas the Landmark reaction coincided almost exactly with the struggle of Baptists to give momentum to their movement. For a time it doubtless aided the churches in their efforts to expand, as such exclusivism usually does. In the end, however, it exacted a high price for the coordination of Baptist effort beyond the congregational level, for Landmark teaching emphasized the local church to such an extent that it left ambivalence about programs and agencies beyond that level.

The Controversy

Knowing the strength of rising opposition to the organized work of the State Convention, James P. Eagle tried to start the annual convention at Paragould in 1901 on a positive note. The report of the Executive Board exulted at "a report incomparably larger in scope and more glorious in results than the one last year."[1] It recounted in tabular form the achievements of a six-year span to highlight the significance of 1901 in money raised, missionaries employed, and baptisms.

At the same time this report gave evidence of alarm over the coming storm. In a long "Statement of Baptist Principles" the Board asserted its adherence to "the time-honored and fundamental doctrine of the absolute autonomy of the churches" as "one point that must ever be jealously guarded."[2] The difficulty, they went on to add, lies in getting people to see that "there is no antagonism between this doctrine and that other sublime and almost equally important doctrine, the co-operation of the churches."[3] The Apostle Paul collected money among his churches "without any surrender of their independence or any violation of their autonomy."[4] Although the Convention is "a voluntary organization through which any church may or may not co-operate," each church assumes certain obligations once it enters into a voluntary arrangement. Each church sends messengers to show "actual and active sympathy and co-operation in practical matters, such as missions and education." The aim is to discharge these tasks "in the way that will most surely and rapidly advance the kingdom of Christ."[5] Organization and system are essential "in no other business more than in a religious business."[6]

Impressive as it sounded, however, the report of the State Board did not meet the approval of a majority at the Convention. Opponents of the plan for coordinating the work through a Corresponding Secretary assembled sufficient votes to send it back to the Executive Committee for revision. Resubmitted, it argued continuity with twenty or more years of history in maintaining the office and that the plan had produced good results. The report continued:

This consideration of our work leads us to this that God has signified his approval of our plans, which were given to us by our fathers, and have been followed by us, that we would fear to change or interrupt the same. We heartily believe that there would be great danger in making any change if the same could be avoided. The wisdom of the fathers, the blessing of God, the judgment of our most experienced and wisest men, now among us, and the almost universal practice of our denomination, wherever active missionary efforts are made, urge the continuance of the plan.[7]

The report noted the re-election of A.J. Barton as "Missionary Secretary" of the Executive Board at a salary of $900 plus travel allowance to be supplemented by $600 more from the Boards of the Southern Baptist Convention. It specified his duties under three headings: (1) doing correspondence and office work for the Board, (2) visiting churches and associations and raising funds for the Board, and (3) doing evangelistic work under the Board's direction.

Although this amended report passed, largely because of the personal influence of James P. Eagle, the issues of a paid "Corresponding Secretary" or "State Missionary" and of the connection between Arkansas Baptists and the Southern Baptist Convention smoldered still. Ben M. Bogard, a newcomer to Arkansas, led the attack on the system. As so often happens in incidents of this kind, however, these were not the immediate cause of the division. The precipitating cause was much more personal. It was connected with the disappointment of W.A. Clark in being passed over for the office of "Corresponding Secretary" in 1899. Clark had served for several years (1881-1884) as State Missionary and as acting Missionary Secretary (1896). He sold controlling interest in the **Arkansas Baptist** to O.L Hailey with expectation of being made Corresponding Secretary. His long years of denominational service doubtless raised strong hopes that he would again be so chosen. When these hopes were thwarted, Clark proceeded to ventilate some of his resentment through the **Arkansas Baptist,** whose control he again assumed in 1899. In 1900 the Committee on Publications issued a severe reprimand for Clark's failure to support the Convention and its programs. Clark agreed to stop his attacks, but then reneged on his promise. The result was a still more explicit reprimand in 1901 which, more than any other factor, triggered the split, with Clark as one of the key Landmark leaders.

The report of the Committee on Publications tiptoed around the issue by noting "with gratitude" "the existence of many useful Baptist newspapers" and praying that "the editors have wisdom and enjoy the confidence of their brethren."[8] A special resolution was more explicit, delineating the whole issue of Clark's unkept promise.

> *Whereas, At the last session of this Convention we recommended the Arkansas Baptist as "our State paper," and*
>
> *Whereas, The same was procured by a solemn and deliberate promise on the part of Dr. Clark that the said paper would neither in editorials nor in correspondence permit any attack upon the plans or employees of the Board until this session of the Convention, and*
>
> *Whereas, Said promises have been wholly unkept and violated, and the same has been further conducted as an organ of his personal views, and those agreeing with him, and in antagonism to the plans of the said Convention, therefore be it*
>
> *Resolved, That the said recommendation be withdrawn.[9]*

The General Association

The pro-Board group led by James P. Eagle won a victory of sorts at Paragould in 1901, but they did not have long to savor it. As they had threatened at this convention, the disaffected anti-Secretary faction gathered in Little Rock April 10-11, 1902 to form the "General Association of Arkansas Baptists." This new organization attracted strong support among the district associations of the state, where the issue had been churning for a long time. Almost half of them voted to cooperate with the General Association in mission work. About a fourth voted to continue cooperation with the State Convention. The remaining fourth, chiefly the larger associations, voted to remain neutral as a result of sharply divided opinion within their own ranks.

State Convention leaders responded to this crisis with understandable uncertainty. On the one hand, they treated the division as an accomplished fact. In order to minimize the impact of divisions both within the Convention and within associations, they changed the basis of representation to the State Convention. Whereas before, associations as well as churches had been allowed messengers, in

1902 the Constitution was altered to accredit only "messengers from regular Baptist churches which are in sympathy with the principles and purposes of this constitution, and which desire to co-operate with this convention."[10] For the Convention itself the new arrangement assured a fairly high level of unity and cooperation in pursuing the Convention's goals. For the associations it opened the way for individual congregations to decide for themselves which of the two organizations they would support. At the same time, however, it eventually necessitated the formation of new associations as the churches made their choices.

Though treating the division as a **fait accompli,** on the other hand, Convention leaders also made strong efforts to conciliate the opposition. At the outset they responded to a plea from the Caroline Association "that the State Convention and the General Association appoint a Conference Committee of twenty, each of representative Baptist (sic) to meet at some time by them appointed, with the view of harmonizing and coming together in our state work."[11] Shortly thereafter at the annual convention in 1902 a committee of three (H. Beauchamp, W.E. Atkinson, and J.H. Kitchens, Jr.) was appointed to name ten persons "who should confer with a like committee appointed by the General Association,"[12] a procedure the Landmarkers later labeled undemocratic. The General Association also appointed a committee, by popular nominations and election, but the two committees never met nor functioned as a single group ironing out their differences. Instead, the General Association Committee set forth six propositions which were to serve as the basis of reconciliation.

1. The scriptural right of individual churches to commission and send forth missionaries.

2. The arranging of missionary methods so that the reports of missionaries shall include only the work actually performed by the missionaries and paid for by missionary contributions.

3. Recognition of each church as a unit and entitled to equal representation with any other church in association or Convention.

4. The absolute abolition of the office and expense of the Corresponding Secretary under whatever title.

5. The right of the churches to instruct their messengers on any subject to be recognized.

6. The abolition of the present plan of co-operation with the Home and Foreign Mission Boards of the Southern Baptist Convention.[13]

The Convention Committee, though thwarted in efforts to meet with the Association Committee, agreed to accept all six of these propositions with two conditions: (1) that the General Association dissolve and recommend that its churches send messengers to the State Convention, and (2) that, after adoption of the recommendations by both the Convention and the Association, the **Landmark Baptist** and the **Baptist Advance** merge under a plan to be mutually agreed upon by a nine-man committee, four members of which would be chosen by each editor, one by the other eight. The Association Committee, still refusing to meet with the Convention Committee, accepted these stipulations but insisted that the Convention approve the arrangement before the Association and thus that the Association continue another year. The result was an extended hassle with charges and counter-charge of "ambiguity" and "evasiveness." These difficulties notwithstanding, a majority of the Committee proceeded to offer to the Convention the original recommendation.

When it met in the Fall, however, the Convention declined to approve the majority recommendation and instead voted overwhelmingly, 176 to 48, in favor of a minority report by T.W. O'Kelley. O'Kelley charged that the General Association had rendered implementation of their resolution to dissolve the Association impossible by voting to continue another year and by instructing its Executive Committee to continue as before. Furthermore, editors of the **Landmark Baptist** (notably W.A. Clark) refused to abide by the agreement unless the propositions were interpreted to mean (1) adoption of "the principles of the General Association" by the Convention, (2) "'the surrender by the Convention of all things peculiar to the organized work," and (3) the end of all cooperation with the Southern Baptist Convention. The report went on to assert that the Convention Committee had never agreed to these conditions and to posit responsibility for the split with the General Association. In concluding, it (1) invited all Baptists to "cooperate with us on the old time Baptist principles and practices of cooperation, for which the Convention has always stood"; (2) expressed regret for the departure of some but recognized their right to do what they wished and wished them well; and (3) requested publication of the report in both papers as well as other daily or weekly papers.[14]

The emerging leader of the General Association was Ben M. Bogard. He had come to the state, as pastor in Searcy, only a couple of years before the split. During these years, he aligned himself fully with the Convention's work. As late as October 9, 1901, he presented himself as a supporter of the State Convention. In the **Arkansas Baptist** he said,

> *Whereas, some have been persistently misrepresenting me in this matter, I beg leave to state plainly that I am heartily in favor, first, of the churches, second, of the associations, and third, of the Baptist State Convention. I want to preserve the Associations, the State Convention and our State Mission Board. Whoever says I am opposed to the State Convention or its work, misrepresents me.*

At Paragould, however, he became the chief spokesman for the anti-secretary forces as they voiced their opposition to the office of Corresponding Secretary. In his argument he called the office "a dangerous innovation leading to Episcopacy of the worst form and going back to the Dark Ages."[15] Subsequently he took an active leadership in the organization of the General Association in Little Rock and, ironically, gradually came to dominate the Association organized out of fear of authoritarianism! As the latter was forming, he hopped from one associational meeting to another to drum up support for it. This kept the associations in an unsettled condition until about 1917 to 1921, when most either aligned themselves fully with the State Convention or split to form new associations.

In the Eye of the Storm

The controversy over the structures of the Arkansas Baptist State Convention stewed for years as the lines dividing the two factions became more and more firm. It left its mark on both churches and associations, but the most easily discernible effect was on the latter.

Immediately after the formation of the General Association, associations were thrust into the uncomfortable role of deciding whether to cast their loyalty and support there or to cast them on the side of the Convention. For a time some associations tried to sidestep the issue, but since several associations were the source of the

179

original objection to a paid Corresponding Secretary, they could not do so for long. By the arrangement of the State Convention regarding membership the churches finally had to decide. In doing so, they forced associations to undertake the painful task of deciding how they would align themselves and their work. At the end of this process the State Convention came out ahead roughly two to one in churches and membership, as the statistics in Table XVII readily reveal.

We will not take time here to look at the trauma experienced by individual congregations; this can be examined in another connection. Since the split had its most immediate and forceful impact on associations, we will do a sampling of the way these wrestled with the problem.

TABLE XVII
BAPTIST GROWTH, 1901-1926

Year	Churches		Associations		Membership		Baptisms	
	Conv.	Assoc.	Conv.	Assoc.	Conv.	Assoc.	Conv.	Assoc.
1901	1,321		47		74,117		5,994	
1902	1,241		47		75,977		4,588	
1903	1,327		47		77,590		5,117	
1904	1,355		49		80,705		5,547	
1905	1,368		49		84,642		5,809	
1906	1,389		49		88,262		7,372	
1907	1,449		49		92,821		7,157	
1908	1,490		50		99,872		7,265	
1909	1,536		50		105,455		6,337	
1910	1,534		51		106,528		7,243	
1911	1,527		50		108,248		5,996	
1912	1,531		50		109,629		4,596	
1913	1,528		50		111,991		4,296	
1914	1,514		50		111,185		6,362	
1915	1,483		52		114,713		7,278	
1916	1,488		54		118,930		7,397	
1917	1,547		54		122,635		6,419	
1918	1,489		56		121,484		4,435	
1919	1,529		56		124,115		3,992	
1920	1,428		71		124,024		6,833	
1921	1,135	507	48	22	98,376	34,271	7,912	1,540
1922	1,174	502	49	24	106,409	36,416	8,910	1,613
1923	998	655	42	32	100,302	47,782	7,132	2,579
1924	920	655	41	31	101,589	47,782	7,674	2,579
1925	953	655	41	31	106,374	47,782	7,988	2,579
1926	1,030		45		112,231		7,165	

According to statistics recorded in **Annuals** of the Southern Baptist Convention, churches leaning toward the General Convention formed new associations only gradually. At the outset both sides evidently hoped for a complete victory—Convention leaders for a complete reconciliation and General Association leaders for the triumph of their viewpoint. Until about 1908, Convention reports regularly claimed growing unity and ignored evidence of a widening rift. In time, however, the pressures on churches to take one side or the other forced the formation of new associations.

The first Landmark association to develop was apparently a second Benton County Association, formed in 1904 under the rubric of the Gospel Mission Plan. From 1907 to 1920 it was designated Benton County Association No. 2 in the SBC Convention **Annuals.** The nine (later ten) churches continuing affiliation with the State Convention immediately renewed their allegiance to the Arkansas Baptist State Convention "for the wise manner in which it has conducted our state mission work through its executive board" and pledged their "hearty support in taking Arkansas for Christ."[16] They also censured the separating body for receiving members of Temperance Hill Church who had been excluded and for "violation of all Christian courtesy" by separating, even though the Association allowed freedom to support mission work through the General Association.[17] Meantime, the twenty-eight (later twenty-seven) churches affiliating with the General Association severed ties with the Home Mission Board of the Southern Baptist Convention for dispossessing the Gethsemane Baptist Church in Havana, Cuba, and their pastor and urged that money for state mission work be sent to the General Association.[18] New Landmark associations formed in a trickle until 1920 when they suddenly puffed out to 22. For the next five years they multiplied rapidly.

During these twenty-five years other associations underwent a great deal of inner turmoil, sometimes bounding back and forth from the Convention to the General Association, sometimes supporting both at the same time, and sometimes remaining passive. A few settled the issue quickly. In 1903, for instance, the Caddo River Baptist Association rejected a motion by A.R. Chitwood that the Association "adopt the plans and principles as set forth by the General Association and that we denounce the Board System as unscriptural."[19] Thereafter, it did not debate the matter again. Most, however, suffered painful disturbances. The White River, Current River, and Greenbrier Associations illustrate the trauma experienced throughout the state.

Prior to the split of 1901 the churches of the White River Baptist Association had already begun to withhold financial support. Between 1898 and 1900 only Mountain Home Church contributed anything to state missions. In 1901, meeting prior to the State Convention, the Association drafted a resolution "expressive of the attitudes of this Association toward the present Board system" which opposed "the present high salaried Board system of Missions" and urged "that the Mission work be carried on by the churches, inasmuch as the church is the highest authority on earth."[20] The next year, the Association withdrew its support from state mission work "owing to the centralizing tendencies and extravagance of the present management" of it and endorsed "the present plan of the general association through which to do our state mission work." It also affirmed the right of local churches to instruct messengers how to vote at the Association or State Convention.[21] For the next several years the work of the Association muddled along as best it could without aid from the State Convention. In 1906, however, the Association evidently relented earlier opposition, for the report on state missions recorded "grateful thanks to the State Board for their timely aid which they have so willingly given, in assisting some of our weak churches and our associated Mission work" and recommended hearty cooperation "with these brethern (sic) in forwarding this glorious work."[22] In 1907 the State Board was paying one-half the salary of an associational missionary, N.C. Danner, the Associational Mission Board, the other half.

Division of sentiment within the White River Association, however, appeared in 1908 in an establishment of ties with the General Association as well as the State Convention. In 1910 the Committee on State Missions acknowledged and commended the efforts of both bodies and added a plea for dual support.

> *Your committee recognizes the perfect freedom of every Baptist church, to contribute to either of these bodies as conscience may direct; but we urge upon every Baptist church, and every member of every Baptist church, within the bounds of this Association, to support one or the other of these mission bodies, or both if they see fit, and let us do our part in the White River Association toward saving lost souls in Arkansas.*[23]

Among other things, the Committee recommended an annual

offering for the homes for orphans operated by both groups—the State Convention at Monticello and the General Association Home at Texarkana, opened the year before. In 1912 the White River Association also commended a high school at Bodcaw supported by the General Association.

The question of affiliation continued to agitate the Association for the next ten years. In 1916, however, the tide began to turn in favor of the State Convention, which proved that it was much more capable of aiding the struggling churches and institutions of this impoverished mountain association. That year there was still sufficient support for the General Association to force an amendment to a state missions report which had deleted any reference to its work. The amendment urged churches and members of churches cooperating with the General Association "to heartily support the State Mission work as carried out by the State Association."[24] Thereafter, support for the General Association gradually dwindled to nothing. Throughout the decade contributions to the Convention were consistently larger. In 1920 the Committee on State Missions noted that "The work of State Missions is carried on by the churches through the Executive Board of the Baptist State Convention."[25] After 1921 minutes of the Association no longer referred to the General Association's orphans' home at Texarkana. The White River Association had fully restored its relationship to the State Convention, but it paid a price. A number of General Association supporters withdrew, though not enough to affect the Association's constituency seriously.

The State Convention did not come out as well in many other associations as it did in the White River Association. The younger Current River Association, organized in 1881, fell under control of the Landmark faction in 1902, recommending cooperation only with the General Association. In 1907, meeting in the Landmark Baptist Church, Corning, the Association adopted a resolution, evidently without debate, to "discontinue any co-operation with the State Convention."[26] At the meeting of the Association in 1911 the Landmark group dominated the proceedings. Ben Bogard preached twice. The Association took an offering only for the orphans' home at Texarkana. As it had for several years, the Committee on Publications recommended only the **Arkansas Baptist** and the **Baptist Flag,** both Landmark papers, and "Arkansas Landmark Literature for our Sunday schools." The Committee on Education recommended only Buckner College, now controlled by the General

Association. By 1917, however, the tide seems to have shifted in this Association as it had in the White River Association. Meeting in the Moark Baptist Church, the Association gave much more attention to Convention matters. The next year, associational reports recommended both Convention and General Association literature and urged support of both orphans' homes. The opposing groups seem to have maintained an uneasy truce until 1922, when churches sympathetic to the General Association withdrew and made plans for a new association. The next year, five of the Association's eighteen churches formed the "Current River Missionary Baptist Association." The latter continued until 1938 when it merged with the Bethlehem Missionary Baptist Association.

The Greenbrier Association experienced a great deal of strife before it eventually reaffirmed its affiliation with the State Convention. In 1902 the Committee on State Missions presented a long report noting long standing "dissatisfaction among some brethren and churches of the State" with the work of the State Mission Board and thus the Convention. They refused, however, to take a stand and, instead, recommended that the churches decide whether to support the General Association or the State Convention.[27] The Association repeated this policy of neutrality for the next several years. In 1909, however, the Committee on State Missions recommended that the Greenbrier Association "do their State Mission work through the General Association."[28] The next year, a stronger report urged churches "that cannot conscientiously work with us on these principles to quietly withdray (sic), and go where they can work, and leave us to work in peace."[29] But this report precipitated a debate lasting from Friday afternoon until Saturday noon and was adopted by a precarious vote of 17 to 16. Two years later, the Association was recommending the dispatching of messengers to either the General Association or the State Convention. By 1915 it was showing signs of a clear shift toward the Convention. The Committee on Literature, for instance, commended only **The Baptist Advance** and Southern Baptist Convention literature. Other committees reported only on State Convention and SBC mission work and recommended only Ouachita and Central colleges. The next year the Greenbrier Association backtracked just slightly, leaving a door ajar for the churches to send money to the General Association for state mission work or for the home at Texarkana, but they pitched the recommendation on a low key. By 1919 the Greenbrier Association was caught up fully in the "75-Million Campaign" and it did not look back thereafter in its support of the State Convention.

On the whole, the evangelistic efforts of Arkansas Baptists did not fare as badly from all of the strife as one might have expected. As Table XVII shows, the State Convention increased its membership nearly a third between 1901 and 1921, when the split had crystalized sufficiently to give separate statistics. By 1926 it had multiplied its constituency about one and a half times. General Association statistics are obviously not complete, but the Association appears to have siphoned off about a third of the total Baptist constituency. If the reports for 1923 can be trusted, the Association attracted smaller churches. Whereas Convention churches for that year averaged slightly over 100 members per church, Association churches averaged slightly under 73 members per church, exactly the average of **rural** churches at the time.

This bit of information helps to verify an interpretation of the split given earlier, that is, its connection with social changes. People in rural areas and in small towns were less prepared to accept the idea of salaried employment than those in urban areas, where the larger churches were located. They thought in terms of payment for clock hours worked, as on a farm or in a factory. They could not comprehend annual salaries, which may have seemed astronomical to many of them, paid to executives or managerial personnel.

Beyond the Storm

The recouping of a large percentage of those churches and associations which at one time joined or leaned toward the General Association represented a surprising turnabout in the Convention's favor. It has been estimated that three-fifths of the churches sided with the General Association in 1904; but by 1925 no more than a third did so. What accounts for the Convention's recovery here?

One fact was the **patient flexibility of Convention leaders,** which, once they discerned that the Landmark faction would not stop short of complete triumph, helped to avert permanent alienation of their critics. Early on, to be sure, they may have acted too flexibly and shown too much willingness to concede to their opponents. The latter took advantage of huge concessions made by the "Peace Committee" and nearly effected a complete destruction of co-operative work between Arkansas Baptists and the Southern Baptist Convention. In the long run, however, patience and flexibility paid off. The avoidance of authoritarian pronouncements and pressures during the first decade after the split neutralized the suspicions of "episcopacy" sown by Ben Bogard and other Landmark leaders. Associational leaders sympathetic with the State Convention capitalized on such sentiment to win defectors.

Another factor was **the Convention's headstart on the General Association.** When the split came, the Convention owned vast amounts of property, operated numerous institutions dear to Arkansas Baptists, had aided in the founding of numerous churches and associations, had developed means of supporting varied programs, and was rendering immense service through these. The General Association tried to compete in missionaries, schools, an orphan's home, and other programs, but, given its late start and opposition to organized effort, its work looked pale by comparison with that of the State Convention.

A still more important factor was **the actual effectiveness of the State Convention's organization as enhanced by connections with the Southern Baptist Convention.** Its approach worked! Undergirding its success was a rapid escalation of income. Unfortunaely we do not have accurate data on the General Association's finances until 1922. As Table XVIII illustrates, however, statistics for the Convention reveal soaring income reaching a peak in the "75-Million Campaign" of 1919-1924.

In and of themselves figures such as these in no way confirm the success of the Arkansas Baptist State Convention, but they help to explain how the Convention gradually won back many disaffected churches or associations. Convention leaders, of course, once they decided to forge ahead, had a vested interest in making their organization work. Some of them, such as James P. Eagle, increased their personal contributions substantially. Some churches which had benefited from the Convention's missionary programs also increased their giving. The Second Baptist Church of Little Rock, for instance, organized by the State Mission Board in 1885 and sustained by it for several years thereafter, gave $935.00 for mission purposes in 1902, a huge sum for that day. By 1904 Convention supporters heralded increased giving, growth in the number of churches, and "the more complete enlistment of the entire organization in our churches" as signs of "a return of confidence in the old methods of doing mission work."[30] The next year, they were exulting over the fact that the troublesome area of state missions was "becoming the rallying point of interrupted confidence," and might soon "be the ground of a happy reunion of our Baptist forces in the State."[31] A year later, for similar reasons, the Missionary and Sunday School Board reported "a mighty swinging back into line on the part of many who have drawn

TABLE XVIII
CONTRIBUTIONS, 1901-1926

| | ARKANSAS BAPTIST STATE CONVENTION | | | GENERAL ASSOCIATION | |
Year	Home Purposes	Missions	Other Benevolences	Home	Missions
1901	$ 84,746.17	$ 13,275.03	$ 4,961.59		
1902	97,336.67	13,897.47	6,735.87		
1903	92,943.89	17,476.96	3,702.66		
1904	103,498.21	19,246.84	9,726.36		
1905	122,443.98	22,029.91	12,612.56		
1906	150,591.68	27,119.77	11,530.97		
1907	175,937.61	34,326.71	14,783.87		
1908	194,765.12	42,005.40	18,590.37		
1909	196,359.51	49,208.86	28,815.38		
1910	268,785.00	58,334.62	32,415.02		
1911	258,580.15	45,786.05	46,385.61		
1912	247,087.93	47,126.80	38,273.45		
1913	278,812.97	45,151.24	24,966.80		
1914	285,891.61	41,715.75	43,615.50		
1915	276,281.96	46,385.74	48,634.13		
1916	304,985.33	55,729.43	50,761.15		
1917	321,792.38	69,558.47	52,460.20		
1918	362,761.80	98,002.94	76,682.41		
1919	353,254.59	115,545.03	56,346.56		
1921	590,347.13	233,816.98			
1922	824,885.44	275,713.23		$33,698.10	$10,077.56
1923	832,229.27	265,607.93		58,456.25	13,961.44
1924	786,453.10	507,269.68		No Report	
1925	891,726.93	324,647.87		No Report	
1926	1,000,102.97	282,398.73		No Report	

away from us, because of misunderstanding" and reassured the Convention that they would "possess" the state "for God and for Baptists."[32]

The optimism of the reports in 1905 and 1906 was obviously exaggerated and would not last. Actually, an economic boom—growth in land values, expansion of business, higher farm prices, more railroads, and new towns—was accompanying and assisting the mission boom. Nevertheless, the Convention did not hurt itself at this point, and we can understand readily why churches and associations were shifting their allegiances and sympathies back between 1906 and 1917. Employing vastly increased financial resources, it regained or won many friends by "sustaining and strengthening" weak churches and getting them more efficiently equipped with Sunday Schools, Training Unions, or other programs. In 1906 the State Missionary and Sunday School Board was helping pay the salaries of six associational missionaries and 100 pastors. It aided "City Mission Boards" in Texarkana and Little Rock. It assigned evangelists to certain "districts" so that they could get to know the people, pastors, and churches better and thus be more effective. It kept numerous churches alive.

State Missions First!

Under such circumstances as these it should not surprise us that Arkansas Baptists concentrated their efforts on the state and toned down their concern for foreign or home missions. This fact stands out clearly in a comparison of expenditures or contributions to these causes. Table XIX indicates a heavy upward turn in expenditures for state missions in 1905 and again in 1919, the year the "75-Million Campaign" got underway. Both dates represent crucial stages in the Convention's efforts to recoup losses in the split of 1901. The Home Mission Board supplemented the work of the State Missionary and Sunday School Board.

A substantial amount of reorganization accompanied the Convention's effort to shore up the state mission program. Initially, as we noted earlier, the Convention yielded to those who opposed the office of "Corresponding Secretary," in 1902 renaming it "Missionary Secretary" and emphasizing the efforts of field missionaries and evangelists.[33] In 1912 and 1913, however, the Convention moved toward a more centralized scheme of management by placing all missionary activity—state missions, home missions, foreign missions, Christian education, ministerial education, publication, the orphans' home, and Sunday school and B.Y.P.U. work—under one

188

Executive Board. This plan, as explained in the annual report of the Executive Board at the annual convention in 1914, called for "one General Secretary who, under the direction of the Executive Board, shall have general oversight of all the interests above mentioned" and "as occasion shall demand, associate with him one or more field men whose business it shall be to represent all the interests of the Convention."[34] The aims of this reorganization, the report noted, were (1) simplification, (2) increasing the effectiveness, (3) reducing the cost of the work, and (4) promoting harmony.[35]

The special pleading of the report shows that the new plan was not likely to achieve the fourth objective; to many it must have seemed a confirmation of their earlier fears of the corporation model.

TABLE XIX
MISSIONS EXPENDITURES, 1901-1926

Year	Spent by HMB	Spent by State	Foreign Missions
1901	$ 2,050.00	$ 3,703.36	$ 2,890.62
1902	3,300.00	5,366.22	2,656.56
1903	4,300.00	4,746.68	4,256.24
1904	5,000.00	6,904.92	4,755.51
1905	5,300.00	14,900.00	4,988.63
1906	5,000.00	19,156.08	5,764.44
1907	5,275.00	17,211.88	10,001.32
1908	5,300.00	25,276.30	10,345.48
1909	5,300.00	20,480.20	12,432.22
1910	5,535.00	34,393.88	13,184.15
1911	8,165.26	28,464.96	7,273.66
1912	6,500.00	25,683.37	10,417.00
1913	10,000.00	35,117.35	9,606.79
1914	10,000.00	14,000.00	10,978.72
1915	9,000.00	11,375.00	8,665.67
1916	11,000.00	29,262.17	10,701.75
1917		13,000.00	8,455.90
1918		18,000.00	23,014.89
1919	1,000.00	80,426.00	29,000.00
1920	27,045.00	57,658.00	20,279.87
1921	18,336.26	22,855.69	38,168.42
1922	16,000.00	No State Report	
1923	20,000.00	26,743.19	39,713.39
1924	20,000.00	18,081.45	29,152.45
1925	18,666.60	23,830.11	16,100.00
1926	15,000.00	21,821.23	18,925.00

Not surprisingly, the Board felt constrained to defend the plan again in 1915 as contributing to denominational solidarity and efficiency. But such fears were not the main reason the plan failed. The main reason, rather, was that no one was capable of doing the work demanded of the "General Secretary." How utterly impossible the demands of the office were is shown by the rapid turnover in secretaries until 1921 when the structure was revamped.

A.J. Barton, charged with the duties of correspondence, office work, fund-raising, and evangelism,[36] stayed approximately two and a half years (1900-1902), resigning to become editor of the **Baptist Advance,** the new voice of the Convention. After a brief interim filled by Benjamin Cox, versatile pastor of the First Baptist Church of Little Rock, J.F. Love took up the reins late in 1902. After about four years he resigned to become Assistant Secretary of the Home Mission Board. R.G. Bowers, pastor of the First Baptist Church of Waco, Texas, held the post two years, then relinquished it to accept a job as financial agent for his alma mater, Ouachita College.[37] J.S. Rogers held the office three times: 1908-1911, 1915-1919, 1921-1929. In the intervening periods it was filled briefly by John T. Christian, pastor of the Second Baptist Church of Little Rock (1911-1913); R.M. Inlow, formerly serving as a pastor in Nashville, Tennessee and in Joplin, Missouri (1913-1915); E.P. Alldredge, pastor of the First Baptist Church of Little Rock (1919); Otto Whittington (temporarily several times between 1919 and 1921); and L.E. Barton (1920-1921). Rogers' third and longest term resulted from a division of labor in 1921, wherein Otto Whitington became Secretary of the State Mission Board and Rogers Secretary of the Executive Board.

Convention leaders sought to soften possible objections to this plan by broadening its constituency. Thus, whereas in 1900 the Executive Board had consisted of thirteen members-at-large plus one member from each association, in 1913 the number was raised to seventy-five, one from each association and the rest from the state at large. Although this arrangement helped to alleviate some objections to centralization, it did nothing to lighten the burden on the secretaries. Consequently in 1921 the Convention returned to a less-centralized plan by which the Convention's work was distributed between an Executive Board, and a State Mission Board as well as a Hospital Commission, Boards of Trustees for Ouachita and Central Colleges and the Arkansas Baptist Orphans' Home, a Board of Ministerial Education, and a State (Women's) Executive Committee.[38] J.S. Rogers became "General Secretary" of the State Mission Board. In 1926 the Convention again merged the work of the Executive Board and the State Mission Board.

The Corporation Comes of Age

We have been witnessing a very important shift in the way Arkansas Baptists went about their task of evangelizing the state. Growing up as the state of Arkansas itself grew up, they increasingly utilized the model which was imposing itself on the whole culture, that of the corporation. Most Arkansans were not able to understand this way of doing things and were unprepared for this transition. That is why it proved to be a painful experience for Arkansas Baptists. Before the present period was over, however, the corporation model had been more or less completely adapted to the needs of the Arkansas Baptist State Convention.

The preeminent concern of any corporation is funding. It is not surprising, therefore, that, in Arkansas as well as in other Southern Baptist states, fund-raising stepped to the center of the stage. Funding, of course, had been a major problem for the State Convention. Not many Arkansas Baptists were wealthy. The state itself was not. Consequently, it is not surprising that churches paid pastors poorly, that associations had to turn to the State Convention or the Home Mission Board of the Southern Baptist Convention for help in paying associational missionaries, that the State Convention relied on the sacrificial commitments of its leaders to provide support and stimulation for churches and associations, and that schools and the orphan's home often floundered.

Early on, Arkansas Baptists had used various strategies for collecting funds. They had employed financial agents for particular projects such as Ouachita College. They had thrust the fund-raising burden on the shoulders of state missionaries, evangelists, and mission or Sunday school secretaries. In addition, from 1888 on, they had gotten massive help from the Woman's Missionary Union, which enlisted even children in the task. The W.M.U. deserves much credit for convincing Arkansas Baptists that they could dream big dreams. More than any other organization, this one pointed the way to a unified effort in funding the Convention's work.

The consolidation of Arkansas Baptist work under a single board in 1913 was aimed essentially, whatever other reasons were given, at more efficient coordination of effort. This meant, above all else, improvement in the system of collecting and distributing funds.

Such is precisely what was implied in the delineation of the Executive Board's work.

> *This Board shall co-operate with the churches in gathering and disbursing funds for evangelization, education, orphanage and hospital work, Sunday School, publication and B. Y.P. U. work and whatever other work this Convention may see fit to engage in not otherwise provided for; except that, without specific orders from this Convention, it shall not be the duty of this Board to raise endowment for educational institutions.*[39]

The plan proposed here prefigured the Cooperative Program, which was inaugurated in 1925 in the wake of the "75-Million Campaign." As the figures given above in Table XIX demonstrate, it proved quite successful. Most Arkansas Baptists, of course, being farmers and backwoods people, still did not understand the corporation approach. If they gave a few dollars a year to support a preacher, they thought they had done enough. Many refused to give anything. But the most troublesome opponents of the plan had already made their exit in 1901, and those who had had reservations now perceived that the Convention's approach did not seriously threaten the local churches or the associations. Quite the contrary, it enabled both to do things they could not do alone. This time, the Convention would ride out objections.

Actual implementation of the plan did not proceed as smoothly as the plan itself intended, but it did not go badly. In 1916 the Committee on State Missions reported that about 700 churches had contributed during the past year, compared to only 511 before the State Mission Campaign began.[40] Each year, moreover, the contributions and the number of state missionaries and other workers multiplied rapidly. Schools and the orphans' home were rescued from near bankruptcy. Table XX shows the vast improvement in finances between 1916 and 1919 and the corresponding improvement in the Convention's capabilities.

Optimism about Arkansas' "Five Year Plan" (1913-1918), spurred on by the post-World War I popular optimism, prepared the way for enthusiastic efforts in the "75-Million Campaign" in 1919. Under the brief but highly skilled leadership of E.P. Alldredge the Executive Board laid out an ambitious plan for Arkansas Baptists not merely to solicit funds but to enlarge all of their work. Alldredge conceded that Arkansas Baptists faced numerous problems: (1)

TABLE XX
EXECUTIVE BOARD WORK, 1916-1918

	1916	1917	1918
Associational Missionaries Assisted			21
Missionaries and other workers	65	91	194
Sunday Schools and B.Y.P.U.s Organized	24	111	136
Churches Organized	18	29	16
Conversions	3,134	4,384	2,253
Soldiers Converted			10,000
Baptisms	2,281	2,242	2,337
Total Additions	3,010	3,470	3,779
Funds Raised:			
For Education	$13,085.09	$ 8,217.75	$ 6,980.78
For Ministerial Education	1,263.53		1,662.37
For Endowment			22,008.00
For Orphanage	18,420.08	29,789.75	13,627.53
For Home Missions	10,100.00	16,405.00	27,000.00
For Foreign Missions	19,072.65	23,631.18	29,948.00
For Mary Forbes Home	88.00	179.65	91.50
For Training School	159.10	1,844.07	1,926.23
For State Missions	25,171.47	44,800.12	56,626.45
For Asso. Missions		22,700.00	27,800.00
Margaret Fund		32.50	
Cone Property		1,799.42	
Hospital Work		322.80	
Old Ministers' Relief		281.21	
Grand Total	$87,359.89	$150,003.35	$187,670.00

inadequate leadership, (2) Landmarkism, (3) insufficient equipment for schools and hospitals, (4) lack of information or widespread misinformation, (5) too many rural churches, (6) inability of many to adjust to a changing America, and (7) inadequate commitment of leaders to Arkansas. But he refused to let these squelch his optimism. Arkansas Baptists had an equal number of things in their favor: (1) a large rural populace receptive to the gospel "as no other class of people in the world," (2) a big numerical lead over other denominations in Arkansas, (3) rapid recent growth, twice that of any other leading denomination, (4) a largely native-born populace who can understand the message, (5) a state "peculiarly free from the great institutions of vice which hinder and hold back the cause of religion in other States," (6) a state constituency "naturally inclined toward the Baptist position," and (7) a climate which allows work 365 days a year.[41]

The 14-point program for the "75-Million Campaign" drawn up by the Executive Board illustrates so well the ambitious aims of the Convention that it merits quotation in full.

1. *75 Associational or County Missionaries Employed For All Time (that is, fulltime).*
2. *100 Student Pastors, Missionaries, and Evangelists Employed For Vacation Work.*
3. *Eight Enlistment Missionaries Employed For All Time.*
4. *Every Church Aided in Securing, Keeping and Supporting a Pastor.*
5. *20,000 New Converts Baptized Every Year.*
6. *$55,000 Expended Yearly in Assisting Churches to Build or Repair Meeting Houses.*
7. *One Million Dollars Expended in Equipping and Endowing Ouachita and Central Colleges.*
8. *Our Four Mountain Schools Equipped and Enlarged and Two or Three More Built.*
9. *Our Orphans' Home Greatly Enlarged and Better Equipped.*
10. *$65,000 Raised For Our Worthy Old Ministers.*
11. *Our Davis Hospital at Pine Bluff Enlarged and a Great Central Hospital at Little Rock Built and Put in Operation.*
12. *Our Sunday School, B.Y.P.U., and Woman's Work Increased 200 Per Cent.*
13. *The Greatest Campaign of Information, Inspiration, and Indoctrination of Our History Waged*

Incessantly.

14. *The Number of White Baptists in Arkansas Increased From 126,000 to 250,000 and 80 Per Cent of Them Fully Enlisted.*[42]

The ambitiousness of the "75-Million Campaign" created immediate and serious problems of indebtedness. In 1920 the Executive Board correctly sized up the difficulty in terms of "too large a programme at the first of the year and an insufficient income during the year to meet the expenditure necessary to put on this programme."[43] The part of the program which suffered most was that to which the Convention assigned the highest priority, namely, state missions. To avoid further embarrassment, the Board asked the Convention to allow it to borrow money to meet pressing obligations, to place direction of associational missions entirely under control of associational boards, to reduce appropriations to missionary pastors and churches to a minimum, to employ up to six "general enlistment workers" who would help in collecting funds as well as do "general missionary work," to employ a staff of evangelists to work under direction of the General Secretary, and to prepare "an adequate, accurate, estimated budget" for the ensuing year covering all areas of the Board's work.[44] A year later, the Executive Board requested a shifting of appropriations from foreign missions, home missions, and various institutions to state missions in order to offset a heavy indebtedness and to strengthen a weak program. The Convention, as we noted earlier, also acted to solve the problem by resurrecting a State Mission Board.

Financially, however, another approach was called for. In 1922 the State Convention authorized the Executive Board to employ J.F. Tull to devote full time "to the promotion of Stewardship, Tithing and Systematic Giving among our people."[45] Tull committed himself unreservedly to the "Unified Budget Plan of Systematic Church Finance" developed by the Southern Baptist Convention. The word "unified" must be underlined here. In recommending this plan to the Convention and the churches in 1923 the Committee on the Budget Plan, of which Tull was a member, argued, "Unification is the one thing needful, and this cannot be accomplished in the local plans of any church when the auxiliaries of the church are left out as separate administrative agencies in money matters." They went on to add, "Church finance is the only and one basis upon which all the life of a church can be unified, and it is the common-cause element of financial support that the church itself should take over and thereby assume its right as well as its privilege to collect and administer all common-cause funds."[46]

With Tull as Stewardship and Budget Director the financial picture brightened. Arkansas Baptists had pledged approximately 2.4 million dollars. An "Every Member Canvass" in the last year of the campaign brought them close to complete success. During the five-year period of the "75-Million Campaign," they contributed $2,228,413.97. In the five years preceding the Campaign, they gave only about a half million dollars. Executive Board debts totaled about $249,000.[47]

The growing number of Baptists loyal to the State Convention did not have long to exult in the successes of the "75-Million Campaign," however. The Campaign had given Southern Baptists an idea about united effort in financing their ambitious programs. Even before they completed it, they put forth their plan for a "Cooperative Program," which would take effect when the Campaign ended December 31, 1924. At the annual meeting of the State Convention in 1923 a Special Committee on Program for 1925 proposed a financial goal of $400,000 for the calendar year, solicited through an "Every Member Canvass." They underlined the values of the unified budget method. "While the right of individuals and churches to designate gifts is recognized, it is earnestly hoped that the contributions will be made to the whole program."[48]

In transition from the "75-Million Campaign" to the Cooperative Program the Convention encountered new difficulties which the depression of the late 'twenties and the 'thirties prolonged. In 1925 the Executive Board reported that only 150 churches had opted for the Cooperative Program. The Convention owed a whopping $850,000. Though debts were counterbalanced by assets of more than three million dollars, plus $145,000 in anticipated income, at this date such a large sum must have been frightening. Just a year before, James F. Dew, editor of the Landmark **Baptist Flag** had charged that E. P. Alldredge had misappropriated $59,000 of the "75-Million Campaign" money when he was Secretary in 1919. Although the Board easily disproved these allegations, they took care in their report in 1925 to reassure Arkansas Baptists that Board policies were "open" and "business-like." They noted further that they spent only a small amount on administration, spending most money "for purely Mission work." Listing various southwide and state programs, they reminded their constituency that the Baptist work was no longer a "peanut business" but "runs on a colossal scale" requiring "huge sums of money."[49] The corporation had come of age.

Promoting the Convention's Programs

It will not be necessary to discuss here the implementation of the numerous Convention programs—increasing the number and improving the training of pastors, aiding work of associations, educating the constituency through Sunday schools and B.Y.P.U.s, fostering benevolent institutions such as the Baptist Orphans' Home and hospitals, influencing the society morally and spiritually through schools and colleges or social and political action, and various direct efforts in evangelism. These will each receive attention in other contexts. Attention does need to be directed here, however, to **The Baptist Advance,** the Convention-affiliated paper which in 1902 supplanted the Landmark-leaning **Arkansas Baptist,** and Arkansas Baptist Assembly.

The Baptist Advance. The importance of a paper sympathetic with the work of the Convention and serving as its voice had long been recognized. The embittered attack of W.A. Clark on the work of the Convention, however, heightened concern for a paper representing the convention's point of view. When Clark failed to abide by a promise to halt his criticisms, the Convention withdrew its recommendation of **The Arkansas Baptist** and Convention leaders moved quickly to create a new Convention voice.

The new paper, significantly named **The Baptist Advance,** was founded, like the old one, on private initiative of M.R. Pittman, then pastor at Fort Smith, M.L. Thomas, pastor of the Second Baptist Church, Little Rock, and A.J. Barton, Missionary Secretary of the State Convention. Barton became the first editor, E.J.A. McKinney and Sam Eaton, assistant editors. Support for the paper came through stock subscriptions in the Advance Publishing Company.

The Baptist Advance, its first issue appearing January 4, 1902, defined its purpose as "For Christ, the Churches, and Co-operation." In an early issue the editor, obviously alluding to the Convention's experience with Clark's editorship, promoted the new paper with the point that "A good Baptist paper will not only make you feel more loyal to your own denomination, but will probably make you feel more kindly toward all who love the Lord Jesus Christ."[50] In a later issue W.L. Compere rejoiced that Arkansas Baptists again had a paper which would let "all the facts, principles and issues involved in our convention work be clearly set before your readers."[51] In 1903 the Committee on Publications commended it as "an indispensable factor in our denominational life" and urged its use because it shows a "loving spirit, loyalty to truth," is "wisely aggressive," "constructive," and "hopeful" and "because it is loyal to those institutions which have come in response to the prayers, the tears, and the toils of our fathers."[52]

Even with strong endorsement among Convention leaders, however, the **Baptist Advance** floundered financially. Important as the paper's purpose was, Arkansas had too few literate people to assure a large subscription, and backers of the paper continually had to plead for help. Early on, it experienced rapid turnover in editors. A.J. Barton resigned after less than three years to become Field Secretary of the Home Mission Board in August of 1904.[53] John Jeter Hurt, Jr. and J.F. Love together lasted less than two years (September 1, 1904 to March 1, 1906). E.J.A. McKinney, the associate editor, continued publication for several months with the aid of Benjamin Cox, then pastor of the First Baptist Church of Little Rock. J.B. Searcy, recently returning to Arkansas from Mississippi, replaced Cox for three months but found the labor so strenuous that he had to relinquish the post.[54] McKinney carried on for the next eleven years, either as sole editor or as an associate.

In 1912 the Advance Publishing Company found itself $6,000 in debt, an accumulation of several years. As a result, the Directors offered to transfer their stock (a large majority of the total) to the State Convention and to aid in securing the remainder if the Convention would assume the debt. The Convention agreed, placing the paper's "future policy" and "management" in the hands of the newly created Executive Board "for final solution."[55] This new arrangement did not solve all of the **Advance's** problems. It still waged a fierce battle to increase its readership to a level comparable with that of the state Methodist paper. Though the vastly improved financial situation connected with the "75-Million Campaign" gave a big boost here, the paper fell victim to over-enthusiasm along with the Executive Board. Beginning 1920 with 11,860 subscribers, it carried about 3,000 of these longer than funds provided for and ended the year with 8,618 and a deficit. Later the Convention approved a resolution that all churches should send the **Advance** to every member, paying for it from the church treasury, the price of subscriptions being reduced accordingly.[56] The plan did not get an enthusiastic reception. In 1923, for instance, only 25 churches and four other organizations included the paper in their budgets. Even with Executive Board support in prosperous times it struggled along with limited subscriptions and substantial indebtedness, having difficulty collecting on unpaid subscriptions. Between 1921 and 1925 the Executive Board reported annual deficits of $4,100.10, $150.00, $2,412.42, $2,042.70, and $944.17. Fortunately, in 1921 the Convention voted to place the **Advance** on an insured financial basis by instructing the Board to cover all debts for it.[57] J.S. Compere, editor from 1919 until 1929, had a much easier task than his predecessors.

For a brief period the state paper was linked with the Baptist Book House. Originally a part of the colportage work of the Convention, in 1911 the Book House was "sold" or leased for five years to A.P. Scofield by the Missionary and Sunday School Boards. In exchange for free rent and encouragement Scofield was to give the Board a "percent on all books."[58] When the Book House reverted to the Convention, its management was consolidated with that of **The Baptist Advance** under the direction of a Commission appointed annually by the Executive Board. This heavy double load was borne by the editor, J.S. Compere, until 1922, when the Book House was placed under the direction of the General Secretary of the Convention. The Sunday School Board of the Southern Baptist Convention held a half-interest in the Book House.

Arkansas Baptist Assembly. Another important means for fostering the denominational program was the development of a state summer assembly. Originally sponsored by the Baptist Young People's Union, the first assembly met in 1905 at Brown Springs under the direction of H.L. Winburn, pastor of the First Baptist Church of Arkadelphia. Despite steady downpouring of rain, flooding the grounds, 419 participated. Among other activities, William Jennings Bryan delivered an address on "Ideals of Christian Citizenship" and Booth Lowry gave his famous lecture, "Simon Says Wigwag."

From 1905 until 1922 the summer assemblies met at Arkadelphia on the campus of Ouachita College. Thereafter it shifted to Siloam Springs. Attendance fluctuated up and down. For the years for which records were kept the following figures were reported:

1905	419	1920	500
1913	600	1922	402
1914	600	1923	553
1915	500	1924	911
1919	300	1925	1,086

The assembly gradually enlarged its offerings. Initially concerned chiefly with B.Y.P.U., in 1911 a Teacher Training Institute was arranged and certificates were issued by the Sunday School Board for work done. In 1912 Clarence S. Leavell, Sunday School Field Secretary, urged that the assembly "be made the greatest factor fostered by the Baptists of Arkansas, for development, improvement, and general efficiency in church life and methods."[59] In 1914 the assembly listed sixteen lecturers, teachers, or other speakers. It issued 361 study awards.

With the election of H.V. Hamilton as B.Y.P.U. Secretary in 1922 interest in locating a permanent home for the assembly quickly came to a head. Hamilton envisioned an attractive location which would induce families to come to the assembly for their summer vacations. The city of Siloam Springs obliged him by presenting a 160-acre site located in a valley near the city. Attendance leaped upwards and so again did the aims of the assembly. The constitution stated that it was the assembly's purpose "to foster all phases of our denominational work."[60] Unfortunately, these ambitious designs soon created financial problems. In 1926 the Convention, noting that the assembly could not finance its growing program, voted to assume responsibility for its debts. With the untimely death of Hamilton at age thirty-four and the onset of a depression the assembly did not meet for two years (1927-1928).

The Churches Inside Out

In studying the history of Arkansas Baptist churches in earlier periods we have had to rely largely on impressions gained from widely scattered sources. For the period now under discussion we are aided by a survey of **Arkansas Baptist Rural Churches** compiled by E.P. Alldredge, General Secretary of the Executive Board of the Arkansas Baptist State Convention in 1919. This survey, focused on the year 1922, enhances greatly the accuracy of our impressions of Baptist church life in Arkansas during this period.

In 1922 ten Baptist bodies nearly equalled all other denominations combined. The five largest denominations ranked approximately as follows:

Baptists (10 bodies)	260,000
Methodists (7 bodies)	195,000
Churches of Christ and Disciples	40,000
Presbyterians (5 bodies)	25,500
Roman Catholics	24,000

Baptists reported the following figures:

Southern Baptists (white)	118,316
Landmark Baptists (white)	35,500
Black Baptists	97,500
Miscellaneous Baptists (7 bodies)	11,935
Total	263,251

Together Baptists constituted approximately fifteen percent of the total state population.

Arkansas' Ruralism

Baptists affiliated with the State Convention, like all other Baptists, were overwhelmingly rural. In 1922 1,127 or 89.5% of a reported 1,260 churches were either open country (800) or village (327) congregations. Correspondingly, the State Convention claimed only 133 urban churches, i.e. in cities larger than 1,000, or 10.5% of the total. Though urban churches claimed a much larger proportion of the total membership (36,045 or 30.4%), they still fell far below the rural churches (82,271 or 69.6%) even in numbers.

As one would expect, rural churches were small, poor, and struggling. None had as many as 400 members. They averaged 73 members. Table XXI reveals that most had less than a hundred, 91.1 percent less than 150.

TABLE XXI
MEMBERSHIP OF RURAL CHURCHES, 1922

Range of Membership	Number
Less than 10	14
11 to 49	419
50 to 99	420
100 to 149	188
150 to 199	51
200 to 299	45
300 to 399	4
over 400	0

Small congregations such as these usually met part-time. In 1922 fifteen were meeting full time, 4 three quarter-time, 228 or 20.2% half-time, and 880 or 78.1% quarter-time. Of the 880 more than a third (365) were without pastors. Many preachers served several churches at the same time. In 1902, for instance, the **Baptist Advance** referred to one person "who was pastor at Esau, Houston, and Casa in Perry County and at Oppello in Faulkner County and supplied at Antioch in Perry County."[61] Lucille Wood, a member of the First Baptist Church at Paragould, recalls that in her early years (1914-1924) Union Grove Baptist Church, near Paragould, held services at 11:00 a.m. and 7:00 p.m. on Saturday. The next day, they met for Sunday school at 10:00 a.m., "preaching service" at 11:00, and evening worship. The preacher spent Saturday night in the home of a member. On off-Sundays a singing was sometimes scheduled or someone would come to play the pump organ for those present. Often, however, members visited other churches in the community on those days. Methodist and Baptist churches usually cooperated in this respect by scheduling their preaching on different Sundays of the month so that they could attend the services of both churches.

Arkansas' rural churches showed their poverty both in finances and in church edifices. According to the Elldredge survey, the average per capita gift of all rural Baptists in Arkansas was only $2.67 for local church expenses, $3.73 for all causes. This figure is not surprising, when we consider the fact that the average per capita income in rural Arkansas was only $210 a year. Nor is it surprising that, despite the pressures of the "75-Million Campaign," only 7.9% of Arkansas' rural churches employed a budget system, an item quite unfamiliar to farm folk. In the Campaign 539 rural churches pledged only $531,664.00 while 122 urban churches pledged $1,851,947.90.

A similar impression is gained from a look at the properties of Arkansas rural churches. In 1922 236 or 20.9% were meeting in school houses and lodge halls, 80 or 7.1% in "Union" church buildings, 811 or 72% in Baptist church buildings, and 316 or 28% had no building. The same year twelve churches were still congregating in buildings which antedated the Civil War, but 65.4% of the churches were built after 1900. Almost all rural buildings (96.4%) were of wood construction; a few were of stone (2.9%) or brick (.7%). Most (746 or 92%) were one-room buildings seating an average of 294 persons. Their average value, including grounds, was $1,542. None was insured. According to Elldredge, 40.6% needed enlargement, 45.6% repairs, and all remodeling.

Revivals continued to play an important role in most rural churches, especially on account of their part-time status. Preachers normally saved evangelistic sermons for the annual revival, and, according to W.O. Taylor, [62] they placed little emphasis on evangelism at other times. Since an increasingly high percentage of converts entered Arkansas Baptist churches through Sunday schools, the effect of revivals was reduced to some extent. But a well-timed revival sometimes brought a dying congregation back to life. The Corning Baptist Church depicted in the preceding chapter, for example, deteriorated badly during the height of the Landmark controversy, 1906-1920. Between 1918 and 1920 it made no reports to the Current River Association. Evidently having no pastor, the congregation let the Sunday school die and did not use their church building for a year or two. In the early spring of 1920, however, D.M. Carter, pastor of the Piggott Baptist Church, preached a revival which resulted in 33 new members—21 by baptism and 12 by letter or statement. The congregation struggled along until 1924, when it again closed its doors, this time for six years. In November of 1930 Golden E. Neely held a revival at the request of his father, F.C. Neely, twice pastor of the Corning Church. This revival, among other things, resulted in the calling of the younger Neely as pastor. In the Fall of 1931 the church reported 29 baptisms, 33 new members, a total membership of 108, 140 enrolled in Sunday school, and total expenditures for the year of $2,069.64. Thereafter, it thrived for a time.

Associations also sponsored revivals. In August, 1905, for instance, the Caddo River Baptist Association held a nine-day meeting on the camp ground maintained by Mountain Home Church. Five preachers took turns preaching. The revival resulted in 41 conversions.[63]

Worship in Arkansas Baptist rural churches underwent little alteration during the period under discussion. Services remained very informal. Men sat on one side of the building and women on the other. Children sat by one or the other of their parents. Young people usually occupied a special pew. There were no nurseries. Preachers simply yelled louder in order to drown out the wails of crying babies. Fathers often helped mothers by holding the babies. If they could not quiet them, they would pass them across the aisle to the mothers.

The ideal of worship was simplicity of spirituality. In 1902 W.L.A. Stranburg described the goal in the **Baptist Advance.**

Simple spiritual worship means destitute of art or constraint. Characterized by plainness, liberty, freedom. Not art or a system of rules, but with ease, joy, and delight should we draw from the wells of salvation.[64]

The key elements were singing, prayer, and preaching.

Singing in the typical rural church, according to Victor I. Masters,[65] left much to be desired. Many smaller churches still had neither piano, organ, nor song leader. At Union Grove, for instance, according to Lucille Wood, someone would start the singing, and the congregation would sing three or four songs without instruments. Most rural churches, recalls James Fitzgerald, a retired pastor and missionary now living in Paragould, used Stamps Baxter type song books with shaped notes.

Some churches had pump organs and a few pipe organs. Every issue of the **Baptist Advance** for 1902 carried ads for Kimball pianos and organs, "the most renowned instruments in the world." According to Clella Bleier, the First Baptist Church of Paragould owned a pipe organ when she joined in 1916 at age twelve. At that early date someone had to man an apparatus in a back room in order for it to be played.

Most churches scheduled a time for prayer requests at the conclusion of the song service. Prayers were typically simple and extemporaneous.

Sermons were much longer than they are today. Often, according to Noah Dearing, a longtime deacon from Harrison, those attending would not get home from the morning services until 2:00 p.m. With this prospect in mind wives cooked Sunday's noon meal on Saturday. Most person, however, were not as time conscious as they are today. Long services filled an important social need.

Preachers emphasized sin, judgment, and hell more in the early 1900s than today. They also gave extended invitations. Many churches had mourners' benches, where the repentant waited for the Spirit to move them toward a decision.

A printed or mimeographed order of service for worship began to appear in some churches during this period. The First Baptist Church of Jonesboro, for instance, has copies of printed bulletins dating back to 1923. Most churches, however, adopted this custom slowly and reluctantly. Many persons, according to J.I. Cossey, thought this innovation left out the leadership of the Holy Spirit.

Most Arkansas churches observed the Lord's Supper infrequently and restricted it to the church family or at least to persons of "like faith and order." At Friendship Baptist Church in Greene County, states Raymond Faulkner, the Lord's Supper was observed but once a year, near Easter, and restricted to the church family. It was interpreted as taking the place of the Jewish Passover. Curiously the whole congregation drank from two glasses, but they shared a common loaf.

Arkansas churches continued to exercise rather strict discipline over their members during this period, at least until 1918, when Southern Baptist Convention **Annuals** no longer reported these on a state-by-state basis. Table XXII indicates a substantial increase during this period in the percentage of persons excluded as compared to those restored. Exactly what caused this may not be determinable.

TABLE XXII
DISCIPLINE IN BAPTIST CHURCHES, 1901-1918

Year	Exclusions	Restorations	Year	Exclusions	Restorations
1901	1574	647	1911	1510	425
1902	1191	503	1912	1511	338
1903	1241	419	1913	1472	243
1904	977	513	1914	1495	489
1905	1039	496		(Exclusions and Erasures)	
1906	1359	473	1915	1632	468
1907	1264	535	1916	1629	337
1908	1169	486	1917	1067	449
1909	1537	526	1918	1062	559
1910	1594	512	1919	Not reported hereafter	

It may be partially connected with the Landmark controversy, but one suspects also that it was related to growth of secularity. Many of those excluded did not let church authority weigh very heavily upon them. It was this which accounts for the gradual abandonment of discipline in Baptist churches everywhere. Disdain for church authority would have been especially strong in areas of private morality to which Baptists usually applied their sanctions—drinking, dancing, gambling, and smoking.

Typical of Baptist piety in this period would have been John William Black. Born December 3, 1858 in Williamson County, Illinois, John William married Mary Logan Gold in 1879. The Blacks moved to Corning, Arkansas, then still a village, in January of 1895. For three years Black farmed, but in the rugged hill country around Corning this venture proved unsuccessful. He then entered the lumber business and succeeded in developing one of the strongest businesses in Northeast Arkansas, where timber abounded. Converted about 1900, he refused to be baptized in the church's usual baptistry, the local lake, and insisted on being baptized in "running water." Responding to his wish, the pastor, O.H.L. Cunningham, baptized him in the nearby Current River. Indicative of his independent spirit, however, Black declined to join the church immediately, insisting that he had first to study Baptist doctrines. After joining he proved a liberal contributor to Baptist causes and took particular pride in assisting churches building new houses of worship. Ordained a deacon in 1934, he served as chairman of the building committee when the Corning Baptist Church erected its new building in 1939. He frequently attended the State and the Southern Baptist Conventions. He died March 21, 1944.

Mary Logan Gold was the daughter of a pioneer Baptist preacher in Illinois. While a student at Ewing College, which was originally founded as a non-denominational school but which became Baptist in 1877 and aligned itself with the Illinois State Baptist Association in 1908, she made a profession of faith and was baptized into the fellowship of the Ewing Baptist Church, Ewing, Illinois. Later she transferred her membership to the Carrier Mills Baptist Church and, after she and her husband moved to Corning, to the Corning Baptist Church. She was instrumental in leading her husband and all six of her children into the Christian faith and membership in the Corning Church. The Blacks regularly entertained visiting preachers. Mrs. Black led in the work of the "Ladies' Aid Society," which raised much of the money needed for the operation of the church. From personal savings she gave the church a communion service. After a lengthy illness she died on May 4, 1941.[66]

Leaders of the Flock

In rural churches pastors were poorly educated, poorly paid, and held short term pastorates. In 1922, according to the Elldredge survey, 62.2% had neither college nor seminary training, 28% college but no seminary training, 1.4% seminary but no college training, and only 8.4% both college and seminary training. Preaching was an avocation, farming a vocation for most; yet most interpreted their ministry as a "Divine Call."[67] J.I. Cossey, a retired pastor, recalls a country preacher in central Arkansas from the years 1900-1910 who could neither read nor write. His wife taught him the

Bible, and, says Cossey, "He became an outstanding country preacher."

Most rural pastors depended on other means of support. In 1922 Arkansas rural churches reported the following salaries:

Full-time	$1,390.00
Half-time	353.93
Quarter-time	128.50

The general average for those serving full-time, only 22.1% of the total, was $655.84. By contrast the general average of urban pastors was $1,706.90.

Tenure in rural pastorates was short. In 1922 the average pastorate was 2 years and 7 months. A major reason for the brevity of service was the "annual call," a custom at the time in 83.3% of the rural churches. In addition, many pastors commuted a considerable distance to their churches. Most lived within twenty miles, but 18.9% lived between 20 and 75 miles and 2.2% from 75 to 150 miles from their charges.

The typical minister's story would not differ a great deal from that of the couple described above except that he would have changed congregations far more often. Instead of trying to characterize the average minister, it will be more helpful here to sketch the life of an exceptional one, James Seth Compere, Sr. Compere was the son of Ebenezer Lee Compere, the distinguished missionary to the Indians in western Arkansas and Indian territory alluded to in an earlier chapter, and Isabella Mullins, an aunt of E.Y. Mullins, President of the Southern Baptist Theological Seminary in Louisville. Born August 9, 1873 in Charleston, Arkansas, he grew up in western Arkansas, his family moving from place to place during his early years. He entered Ouachita College in 1892, having as yet made no profession of faith. In the spring of 1893, however, he was converted during a revival meeting conducted by T.S. Potts in the First Baptist Church of Arkadelphia and baptized in the Ouachita River by E.B. Miller, pastor of the Church. The next academic year, 1894-1895, he continued his study at Mercer University in Macon, Georgia. Shortly thereafter, June 7, 1896, he married Pen Lile of Waldo, Arkansas in a ceremony performed at Central College in Conway. After a brief interruption of his studies he returned to Ouachita and graduated at the head of his class in 1901, receiving the A.B. degree. Ordained on January 2, 1901, in the First Baptist Church of Arkadelphia, he went on to graduate from the Southern

Baptist Theological Seminary in Louisville with the Th.M. degree in January, 1905. After a brief pastorate in the Warren Baptist Church in Arkansas he went in 1905 to Nigeria under the auspices of the Foreign Mission Board of the Southern Baptist Convention. Mrs. Compere, however, contracted a fever which forced them to return home. Although her health improved rapidly thereafter, the Foreign Mission Board declined to reappoint them.

On their return Compere served simultaneously as pastor of churches in Magnolia, Fordyce, Lewisville, and Stamps. Subsequently he filled several important state posts. Between 1912 and 1914 he headed the Bible Department of Ouachita College. From 1917 to 1919 he served as Assistant General Secretary of the Arkansas Baptist State Convention. Then, as we stated earlier, from 1919 until 1929 he edited the **Arkansas Baptist,** the official state Baptist paper. Thereafter he returned to the pastorate: First Baptist Church, Charleston, Missouri (1930-1933); First Baptist Church, Hayti, Missouri (1933-1934); Corning Baptist Church (1934-1939); and again in Hayti (1939-1941). Failing health forced his retirement in 1941. He died on September 21, 1957.

Pen Lile, daughter of Luther Rice and Lydia Lile, was born June 2, 1876 in Columbia County, Arkansas. Her great grandparents, Robert H. Warren and Lydia Minter Warren, were pioneer settlers in that county, migrating there from Tippa County, Mississippi in 1847. Already Baptists, they donated land and built the first house of worship for Beech Creek Baptist Church shortly after they arrived. Pen Lile made a profession of faith at age fifteen and received baptism as a member of this church. The same year, she entered Ouachita College, graduating in 1899. She studied later at Southern Seminary.

Like other ministers' wives, Mrs. Compere took an active role in her husband's work. In pastoral situations she devoted much of her time to youth work. As a missionary in Nigeria, she worked with children—clothing, feeding, and educating about twenty committed to her care by parents. During Compere's thirteen years in State Convention work, she took an active part in the Woman's Missionary Union in Little Rock. In that connection she led in the planning and implementing of the first Daily Vacation Bible School held in Arkansas, sponsored by the W.M.U. While Compere served as pastor in Missouri, Mrs. Compere served on the Board of Trustees of the Woman's Missionary Union Training (later Carver) School, Louisville, and as a member of the Missouri Baptist Executive

Board. For many years, too, she was a member of the W.M.U. Executive Board for the state of Arkansas, in 1929 being made a life member of this Board. Several times she served as superintendent of associational Woman's Missionary Unions—in Hope Association, Pulaski County Association, Current River Association (3 times), and Madrid Association in Missouri. She died on September 21, 1948.

Training the Flock

Vigorous effort by Sunday School secretaries and field workers, aided by the pump-priming of the Sunday School Board of the Southern Baptist Convention, gradually increased the number and constituency of Sunday schools to a level commensurate with the number and constituency of the churches. Table XXIII, based on

TABLE XXIII
SUNDAY SCHOOLS IN ARKANSAS CHURCHES, 1901-1926

Year	Sunday Schools		Churches—ABSC		Sunday Schools—GA	
	Number	Enrlmnt.	Number	Mbrship.	Number	Enrlmnt.
1901	414	21,612	1,321	74,117		
1902	430	22,686	1,241	75,977		
1903	504	25,480	1,327	77,590		
1904	475	23,569	1,355	80,705		
1905	464	24,213	1,368	84,642		
1906	500	27,702	1,389	88,262		
1907	544	30,014	1,449	92,821		
1908	628	38,122	1,490	99,872		
1909	630	36,897	1,536	105,455		
1910	648	41,047	1,534	106,528		
1911	651	41,418	1,527	108,248		
1912	665	42,815	1,531	109,629		
1913	656	45,519	1,528	111,991		
1914	758	51,519	1,514	111,185		
1915	758	57,865	1,483	114,713		
1916	786	59,243	1,488	118,930		
1917	790	61,359	1,547	122,635		
1918	761	65,965	1,489	121,484		
1919	784	59,189	1,529	124,115		
1920	726	55,975	1,428	124,024		
1921	618	56,582	1,135	98,376	179	9,386
1922	681	67,110	1,174	106,409	217	12,571
1923	655	65,518	998	100,302	314	19,319
1924	650	74,370	920	101,589	325	19,617
1925	774	87,206	953	106,374	325	19,617
1926	798	89,440	1,030	112,231	No Report	

reports to the Southern Baptist Convention, reflect a significant jump in the number of churches having regular Sunday Schools in 1908 and 1914 and a steady rise during this entire period. It is necessary, however, to upgrade even these statistics, for many small churches failed to report. In 1922, for instance, when only 681 churches reported schools, E.M. Alldredge found there were actually 138 or more urban schools and approximately 680 rural ones. At least five of the 133 churches classified as urban were maintaining mission Sunday schools in addition to their own.

In rural areas Sunday schools showed mixed results. Out of the 680 schools 91 or 13.4% operated only during the spring and summer months. Like rural churches, rural Sunday schools were small, 549 or 80.7% enrolling less than 100 pupils, 110 or 16.3% 100-199, 20 or 2.9% 200-299, and only 1 over 300, none as many as 400. Though the average enrollment throughout the state was 71, nearly equalling the average of 73 for each church, average attendance was a meager 46.

In 1922 rural Sunday schools still functioned with limited structure and resources. Most (531 or 78.1%) were meeting in one-room church buildings and only a fraction (65 or 9.5%) had separate rooms. A few (84 or 12.4%) used curtains strung on wires to partition a church building, thus assuring some privacy. A majority (375 or 55.1%) were not graded or departmentalized.

Teachers in these schools had little preparation for the task. Among all of the rural schools Alldredge found only 637 teachers who had studied the manual designed for their work and only 144 had received a certificate called the "Normal Diploma."

Despite some apathy toward Sunday schools still, a carry-over from an earlier period, Elldredge found the results of their work clearly manifest in two areas. First, they accounted for 55% of all baptisms reported by Arkansas rural Baptist churches. Second, they accounted for a fair amount of rural contributions.

The Baptist Young People's Union, which had gotten off on wobbly legs during the preceding period, gained in importance in the training of church leadership during the period now under discussion. More than half of the B.Y.P.U.s, however, were in urban churches when Alldredge made his survey in 1922. They accounted for 175 Unions, whereas rural churches reported only 141, or 162 counting churches which had more than one Union. These 162 rural B.Y.P.U.s enrolled 5,022 young people, an average of 31 persons per unit.

Although B.Y.P.U.s were enrolling only about 80.3% of the young people then living in rural church areas, they were laying foundations for future leadership in modest ways. Among other things, they accounted for 122 volunteers for the ministry and mission work in 1922. They claimed some responsibility for 21 missionaries and 94 young ministers already serving and for 299 young persons attending some Baptist college. They were enlisting others in study courses and encouraging daily Bible reading.

Baptists in the City

It would be a long time before Arkansas Baptists would have a predominantly urban constituency. To the present time, the number of small, rural churches far outnumbers that of urban churches. Already in the period under discussion, however, we can discern the growing importance of the latter. The future direction of the Arkansas Baptist State Convention was being determined by these churches, which were better trained, more affluent, more completely structured, and better equipped to lead. Table XXIV shows why.

The figures in this Table suggest that, while rural churches dominated numerically, both in churches and membership, they

TABLE XXIV
RURAL AND URBAN CHURCHES COMPARED, 1922

Items	Rural Churches	Urban Churches	Total
No. of Chs.	1,127-89.5%	133-10.5%	1,260
Membership	82,271-69.6%	36,045-30.4%	118,316
Baptisms	5,799-65.1%	3,111-34.9%	8,910
No. of SSs	680-83.7%	138-16.3%	818
SS Enrollment	48,280-59.6%	32,830-40.4%	81,110
No. of BYPUs	162-48.3%	175-51.7%	337
BYPU Enrollment	5,022-46.2%	5,846-53.8%	10,868
No. of WMSs	282-64%	159-36%	441
75-Million Campaign Subscription	$531,644-23.2%	$1,851,947-76.8%	$2,283,611

were losing ground rapidly to urban churches in areas where leadership existed or was being shaped and, still more dramatically, in financial matters. The superiority of urban churches stands out starkly in B.Y.P.U., which at this time laid claim to the cream of the younger constituency, those supplying the next generation's pastors and lay leaders. It is clearly evident also in contributions to the "75-

Million Campaign." Leadership and financing, however, need to be construed in much broader terms. They assured far more effective work in all areas, a fact confirmed by the proportionately higher percentage of baptisms in urban than in rural churches. Rural churches suffered heavily from part-time ministry and, accordingly, from lack of continuity. What they did, they often did haphazardly and ineffectively. They could scarcely match their urban counterparts in anything except good intentions.

The advantages of the larger urban churches may be readily put in bas-relief by looking at one example, the First Baptist Church of Fort Smith. As we saw in the preceding chapter, this church benefited immensely from the state mission program in being able to employ capable pastors almost from its beginning in 1857. In the period we are now discussing, it was served by only three persons, two of whom received both college and seminary training and held long terms of service. Finley F. Gibson served thirteen and half years (1902-1916), B.V. Ferguson thirty-four (1916-1950). Gibson, a convert from Methodism, was educated at Ouachita College (B.A. 1897) and the Southern Baptist Theological Seminary (Th.M. 1900). After two years as pastor of the First Baptist Church, Malvern, where he received a salary of $600 a year, he moved to Fort Smith, where he received a salary of $1,500. Shortly after he arrived, the church purchased a lot and started a mission which resulted in Lexington Avenue Baptist Church, organized in 1906. In 1909 the church granted letters to numerous members to form the Calvary Baptist Church in Fishback Addition to Fort Smith.

The First Baptist Church expanded and refurbished its own property during this period. In October of 1903 the congregation occupied the new stone sanctuary replacing the original frame building demolished by a tornado in 1898. In 1913 they installed a new Kimball pipe organ costing $3,500, in the process rearranging the choir gallery in tiers. They also added a system of indirect lighting, the first of its kind in a Baptist church in the South, and a ventilating system which cooled the entire plant and allowed the congregation to worship without interference from outdoor noises. In addition to direct improvements to the church buildings, the congregation purchased a lot and built a home for the pastor on an adjoining lot in 1907. When Gibson resigned to accept a call from the First Baptist Church of Bowling Green, Kentucky, the church had grown to approximately 500 members.

Gibson's successor, Barbour Vaughn Ferguson, received similar training and proved even more successful during a period of dramatic growth in the size of Fort Smith. Educated at Wake Forest College and Southern Seminary, he came to Fort Smith from the First Baptist Church of West Durham, North Carolina, his only other pastorate. By this time the pastor's salary had grown to $2,100 plus parsonage. His successor, J. Harold Smith, started at $7,500 a year. Accentuating evangelism, Ferguson led the church in a massive program of growth. During his tenure, membership increased from about 500 to over 4,000; Sunday school enrollment from a little over 500 to over 2,100; Training Union enrollment from 50 to over 900. The First Baptist Church started two other mission churches, Bethlehem and Spradling. They led the city in two community-wide evangelistic campaigns directed by Mordecai Ham, a noted Baptist revivalist.

The congregation also expanded their physical facilities extensively during Ferguson's pastorate. They replaced the 350-seat sanctuary dedicated in 1903 with one seating 1,500. In 1926 they erected a three-story educational building, to which they added another wing in 1950. In 1950 church properties covered three-fourths of a block and were valued at $750,000.

Such matters as these, of course, in no way describe what was really happening in the First Baptist Church of Fort Smith. They do illustrate why urban churches like this one assumed increasingly prominent roles of leadership. Smith served two terms as president of the Arkansas Baptist State Convention (1936-1937) and as a trustee of the Relief and Annuity Board of the Southern Baptist Convention and of Southern Seminary. Other Arkansas churches had to look to churches such as this for leadership.[69]

Baptists and Their Peers

Baptist relations with other Protestants were usually cordial during this period. Locally churches cooperated in sponsoring revivals. Often they shared facilities during periods of stress. Members of one denomination also visited one another's churches. Until 1916, when the Convention changed its schedule, Baptist leaders attending the Arkansas Baptist State Convention regularly preached in Methodist, Presbyterian, and Disciples' churches as well as other Baptist churches, both white and black.

It is significant of Baptist attitudes toward others that Arkansas Baptists cooperated with them in support of temperance and

213

prohibition. In 1903 the Committee on Temperance urged every true Christian to "align himself unequivocally with every force that has for its purpose the elimination of this fearful traffic of lands, and the institution and protection of a pure ballot."[70] The rivalry of Baptists with other groups may have weakened this kind of cooperation on occasion. In 1906, for instance, the Convention agreed to support all temperance groups except the "Inter-Church Temperance Federation." This reservation may have been connected with the views of the Federation rather than ecumenism, however, for the next year the Convention agreed to support "every temperance organization which have for their object the complete annihilation of the liquor business."[71] In 1910 seven Baptists served on the 24-member Board of the Anti-Saloon League of America. In 1915 and for several years afterwards the Convention voted to name five representatives to the State Anti-Saloon League.[72]

Inevitably Landmark influence restricted Baptist relations with others. In the midst of the controversy with the General Association the Convention adopted a resolution, offered by A.H. Autry, requesting the Foreign Mission Board of the Southern Baptist Convention to withdraw missionaries who advocated or practiced "alien immersion." The same resolution also noted that "the practice of holding union meetings, as is done by some Baptists, is subversive of Baptist principles, and should be discouraged."[73] Associational and Convention statements frequently reiterated the finality of Baptist claims over against those of other denominations.

The group which aroused Baptist suspicions and hostilities most were Roman Catholics. Baptists blamed the latter for the decay of "Christian" customs in America. They indicted them for encouraging the sale and consumption of liquor, gambling, dancing, and erosion of sabbath observance. In 1915, for instance, the Committee on Lord's Day Observance of the State Convention lamented that "the holiday Sabbath of Roman Catholic countries is becoming very popular in our own so-called Protestant America."[74]

The Convention adopted a strongly worded anti-Catholic statement on the "Patriotic Press" in 1914. The resolution classified Roman Catholicism with "various other un-American ideas and institutions" and urged the development of a "news-gathering agency and assembling of capable and scholarly men" who could write pamphlets, articles, and books "upon every phase of American Romanism and other un-American ideas and institutions." It also encouraged "the formation of lecture bureaus, the circulation of patriotic papers, the enactment of legislation which will safeguard American principles, and the election of officers of the law who stand for American ideas."[75]

Baptists in Arkansas Society

The present period was one of ferment in Arkansas as in the rest of the nation. Although most Baptists, limited in education and cultural advantages, tended to show a natural reserve in social and political matters, they found themselves drawn deeper and deeper into the life of their state. Increased participation can be attributed in part to Baptist growth, as we have seen earlier, for, by now, the three largest Baptist bodies together represented the largest denomination in Arkansas. But it also entailed a growing sense of responsibility for the state's well being and an increased awareness that religion was not a purely private and personal affair.

Baptists in Politics

In the political area Baptists have to take some credit (or blame) for a wide variety of politicians, diverse as the populace of the state itself. On one end of the spectrum would stand Jeff Davis, champion of the "hill billies" and opponent of big-business, railroads, and "city-slickers." In many ways he typified the highly individualistic piety and demeanor of the "hardshell" Baptists he identified with.

Born in Little River County in southwest Arkansas on May 6, 1862, his family moved to Pope County early in his life. His father functioned there as a small-town lawyer and a local judge, but the family was extremely poor. There is some uncertainty about Jeff Davis's education, but at nineteen he passed an exam for the local bar at Russellville. In 1890 he ran successfully for prosecuting attorney for his district. He married immediately afterwards, and his wife bore him twelve children, eight of whom survived infancy.

In 1898, retiring from the prosecuting attorney's office, Davis ran for state attorney general. He campaigned weakly against F.M. Goar, an old professor of law at the state university, and planned to give up when Goar suddenly dropped dead while delivering a speech on April 7, 1898. Davis thus became automatically the democratic nominee, which in Arkansas assured election.

As attorney general, Davis gained a reputation through his rigorous enforcement of anti-trust legislation. He sued one corporation after another: insurance companies, express companies, tobacco companies, cotton-seed oil companies, and railroads. He threatened to drive every "foreign-born" corporation from the state, and the onslaught of his opponents emboldened him all the more and increased his support with the still predominantly rural public.

Davis ran for the governor's office on the same platform. To the delight of his backers, he campaigned with no holds barred, capitalizing upon his own impoverished roots and vilifying opponents for support from "the high-collared roosters" and the "silk-stocking crowd." Three times he won handily. In 1906 he was elected United States Senator.

Jeff Davis did not fare as well as a Baptist as he did as a politician. In 1901, following his first gubernatorial victory, the Arkansas Baptist State Convention elected him Vice-president, an honor perhaps more or less automatic in view of the long and faithful service of Governor James P. Eagle. Davis reciprocated by appointing Eagle, President of the Convention, a member of the new capitol commission. Because of Eagle's opposition during his second term, however, Davis demanded his resignation. Eagle refused. Davis published a proclamation removing him. The Board of Deacons of the First Baptist Church, where both held membership, responded by excluding Davis. He laughed at this, declaring himself a "pint Baptist" while the others were "quart Baptists."[76]

In 1904 Davis ran against Carroll D. Wood, a Justice of the Arkansas Supreme Court from 1893 until 1929, also a prominent Baptist, as well as A.F. Vandeventer, a lumber dealer from Morrilton and former member of the House of Representatives. The campaign was noted for its backwoods invective. Davis ridiculed the fact that Wood sang in the choir of the First Baptist Church of Little Rock. To gain backwoods support, he made much of Wood's support among Prohibitionists and the fact that he was a teetotaler. He called him "Aunt Priss" or "Aunt Julie." During a platform debate at Hope, Wood became so enraged by the taunts that he struck Davis with his fists. The latter retaliated by cracking Wood over the head with a gold-headed cane.

In the United States Senate Davis soon became a buffoon and failed to achieve his vaunted goal of stopping trusts and railroads.

On the other end of the spectrum would stand Charles Hillman Brough, Governor from 1917 to 1921. Born at Clinton, Mississippi on July 9, 1876, Brough was reared by an aunt and uncle, Dr. and Mrs. Walter Brough, after the death of his mother when he was nine. He graduated with honors from Mississippi College at age seventeen. Five years later, he completed a Ph.D. at John Hopkins, where he studied under Woodrow Wilson. After serving two years as professor of history and economics at Mississippi College, he entered law school, receiving an LL.B in 1902. He taught one year at Hillman College, then was elected to the chair of economics and sociology at the University of Arkansas. June 17, 1908 he married Anne Wade Roark, a native of Franklin, Kentucky.

Brough guided the state through four difficult years, helping to put it on a sound fiscal footing. As a Baptist, he took an active role in church activities. He served as a Baptist deacon both in Fayetteville, while a professor at the University, and in Little Rock, while governor. At Fayetteville he also taught a Sunday school class of 125. He was elected Vice-President of the Southern Baptist Convention in 1918. He served one year (1928-29) as president of Central College, Conway, but resigned when his support of Al Smith, a Roman Catholic, stirred controversy. In March, 1934 President Franklin D. Roosevelt appointed him Chairman of the District of Columbia-Virginia Boundary Commission to arbitrate a long-standing boundary dispute between the District and the state of Virginia. He died in Washington, D.C. on December 26, 1935.

Mrs. Brough, educated at Hollins Institute in Virginia and at the University of Arkansas, also took an active part in Baptist affairs. A member of the Second Baptist Church of Little Rock, she served on the Executive Board of the Woman's Missionary Union of Arkansas and as liaison officer between the Baptist Hospital and the WMU.[77]

Baptists expected and evidently got a sympathetic ear from Brough during his tenure as Governor. In 1917 the State Convention sent him a petition asking that "he use all the power at his command to prevent, during his term of office, a repetition of the debauchings thrust upon the people of our fair state under the guise of the 'Hot Springs Races of 1917'."[78] During Brough's first term, the Arkansas legislature passed a state prohibition law, for which Baptists had worked feverishly for two decades. In 1919 they put added "teeth" into prohibition with the "bone dry law."

Prohibition

No issue inspired Arkansas Baptists more than prohibition. Already by 1900 they were catching the scent of their quarry and moving in for the kill. Church convenants regularly incorporated an oath "to abstain from the sale and use of intoxicating liquors as a beverage," and churches took quick action to exclude offenders. Associations, such as the ancient White River Association, kept the pressure on member churches to "carefully discipline their members who are addicted to drinking and who deal in any way with intoxicating liquor. . .."[79] In the heat of the prohibition campaign, moreover, White River urged Baptist voters to refrain from voting for "all individuals for political preference who drink or deal in intoxicants in any way."[80] Further, they took the highly unusual step of denouncing a local newspaper, the **Cotter Courier,** because of its temperance stand and recommended that Baptists of the White River Association "stop reading it until such time as it shall take a firm stand against the saloon curse, and stand for the homes of our country."[81]

The State Convention too laid aside virtually all of the customary Baptist reservations about the use of political means to obtain a goal. Baptists wanted prohibition, and they would do everything they could to get it.

One tactic was to link up with organizations such as the Anti-Saloon League and Woman's Christian Temperance Union which also sought prohibition. As we have seen, Arkansas Baptists hesitated to support only those groups which would be willing to stop short of national prohibition. In 1910 and 1911 they experienced some "discord" and "friction" either over which groups to support or over the propriety of political action. But they did not falter long. By 1914 they presented a solid front as their goal hove into sight.

As the drive gained momentum, Arkansas Baptists increasingly resorted to political action. Early on, they sandpapered the conscience of a voting public. "The guilt of the saloon is at the door of the Christian voter," the Committee on Temperance declared to the State Convention in 1902, "and God, in that great and notable day, will by no means spare the guilty."[82] In 1911 the Convention employed L.L. Abbott as an "evangelist of temperance" who worked tirelessly to get signatures for a "Three-Mile Petition" for state prohibition. Arkansas Baptists also organized their efforts in behalf of their cause. In 1907 the Convention appointed a committee of five "to memorialize the next Legislature to give us state-wide prohibition."[83] A year later, the Committee on Temperance called for more **"organic, concerted** and **emphasized action"** by Baptists.[84] As we noted above, this policy may have produced some friction, curtailing the work of a "Temperance Commission" appointed in 1910. If so, the setback proved temporary. In 1911 the Convention decided to continue the Commission and to form a "State-wide organization of Baptist temperance forces."[85] The next year, they voted to send E.J. A. McKinney, Editor of the **Baptist Advance** and a member of the Temperance Commission, to

Washington "in the interest of the Sheppard-Kenyon Bill, which proposes to prohibit the shipment of liquor into dry territory" and collected $74.80 in cash and pledges for his trip. The **Advance** fervently promoted prohibition.

For the next several years Arkansas Baptists celebrated one victory after another in the state and national legislatures. In 1913 the state Senate passed a strong prohibition bill for which Frank Barrett, Secretary of the Anti-Saloon League, and E.J.A. McKinney, among others, had lobbied. This bill even precluded "Italians and others than the white race" from signing petitions in favor of saloons! Over the veto of President Taft, the national legislature passed the Webb bill, which forbade interstate transportation of liquor. Exulting in such triumphs, the State Convention pledged in 1914 not to rest until all persons in the nation were "under the protection of National Constitutional Prohibition." They proceeded to appoint a committee to suggest measures the legislature should enact.[87]

This concerted effort proved effective. In 1917 the state legislature voted state-wide prohibition. December 18, the National Congress adopted the Eighteenth Amendment, forbidding the manufacture, sale, or transportation of alcoholic liquors, and submitted it to the states for ratification. By January 29, 1919 the requisite number of states had approved the amendment and it became operative in January, 1920. Thereafter, Arkansas Baptists turned their attention to enforcement. As early as 1921, the State Convention warned against a national movement to repeal the Volstead Enforcement Act and complained that too many prohibitionists had ceased to fight. Five years later, they urged election of people who would sustain prohibition. In 1933, however, their appeals notwithstanding, they saw their hard won victory slip away as the Amendment was repealed.

Sabbath Observance

Arkansas Baptists did not focus their energies on other social or political issues with the same intensity they applied to prohibition. They did have other concerns, however, and frequently articulated them in their churches, associations, and the State Convention. They gave passing attention to gambling, dancing, divorce, and several other social evils. They dealt at greater length with tobacco smoking, which some sought to have outlawed with liquor. In 1916, for instance, the State Convention's Committee on Temperance urged enforcement of a law against the sale of cigarettes.[88] Occasionally, as in 1904, they expanded concern for temperance to include "the misuse of opiates, such as morphine, cocaine, and bromidia. . . as a great and growing evil, ..."[89] Neither tobacco nor drug abuse, however, generated a campaign.

An issue to which they did devote an increasing amount of attention was sabbath observance, a practice threatened by the growth of industry and business in the South. Disregard of the sabbath had become an issue earlier in the North, where industrialization and urbanization advanced much more rapidly. There, however, the major problem was the abuse of labor with the twelve-hour, seven-day work week, and exponents of "applied Christianity" worked assiduously to eliminate this inhuman schedule. In the South the sabbath was defended on much more traditional grounds.

What troubled devout Baptists, as the first Committee on Sabbath Observance for the State Convention made clear in 1909, was treatment of Sunday as "a mere holiday to be spent in amusement."[90] As time passed, committees accumulated a long list of activities which "desecrated" the "Holy Day": auto riding, excursions, dances, theaters, "picture shows," football or baseball games, picnics, hunting and fishing, open ice cream parlors and cold drinks stands, and business for profit.[91]

Baptists leaders did not denounce all of these items indiscriminately. In addition to concern about the sabbath, they were vigilant regarding abuses in the nascent motion picture industry. In 1916, for instance, the State Convention urged good rather than evil uses of movies and called for a conference of leaders of all denominations in Arkansas to discuss this and related subjects of social and moral character. They also requested that the matter be brought to the attention of Governor C.H. Brough, requesting the creation of a Board of Censors to pass on all films before exhibition.

For the most part, sabbath proponents waged a losing battle. Not only did they not obtain legal enforcement of the sabbath, they could not persuade their own constituency to observe it. They did win an occasional victory. In 1925, for instance, Governor Terral, a Baptist, vetoed a Sunday baseball bill.[92] But such occasions were few. Sabbath observance efforts proved ineffective for several reasons. One was the ambivalence of Baptists themselves. Some favored the custom, but just as many did not. Behind this diversity of opinion lay rapid changes in religious outlook as the state of Arkansas underwent urbanization and industrialization. Arkansas Baptists themselves discerned the importance of the automobile here. In rural areas church attendance increased, for the car allowed people to attend more readily. In urban areas, however, it decreased, for the car encouraged them to do other things. More important still, urbanization was creating a more secular outlook, a spirit of indifference which no amount of threatening or cajoling could alter. By the end of the First World War, which helped to hasten the secularization process, the "Christian sabbath" existed more in law than in reality.

Baptists in World War I

When the United States entered the First World War on the side of England in 1917, Arkansas Baptists responded with predictable patriotic fervor. For many years previously they had been reacting with some alarm to the invasion of their "Anglo-Saxon" territory by "foreigners." The war gave them an opportunity to demonstrate their devotion to country.

Baptist backing of the war effort took tangible, physical form. At the urging of the State Convention pastors and churches promoted the sale of "War Savings Certificates" or "Liberty Bonds."[93] In 1917 the Convention, after hearing the pleas of Lieutenant Pat Murphy, Chaplain of the National Army, for equipment, collected $1,125, a typewriter, 500 song books, and one Bible.[94] Along with others, Baptists tightened their belts to conserve food, money, and energy in support of the war effort.

Baptists also pounced upon evangelistic opportunities opened to them by the War. Unfortunately they found themselves frustrated by government restrictions. In 1918 B.V. Ferguson, Pastor of the First Baptist Church of Fort Smith, turned to his church for advice and support when War Department orders slammed the door on certain evangelistic opportunities at Camp Pike. The deacons expressed full sympathy with "his desire to be of the greatest service to his country as a patriot and a minister of the Gospel" and acknowledged the need for religious work among soldiers. But they went on to affirm his decision not to go and "urge and request him to remain with this church" in order to assure a warm "Home Coming" for the troops.[95]

District associations left active efforts to minister to the soldiers stationed in Arkansas to the State Convention or the Home Mission Board of the Southern Baptist Convention. The work of the latter did not have the formal recognition of the army which it assumed later during World War II. Under State Convention sponsorship in 1917 J.O. Johnston made 33 trips to camps, holding conferences, distributing tracts and "Flag Testaments," writing letters, and visiting hospitals. He preached sixteen times to whites, twice to blacks, to a total of 16,700, reporting 1,416 "old time conversions" in one and one-half months. He also helped organize Bible schools and classes.[96] In 1918 the State Executive Board reported 10,000 professions of faith at Camp Pike under ministry of four Baptist preachers and quoted with pride the praise of a Y.M.C.A. Secretary that "Baptists have done more for the soldiers in that camp than all the other denominations put together."[97] The same year, the Sunday School Board also contributed "Khaki Testaments" and Sunday School quarterlies for the camp.[98]

Their wartime experiences made Arkansas Baptists very vigilant about religious liberty, particularly about restrictions on the free exercise of religion in the camps. Prior to the entry of the United States into the war, they got a taste of restriction of this freedom in the "General Funston Incident." In 1916 General Funston, commander of troops along the Texas/Mexico border, instructed J.B. Gambrell, Secretary of the Home Mission Board, that Baptists could hold religious services among the troops only if preachers did not tell them they were lost and did not promote revivals. The Arkansas Baptist State Convention denounced this as blatant interference with religious freedom and urged that the incident be "widely publicized and soundly condemned."[99] They got a second taste of restriction in 1919, when the War Department limited religious activities at military camps. On this occasion the Bartholomew Regular Baptist Association, among others, sent a sharply worded letter to D.F. Keppel, Third Assistant Secretary of War, protesting removal of camp pastors and demanding that the order be revoked "in keeping with the principle of religious freedom which has made our country what it is, and in justice to our denomination which has ever been among the most loyal supporters of our government, ..."[100]

It is not surprising that, after the war ended, the Arkansas Baptist State Convention memorialized the Paris Peace Conference "concerning the freedom of religion throughout the world." Quoting the Bill of Rights, they appealed to the conferees, "as the arbiters of the world's destiny, to guard and conserve these inalienable rights of conscience for all men."[101] In addition, they sent copies of another freedom statement, entitled "A Declaration Concerning Very Weighty Matters," to the President of the United States, the Secretary of War, Mr. Keppel, John R. Mott, and their Arkansas senators and representatives. After emphasizing the need for revival on a worldwide scale the **Declaration** proceeded to sound an alarm about restriction of religious freedom.

> *We look with grave apprehension upon the government, through the War Department, functioning in the field of conscience and religion. For the Secretary of War to admit certain religious organizations to the army camps and exclude others, is prohibiting the free exercise of religion. For the government to seek to control and monopolize religious instruction in the army camps, through its chaplains, is a limitation of the free exercise of religion. In fact the very appointment of chaplains by the government is contrary to the spirit of the constitution, and a violation of the principle of separation of church and state.*

After citing the General Funston incident the document went on to charge intimidation, proscription, and persecution. It took umbrage at Keppel's statement that "the whole desire and trend of the (War) Department, is in the interest of breaking down, rather than in emphasizing, denominational distinctions" as "one of the most objectionable and meddlesome utterances spoken by any public man in American life, in recent years." Then, it added, "To put it bluntly, it is no concern of the state whether the citizen is religious or irreligious. The State's only sphere and obligation with respect to religion is to protect all men in their God given right to worship as they please, or not to worship at all."[102]

Fervency of Arkansas Baptist patriotism should not be construed as a single-minded hawkishness. During the War, State Convention statements expressed concern about the "salvation" of "enemies" as well as allies.[103] Although some persons acknowledged "the marvelous religious benefits" of the war, i.e. in evangelistic opportunities,[104] they also depicted it as "the most horrible nightmare in all history."[105] Moreover, they laid plans for alleviating the distress of people in war-torn nations. In 1918, for instance, the Committee on Woman's Work issued a strong call to meet the religious needs of nations freed by war.[106] In 1919 Arkansas Baptists responded to an appeal from Lee R. Scarborough, President of Southwestern Baptist Theological Seminary, to help Belgian families in need of food, clothing, and shelter.[107] In 1920 the State Convention responded to an appeal from Claude W. Kelley, state manager of the European Relief Council, to aid distressed Europeans and Chinese. Noting the "great suffering" of war-torn

Europe and famine-stricken China, a special committee designated Sunday, December 19 or 26 for a special collection of money and clothing to be sent to the Foreign Mission Board of the Southern Baptist Convention. They added, however, that "while sending our own contributions through our own Baptist agencies, we give all possible encouragement to other well-authenticated agencies that are working at the same worthy cause."[108]

Expanding the Range of Love

During the quarter-century we are considering now, Arkansas Baptists expanded their social vision considerably beyond its earlier range. Up to this era, they had envisioned little beyond the care of orphans and aged ministers. As they grew more affluent during and after World War I, however, they began also to lay plans for a hospital ministry in the state of Arkansas.

The orphan's home, of course, continued, struggling to keep its head above water financially and fluctuating up and down in enrollment. In 1909 sentiment arose in favor of moving it from Monticello to a more central location. Although the issue burned for several years, not being finally resolved until 1923, the Convention decided eventually to leave it where it was. By this time the financial picture brightened as the State Convention paid off the home's indebtedness and launched a campaign to raise $75,000 for two dormitories. In 1924 the Bottoms' family gave a substantial contribution, and the home was renamed in their honor. In 1926 the Convention officially approved the Thanksgiving offering, long a means of financial support for the home.

The population of the home varied widely. Until 1910, when the General Association of Arkansas Baptists decided to establish a home in Texarkana, it stayed under a hundred. In 1911, however, it suddenly shot upwards—to 116 in 1911, to 157 in 1912, to 176 in 1913, to 186 in 1914, and to 192 in 1915. Facing complete financial collapse and starvation, the Board of Trustees immediately sought to place as many children as possible in foster homes. As a result, the enrollment dropped to 98 by December of 1916, to 62 in 1917, and then gradually upward to 88 in 1925. An interesting aside on worsening racial conditions was the decision in 1913 to restrict admission to children born of white parents.[109]

A scandalous area of neglect among Baptists was care of aged ministers and their widows. From time to time churches, associations, or the State Convention had responded to urgent appeals for help with token collections. It was not until 1902, however, that the

State Convention started a fund for relief, asking individuals, groups, and churches to make pledges and pay in five installments. The next year, the Committee in charge of this Fund doled out approximately $4.00 a month to six retired ministers and one widow. The situation improved little until 1918, when the Southern Baptist Convention founded the Relief and Annuity Board with offices in Dallas. Although the financial picture for Arkansas brightened markedly during World War I, assistance remained embarrassingly meager. In 1917 it was only $281.21, in 1918 only $103.50.

The vast improvement of assistance through the Relief and Annuity Board combined with the momentum of the "75-Million Campaign" resulted in a huge jump in contributions to this cause. By 1922 the Arkansas Executive Board was collecting respectable sums to send to Dallas: $5,022.97 in 1922, $3,765.96 in 1923, $3,005.59 in 1924, and $4,117.94 in 1926. Relief and Annuity helped 40 ministers or widows in 1922, 60 in 1923, 55 in 1924, 49 in 1925, and 58 in 1926. Allotments ranged from $5.00 to $20.00 monthly. In a poor state such as Arkansas, as these figures indicate, the denominational connection proved very helpful; in 1924 the Relief and Annuity Board complained that Arkansas had received $7,481.50 more from the Board than it had paid in during the five years since the Board began. Besides Arkansas, only Louisiana received more than it paid into the fund.

The benevolent concern which most strongly captured the attention of Arkansas Baptists during this era was health care. Their entry into this area took flight in 1908 as a joint venture with Baptists in Tennessee and Mississippi in sponsoring Memorial Baptist Hospital in Memphis. Arkansas Baptists, however, never contributed significantly to the Memphis hospital and benefited from it less than their counterparts in the other states. By 1911, for instance, the year before the hospital opened, Arkansas Baptists had given only $6,500 while Baptists in Tennessee had given $65,000 and those in Mississippi $43,000. An estimated ten percent of the hospital's patients came from Arkansas. By 1915 Arkansas Baptists were building up sentiment in favor of a state Baptist hospital. In that year the State Convention unanimously adopted a resolution calling for the appointment of a five-man commission to secure land and donations for such a hospital. The motion argued that this "distinctly religious work" should not be "left entirely to the Catholic Church" or to "fraternal orders."[110] The War delayed these plans for a few years. Meantime, the Convention assumed responsibility for the operation of Davis Hospital in Pine Bluff, donated in 1919 but not opened until February 15, 1920. It also took control of Josephine Hospital in Hope on January 22, 1921, but returned it to Dr. G.E. Cannon on July 29. Work on the State Baptist Hospital in Little Rock began in 1920, but the hospital did not begin operation until 1921 and was not completed until 1924.

As we have seen in an earlier section, the huge program which Arkansas Baptists plunged into put them heavily in debt. In 1925 Baptist State Hospital owed $380,000 in loans and interest. The State Executive Board agreed to pay off an indebtedness on Davis Hospital in the amount of $10,844.70. It also assumed a substantial part of the State Hospital burden. But in 1926 the Executive Committee had to plead that the debts of these two institutions as well as those of the schools and orphanages be removed from its budget and put on their own. The crash which followed a year or two later multiplied the problems many times over.

Such problems notwithstanding, Baptist sensitivities to health problems had been aroused and would not subside. Besides these hospitals, Arkansas Baptists turned their attention to special medical concerns such as tuberculosis, a growing problem in the state. In 1918 the Convention hired W.J. Hinsley, pastor at Booneville, to do religious work in the state TB sanatorium. It lent its enthusiastic support to the Southern Baptist Tuberculosis Sanatorium which opened at El Paso, Texas in February of 1919 and to the Christmas seals campaign that year. In 1922 it memorialized the governor and the legislature in behalf of the establishment of a "negro" tuberculosis sanatorium.[111] In addition, it backed the establishment of a National Baptist Hospital at Hot Springs.

Baptists in Arkansas were conscious of and exploited the evangelistic gains which their hospital ministry could bring. It was evidently this which caused them to cast a wary eye toward Roman Catholic institutions. With a tenth as many constituents as Baptists, the Committee on Hospitals challenged in 1919, Catholics were operating six hospitals and Baptists none. Baptists must act![112] But Arkansas Baptists acted also from more directly charitable aims as well. In 1918 the Committee appointed to examine the feasibility of establishing a state Baptist Hospital urged the project on the grounds that "in our opinion, no greater philanthropy can be thought of for Baptist people to contribute to, than the building, equipping and maintaining a Hospital."[113] Early on, the hospitals received many more outright or partial charity patients than today. In 1925, for instance, Davis Hospital in Pine Bluff reported 67 free and 27 partial-paying cases out of 837; the State Hospital 148 free cases out of 1,503. Such a heavy burden overloaded an already strained financial system and resulted in appeals to churches to take collections to help defray expenses of charity cases sent to the hospitals.

Baptists and Education

In his history of **Arkansas** John Gould Fletcher issued a harsh indictment of Baptists in the Ozarks and Ouachitas. "The all-prevailing Baptist Church, as well as its direct descendant, the Pentecostal," he decided, "has unfortunately tended to keep their minds narrow rather than to open them." Though conceding the importance of the moral impact made by Baptists and Methodists, he went on to add, "These sects encouraged, and still do encourage, continued reading and study of the Bible as interpreted in the fundamentally literal sense recommended by the guardians of the faith. But the philosophy of these teachers of the backwoods creed is none the less, fatal to all intellectual advancement."[114]

Fletcher's judgment is partially true, but it is neither accurate nor fair. Even in the mountains Arkansas Baptists made a vigorous effort to educate their constituency. They did so not merely to inculcate a creed, to which Baptists in the South have had strong resistance, but to prepare them to function effectively within their cultural setting. If they had no more success than they did, the fault lies in the culture and not merely in the Baptist outlook and ethos. Actually it would be much fairer to fault Arkansas Baptists for trying to do too much, given their meager resources, than for trying to do too little.

Focusing the Sights

The major challenge for those interested in education was to fix their sights on a realistic target. During the late nineteenth century, Arkansas Baptists had developed a strong suspicion of public educational institutions which, as we have seen, pushed them in the direction of a Baptist parochial system. Throughout the first quarter of the twentieth century, as a result, they struggled to bring their institutions into line with their limited resources. By the end of this period financial realities had narrowed their aims to more manageable proportions.

The preparation of an educated ministry, of course, continued to be a major concern in Arkansas. As we saw in an earlier section, only a small percentage of Arkansas Baptist ministers were trained at the college or seminary level; many had no education. The surprising thing is that tangible support for ministerial education was so limited. Despite much special pleading by the colleges, committees on ministerial education, and state secretaries, the churches supplied only a trickle of funds for student aid. One wonders whether J.S. Rogers was not engaging in wishful thinking rather than stating a fact when he observed in 1911, "It is a source of gratification to know that the old revulsion of feeling against an educated ministry is rapidly passing away."[115]

As in earlier periods, the main objective for Arkansas Baptist schools was becoming increasingly evangelistic or missionary. To be sure, Baptists could still articulate their aims in broader terms. They could talk about an "educated citizenship"[116] or about Baptists being always "athwart the world's great movements for the enlightenment of the races of the earth."[117] They could also see educational institutions as a bulwark against "worldliness,"[118] offering "religious environment" and "spiritual atmosphere" desired by Baptist parents but lacking in state schools.[119] Or they could envision them as citadels of orthodoxy, standing firm against the onslaughts of heresy or "modernism" during the evolution controversy.

In the main, however, Arkansas Baptist leaders and the schools themselves envisioned their purpose in relation to the missionary aims of the Convention. In 1901 the Trustees of Ouachita articulated the College's chief aim in these terms:

> *The largest function of the Christian College is to make ascendent and controlling the ideas and forces which Christ introduced into the world and which are vitally related to culture and human progress for all time. Christian schools are the medium through which churches secure efficient leadership in the realization of Christian ideals and the evangelization of the world; hence the fundamental idea is Missionary. Our highest ambition at Ouachita College is to prepare young men and young ladies for larger and more efficient work in the Church.*[120]

In 1905 the Board of Ministerial Education, likewise, commended the academies in the Ouachita-Central System as "wisely located" and "becoming great missionary centers."[121] Mountain schools were put directly under control of the State Missions Board.

The statements quoted above, of course, are always somewhat self-serving, directed to the ears of those who pay the bills. Educators realized and sometimes admitted that educational institutions did not bear immediate and direct fruit in the mission enterprise. Colleges were an investment for the future, not a business paying off in the present.[122] Or, as the Trustees of Ouachita put it, they were "a denominational fertilizer."[123] Yet, considered on the whole, the schools which Arkansas Baptists tried to support did mesh with the Convention's missionary aims, often to the extend that their contribution as educational institutions was hampered.

The Ouachita-Central System

From 1901 until 1911 the State Convention consolidated its educational program under a single umbrella, called "The Ouachita-Central System of Colleges and Academies." Under this plan a single board of trustees, composed of fifteen members nominated first by the existing boards of Ouachita and Central and thereafter by the Convention, assumed responsibility for the two colleges and for four academies: Mountain Home, Bentonville, Maynard, and Magazine. In the transaction Mountain Home's status was reduced from college to academy level. The Board was to see that each institution was properly equipped and received an equitable apportionment of funds.[124]

Although hailed by leaders for its coordination of educational effort and peacekeeping in the educational family, the ambitious project soon ran into severe financial difficulties, and no amount of special pleading could rescue it. Bentonville Academy, established in 1901, was plagued with financial problems from the start and closed in 1911. Magazine Academy, also established in 1901, fared better for a few years, but the growth of the public school system caused an erosion in its enrollment and it closed in 1911. The property of both schools was sold to their respective communities for a nominal sum. Maynard Academy, opening in 1900, lasted until 1927, but only because of the mountain schools program. After the Ouachita-Central System collapsed local parties tried to operate it for four years. In 1916 the Home Mission Board incorporated it into its mountain schools program, jointly supporting it with the Arkansas Baptist State Convention. Mountain Home, originally supported by the White River Baptist Association, also became a mountain school in 1916. Offered to the Home Mission Board in 1910, it was declined. From 1912 until 1916 it was reopened under private auspices as a non-sectarian high school and junior college. Agitation

229

in the White River Association led to its return to Baptist affiliation and acceptance as a mountain school by the Home Mission Board and the State Convention.

The failure of the Ouachita-Central System should not be attributed solely to the system itself. It coincided with the increasing effort to coordinate financial support for all Convention programs. The problem was, it attempted to do too much in a day when public education was replacing private and church-sponsored education at the elementary and secondary levels. A number of associational schools also fell at this time as a consequence of the drift of education to public support. Judson Baptist Academy at Fordyce, founded in 1894 at Holly Springs as Judson High School, became a part of the Ouachita-Central System for one year (1907-1908) but folded in 1908 for financial reasons. Friendship High School, opening in 1899 at Star City under sponsorship of the Friendship Baptist Association, ran fairly smoothly until 1908 when its dormitory burned. When the classroom and administration building also burned less than a year later, the school closed temporarily. Efforts to find a new location proved difficult, and the Association transferred its holdings to the Star City Church. The school discontinued permanently in 1911. Union High School at Bodcaw, founded in 1896 by the Union Baptist Association, experienced a steady growth in enrollment until 1907, when A.N. Hollis resigned as principal. After his departure it went steadily downhill, closing also in 1911. Mount Vernon High School—also known as Trenton Baptist High School, Brinkley Baptist High School, and the Collegiate Institute—was established at Trenton in 1900 by the Mount Vernon Baptist Association as a boarding school for girls. The school never had a large enrollment. Although hopes for survival mounted in 1906 when the school completed a new girl's dormitory, they were quickly dashed when fire destroyed the administration and classroom building. Reconstruction of this building, supported also by the Grand Prairie and White River Valley Associations, began in 1909, but, before its completion, a cyclone demolished the unfinished structure. The disheartened Mount Vernon Association gave up on the project and deeded the remaining property to the Brinkley Baptist Church.[125]

By 1912, then, when the Ouachita-Central System closed shop, the day of church-sponsored academies was past. There was one delayed but unsuccessful effort in the early 'twenties. Caledonia Academy, which opened in 1920 under sponsorship of the Liberty Baptist Association and Caledonia Baptist Church, turned quickly to the State Convention for help. Although both pleas failed, the Convention did contribute some funds in 1925. By this time the school was on its last leg. Averaging only forty pupils per session, it closed its doors in 1926.

Narrowing the Scope

By the end of the period under discussion Arkansas Baptist leaders were recognizing fully the need to narrow the scope of their own educational efforts. Financially they could not compete with the public school system. In 1924 the Commission on Education took note of this fact, remarking that Baptists should be active in higher education but not compete with the public school system at lower levels. On the contrary, without accepting any funds to operate their own schools, they should work closely with the public school system to see that it adequately met the needs of all persons.[126]

The impoverished schools struggled to raise their standards and adjust their programs as they competed with public-supported institutions. In 1915 Central College developed classes to help rural churches function more effectively. Later it adapted its curriculum to train women in home economics and education. Ouachita, too, accomodated its programs. In 1918 it contracted with the United States War Department for a Students' Army Training Corps. Both schools obtained membership in the North Central Association of Colleges—Central in 1925, Ouachita in 1927.

The schools which remained in 1912—Ouachita, Central, Mountain Home, and Maynard—were in desperate financial straits. The solution to the difficulties of Mountain Home and Maynard was to put them under Home Mission Board and State Convention joint sponsorship in 1916. Maynard, as we have seen, continued in this relationship until 1927. Mountain Home, the oldest and best established of the academies, continued as an academy until 1923, when it reverted to State Convention control and became a junior college. Under the presidency of H.D. Morton from 1918 until 1929 it prospered, enrolling 180 in 1923. Unfortunately the depression affected it severely. In 1932 it enrolled only 38 students in the high school, ten in the college. Though hopes for its revival persisted until 1947, it ceased to operate in 1933.[127]

Ouachita and Central were both in desperate financial straits in 1912. Ouachita, bearing the main burden of the System, was near bankruptcy. In 1913 a Special Committee on Ouachita College formulated a plan to raise $60,000 immediately to avert foreclosure. This plan included securing $30,000 from citizens of Arkadelphia and the other $30,000 from a canvass of the state in six sections. The campaign worked. The next year, the Convention celebrated "Ouachita's Deliverance," duly noting it in the Convention's **Proceedings**. But this was not the end of the crisis. Year by year, the colleges had to plead for special assistance. By vigorous effort, beginning in 1916, Ouachita secured more than $400,000 in endowment, but $200,000 came from outside sources—$100,000 from the Education Board of the Southern Baptist Convention and the other $100,000 from the General Education Board of New York. Central undertook a more modest endowment campaign of $60,000.

Meantime, the State Convention also sought to assist the schools by supplying more funds and limiting their objectives. In 1922 Central College, like Mountain Home, was reorganized as a junior college. Unfortunately the Convention's hopes for the "75-Million Campaign" did not match its programs. The financial crisis worsened as the depression loomed ahead.

Mountain Schools

Much of Arkansas is mountainous. In the uplands the need for schools at various levels remained for many years after the rest of the state had developed public education. To meet this need Arkansas Baptists plugged into the Home Mission Board's mountain schools program. From this joint effort came a system of mountain schools and a couple of junior colleges.

In addition to Mountain Home College and Maynard Academy the mountain schools included Montview Institute at Blue Eye, Missouri; Mount Ida Academy; New County Academy at Parthenon; and Hagarville Academy. H.D. Morton served as superintendent of the six schools until 1923, when he resigned that post to become president of Mountain Home Junior College. Unfortunately the mountain schools program ran aground in 1928 when it was discovered that Clinton S. Carnes, treasurer of the Home Mission Board, had embezzled $909,461 in principal and interest.

Montview Institute, founded in 1918, was jointly sponsored by the Arkansas Baptist State Convention and the Home Mission Board until 1925. Under severe financial strain the State Mission Board decided to deed the school to the Home Mission Board, since it served both Missouri and Arkansas. When the Home Mission Board ran out of funds in 1928, the school struggled along on its own for two more years. In 1930 the property reverted to the State Convention, which sold it to pay indebtedness.

Mount Ida Academy in Montgomery County, established in

1920, floundered quickly when funds did not come in as expected from the "75-Million Campaign." Although enrolling about 100 students through most of its life, the Academy had difficulty obtaining a permanent location. Classes were conducted in the local school building and teachers' salaries were paid from local taxes. The school closed in 1929.

New County Academy at Parthenon, also established in 1920, prospered its first four years, averaging 125 in enrollment. Thereafter, attendance dropped to about forty-five. With almost no income its last two years it closed in 1930 and the property was sold to the Parthenon School Board.

Hagarville Academy in Johnson County, which opened in 1919, merged with the public school in 1923. After the two systems were separated two years later, the enrollment plumeted from about 160 to 66. The Academy folded in 1927.

Besides these academies, the mountain education program also provided for education at the junior college level. We have examined this already in connection with Mountain Home. There remains one other college to be mentioned in connection with the expansion of Southern Baptist work during the "75-Million Campaign," i.e. Jonesboro College. The foundation for Jonesboro College was laid by Woodland College, established in Jonesboro by interested persons in the Mount Zion Baptist Associaiton in northeast Arkansas. Opening in 1903, Woodland floundered around until 1912 when, with only twenty students enrolling, it was forced to close. Efforts to reopen it proved unsuccessful until 1920, when it was revived in plans for Jonesboro.

The latter held its first session in 1924 under sponsorship of the Home Mission Board and totally independent of the State Convention. Although poorly financed, the college mushroomed from 250 in 1925 to 446 in 1926 to 475 in 1927. The Carnes defalcation of Home Mission Board funds deprived the college of about $15,000 a year in operating expenses. In 1930 the Home Mission Board severed its connection with the school and deeded the property to the "Baptists of northeast Arkansas." Although delegates of sixteen counties tried to keep the school going, it closed permanently in the spring of 1935. Subsequent attempts to reopen it failed.[128]

The Fundamentalist Crisis

As if a financial crisis was not enough, Arkansas Baptist colleges also suffered the ravages of the fundamentalist movement led by J. Frank Norris, pastor of the First Baptist Church of Fort

Worth, Texas. Hints of fundamentalist influence began to appear as early as 1915. In that year an Executive Board statement warned that "if our colleges are heretical and crooked doctrinally, the whole denomination will soon go awry."[129]

By the early twenties the Norris agitation was in full swing. In 1919 he led his church to accept a quota for the "75-Million Campaign," then openly criticized it. A year later, he induced his church to discontinue use of Convention literature. Then in 1921 he attacked Baylor University on the charge of teaching "evolution and infidelity." The general furor led the Southern Baptist Convention to adopt the first Baptist Faith and Message in 1925.

The full blast of the storm hit Arkansas in 1923 and 1924. In 1924 a report from the Ministers' and Laymen's Conference to the State Convention asked the Convention "to take such steps as will forever safeguard against this God-dishonoring error (i.e. evolution), all the schools fostered by the denomination in Arkansas."[130] Responding to this memorial, the Convention adopted a strong "Anti-evolution Resolution" affirming the biblical creation account and repudiating the Darwinian theory whether "materialistic or atheistic or theistic." The resolution required elimination of "all teachers and teachings of evolution, whether materialistic, agnostic or theistic evolution" from schools and colleges backed by the threat of withdrawal of financial support and holding trustees and presidents accountable. It required the signing of the following fundamentalist creed:

> *I believe that the Bible IS God's revelation to man; that it does not only contain God's Word, but that it is really and actually God's revelation of Himself to man. I believe that it is divinely inspired, being written by men who were moved by the Holy Spirit. I accept unreservedly and unqualifiedly the Genesis account of Creation as both accurate and true, and that the language here used is "neither allegorical, nor figurative, nor hypothecal (sic), nor inferential," but gives the plain, simple, direct account of God's Creative Act. I believe that the miracles recorded in the Bible were actually performed as they are recorded. I believe that Jesus Christ was born of the Virgin Mary through the power of the Holy Spirit, and that He is very God; that His death was vicarious, His resurrection bodily, and His return will be personal.*

234

I do not believe in Darwinian Evolution or Mate-rialistic, Atheistic or Theistic or any other theory of Evolution by whatever name called which proposes to teach that there is, or has been, such a thing in Nature as the transmutation of species, or the evolution of life from one species to another, or that man came from the anthropoid ape, or from any lower form of animal life, or that man is derived from a common ancestor with other so-called primates. I believe that Man is the direct creation of God and not the product of some form of evolved life.[131]

The five fundamentals—plenary verbal inspiration, virgin birth, substitutionary atonement, bodily resurrection, and literal second coming— are clearly evident in the first article. Most employees of state agencies signed without murmur. At Ouachita College, however, President C.E. Dicken and six other faculty members refused to sign. All seven professed their orthodoxy, but they refused on the ground that they should not be forced to "sign" to prove it. Dickens' resignation evoked a student petition asking that he reconsider and urging the Convention to deal prayerfully with the problem and persuade him to continue as President.[132] The Convention, however, accepted his resignation. Twelve faculty members signed, but they prefaced their signatures with an explanatory note: "At the request of the Board of Trustees, I have signed the above statement with the understanding that it is to be interpreted to mean that I am in harmony with the masses of our people in regard to the fundamentals of our religious belief."[133]

Campus Ministry in Secular Settings

Arkansas Baptists had long kept a watchful eye on the state university at Fayetteville. Educators capitalized on popular sus-picions of its secular character to promote Baptist institutions. In 1910, for instance, the White River Baptist Association decried the fact that while the public schools required higher scholastic achievements of their teachers, they neglected moral and religious qualifications. As a consequence, many teachers "smoke cigarettes, use intoxicating liquors and openly take the name of God in vain." The Association recommended that, though Baptists "cannot afford at the present time to oppose our free school system," they should see that the County Examiner and School Directors have high moral standards. It went on to urge support for Mountain Home, Ouachita, and Central.[134] By 1900, however, public higher education was already taking the lead throughout the United States, and there was little Baptists could do to claim their whole constituency. They simply did not have the resources to offer education without tuition, as the state schools did. This meant that an increasing number of students of Baptist persuasion chose public institutions over denominational ones. In 1923 the State Convention took note of the fact that the University of Arkansas at Fayetteville enrolled 300 Baptist students, State Normal at Conway 150. A committee recommended definite action "to conserve the students to our denominational life." It proposed that the State Mission Board employ pastors' assistants in these two colleges "or otherwise take steps as may be deemed necessary to properly care for the student groups at the above places."[135] This work proved fairly successful. In 1925 E.N. Strother, the student pastor at the State University, reported an average attendance of 150 in church and, since the work began, 23 conversions and 40 additions.[136]

Considering the vigor of Arkansas Baptists' efforts to keep their colleges going, it is not surprising that they were slow to foster a ministry to state college campuses. They did remain vigilant, however. In 1924, for instance, the State Convention warned against religious instruction in state schools. "Any arrangement whatever that provides by law for the necessity of teaching the Bible in state schools of any grade would be a dangerous isolation of the law of freedom of conscience in religion and ought to be vigorously opposed by all Baptists."[137] In 1926 the Convention passed a resolution urging the state legislature to prohibit the teaching of evolution in tax-supported public schools in Arkansas.[138]

The exact date at which Arkansas Baptist students began to organize for mission action is uncertain. A Baptist Student Missionary Movement got underway in 1915 at Fort Worth, Texas, under the leadership of Professor Charles Ball. According to the **Baptist Advance,** Arkansas students held a "second" conference at the First Baptist Church of Russellville on November 6-8, 1925.[139] The "first" such conference probably met the year before, but we have no precise information on it. The second conference endeavored to help "in intensifying the religious life of our Baptist students not only in our own schools but those who attend state schools also." Mountain Home College evidently organized the first Baptist Student Union in 1926-1927. Its president was Bessie Hicks, now Mrs. George Blackman.

Men and Women in Arkansas Baptist Churches

The women of Arkansas, as we have noted occasionally in preceding discussion, continued to make an immense contribution to the Convention's work. They organized support for missions not only among women but also among children and in time inspired a similar movement among men.

The women's missionary program was rounded out during this period. Its major aims included individual and corporate prayer, Bible study, soul-winning, enlistment, missionary study, organized personal service, and systematic and proportionate giving.[140] Of these diverse objectives the collection of funds stands out. Women raised from a third to a half of the Convention's budget. Table XXV shows a rapid rise in contributions obtained by the W.M.U. during the first quarter of the twentieth century, the biggest jump coming in connection with the "75-Million Campaign."

TABLE XXV
W.M.U. CONTRIBUTIONS, 1901-1926

Year	Amount	Year	Amount
1901	$ 9,329.57	1914	$ 20,654.54
1902	7,117.57	1915	33,134.25
1903	11,801.50	1916	34,301.48
1904	7,803.77	1917	47,256.35
1905	12,241.00	1918	53,182.53
1906	12,690.28	1919	65,279.52
1907	19,412.77	1920	70,884.56
1908	20,131.69	1921	142,138.73
1909	23,252.42	1922	116,413.41
1910	25,823.20	1923	126,475.77
1911	35,102.01	1924	159,171.37
1912	38,831.06	1925	215,754.19
1913	35,749.56	1926	185,286.11

As significant as women's work was, however, they labored hard to obtain recognition. Until 1917 men headed the committees on woman's work of the State Convention and read reports. Judging by special pleading on behalf of women's societies, etc., many pastors still dragged their feet regarding the involvement of women in church life. The "helpmeet" image still prevailed. In 1906 the Committee on Woman's Work explained to the Convention that this term "implies that the work is primarily man's work" and "also that the woman has her specific place in the accomplishment of the life of duty."[141]

This outlook was challenged during and after World War I. As in the Civil War, so also in this one women stepped to the foreground, assuming roles they normally did not fill, as able-bodied men marched off to war. When the war ended, women were not prepared to relinquish gains they had made without murmur. Nationally a woman suffrage movement led to the adoption of the nineteenth amendment to the Constitution, granting women the right to vote.

One may see the effects of this movement in Arkansas Baptist churches. For the first time since Mrs. James P. Eagle stepped aside as Secretary of the Woman's Missionary Union, a woman presented the Woman's Report at the annual Convention in 1917. The next year, Mrs. C.M. Roberts, Chairman of the Committee on Woman's Work, praised the efforts of women, reminding the Convention that "when women are lifted, men and young people are lifted with them. No community is higher than the spirit of its women for women preside over the citadel of civilization—the home."[142] By 1922, riding the wave of enthusiasm for participation of women which accompanied ratification of the nineteenth amendment in 1920, the Arkansas W.M.U., in a memorial read by Pastor T.D. Brown, requested "a fair representation of women on the Boards of the Arkansas Baptist State Convention." The Convention, however, unprepared to go that far, would approve only an amended motion "instructing nominating committees in the future to take notice of this memorial, and to make no distinction in the matter of sexes in nominating boards."[143] In ensuing years women gained slowly in the way of actual involvement.

To a considerable degree, the force of the woman's movement was being siphoned off into the Laymen's Missionary Movement, which was developing concurrently. This Movement, inaugurated in 1907 at the meeting of the Southern Baptist Convention, was just beginning to make an impact in Arkansas during these years. Although Arkansas Baptists established no organization to promote the Movement until 1926, they held ministers' and laymen's conferences in 1916, 1918, 1920, 1922, 1923, 1924, and 1925. The conferences dealt with a variety of topics of current interest, but, as one might expect, they emphasized financial responsibility of laymen more consistently than anything else.

In 1917 a Committee on the Laymen's Movement urged pastors to put forth increased efforts to organize men in their churches, but this did not result in an immediate statewide program. Rather, the financial crisis which loomed so large in 1925 showed the absolute necessity of strong lay support for Convention programs. On recommendation of S.E. Tull, State Stewardship Secretary, the Convention appointed a Commission composed of four laymen and three pastors to study the Convention's financial problems and devise the best means for paying its debts by 1928. The next year, Arkansas Baptist men formed a statewide organization, renamed the Baptist Brotherhood of the South. The men of the state took their stand alongside the women in support of the ambitious mission program of Southern Baptists.

White and Black

Relations between white and black Baptists remained cordial during this period despite the worsening economic situation of blacks and a serious racial disturbance in Phillips County in 1919 which carried over into the next several years. As before, whites offered a limited amount of financial assistance for the religious work of their struggling black counterparts. Although they did little to alleviate the generally distressed condition of blacks, the Phillips County affair forced them to work to improve black-white relations.

Black churches grew steadily during this era. As in earlier periods, we lack accurate statistics regarding church growth, but the number of churches and church membership nearly doubled between 1901 and 1926 (see Table XXVI). After 1917 statistics reported in the **American Baptist Year-Book** are quite incomplete and inconsistent. The disruptions which accompanied and followed the war and post-war years probably account for much of the difficulty. Since black churches were directly involved in the racial strife, many of them stopped reporting; some even closed. Something similar happened in associations. By 1921, the worst over, both churches and associations resumed their normal functions.

The state National Baptist Convention and the Arkansas Baptist State Convention continued as before to exchange greetings and messengers, blacks doing so more consistently than whites. The chief black liaison with the Arkansas Baptist State Convention was through Joseph A. Booker, President of Arkansas Baptist College in Little Rock and, after 1919, Secretary of the National Baptist Home Mission Board. If he could not speak in person, he regularly sent telegrams congratulating or expressing appreciation for the prayers and financial assistance of white Arkansas Baptists. Convention leaders reciprocated by heaping praise on Booker.

TABLE XXVI
BLACK CHURCH GROWTH, 1901-1926

Year	Associations	Churches	Total Mbship.	Baptisms
1901	30	887	62,422	3,084
1902	30	929	63,404	2,897
1903	30	923	63,690	2,780
1904	32	974	67,731	3,009
1905	32	1,009	69,276	3,394
1906	33	1,015	69,768	3,281
1907	33	1,036	70,846	3,475
1908	33	1,048	73,136	3,788
1909	33	1,055	80,233	3,909
1910	33	1,100	82,878	3,834
1911	33	1,101	81,752	3,860
1912	33	1,110	81,992	4,067
1913	33	1,090	83,417	4,018
1914	33	1,173	96,132	3,755
1915	33	1,174	96,070	3,846
1916	33	1,177	96,406	275
1918	.... No Report.......................			
1919	22(?)	1,000	96,406(?)	4,794
1920	.... No Report.......................			
1921	34	1,487	120,000	....
1922	34	.... No Report		4,437
1923	.... No Report			
1924	34	.... No Report		
1925	34	.... No Report		
1926	34	....	125,000	....

In 1911, on invitation of the Arkansas Baptist State Convention to hold a joint session, the National Baptist Convention sent a delegation to meet at Helena with the white Convention. E.C. Morris, President of the NBC, delivered an address which modern ears will have difficulty interpreting. Knowing the desperate situation of blacks at the time, one suspects that he was engaging in a bit of racial gamesmanship and "playing to the galleries," if not being insincere.

He expressed both astonishment and appreciation for the invitation extended the year before, regretting that, due to the National Convention meeting the next week, a larger delegation could not come. He lauded the "encouragement," "inspiration," and "substantial aid to our educational work" given by white Baptists in the preceding forty years. After noting their mutual friendship, he proceeded to lament that misunderstanding had arisen from the races "talking about" rather than "talking to" one another. He cited particularly the assumption that blacks sought social equality. Rather, he insisted, "intelligent negroes nowhere in the country are seeking, or even desire, the social intermingling of the races, but, to the contrary, are striving hard to maintain that peculiar racial identity bestowed by an All-Wise Creator." They fully recognized that they were "the weaker of the races" and thus "dependent upon the stronger race, . . . " White had helped blacks a lot. However, they should not forget that some blacks, such as Booker T. Washington, had achieved notable things. Nevertheless, blacks loved the South and the southern white person. Southern blacks and whites had a "peculiar friendship . . . that does not exist between the white man and the men of any other nationality." Blacks especially owe a debt, which they are beginning to repay, to the Christian white in the South. They are helping to conserve "the fires of religious enthusiasm" being dampened elsewhere. For "as long as the negro cook and negro nurse is employed in the homes of the Southern white people and they continue to hum and sing in the ears of your children the quaint spiritual songs, so long will the fires of the gospel be ablaze in the white ministers of the South, and they will convey it to their white brethren in the North and East." Blacks will keep a warm place in their hearts for whites and "look for your aid in our struggles to build up our race and denomination."

Whites were highly complimented by Morris's speech, sufficiently so to preserve it in the Convention **Proceedings.** Examined closely, however, it interlaces with the flattery a message which blacks desperately wanted whites to hear. Despite their second-class status, they too could achieve something, and, although they had limited material means and needed white help, they were contributing something whites could not buy. Whites needed blacks as much as blacks needed whites!

The tangible help which white Baptists gave blacks consisted chiefly of support for education and evangelism or missions. Most associations seem to have done little. Their minutes reflect scanty acquaintance with help being given by other organizations. Occasionally, an association, such as the Hope Missionary Baptist Association, expressed sympathy for the Home Mission Board's work "among the negroes and Indians, and among the foreigners"[144] or acknowledged that "we (the Baptists of Arkansas and of the SBC) are also co-operating with the Negro Convention in the work of their own people."[145]

241

The State Convention relied more and more heavily on the Home Mission Board, which increased its efforts in Arkansas after the election of Arthur James Barton as Field Secretary and Superintendent specially charged with developing a ministry to blacks.[146] A Committee on Negro Work of the SBC in 1905 decided that the socio-economic problem of blacks was not its business. Instead, it would develop a program that was chiefly personal and directed to individuals. Secular education would be left to others. The Convention would aid in the education of the better qualified black ministers. The Home Mission Board was charged with responsibility for details of the work and leadership for it.[147]

Until about 1910, assistance to blacks fluctuated up and down. In 1901 Baptists recommended continued support of Benjamin Cox's teaching at Arkansas Baptist College and suggested financial backing for it from the State Mission fund or a special fund. The next year, as often before, the State Convention collected $85.30 for the College. In ensuing years, however, assistance lagged. In both 1904 and 1905 the Committee on Colored Work reported no "definite work done by our State Convention" and in lieu of that urged white ministers to "preach and lecture for the colored people whenever possible."[148] Meantime, racial tensions mounted, exacerbated by activities of the Ku Klux Klan and other white supremacist organizations. Whites were uncertain about the course they should pursue but finally decided to assure black Baptist leaders such as Morris and Booker of their support, sympathy, and assistance and to "bend every nerve and spare no means to make the negro a better citizen, and a more efficient Christian worker." The chosen means was preaching.[149]

From 1909 on, Home Mission Board effort became increasingly visible in Arkansas. As it did, Arkansas Baptists began to grasp a special sense of mission. "Upon Southern Baptists," a Committee on Colored Work reminded the State Convention in 1910, "God has laid the responsibility for the evangelization and training of the negroes in our midst more than any other people. In the providence of God they have been laid at our doors, and in his simple faith the negro is naturally a Baptist. The call to Baptists to this work, then, is the call of Providence on the one hand, and the deep need and ready response of the negroes on the other."[150] Momentarily the mission to blacks caught fire. This Committee encouraged further effort to distribute books and literature in black schools, recommended the sending of five delegates to the black convention, commended the cooperative relationship of the Home Mission Boards of the SBC and NBC, and, as we saw above, proposed a joint meeting of the two Conventions. A year later, the Convention not only entertained a delegation of blacks but reported its joy over a meeting of black and white pastors in Little Rock.

The next several years, with Home Mission Board encouragement, the idea of a providential mission to blacks continued to excite Baptists in the State Convention. They repeatedly hymned the praises of the efforts of the Home Mission Board, which in 1916 was cooperating with the Home Mission Board of the National Baptist Convention in supporting thirty missionaries throughout the South.[151] In 1918 the Arkansas Baptist State Convention began to help support W.M. Brewster, a black missionary. In 1919 and 1920 it contributed $500 toward his salary and $400 toward the salary of the NBC Missionary Secretary, J.A. Booker. The same year the Southern Baptist Convention gave $200,000 to the black seminary in Nashville.[152] From 1921 through 1923 the Arkansas Baptist Convention supplemented the salaries of the NBC Missionary Secretary and of a professor of religion at Arkansas Baptist College.

The strife in Phillips County in 1919, however, placed a strain on the already confused black-white relations. The problem evidently originated in trouble blacks had in getting settlements for their labor on cotton plantations owned by whites. They met in a black church to discuss ways to obtain proper settlements. On October 1, a deputy sheriff, accompanied by another white, stopped near the church because of alleged car troubles. Accounts differ as to whether whites or blacks opened fire first, but the deputy was wounded and his companion killed. The next day, when other officers attempted to arrest those who fired on the two whites, they were fired upon and one killed. Panic broke out in the predominantly black county and violence continued for several days, resulting in the deaths of five whites and at least twenty-five blacks. Governor Brough sent United States troops to Helena to restore order and appointed a committee of seven whites to investigate the disturbance. Their report, claiming a pre-meditated plan of insurrection by blacks against whites, made the situation worse. Eleven blacks were sentenced in Phillips County to the electric chair and several others to the pententiary. The National Association for the Advancement of Colored People obtained first-class legal aid for the accused. The cases dragged on for three years. Two days before the date set for the executions, June 8, 1921, the Chancery Court of Arkansas issued an injunction against them. The State Supreme Court ruled that the Chancery Court had no jurisdiction. Next, a Federal Court refused to issue a writ of habeas corpus against the penitentiary warden. On appeal to the United States Supreme Court, Justice Oliver Wendell Holmes reversed this decision. When two terms of the court passed without a trial, Justice Carroll D. Wood, speaking for the Arkansas Supreme Court, ordered the sheriff of Lee County to release the prisoners.[153]

White Baptists reacted with cautious sympathy. Meeting November 12-14, a month and a half after the original storm broke, the State Convention did not comdemn the blacks. Noting the "temporary outbreaks which have been so distressing" they concluded that Arkansas Baptists, "as the stronger race, and having many advantages" needed "to be very patient and considerate toward the negro" who had "insidious enemies whom we must help to overcome."[154] In 1920, trouble still brewing, the Committee on Work among Negroes suggested that white Baptists "frown down upon all mob spirit," urged the Executive Board and all local pastors to work for "better understanding and relation between the races," and recommended continuation of assistance for blacks through the Board and of cooperation with the Southern Baptist Convention in its "splendid attempt to meet the needs of our brother in black."[155] As we have seen, support continued strong for the next several years.

The Turning Point

The painful split of 1901 turned out to be a turning point in Arkansas Baptist history. It exacted its price in ruptured personal relationships, rending of churches and associations, institutional confusion, and the formation of a new Baptist denomination. Nevertheless, it was not entirely a loss insofar as the Arkansas Baptist State Convention was concerned. Amputation of the severest and most disruptive critics of the Convention's methods cleared the way for harmonization of outlook and consolidation of effort never previously experienced by Arkansas Baptists. It is evident that the coordination proceeded at a too rapid pace and had to be slowed, but, from the point of view of achieving the Convention's objectives, it moved in the right direction. Before this period ended the corporate model was more or less complete.

Meanwhile, Arkansas Baptists were becoming increasingly conscious of their vast potential if they coordinated their effort. Indeed, their dreams outstripped the realities of their situation. Often they overreached themselves in missions, education, and benevolence—all three of the areas in which they visualized their responsibility. In their impoverished state funding was always a problem. Early in this period, they lacked not only a plan for financing their programs but also an awareness of its importance. The consolidation of effort under the Executive Board in 1913 signaled an awakening to this reality. Thereafter, the corporation rapidly came of age. Arkansas Baptists' first "Five Year Plan" glided over into the "75-Million Campaign" of the Southern Baptist Convention and, aided by an economic boom after World War I, carried their hopes higher and higher. Unfortunately, like other Southern Baptists, they tried to do too much too soon. Their haste left them in a precarious position on the eve of the terrible depression of the late 'twenties and early 'thirties.

Yet, although Arkansas Baptists teetered on a precipice, they came to the end of the first quarter of the new century with bright prospects. They were already beginning to feel some of the waves of economic insecurity, but they still had reason for optimism. They had gained experience and self-confidence in framing programs, starting institutions, and funding. Though they would soon enter a new period of travail, therefore, they would find strength and courage to carry on.

NOTES

[1] Proceedings, ABSC, 1901, p. 18
[2] Ibid., p. 26.
[3] Ibid., pp. 26-27.
[4] Ibid., p. 27.
[5] Ibid., pp. 27-28.
[6] Ibid., p. 28.
[7] Ibid., p. 51.
[8] Ibid., p. 58.
[9] Ibid.
[10] Proceedings, ABSC, 1902, p. 6.
[11] Minutes, Caroline Association, 1902, pp. 15-16.
[12] Proceedings, ABSC, 1902, p. 19. The Committee included A.H. Autry, W.A. Freeman, W.H. Sledge, F.E. Briggs, T.W. O'Kelley, W.S. Roney, H.T. Bradford, M.T. Webb, Dr. E.C. Ellis, and H. Beauchamp.
[13] Proceedings, ABSC, 1903, p. 16.
[14] Proceedings, ABSC, 1903, pp. 26-27.
[15] Baptist Argus, Louisville, Kentucky, November 23, 1901,

p. 6.
[16]Minutes, Benton County Baptist Association, 1904, p. 3.
[17]Ibid., pp. 5-7.
[18]Minutes, Benton County Baptist Association (Gospel Mission Plan), 1904, unpaged.
[19]Minutes, Caddo River Baptist Association, 1903, p. 4.
[20]Minutes, White River Baptist Association, 1901, pp. 4-5.
[21]Minutes, White River Baptist Association, 1902, p. 4.
[22]Minutes, White River Baptist Association, 1906, p. 6.
[23]Minutes, White River Baptist Association, 1910, p. 7.
[24]Minutes, White River Baptist Association, 1916, p. 9.
[25]Minutes, White River Baptist Association, 1920, p. 5.
[26]Minutes, Current River Baptist Association, 1907, p. 10.
[27]Minutes, Greenbrier Baptist Association, 1902, unpaged.
[28]Minutes, Greenbrier Baptist Association, 1909, p. 8.
[29]Minutes, Greenbrier Baptist Association, 1910, p. 4.
[30]Minutes, ABSC, 1904, p. 23.
[31]Minutes, ABSC, 1905, p. 24.
[32]Minutes, ABSC, 1906, p. 28.
[33]Constitution, Art. V, Sec. 2.
[34]Proceedings, ABSC, 1914, p. 21.
[35]Ibid., pp. 21-22.
[36]Arkansas Baptist, November 27, 1920, pp. 1ff.
[37]Baptist Advance, November 1908, p. 8.
[38]Constitution, Art. V.
[39]Constitution, Art. V, Sec. 4; Proceedings, ABSC, 1913.
[40]Proceedings, ABSC, 1916, p. 45.
[41]Proceedings, ABSC, 1919, pp. 66-67.
[42]Proceedings, ABSC, 1919, p. 63.
[43]Proceedings, ABSC, 1920, p. 78.
[44]Ibid., pp. 78-79.
[45]Proceedings, ABSC, 1922, p. 74.
[46]Proceedings, ABSC, 1923, p. 51.
[47]Proceedings, ABSC, 1924, pp. 68-77.
[48]Proceedings, ABSC, 1923, p. 71.
[49]Proceedings, ABSC, 1925, p. 25.
[50]Baptist Advance, January 25, 1902, p. 8.
[51]W.L. Compere, "Turn on the Light," Baptist Advance, February 15, 1902, p. 2.
[52]Proceedings, ABSC, 1903, p. 33.
[53]Baptist Advance, September 1, 1904, p. 8.
[54]Baptist Advance, August 22, 1907, p. 4; January 2, 1908, p. 6.
[55]Proceedings, ABSC, 1913, p. 49.

[56] Proceedings, ABSC, 1920, p. 84.

[57] Proceedings, ABSC, 1921, pp. 15-16.

[58] Proceedings, ABSC, 1911, p. 43.

[59] Proceedings, ABSC, 1912, p. 47.

[60] Proceedings, ABSC, 1925, p. 78.

[61] Baptist Advance, January 25, 1902, p. 6.

[62] The Old Timers Did It This Way (Melbourne, Ark.: The Author, 1976), p. 77.

[63] Minutes, Caddo River Baptist Association, 1905, pp. 7-8.

[64] W.L.A. Stranburg, "Church Life," Baptist Advance, March 1, 1902, p. 3.

[65] Country Church in the South (Atlanta: Home Mission Board, SBC, 1916), pp. 171-2.

[66] Data for both sketches taken from Tedford, op. cit., pp. 40-42.

[67] Taylor, op. cit., p. 80.

[68] Data for both J.S. and Pen Lile Compere adapted from Leroy Carson Tedford, A History of the Corning Baptist Church (Poplar Bluff, Mo.: The Author, 1947), pp. 43-46.

[69] Data compiled from First Baptist Church, Fort Smith, Arkansas, compiled by Roy Gean, et al., and Pat Murphy, "Ferguson, Barbour Vaughn," Encyclopedia of Southern Baptists, I, 438.

[70] Proceedings, ABSC, 1903, p. 54.

[71] Proceedings, ABSC, 1907, p. 54.

[72] Proceedings, ABSC, 1915, p. 27.

[73] Proceedings, ABSC, 1909, p. 40.

[74] Proceedings, ABSC, 1915, p. 32.

[75] Proceedings, ABSC, 1914, p. 62.

[76] John Gould Fletcher, Arkansas (Chapel Hill, N.C.: University of North Carolina Press, 1947), pp. 306f.

[77] Mrs. C.H. Brough, "Brough, Charles Hillman," Encyclopedia of Southern Baptists, I: 199; J.S. Rogers, A History of Arkansas Baptists, pp. 226f.

[78] Proceedings, ABSC, 1917, p.111.

[79] Minutes, White River Baptist Association, 1908, p. 8.

[80] Ibid.

[81] Minutes, White River Baptist Association, 1906, p. 6.

[82] Proceedings, ABSC, 1902, p. 45.

[83] Proceedings, ABSC, 1907, p. 54.

[84] Proceedings, ABSC, 1908, p. 18.

[85] Proceedings, ABSC, 1911, p. 22.

[86] Proceedings, ABSC, 1913, p. 58.

[86] Proceedings, ABSC, 1913, p. 58.

[87] Proceedings, ABSC, 1914, p. 18.

[88] Proceedings, ABSC, 1916, p. 18.

[89] Proceedings, ABSC, 1904, p. 50.

[90] Proceedings, ABSC, 1909, p. 54.

[91] Proceedings, ABSC, 1917, pp. 27-28; **1918**, pp. 24-25.

[92] Proceedings, ABSC, 1925, p. 95.

[93] Proceedings, ABSC, 1917, p. 35.

[94] Ibid., p. 53.

[95] Minutes, First Baptist Church, Fort Smith, Sept. 29, 1918.

[96] Proceedings, ABSC, 1917, pp. 67-68.

[97] Proceedings, ABSC, 1918, p. 53.

[98] Ibid., p. 54.

[99] Proceedings, ABSC, 1916, pp. 39-40.

[100] Minutes, Bartholomew Regular Baptist Association, **1918**, p. 3.

[101] Proceedings, ABSC, 1918, p. 17.

[102] Proceedings, ABSC, 1918, pp. 20-21.

[103] Proceedings, ABSC, 1917, p. 112.

[104] Proceedings, ABSC, 1918, p. 57.

[105] Proceedings, ABSC, 1917, p. 54.

[106] Proceedings, ABSC, 1918, pp. 77-78.

[107] Proceedings, ABSC, 1919, pp. 26-27.

[108] Proceedings, ABSC, 1920, p. 85.

[109] Minutes, Board of Trustees, pp. 95-97.

[110] Proceedings, ABSC, 1915, p. 23.

[111] Proceedings, ABSC, 1922, pp. 85-88.

[112] Proceedings, ABSC, 1919, pp. 95-96.

[113] Proceedings, ABSC, 1918, p. 27.

[114] John Gould Fletcher, op. cit., p. 321.

[115] Proceedings, ABSC, 1911, p. 33.

[116] Proceedings, ABSC, 1901, p. 38.

[117] Proceedings, ABSC, 1907, p. 27.

[118] Proceedings, ABSC, 1910, pp. 24-25.

[119] Proceedings, ABSC, 1912, p. 18.

[120] Proceedings, ABSC, 1901, p. 41.

[121] Proceedings, ABSC, 1905, p. 31.

[122] Proceedings, ABSC, 1910, pp. 24-25.

[123] Proceedings, ABSC, 1916, p. 65.

[124] Proceedings, ABSC, 1901, pp. 58-59.

[125] Detailed data on these schools can be found in Garland H. Allen, "A History of the Arkansas Baptist Convention, 1900-1950," pp. 145-151.

[126] Proceedings, ABSC, 1924, pp. 42ff.

[127] See Allen, op. cit., pp. 127-130.

[128] For further data on the mountain schools see Allen, op. cit., pp. 132-134, 151-156.

[129] Proceedings, ABSC, 1915, p. 46.

[130] Proceedings, ABSC, 1924, p. 66.

[131] Proceedings, ABSC, 1924, p. 67.

[132] Baptist Advance, November 12, 1925, p. 8.

[133] Proceedings, ABSC, 1925, p. 55.

[134] Minutes, White River Baptist Association, 1910, pp. 10f.

[135] Proceedings, ABSC, 1923, p. 48.

[136] Baptist Advance, November 19, 1925, p. 9.

[137] Proceedings, ABSC, 1924, pp. 41-2.

[138] Proceedings, ABSC, 1926, p. 94.

[139] Baptist Advance, November 5, 1925, p. 14.

[140] Proceedings, ABSC, 1925, p. 56.

[141] Proceedings, ABSC, 1906, p. 48.

[142] Proceedings, ABSC, 1918, p. 79.

[143] Proceedings, ABSC, 1922, p. 83.

[144] Proceedings, Hope Missionary Baptist Association, 1908, p. 8.

[145] Ibid., 1915, p. 10.

[146] HMB Minutes, IV (July 5, 1904), p. 125.

[147] For a fuller discussion of the Home Mission Board's work see John E. Hughes, "A History of the Southern Baptist Convention's Ministry to the Negro: 1845-1904," Ph.D. thesis, Southern Baptist Theological Seminary, 1971, especially pp. 240ff.

[148] Proceedings, ABSC, 1904, p. 41; 1905, p. 45.

[149] Proceedings, ABSC, 1909, p. 44.

[150] Proceedings, ABSC, 1910, p. 54.

[151] Proceedings, ABSC, 1916, pp. 57-59.

[152] Proceedings, ABSC, 1919, pp. 101f.

[153] Paraphrase of David Y. Thomas, ed., Arkansas and Its People (New York: The American Historical Society, Inc., 1930), I: 293-4.

[154] Proceedings, ABSC, 1919, p. 101.

[155] Proceedings, ABSC, 1920, p. 94.

Chapter VI

LEAN YEARS AND FAT YEARS

1927-1950

The great Depression sent Arkansas Baptists reeling. Staggering under a heavy burden of debts even before the blow came as a result of their own ambitious programs, they faced a decade of crushing poverty equaling and perhaps surpassing that during Reconstruction. Had they not been well disciplined by past experience and effectively led, recovery would have taken much longer. Though knocked down, they were not knocked out by the Depression, and by 1938 they were up again, even if on wobbly legs, ready to go another round.

Surprisingly, economic hardships notwithstanding, Arkansas Baptists grew steadily during these years. While the general population growth rate slowed and then reversed itself, their growth rate speeded up. Between 1910 and 1920 population increased from 1,574,449 to 1,752,204, a rate of 11.3%. By 1930 it increased to 1,854,482, a rate of 5.8%; and by 1940 to 1,949,387, a rate of 5.1%. By 1950, however, it dropped to 1,909,511, a decline of 2.0%, starting a trend which would continue until the late 'sixties. Arkansas Baptists, meanwhile, registered the reverse trend. They advanced from 102,914, a decline of 3.4% from the 106,528 of 1910 by virtue of the split of 1901, to 108,860 in 1930, an increase of 5.8%; to 154,635 in 1940, an increase of 42.5%; and to 253,306 in 1950, an increase of 52.2%. This dramatic rise in growth rate parallels that of the Southern Baptist Convention as a whole, which jumped from 2,149,346 in 1920 to 3,850,278 in 1930, to 5,104,327 in 1940, and to 7,079,889 in 1950. Between 1920 and 1950 both the Arkansas Baptist State Convention and the Southern Baptist Convention increased roughly 125%. To be precise, Arkansas Baptists outstripped the SBC just slightly, 128.6% to 124.8%.

Rapid growth brought new opportunities and new problems. In Arkansas these were connected closely with the rural character of the state. Although a drift from the countryside to larger towns occurred during this period, it took place more slowly than in the rest of the nation, leaving Arkansas grossly impoverished. The following census figures reflect the turtle's pace of Arkansas urbanization prior to World War II:

Date	Urban Population		Rural Population	
1900	111,733	8.5%	1,199,831	91.5%
1910	202,681	12.9	1,371,768	87.5
1920	290,497	16.6	1,461,707	83.4
1930	382,878	20.6	1,471,604	79.4
1940	431,910	22.2	1,517,477	77.8
1950	617,153	32.3	1,043,403	68.4

It was not until after the War that the population shifted sufficiently to alleviate overpopulation in rural areas and to allow improvement in income.

Cash farm income plumeted downward during the depression and did not rise significantly until World War II. The plight of the rural poor is evident in rural cash income figures during these years. From about $190 in 1928 and 1929 cash farm income dropped to about $50 in 1933. Reversing in 1934, it climbed slowly upwards to $206 in 1940. Farm tenancy was a continuing severe problem which resulted in the exodus of vast numbers of Arkansans during and after the War. In 1935 tenants outnumbered owners 151,759 to 100,662. By 1940 the ratio had dropped to 115,442 to 100,636.

But figures such as these tell far less about the situation than Brooks Hays' eyewitness depiction of the Ozarkers' plight. In an address to the Christian Rural Fellowship in New York City in December, 1935, he said:

> In recent months I have covered quite a bit of the Ozark country and I tell you today that the people of those mountains are not the happy and carefree folk that are often pictured to you. There are certain compensations, of course, for their lack of a cash income, but they are really in trouble. Their fields have eroded, the soil's fertility is vanishing, their markets have all but disappeared, and the institutions which they once enjoyed, their schools and churches, have suffered terrifically. [1]

In his work with the Farm Resettlement Administration, Hays went on to relate, he found "scores of families who had had cash incomes of less than $75 last year."[2] Some earned daily wages of $.60, few above a dollar. Especially in the lowlands they suffered from pellagra, malaria, tuberculosis, syphilis, and hookworm.

Where whites suffered, blacks suffered doubly. Black tenant farmers outnumbered white three to one. Only one in five blacks owned land. In 1950 when median income in the state rose to $920, whites were getting $1,117, blacks $488. Divided by areas, the figures looked worse. Whereas income of whites was $1,720 in urban and $862 in rural areas, that of blacks was $698 and $429 respectively. In assuming a position as legal adviser in the Arkansas office of NRA in 1934, Mr. Hays found an Arkansas garment factory employing Negro workers at a weekly wage of $5.00 to $7.00.[3] Blacks experienced disadvantages in education, and, until World War II, the poll tax virtually cancelled their voting franchise.

Claiming about forty-five percent of the church-goers in their state, Arkansas Baptists assumed everywhere a more visible place and a heightened responsibility for the shaping of their society. Given the bifurcated nature of their constituency, it is understandable that here too they responded in ambivalent ways. But both depression and war are profound teachers. More than any other comparable span of their history, this one taught Arkansas Baptists something about themselves and their work in Arkansas and in the world.

Arkansas Baptists in Economic Crisis

The external effects of the depression on Arkansas Baptists are easy enough to see in records of their financial contributions between 1927 and 1937, when they again reached solid ground. A glance at either the Liberty Baptist Association or the State Convention reports in Table XXVII tells the same story. The downward slide began in 1927, bottomed out in 1933, and then started upward, first slowly and then more rapidly. With it slid programs and institutions supported by these contributions.

Schools such as Mountain Home, Jonesboro, and the few remaining academies and mountain schools folded. Central College limped along with heavy indebtedness. Even Ouachita, at one time well endowed, plunged heavily into debt and lost its accreditation when it used its endowment income to bail itself out. The Orphans' Home, virtually severed from the Convention, struggled to stay afloat. Only the hospitals—Arkansas State and Davis—thrived. Missions and evangelism came to a virtual standstill with the dismissal of employees for lack of funds. Contributions to southwide causes—home and foreign missions, seminaries, hospitals—all but dried up. In January, 1934 the Woman's Missionary Union report to the State Convention summed up the sentiment of the times when it

252

depicted the situation as the "worst economic and social crisis our generation has known."[4]

TABLE XXVII
CONTRIBUTIONS, 1927-1950

Year	Liberty Association	State Convention
1927	$132,063.65	$1,215,464.82
1928	111,298.59	1,205,423.28
1929	112,445.00	1,241,608.93
1930	103,784.25	1,218,693.82
1931	87,735.08	943,673.19
1932	64,393.17	778,897.49
1933	58,398.50	685,017.10
1934	74,495.80	746,220.18
1935	63,956.22	783,863.23
1936	75,697.70	878,647.57
1937	84,640.86	1,059,688.11
1938	83,177.23	1,032,898.35
1939	91,688.71	1,143,720.85
1940	90,251.65	1,283,944.83
1941	106,348.03	1,461,883.76
1942	156,475.89	1,745,615.43
1943	166,948.81	2,221,477.74
1944	342,149.44	2,491,200.07
1945	297,327.25	3,314,104.00
1946	381,157.91	4,058,590.00
1947	391,859.22	4,601,799.00
1948	454,280.35	5,453,836.00
1949	800,681.17	6,365,568.00
1950	615,655.27	7,100,016.00

Behind the Crisis

Of itself the depression which hit in 1928 was sufficient to account for the financial crisis which struck Baptists throughout the South with such stunning force. Its effects in Arkansas, however, were magnified by the state of transition from the "75-Million Campaign" to the Cooperative Program and by the heavy burden of debt already accumulated on the eve of the depression.

It is evident that Baptists in Arkansas were not ready for the Cooperative Program, despite the experience they had had with both their "Five-Year Plan" (1913-1918) and the "75-Million Campaign." In the first year of the Cooperative Program the

Executive Board reported that only 150 churches had adopted it. To the contrary, hundreds of churches took no collections for missions or other causes, and continuous debate about the Program went on in the **Baptist Advance** and various meetings. In 1926 the Board complained that the number of contributing churches had risen only to 162, that very few associations or churches would adopt a definite quota for the year, and that too many churches considered other causes their preferred obligations and gave the Program only what they had left.

In retrospect, it is easy to see where the problem lay. The Cooperative Program called for pledging and budgeting. Pledges were not to be designated. Receipts were to be distributed on a percentage basis to state and southwide causes. Being predominantly a rural constituency, Arkansas Baptists were ill-prepared even to understand this approach, much less to support it with enthusiasm. As we have seen above, cash farm income in this period was meager and uncertain. Few farmers could be expected, therefore, to pledge a certain amount and contribute on a regular basis. It was not until farm income got some kind of guaranteed base, about 1935, that this situation changed. In rural areas, moreover, budgeting was a strange practice. Farmers bought when the money came in, as they sold hogs, cattle, or crops. With only a hundred dollars or so in cash passing through their hands in a year they had little need for budgeting and long-range planning. In addition to these reservations, the development of the Cooperative Program raised anew Arkansas Baptists' deeply engrained suspicions of organization. As late as 1938, some were construing the Program as "a plan handed down from some super-church organization."[5]

Against such a background as this it is not hard to see why support for the Cooperative Program crystalized slowly in Arkansas and required much special pleading. It was not until Arkansas' economy improved significantly during the Second World War that the Program became an established part of Arkansas denominational life. Meantime, Arkansas Baptists floundered financially, having overspent during the bouyant days of expansion prior to the depression. Coupled with the drop in income which accompanied their transition to the Cooperative Program, the debt became overwhelming.

In 1925 the Secretary of the Executive Board, J.S. Rogers, reported an indebtedness of $850,000. More than half of that amount ($380,000), however, was owed on Baptist State Hospital, which eventually proved capable of paying its own way. By 1928 the debt had risen to $1,206,213.87. Though reduced by means of a stringent, austere budget and frantic fund raising, in January of 1934 it was still $1,126,155. Eventually a cash settlement of $.35 on the dollar was made and financed through a bond issue. By December of 1938 the Convention had settled all debts and paid off all but a few bonds, vowing "NEVER" to commit itself to any more "legal indebtedness."

Dealing with Debt

The Convention scrambled in many directions to find funds to pay off its colossal debt. On recommendation of its Debt-Paying Commission in 1926, it sliced the debts of Ouachita, Central, Mountain Home, Bottoms Orphans' Home, State Baptist Hospital, and Davis Hospital from its budget and put each of these institutions on its own resources to pay off its debts. For the hospitals this proved satisfactory, but the other institutions lacked effective means for generating revenue. Mountain Home, as we have seen, had to close its doors in 1932. Ouachita eventually consumed much of its endowment income to pay its debts. Central College and Bottoms Orphanage barely managed to stay afloat. The **Arkansas Baptist,** as the paper was again named in 1933, was leased. The Executive Board then paid $1,000 a year to use the back page, the Sunday School and Baptist Training Union Department $1,000 for another page. The Sunday School Board of the Southern Baptist Convention funded most of the work the Sunday School and B.Y.P.U. or B.T.U. Department from 1928 until 1937. It also assumed responsibility for the State Convention's half-interest in the Book Store, a losing operation part of the time.

On the basis of a joint recommendation by its Debt-Paying Commission and a Special Committee of fifteen appointed in 1926, the Convention once again consolidated its Executive and Mission Boards, placing all financial matters in the hands of the Executive Board.[6] At the same time it authorized the Board to borrow up to $950,000 by sale of bonds redeemable in twenty years to pay off indebtedness.[7] In 1927 the Board laid out a plan to avert further debt and to retire current indebtedness. (1) Any institution or Board incurring more debt would "forfeit its right to the support of this Convention. . ." (2) The Board would not assume "another dollar of indebtedness for any institution or interest of this Convention, except Orphanage and then only for current support,. . ." though it would pay the current debt of Mountain Home College. (3) It would pay interest and principal due for current debts, "leaving a safe margin in the light of receipts from the churches the previous year." (4) It requested permission to "take whatever course is necessary" to raise funds to pay interest and part of the principal on $250,000 unbonded debt. (5) It recommended a stringent budget for 1928 and urged all churches to do an every-member canvass for local expenses and the Cooperative Program. (6) It urged also solicitation of pledges from every church member and the use of weekly offering envelopes. (7) Finally, it implored churches to contribute 40 percent of their total budget, exclusive of building obligations, to the Cooperative Program.[8]

For a time, as contributions dipped, the Executive Board continued to overspend its receipts, despite its pledge not to. Alarmed at this, in 1930 the Liberty Association memorialized the State Convention "to take such action as may be legally required authorizing the readjustment of our denominational enterprise on a sounder business and economic basis." This included possible sale of property.[9] In reply the Convention appointed a committee of seven to formulate plans which could solve the problem. A year later, however, the economy dipped further and the Plans and Policies Committee had to report that efforts to sell certain properties had failed.[10] By that time the Convention and its agencies were in such desperate straights that they were operating on a monthly basis as they received funds. In 1932 the Executive Board recommended a bare bones budget of $45,000 for 1932-1933, roughly equal to receipts in the preceding year, and inaugurated a debt-paying campaign in conjunction with that of the Southern Baptist Convention. It secured an agent to assist in selling bonds.

After the depression had bottomed out in 1933, a year in which the Convention did not meet, Arkansas Baptists participated in and devised an assortment of fund raising efforts: the "100,000 Club," designed to reduce indebtedness of the Southern Baptist Convention; the "Crucible Campaign," a collection of old gold and silver, half of whose proceeds would be applied to state debts; "God's Acre Plan," a scheme to get farmers, with their small cash flow, to raise crops to be sold and allocate proceeds to the "Every-member Canvass"; the "Prove Me" movement, an effort to secure 10,000 tithers; and the "Belmont Covenant Plan," which encouraged non-tithers to try tithing for thirteen weeks. In the end, however, the solution to the crisis required compromise and improvement of the economy itself.

In its January, 1936 meeting the Convention adopted the

256

recommendation of the Executive Board and Debt-Paying Commission that it mount a special campaign to pay 35% on its bonds, roughly $800,000.[11] The Board set the target at $350,000. It asked the State Baptist Hospital, which had paid off its own indebtedness and begun to assist the Convention with its floating debts, to finance $150,000. The remainder was to come from a fund-raising campaign. In December, 1937 a Committee on the Debt Redemption Campaign reported $186,236.19 in cash and "assurances." A final settlement, contested by only one or two bondholders, was held up until the Hospital received permission to borrow the remainder. The difficulty here originated from the Convention's caution about additional debt. In eagerness to forestall future financial crunches like the one they had just been through in January of 1937 the Convention had revised its Constitution so as to require any proposal for borrowing money—whether by the Convention, its boards, institutions, or agencies—to obtain approval in two successive annual sessions of the Convention, "except when three-fourths of the members of the Convention present and voting shall decide that an emergency exists which makes immediate authorization necessary."[12] When the Convention made it clear that this article did not apply to the hospitals, the State Baptist Hospital obtained a loan from the Trustees of Ouachita College and supplied the money.

From this point on, the Arkansas Baptist State Convention was able to apply its energies to restoring shattered programs and developing new ones. As important as 1937 was for debt-cancellation, however, it was not a good year for other finances. Ben L. Bridges, General Secretary from 1931 on, offered five reasons for this in the Executive Board Report: (1) Financial support for current work was not vigorously promoted because of debt payment. (2) Churches gave heavily to the Redemption Fund. (3) Late in the year, some lost faith in the possibility of paying the Convention's debts. (4) Many churches paid on their own overdue notes. (5) Many leaders "have not recognized missions as a part of the Divine Plan and program."[13]

The future, however, was destined to be much brighter. Although legally free of debt, in 1943 the Convention voted to pay ten percent each year on the other $.65 due "former noteholders, their heirs and assigns."[14] The State Baptist Hospital balked at a $30,000 levy which the Executive Board handed it as its portion. The Board of Trustees of the Hospital, arguing that the transfer of funds would be "legally impossible," took the case to court. The Pulaski County

Chancery Court sided with the Hospital Board, but the State Supreme Court reversed this decision, thus freeing the funds for Convention use.[15] The General Secretary, Ben L. Bridges, and the Convention Bookkeeper, Ruth DeWoody, tracked down those to whom the Convention owed money. Payments began in 1944 and were completed in 1952. A "Baptist Honor Club" raised a substantial amount. So also did the Arkansas Woman's Missionary Union, who supplied the last $2,000.

Retrenchment and Expansion

During the crunching years of depression, Baptist work in Arkansas marked time. "Bowed down by debt," as J.S. Rogers phrased it, churches, associations, and the State Convention were forced to take the route of retrenchment.

The direct connection between financial support for programs and the ability to implement them is clearly evident in church and membership statistics during this era. As seen in Table XXVIII, the number of churches dwindled. Although a few of these were trickling into the General Association, most were casualties of the depression, hitting bottom in 1932 and not recovering fully until the 'forties. The number of associations remained relatively stable, but their programs sagged badly. Deprived of State Convention assistance little by little, the work of many stood still. In 1925, the Convention supplemented salaries of eighteen associational missionaries and 74 pastors. The next year, it decreased supplements to 14 and 51, and in 1927 to 11 and 28 respectively. By 1930 it could offer no supplements and had to restrict its limited funds to direct state causes. This situation did not change until 1935 when improvement in the financial situation allowed the Executive Board to supplement some associational missionaries' salaries again. In 1937 it added to the salaries of ten; by 1940 it was assisting 22 and by 1950 it was helping 40.

The entire state mission enterprise reflects the same pattern. The Convention was forced by lack of funds to cut back in every phase of its work. In June of 1927 it discontinued the ministry of E.N. Strother on the campus of the University of Arkansas. In September it dismissed four general evangelists, two district missionaries, one lay secretary, and one gospel singer in its employ. Subsequently it retreated to a plan of evangelism, similar to that used during Reconstruction, which would not weigh heavily on the

TABLE XXVIII
BAPTIST GROWTH, 1927-1950

Year	Associations	Churches	Membership	Baptisms
1927	45	961	108,961	6,936
1928	44	917	106,804	6,427
1929	45	854	108,137	6,123
1930	45	827	108,860	6,848
1931	44	820	110,962	7,691
1932	42	803	112,815	8,668
1933	42	824	119,876	9,423
1934	41	822	125,827	8,414
1935	42	853	129,903	7,458
1936	40	872	132,870	7,462
1937	40	864	135,854	6,965
1938	40	892	145,386	10,501
1939	40	929	152,773	11,854
1940	40	903	154,959	11,636
1941	40	904	167,431	8,923
1942	40	973	170,017	8,046
1943	40	964	175,724	7,850
1944	40	975	180,088	7,729
1945	41	994	188,948	9,591
1946	42	986	195,860	8,874
1947	42	1,000	200,843	11,460
1948	42	1,002	214,704	13,763
1949	42	1,019	223,947	14,737
1950	42	1,041	239,049	16,600

Convention's meager budget.

In 1928 the Convention set up a Department of General

Evangelism under the Executive Board. This Department seems to have been virtually immobilized, however, in the heart of the depression, for we have no report on its work until January, 1934. At that Convention the Executive Board drew a pitiful picture of state evangelistic work. Although it allocated $5,833 for evangelism in 1933, it raised only $1,500.94. Due to fears of adding to its mountain of debts, it discontinued the employment of missionaries in the summer of 1933 when receipts did not appear to be coming in. Evangelistic efforts were confined "to the most needy fields under our observation" i.e. where there were few Baptists. The net result was 25 revivals, 180 professions of faith, and only $2.00 collected for state missions.[16]

Mission prospects brightened in 1934 and 1935. The General Secretary, B.L. Bridges, employed students as evangelists at a salary of $25.00 per month. By 1934 the Board was again supplementing salaries of associational missionaries and employing two state missionaries. In January of 1936 Bridges exulted that the Convention had accomplished more in "Kingdom building" in 1935 than at any time in the past decade and had engaged in the most extensive evangelism campaign.[17] In December, 1937 he proposed a bold campaign to reach "ALL the churches in ALL the program," a move which helped to overcome the "inferiority complex" induced by the depression.

This three-year plan, among other things, called for: (1) doubling appropriations to supplement salaries of associational missionaries, (2) increasing the number of general missionaries from three to five, "each residing in a designated section of the state to promote the WHOLE program in that respective section," i.e. evangelism, stewardship, missions, and education; (3) increasing the number of baptisms (from 14,000 in 1938 to 20,000 in 1940), tithers (from 25,000 in 1938 to 40,000 in 1940), and churches giving regularly to the Cooperative Program (from 600 in 1938 to 800 in 1940); (4) enlarging the state missions budget from $14,000 in 1938 to $25,000 in 1940; (5) overcoming handicaps to the Convention's work such as pastorless churches, churchless preachers, inadequate contributions, etc.; (6) nurturing a "co-operative spirit" and effecting a "co-ordinated program"; and (7) appointment of a committee "to encourage, to enlist and probably to assist our colored brethren in an enlarged missionary program among their people in this state."[18]

The "Three Year Plan" proved remarkably successful in this recuperative period. There were 9,199 baptisms in 1938. In 1939 the Executive Board hailed the Convention's greatest year in evangelism, reporting 11,592 baptisms, not quite achieving the goal of 14,000 but baptizing the most ever in one year and a ten percent increase over the preceding year. They envisioned themselves "on the brink of an immense future" with "absolutely unlimited" opportunity.[19] In 1940 the Board took inventory of the preceding three years. They had by no means achieved all their goals, but they had reached far in that direction. They had upped the number of district missionaries from three to five, enlarged the number of associational missionary supplements from ten to twenty-two, baptized approximately 37,000 (against a goal of 50,000), increased the state mission budget to $20,100 (against a goal of $25,000), and added 145 churches to the Cooperative Program plan (against a goal of 800).[20]

The success of the three-year plan encouraged formulation of a four-year program which was to close just prior to the centennial of the Southern Baptist Convention in the spring of 1945. This ten-point program opened still wider vistas before a people hungering for the main meal after an appetizer. With depression clouds lifting and war clouds descending it called for attention to (1) the needs of Camp Robinson, (2) the "government colonies and rehabilitation projects together with the seasonal migrant problems," (3) improvement of stewardship and budgeting, (4) continuation of the state-wide evangelistic campaigns each year with at least one revival in each needy place and a goal of 60,000 baptisms in the four-year period, (5) four major mission offerings each year (home, associational, state, and foreign), (6) encouragement and assistance of "our colored brethren in an enlarged mission program" among their own people, (7) leading the state in "aggressive co-operative enlargement and enlistment campaigns" for Sunday school and Training Union, (8) increasing the number of missionaries "as rapidly as funds will justify," (9) continuation of the "District Bible Conference," and (10) enlarging the state mission budget to $40,000 by 1944.[21]

The Second World War disrupted these plans to some extent, but they produced an important by-product in the fact that Arkansas Baptists became increasingly cognizant through their efforts of the importance of planning. Following the War, the Convention pursued its mission work along five lines: (1) through five state (formerly district) missionaries, who served as preachers, conducted revivals,

261

stewardship campaigns, and enlargement campaigns, and assisted weak and pastorless churches or associations; (2) through supplemenal payments to associational missionaries (38 in 1945); (3) through financial assistance to weak churches; (4) through assistance to small churches in erecting church buildings; and (5) through support of a Baptist Student Union program at Fayetteville.[22]

Meanwhile, prodded by the Home Mission Board of the Southern Baptist Convention, Arkansas Baptists awakened to the strategic importance of the fact that Arkansas was predominantly rural. Acting on a recommendation of the State Missions Committee in 1945 the Convention employed Otto Whitington as Superintendent of Rural Missions. The next year, the State Missions Committee pointed squarely to the rural mission as the prime concern of Arkansas Baptists. Despite the fact that the state population was 78% rural, rural people affiliated with the State Convention constituted only a fraction of the population. Associations in which cities were located claimed a much higher percentage of the population than rural associations. The Pulaski County Association enrolled 18% of the people in its area, surrounding rural counties only 4 to 7%. Yet "evangelistic efforts are more fruitful in rural areas." On the basis of these data, the Committee proceeded to recommend the creation of a Department of Rural Missions under direction of the Executive Board. Through this Department the Board would conduct surveys and "give assistance to the territories where evangelistic and mission opportunities are afforded by establishing pioneer missionaries, pastor missionaries, and aiding the churches in any way possible." Further, because of financial weaknesses in rural areas, the Department would emphasize stewardship along with evangelism and lead churches to adopt tithing methods. The Committee also recommended the establishment of a "planning, co-ordinating, and steering committee" charged "to co-ordinate training in our denominational schools with the educational needs of the mission program." The Superintendent and his staff were to "work in closest co-operation with the pastors of the churches and the associational missionaries."[23] C.W. Caldwell, Pastor of the First Baptist Church, Fordyce, was chosen Superintendent of Rural Missions, picking up the reins in February, 1947.

The rural-oriented mission program of the State Convention was undergirded by the Home Mission Board of the Southern Baptist Convention. A lengthy "Agreement between the Arkansas Baptist Executive Board and the Home Mission Board, Southern Baptist

Convention" set out a detailed "plan of work for doing rural missions in Arkansas." We cannot take time to examine the plan in detail, but it included: (1) discovering and publicizing "conditions, needs and accomplishments" of rural churches; (2) cooperating with associational workers in sponsoring simultaneous revivals, making associational surveys, suggesting and adopting definite goals, and, framing a workable financial plan; (3) establishing strong church centers in weak or pioneer fields; (4) helping rural pastors to obtain adequate training, financial support, literature, and appreciation; (5) erecting better church buildings; (6) cultivating better understanding of the denominational program; and (7) cooperating with other agencies to effect these goals. The plan also called for a staff of eight persons—Superintendent of Rural Missions, three general field workers, three pioneer missionaries, and a secretary for the Superintendent—and a budget of $47,500. Other recommendations concerned the larger scope of missions in Arkansas: purchase of property for a Baptist Student Center at Fayetteville, employment of a chaplain for the State Sanatorium at Booneville, and establishment of a statewide Department of City Missions to be financed by the Home Mission Board. In time each of these would receive greater attention, but at this point the rural mission claimed top priority.[24]

The net effect of the massive reprograming effort which the State Convention engaged in after the depression is clearly visible in Table XXVIII. After standing still until 1933 churches and church membership spurted ahead again. The "Three-year Plan" (1937-1940) resulted in a net gain of more than 30,000 members. World War II slowed the progress of the "Four-year Plan" (1940-1945). In that period membership grew by only about 20,000. After the War, however, statistics shot upwards again as Arkansas Baptists targeted the rural areas as their main goal. Between 1945 and 1950 they added more than 50,000 persons to their rolls. A new day of prosperity was opening before them.

Arkansas Baptists and the SBC

We will return to examine other matters relative to the expansion of Baptist work in Arkansas at a later juncture. Presently it will add to our understanding of the growth process during this period to take note of the increasing interconnection and interdependence of the Arkansas Baptist State Convention and the Southern Baptist Convention. To a considerable degree, we must attribute this development to the Cooperative Program, which was designed to coordinate diverse activities and concerns around a single, unifying effort.

Prior to 1925, Arkansas Baptists had at best, an ambivalent relationship to the SBC. They received much more than they gave. On the one hand, they contributed modest sums to foreign and home missions, Southern Seminary, Southwestern Seminary, the Baptist Hospital in New Orleans, the Tuberculosis Sanatorium in El Paso, and occasionally other southwide causes. They promoted SBC programs with only a modicum of enthusiasm. On the other hand, they obtained immense help from the Home Mission Board in their state mission work and, after 1891, from the Sunday School Board in their Sunday school and B.Y.P.U. or Training Union work. All along, appeals were being sounded for more of a **quid pro quo** exchange, but this seems seldom to have been heard.

In the split of 1901 Convention Baptists turned a corner in their relationship with the Southern Baptist Convention. Momentarily they appeared ready to surrender even SBC ties for the sake of peace and harmony within their own state. Enough persons, however, queried the wisdom of such a move that the Convention was led to vote against peace at the price of their connection with the Southern Baptist Convention.

It is perhaps significative of a new phase of the Arkansas Baptist Convention relationship with the SBC that Governor James P. Eagle presided over both for three years at the turn of the century, for it was he, more than any other, who steered the State Convention down the SBC road. He served as President of the Southern Baptist Convention from 1901 to 1904. Nevertheless, we must be candid to observe that Eagle was not the typical Arkansas Baptist, even as he was not the typical Arkansan. He and his wife, Mary, anticipated the day of effectively organized Baptist work by at least a quarter century. Most other Baptists in Arkansas, even those affiliated with the State Convention had a much more restricted grasp and took much less thought for the Southern Baptist Convention and its worldwide programs. They lived in a smaller world.

The First World War began to enlarge the world view of Baptists in Arkansas as in the rest of the South. On its heels came the "75-Million Campaign" and the vision of a new potential in Baptist work. Then came the Cooperative Program, promising to gather together all of the loose ends.

In time the Cooperative Program proved to be the cement which bound the Arkansas Baptist Convention more and more tightly to the Southern Baptist Convention. At the outset, however, that was not true. Many churches, as we have seen, balked at suppport of the Cooperative Program, claiming it was handed down by some "super-church organization" and preferring "causes" to a "Program." Then, the depression shattered them financially. As a result, it was not until 1936 that Convention leaders resumed their initial campaign on behalf of the Cooperative Program. It took years of skilled promotion to convince Arkansas Baptists that cooperation with the Southern Baptist Convention was the best way to effect **their** aims as well.

As often happens in history, an unfortunate experience, the depression, may have supplied the strongest impetus for closer cooperation with the Southern Baptist Convention. More than any other source during the depression, SBC agencies bailed out ABSC agencies. The Sunday School Board, for instance, came to the aid of the State Convention in its Book Store operation and in Sunday school and Training Union work. Between 1931 and 1935 the Board supplied two-thirds of funds on which the State Sunday School and B.Y.P.U. Department operated. It carried a heavy part of the burden between 1929 and 1938. Had it not been for the Carnes embezzlement of funds, the Home Mission Board would have kept the mountain schools program alive. With some justice, then, in January of 1937 Ben L. Bridges argued his case for the Cooperative Program with the statement that "But for the Cooperative Program we doubt if our organizations could have survived the depression."[25]

In Arkansas, however, with its burdensome heritage of Landmarkism and Hardshellism, suspicions of organized effort persisted. Leaders had to plead patiently and painstakingly for undesignated funds to be sent so that they could be applied to the Cooperative Program. Starting with 150 churches giving directly to it in 1925 and only 162 in 1926, the Cooperative Program got derailed by the depression. For several years it did not receive mention in annual meetings. The big push for it, which resumed in 1935, began to produce results by 1941. We lack complete statistics regarding churches participating in the Program, but those we have show a steady upward trend from 1941 on with occasional exceptions: 621 in 1941, 652 in 1942, 668 in 1943, 732 in 1946, 840 in 1947, 800 in 1948, and 893 in 1949 and 1950. As late as 1950, however, about fifteen percent of the churches were not contributing through the Cooperative Program.

Reservations such as these aside, the bonds between Arkansas Baptists and the Southern Baptist Convention were being forged more and more strongly. Attendance at the annual meetings of the SBC; participation in assemblies at Ridgecrest; education of ministers in the SBC's seminaries; involvement of Arkansans on SBC boards, commissions, agencies, and committees; advice and assistance obtained through the Home Mission Board and the Sunday School Board—all were drawing them deeper and deeper into the work of the SBC and beyond the confines of their own state. In Arkansas as elsewhere in the South the Southern Baptist Convention was displaying its gift for pump priming and involving masses of people in its own evangelistic and missionary dreams and hopes. Increasingly in this era Arkansans proved they could offer reciprocal help in fabricating and achieving some of the bold plans of the SBC.

The Churches Inside Out

We turn now to look at Arkansas Baptist churches during the lean and the fat years, 1927-1950. For most of this period, as one would expect, we will not discern a great deal of change in their ethos. First, the depression, then the War prevented or inhibited change. Until after World War II, as we have seen earlier, Baptist churches remained predominantly rural in constituency and outlook.

We lack precise statistics regarding location of churches until 1946, when the Southern Baptist Convention began to publish such information in its **Handbook.** In 1922, you will recall, the Alldredge survey showed 800 open country, 327 village (under 1,000 population), and only 133 urban (over 1,000 population) churches. By 1946 these figures had changed but not as significantly as one might suppose, except for diminishment of the number of open country churches. As Table XXIX discloses, most Baptists still resided in small towns and rural areas.

TABLE XXIX
LOCATION OF CHURCHES, 1946-1950

Year	City (over 2,500)		Town (500-2,500)		Village (under 500)		Open Country		Total
1946	186	18.9%	173	17.5%	188	19.1%	437	44.4%	984
1947	191	19.1	175	17.5	190	19.0	442	44.3	998
1948	124	12.4	163	16.3	227	22.7	488	48.7	1,002
1949	141	13.8	161	15.8	239	23.5	478	46.9	1,019
1950	149	14.3	156	15.0	221	21.2	515	49.5	1,041

The Plight of Rural Churches

In 1928 Brook Hays proposed and got unanimous approval for a Rural Church Commission to survey rural church conditions and recommend Convention policy changes which might help them. The next year, this Commission—composed of Hays as chairman, H.G. Thomasson, L.B. Jackman, P.A. Squyres, and Helen Shaw—called attention to the "great destitution" which existed "in this department of our denominational life." Though expressing confidence that Arkansas Baptists could deal with the problems, they handed down the bleak judgment "that Arkansas Baptists have literally lost the rural sections, . . ." This loss threatened the Convention's leadership supplies, which came largely from the countryside. The Convention could not wait for the economic situation to improve but rather "must destroy the fear that economic conditions can retard us."

In examining records of the State Mission programs for the previous fifteen years the Commission found that, despite sacrificial and heroic leadership, "startling mistakes" had been made, above all, in "the absence of a definite and permanent policy in regard to the rural church." Rural churches were grossly neglected in the apportionment of state mission funds.

The Commission spelled out the problem of the rural churches in terms of missions, education, and organization on a southwide basis. With reference to the **mission problem** they pointed out that it was the Convention's task "not merely to inspire, but to provide sound plans and substantial material assistance in the rebuilding process." Arkansas Baptists needed to "think in terms not of what the rural churches can do for the program, but what the program can do for rural church." With reference to the **educational problem** rural churches required more than evangelism, vital as that is; they needed "a balanced and comprehensive program for each local unit" in evangelism, training, religious instruction, and social service. Above all, the Commission found, vigorous efforts must be made to provide full-time pastors. With reference to the **organizational problem** the Commission noted that "there are far too many rural Baptist churches in Arkansas today, . . ." and urged a "timely movement for voluntary consolidations." In addition, the State Convention and associations needed to unify their efforts. Hopefully, concern for unity might reach out to include a reunion with the General Association. Whatever Arkansas Baptists would do, however, they could not succeed "without the active participation of South-wide Baptist agencies." Seminary students needed to be trained in the problems peculiar to rural churches.

In the interest of a coordinated program the Commission recommended (1) establishment of a Department of Rural Church Life under direction of the Executive Board "for the purpose of directing all rural church work authorized by this Convention"; (2) transference of "all functionaries now engaged strictly in rural work" to this Department and appropriation of such funds "as receipts and relative needs will justify"; (3) consideration of "only those local situations which give assurance of effectual and continued results" in establishing a policy for assisting rural churches; (4) memorializing the SBC in 1930 "to appoint a commission for the purpose of making a comprehensive survey of rural church conditions throughout the South"; and (5) continuation of the Rural Church Commission for one more year.[26]

Leaders of the Flock

Already groaning under the burden of depression, neither the Arkansas Baptist State Convention nor the Southern Baptist Convention acted immediately to carry out the recommendations of the Rural Church Commisssion. Rather, it was 1943 before the Home Mission Board of the Southern Baptist Convention inaugurated a Rural Church Program under the direction of Courts Redford, Assistant Executive Secretary. The next year, it organized a Department of Rural Church Work headed by John D. Freeman. This Department stimulated Arkansas Baptists to direct their energies toward the rural mission.

A study of the **Country Church: Its Problems and Their Solution,** prepared for the Home Mission Board by Freeman, once a missionary in the Ozarks of Arkansas, assigned strategic importance to pastoral leadership, and we can see a vast improvement in this area after World War II, when the number of full-time pastors quickly overtook the number of part-time. Within a five year period, the number of full-time pastors increased by 223 while the number of part-time pastors declined by 169. The biggest drop was in quarter-time churches, reduced to less than a hundred. Half-time churches remained relatively stable.

This radical shift in the number of ministers devoting full-time to their work helps to explain the quantum increase of more than 50,000 in the size of the State Convention during these years. Full-time employment assured better trained ministers capable of organizing a complete program of evangelism, education, leadership training, stewardship, and community involvement: all problem

TABLE XXX
TYPES OF CHURCHES AND AVERAGE PASTOR'S SALARIES

| Year | Full Time | | 3/4 Time | | 1/2 Time | | 1/4 Time | |
	No.	Avg. Sal.	No.	Avg. Sal.	No.	Avg. Sal.	No.	Avg. Sal.
1945	361	$2,144	3	$ 825	315	$336	308	$158
1946	369	2,524	4	1,198	339	608	274	311
1947	422	2,602	6	1,215	327	650	245	390
1948	464	2,115	6	755	384	385	148	121
1949	535	2,115	1	....	356	411	127	126
1950	584	2,119	9	....	349	456	99	135

areas in part-time rural churches.[27] It also allowed them to apply their energies to preparation of sermons, planning and implementing of programs, pastoral and evangelistic visitation, and the many other duties which rest upon a pastor's shoulders.

A key factor in expanding the number of full-time pastors was the association and the associational missionary, both of which began to recoup some of the importance they had let diminish in previous decades. In their efforts to put more churches on a full-time schedule, both the State Convention and the Home Mission Board worked through associations, supplementing salaries of missionaries and pastors and supplying building funds. We can see the net effect of their coordinated effort in Table XXXI, which shows the progress of churches in the Liberty Baptist Association toward full-time. Whereas in 1930 less than one-third of the churches were full-time, in 1949 fully two-thirds were. Often churches of considerable size, such as Junction City, remained part-time much longer than necessary, afraid to trust their wings. Others did not become large enough to support a pastor until they went full-time. In both cases the encouragement of the association, State Convention, and Home Mission Board proved crucial.

We are fortunate to have a case history of the Three Creeks Church in the Liberty Association to illustrate the struggle which churches sometimes experienced in this period. According to Carl

A. Clark, the sandy soil in the Three Creeks area had become increasingly unproductive. During the depression and into the early years of the Second World War, most farmers barely made a living. During the War, they gradually secured other kinds of employment in industries of nearby towns or in the oil fields. A large percentage of the local population moved away, many to the towns where they worked. In one twelve-month period eighteen members of Three Creeks, including three deacons and their families, moved out of the community.

To offset this kind of problem the church had to have effective leadership and apply itself more consistently in the training of new leaders and in the development of programs. In 1943, their church building having burned, they were meeting in a dilapidated one-room school building with no modern facilities or equipment. They met irregularly, sometimes quarter-time but never more than half-time. A neighboring pastor held a revival there, but the church continued to go downhill.

In an effort to hold the congregation together the associational missionary, J.E. Cox, began conducting services one Sunday afternoon a month. These drew an average of fifteen to eighteen. The church had two elderly deacons, one ill. In 1944 the missionary persuaded the church to try half-time services and arranged for a Ouachita student, Paul Shipman, to come without a stated salary. Following the missionary's advice, the young pastor took a religious census and found 295 prospects. By zealous effort he launched a successful enlistment campaign. In 1948 the church, reporting over 170 members, went full-time. The congregation purchased property and erected a new building to replace the one which had burned. Whereas in 1943 they had given $395.70 to all causes, in 1948 they gave $6,166.35. Although they moved with uneven steps, ten years later they averaged 75 to 100 in Sunday School and were building a pastor's home and had a budget of $10,000.[28]

Worship and All That

The basic character of Baptist church life altered little until after the Second World War. The depression, as we have remarked before, caused church life, like everything else, to mark time. The War, though improving the financial situation, created shortages of materials and diverted labor into other channels. The post-War years, therefore, represented a time of release for pent-up energies long held in check.

The deleterious effects of depression and war were especially

TABLE XXXI
LIBERTY ASSOCIATION PROGRESS TOWARD FULL-TIME

Church	1930		1935		1940		1945		*1949	
	Size	M.D.	Size	M.D.	Size	M.D.	Size	M.D.	Size	M.D.
1. Caledonia	118	2/4	130	3	177	2/4	152	F	133	1/3/4
2. Calion	54	F	67	2/4	106	1/3	148	F	99	F
3. Camden	903		741	F	1,388	F	867	F	1,674	F
4. Champagnolle	32		38	2						
5. Cross Roads	132	2/4	154	1/3	166	F	126	F	125	1/3
6. Cullendale	38	2/4	207	1/3	249	F	458	F	795	F
7. Ebenezer	161	1/3	112	1/3	129	1/3	150	F	160	F
8. El Dorado First	1,258	F	1,166	F	1,798	F	1,958	F	2,420	F
9. El Dorado Emmanuel							499	F	840	F
10. El Dorado Parkview							55	F	143	F
11. El Dorado Second	805	F	1,294	F	1,484	F	1,866	F	1,946	F
12. El Dorado W. Side	199	F	214	F	310	F	535	F	654	F
13. Elliott	77	1	80	1/3	86	1/3	135	F	224	F
14. Felsenthal	32	1/3	80	4	56	5	78	1/3	73	2/4
15. Galilee	100	2/4	83	2/4	161	2/4	167	F	236	F
16. Huttig	255	F	223	F	287	F	356	F	358	F
17. Joyce City			106	1/3	185	F	211	F	319	F
18. Junction City	329	1/3	386	1/3	396	1/3	277	F	391	F
19. Knowles Chapel	43	1	64		58	1/3	58	1	72	F
20. Lapile									31	2/4
21. Lawson	91	2/4	89	4	111	4	102	2/4	92	F

22. Liberty	97	2/3	137	1	146	2/4	101	1/3	140	F
23. Lisbon									38	3
24. Lone Oak			57	4	34	1				
25. Louann	313	F	161	2/4	55	2/4	158	F	152	F
26. Midway	202		255		90	3	93	1/3	96	1/3
27. New London			31	4	50	1	55	2/4	60	2/4
28. Norphlet	288	F	598	F	533	F	544	F	643	F
29. Norris Chapel					40	3			28	3
30. Philadelphia	81	2	84	3	79	4	74	1/4	94	F
31. Salem					130	1/3	121	1/3	108	1/3
32. Shuler					42	1/3	65	1/3	1/3	
33. Smackover	218	F	452	F	617	F	689	F	794	F
34. Snow Hill							100	F	101	F
35. Stephens	275	F	311		217	F	267	F	407	F
36. Strong	158	1/3	177	F	311	F	225	F	290	F
37. Three Creeks	336	1/3	396	1/2/3	177	3	184	1/3	158	2/4
38. Union	45	3	83	2	384	F	318	F	337	F
39. Union Chapel	121	2/4	162	1						
40. Urbana					135	F	184	F	218	F
41. Village							207	F	253	F
42. Wesson	58		39	4	50	3	82	F	97	F

M.D.—Sundays of the month on which churches were meeting.
F.—Full-time
*Figures for 1950 not available

evident as regards church edifices. Churches which had built new buildings in the prosperous era just before the depression had immense difficulty paying off their indebtedness. In 1927, the First Baptist Church of Harrison, for instance, borrowed $15,000 to erect a new building which they occupied in December 1929. As the depression hit, they defaulted on one annual payment of $1,000 and thus needed to make two payments at once. Through a drive for subscriptions and gifts they raised the balance of their payment on one high attendance Sunday and deposited it in a local bank on Monday. Sadly the bank closed on Tuesday and wiped out the deposit. Not until 1934 did a "Prove Me" tithing campaign restore the congregation's financial stability. Thereafter they managed to meet their obligations without serious difficulty, erasing their full indebtedness by 1944.[29]

The cloud over church building activities lifted about 1938 as the depression began to recede. In 1939 the Committee on Sunday Schools, Baptist Training Unions, and Baptist Student Unions reported "a year for building new church buildings or repairing and adding to those already in use." That year, 25 churches had expanded their facilities to make room for Sunday Schools and B.T.U.s.[30] The Second World War, as expected, soon disrupted this mini-boom in construction, but it resumed on a major scale in 1946.

Not all aspects of church activity deteriorated during the depression. There is widespread agreement among persons who lived in Arkansas during that era that revivalism thrived. At the associational and state levels, as we noted earlier, revivalism stepped in to fill a gap left by the fuller programs which Arkansas Baptists had been using, thus alleviating a financial pinch. High unemployment doubtless encouraged attendance at revival meetings, for most persons had few other things to occupy their time. In addition, as we have seen in earlier chapters, depressions and wars tend to bring out religious inquiry and concern. The Harrison Church mentioned above, for instance, reported to the Crooked Creek Association 99 baptisms in 1936 and 53 in 1937. Two preachers, Arden P. Blaylock and Purl Stockton, conducted a revival meeting in 1935 which resulted in 66 baptisms and several other decisions.[31] James Fitzgerald, a retired minister now living in Paragould, feels that the dire circumstances of the depression years caused many people to be more God-conscious. All one needed to do to get a crowd was to announce the meeting a few days ahead of time, and the community would turn out to support it.

Baptist worship retained the fundamentals of previous days—preaching, prayer, and singing. The principal change in it, coming during the late 'thirties and early 'forties, had to do with the enlistment, training, and use of music groups. Larger churches led the way in this development.

Meantime, church music got a strong boost from the Southern Baptist Convention and the State Convention. In 1940 the SBC published the **Broadman Hymnal** and pushed its use in the churches. It also encouraged the development of music organizations. In Arkansas church musicians gathered for a "Statewide Church Music Conference and Festival" on September 2, 1941 and formed the "Arkansas Baptist Church Musicians," electing Mrs. B.W. Nininger, music director at First Baptist Church of Little Rock, their president. This group, the first of its kind in the SBC, outlined the following objectives:

(1) To glorify Christ in all church music. (2) To encourage a closer relationship between all musicians in Arkansas. (3) To encourage our colleges to offer courses in church music leadership. (4) To discover and develop leaders among our young people who do not attend college. (5) To reach every church in Arkansas with a training program. (6) To hold music clinics, festivals and training schools whenever advisable. (7) To develop appreciation and zeal for the best in church music. (8) To encourage a better grade of evangelistic singing. (9) To bring about the right kind of community sing-songs in church music. (10) To cooperate with the public school system in teaching better church music. (11) To encourage a close relationship between pastors and music leaders in bringing to pass the above objectives.[32]

For two years Mrs. Nininger served without salary as "Approved State Music Director for Arkansas," conducting institutes of church music, holding hymm-sings, assisting in revival meetings, working at summer assemblies, speaking on radio, providing music for the Baptist hour, and doing many other things to promote better church music in Arkansas churches. In 1942 she traveled nearly 6,000 miles. January 1, 1944 she was designated Church Music Secretary for Arkansas with the notation by the Convention that, since she did not receive adequate salary from the Department, she would "continue to receive honorariums and expenses from the churches served."[33]

After the War interest in church music continued to grow. Ouachita College, which had offered music in its curriculum from the beginning, sponsored a Youth Choir Festival in 1947. The Festival brought guest clinicians to listen to the youth sing and to offer suggestions for improvement. More than 200 hymn-sings were held in 1949.[34]

The accent put on church music tended to add to the quality and orderliness of Baptist worship services. New elements included calls to worship sung by the choir, prayer responses following the pastoral prayer, and doxologies. Worship hymns and anthems balanced gospel songs so popular in an earlier day. In addition, pastors and musicians began to pay attention to the details of worship, particularly as they broadcast or, later, televised services.

Printed bulletins were more widely accepted in the 'thirties and 'forties than in the 'twenties. James Fitzgerald, for instance, recalls that, when he became pastor of the First Baptist Church of Stamps in 1939, members of the congregation were asking why they couldn't have a mimeographed order of service, as Beech Street Church of Texarkana or First Baptist Church of Shreveport, Louisiana. They responded enthusiastically when Fitzgerald printed their first bulletin.

The Second World War influenced Baptist worship in several ways. One was through making people more time-conscious. The day of one or two-hour sermons had passed, as congregations pressed for dismissal by 12:00 noon on Sunday. As the time devoted to music and other items increased, preaching time decreased. The preacher had to read his scripture, preach his sermon, give an invitation, welcome new members, and dismiss the congregation by noon.

Another was through improvement of communications. Larger churches quickly installed public address systems when they became available during and after the War. By the 'sixties even small churches were using them. At the same time some churches extended their worship services by means of radio. The First Baptist Church of Paragould, for example, has broadcast its Sunday morning services over the local station ever since the latter opened in 1947.

A third was through its emphasis on youth. War touches the lives of young people more radically than it does others. Accordingly, the Second World War heightened consciousness of the role of youth in our society and in its institutions. Churches responded to the

275

youth movement with activities such as fellowships, softball teams, and youth camps. Religion became an "in" thing among youth. And as they came, they brought new ideas and ways of doing things, for which the payoff would come in the 'fifties and 'sixties, as youth assumed leadership roles in the churches.

The setting of worship improved steadily once Arkansas Baptists got out of the grips of the depression. Buildings erected during the late 'thirties and 'forties catered to more affluent tastes, reflecting much greater concern for both comfort and artistic appeal. Stained glass windows became more common. Churches of medium size almost always included baptistries.

The rigorous discipline of frontier days continued its disappearing act during the period being discussed. Churches, to be sure, went on admonishing their members about such "worldlinesses" as dancing, gambling, card playing, mixed bathing, sabbath-breaking, movies, and especially drinking. Until 1945, they regularly reported exclusions and restorations to their associations. Occasionally serious discipline problems surfaced even in the associations. In 1933, for instance, the Louann Baptist Church petitioned the Liberty Association to investigate "rumors reflecting on the character" of a former pastor then serving as pastor of the Galilee Church in the same association. Louann requested Galilee to convene a council within thirty days and examine the allegations. The matter was referred to the Executive Committee with power to act, and the moderator appointed a committee to investigate and report to the Executive Board within thirty days.[35]

Steady decline in the number of exclusions reported in associational minutes throughout this period, however, indicates that stern discipline already belonged to the past even before 1945. The War especially reshaped the Baptist outlook and made people of necessity more tolerant. Although a substantial number of dismissals still occurred in the 'thirties, there were few in the early 'forties.

Along similar lines, the mourners' bench, a common sight in earlier days, started to disappear from Baptist churches in the 1930s. According to James Fitzgerald, this was connected with prosperity, education, and sophistication. In addition, more persons entered the churches via some form of Christian nurture rather than the sawdust trail.

Training the Flock

One of the major stabilizing factors in Arkansas Baptist churches during the trying years of depression and war was their training organizations, particularly Sunday Schools and B.Y.P.U.s or, after 1935, Baptist Training Unions. Whereas many other programs lapsed, these did not. Thanks to assistance supplied by the Sunday School Board of the Southern Baptist Convention from 1928 on, the state Sunday School and B.Y.P.U. Department, directed by J.P. Edmunds, continued a vigorous effort to promote these organizations and their programs. By 1937, when Edmunds took a position with the Sunday School Board, the State Convention was again prepared to stand on its own feet.

Edmunds pressed continually to enlarge the number of persons involved in church training programs. At the outset of his appointment he undertook enlargement campaigns as the "finest tonic for any Sunday school."[36] The campaigns involved an eight-day program in which trained workers (1) conducted a census and tabulated its results, (2) taught officers, teachers, and members Sunday school methods and principles for five nights, (3) enlarged the Sunday school organization, and (4) laid out plans for reaching prospective members. The Department also conducted Vacation Bible Schools, the first in Arkansas being held in 1926, and an Intermediate Sword Drill, the Arkansas winner participating in the Memphis Southwide Conference in December, 1929. After several years of strenuous personal efforts, in 1934 Edmunds, recognizing his inability to promote church training in all churches in the state, began to place major emphasis on associational promotion.

Edmund's successor, Edgar Williamson, concentrated on promotion of Training Union. Early in his administration, he inaugurated a volunteer summer field work program to promote Training Union in rural churches, a desperate need in Arkansas. His plan called for thirty college students, trained at the State Assembly, to spend a week in teams of two in six churches organizing new unions. During the first year (1938), the volunteers organized 169 new unions, enrolled 4,452 in night classes, and issued 1,694 study course awards.

Throughout this period the State Assembly served as a kind of rallying point for church training endeavors. Revived in 1928 under direction of the state Sunday School Secretary, it struggled to gain fiscal stability. After 1937 it expanded both programs and facilities in order to reach an even wider audience of Arkansas Baptist leaders. Originally a one-week meeting, in 1947 it expanded to two one-week assemblies; the first structured around Sunday School, W.M.U., and Brotherhood; the other around Training Union, Baptist Student

Union, and Church Music. Records are incomplete, but extant reports on attendance indicate steady interest in the Assembly at Siloam Springs.

1929	353
1934	1,000
1935	1,000
1937	820
1940	1,056
1941	1,264
1942	1,150
1943	903
1948	1,300

The effectiveness of these combined promotional efforts is evident in Table XXXII. Little by little, the active core of Arkansas Baptist churches were being engaged in Sunday School, Training Union, and related programs. Except for the war years, both Sunday School and B.Y.P.U. or Training Union grew steadily.

In a state such as Arkansas, where education lagged, the expansion of the Training Union was of paramount importance, for this program was designed to enlist and train church leaders. At the beginning, as we have seen in earlier chapters, it was aimed at and restricted to young people. In time, however, it became clear that churches needed to prepare their entire constituencies for effective participation and leadership in their activities. Consequently, in 1935, Baptist Young People's Union became Baptist Training Union. The long-range effects of this decision could not be measured until after World War II, but an obvious outcome was enlargement of the program itself. Thus, whereas only about 10.6 percent of the church constituency was involved in B.Y.P.U. in 1927, in 1950 28.25 percent was involved. During the same period, the Sunday school remained relatively stable, enrolling about 75 to 80 percent of the church membership.

In 1944 the department was renamed the "Religious Education Department." It now embraced not only Sunday School and Training Union, but also Student Union and Church Music. Student work, which we will discuss in another context, came under the Sunday School and B.T.U. umbrella in 1937. Church music, as we noted above, had an **ad hoc** relationship to the Convention when the "Arkansas Baptist Church Musicians" organized in 1941. Its promotion became a responsibility of the Religious Education

TABLE XXXII
CHURCH TRAINING PROGRAMS, 1927-1950

Year	Sunday School		Training Union		Vacation B.S.		Church
	No.	Enrolled	No.	Enrolled	No.	Enrolled	Mbship.
1927	765	88,686		11,578			108,961
1928	701	85,875		14,800			106,804
1929	682	81,682	719	14,239	16		108,137
1930	676	84,339		16,200			108,860
1931	706	86,247	783	17,957			110,962
1932	754	87,995		20,474			112,815
1933	728	89,993		21,730			119,876
1934	722	90,985	1,033	22,092			125,827
1935	769	96,566		23,852			129,903
1936	797	99,182		23,393			132,870
1937	831	99,831		23,678			135,854
1938	859	108,089		26,025			145,386
1939	900	118,055		32,440			152,773
1940	893	122,864		41,462			154,959
1941	835	117,126		39,953			167,431
1942	955	118,526		28,788			170,017
1943	956	114,206		26,712			175,724
1944	952	114,296		28,025			180,088
1945		120,245		33,278			188,948
1946		128,308		39,507			195,860
1947	988	135,857		43,296		31,254	200,843
1948	994	149,343		51,015		36,375	214,704
1949	969	161,809		61,462		39,285	223,947
1950		174,840		67,546		43,706	239,049

Department in 1944.

Baptist Piety in a New Day

The new day which was dawning for Arkansas Baptists with the Second World War will not have left as tangible traces on personal piety as on institutions and programs, but its impact was no less real and forceful there. With its demand for technology the War speeded up the pace of change already taking place in American society. It hastened urbanization as the populace shifted to the cities to take employment in wartime industries. It widened American contacts with the rest of the world. It created a demand for education. It laid the groundwork for radically different lifestyles.

Prior to World War II, the piety of Arkansas Baptists remained simple, individualist, highly personal, and Bible-entered. The devout read their scriptures daily, prayed, went to church, and helped their neighbors. There was even a kind of negative slant to their devotion—don't dance, drink, smoke, play cards, gamble, violate the sabbath, curse, go to movies, or live indiscretely.

As we have seen in looking at discipline, however, the War crumbled and confused many of these perceptions. Thousands who went abroad were exposed to other customs, including religious ones. For many, what had been "worldly" now became acceptable. Already during the depression, moreover, more persons began to see the religion had to do not merely with the private and personal sphere but also with the social. They wanted a faith which spoke not merely to individual responsibility but to corporate responsibility as well.

Baptists and Their Peers

Baptist relationships with other Protestants continued to be cordial and often cooperative but were sometimes strained as a result of competitiveness and Landmarkism. Generally speaking, competition remained friendly, even if vigorous. Baptists and other groups enjoyed swapping yarns about one another and even on themselves. Brooks Hays relates a favorite about "Brother Tucker," a middle-aged deacon in the little congregation at Russellville. When a merger of the Baptist and Christian churches was proposed, Brother Tucker replied in no uncertain terms: "I'm a **Baptist,** and nobody's gonna make a Christian out of **me!**"[37]

Landmarkism, of course, continued to keep a strong grip on the minds of most Baptists in Arkansas, the departure of some to the American Baptist (General) Association notwithstanding. Its high churchism muddied relationships with other Christians. In December, 1937 the Convention voted to notify John R. Sampey, President of Southern Seminary and also of the Southern Baptist Convention, that "the teaching of alien immersion and open communion (at the Seminary) is objectionable to the Arkansas Baptist State Convention."[38] Sampey replied that he had not heard of any teaching of open communion at the Seminary, which would be "contrary to the Abstract of Principles signed by each professor in the Seminary at the time of his inauguration." But he refused to acknowledge that a certain position on alien immersion should constitute "a test of church fellowship." Each church in the SBC had a right to form its own conclusions on this question.[39] Landmark ecclesiology, however, won a stunning victory in Arkansas in 1949 and 1950, when the Convention voted to "refuse to seat any messenger from any church that accepts alien immersion; practices open communion; or affiliates with any branch of the Federal Council of Churches; World Council of Churches; or any other organizations similar to, or growing out of such."[40]

Baptist successionism also held on in Arkansas. In 1945, celebrating the centennial of the Southern Baptist Convention, Ben L. Bridges, the General Secretary, explained, "Of course, Baptists and Baptist churches have been in existence since the days of Jesus on earth, but the Southern Baptist Convention Organization was not effected until 1845."[41]

A narrow ecclesiology, however, may have been more theoretical than actual, for Arkansas Baptists maintained a cooperative relationship with most other denominations except Roman Catholics. In many areas they could do so without serious threat. Baptist Ministers belonged to Protestant ministers' associations.[42] The Baptist Hospital in Little Rock, whose patients were only about one-fourth Baptists, worked out a relationship with Methodists to handle Methodist charity patients and be reimbursed from their Golden Cross Funds.[43] In 1928 the Hospital reported 882 Baptist, 444 Methodist, 44 Presbyterian, 37 Roman Catholic, 181 "other religious," and 534 "no religious" preferences among its patients.[44]

In two matters of concern Baptists found themselves closely linked with other Protestants, especially Methodists, the next largest denomination in the state. One of these had to do with a drive to prevent the teaching of evolution in public schools, the other with the presidential election of 1928. In both pragmatism overcame whatever reservations they might have had about ecumenical relations.

We have witnessed in the preceding chapter a buildup of anti-evolution sentiment in Arkansas in the early 'twenties as a result of Fundamentalist influence. In 1926 the Convention unanimously adopted a memorial introduced by J.S. Compere petitioning the state legislature to pass a law prohibiting the teaching of the theory of evolution in tax-supported schools in Arkansas.[45] Other denominations issued similar petitions. In 1927 the lower house of the Arkansas legislature, after a "desperate fight," voted 50 to 47 in favor of an anti-evolution bill which they had at first rejected. The Senate tabled the House bill and later voted 17 to 14 against further consideration of it.[46] Anti-evolutionists, however, did not let the matter rest. Ben M. Bogard, scion of the American Baptist Association, assembled enough signatures on a petition to place the question on the fall ballot in 1928. The referendum called for outlawing the teaching of Darwinism in public schools, prohibition of the use of textbooks containing the theory, and fining offenders up to $500.[47] It passed 108,991 to 63,406, but it was never actively enforced.[48]

Opposition to the candidacy of Al Smith in 1928 was a much more complicated and vexing affair. It illustrates well the mixture of attitudes and concerns which entered into Baptists' relationships with other Christian groups. Initially the concern was conservation of prohibition, for which Baptists and Methodists, among other Protestants, had fought hard. Following up on a Southern Baptist Convention resolution, in 1926 J.S. Compere, Editor of **The Baptist Advance,** issued warnings about the dire consequences of the nomination of a known "wet" like Al Smith, Governor of New York, as the candidate of the democratic party. In 1927 the State Convention went on record as opposing

> *any man as candidate for the presidency of the United States, no matter what may be his party affiliations, who is opposed to a strict enforcement of the eighteenth amendment to the Constitution, and we serve notice on the political leaders of both parties that we will not compromise our consciences by voting for such outstanding foes of prohibition as Gov. Al Smith, Senator Jim Reed, or Gov. Albert C. Ritchie.*[48]

Many associations followed suit the next year.[50] To this point, the fact that Smith was a Roman Catholic seems not to have entered the picture. After his nomination in June, 1928, however, his religious affiliation quickly became an issue. It was evidently Smith's supporters who lighted this fuse by charging that opponents acted on the basis of motives of "intolerance" and "bigotry." Such charges were all that Protestants, deeply suspicious of Roman Catholics, needed to bring out the worst in their invectives. B.V. Ferguson, Pastor of the First Baptist Church of Fort Smith, flicked off the accusations by calling them "the cheapest sort of demagoguery." He went on to point out that

> *The Catholics in the Republican party will, without doubt, vote for Governor Smith on one ground only, that he is a Catholic. They will grant and expect the same privilege to be used by Protestants, which means that Protestants have a perfect right to vote against Al Smith because he is a Catholic, and if the Protestant's faith is as*

282

strong as the faith of the Catholic, he will do so.[51]

August 2, 1928 the **Advance** featured a cartoon of Al Smith leading Arkansas Senator Joe Robinson to kneel at the feet of the pope.

Arkansas Baptists had strong Protestant allies in their anti-Smith stance. Just after the democratic convention, A.J. Barton, Chairman of the Social Service Commission of the SBC from 1910 to 1942 and also of the National Executive Committee, Anti-Saloon League of America from 1924 to 1934, and Methodist Bishop James M. Cannon, Jr., organized a Conference of Anti-Smith Democrats. The **Baptist Advance** featured the platform of this group on its front page on July 26, 1928. It also applauded A.C. Millar, Editor of the **Arkansas Methodist,** when he withdrew as democratic candidate for Lieutenant Governor to protest the candidacy of Al Smith.[52]

Throughout the period being discussed Catholics frequently served as a handy object for invidious comparisons. In 1938 the Committee on Hospitals, like earlier committees, promoted the Baptist Hospital in Little Rock by remonstrating Baptists for their late start. For Baptists to go to Catholic hospitals, the Committee said, was like Israelites going to the Philistines to get axes sharpened.[53] In 1939 the Executive Committee chided Arkansas Baptists about their poor record of aid to blacks with the query: "When will we step into the Negro race and do as much for them as the Catholics are doing?"[54] In their dispute with the Baptist Hospital over funds to pay off remaining indebtedness the Executive Board put down the Board of Trustees of the Hospital with the comment that "'The powers that be' have also seemingly catered to Catholic methods and ideals and demands, . . ."[55] In 1947 J.S. Rogers promoted his forthcoming **History of Arkansas Baptists** at the State Convention with the promise that it would "Help stop any leaks in orthodoxy and tend to steel us against adroit counterfeit doctrines." "Remember," he explained further, "Catholics largely control the press, radio and motion pictures."[56]

Though Catholics were the main "whipping boy," Arkansas Baptist leaders also registered clear opposition to Protestant ecumenism when it went beyond cordiality and cooperation. In 1940 for instance, the Executive Board insisted that Baptist principles needed a new emphasis. Among the major reasons given for this, the chief was: "Our answer to the periodical approach of unionizers should be a fervent campaign of indoctrination."[57] In 1946, moreover, the Radio Commission of the State Convention, formed in

1944, noted with approval the fact that Southern Baptists had joined with southern Presbyterians and southern Methodists in forming the Southern Religious Conference because "radio chains are giving time alloted for Protestants to the Federal Council of Churches."[58] Then, as the Southern Baptist Convention debated whether to join the newly formed World Council of Churches in 1948, the Executive Board forcefully articulated its own conclusion: "Baptist Churches should keep themselves free from entangling alliances and keep themselves out of interdenominational organizations."[59] The next year, as we saw above, the Convention passed a still stronger anti-ecumenical statement.

Such ecumenical reserve, however, did not carry over into relationships with other Baptist groups, perhaps because the latter did not press for formal ties. Arkansas Baptists participated in and reported with pleasure on the Baptist World Alliance. They periodically ventilated their hopes for an eventual reconciliation with the American Baptist Association, and, as we will see shortly, they maintained some ties with black Baptists in their state. To a people whose minds were firmly infused with the finality of their own tradition, however, too close association with non-Baptists would not have seemed wholesome.

Baptists in Arkansas Society

Depressions and wars, those "times that try men's souls," offer opportunities for deepening and widening human perceptions. Both the Great Depression and the Second World War had that effect on Arkansas Baptists, as it did on most American Christians. The experiences of these years sharpened their sensitivities to human suffering and deprivation and extended their world vision. Shattering events forced them out of an often too simplistic and too individualistic moral stance toward a broader social concern. If they were quick to repudiate the phrase "social gospel," they were not so quick to slough off some of the gospel's implications for society in the face of human hurt.

Baptist Social Perceptions in the Great Depression

The long, painful depression expanded the social perceptions of many Arkansas Baptists immensely. To be sure, whatever other matters came in for discussion, temperance or prohibition remained throughout the depression at the top of the list of social concerns. Even when from time to time temperance shared the marquee with other issues, it usually got top billing. As regards the depression, that was the case just before revocation of the Eighteenth Amendment and the Volstead Act in 1933. In 1928 the State Convention's Committee on Temperance became the Committee on Temperance and Social Service and dealt with such concerns as war, lawlessness, the rise of salacious literature, and increased number of divorces. The next year, the name reverted to "Temperance Committee." By 1931 this Committee hammered away at a single concern, preventing the revival of the liquor industry and rallying forces to oppose it. In 1934, the Eighteenth Amendment already repealed, the Convention once more broadened this Committee's title and business. Although declaring itself unready to give up the fight for prohibition, despite losing the battle over the Amendment, in January, 1934, the Committee on Temperance and Social Service addressed themselves also to the threat of war, military training in denominational colleges, unwholesome movies, divorce, racial problems, and gambling.

Commitment to a broader social perspective, however, also fluctuated up and down, depending upon particular persons as much as upon the times and circumstances. Some associations maintained greater consistency than the State Convention. The Liberty Baptist Association, for instance, retained the name "Social Service" for its committee even when concern for temperance and prohibition dominated in 1931 and 1932. In the State Convention the Temperance and Social Service Committee put forth a vigorous rationale for application of the gospel to social matters while Clyde V. Hickerson served as its chairman from January, 1934 to January, 1936. The Hickerson committee stressed commitment to the "whole Gospel," contending, "It is not true to say that if we could only get men converted we would solve all our problems."[60] They pointed out that "Some of our people make the unfortunate mistake of setting what is called the 'individual' gospel over against what is termed the 'social' Gospel." Such an understanding, they went on to argue, is erroneous. "He who appreciates the Gospel in its fullness and power knows that it has and is working in the regeneration of individual hearts and in the combating of destructive forces in the larger life of society."[61] In support they ticked off one by one "the liquor evil," with its contribution to deaths and accidents on the highways, gambling, "the widespread divorce evil" created by lax divorce laws in Arkansas, racial tensions, war, and "compulsory military training in denominational colleges." Indicative of the mixed response such a strong statement got, it was amended before being passed.

The next two committees reversed the potent social thrust of the Hickerson committees. In January, 1937 a committee comprised of E.S. Elliott, V.H. Coffman, Mrs. F.E. Goodbar, J.F. Queen, and Mrs. E.L. Cole prefaced its report with a reassuring word about the adequacy of personal religion. "Where the whole Gospel is preached and lived God's word cuts crime asunder as the sword does the enemy in battle," they asserted. Later they added, "In Christ we have the answer and this generation has a right to look to the church for help." Though citing the same evils as previous committees—crime, liquor, road houses, immoral movies, gambling, divorce, race relations, and war—they made recommendations only regarding more personal ones (gambling, divorce, movies, and liquor) and called on the Convention to "pledge ourselves to expose and use every effort to defeat Communism with all of its hellish teachings in the State of Arkansas."[62] The next committee, chaired by Coffman, did a virtual verbatim.

We will not take time to note all of the about-faces social service reports did subsequently. Of greater moment here are the experiences of hurt and deprivation which were shaking Baptists and broadening their social outlook and involvement. A Social Service report to the Liberty Baptist Association in 1930 spells it out for us. "As a result of the financial depression at this time; and there is evidence of a possibility of hunger and suffering among us; we recommend that our people give much concern to properly care for local needs."[63] The next year, among other things, the same committee urged members of the Association to heed the cries of persons in distress. They also took note of the problem of unemployment and its consequences, exhorting the churches to provide entertainment for young people, knowing they would seek it elsewhere if not provided.[64] In 1935 the Association's Social Service Committee ranged even farther. Alongside the usual denunciation of liquor and gambling, they discussed injustice in employer-employee relationships in industry. This statement, drafted by E.L. Compere and Mrs. L.G. Mosley, indicated abuses of the free enterprise system:

> The generally accepted theory of industry is that it is carried on for the purpose of making profits for owners of the business. The profit motive may be a necessary incentive in business, but certainly employers and business men have a vital responsibility beyond that of

paying such profits. The welfare of employees and their families must be given adequate consideration. Men are enjoined to be honest, just and merciful in all of their dealings with each other. Christianity places this obligation squarely upon everyone alike, regardless of his station in life.[65]

The next year, they commended Mormons for taking people off the relief roles. "Whether or not this great church succeeds in this commendable undertaking," they added, "Southern Baptists cannot evade the fact that we as a denomination need to direct our thinking and activities along similar lines."[66]

Baptists in World War II

The Second World War was to reshape further the social perceptions of Arkansas Baptists but in rather curious ways. On the one hand, the scope of social pronouncements narrowed during and after the War, drawing back to an almost exclusive preoccupation with temperance and prohibition. On the other hand, while decrying war, patriotism drew Arkansas Baptists into the war effort and by that route into a more intimate relationship with American government and society. When the War ended, there was no climbing back over "a wall of separation" and keeping church and state wholly isolated, if they ever had been.

Renewal of concern for temperance and prohibition was directly connected with a sharp upswing in alcohol consumption and drunkenness during the War. Arkansas Baptists, of course, had not stopped their fight with the liquor industry after the repeal of prohibition. In the interim years between 1933 and the War, however, they had toned down their pronouncements and balanced them with other issues. Then, as the War approached, they narrowed these again. In 1941 the Committee on Temperance and Social Service became the Committee on **Prohibition** and Social Service, and from 1943 until 1948 the Prohibition or Temperance Committee. In 1942 Arkansas Baptists once again found themselves linking arms with the Anti-Saloon League of America in a prohibition campaign. This time, the aim was not national prohibition but Initiated Act No. 1, which simplified local option legislation by bringing all kinds of liquor under one law and by lowering the percentage of votes required for a local option petition (from 35% to 15%).[67] The next year, they celebrated thirty-two victories by "drys" in forty local option elections.[68] At the same time they

287

pressed to halt sale of liquor "in or near" army bases, where alcohol abuse led to many other problems.[69]

The increasing stridency of pronouncements would indicate, however, that Baptists sensed they were fighting a losing battle with booze. In 1945, after giving an intentionally alarmist recitation of facts about the alcohol "menace," the Committee on Temperance urged all to lick this "INSIDE ENEMY" as they had licked "OUTSIDE ENEMIES"—"Japs" and Germans.[70] But times and moral perceptions were changing. Not even all Baptists were teetotalers any longer, judging by pleas in various reports. At the State Assembly in 1949, moreover, only 609 out of 791 persons making "definite decisions to serve the Lord in a better way" pledged themselves to "no drinking, no smoking, no dancing and no desecration of the Lord's Day."[71] November 7, 1950 the prohibition cause suffered a major defeat at the polls as Arkansans voted to allow liquor sales. The Convention's Prohibition Committee described this as "truly a dark day for Arkansas."[72]

We can see here the subtle way in which American culture was stamping its imprint on Arkansas Baptists as on other Americans. War-time and post-war culture rolled on. As it did, it left its tread on everything.

In a wartime situation, a nation even a democratic one, of necessity tightens its control over all institutions or bodies within and implicates them in what it is doing, as it summons all reserves for the fight. Unless churches adopt a strong stance over against the war and the policies or the actions of the government, they too are drawn into the net. As in the case of Arkansas Baptists, they may go willingly, not wanting to appear unpatriotic and valuing certain benefits from "serving their country."

There is a strong touch of irony in this. When they knew about the possibility of war only by distant beat of drums, in 1928, Arkansas Baptists condemned it.[73] As the sounds in Europe grew louder and more ominous with Hitler's takeover in Germany, they issued strong appeals for world peace and urged support of persons working to effect it. Following an SBC resolution, they went on record against compulsory military training in denominational colleges, querying whether "such training is consistent with the highest ideals of Christian education."[74] Less than a month before Pearl Harbor, the Committee on Prohibition and Social Service urged the use of "every honorable means looking toward the cessation of hostilities and toward an equitable and lasting peace."

They expressed confidence that a "just solution" without "further resort to arms" was still possible and petitioned Congress to help the "unfortunate of Europe in danger from want and hunger."[75]

When America went to war, however, their stance shifted too, and as it did they found themselves intimately involved in state affairs. We can see this quite clearly in service contracts between Ouachita College and the federal government. In 1943 the College contracted with the government to train 250 aviation cadets apart from its regular student body. The government aided the college not only by paying for the program but by supplying money to repair buildings.[76] Similarly, for several years after the War, the College benefited from enlarged enrollment of G.I.s on the G.I. bill and, in 1947, from materials for three new buildings furnished by the government.[77] In 1949 College officials estimated that, since 1942, the government had "been carrying up to 40% of the financial load, both capital and operation" through the R.O.T.C., Air Cadet program, and G.I. bill.[78]

Government assistance, however, created an unnatural dependency which came to endanger the existence of Ouachita, as it did that of other colleges. When the government no longer needed the services of private or church-related colleges, Ouachita was stranded, desperately in need of supplementary income, as we will note later. With public schools also expanding with much better financial support Arkansas Baptists were hard put to maintain even one school, much less two or three.

We will examine in some detail the efforts of Arkansas Baptists to address the racial situation in another section. One item, however, calls for special comment in this context. In connection with the resettlement of aliens living in the United States, in 1942 the Convention issued a counsel on the side of tolerance. "With the coming of the Japanese Colonies (to Arkansas) race prejudice again crops out and it is well for us to hear again the admonition of the great Apostle, 'Let this mind be in you which was also in Christ Jesus'."[79] The War, of course, tested such feelings severely, but it is worthy of note that, in 1943, the Convention entertained three guests with Japanese names, two from "Relocation Centers."[80]

A Baptist in Politics

Before concluding our consideration of Arkansas Baptists in their social setting, it will be useful to look biographically at a distinguished political figure of this era, Brooks Hays. Better than any other, I think, Hays exemplifies the fruits of Baptist piety in both religious and political life. Although not the preacher-politician that James P. Eagle was, he still has blended together in a fashion not unlike Eagle did his service of God through the Church and his service of God through his country. Personal faith, nurtured in Baptist churches, has helped to inform and shape political perceptions throughout his career even as it has sustained him personally. Arkansas Baptists might appropriately recognize in him some of the ways in which their own better Christian perceptions have been infused into the body politic.

Born in Russellville August 9, 1898, Hays studied at the University of Arkansas (B.A., 1919) and the law school of George Washington University (J.D., 1922). Admitted to the Arkansas bar in 1922, he practiced law in his hometown for three years, then served as Assistant Attorney General of Arkansas (1925-1927). He was twice defeated in Arkansas gubernatorial races (1928, 1930), running second each time, but he ran well enough to be elected Democratic National Committeeman in 1932. In 1933 he lost a congressional race by way of a voting fraud. Being closely in touch with the plight of folks in rural areas, in 1934 he took a position in the National Resettlement Administration and then in the Farm-Security Administration. In 1942 he ran successfully for congress in the Fifth District. Holding his seat eight terms, he was defeated in 1958 on account of his moderate views on integration. Since 1958 he has served, among other positions, on the Board of Directors of the Tennessee Valley Authority, as Assistant Secretary of State for Congressional Relations in the U.S. State Department, Special Assistant to the President of the United States, Presidential Consultant, and as a visiting professor at Vanderbilt, Rutgers, and the University of Massachusetts.

Hays has interlaced his political career with a religious one. The grandson of a Baptist preacher, his mother, Sallie Butler Hays, took him to the little Baptist Church in Russellville every time the doors opened. Early on, he earned the nickname "deacon" from some of his friends. While a student at the University of Arkansas, he taught a Sunday school class, served as president of the Y.M.C.A., and worked in a mission. After he returned to Russellville, the Church ordained him as a deacon. In 1925, moving to Little Rock, he began teaching a Bible class which now bears his name in the Second Baptist Church.

From 1928 on, Brooks Hays' religious involvement expanded along with his political horizons. In 1929 and 1930 he served as chairman of the Rural Church commission of the Arkansas Baptist State Convention which drafted proposals for a revamping of Arkansas Baptist work. While working in his own law firm in Little Rock (1928-1933), he was on the Board of Directors of the Little Rock Y.M.C.A. and the Arkansas Tuberculosis Association and served as president of the Arkansas Children's Home and Hospital. From 1932 to 1935 he was also president of the Arkansas Conference of Social Work, which was devoting its attention to rural problems.

In 1951 Brooks Hays was elected Second Vice-president of the Southern Baptist Convention. Always keenly interested in race relations, from 1954 to 1957 he served as a member and chairman of the Southern Baptist Convention's Christian Life Commission. Indeed, he was chairman in 1956 when the Commission issued "An Appeal for a Christian Spirit in Race Relations" and urged the Convention to support the "awakening of the submerged peoples of the world to their personal destinies and inherent freedoms."[81] In 1957 he was elected President of the Southern Baptist Convention, an honor which he labeled "the culmination of my religious life and work."[82] He was reelected the next year.

From 1969 until 1973 Hays served as Director of the Ecumenical Institute at Wake Forest University. While this will seem little short of astonishing in light of the history of Arkansas Baptists, he had good preparation for it. His repertoire is filled with good-natured ecumenical anecdotes dating back to his childhood in Arkansas. In 1922 he married a Methodist, Marion Prather. Then, during his second term as President of the Southern Baptist Convention, he and Marion had an audience with Pope John XXIII, as it were, ushering in the new era in Baptist and Catholic relations.

This resume of Brooks Hays' career, of course, stays too near the surface for us to see how his Baptist piety informed his politics. Fortunately his own speeches and writings help us to go deeper. In his reflections upon his frustrating defeat in the special election for Congress in 1933 we can get a better measure of the man. Hays had a lead of 595 votes outside of one county. Because the political leaders of that county were angry at him, they used the occasion to get even. They gave him 616 votes, his opponent 1,850—in a county with only 1,632 registered voters! A long and tedious lawsuit ended in dismissal on technicalities. Many would not have been able to handle such a vexing experience, especially as a sequel to two previous election defeats. Quite candidly, Hays later admitted, ". . . I struggled against human reactions that would impair my faith." Nevertheless, "my faith in God and in my fellow man survived that bitter experience. It served to give me a further understanding of the difficulties of a minority group in achieving recognition and proper legal safeguards, and it strengthened my dedication to the cause of universal suffrage and honest elections."[83]

In the civil rights struggle of the 'fifties, in which he played a leading role, he retained a strong sense of confidence in the churches, with all of their limitations. "In the last analysis," he wrote in 1959 after his defeat in the congressional race, "it will be the churches and the local community organizations that will provide solutions to the problems of civil rights."[84] In a defense of his signing of the "Southern Manifesto," a protest of the Supreme Court Decision in 1954, he pointed especially to its provision for the use of coercion. He was convinced, he said, that "our honest disagreements could be reconciled on the basis of social, religious, and political actions of an educational nature, rather than by the utilization of the coercive powers of government,. . ." His Baptist heritage, he insisted, led him to this conviction. "In maintaining this view I was putting into practice the Baptist doctrines of my belief, recognizing the obligation to urge my fellow citizens to take the actions necessary for a final reconciliation."[85]

In 1957, while serving a first term as President of the SBC, Hays was thrust into the highly volatile position of liaison between federal officials and Governor Orval Faubus, also a Baptist, in the Little Rock school desegregation crisis. He did not act as President of the Convention in arranging a Newport conference between Faubus and President Dwight D. Eisenhower, he observed: "But as the crisis dragged on, I saw that I had a triple role: I was attempting to mediate. . . .; I was acting in my capacity as a congressman; and partly because I was a Baptist official, I found that the role of moralist was inescapable."[86] The churches, he concluded, could do three things to effect the reconciliation which the gospel entails: "(1) seek a non-violent solution, (2) avoid economic, political, or social pressures upon the preachers to prevent their saying what conscience directs, and (3) seek to promote justice in specific situations."[87] It is surely significant of Hays' faith that he did not lose confidence in the churches when so many things they were doing at this time showed so little promise of reconciliation. Perhaps his experience in Arkansas taught patience. In 1922 his pastor in Russellville was a klansman.

292

Social Service

During the period under discussion, Arkansas Baptists continued the social ministries begun earlier with little alteration.

Bottoms' Orphans Home calls for little comment. As noted earlier, the Home struggled along without explicit Convention assistance during the depression. Due to lack of funds, it made few improvements on its buildings and, in 1932, had to beg its supporters to send anything the home could use.[88] In 1934 its population dropped, it was theorized, as a consequence of "the fact that the more dependents a man had, the better chance he had for federal help."[89] As economic conditions improved in 1936, however, the Home was put in the State Convention's budget. Subsequently it began to receive Cooperative Program funds, but drought, fires, and other calamities kept it on the edge of a financial precipice until the Second World War. In 1949 the Cooperative Program was supplying 25% of the operating budget; the rest came from special offerings.

The hospitals had a much easier time financially during the depression than other Convention institutions. Apart from an increase in the number of charity patients they treated, they experienced less strain on resources than they did during World War II, when the War sapped them of personnel and escalated costs. As we have seen above, the State Baptist Hospital in Little Rock had sufficient funds to pay off $150,000 of the Convention's bonded debt and some of its "floating" debt also. Although for a brief period the Convention assumed some of the indebtedness for Davis Hospital, the latter subsequently paid its own way without serious difficulty, until the Convention, unable to fund needed improvements, transferred title to the city of Pine Bluff in 1942.[90]

We can see here once more how the depression and War complicated relationships between state and church. During the depression, the State Hospital secured contracts with the United States Army, Citizens Military Training Camps, and Civilian Conservation Corps Camps.[91] With the onset of the War, being the largest "voluntary" hospital in Arkansas, it obtained additional contracts with the railroads and defense plants. In 1943 it related its School of Nursing to the "Nurses Training Corps," which provided wartime assistance to student nurses.

The War, of course, dumped a weighty burden on hospital facilities and personnel. The Board of Trustees reported throughout the War on the construction of one building after another. They complained repeatedly about resources being "taxed to the limit."

293

There were shortages of nurses and doctors. In 1942 thirty staff doctors were inducted into the Army. Other personnel left for higher paying jobs in defense industries.

The increase of the State Baptist Hospital's relationships with the Federal Government complicated its relationships with the Arkansas Baptist State Convention, eventually producing some disagreements regarding control and generating hard feelings. This emerged quite clearly in the question of transferring funds from the Hospital to the Convention, a matter which had to be settled in court. To all intents and purposes, of course, the Hospital had come to conceive of itself as a private corporation, receiving little direct aid from the Convention but, since legally related, giving quite a lot in return. The Supreme Court ruling in 1944 proved, however, that the Convention could still tell the Board of Trustees of the Hospital what to do. Significative of the whole undercurrent of uncertainty here, in 1948 the Convention changed the hospital's name to Arkansas Baptist Hospital to end the problem of people thinking it was a "state" institution. The next year, the Hospital Board reported that the hospital "majored on public relations" with the result that "Many misunderstandings have been cleared up."[92]

Meanwhile, with the release of Davis Hospital, Arkansas Baptists turned up the burner on a usually casual interest in the Baptist Memorial Hospital in Memphis. The expansion of this tri-state facility also aroused some anxiety in Arkansas when it reached out to build an orphan's home in Memphis. A special committee appointed to study the matter concluded that the hospital had overstepped the bounds of its own authority in 1942 in creating and funding the orphanage. Though it had acted in good faith, the Committee said, it "assumed an independence that violates Baptist democracy and the rights of the states who own the hospital." The result was "friction" and "unpleasantness." The orphanage should be separated completely from the hospital. If Tennessee Baptists wanted an orphanage in Memphis, they should study the matter and establish one "properly."[93]

At least one feature of hospital ministry merits special comment at this point. During and after the Second World War, racial barriers began toppling, particularly through connections with the military, which emphasized integration. The effects of this movement soon registered in the hospitals. Baptist reactions appear mixed. On the one hand, a year before the Convention released it, Davis Hospital took over management of Brewster Memorial Hospital in Pine Bluff, using it for treatment of "both colored and white crippled children" as well as other patients.[94] In 1943, moreover, the Baptist Memorial Hospital in Memphis was laying plans for "a negro branch" located near the hospital, "largely built for negro charity patients that live outside of the city and can not come to the City Hospital."[95] On the other hand, in 1944 the State Convention declined to assume operation of an existing hospital which had been closed as proposed by the Dardanelle-Russellville Association. Among other arguments given for this proposal was that the area included 60,000 people "nearly all of whom are white,. . ."[96]

Baptists and Education

In the preceding period we saw the decline and disappearance of Baptist elementary and high schools as public education, with far superior resources, moved in to replace them. In the present period Baptist colleges, crippled by the depression, came near to meeting the same fate. Mountain Home barely survived 1927 and 1928 with token help from the State Convention. In 1929 it closed because it could not obtain operating funds either from the Convention or from the Home Mission Board on account of the Carnes embezzlement. It reopened in 1930 with assurance of $4,000 from the Executive Board of the Convention, but only 38 students enrolled in the eleventh and twelfth grades of high school and first year of college.[97] In the 1931-1932 school year it upped its enrollment to 78 but operated with a $3,000 deficit.[98] In the next session the high school had 32, the college 10 students. Income paid groceries and running expenses. Five full-time and one part-time faculty members received $2.00 each.[99] Although the Convention sustained some hope of reopening the college, appointing a Board of Trustees for it year by year, it closed permanently in 1933.

Meanwhile, both Central and Ouachita had to fight hard to avert a like fate. Central lost its battle in 1950. It fought a losing fight all along, first to the depression and then to its ever-expanding competitors in higher education. Ouachita was aided, as we have seen, by government-service contracts during the War, but it too nearly drowned a few years afterward in the tide of public education. Only a strongly contested decision to close Central and concentrate on the survival of Ouachita saved it for another day.

The Saga of Central

The enrollment of Central, a women's high school and junior college located away from the center of Arkansas and its increasingly urban culture, declined steadily. The following figures reflect the dimming of its prospects:

1927-28	226	1939-40	116
1928-29	200	1940-41	107
1929-30	141	1941-42	"Down"
1930-31	133	1942-43	103
1931-32	123	1943-44	90
1932-33	138	1944-45	96
1933-34	142	1945-46	No Report
1934-35	135	1946-47	No Report
1935-36	230 (?)	1947-48	No School Held
1936-37	151	1948-49	128 (Little Rock)
1937-38	123	1949-50	285 (Little Rock)
1938-39	126	1950-	Closed

Finances were, of course, equally problematic. Forced to fend for itself during the bleak years of the depression, soliciting funds either from individuals or churches without disrupting the Cooperative Program, it had to call on the citizens of Conway to bail it out of debt in 1929 and 1930. Despite this aid and stringent budget measures by J.S. Rogers, president from 1920 to 1940, the school ran behind in operating expenses and salaries for teachers and repeatedly had to solicit special help during the worst part of the depression.

But the depression was not Central's worst nemesis. By 1937 it was again managing to pay its bills with aid from the Convention. A much more powerful adversary was the rapid shift of support to public higher education which preceded and followed the Second World War. Even Baptist students had difficulty buying arguments for the special value of education in church-related colleges when they received free tuition in state colleges. The same foe did not strike Ouachita such a powerful blow quite as soon, thanks to government service contracts and the G.I. bill. But Central, being a women's college and a two-year one at that, did not share this bounty. Consequently the steep slide of its enrollment during the depression continued during and after the War.

The plan to relocate came too late to save Central's life, therefore. As enrollment kept on declining after the War, the first strategy was to attract more students by improving facilities. When a half-million dollar fund-raising proposal got a cool reception, the Board of Trustees decided to move to Little Rock, following population trends and "momentum," and establish a coed school.[100]

Unfortunately they encountered delays in selling their property in Conway and in negotiating for the purchase of property in Little Rock. By the time they got moved to the new site, the "base hospital area" of Camp Robinson, in 1948, Ouachita was experiencing the belated financial crunch that came when most of the G.I.s were graduating. The Convention reluctantly authorized Central to approach "friends and churches" to raise funds for current needs but not to undertake a general solicitation.[101] In 1950, however, with Ouachita reporting current liabilities of $64,332.43 and Central of $78,170.73, the Executive Board called for a special session of the Convention to consider Central's future.

The Executive Committee recommended "that the operation of Central College be permanently discontinued" and "all the assets of the institution be placed in the hands of the proper agency for the liquidation of all financial obligations against the College."[102] A substitute motion which would have rallied Convention support for the College failed.

Ouachita's Story

The survival of Ouachita was a consequence of several factors: history, endowment, sacrifices of faculty and administration during and after the depression, government service contracts before and during the War, and the G.I. bill. The story of these years, however, is a painful one.

The successful $400,000 endowment campaign assured Ouachita of about $20,000 a year in income even during the worst days of the depression. To compete with state-financed colleges in attracting students, however, the College awarded free tuition to an inordinately large number of students. In 1930-1931, with only 248 students enrolled, for instance, it handed out 75 freshmen scholarships and free tuition to 23 ministerial students and to 20 sons and daughters of ministers. In 1934-1935, with 487 enrolled, it gave free tuition to 60 ministerial students, 14 missionary students, 7 special students in religious education, 4 evangelistic singers, 9 wives of ministerial students, 34 sons or daughters of ministers, and 80 class valedictorians or special honor students. It also allowed 100 to attend who could not pay or who worked for their tuition.[103]

Such a generous tuition plan obviously achieved its main object, that is, to attract more students. Unlike Central, Ouachita experienced a steady rise in its enrollment, except in 1936-1937 when the Trustees limited it, until the Second War siphoned off prospective male students.

1927-28	318	1938-39	560
1928-29	302	1940-41	608
1929-30	327	1941-42	630
1930-31	248	1942-43	460
1931-32	241	1943-44	800
1932-33	424	1944-45	539
1933-34	487	1945-46	850
1934-35	510	1946-47	850 (1,123 counting summer)
1935-36	(over 500)	1947-48	1,100
1936-37	409	1948-49	698
1937-38	510		

In bleak financial circumstances, however, the College's student boom loaded a heavy burden on the faculty. To finance scholarships, the school cut faculty salaries. In January, 1935 President J.R. Grant expressed the hope that Ouachita could pay half of the salaries for the whole year. At this time endowment income was paying off a $60,000 note. Salaries began to improve in 1937, but until 1940 Grant repeatedly reminded the Convention that the school could not guarantee its salaries.

Cumulatively, these things—use of endowment income to pay off debts, too many tuition-free students, poor faculty remuneration—caused Ouachita to lose its accreditation with the North Central Association in 1935.[104] It did not regain accreditation until 1942.[105] In 1949 it again received a "rather severe and critical" report from the Association, noting that its faculty were underpaid, its library was "deplorably weak," it had inadequate "educational policies," and it lacked sufficient "budget control."[106] Ouachita's post-War financial pinch came at a bad time; it was awaiting a full accreditation study in 1950. In 1951 it again dropped from the accredited list of the North Central Association.

The reduction of Arkansas Baptists' colleges to one had been proposed actually at a much earlier date. In 1931 the Education Commission of the State Convention, chaired by Otto Whitington, did a thorough survey of Arkansas Baptist educational experience and made some far-reaching recommendations. Among other things, the study candidly highlighted the decrease in number of Baptist schools, the increase in number of public institutions of higher learning (twelve in 1931), the corresponding increase of Baptist students in state schools as a result of free tuition there and high tuition in Baptist schools, the proximity of state schools to every Baptist college in Arkansas, the nationwide trend from church-related colleges to state colleges, the introduction of religion courses in state schools, and the great burden of operating Baptist schools with limited enrollments. On the basis of these data the Commission proposed (1) coordination of all Convention controlled schools "into one large Baptist University," (2) location of it "near the center of the population of the state," and (3) development of a curriculum "to meet the demand and supply the education need of this and future generations of a great and growing commonwealth" while "preserving and maintaining absolute allegiance to Christian Education and denominational support and control." These items were to be carried out "as soon as practicable and possible" through a nine-member Education Commission. Boards of Trustees were "instructed to cooperate with the Commission and the Executive Board in carrying out the above recommendations."[107] As one would expect, the Commission got into serious difficulty trying to decide between two proposals on location—one from Little Rock, the other from Arkadelphia.[108] After another year of discussion the proposal was quietly ignored when the Convention met again after more than a year in January of 1934. Ouachita and Central carried on their battles for survival separately, until the inevitable happened in 1950.

The one bright ray peeking through these dark clouds is that the arduous trials of the period forced Arkansas Baptists to come up with a more compelling **raison d'être** for Baptist higher education. Before the public education system had developed fully, it sufficed for them to berate the limitations of public education and to laud the advantage of Christian education. By this era they had to spell out more clearly the peculiar contributions of every educational institution they retained. Their rationales varied considerably, but they invariably pointed to the distinctiveness of Christian as opposed to secular education. In 1938, for instance, the Christian Education Committee, conceding that the increase of state involvement had muddied the role of the churches in general education, went on to emphasize support for Christian colleges because of their contribution to truth and character. They noted, too, that church colleges relieved the state of a financial burden. The major question for Christians today, they added, was how to provide "religious and moral instruction" in elementary and secondary schools "without infringement upon the fundamental principle of the separation of Church and State."[109]. Another, we might observe in light of Arkansas Baptist history, is whether and how Christian colleges can compete in terms of quality education with such limited resources.

Southern Baptist College

Considering the sad end of Central College, it is perplexing that Arkansas Baptists would take another college under wing in the very year their other two colleges had reached a point of crisis. The explanation perhaps lies largely in the fact that the State Convention expected people in the northeastern part of the state, who had yearned for their own college since Jonesboro folded in 1935, to continue to give strong support. The Convention itself allotted approximately $20,000 a year.[110]

Officially opened in Pocohantas in September, 1941, with H.F. Williams as its first President, it grew slowly from 42 its first session to 128 in 1944, then mushroomed after the War. In 1947 it moved to the air base near Walnut Ridge. From the first, the College concentrated on the educational needs of rural ministers in the area, creating the "first rural ministerial training course in the United States designed to fully equip the rural minister for his task."[111] It embarked also upon an extensive missions program in the area. The Black River Baptist Association recorded the highest percentage of baptisms in the state shortly after the college moved to Walnut Ridge, attributing the phenomenon chiefly to the College's students who were serving as ministers throughout the region.[112] After World War II Southern Baptist College developed a vocational arts program designed to provide ex-military personnel with needed job skills. In 1949 it reported a record enrollment of 1,110, many in the industrial arts program.

Campus Ministry

In surveying the problems of Baptist colleges in this period we have repeatedly taken notice of the shift of Baptist students to state colleges. In 1931, for example, eighty percent of Baptist students were studying in one or another of the twelve tuition-free schools in the state. The trend has not abated since.

Unfortunately, after the discontinuance of the pastoral services of E.N. Strother at the University of Arkansas in June of 1927, student ministry got only token attention until 1937. In the interim, of course, B.S.U.s were organized on Baptist college campuses, for instance, at Ouachita in 1928.[113] Baptist students attended southwide conferences. But it was not until January, 1937 that Baptist student ministry was revived on a significant scale. At that time the State Convention passed a resolution instructing the Executive Board to "provide for personnel and program to integrate the Student Work in the state" and to organize Unions at all colleges.[114]

In December, at its own request, the Baptist Student Union became a part of the Sunday School and Church Training Department, so as to have a "more vital connection with the Convention."[115] The B.S.U.

continued in this relationship until 1951 when it became a separate department.

According to their own definition, the Unions sought to help Baptist students to live a Christian life on campus and to enlist students in the work of local churches. Early on, however, the part of their program which caught the eye of the State Convention was summer field work, which as we saw earlier, enlisted volunteers to promote Training Union in rural churches. Four years in a row Department reports lauded Summer Field Work as the Baptist Student Union's "most fruitful outcome."[116] In 1943, due to the War, there was no summer work, but the B.S.U. did start a paper, **The Challenger.**[117] In 1939 the Department organized Unions on twelve college campuses. By 1944 the number had risen to fifteen. After the War, for some reason, the number declined. Only thirteen were reported in 1946, "some not active."[118] By 1949, however, Baptist Student Union was extending its range to include business and professional schools, employing more full-time secretaries, establishing student centers, and encouraging the establishment of Bible chairs on state college campuses.[119] In addition, some churches were hiring staff members to work with students and building student centers on nearby campuses. The First Baptist Church of Russellville, for instance, hired a student director, purchased land, and built a Baptist Student Center at Arkansas Tech. The First Baptist Church of Monticello also employed its own B.S.U. director.

Women and Men

The Women's Movement

At the outset of this period women were calling attention to the inequities of their situation. In 1927 the Committee on Woman's Work, chaired by J.F. Tull, for example, cited Matthew 19:4-6 to point out that Jesus "did not even quote Genesis 3:16, or mention anywhere woman's subordination or inferiority to man, but lifted him clear over the whole Woman Question controversy back into the original place of **absolute equality with her husband,** and there is exactly where he left her when he went back to glory."[120] This document went on to denounce those who overemphasized Genesis 3:16 and thus "not only cheated woman out of her high place of honor and service" but "hampered the progress of God's Kingdom in a thousand ways and forced upon Christian women a struggle for liberty which is unmatched for heroism in all annals." But the vigorous women's movement which this statement reflects faltered during the depression, as Baptist women again channeled their energies into saving the Convention's programs and institutions.

We cannot take time to give a detailed report of the immense contribution the Woman's Missionary Union made financially. During the years of struggle to pay off the huge indebtedness of the Convention and its institutions, they raised massive sums as indicated in the following financial summary:

1929	$231,494.23	1940	$266,047.68
1930	177,632.24	1941	279,596.48
1931	186,584.84	1942	316,964.82
1932	134,547.47	1943	356,242.40
1933	116,938.81	1944	418,036.44
1934	123,589.52	1945	532,310.49
1935	127,025.72	1946	567,504.13
1936	166,739.78	1947	677,958.75
1937	201,264.30	1948	793,648.98
1938	204,007.52	1949	846,546.08
1939	225,211.65		

It was altogether appropriate that the W.M.U. should supply the final $2,000 toward the retirement of the Convention's bonded indebtedness in 1938.

Of more current interest at this point is the extent to which the State Convention followed up on its resolve in 1922 to give women a more prominent place on committees, boards, and commissions. Careful tabulation of the number of women serving on these between 1927 and 1949 reveals that women **did** extend their influence and recognition beyone the range they had enjoyed earlier. As indicated by Table XXXIII, they obtained places on most of the standing committees and boards and a few special ones.

These appointments, however, do not indicate a vast improvement in recognition of women. The frequency of female appointments to certain positions, such as the Boards of Trustees of Bottoms Orphanage and Central College, suggests that Arkansas Baptists tended to distinguish between "men's" and "women's" work. Moreover, a woman chaired a committee (the Orphanage Committee in 1944) only once, and no women were elected to the Executive Board, the most prestigious of the appointments. They

302

were, however, represented on the Planning, Coordinating and Steering Commission in 1947 and after, a possible sign of gains registered during the Second World War.

The Men's Movement

The men's movement which got off to a flying start after the First World War faltered, died, and was revived with difficulty after the Second World War. In 1927 I.E. Taylor, Laymen Secretary of the Arkansas Baptist State Convention, gave a spectacular report of work done between February 1, 1926 and September 1, 1927. He had assisted in more than 75 county-wide rallies on behalf of the denominational program, secured more than 2,500 new subscribers to the **Baptist Advance,** raised $25,000 for the Orphans' Home, spoken to more than 25 district associational meetings, "securing the adoption of a definite program for laymen's work in most," helped organize 30 "Brotherhood" organizations in the state, distributed several hundred copies of a book on stewardship and missions, supplied in a dozen pulpits, obtained "the appraisal of nearly all of the denominational property for the refinancing of this indebtedness," delivered more than 300 addresses in churches, and traveled thousands of miles by car or train to promote the work.[121]

Although the Laymen's Work Committee which prepared this report urged continuance of Taylor as a full-time secretary, the Convention's growing deficit rendered that impossible. Arkansas was not to employ a staff person specifically assigned to promotion of the men's movement until 1946, when a Brotherhood Department was established at last. Meantime, committees on "laymen's work," "men's work," or "brotherhood," as this area was variously named, made repeated appeals for action as they watched the work flounder helplessly. In 1930 they recommended the appointment of W.A. Jackson as Laymen Director serving without pay.[122] Five years later, after a complete lapse in state promotion, they urged election of a "consecrated layman" as State Brotherhood Secretary at the earliest possible date to serve at least half-time. In January, 1937, reporting that the laymen's movement was at a "complete standstill" due to lack of interest and funds for promotion, they pleaded for a revival of aggressive promotion at all levels through inclusion of the work in the Convention budget. As late as 1942, despite election of a Brotherhood President in 1941, they were lamenting that "So far as we are able to learn, there is no definite Baptist Brotherhood in our

303

TABLE XXXIII
WOMEN ON COMMITTEES, 1927-1948

	1927	1928	1929	1930	1931	1932	1934	1935	1936	1937
BOARDS:										
Bottoms Orphanage	2	2	2	3	3	1	1	2	2	2
Davis Hospital										1
Memorial Hospital									1	
State Hospital		1	1	1	1	1	1	1	2	2
Central College			2	3	2					2
Mountain Home College		1	1	1	1	1	1			
Ouachita College			1	1	1					
COMMITTEES:										
Christian Education, Ect.	1	1								
Church Music										
Cooperative Program	1								1	
Debt-Paying Campaign									1	
Foreign Missions			1	3		3			2	1
Gambling									1	
Home Missions	1	1		2		2	1		1	1
Hospitals	1	2	4							
Hundred Thousand Club									3	
Lord's Day Alliance			1							
Ministerial Education		1				3				
Ministerial Relief		1		2		3				
Mountain Home College				3						
Nominations	1	1						1	1	1
Obituaries	1		2	5		2			1	
Order of Business			1							
Orphans' Home	1	2	3							1
Publications, **Ark. Baptist**		1		2		3			1	
Publicity										
Resolutions										
Rural Church Conditions		1								
Seminaries										
Special B.Y.P.U.		1								
State Missions	1								3	
Stewardship						3				
Sunday School and B.Y.P.U.	3	4	5			3	1			
Temperance and Social Services	1	1	3						1	3
SPECIAL COMMITTEES:										
Comm. of 5 to Cooperate with Ark. Cent. Comm.									2	
Anti-Saloon League					1	1	1	2	1	1
Central College Comm.										

TABLE XXXIII
WOMEN ON COMMITTEES, 1927-1948

	1938	1939	1940	1941	1942	1943	1944	1945	1946	1947	1948
BOARDS:											
Bottoms Orphanage	2	2	3	3	4	3	2	3	3	5	4
Davis Hospital											
Memorial Hospital											
State Hospital	1	1						1	1	1	
Central College	2	1	3	4	5	5	5	5	5	5	4
Mountain Home College											
Ouachita College								1	2	2	
COMMITTEES:											
Christian Education, Etc.			1				2	1			
Church Music					2	1					
Cooperative Program			2								
Debt-Paying Campaign											
Foreign Missions			1	3							
Gambling											
Home Missions		1	1								
Hospitals				1							1
Hundred Thousand Club											
Lord's Day Alliance											
Ministerial Education											
Ministerial Relief											1
Mountain Home College											
Nominations											1
Obituaries		2							1		2
Order of Business											
Orphans' Home		1		7		1	1				
Publications, **Ark. Baptist**	1										1
Publicity											
Resolutions			1	1							
Rural Church Conditions											
Seminaries			1					1			
Special B.Y.P.U.											
State Missions		1									
Stewardship			2	2							
Sunday School & B.Y.P.U.	1		1	4					2		
Temperance and Social Services											
SPECIAL COMMITTEES:											
Comm. of 5 to Cooperate with Ark. Cent. Comm.											
Anti-Saloon League	1	2	1	1	1	1	1	1	1		1
Central College Comm.									1		

State."[123]

The laymen's movement encountered not only lethargy but direct opposition, probably in relation to lack of clarity as to its purpose. Early on, the movement was envisioned as the male counterpart of W.M.U., meaning an auxiliary in promoting the Convention's total program and in raising funds. In January, 1937, for instance, the Baptist Brotherhood Committee proposed the organization of the brotherhood around prayer, stewardship, and social activities.[124] Such a program, however, evidently did not capture the interest of many men, who perhaps regarded them as belonging to the women's sphere. At any rate, in 1941 the State Brotherhood President, C.L. Durrett, complained that most laymen had a "passive attitude" and were not as interested in religious as in business, civic, or other activities.[125] A year later, the Division of Men's Work Committee reported "criticism and objections" due to "misunderstanding of the methods and motives" of the brotherhood. "Contrary to popular comment," they replied, "we are not over-organized."[126] Subsequently, a Brotherhood Committee charged that "The reason we are not promoting this work is because we are either afraid of the movement, or we are not entirely sold on its value."[127]

An about-face in definition of purpose occurred with the establishment of a Brotherhood Department in 1946. Besides promoting brotherhoods, the new secretary emphasized evangelism and expanded the membership to include ministers as well as laymen. The shift in approach proved effective. From a meager 53 local brotherhoods in 1946, the Brotherhood jumped to 134 in 1947, 160 in 1948, 197 in 1949, and 251 in 1950. Simultaneously the secretary reported numerous additions to churches by virtue of brotherhood-sponsored revivals: 513 in 1947 and 500 in 1948. In 1949 he published a tract on "Essential Steps in Personal Salvation." By 1950, however, the organization was broadening out again, devoting much energy to the Arkansas prohibition campaign. "Brotherhood," the State Convention Committee declared that year, "is simply MEN AT WORK at the tasks of their church and denomination."[128]

One interesting aside on the laymen's movement: In January, 1935 a special committee appointed by the Pastor's and Laymen's Conference in the preceding year (consisting of L.D. Summers, E.P.J. Garrott, and Otto Whitington) delivered a virtual indictment on "the low standard, or no standard, of church membership" in their denomination. Among faults they noted (1) the majority's lack of a sense of obligation to support missionary, benevolent, and educational programs; (2) the lives of many members "not only wholly unfruitful, but openly scandalous;" (3) many members "in league with those forces in the community which are subversive of decent moral standards"; (4) high absenteeism from church services; and (5) too few devoting themselves "with joy to worship, to witnessing and to sacrificial living and giving." The Committee proceeded to summon churches to pledge "to counteract the shallow evangelism that appears to be interested in quantity rather than in quality," to pursue a stricter policy regarding church membership, and to obtain genuine Christian commitment reflected in the way people lived.[129]

Black and White

The years of depression and war disrupted relationships between blacks and whites in Arkansas even more severely than it did other activities. Overpowered by its own indebtedness, the State Convention had to stop supplements it had been sending to Arkansas Baptist State College and the National Baptist Home Mission Board. After only a year, in 1927 it withdrew its endorsement and support of the National Baptist Hospital in Hot Springs.[130] From 1927 until 1938 it appointed no standing committee on work with blacks and sent no specific contributions. Although the Convention voted in January of 1935 to endorse the movement of Arkansas Baptist College to pay their debt, we have no record of actual assistance.[131]

This is not to imply that white Baptists took no thought for their black brothers. Of necessity, as the dreadful situation of blacks generated unrest and strife, individuals, churches, associations, and the State Convention came alive to the crisis. Three Convention Committees on Temperance and Social Service (1934, 1935, 1936), for instance, rejoiced that Arkansas had had no lynchings and urged greater understanding between the races. They placed the responsibility squarely on their own shoulders "because of the large number of colored people who are our fellow Baptists." They commended efforts of "some groups and churches to create a better understanding between black and white races." The solution to racial problems, they insisted, lay in "brotherhood as taught and practiced by Jesus. . ."[132] They expressed the hope that the time was not far off when blacks would have equal protection by law and equal justice in courts.[133]

Not all Arkansas Baptists by any means held such enlightened views or assumed such direct social responsibility. As we have seen earlier, subsequent Committees on Temperance and Social Service toned down the "social gospel" thrust of the Hickerson committees. In January of 1937, for instance, the Committee thrust the responsibility upon fathers and mothers to teach "respect for law and order" as an antidote to lynchings, which had increased nationwide and two of which had occurred in Arkansas in the previous year.[134] In December, however, racial strife worsening, they resumed a slightly bolder stance, urging "equal protection and equal justice in our courts" and favoring "every movement that will promote brotherly feeling and better relationship between races of our state and nation."[135]

Although in some ways the Second World War helped to prepare for advance in racial relations, especially through the policy of the armed forces, momentarily it sidetraced all serious efforts, at least by Arkansas Baptists. After 1939 war and temperance dominated Arkansas Baptist social thinking until 1948. Save for concern expressed in 1943 about "racial prejudice" toward Japanese internees of "Relocation Centers," Convention ethics committees did not refer to racial injustice; it was a problem which had receded into the background

By 1948, however, the civil rights movement was in full swing and could not be dodged any longer. By this time Arkansas Baptists, like most southerners, were prepared to grapple with the immense problem only in the most conservative way. Though manifesting awareness of the magnitude of the issue, in 1948 the Committee on Social Service envisioned no tangible strategy.

> *In the midst of agitated political issues dealing with the Negro problem in our Southland, they said, we recommend to the churches in our Convention that we hold to the one guiding New Testament principle of Love as the surest way of two racial groups solving the problems incurred in a Christian democracy. We recommend the Spirit of Christ and His patience in meeting the troublesome issues of the day and hour. We will make progress on this road and keep the peace.[136]*

The next year, alluding to "race riots," the Committee posited a solution "in experimental, spiritual religion—experienced in the heart of man and practiced in the conduct of this product."[137] Unfortunately stepping around the problem left it to grow for more painful solutions a few years hence.

On the brighter side, a once again solvent Convention renewed its financial assistance to National Baptists in 1938. A Committee on Negro Baptist Work, noting the need of blacks for better trained ministers, encouraged whites to send scholarship money to the American Baptist Seminary in Nashville, directed at the time by E.P. Alldredge, former Secretary of the State Convention. At the same time the Executive Committee budgeted $1,000 for black Baptists' work.[138] Actual support, of course, was often still tokenish. In 1940, for instance, when P.W. Coggs, President of Arkansas Baptist College, spoke and the College Glee Club sang, the Convention collected $23.13 for the College.[139] But in 1945 the Executive Board began sending $500 to $1,000 a year to the College.[140] In 1947 the Convention contributed $10,000 to start a National Baptist School of Nursing in Hot Springs.[141]

At the same time the Woman's Missionary Union of Arkansas initiated sponsorship of work among blacks in October, 1947. Through a specially designated gift to the State Missions offering the Mission Department hired Gwendoline Luster, a graduate of the National Training School for Negroes in Nashville, to work with black Baptist women and young people. The W.M.U. also allocated money to promote camps for black children.[142]

Looking Ahead

During the period we have been discussing, Arkansas Baptists slid deep into a valley and had to climb a steep hill on the other side. Numerically they held their own during the descent, but economically they were shattered. Only a radical turn around in the economic circumstances of the country sufficed to allow them to reascend. Not until the Second World War did they recover fully, and even then they had a mountain of debts they wanted voluntarily to settle.

By 1950 Arkansas Baptists had reached a kind of plateau. Their remarkable post-war expansion was leveling off to more normal proportions. Programs and plans were running smoothly with adequate funding.

Already, however, some of the terrain they were crossing was becoming rocky. That was especially evident as regards the institutions related to the State Convention, the hospitals and the colleges. As a result of government contracts and connections, the Baptist State Hospital was already operating in a quasi-independent fashion. The major difficulty at the moment, however, had to do with the schools. In competition with richly funded public institutions, Baptists of Arkansas, though more affluent than ever before, could not save two colleges. They killed one and concentrated on resuscitating the other.

Against this background the Executive Board of the State Convention took steps, as they had many times in the past, to assure "better planning, better support, and co-ordination of the institutional life" of the Convention. In 1946 they proposed the creation of a Planning, Coordinating and Steering Commission. The duties of this Commission were:

1. *To make plans for development of our Baptist institutions over a long period of time.*
2. *To co-ordinate plans for institutional development in such a manner as to represent the full and impartial needs of our full constituency.*
3. *To keep fully informed at all times as to the welfare, needs and plans of all of our institutions and to call such matters to the attention of the Board from time to time.*
4. *To examine and evaluate all claims and plans of said institutions and to recommend or disapprove said plans for general presentation to the Board and Convention.*
5. *To steer such plans and policies before the Board for presentation to the Convention.*[143]

This Commission, composed initially of two representatives of each Convention-operated institution but revamped in 1947 to consist of seven men and two women, none of whom could be employees of the Convention except the General Secretary,[144] were delegated the colossal task of studying the number and location of "Institutions and Camp Grounds and Assemblies," the character of the work they do, the needs of the constituency, and whether the institutions, etc. are properly located and if new ones are needed. In effect, this meant advising the Executive Board on the fate of the colleges and whether to launch further institutions. In 1949, looking at the budget, the Commission concluded that "no new enterprises could now be launched."[145]

In 1950 the rear view from the plateau was spectacular. But the way ahead looked rough.

NOTES

[1]In Brooks Hays, **The World: A Christian's Workshop** (Nashville: Broadman Press, 1958), p. 25.
[2]Ibid., p. 26.
[3]Brooks Hays, **A Southern Moderate Speaks** (Chapel Hill: University of North Carolina Press, 1959), p. 17.
[4]**Proceedings, ABSC, 1934,** p. 15.
[5]**Proceedings, ABSC, 1938,** p. 46.
[6]**Constitution, 1926,** Art. VI.
[7]**Proceedings, ABSC, 1926,** pp. 81-83.
[8]**Proceedings, ABSC, 1927,** pp. 24-25.
[9]**Proceedings, ABSC, 1930,** p. 8; **Minutes, Liberty Baptist Association, 1930,** p. 15.
[10]**Proceedings, ABSC, 1931,** p. 61.
[11]**Proceedings, ABSC, 1936,** pp. 43-68.
[12]**Proceedings, ABSC, 1937,** p. 91.
[13]**Proceedings, ABSC, December, 1937,** p. 41.
[14]**Annual, ABSC, 1943,** p. 61.
[15]**Annual, ABSC, 1944,** pp. 58-59; **1945,** p. 57.
[16]**Proceedings, ABSC, January, 1934,** pp. 43-44.
[17]**Proceedings, ABSC, January, 1936,** p. 38.
[18]**Proceedings, ABSC, December, 1937,** pp. 70-71.
[19]**Proceedings, ABSC, 1939,** pp. 18, 22.
[20]**Proceedings, ABSC, 1940,** pp. 40-41.
[21]**Proceedings, ABSC, 1940,** pp. 41-42.
[22]**Proceedings, ABSC, 1946,** pp. 57-58.
[23]**Proceedings, ABSC, 1946,** pp. 45-47.
[24]**Proceedings, ABSC, 1946,** pp. 24-28.
[25]**Proceedings, ABSC, January, 1937,** p. 55.
[26]**Proceedings, ABSC, 1929,** pp. 84-90.
[27]See John D. Freeman, **Country Church: Its Problems and Their Solution** (Atlanta: Home Mission Board, SBC, 1943), pp. 11-27.
[28]Adapted from Carl A. Clark, **Rural Churches in Transition** (Nashville: Broadman Press, 1959), ppp. 16-19.
[29]Roger V. Logan, **History of the North Arkansas Baptist Association** (Harrison, Ark.: Pine Tree Press, 1978), p. 99.
[30]**Proceedings, ABSC, 1939,** p. 42.
[31]Reported in Logan, op. cit., pp. 206-7.
[32]**Proceedings, ABSC, 1941,** p. 88.
[33]**Proceedings, ABSC, 1944,** p. 32.

[34] Proceedings, ABSC, 1949, p. 53.

[35] Minutes, Liberty Baptist Association, 1933, pp. 5-6.

[36] Proceedings, ABSC, 1928, p. 85.

[37] Brooks Hays, A Hotbed of Tranquility: My Life in Five Worlds (New York: MacMillan Co., 1968), pp. 167f.

[38] Proceedings, ABSC, December, 1937, p. 57.

[39] Cited in Proceedings, ABSC, 1938, p. 44.

[40] Annual, ABSC, 1949, p. 92; 1950, p. 52.

[41] Annual, ABSC, 1945, p. 60.

[42] The Baptist Advance, July 19, 1928, p. 1, has a petition against any anti-prohibition candidate signed by the "Protestant Ministers' Association of Fort Smith." It contains names of Baptist, Presbyterian, Methodist, Christian, and Nazarene ministers in the city.

[43] Proceedings, ABSC, 1936, p. 72.

[44] Minutes, Liberty Baptist Association, 1928, p. 14f.

[45] Proceedings, ABSC, 1926, pp. 91-92.

[46] Arkansas House Journal, 1927, pp. 323-325; Senate Journal, 1927, pp. 317, 351.

[47] Arkansas Laws, 1929, II, 1518-19.

[48] See Kenneth K. Bailey, Southern White Protestantism in the Twentieth Century (New York: Harper & Row, 1964), p. 87.

[49] Baptist Advance, July 19, 1928, p. 4.

[50] See Minutes, Liberty Baptist Association 1928, 2p. 21.

[51] Baptist Advance, July 12, 1928, p. 12.

[52] Baptist Advance, July 12, 1928, p. 4. On Millar's death in 1940 the State Convention eulogized him, noting especially his prohibition work and "kindly attitude" toward Baptists. (Proceedings, ABSC, 1940, p. 97).

[53] Proceedings, ABSC, 1938, p. 50.

[54] Proceedings, ABSC, 1939, p. 22.

[55] Annual, ABSC, 1944, p. 51.

[56] Annual, ABSC, 1947, pp. 40f.

[57] Proceedings, ABSC, 1940, p. 27.

[58] Annual, ABSC, 1946, p. 91.

[59] Annual, ABSC, 1948, p. 72.

[60] Proceedings, ABSC, January, 1935, p. 70.

[61] Proceedings, ABSC, January, 1936, p. 76.

[62] Proceedings, ABSC, January, 1937, pp. 72-75.

[63] Minutes, Liberty Baptist Association, 1930, p. 13.

[64] Minutes, Liberty Baptist Association, 1931, p. 14.

[65] Minutes, Liberty Baptist Association, 1935, p. 14.

[66] Minutes, Liberty Baptist Association, 1936, p. 7.

[67] Annual, ABSC, 1942, p. 92.

[68] Annual, ABSC, 1943, p. 87.
[69] Annual, ABSC, 1942, p. 94.
[70] Annual, ABSC, 1945, pp. 43-45.
[71] Annual, ABSC, 1949, p. 55.
[72] Annual, ABSC, 1950, p. 73.
[73] Proceedings, ABSC, 1928, pp. 70-73.
[74] Proceedings, ABSC, January, 1934, p. 32.
[75] Proceedings, ABSC, 1941, p. 84.
[76] Annual, ABSC, 1943, pp. 51, 53.
[77] Annual, ABSC, 1947, pp. 44-45.
[78] Annual, ABSC, 1949, p. 70.
[79] Annual, ABSC, 1942, p. 93.
[80] Annual, ABSC, 1943, p. 18.
[81] Cited by Brooks Hays, **A Southern Moderate Speaks,** p. 203.
[82] Ibid., p. 210.
[83] Ibid., p. 17.
[84] Ibid., p. 195.
[85] Ibid., pp. 209f.
[86] Ibid., p. 211.
[86] Ibid., p. 212.
[87] Proceedings, ABSC, 1932, p. 46.

[88] Proceedings, ABSC, 1932, p. 46.
[89] Proceedings, ABSC, January, 1934, p. 55.
[90] Proceedings, ABSC, 1941, p. 61; 1942, p. 33.
[91] Proceedings, ABSC, January, 1936, p. 70.
[92] Annual, ABSC, p. 72.
[93] Annual, ABSC, 1948, pp. 42-44.
[94] Proceedings, ABSC, 1941, p. 71.
[95] Annual, ABSC, 1943, p. 44.
[96] Annual, ABSC, 1944, p. 71.
[97] Proceedings, ABSC, 1930, pp. 10-11.
[98] Proceedings, ABSC, 1931, p. 10.
[99] Proceedings, ABSC, 1932, p. 43.
[100] Annual, ABSC, 1946, p. 19.
[101] Annual, ABSC, 1948, p. 29.
[102] Annual, ABSC, 1950, p. 19.
[103] Proceedings, ABSC, 1931, pp. 12-16; January, 1935, pp. 16ff.
[104] Proceedings, ABSC, January, 1936, p. 21.
[105] Annual, ABSC, 1942, p. 70.
[106] Annual, ABSC, 1949, p. 69.
[107] Proceedings, ABSC, 1931, pp. 31-32.

108 Proceedings, ABSC, 1932, pp. 24-25.

109 Proceedings, ABSC, 1938, p. 33.

110 Annual, ABSC, 1948, p. 27.

111 Annual, ABSC, 1951, p. 50.

112 Annual, ABSC, 1949, p. 65.

113 Proceedings, ABSC, 1928, pp. 43-45.

114 Proceedings, ABSC, January, 1937, p. 71.

115 Proceedings, ABSC, December, 1937, p. 84; also p. 39.

116 Proceedings, ABSC, 1939, p. 43; 1940, p. 47; 1941, p. 75; and 1942, p. 58.

117 Annual, ABSC, 1943, p. 23.

118 Annual, ABSC, 1946, p. 34.

119 Annual, ABSC, 1949, p. 52.

120 Proceedings, ABSC, 1927, p. 44; my italics.

121 Proceedings, ABSC, 1927, pp. 57-58.

122 Proceedings, ABSC, 1930, pp. 45-46.

123 Annual, ABSC, 1942, p. 76.

124 Proceedings, January, ABSC, 1937, p. 32.

125 Proceedings, ABSC, 1941, p. 22.

126 Annual, ABSC, 1942, p. 7.

127 Annual, ABSC, 1943, p. 86.

128 Annual, ABSC, 1950, p. 78.

129 Proceedings, ABSC, January, 1935, pp. 32-34.

130 Proceedings, ABSC, 1927, pp. 66, 91.

131 Proceedings, ABSC, 1935, p. 61.

132 Proceedings, ABSC, January, 1936, p. 78.

133 Proceedings, January, ABSC, 1935, p. 73.

134 Proceedings, ABSC, January, 1937, p. 82.

135 Proceedings, ABSC, December, 1937, p. 82.

136 Annual, ABSC, 1948, p. 96.

137 Annual, ABSC, 1949, p. 84.

138 Proceedings, ABSC, 1938, p. 79.

139 Proceedings, ABSC, 1940, p. 107.

140 Annual, ABSC, 1945, p. 59.

141 Annual, ABSC, 1947, pp. 69, 81.

142 Annual, ABSC, 1947, pp. 29-30.

143 Annual, ABSC, 1946, p. 69.

144 Annual, ABSC, 1947, p. 67.

145 Annual, ABSC, 1949, p. 81.

Chapter VII

ACROSS A PLATEAU

1951-1978

Most of the history of Arkansas Baptists runs up and down hills as steep as the Ozark mountains. The present period is an exception. Although the path ahead did not lack bumps, it lay for the most part across a plateau.

As in the preceding period, Arkansas Baptists experienced continued growth, despite decline of population until the mid-sixties for the state as a whole. While the general population was dropping 6.5 percent (from 1,909,511 to 1,786,272) between 1950 and 1960, the membership of the churches connected with the State Convention was going up 29.3 percent. Between 1960 and 1978, as the trend reversed itself, Baptists continued to increase. Between 1960 and 1970 the general population grew 7.7 percent (to 1,923,295); since 1970 it has increased at an estimated rate of 1.8 percent per year, standing near 2,220,000 at the time of writing. In the meantime, between 1960 and 1978, membership in churches affiliated with the State Convention increased 38.7 percent, an annual rate of 2.15 percent, exceeding still the most rapid growth rate of the state population as a whole.

The financial situation of Arkansas Baptists also eased during this period, as income mounted nationally and the population shifted from the farm to the city. Having a "rural problem" until the 'fifties, the State Convention now began to find itself confronted with an "urban problem." Whereas in 1950 the population was 67.0 percent rural, by 1960 it was 57.2 and by 1970 only 50.0 percent rural. Altogether the trend proved financially beneficial. Whereas in 1951 Arkansas Baptists gave $778,251 to the Cooperative Program, in 1978 they gave $6,040,919. Simultaneously the number of part-time churches dwindled away to nothing by 1967. Most church programs thrived.

Some difficult times, however, did loom up to vex both church and society. In the mid-fifties the whole nation focused attention on Little Rock as the schools there became the showcase for applying the United States Supreme Court decision of 1954. Racial tensions, sometimes subdued and sometimes openly erupting, shattered the "ease in Zion." While Arkansas Baptists responded in mixed ways,

315

they deserve some credit for the efforts of persons such as Congressman Brooks Hays to secure acceptance of the law and to work toward peaceful implementation. In addition, church leaders obviously stepped up their long even if modest efforts to create a closer working relationship with black Baptists. At the time of writing, in cooperation with the Home Mission Board of the Southern Baptist Convention, Arkansas Baptists were developing an increasingly close and well-funded cooperative relationship with two National Baptist groups.

Meantime, church-state relationships, already becoming complex in the preceding period, grew still more vexatious. Ouachita College, on the brink of extinction at the beginning of this period, recovered and thrived during the 'fifties and 'sixties. To compete with institutions of higher learning supported by public funds, however, it was forced to decide whether to expand its participation in the public bounty or to find vastly enlarged support from church sources. Arkansas Baptist Hospital, already private in all but name, was released by the Convention in 1966 so as to permit it to solve problems stemming from federally subsidized health programs.

As often happens in periods of relative prosperity, internal strife arose, presenting Arkansas Baptists with the most serious challenge to cooperative effort since 1901. As in the latter period, this resurgence of Landmark views again posed starkly the question of Baptist identity. By Convention vote the cherished Landmark tenets concerning "closed communion" and "alien immersion" became tests of fellowship. For a time four churches were excluded from the Convention.

Consolidating the Corporation

The post-war years were a time of consolidation in the Arkansas Baptist State Convention. Since organization has figured so prominently in the success of the Convention, it will be worth our while to examine briefly the major lines along which consolidation occurred.

The trend toward consolidation of the Convention's work under an Executive Board which was begun in the nineteenth century continued during this period. Although Arkansas Baptists pulled back from this briefly in 1921, when they revived the Missions Board momentarily, they resumed it again in 1926. The depression, of course, derailed the fiscal gains which this move entailed, and it was not until after the Second World War that economic circumstances allowed Arkansas Baptists to resume their consolidation efforts. In the interim, as we saw in the previous chapter, they expended most of their energies paying their debts.

As soon as the War ended, they resumed their consolidation. In 1946 the Convention, updating its Constitution, added a set of By-Laws which, among other things, spelled out explicitly the powers of the Executive Board to make decisions and to act on the Convention's behalf between sessions, "provided that it shall never exercise any authority contrary to the expressed will of the Convention." This lengthy article merits quotation in full:

> *The Executive Board, being the legal trustees of the Convention shall be empowered by the Convention to administer all business committed to it by the Convention.*
>
> *The Executive Board is empowered to act for the Convention between sessions of the Convention, provided that it shall never exercise any authority contrary to the expressed will of the Convention.*
>
> *When any unforeseen emergency occurs in any of the affairs of the Convention, or in any of the interests it controls, that in the judgment of the Executive Board requires action before the next session of the Convention, the Executive Board shall have full authority to take such action as may seen necessary, and all interests concerned shall be governed by such action, provided the Executive Board shall make full report of all matters pertaining thereunto to the next session of the Convention for its approval, and provided further, that nothing in this article shall be construed as giving the Executive Board authority to execute any matter already committed by the Convention to any of its Boards of Trustees of its Institutions unless such Board when so commissioned shall decline to act on the orders of the Convention.*
>
> *All proposals requiring the expenditure of money by the Convention, or the Executive Board of the Convention, from the annual budget, shall be considered by the Executive Board, before being presented to the Convention.*
>
> *This Board shall be charged with the responsibility to have the books and financial affairs of each and all of the Boards and Institutions of the Arkansas Baptist State*

317

*Convention audited annually by an accredited firm of
auditors, all audits to be accessible to the Executive
Board at its budget planning session, and to be included
in the Institutions Report to the Convention.*

*Members of the Executive Board, having served one
term of three years shall not be eligible for re-election
until as much as one year has elapsed.*[1]

Since 1946, the powers of the Executive Board have remained
intact, but its composition has changed. Consisting since 1926 of 15
members at large plus one additional member "from the bounds of
each co-operating Association," in 1954 the Board was revamped.
Thenceforth it was to consist of one member "from the bounds of
each co-operating association with a membership up to 5,000, and
one additional member for each additional 5,000 constituency, or
major fraction thereof," provided that no association would have
more than five members. In 1969 the constituency was enlarged by
including "one lady from the bounds of each of the eight districts in
the state."

More important for effecting the objectives of the Convention,
the managerial structures have undergone several revisions. It will
not be necessary or possible to note the many minor shifts which
occurred through the years, but two significant changes may be noted
in connection with the appointment of new executive secretaries.
Following the retirement of Ben L. Bridges after twenty-seven years,
the Executive Board voted to do a self-survey, using a committee
made up of Board members, members of the staff, the new Executive
Secretary, S.A. Whitlow, and his Associate.[2] The survey led to the
addition of a business manager and a field representative for
retirement plans, a program jointly operated with the Annuity Board
of the SBC, and reorganization along lines of the division plan
represented by Diagram A. This plan called for representatives from
each of the divisions—Religious Education, Missions, Business
Management, and the **Arkansas Baptist Newsmagazine**—to work
in the eight districts of the state. A pilot project with this plan in the
Division of Religious Education, however, led to its termination
before its four-year trial period was over (1962-1966). Among the
reasons cited for its failure were: (1) lack of information about it, (2)
too rapid turnover in personnel, and (3) negative responses from
some associations.

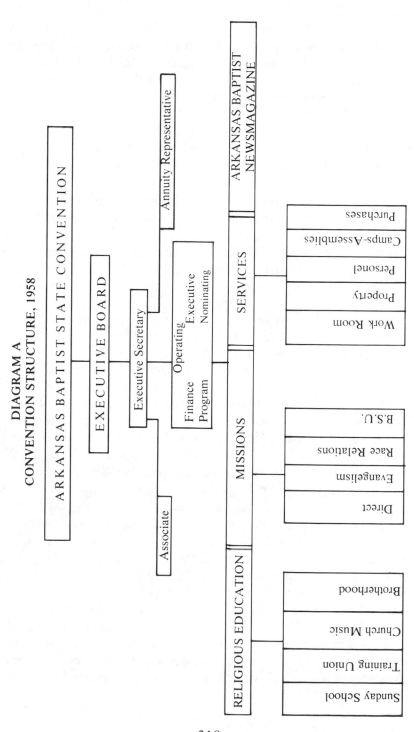

DIAGRAM A
CONVENTION STRUCTURE, 1958

ARKANSAS BAPTIST STATE CONVENTION

EXECUTIVE BOARD

Executive Secretary

Associate

Annuity Representative

Finance
Operating
Executive
Nominating
Program

ARKANSAS BAPTIST
NEWSMAGAZINE

RELIGIOUS EDUCATION

MISSIONS

SERVICES

Sunday School
Training Union
Church Music
Brotherhood

Direct
Evangelism
Race Relations
B.S.U.

Work Room
Property
Personel
Camps-Assemblies
Purchases

Following the employment of Charles Ashcraft as Executive Secretary-Treasurer in 1970, the Executive Board again revamped the structure of the staff, as indicated in Diagram B. The most noticeable changes from the 1958 model are the abandonment of the divisional structure in favor of a departmental one under the direction of the Executive Secretary-Treasurer and expansion of the role of Assistant or Associate Executive Secretary-Treasurer. One may notice at a glance the program emphases of the Convention. These obviously represent the culmination of more than a century of development.

One new development of this period, the Arkansas Baptist Foundation, merits special comment. The leading factors in its formation after the Second World War included: (1) the Convention's experiences of financial reversals, (2) the closing of the Bottoms' estate, which brought into focus the potential gifts available for Baptist causes, and (3) a growing recognition of the importance of common planning for the support of Baptist institutions.

Though originally proposed in 1946,[3] the Foundation was not chartered until 1948 and did not get its first director until June of 1950. Its stated purpose was to "secure and invest trust funds for the best interests of all concerned," specifically "as directed by the donor" or, if undesignated, as decided by the Convention.[4] As Table XXXIV indicates, the Foundation idea caught on slowly. Its first three directors served short terms, the last part-time and without pay for part of his term. In 1960 the Foundation report sounded a note of frustration with its inability to obtain "the proper director for the Foundation work," but it concluded on an optimistic note.[5] The next Executive Secretary, Ed F. McDonald, stayed with the job eleven years (1961-1972), but the plan did not jell fully even then. Foundation minutes reveal a carryover of uncertainty and confusion about its aims and efforts. The election of Charles Ashcraft as Executive Secretary-Treasurer of the Executive Board, however, brought a new impetus in the 1970s. Organizer of the Baptist Foundation in New Mexico, he had sufficient enthusiasm for Foundation work to generate a new confidence in its value and appropriateness. During the 'seventies, the Foundation rapidly multiplied its assets and income under Interim Executive Secretary Roy Lewis (1972-1974), the Assistant Executive Secretary-Treasurer of the Executive Board, and President Harry D. Trulove (1974-   ).

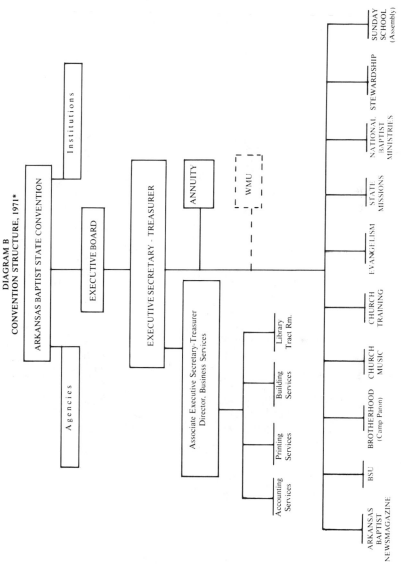

DIAGRAM B
CONVENTION STRUCTURE, 1971*

ARKANSAS BAPTIST STATE CONVENTION

Institutions

Agencies

EXECUTIVE BOARD

EXECUTIVE SECRETARY - TREASURER

ANNUITY

WMU

Associate Executive Secretary-Treasurer
Director, Business Services

Accounting Services

Printing Services

Building Services

Library Tract Rm.

ARKANSAS BAPTIST NEWSMAGAZINE

BSU

BROTHERHOOD
(Camp Paron)

CHURCH MUSIC

CHURCH TRAINING

EVANGELISM

STATE MISSIONS

NATIONAL BAPTIST MINISTRIES

STEWARDSHIP

SUNDAY SCHOOL
(Assembly)

*Adopted 1969; amended 1971, 1973, 1974, 1975, 1976.

321

TABLE XXXIV
FOUNDATION ASSETS AND INCOME, 1949-1978

Year	Assets	Income
1949	.00	.00
1950	.00	.00
1951	200.00	6.71
1952	924.00	7.00
1953	7,018.94	330.46
1954	10,556.00	405.18
1955	26,857.00	627.05
1956	42,407.00	1,658.53
1957	41,354.00	2,508.84
1958	44,892.00	2,304.68
1959	57,151.00	2,416.48
1960	68,758.00	2,517.24
1961	74,357.00	2,976.23
1962	89,536.00	3,841.22
1963	119,002.00	4,753.86
1964	137,412.00	4,441.68
1965	139,428.00	5,798.13
1966	215,304.00	5,786.97
1967	240,186.00	8,871.10
1968	258,432.00	9,870.46
1969	258,445.00	9,477.55
1970	289,247.00	16,224.42
1971	371,419.00	15,256.41
1972	412,140.00	17,620.74
1973	713,205.00	24,809.00
1974	977,109.00	55,231.00
1975	1,322,904.00	75,174.00
1976	1,686,860.00	112,373.00
1977	2,195,071.00	116,151.00
1978	2,757,547.00	

Baptist Expansion

Growth of Arkansas Baptist churches was steady if not spectacular during these years. As Table XXXV shows, the number of churches remained relatively stable. Overall membership, however, increased more than 70 percent, which indicates that the size of individual churches swelled.

TABLE XXXV
BAPTIST GROWTH, 1951-1978

Year	Associations	Churches	Membership	Baptisms
1951	45	1,064	248,080	14,612
1952	45	1,084	258,001	14,924
1953	45	1,115	265,478	13,418
1954	45	1,136	274,661	14,668
1955	45	1,146	283,820	15,037
*1956	45	1,170	292,165	13,428
1957	44	1,147	291,370	12,218
1957	44	1,147	291,370	12,218
1958	44	1,151	296,088	12,906
1959	44	1,155	298,428	12,758
1960	44	1,162	304,262	11,838
1961	44	1,163	310,504	12,787
1962	43	1,170	315,689	11,217
1963	43	1,171	321,229	10,202
1964	43	1,181	322,786	10,452
1965	43	1,195	327,759	10,435
1966	43	1,192	332,227	10,407
1967	43	1,193	337,122	11,614
1968	44	1,187	342,414	11,370
1969	44	1,187	346,422	10,731
1970	44	1,190	349,724	11,195
1971	44	1,186	356,674	12,331
1972	44	1,192	367,020	14,551
1973	44	1,197	378,117	13,899
1974	44	1,198	390,333	14,606
1975	43	1,201	398,166	14,086
1976	42	1,213	406,878	13,273
1977	42	1,229	416,338	11,492
1978	41	1,233	422,146	11,822

*Includes many churches in Michigan

An Overview

By this period we are able to make a fairly accurate comparison of the Arkansas Baptist State Convention with its peers. According to a county by county survey of the **Churches and Church Membership in the United States** for 1971 made by the Glenmary Research Center in Washington, D.C., the State Convention claimed from 25 to 35 percent of the population of 23 of Arkansas' 65 counties. In only five did it claim less than ten percent.

A comparison of Baptist growth with that of other denominations in Arkansas between 1906, when the U.S. Department of Commerce and Labor took the first of four religious censuses, and 1971 points up the remarkable character of the State Convention's story. Assessed by any standard, the growth was phenomenal. As Chart 1. indicates at a glance, whereas most of the larger religious bodies in Arkansas grew slowly, after 1936 the Convention shot skyward like a rocket. Actually, only the Roman Catholic and United Methodist Churches experienced significant increases during the same period. The Catholic Church, of course, benefited from migration back toward the South as well as its own missionary efforts. The United Methodist Church owed a significant part of its numerical upsurge to mergers, concluded recently with the union of the Methodist Church and the Evangelical and United Brethren.

How does one account for the astonishing increase of the Arkansas Baptist State Convention between 1936 and 1971? Recently Fundamentalists have been arguing that it is due to commitment to biblical inerrancy. However, all of the data we have compiled here would make that a negligible consideration at best. Most Arkansas churches fit a conservative mold, and the figures compiled in Appendix H-1 prove that many denominations more conservative than Southern Baptists, among them Missouri Synod Lutherans, have made little headway in Arkansas. On the contrary, many have withered on the vine. We must look elsewhere for an answer.

Since Methodists and Baptists have competed on fairly equal terms during much of their history in Arkansas, part of the answer lies in what they had in common. Three things stand out here: First, both got an early start in Arkansas. Yet we must not press this point too strongly, for Presbyterians also got an early start but have had limited numerical success. Far more significant, Methodists and Baptists both entered Arkansas with an intense evangelistic or missionary drive. Until the 1930s, Methodists maintained a more or less single-minded commitment to evangelism, just as Southern Baptists did. In the late 'thirties, however, they bifurcated their aims as they turned their attention toward reunion of divided Methodist bodies. The first major step occurred in 1939 with the merger of three Methodist groups: Methodist Episcopal Church, Methodist Episcopal Church South, and Methodist Protestant Church. Subsequently Christian unity has tended to occupy the more prominent place in Methodist thinking, and Southern Baptists, never wavering in their missionary zeal, have outstripped them.

CHART I.
COMPARATIVE CHART OF GROWTH OF RELIGIOUS BODIES

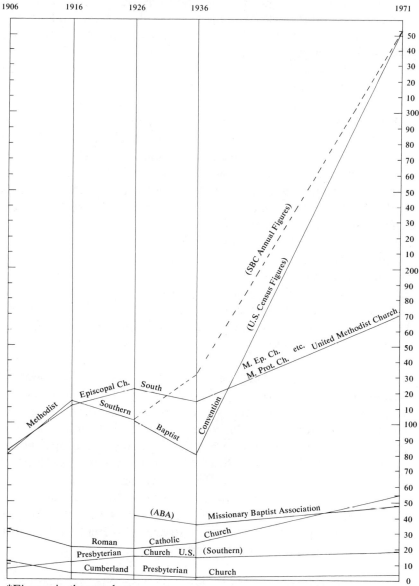

*Figures in thousands.

Figures for 1906, 1916, 1926, 1936 from U.S. Dept. of Commerce, Bureau of the Census, **Religious Bodies;** for 1971 from Douglas W. Johnson, et al., **Churches and Church Membership in the U.S.**

A third factor which these two groups have shared is the organization to carry out evangelistic aims. Early on, Methodist circuit riders and Baptist farmer preachers planted the seed all over the frontier. Niether group let the problem of distance stand in the way. Subsequently both developed organizations which would continue the work of evangelism and church planting. These organizations touched all levels. Southwide and statewide organizations served to prime the pump, as we have noted several times before, at local levels. They enabled Methodists and Baptists to develop and sustain subsidiary agencies such as schools and hospitals which would have been impossible with local effort alone.

The importance of such coordinated effort for Baptist expansion is readily demonstrated by comparing the figures for the Arkansas Baptist State Convention and the American Baptist Association or, as it is now called, the Baptist Missionary Association. The latter has scarcely grown at all since its formation. Indeed, it probably claimed more churches and members in 1905 than it did in 1971. At any rate, whereas, according to the 1926 census, the ABA reported 560 churches and 41,281 members, in 1971 it claimed only 370 churches and 48,716 members. During the same time span, the Arkansas Baptist State Convention leaped from about 80,000 (or 135,000, using Convention statistics) to almost 360,000! Furthermore, this remarkable growth was spread more or less evenly over the entire state. Maps 8 and 9 reveal that whereas the BMA showed strength by claiming above ten percent of the populace in only eight of the 65 counties of the state, the SBC manifested such strength in 60 out of 65. More precisely, whereas the BMA could claim no county in which it registered more than 25 percent, the SBC could claim 23. The ABA counted 20 to 25 percent in only one, 15 to 20 percent in only three, and 10 to 15 in only four.

The soundest conclusion to reach regarding the expansion of the Arkansas Baptist State Convention is that it was due chiefly to unflagging commitment to the winning of adherents channeled into effective organized effort.

Mission Strategy

It would be impossible to explain fully how this expansion took place. We will have occasion later to note again the contribution of individual churches and associations. At this point our task is to call attention to the evolving strategy of the State Convention, which served, as it were, to prime the pump in the churches and associations.

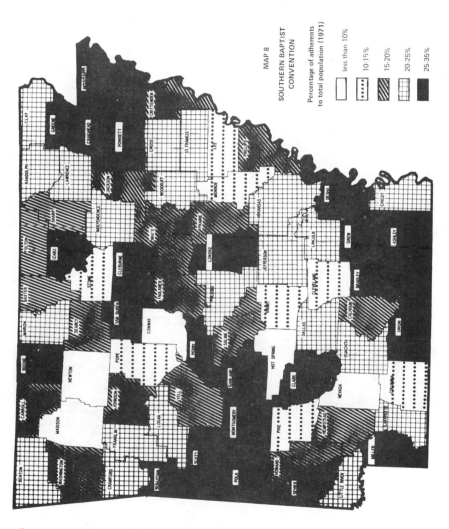

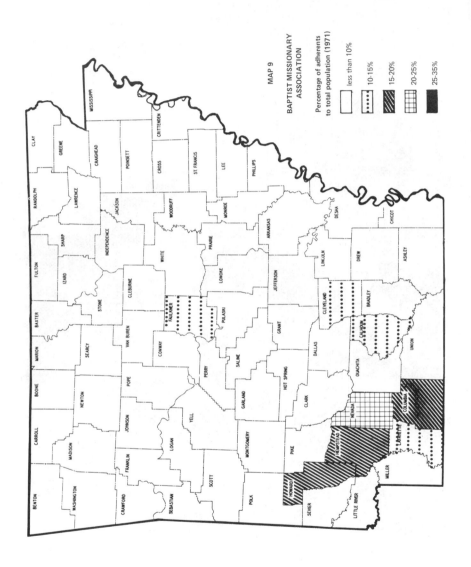

Source: Johnson, Douglas W., Paul R. Picard and Bernard Quinn. **Churches and Church Membership in the United States.** Washington, D.C.: Glenmary Research Center, 1974.

328

In the 'forties, it will be remembered, the Convention focused its sights on the rural population, recognizing the essentially agrarian character of the state. This proved to be a wise and well-timed move. But the rural areas could not remain the center of attention, for, in the 'fifties, the population began a rapid shift to urban areas. By 1970 rural and urban populations were almost equal; by 1978 the urban populace exceeded the rural.

Already in 1951, C.W. Caldwell, formerly Superintendent of Rural Missions, expanded the scope of state missions. His program included some items of longstanding concern such as supplements for salaries of associational missionaries and pastors, financial aid for church building, a chaplain at the State Sanatorium at Booneville, evangelism, and pioneer missions. But indicative of his sensitivity to the changing face of Arkansas society, the Secretary of Missions added some new emphases, notably on city missions, "services for the silent," work among migrants and work among blacks.

For **urban work** the Department of Missions employed a Superintendent of City Missions to organize mission efforts in Little Rock and other cities or large towns throughout the state. For the **deaf** it paid expenses of workers to travel from Little Rock to other cities to translate sermons into sign language. For **migrants** it prepared a program of evangelism and ministry when they entered the state during the berry and cotton-picking seasons. For **work among blacks** it employed Gwendoline Luster, whose salary formerly was paid by the W.M.U., to continue work with black women and youth; gave financial help to Arkansas Baptist College in Little Rock and to Morris-Booker Memorial College in Dermott; planned a special "dollar days offering" for Christian education of blacks; and sponsored leadership conferences.[6]

In the wake of the Little Rock school crisis the State Convention shifted its priorities in black-white relationships. In 1958 it removed work among blacks from the Department of Missions and created a separate Department of Race Relations, whose tab was jointly paid by the Convention (60%) and the Home Mission Board of the Southern Baptist Convention (40%). We will look more closely at this new program in a later section.

During this same era, the Department of Missions expanded its **institutional outreach.** As we have noted, it had long employed a chaplain at the State Sanatorium. In 1952 it hired a chaplain to serve at the Boys Industrial School in Pine Bluff. In 1968 the Convention secured a full-time Director of Chaplaincy in cooperation with the

Home Mission Board. In 1970 it added two more chaplains, one for Cummins Prison and the other for the Arkansas Children's Colony. By late 1972 it employed five full-time chaplains to work in state institutions. In addition to the TB Sanatorium, the Boys Training School, and Cummins, cooperative arrangements were made with the Girls Training School at Alexander and the Hot Springs Rehabilitation Center. In addition, other Baptists were employed as chaplains in hsopitals, institutions, industries, and at the Air Base in Little Rock.

In the late 'sixties the Missions Department awakened to a new field in Arkansas' popular resort areas. With Home Mission Board assistance, in 1969, it hired six summer missionaries to work in this ministry.[7] Simultaneously it zeroed in on week-day ministries such as day-care centers or kindergartens, youth "rap-in" centers, mothers' clubs, after-school care centers, senior citizens groups, literacy classes, etc.

In the 'seventies, the Department of Missions reinforced its long term commitments: assistance to churches, salary supplements for associational missionaries and pastors, chaplaincy, deaf ministries. In cooperation with the Home Mission Board, however, it accentuated church extension and language missions. Church extension involved employment of a Field Missionary for Church Extension to investigate and process applications for building aid grants and loans to churches with less than 300 members and to work with associations and churches in securing new sites for establishing churches. The language division continued the Department's ministry to the deaf, but it also added work among Spanish-speaking peoples and Vietnamese refugees.[8]

Evangelism

Although we have not devoted special attention to it heretofore, it would not be appropriate to gloss over the role of evangelism in the efforts of Arkansas Baptists to win their state. As a program, however, evangelism has had considerable difficulty establishing a distinct identity. The State Convention, of course, had employed "evangelists" or "missionaries," the titles being frequently interchanged, to travel about the state and hold revivals, revive churches, or do other things to foster Baptist work. During the depression, moreover, the financially strapped organization reverted to the employment of part-time evangelists as the most economical means of doing missions. But with the resuscitation of the Department of Missions evangelism again assumed a subordinate role.

330

In 1949 the Executive Board revived the question of a separate department for evangelism but reached no definite decision. With a promise of a salary supplement from the Home Mission Board a separate Department was set up in 1952. Following the retirement of I.L. Yearby as Secretary in 1958, however, the Department of Evangelism was quietly merged with the Department of Missions, both departments being headed by C.W. Caldwell. In 1969 it was again separated from the latter and Jesse S. Reed who had served several years without title, became Associate Superintendent and then Secretary.

Evangelism has been promoted on a state-wide basis in a number of ways. Early on, the chief means was the church, city-wide, or area-wide revival. Although effective in rural areas, by the present period the shift of the populace to urban areas required other emphases. As other programs, evangelism too came to depend on training and organization, not merely of professionals but of all church members. Secretary Reed thus sought to promote evangelism through WIN ("Witness Involvement Now"—lay centered evangelism) schools; WOW ("Win Our World," aimed primarily at youth); renewal evangelism; statewide, associational, and area evangelism conferences and clinics; Joy Explo Youth Evangelism Conferences; and evangelism workshops; as well as revivals.

Organizational Evangelism

To stop here, leaving the impression that Arkansas Baptists achieved their remarkable success only through direct missions or evangelism, would be misleading in the extreme. The fact is, as we have had occasion to note several times already, they effected evangelistic aims through their whole complex array of programs and institutions, which increasingly intersected with programs and institutions of the Southern Baptist Convention. Not only did they win converts, they drilled the mission idea and motive into every convert. "Each one win one" became a battle cry in generation after generation passing through Sunday school, Training Union, Girl's Auxiliary to the W.M.U., Royal Ambassadors (boys counterpart of G.A.s), W.M.U., Brotherhood, and all the rest of the Southern Baptist organizations and programs. Over and over, the faithful heard the evangelistic refrain in their churches, in giant "M-Night" ("Mobilization-Night") rallies sponsored by the Training Union, in Sunday school or other types of clinics and schools, in literature, in camps—everywhere.

Baptist use of camps offers real insight into the Southern Baptist genius for tapping popular activities to serve their missionary aims. Camping became exceedingly popular in America following the First World War. Arkansas Baptist women were among the first to seize upon this movement to foster the concerns of the W.M.U. Individual churches, associations, and the State Convention held camps first for young women (Young Woman's Auxiliary), then girls (G.A.s) and boys (R.A.s) with two objectives paramount: to effect conversions and to instill a love for missions and a sense of obligation to witness anywhere in the world. Out of these camps came not only numerous converts but also many volunteers for missions or other kinds of "full-time Christian service."

In time camp programs expanded and grew both more sophisticated and more effective. In 1953 the Brotherhood, which by this time was beginning to get its own essentially missionary vision in focus, joined the W.M.U. as sponsor of R.A. work. Three years later, it assumed full responsibility for that work.

Recognizing the value of camps and assemblies to its total program, in 1958 the State Convention placed both activities under supervision of the Executive Board with instructions to provide adequate facilities. As Arkansas Baptists outgrew their early facilities and demanded new and better accomodations, commensurate with their move up the social ladder, the Board increased appropriations and personnel for this work. At the state level this resulted in Camp Paron, construction of which was inaugurated in 1962 but not completed until 1964. Testimony of the escalating importance of camping, in 1966 Camp Paron was put on a year-round schedule. The original campers—R.A.s and G.A.s—were scheduled for the summer, other denominational and church groups for the rest of the year.

The contribution of the camps to the evangelistic and missionary goals of Arkansas Baptists are readily evident in Table XXXVI, a report from Arkansas Baptist Assembly at Siloam Springs for the years 1960 to 1977. The Assembly has made evangelistic and vocational decisions its major objectives. Bible study periods, morning devotions, and even preaching services all zeroed in on evangelism and missions.

Along with other Southern Baptists, during these years Arkansas Baptists constantly came up with new programs in camping. In 1958, following the eruption of racial strife, they developed a special facility for black children, called "Hart of the Hills" after Clyde Hart, the first Secretary for Race Relations.

Between 1960 and 1965 1,310 black children attended the camps; 54 made "professions of faith." In 1971 blacks held their first music camp. The same year, however, the State Health Department condemned "Hart of the Hills." Consequently, the next year, Arkansas brought blacks to Camp Paron as they moved toward an ever close cooperative relationship with National Baptists.

In 1969 the Arkansas Baptist Student Union and Women's Missionary Union sponsored their first International Students' Conference, attended by eighty persons. Although low key, this

TABLE XXXVI
ARKANSAS BAPTIST ASSEMBLY, 1960-1977

Year	Number of Weeks	Attendance	Conversions	Church Related Vocations
1960	4	1557	15	36
1961	3	1555	11	60
1962	3	1676		
1963	3	1790	27	81
1964	3	1721		
1965	3	1895	53	
1966	3	2115		
1967	3	2284		
1968	3	2169	57	84
1969	3	2170		
1970	3	2196	99	90
1971	3	2416	117	58
1972	4	3486	188	77
1973	4	4181	253	78
1974	5	4896	192	58
1975	5	5654	256	42
1976	5	5392	234	33
1977	5	5421	184	74

conference widened a little more the evangelistic outreach of Arkansas Baptists. But they were also keeping their eyes open to needs and opportunities at home. In 1971, responding to a surge of concern about family life, the Royal Ambassadors held their first father-son camp at Paron. In 1976 the Girls' Auxiliary followed suit with a mother-daughter camp.

Evangelism Through Nurture

One of the obvious trends among Southern Baptists in Arkansas as elsewhere during this post-War period was a lowering of the age for baptisms. Such a trend was directly connected with the increasing reliance on organized effort, especially the Sunday school, to effect the aims of the churches which we have been describing. Through instruction, as it were, children were being nurtured toward "decisions" at an earlier and earlier age.

Arkansas Baptists responded cautiously to this phenomenon. Indeed, to this date, Southern Baptists have not come to grips with its implications for their traditional understanding of baptism. Prior to 1900, when Sunday school work was still struggling to gain acceptance, it was customary for youths to make professions of faith in their twenties. As the Sunday school and then the B.Y.P.U. or other programs got a better footing, the age for "profession of faith" started dropping. In 1953 Gaines S. Dobbins, Dean of the School of Religious Education at the Southern Baptist Theological Seminary, published a rationale for directing evangelism to children, entitled **Winning the Children.** Although he made no reference to very young children, he did note that most commited members of Southern Baptist churches responded during childhood and early youth. Out of 1,000 persons polled at Ridgecrest Assembly, 30 or 40 indicated that they came before age 9, about 500 between 9 and 12, 300 between 13 and 16, 100 between 17 and 24, only 50 or 60 between 25 and 50, and not one person after 50.[9]

Since the 'fifties, an increasing number of children make decisions before age nine, some as early as the Beginners' Department in Sunday school (age 3-5). There is a nagging suspicion, of course, that such young children cannot yet make the responsible decision Christian faith requires, but the nurturing process certainly prepares them for this earlier than at any time in the past.

The Churches Inside Out

We have had occasion already to observe the shift of population in Arkansas toward towns and cities, a matter of grave consequence for the ministry of Arkansas Baptists. If previously they had to worry about Arkansas ruralism, from now on they would have to take careful notice of Arkansas urbanism. Henceforth they would have to target the cities.

Growing Urbanism

Table XXXVII indicates that the major increase in number of churches was in the cities, that is, with populations larger than 2,500. Whereas the number of open country churches declined by 21 and the number of village (under 1,000) or town (1,000-2,500) churches remained almost even, the number of city churches multiplied more than 222 percent.

The full import of this fact cannot be recorded on paper, for urbanization entails a change of outlook, ethos, and lifestyle which it is impossible to measure. As far as the churches are concerned, the most obvious consequence is that urban churches will be much larger on the average than rural ones. As Table XXXVII shows, urban churches, though fewer in number, accounted for a much larger percentage of the constituency than rural churches by 1978. Whereas in 1951 they reported less than 49 percent of the total church membership, in 1978 they claimed almost exactly 60 percent. Correspondingly, whereas in 1951 rural churches averaged less than 140 members, urban churches averaged over 782. In 1978 rural churches averaged 190, urban churches 727, a drop perhaps related to urban sprawl, causing absorption of rural or semi-rural congregations within a city area.

Increased size is generally beneficial to church programs and institutions, although, as we will note later, its long term effects will depend on extent of secularization. First to be noted here is that part-time church services all but ended during this period. The push for this, as we saw in the preceding chapter, followed World War II, but as Table XXXIX demonstrates, forty percent of Convention churches were still part-time in 1951. By 1978 that percentage had fallen to 3.5 percent, thanks to the cooperative efforts of associations, the State Convention, and the Home Mission Board of the Southern Baptist Convention. Financial affairs of the churches, always a matter of intense concern, also benefited from the urban environment. The benefit in gross income is, of course, readily evident in Table XL. Per capita, the size of contributions increased in direct proportion to size of cities, as should be clear from Chart 2. Greater income, in turn, resulted in increased gifts to missions, improved physical facilities, enlarged pastor's salaries, multiple church staffs, and more specialized programs in evangelism, education, and social ministries.

We will not take time to look at each of these areas here. Tables XLI and XLII, respectively record church property values by

TABLE XXXVII
NUMBER OF CHURCHES BY LOCATION, 1951-1978

Year	Total	Open Country	Village	Town	City	2,500 to 9,999	10,000 & up, downtown	10,000 & up, neighborhood	10,000 & up, suburban
1951	1064	500	224	181	155				
1952	1084	489	236	182	174				
1953	1115	498	238	186	193				
1954	1136	500	243	183	210				
1955	1146	511	253	163	219				
*1956	1170	514	261	158	237				
1957	1137	527	259	153	208				
1958	1151	535	250	147	219				
1959	1155	528	248	150	229				
1960	1162	536	242	147	237				
1961	1163	528	252	152	231				
1962	1170	525	256	152	237				
1963	1173	499	265	148	259	96	31	91	41
1964	1181	495	272	147	267	98	25	104	40
+1965	1195	477	275	153	290	103	30	109	48
1966	1192	475	276	160	281	106	32	98	45
1967	1193	470	269	167	287	116	20	96	55
1968	1189	472	268	159	290	107	24	102	57
1969	1187	472	271	154	290	102	22	104	62
1970	1190	473	270	158	289	101	22	103	63
1971	1186	469	265	155	297	94	26	115	62
1972	1192	466	263	161	302	96	27	114	65
1973	1197	458	266	166	307	99	28	112	68
1974	1198	460	250	174	314	97	31	107	79
1975	1201	465	230	182	324	102	32	111	79
1976	1213	480	225	178	330	107	32	111	79
1977	1229	475	234	178	342	108	37	107	90
1978	1233	479	234	175	345	112	35	108	90

*Includes churches now in Michigan.
+Begins to include inactive churches.

TABLE XXXVIII
MEMBERSHIP BY LOCATION, 1951-1978

Year	Total	Open	Village	Town	City	Suburban
1951	248,080	53,303	26,123	46,163	121,298	1,193
1952	258,001	52,933	28,077	47,887	128,556	549
1953	265,478	55,070	27,934	48,146	134,328	
1954	274,661	57,215	29,290	48,805	139,351	
1955	283,820	59,636	32,131	49,974	142,079	
*1956	292,165	59,391	32,366	48,205	152,203	
1957	291,370	61,518	32,845	48,600	148,407	
1958	296,088	62,502	32,929	47,259	153,498	
1959	298,428	64,334	32,857	47,506	153,731	
1960	304,262	65,434	32,708	48,404	157,716	
1961	310,504	66,968	34,263	51,717	157,556	
1962	315,689	67,605	35,433	52,967	159,684	
1963	321,229	65,108	37,154	52,745	167,222	
1964	322,786	64,471	37,850	50,078	170,387	
1965	327,759	57,304	38,152	50,832	181,168	
1966	332,227	58,328	37,426	52,295	184,168	
1967	337,122	59,788	36,477	54,709	186,148	
1968	342,414	58,810	38,265	54,717	190,622	
1969	346,422	58,952	39,542	54,052	193,876	

Year	Total	Open Country & Village	Town	City 2,500-9,999	City 10,000-49,999	City 50,000 & up
1970	349,724	99,243	53,518	58,916	71,479	66,568
1971	356,674	99,782	52,643	55,284	80,489	68,476
1972	367,020	99,159	55,742	57,518	82,003	72,598
1973	378,117	101,582	57,596	60,615	80,276	78,048
1974	390,333	102,719	59,750	60,197	90,567	77,100
1975	398,116	101,404	62,641	63,135	96,117	74,869
1976	406,878	105,313	62,338	64,477	99,207	75,543
1977	416,338	106,005	63,051	66,414	98,848	82,020
1978	422,146	109,403	60,661	69,430	102,488	80,164

*Includes churches now in Michigan.

TABLE XXXIX
CHURCHES CHARACTERIZED BY NUMBER OF SERVICES

Year	Total	¼-Time	½-Time	¾-Time	Full-Time	No. Svcs.	Inactive
1951	1,064	106	321	7	630		
1952	1,084	74	307	4	697	2	
1953	1,115	72	272	5	766		
1954	1,136	50	277	4	793	12	
1955	1,146	57	238	4	837	10	
1956	1,170	26	243	5	885	11	
1957	1,147	22	224	3	893	5	
1958	1,151	20	210	5	913	2	
1959	1,155	19	164	5	965	3	
1960	1,162	19	149	2	986	6	
1961	1,163	16	131	1	1,012	3	
1962	1,170	13	115	3	1,038	1	
1963	1,173	15	108	3	1,043	2	
1964	1,181	13	90	1	1,076	1	
1965	1,195	15	91	2	1,076	1	10
1966	1,192	12	75	3	1,088	2	12
1967	1,193	13	68	6	1,096	1	9
1968	1,189				1,072		
1969	1,187				1,067		
1970	1,190				1,080		
1971	1,186				1,088		
1972	1,192				1,109		
1973	1,197				1,135		
1974	1,198				1,150		
1975	1,201				1,149		
1976	1,213				1,160		
1977	1,229				1,185		
1978	1,233				1,190		

*Includes churches now in Michigan.

location and mission gifts. For those who have read this history from beginning to end, the striking feature of property values will be the affluence of Arkansas Baptists by comparison with their poverty as late as the Second World War. Between 1951 and 1978 their property increased in value almost 100 times. Part of the increase, of course, would have resulted from inflation in the American economy. In addition, however, hundreds of churches built new buildings and expanded their old ones. A similar boom occurred in institutions owned and operated by the State Convention.

TABLE XL
CONTRIBUTIONS BY LOCATIONS, 1951-1978

Year	Total	Open Country	Village	Town	City
1951	$ 7,527,641	$ 793,235	$ 516,506	$ 1,242,322	$ 4,932,791
1952	8,425,289	$ 904,956	608,513	1,405,784	5,481,945
1953	9,384,276	1,035,388	673,268	1,532,091	6,143,529
1954	9,904,377	1,091,865	712,499	1,567,442	6,542,571
1955	10,696,915	1,169,763	849,543	1,646,442	7,031,167
*1956	11,872,437	1,337,788	937,911	1,666,551	7,930,187
1957	11,749,187	1,376,359	984,280	1,722,947	7,665,601
1958	12,102,125	1,435,234	951,173	1,605,335	8,110,383
1959	12,220,408	1,589,840	925,274	1,734,053	8,971,241
1960	13,614,524	1,690,074	955,069	1,842,242	9,127,139
1961	14,353,878	1,765,435	1,040,336	2,095,509	9,462,598
1962	15,726,534	1,976,091	1,153,416	2,310,493	10,285,534
1963	16,134,920	1,915,978	1,231,042	2,218,225	10,769,675
1964	17,076,736	2,020,973	1,379,086	2,304,113	11,372,564
1965	17,042,629	1,755,047	1,350,915	2,489,411	12,347,256
1966	18,909,841	1,819,246	1,438,453	2,601,025	13,051,117
1967	20,533,828	2,172,068	1,562,148	2,734,313	14,065,295
1968	21,791,986	2,331,907	1,755,608	3,018,272	14,686,199
1969	23,365,039	2,430,513	1,847,185	2,967,126	16,120,215

Year	Total	Open Country & Village	Town	City 2,500-9,999	City 10,000-49,999	City 50,000
1970	$24,271,258	$ 4,463,943	$3,128,539	$ 4,443,412	$ 6,048,663	$ 6,186,701
1971	26,535,074	4,985,535	3,395,554	4,437,483	6,990,407	6,726,095
1972	29,942,518	5,450,374	3,959,026	4,945,288	7,905,787	7,682,043
1973	33,316,149	6,105,620	4,460,665	5,700,886	8,253,962	8,785,016
1974	38,613,987	7,434,031	5,171,105	6,336,007	10,065,079	9,607,765
1975	42,974,406	7,830,738	5,680,017	7,318,935	11,847,604	10,297,112
1976	49,053,439	9,056,992	6,641,429	8,211,177	13,575,219	11,568,622
1977	53,933,303	9,913,231	7,135,621	9,088,602	14,719,086	13,076,763
1978	61,215,545	11,303,912	7,584,894	10,367,369	17,194,912	14,764,458

*Includes churches now in Michigan.

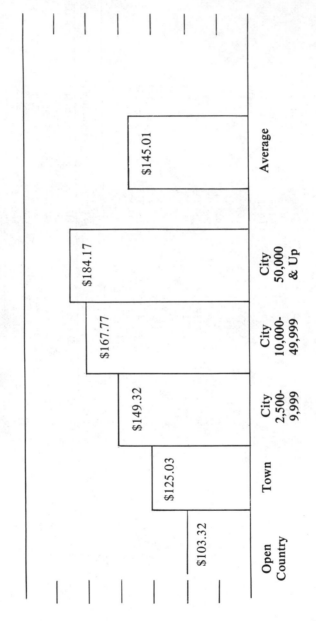

CHART 2.
CONTRIBUTIONS AND CITIES, 1978

Open Country — $103.32

Town — $125.03

City 2,500-9,999 — $149.32

City 10,000-49,999 — $167.77

City 50,000 & Up — $184.17

Average — $145.01

TABLE XLI
CHURCH PROPERTY VALUES BY LOCATION, 1951-1978

Year	Total	Open Country	Village	Town	City
1951	$ 25,609,281	$ 2,214,881	$ 1,433,449	$ 4,304,462	$17,566,489
1952	29,853,052	2,418,569	1,727,871	4,784,372	20,874,240
1953	34,515,448	2,846,740	1,931,179	5,618,472	24,118,857
1954	37,283,086	3,209,910			
1955	41,438,545	3,535,537	2,504,796	6,540,245	28,857,967
*1956	46,676,463	3,876,260	2,809,286	6,849,880	33,228,037
1957	48,663,295	4,268,331	3,021,062	7,201,072	34,172,830
1958	53,726,171	4,764,672	3,090,297	7,181,515	38,689,687
1959	57,887,934	5,241,802	3,223,926	7,545,644	41,876,562
1960	61,056,837	6,200,394	3,416,260	7,984,744	43,455,439
1961	64,909,872	6,465,042	3,663,458	9,349,454	45,431,918
1962	70,517,141	7,053,946	3,823,376	10,289,880	49,369,939
1963	76,278,640	6,961,817	4,421,294	10,062,297	54,833,232
1964	81,309,653	7,516,630	5,078,488	10,237,752	58,476,783
1965	84,024,094	6,240,594	5,295,400	10,496,040	61,992,060
1966	92,180,559	6,238,536	4,937,750	11,459,693	69,544,580
1967	97,933,803	7,083,534	5,404,074	12,021,251	73,424,948
1968	101,418,714	7,853,749	5,632,163	12,499,872	75,432,930
1969	109,713,397	8,150,835	6,634,993	13,083,708	81,843,861

Year	Total	Open Country & Village	Town	City 2,500-9,999	City 10,000-49,999	City 50,000 & Up
1970	$113,761,898	$15,577,108	$13,750,814	$22,168,965	$31,916,747	$30,348,264
1971	119,949,146	16,173,853	14,111,539	21,184,636	35,107,929	33,371,189
1972	126,828,907	17,056,258	15,283,052	22,634,390	35,598,082	36,257,125
1973	137,574,301	18,582,127	16,060,470	24,606,317	37,823,712	40,496,675
1974	154,653,737	20,631,806	17,699,077	26,714,937	45,377,617	44,230,300
1975	170,103,869	22,749,668	19,596,709	29,942,515	50,569,007	47,245,970
1976	189,890,847	26,069,627	21,994,361	32,364,261	57,386,229	52,076,369
1977	214,659,968	30,237,204	25,713,822	36,860,254	60,868,571	60,980,117
1978	248,416,508	35,902,903	29,087,676	44,089,735	72,239,302	67,096,892

*Includes churches now in Michigan.

TABLE XLII
MISSION GIFTS, 1951-1978

Year	Total	Open Country	Village	Town	City
1951	$ 1,210,824	$ 77,998	$ 56,519	$ 186,306	$ 883,331
1952	1,524,479	112,886	83,776	235,136	1,091,127
1953	1,600,499	102,398	82,446	238,082	1,177,573
1954	1,728,529	117,493	87,078	267,805	1,256,153
1955	1,872,565	130,378	107,816	291,852	1,342,519
*1956	2,110,379	151,790	129,845	299,084	1,529,660
1957	2,255,040	159,349	131,612	314,242	1,649,837
1958	2,231,653	162,760	127,117	289,515	1,652,261
1959	2,322,594	173,485	117,550	308,096	1,723,463
1960	2,414,379	183,672	119,191	333,534	1,777,982
1961	2,488,991	198,008	122,932	377,756	1,790,295
1962	2,757,055	211,666	135,867	419,057	1,990,465
1963	2,860,607	207,725	147,606	425,358	2,079,918
1964	3,027,659	231,006	164,833	427,849	2,203,971
1965	3,150,094	196,073	170,517	407,481	2,376,023
1966	3,401,756	217,781	179,601	458,594	2,545,780
1967	3,586,044	244,135	191,331	486,618	2,663,960
1968	3,889,627	274,027	213,703	533,304	2,868,593
1969	4,036,304	283,228	240,589	520,405	2,992,082

Year	Total	Open Country & Village	Town	City 2,500-9,999	City 10,000-49,999	City 50,000 & Up
1970	$ 4,180,078	$ 563,543	$ 541,281	$ 902,955	$1,050,599	$1,121,700
1971	4,915,221	651,930	652,553	980,574	1,346,986	1,283,178
1972	6,048,726	713,095	739,091	1,069,582	1,499,604	2,027,354
1973	6,451,592	805,591	800,816	1,218,450	1,542,129	
1974	7,709,938	990,175	961,881	1,397,624	2,054,968	2,305,290
1975	8,327,892	1,098,327	1,061,425	1,601,840	2,204,418	2,361,886
1976	9,180,311	1,258,608	1,221,695	1,620,168	2,508,687	2,571,153
1977	10,862,849	1,441,793	1,290,610	1,809,678	2,638,643	3,682,125
1978	13,114,272	1,604,271	1,347,871	2,012,507	2,917,877	5,231,746

*Includes churches now in Michigan.

Gifts to mission causes reflect a curious pattern by comparison with total contributions. Whereas the latter increased in proportion to the size of the city, the former varied radically in larger metropolitan areas, but not in smaller ones (under 50,000). Chart 3. illustrates that per capita mission giving in cities over 50,000 quadrupled open country, almost tripled small town, and doubled smaller city gifts. Exactly what lies behind these facts is uncertain, but they appear to confirm that urbanization works in favor of the Cooperative Program. Baptists in large urban areas obviously give more disinterestedly, that is, without regard to persons or causes, than Baptists in rural areas or small towns and cities. It should be remembered that a major objection to the Cooperative Program at the beginning was that some preferred giving to "causes" rather than a "program." In metropolitan areas Baptists seem to have lost some of their partiality and come nearer the New Testament virtue of **agape**-love than when they were largely a rural people.

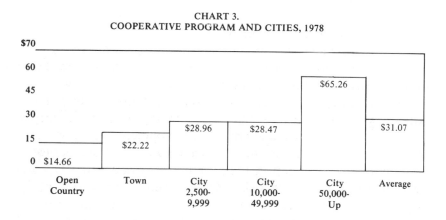

CHART 3.
COOPERATIVE PROGRAM AND CITIES, 1978

Urbanization has also helped to increase pastors' salaries in Arkansas, but, by comparison with those in the SBC as a whole, they remained woefully small. We lack complete data here, but Table XLIII reveals that, for years where information is available, the average of salaries of Arkansas pastors was at least 15 percent under the SBC average. This can be attributed partially to lower per capita income in Arkansas, but it may also show some residual "hardshell" sentiment, especially in rural areas.

TABLE XLIII
AVERAGE PASTOR'S SALARY, 1951-1969

Year	Full Time		Half Time		Quarter Time	
	SBC	Ark.	SBC	Ark.	SBC	Ark.
1951	$2,340	$2,182	$550	$409	$232	$202
1952	2,498	2,347	590	444	259	181
1953	2,666	2,520	610	488	259	188
1958	3,618	2,808				
1959	3,300	2,823				
1960	3,401	2,981				
1961	3,470	2,967				
1962	3,559	3,065				
1963	3,644	3,142				
1965	3,814	3,227				
1966	3,970	3,497				
1967	4,150	3,644				
1968	4,515	3,866				
1969	4,707	4,077				

Training in Town and Country

From a financial standpoint, then, the move toward the city has benefited the churches. What about their organizational life? Have they experienced a lift there too as a result of urbanization?

Generally speaking, the answer to this question is a mixed one. Affluence obviously has helped church programing, particularly in opening the way for new and creative developments. A comparison of participation in various church organizations with percentage of total church membership in the various areas between 1973 and 1978, however, as seen in Table XLIV, reveals some variations by area but not favorable to one over another overall. All had about the same percentage of Sunday school enrollment as they did of total church membership. Open country and village churches reflected a much higher percentage of participation in Church Training than churches in cities over 50,000. Churches in towns or cities under 50,000 enrolled more women in the Women's Missionary Union than those in open country and villages or cities over 50,000. Churches in cities with populations between 2,500 and 50,000 claimed more men for Brotherhood than the other three areas.

It would be difficult to explain all of these variations with precision, but they doubtless had something to do with variations in

TABLE XLIV
ORGANIZATION SUPPORT, 1973-1978

	1973					1974					1975				
	C.M.	S.S.	C.T.	W.M.	Br.	C.M.	S.S.	C.T.	W.M.	Br.	C.M.	S.S.	C.T.	W.M.	Br.
Open Country & Village	29.9	24.8	30.4	15.7	17.2	26.3	24.6	30.7	15.7	17.3	25.5	24.0	29.8	16.6	17.7
Town	15.2	14.4	15.1	17.3	15.0	15.3	14.5	15.5	17.9	11.8	15.7	14.5	15.7	16.8	12.0
City 2,500-9,999	16.0	16.8	15.7	23.2	25.1	15.4	16.1	15.3	21.6	24.0	15.9	16.6	15.6	22.1	21.0
City 10,000-49,000	21.2	22.7	20.1	22.6	20.2	23.2	24.6	21.1	23.7	24.3	24.1	25.2	23.0	25.4	29.9
City 50,000 & Up	20.6	21.2	18.7	20.8	22.5	19.7	20.2	17.4	20.5	22.6	18.8	19.6	15.9	18.9	19.3

	1976					1977					1978				
	C.M.	S.S.	C.T.	W.M.	Br.	C.M.	S.S.	C.T.	W.M.	Br.	C.M.	S.S.	C.T.	W.M.	Br.
Open Country & Village	25.9	24.4	31.1	16.8	16.6	25.5	23.8	30.2	15.2	17.2	25.9	24.2	30.7	15.9	16.4
Town	15.3	14.2	15.6	16.2	12.9	15.1	14.8	15.9	16.4	12.6	14.4	13.2	15.0	15.8	13.0
City 2,500-9,999	15.8	16.2	15.8	22.0	18.5	15.9	16.7	15.3	21.6	19.5	16.4	17.3	16.2	22.1	22.6
City 10,000-49,999	24.4	25.5	22.8	26.9	30.9	23.7	24.9	21.8	28.2	32.6	24.3	25.5	22.2	27.8	30.4
City 50,000 & Up	18.6	19.3	14.8	18.1	21.0	19.7	20.2	16.7	18.6	18.3	19.0	19.8	15.9	18.4	17.6

C.M.=Church Membership   S.S.=Sunday School   C.T.=Church Training   W.M.=Woman's Missionary Union   Br.=Brotherhood
All figures represent percentages of total participation in these organizations.

345

TABLE XLV
SUNDAY SCHOOL ENROLLMENT BY LOCATION, 1951-1978

Year	Total	Open Country	Village	Town	City
1951	176,008	39,096	18,120	34,423	87,280
1952	182,471	35,186	19,772	33,201	93,777
1953	188,383	37,036	19,501	33,534	98,312
1954	203,311	39,542	20,981	35,767	107,021
1955	206,455	40,476	22,476	35,170	108,333
1956	210,740	40,115	23,020	33,515	114,090
1957	205,211	40,546	22,646	33,087	108,932
1958	208,013	41,309	22,293	31,730	112,681
1959	210,036	42,683	21,413	32,226	113,714
1960	211,936	42,468	21,676	32,004	115,788
1961	215,137	43,142	22,880	34,705	114,410
1962	217,167	42,808	23,183	35,060	116,107
1963	217,048	40,126	23,698	33,535	119,689
1964	217,300	40,022	24,425	32,074	120,779
1965	214,146	34,184	22,815	32,477	124,670
1966	213,256	34,407	22,629	31,780	124,440
1967	212,393	34,498	21,427	32,015	124,453
1968	212,914	33,961	21,761	31,484	125,708
1969	209,219	33,139	22,078	29,597	124,405

Year	Total	Open Country & Village	Town	City 2,500-9,999	City 10,000-49,999	City 50,000-Up
1970	207,165	54,654	29,415	36,799	45,053	41,244
1971	205,856	53,703	28,591	33,632	48,109	41,821
1972	212,555	53,311	30,528	34,892	50,344	43,750
1973	215,927	53,678	31,175	36,301	48,983	45,790
1974	222,551	54,751	32,224	35,752	54,811	45,013
1975	226,387	54,367	32,915	37,613	57,023	44,469
1976	233,211	56,899	33,146	38,621	59,402	45,143
1977	232,694	55,496	33,366	38,817	58,003	47,012
1978	232,935	56,364	30,871	40,272	59,366	46,062

culture and lifestyles in the different areas. Sunday school had become sufficiently well established by this period that it could hold its own in all five. It should be noted, however, that the percentage of people enrolled in Sunday schools did a steady downward slide after 1954, as indicated in Table XLV and Chart 4. This trend, already visible during and after the Second World War, represents the 'negative side of urbanization, much more than the disturbances of the Vietnamese War era. If the turbulence of the 'sixties had been the main cause, there would have been a steeper drop at that time. As many recent studies of the urbanization process have indicated, the secular city rearranges the clock, the calendar, and the priorities of its citizens. It also discourages long term commitment to organizations, including Sunday schools, and encourages a more **ad hoc** relationship.

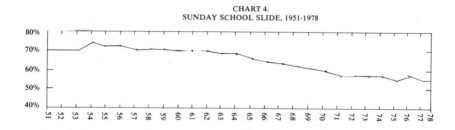

CHART 4.
SUNDAY SCHOOL SLIDE, 1951-1978

The preference of open country or village church members for Church Training is probably to be attributed to level of education as well as the fact that most of them would have fewer competing activities available on Sunday evening. Church Training, it will be recalled, was designed to supply leadership for the churches. In Arkansas it proved extremely useful for a largely rural constituency with limited education, but, as the educational level went up, interest in Church Training declined. Since the early 'sixties, as Table XLVI indicates, not only the percentage but even the number of participants has dwindled, particularly in the larger cities, where the educational level will be the highest. A revision of the program in 1971 has failed thus far to stop the decline as urbanization rolls on.

347

TABLE XLVI
TRAINING UNION ENROLLMENT, 1951-1978

Year	Total	Pct.	Open Country	Village	Town	City
1951	72,269	29.1	18,922	8,373	13,672	30,853
1952	76,249	29.5	19,391	9,623	14,239	32,725
1953	83,097	31.3	21,307	10,340	15,105	36,345
1954	90,582	33.0	22,926	11,021	15,722	40,913
1955	94,452	33.3	23,355	12,719	15,312	43,066
1956	95,663	32.7	22,854	12,490	14,766	45,553
1957	92,695	31.8	23,228	12,071	14,182	43,214
1958	93,534	31.6	23,683	11,944	14,465	44,442
1959	95,872	32.1	24,829	11,461	14,162	45,420
1960	97,604	32.1	24,863	11,430	14,291	47,020
1961	99,028	31.9	25,009	11,841	15,145	47,033
1962	99,025	31.4	24,471	12,297	15,332	46,925
1963	98,799	30.7	22,971	12,089	14,654	49,085
1964	97,030	30.1	22,235	12,173	13,589	49,033
1965	93,250	28.4	18,246	10,512	13,533	50,959
1966	91,827	27.6	17,612	10,406	13,819	49,990
1967	91,970	27.3	18,045	10,318	13,918	49,689
1968	91,926	26.8				
1969	87,782	25.3				
1970	85,494	24.4				
1971	84,326	23.6				
1972	84,772	23.1				

Year	Total	Pct.	Open Country & Village	Town	City 2,500-9,999	City 10,000-49,000	City 50,000 & Up
1973	84,009	22.1	25,506	12,723	13,199	16,898	15,683
1974	83,364	21.3	25,595	12,929	12,731	17,556	14,553
1975	83,514	21.0	24,887	13,112	13,007	19,237	13,271
1976	83,173	20.4	25,861	12,952	13,114	18,958	12,288
1977	80,321	19.3	24,246	12,812	12,279	17,542	13,442
1978	80,105	19.0	24,636	11,984	13,013	17,749	12,718

Larger Woman's Missionary Union and Brotherhood enrollments in cities ranging between 2,500 and 50,000 (Tables XLVII and XLVIII) is probably to be explained by the small city atmosphere. Open country, villages, and towns may have too few residents to encourage this type of activity. On the other hand, larger cities offer many additional options. Smaller cities have sufficient population and yet do not offer too many competing activities. As regards W.M.U., moreover, women in rural areas and in large cities are more likely to be employed full-time outside the home than women in intermediate size cities.

Both W.M.U. and Brotherhood suffered serious erosion during this period. It is likely that this decline was due not only to the social factors mentioned but, as was true of Church Training, to lack of a clear purpose. As we saw in the preceding chapter, the Brotherhood had great difficulty defining its purpose so as to make it attractive to Baptist laymen in Arkansas. To be the counterpart of W.M.U. was not adequate. In the late 'forties it found a **raison d'être** in evangelism and prospered until the early 'sixties. Even a reorganization in 1960, however, failed to keep Brotherhood from sliding downhill thereafter.

From its beginning in 1888 the W.M.U. had had a clear challenge and purpose—to raise funds to support the missionary or other endeavors of the State Convention and the Southern Baptist Convention. It carried a major part of the Convention's financial load during the latter's most trying years. When the Convention finally settled its huge depression debt in 1952, the W.M.U. supplying the last sum, a new but not very promising day dawned for the W.M.U. Although it could spell out some major areas of concern—prayer, study of missions, stewardship, community missions, and missionary education of young people—it lacked henceforth the do-or-die challenge of the past. The Convention no longer existed marginally as it had for many years. Even with a revamping of the whole W.M.U. program in the 'sixties the organization failed to stop the drain on its rolls caused by a rapidly changing social situation.

TABLE XLVII

W.M.U. ENROLLMENT BY LOCATION, 1951-1978

Year	Total	Open Country	Village	Town	City
1951	31,827	2,733	2,480	7,267	19,105
1952	34,439	3,309	2,594	7,721	20,641
1953	35,226	3,531	2,686	7,571	21,438
1954	38,505	4,545	2,901	8,264	22,795
1955	36,574	4,344	2,676	7,743	21,811
1956	36,375	4,163	2,818	7,097	22,297
1957	36,459	4,295	2,653	7,195	22,316
1958	37,907	4,774	3,075	7,284	22,774
1959	38,931	5,154	2,894	7,467	23,416
1960	38,109	5,002	3,076	7,176	22,855
1961	38,136	5,057	3,200	7,560	22,319
1962	37,303	5,242	3,439	7,584	21,038
1963	37,735	4,534	3,536	7,087	22,314
1964	36,615	4,250	3,321	6,723	22,071
1965	35,842	3,281	2,581	6,376	23,447
1966	34,208	3,122	2,523	6,014	22,312
1967	34,687	3,236	2,495	6,037	22,668
1968	34,993	3,306	2,618	5,728	23,160
1969	31,672	2,762	2,507	5,069	21,204

Year	Total	Open Country & Village	Town	City 2,500-9,999	City 10,000-49,999	City 50,000 & Up
1970	28,835	4,682	4,520	6,698	7,141	5,674
1971	27,606	4,598	4,275	5,861	7,263	5,434
1972	27,184	4,503	4,139	6,192	6,855	5,400
1973	26,103	4,111	4,524	6,070	5,892	5,431
1974	26,296	4,131	4,716	5,694	6,230	5,400
1975	26,276	4,356	4,416	5,822	6,676	4,961
1976	26,298	4,411	4,253	5,785	7,081	4,768
1977	26,958	4,093	4,433	5,814	7,593	5,025
1978	25,499	4,057	4,031	5,645	7,081	4,685

TABLE XLVIII
BROTHERHOOD ENROLLMENT BY LOCATION, 1951-1978

Year	Total	Open Country	Village	Town	City
1951	6,564	684	401	1,005	4,474
1952	7,522	929	565	1,265	4,763
1953	8,436	1,095	572	1,519	5,250
1954	9,191	1,123	942	1,618	5,508
1955	8,718	1,632	836	2,035	7,439
1956	8,781	1,463	751	2,030	7,830
1957	9,419				
1958	10,829	1,371	790	1,788	6,880
1959	11,425	1,623	696	1,818	7,288
1960	10,895	1,538	816	1,648	6,893
1961	10,180	1,610	761	1,737	6,072
1962	9,730	1,515	646	1,785	5,784
1963	9,601	1,314	522	1,709	5,969
1964	9,605	1,313	641	1,540	6,111
1965	6,712	701	414	885	4,712
1966	5,979	636	274	944	4,125
1967	6,136	626	291	793	4,426
1968	5,736	501	350	829	4,056
1969	5,114	423	251	602	3,838

Year	Total	Open Country & Village	Town	City 2,500-9,999	City 10,000-49,999	City 50,000 & Up
1970	4,518	638	502	1,402	986	990
1971	9,001	1,472	988	2,300	2,293	1,948
1972	9,324	1,564	1,255	2,538	1,940	2,027
1973	8,645	1,489	1,295	2,174	1,745	1,942
1974	8,491	1,471	1,004	2,036	2,061	1,919
1975	8,940	1,584	1,074	1,881	2,672	1,729
1976	9,016	1,500	1,164	1,665	2,793	1,894
1977	9,644	1,655	1,216	1,882	3,146	1,765
1978	9,214	1,508	1,199	2,085	2,802	1,620

Urbanization and Worship

Urbanization left its stamp on many facets of Arkansas Baptist church life, including worship. During the 1950s, youth took an increasingly prominent leadership role in it. Many churches began to observe youth week, calling on young people to testify, sing, pray, preach, and lead in worship. Youth revival teams fanned out from the colleges to hold "youth revivals." In the 'sixties and 'seventies guitars, banjos, saxophones, drums and a variety of musical ensembles became acceptable in many churches. The guitar was especially popular. Moreover, folk songs and gospel music, adapted from pop music of the era, made inroads into the churches. In some areas of the state Stamps-Baxter music, once on the way out, experienced a revival. Some churches in northeast Arkansas were putting Stamps-Baxter and Baptist hymnals side by side in the pew racks on the backs of their pews. Baptist worship had turned full circle.

Arkansas Baptists continued to whet their musical appetites during the period under discussion. In 1952 the Convention created a separate Church Music Department, "operating on an equal basis with all other departments of Arkansas Baptist activity."[10] That same year, the Department held its first summer Youth Music Camp. More and more churches hired professional ministers of music, developed graded programs in music for all ages, assembled orchestras and handbell groups, outfitted choirs in robes, and added in many other ways to the formalities of worship. In 1965 Arkansas churches reported 22,909; in 1977 29,429 persons enrolled in choirs.[11] Reflective of burgeoning music appreciation and tastes, whereas in 1965 they reported 48 persons devoting their time to music alone or music in combination with other roles, in 1977 they counted 113. For the latter year this total broke down into 15 full-time ministers of music, 70 full-time ministers of music and youth, 11 full-time ministers of music and education, four full-time ministers of music and administration, one youth music director, and ten other persons working as ministers of music with other responsibilities.[12]

True to the general thrust of the Southern Baptist program, Arkansas musicians tied their work to missions and evangelism. At the Junior Music Camp held at Ouachita College in 1966, for instance, participants collected funds to send a set of twenty-five handbells to missionaries in Recife, Brazil.[13] In 1972 twenty men and seven women journeyed to Alaska to assist in revivals and to lead in church music advancement in that state as a part of the Alaska

Cooperative Mission Project.[14]

During the 1950s and 1960s, Sunday morning worship in Arkansas Baptist churches continued its trend toward greater formality, though evening services remained more or less informal. In 1963, Brooks Hays and John E. Steely, both Arkansans, remarked, "Now becoming more common, and probably representing the dominant trend among Baptist churches in America, is the Sunday morning service which is carefully planned in detail."[15]

In the late 'sixties and 'seventies even smaller Baptist churches reflected the affluence which came with urbanization. Many churches acquired baptistries, organs, padded pews, carpeted floors, choir robes, printed bulletins, stained glass windows, nurseries, trained song leaders if not choir directors, well educated pastors, and other features which added to the enjoyment and beauty of worship.

Capitalizing on the post-War technological boom, some churches began televising their Sunday morning worship services in the late 1950s and early 1960s. Some, taking advantage of the fact that they were located in cities having television stations, shared their worship hour with areawide audiences.

In order to reach an increasingly mobile population with irregular schedules, many churches began scheduling early Sunday services at 8:30 a.m. before Sunday school or, in a few cases, shifted to an early schedule altogether during the summer. Some set up special services at local motels or hotels to accomodate travelers or, during the summer, arranged for evening services at nearby parks and resorts.

Ministers and Urbanization

Urbanization has eased many burdens, but it has also created new ones and placed them on the backs of people in the cities. Among those who reflected the stress of the new social situation were ministers. During the 'fifties and 'sixties, an ever larger percentage of ministers resigned their churches and took employment elsewhere, unable to cope with the demands, strain, and conflict of church situations.

Arkansas, being behind much of the nation in the urbanization process, did not take note of the "crisis" in ministry until the early 'seventies. In 1974, however, the State Convention appointed a Study Committee on Ministry composed of four lay persons, two associational missionaries, six pastors, a faculty member in the religion department at Ouachita and in Southern Baptist College, and two members of the Executive Board. The Committee was instructed (1) "To survey available literature and current efforts being made in the provision of helps for pastors and persons in other Church related vocations, and their families"; (2) "To consider several approaches to help the above persons"; and (3) after study, to make appropriate recommendations to the Convention.[16]

The committee's study, reported at the 1975 Convention, delineated areas of stress for both pastors and their wives. As regards **pastors,** it called attention to inadequate prayer time and prayer life, insufficient Bible study, "feelings of inadequacy" in fulfilling demands of their calling, overwork, tensions in administration and staff relations, problems with deacons, too many church services, lack of provision for continuing education, financial problems, family difficulties, and lack of time to spend with families. As regards **wives** of pastors, it noted feelings of loneliness and isolation with no one to talk to in times of stress, ambivalence regarding the role of the pastor's wife, feelings of being "left out" of conferences and conventions, financial inadequacies, and marital conflict due to lack of time with husbands.

The committee posited the "basic" solution in "the indwelling Lord Jesus Christ." But it also made some practical recommendations: (1) continued study of the problem by a committee appointed by the Convention president; (2) "the development of seminars, institutes, and conferences to assist the ministry of our churches in meeting the challenge of stress," giving primary attention to "the prayer life of the minister and his family," "the Biblical approach to stress solutions," and "the minister's family life"; (3) provision of funds for pastors' and staff members' wives to attend conventions with their husbands; and (4) further study of such areas of "supportive pastoral help" as continuing education, available resource materials and persons, and sources of professional help in situations requiring it. In addition, the committee recommended, from the negative side, "That no new staff person be employed or office be created by our State Convention to deal with this problem."[17] The latter recommendation bears an obvious reference to an Executive Board effort to set up an "Office of Information Services" in 1973, a proposal which the Convention rejected.[18]

Baptists and Their Peers

One would expect evidences of the impact of urbanization noted in the preceding section—on finances, programs, worship, and the ministry—to turn up also in Baptist dealings with their peers. Recent sociological studies of religion have shown, among other things, that the typical urban congregation is a composite of many denominations. The average Baptist congregation, for instance, will consist of persons of Presbyterian, Luthern, Methodist, Episcopal, or even Roman Catholic background and basic outlook. A larger percentage may have Baptist backgrounds and have stronger commitment to the Baptist tradition, but the constituency is highly diversified. The same will be true of the other denominations as well.

The effects of pluralism should be fairly obvious. Church members usually are more tolerant of the views of others and less dogmatic about their own. They participate more readily in ecumenical ventures, for example, to promote a higher level of public morality. But, perhaps surprisingly at first glance, they do not have a greater intensity of concern for merging with others; they are experiencing enough church unity the way things stand.

As on so many other issues, here too Arkansas Baptists present a mottled picture, vividly colored by their Landmarkism. Early on in this era, they often reiterated the "non-cooperative" stance of earlier years. In 1951, for instance, the Executive Board observed that it declined to "co-operate with movements other than those under the direction of Baptist churches."[19] Two years later, they urged, "Let us pray that our Foreign Mission Board will never yield to the clamor of Pedo-baptists and ecumenical movements to divide up the world and let Baptists of the South take a minor segment of the Mission field."[20]

Practical necessity, however, did not encourage non-cooperation. Arkansas Baptists, suspicious as they were of ecumenical groups, were quite capable of linking up with others when it served their purposes. For years, as we saw in the preceding chapter, they lent their support to the Anti-Saloon League of America. They also rallied behind its successor, the Temperance League of Arkansas. In 1958 S.A. Whitlow, newly appointed Executive Secretary of the Arkansas Baptist State Convention, was among the leaders of a merger of the latter organization with the Arkansas Civic and Morality Foundation to form the Christian Civic Foundation of Arkansas. The first officers of this organization included three Baptists: Tom Digby, Jr. as President, Rheubin L. South as Second Vice-President, and Paul Meers as Third Vice-President. All presidents of the organization except one have been Baptists; all three Executive Directors—William E. Brown, W. Henry Goodloe, and Edward W. Harris—Methodists. For a number of years Arkansas Baptist churches engaged in friendly rivalry with Methodists to see who could offer the largest financial support to the Foundation. Baptists also played a prominent role in the organization of the Churches United Against Gambling (CUAG) in 1964. Ralph Phelps, Jr., President of Ouachita, served as the first president. Five Baptists held places on the nineteen member executive committee. CUAG dedicated itself to doing "everything in our power to keep legalized gambling out of Arkansas." As so often in earlier periods, Arkansas Baptists appealed in 1968 "to all the Baptists of Arkansas and all Christians" to join in fighting a mixed-drink bill which was about to be submitted to the Arkansas legislature.[21]

Baptists and Roman Catholicism

The one area of ecumenical relations where one would expect to find the least change would be in Baptist-Catholic encounters. Baptist watchfulness regarding the separation of church and state almost assured that they would deal cautiously with Catholics. Nevertheless, in the present period, some changes of attitude are visible on both sides.

In a later section we will discuss the thorny problem of church and state in which Baptists had to be careful not merely for Roman Catholics but also for themselves. More illuminating for Catholic-Baptist relations is the 1960 presidential election. Whereas in 1928 Arkansas Baptists had initially opposed Al Smith on the grounds of his opposition to prohibition, this time they sounded their alarm about John F. Kennedy on the grounds that he was a Roman Catholic. In 1959, when Kennedy's candidacy was merely being rumored, the State Convention went on record as opposing "the candidacy of any Roman Catholic for President of the United States, in the interest of religious liberty." The resolution proceeded to clarify that the opposition was "not directed at the freedoms of the Catholic people but at the allegiance they have to a foreign person who is outside the United States, and above the laws and governing forces of the United States."[22] The next summer, the Executive Board of the Convention named a committee composed of the President of the Convention, the President of the Executive Board, the Executive Secretary of the Convention, and the Editor of the **Arkansas Baptist** "to do what it could to alert the Baptists of the state to certain threats to religious liberty should a Catholic be elected President of the United States."[23] The committee sponsored a mass meeting on religious liberty in Little Rock on September 3, 1960, inviting Glenn L. Archer, Executive Director of Protestants and Other Americans for Separation of church and State, and an attorney and active Methodist layman, to speak.

Not all Arkansas Baptists took such a decisive stance. Only about 500 to 600 persons turned out for the rally in Little Rock on September 3.[24] To Baptists' credit, moreover, after Kennedy's election the State Convention pledged him "prayers and support

356

toward improving the total well-being of our nation and to maintaining peace throughout the world" and especially "efforts in the interest of maintaining our cherished American heritage of religious liberty."[25]

From this date on, some of the earlier stridency in the tone of references to Roman Catholicism diminished as Roman Catholics improved their image during the pontificate of John XXIII (1958-1962) and through the Second Vatican Council. Kennedy, of course, helped by adhering carefully to a promise to uphold separation of church and state. Nevertheless, Arkansas Baptists remained vigilant about the church-state issue, if for no other reason than that they were battling it themselves in connection with their schools and hospitals. In 1972 the State Convention gave a hint of old suspicions of Roman Catholicism when it issued a reminder to persons seeking public office that they opposed the use of public monies for the support of private or parochial education.[26]

In at least one area Arkansas Baptists leaned toward Roman Catholics, reflecting the potpourri which characterized the religious scene in the 1970s and the extensive cross fertilization taking place in the secular city. In 1978 the State Convention adopted a "pro-life" statement on abortion. The wording of the resolution itself reflects a mixture of Baptist and Roman Catholic traditional phrases and ideas.

> *WHEREAS, Baptists are "People of the Blood", and*
>
> *WHEREAS, the Bible teaches that all life is of God (Jer. 1:4-5; Ex. 21:22-26) from the moment of conception, and*
>
> *WHEREAS, the practice of abortion wantonly destroys fetal life, dulls our society's moral sensitivity, and leads to a cheapening of all human life, and*
>
> *WHEREAS, the practice of abortion encourages and supports the practice of permissive sex outside of marriage, therefore be it*
>
> *RESOLVED, that the presiding officer of this convention write the Arkansas Hospital Association, the State Medical Board, and Arkansas News-Media, informing them of our position, and be it further*
>
> *RESOLVED, that we as pastors and churches of this convention inform our people of the wrong of this practice.*[27]

Resurgence of Landmarkism

In the context of the kind of evolution of attitudes toward other denominations visible here it is curious at first glance that Arkansas Baptists would experience a resurgence of the Landmark blood which courses through their veins. On fuller reflection, however, this should not come as a surprise. Religious groups always experience opposite tendencies in times of rapid change. Roman Catholics, for instance, "opened the windows," as Pope John XXIII called the renewal movement, at the Second Vatican Council; since that date (1962-1965), they have oscillated between reactionary and progressive poles. Arkansas Baptists did the same in the period under discussion.

During the early 'sixties, several Arkansas churches were loosening up on the Landmark rejection of "alien immersion" (that is, immersion on profession of faith in non-Baptist churches) and "open communion" (that is, communion with persons not of "like faith and order"). The First Baptist Church of Russellville did so formally after an in-depth study of the New Testament regarding the ordinances led by the pastor, Charles B. Thompson. As a consequence of their study, they adopted a position on baptism and communion shared by many other Southern Baptist churches but which in Arkansas, so effactually molded by the teachings of J.R. Graves, evoked controversy.

The Church concluded that the **validity** of both baptism and the Lord's Supper depended **objectively** on "the conditions of the command of the Lord Jesus Christ and the principles set forth in the New Testament" and **subjectively** on the fact that "the person participating understands and complies with these principles." This means that both baptism and the Lord's Supper are "primarily the act, not of the administrator (as J.R. Graves had insisted), but of the person participating." On the basis of this theological judgment the Church decided to receive into its fellowship persons "who give credible testimony that they have complied or are willing to comply with" principles set forth from the New Testament and not to require baptism "in those instances where it is determined that the applicant has been properly baptized." Similarly it voted to "bar no one from the Lord's Supper who believes that he is in compliance with the command and the conditions of the Lord Jesus Christ."[28]

The storm broke first in the annual meeting of the Dardanelle-Russellville Association, October 15, 1965, held in the First Baptist Church of Russellville. After lengthy debate on a motion made by the pastor of the First Baptist Church of Dardanelle, Anton C. Uth, the Association voted by the required two-thirds majority to withdraw fellowship from the Russellville Church. Arguments that neither the State Convention nor the Southern Baptist Convention restricted fellowship on grounds being laid down by the Association proved unavailing. On the contrary, it was pointed out, the Association is an autonomous body which can establish its own requirements for membership. After messengers of the host church departed the Association voted to move to Dardanelle for the remainder of its annual meeting.[29]

The issue exploded again in November at the annual meeting of the State Convention. At the first session, on motion of Amos Greer, Pine Bluff, the Convention voted to seat all messengers except those from the First Baptist Church of Russellville, whose credentials were sent to the Credentials Committee for investigation. Subsequently the Convention, its mind made up, showed that it was in no mood to temporize as it defeated a recommendation of the Credentials Committee "that the messengers be seated, and that the matter be referred to a committee for careful study and recommendation next year."[30]

More consequential in the long run even than action taken with reference to the First Baptist Church of Russellville, the Convention set in motion a movement which would eventually lead to a Landmark interpretation of the phrase "regular Baptist Churches" in the Constitution. After defeating a motion by Don Harbuck, pastor of the First Baptist Church of El Dorado, to refer the matter to the Executive Board for study and report at the next meeting of the Convention, it adopted a strongly Landmark resolution formulated by Don Hook, pastor of the Baptist Tabernacle Church of Little Rock, who was subsequently elected President of the Convention. The resolution, cited in full, said:

> WHEREAS, in the past, the most general inter-pretation of the New Testament, and the most general interpretation of the word "principles" as it is used in Article 3, Section 1 of our constitution, and the most prevalent practice of Baptist churches in Arkansas with reference to the church ordinances, has been what is commonly called "close baptism" and "close communion", and
>
> WHEREAS, it is recorded on page 57 of the Minutes of the Arkansas Baptist State Convention meeting in Fort Smith in 1937 that the Convention officially objected to the teaching of alien immersion and

open communion in one of our Seminaries, thereby establishing a precedence for future Conventions, therefore

BE IT RESOLVED that the Arkansas Baptist State Convention, meeting in its 112th annual session, go on record as objecting to the reception of alien immersion and the practice of open communion, and

BE IT FURTHER RESOLVED that we urge churches everywhere to re-examine the New Testament teaching on baptism and the Lord's Supper, and

BE IT ALSO RESOLVED that, in addition to becoming a part of the regular minutes, this resolution, if passed, be published in the **Arkansas Baptist Newsmagazine.**[31]

The issue of the First Baptist Church of Russellville's relationship to the Arkansas Baptist State Convention continued to occupy the attention of the Convention until 1974, when the Church attempted to regain its affiliation on the basis of policy change. Meantime, in 1968, three other churches—University Baptist in Little Rock, First Baptist in Malvern, and Lake Village—were excluded on account of their policies regarding "alien immersion" and "open communion."[32] After the Convention voted 491 to 312 to "withdraw fellowship" from these churches the Convention parliamentarian, Burton Miley, ruled out of order a second motion which would have instructed the Executive Secretary not to accept mission gifts from the churches excluded.

The Convention, by no means achieving consensus on the issue, took conciliatory steps which eventually resulted in the restoration of fellowship with two of the four churches on Convention terms. In 1965 it passed a motion by L.H. Coleman that the Convention "make every effort to stay in communication with and offer assistance to this great (Russellville) church to the end that eventual fellowship can be restored between the church and our State Convention."[33] In 1966 John McClanahan, pastor of the First Baptist Church of Pine Bluff, proposed that the Convention "go on record as inviting the First Baptist Church at Russellville to attend any remaining sessions of this convention and/or future conventions."[34] But the Credentials Committee professed themselves "powerless to act since the Russellville Church has not sought to be received"[35] Following the exclusion of the other three churches in

360

1968, the Convention unanimously endorsed the formation of a "Reconciliatory Committee," which would "be available upon request, to serve in dealing with current frictional situations in churches where fellowship has been withdrawn." The motion stipulated, however, that restoration would have to follow guidelines laid down by majority vote of the Convention "concerning modes and manners of observing the Lord's Supper and receiving membership into local churches."[36] In 1971 the Convention voted to make

> *every effort to encourage the churches previously excluded from our convention to comply with our convention's stated policies for fellowship and upon evidence of their so doing their messengers be admitted as messengers of 'regular' Baptist churches upon the recommendation of the convention Credentials Committee.*[37]

By 1973 two of the excluded churches were again within the good graces of the Convention. University Baptist in Little Rock reorganized as the Lakeshore Drive Baptist Church. In 1971 it was in full fellowship with the Pulaski Baptist Association and the State Convention. Lake Village, First Baptist Church of Malvern, and First Baptist Church of Russellville sent messengers to the Convention in 1971 who were not challenged, but the churches' status remained in dispute. In 1973 the Credentials Committee overrode a challenge to seating of messengers of the First Baptist Church of Malvern on the grounds that the Church was "not in violation of the constitutional requirement for membership in the convention."[38] The First Baptist Church of Russellville had not sent messengers. In 1974, however, responding to a letter assuring "continued prayers and concern that this great Church soon be associated" with the Convention as before,[39] it did. After being inconspicuously enrolled with other messengers their seating was challenged. The Credentials Committee, after investigation, recommended seating "on the basis of the church's present practice of continuing effort to bring all past policies and resolutions into harmony with such practices, . . ."[40] Before a vote was taken, however, the messengers of the Church withdrew voluntarily "in the interest of harmony in the convention," promising to "continue to support the convention financially."[41] The First Baptist Church of Russellville sent messengers again in 1975.

In the meantime, proponents of the Landmark interpretation of the ordinances sought to establish an official sanction for their views.

In 1967, after considerable debate, the Convention approved a motion made by Carl Overton, an associational missionary, ordering search of convention minutes to discover "policies and Constitutional interpretations adopted by this convention in past years" and to append these to the Convention's Constitution and Bylaws.[42] This motion set the stage for a strict enforcement of doctrinal requirements vis-a-vis the ordinances at the next annual convention.

In 1969, on motion of Dillard S. Miller, Chairman of the Credentials Committee, the Convention authorized appointment of a committee of twenty-five persons, representing all eight of the Convention's districts, to "clarify, specify, and recommend policies regarding membership to this Convention."[43] The next year, the Committee was prepared only to recommend "AS A FIRST STEP. . . the adoption of the 1963 SBC statement of faith as DOCTRINAL GUIDELINES for the convention."[44] In 1971 the committee presented a more precise recommendation to amend the Constitution so as to define "Regular Baptist Churches" in line with the **Baptist Faith and Message.** The proposed amendment read: "Regular Baptist churches are those Baptist churches which in doctrine and in practice adhere to the principles and the spirit of 'The Baptist Faith and Message' as adopted by the 1963 session of the Southern Baptist Convention."[45] This proposal, however, did not satisfy Landmarkers. On motion of Wayne B. Davis, pastor of the Oak Grove Baptist Church, Van Buren, the Convention voted 389 to 263 to amend the Committee's recommendation, adding, ". . . and 'The Baptist Faith and Message' shall not be interpreted as to permit open communion and/or alien immersion."[46]

Formally, then, the Landmark perspective on church membership triumphed in the State Convention. It would not be right to conclude from this, however, that the victory was complete or permanent. In the decade of controversy there were a number of signs that the escalation of tolerance mentioned at the beginning of this section was making an impact. For one thing, the votes on withdrawal of fellowship in 1965 and 1968 show a large minority who opposed the Convention action. Furthermore, the amendment mentioned above carried by less than a sixty percent majority. For another thing, many churches were maintaining more open practices without formalizing their policies, a fact which assured enforcement difficulties. In 1968, for instance, John McClanahan, pastor of the First Baptist Church of Pine Bluff, queried whether the Convention was drawing a line only on churches which had voted to observe open communion or also on those with no formal policy but which practiced it. He named several churches in Arkansas to which he had belonged or which he had served as pastor, including the First Baptist Church of Pine Bluff, which actually practiced open communion. The President, Thomas A. Hinson, ruled that this was not the matter before the Convention.[47] When such considerations as these combine with such practical matters as the obstacles "close baptism" and "close communion" put in the way of fellowship and church growth in urban settings, they will create a stiff challenge to the new policy.

From a slightly different angle some were questioning whether Landmarkism did not stand opposed to itself here. It has always emphasized local church autonomy; here it threatened that very principle. In line with this many persons queried the constitutionality of the Convention's action, citing Article IV of the Constitution:

> *While independent and sovereign in its own sphere, this Convention shall never exercise any authority whatever over any church, nor shall it in any way interfere with the constitution of any church, or with the exercise of its functions as the only ecclesiastical body, but will cheerfully recognize and uphold the absolute independence of the churches.*

In the annual meeting of the Southern Baptist Convention in 1966 Wayne Dehoney, the Convention President, refused to allow a motion challenging the seating of messengers from the First Baptist Church of Russellville on the grounds that the SBC had no authority to tell member churches what they could or could not do regarding baptism or the Lord's Supper.[48]

Overtures to Other Baptists

While Baptists associated with the State Convention were feeling their way ecumenically with other denominations, they were also making overtures to other Baptist bodies, namely, the Missionary Baptist Association and the two National Baptist bodies. Since we will be examining the development of cooperation with the latter in another context, we will focus here on the exchange with the former.

In 1953 the Convention voted to appoint a committee to express to the Missionary Baptist Association (NABA) "appreciation for their progressive attitude and their sound Bible preaching and convictions" and "convey to them an expression of our willingness to renew fellowship with them." The committee consisted of T.L. Harris, B.H. Duncan, E.P.J. Garrott, L.C. Tedford, and J.S. Rogers.[49]

The action evidently raised the question of a possible merger in the MBA, for, in a letter addressed to the latter in the annual meeting the next year, the committee assured them that "We do not interpret this action of our Convention as a bid to you to merge your association with our Convention, nor to sacrifice any of your principles and convictions in order to find a basis of Christian fellowship." They went on, however, to quote with approval the interpretation of D.N. Jackson, editor and publisher of the **American Baptist:** "The state convention did extend felicitations to our missionary Baptist group, and in doing so, opened the door to negotiations."[50] They also noted their concurrence with an opinion expressed in the same paper by T. Sherron Jackson that

> *If there are churches and pastors who desire to work with the Convention, then go to it. And vice versa. The only way that any of our people could work with the Convention would be on an individual, church by church, preacher by preacher basis.*[51]

The Committee concluded their letter on the same note:

> *It is therefore in the spirit of Christian fellowship that we extend to you the greetings of the Arkansas Baptist State Convention and at the same time recognize the freedom of both individuals and the churches of our respective organizations to determine their affiliations with denominational bodies and to direct their support to denominational institutions.*[52]

The MBA responded with a formal resolution which accepted "the Convention's greetings in a brotherly spirit" and concurred in the committee's interpretation of the Convention's action. Restating this interpretation, the Association clearly ruled out a reunion. Their "acceptance of the interpretation," they said, was

> *to be understood by the churches of our Association (as) not tending toward an organic merger of the two state groups, but toward a rightful and brotherly understanding of each other's (views) touching our church government and doctrine and our respective efforts in the promotion of Christian education, benevolence and world-wide search in soul-winning; . . .*[53]

Baptists in Arkansas Society

The period under discussion confronted Arkansas Baptists with some of the most serious social challenges they had faced. As urbanization and secularization rolled on, they produced radical changes in lifestyle and moral outlook. Attitudes changed, not only outside but even inside the churches, toward the use of alcohol, gambling, publication and sale of sexually explicit magazines and books, increase of violence and sexual explicitness in movies and on television, and other customs. Violent crime, divorces, juvenile delinquency, and other problems multiplied as urban populations mushroomed. The long brewing cauldron of racial strife, poorly tended, boiled over. The Vietnam War generated massive unrest among youths and minority groups on whom the burden of military service fell heaviest. Church-state relations grew more and more complex as governments at all levels called on the churches to assist in dealing with the problems of society.

Widening Social Vision and Responsibility

Arkansas Baptists should not be faulted for the ambivalence which they displayed in responding to the accelerated pace of social change which this period brought. Like other religious groups, they too lacked experience in dealing with many of the new problems. To their credit, they laid aside many conventional reservations about dealing with society's woes and, along with other Southern Baptists, waded in. This era of their history is striking for the number of new issues they grappled with and the multiplication of corporate effort in doing so. Whereas during and after World War II they had narrowed their social vision to one or two items, notably drinking and gambling, in this period they expanded it immensely. Relations between blacks and whites, which we will consider later, took the center of the stage, but numerous other issues received plenty of attention.

The manufacture, distribution, sale and use of alcoholic beverages, of course, continued to stand at the forefront of Baptist concern as it had since the Civil War. Early in this period, Baptists tended to associate alcohol abuse with a whole array of social ills—highway accidents, increase of violent crime, the number of women sentenced to prison, broken homes, divorces, juvenile delinquency, and others.[54] Later, they isolated other problems and attempted to address them in a more specific and thoroughgoing way.

Baptist alarm over dog and horse racing also rose significantly during this period, as Arkansans sought to capitalize on revenues generated by betting. As in the past, here too Baptists set themselves

365

firmly against this invasion. In 1955 they commended Governor Orval Faubus for the stand he took against gambling and urged him "to use his influence to refuse a franchise to anyone until after the 1956 general election."[55] At the same time they went on record "as favoring the initiation of an amendment to the constitution of the State of Arkansas prohibiting the establishment and the operation of legal gambling in **any form** whatsoever in this State."[56] Year by year, they issued resolutions against parimutuel betting at racetracks.

Intensity of concern about these two matters, combined with a growing recognition of the need for united Christian effort, led in 1958 to the formation of the Christian Civic Foundation of Arkansas, Inc. This lineal successor of the Anti-Saloon League set itself "to promote abstinence, by education, legislation and re-habilitation, through the united efforts of the churches of Arkansas." To liquor it added gambling and pornography and salacious lit-erature.[57] Whatever ecumenical reservations Arkansas Baptists normally had, they laid them aside to slow or halt the state's traffic in liquor and gambling as they had done in the prohibition drive. Through the Christian Civic Foundation they also divested them-selves of inhibitions they sometimes manifested regarding the use of organized political pressures. The Foundation sought to educate youth about the dangers of alcohol, narcotics, gambling, and salacious leterature through the school systems and Parent Teachers Associations. Foundation officials sent questionaires to candidates for public office and distributed their answers through news letters. They lobbied to secure passage of legislation against liquor sales, gambling, etc. They dismissed the popular judgment that "You can't legislate morality" with a list of things legislation could do to discourage immorality.[58] They linked up with "Marion County Drys" to test the constitutionality of Act 132 in the Arkansas Supreme Court. Act 132 made legislation concerning mixed-drinks a local option, resulting in legalization in three counties.[59]

As urbanization undermined the Christian calendar, Arkansas Baptists also protested the passing of Sunday as a day of rest but without the old fire, perhaps conceding the inevitable. From time to time, they registered their "vigorous protest to and abhorrence of Sabbath desecration" with no elaboration.[60] In 1958 they aired their concern in more precise terms when some officials proposed holding general elections on Sunday. Reaffirming their belief that Sunday is "a sacred and holy day," they registered "staunch disapproval" of the proposal.[61] Similarly, in 1968 they bridled when they learned of a bill before the United States Congress which would have fixed certain national holidays on Monday and thus, as they saw it, "encourage further disregard of Sunday as the Lord's Day."[62] A year later, they urged Baptists "to put forth a concerted effort to reclaim the Lord's Day from the commercial clutches of our materialistic society and restore it to its Biblical place as a day of rest and worship; . . ."[63]

Many other issues, however, were more pressing than preservation of the sabbath. One was created by a rapid shift in public judgments about how explicit literature, movies, or television should be in regard to sex and violence and how far they should go in exercising free speech. In the preceding period Arkansas Baptists had taken a critical look at movies, sometimes repudiating them altogether and sometimes working for improved morality. Now they found a much larger problem. In 1954, for instance, they called on senators and representatives to pass laws against "immodest and suggestive picture shows, indecent funny books, impure and salacious literature, nudist colonies and their magazines."[64] From 1958 on, as noted above, the Civic Morality Foundation made pornographic or salacious literature one of its chief targets, and the Convention repeatedly backed it up with supportive resolutions. In the late 'sixties, in line with the action of Southern Baptists elsewhere, Arkansas Baptists began to take exception to violence as well as immorality and illicit sex in movies and on television. In 1970 they denounced the report of the President's Commission on pornography, which had taken a light view of changing mores, as "irresponsible, misleading and in tragic error."[65] The next year, they put themselves on record against "the use of any 'four letter' words or other offensive language on a TV series or cartoons that are slanted at children or youth."[66] In 1978 they petitioned major networks, Arkansas Television stations, and the Federal Communications Commission concerning "illicit sex, casual violence, alcohol promotion, vulgarity, and profanity." At the same time they commended the President of the University of Arkansas for vowing not to allow "sexually explicit films" to be shown at the University again.[67]

Drug abuse, a growing problem in the era under discussion, frequently came to the attention of Arkansas Baptists. In 1953 the Social Service Commission noted the ready availability of marijuana and heroin to teenagers. Pushed by racketeers, youth were using it for emotional release, "brought on by unsatisfactory home life and maladjustments," and turning to crime to obtain supplies. The Commission went on to remark that, because Church and Community leaders had been slow to recognize the problem, adequate facilities for dealing with it were lacking.[68] Although the State

367

Convention subsequently made passing mention of the drug problem, it did not set up a specific means for handling it apart from the Christian Civic Foundation, which gave it low priority. Its most serious action was a resolution drafted in 1970 calling on "all our elected officials and law enforcement agencies to strictly enforce all existing laws" and asking them "to pass more stringent laws regarding the use and abuse of drugs."[69] A more constructive approach came from the Liberty Association, which helped to finance a curriculum guide on drug education to be used in public schools.[70]

Breakdown of the family also occupied the attention of Arkansas Baptists. In the preceding period, they had directed their attention chiefly to escalation of the divorce rate and Arkansas' lax divorce laws. In the present period they began to discover that the problem went much deeper and had much wider ramifications. They, of course, still denounced "the divorce evil" and, as late as 1978, vigorously opposed "no fault" divorce laws, which allowed divorce on grounds only of "irreconciliable differences, which have caused the irremediable breakdown of the marriage." At the same time, however, they were exhorting their churches "to utilize every means to strengthen and sustain the unity and sanctity of family life."[71] In line with the broadening of perspective here the Arkansas Baptist Home for Children (formerly Bottoms' Orphans Home) evolved into Arkansas Baptist Family and Child Care Services. As it changed its name in 1971, this agency asserted that it "continued to place emphasis on the total family." It listed, among its many programs, "counseling service for families and children, a treatment and guidance program at Monticello, referral services, foster care for individuals, group homes for children, and other related services."[72]

Cries of hunger caught the ear of Arkansas Baptists early. In 1953 a sensitive Committee on Public Morals noted that two-thirds of the world's population was suffering from malnutrition. No organized effort to deal with the problem developed, however, before the mid-seventies, for national social concerns shoved international ones aside. In 1975, Vietnam and other crises now behind, Arkansas Baptists took their first world hunger offering.[73] In 1977 they established a World Hunger Committee in conjunction with an SBC push in this direction.[74] A year later, this Committee reported a collection of more than $35,000 between January 1 and September 30, 1978.[75]

Abortion also became an issue in the 'seventies, connected with the Supreme Court decision to overrule state laws prohibiting or restricting a woman's right to obtain an abortion during the first three months of pregnancy. The ruling permitted states to "regulate the abortion procedure in ways that are reasonably related to maternal health" during the second three months and to prohibit abortions thereafter. On this issue we may detect a growing conservatism in Arkansas Baptist pronouncements. In 1972, **before** the Supreme Court handed down its decision on January 1, 1973, the Convention adopted a cautious statement urging "all agencies and personnel responsible for authorizing abortions. . . to give scrupulous regard to the letter and intent of the new laws, and particularly . . . give every resistance to making abortions available simply on demand."[76] In 1978, as the number of abortions vaulted upwards, the Convention issued the strong anti-abortion statement cited earlier.

References to many other social issues could be added. What should be observed here, however, is the evidence which the data compiled above supplies regarding the development of a more and more positive sense of responsibility for society. This evidence, moreover, is undergirded by more self-conscious and explicit statements to this effect. In 1955, for instance, the Convention's Social Service Committee explicitly urged the churches to "actively engage in a promotion of civic and community projects that better social conditions" and "build a more positive program to meet the social needs of the community."[77] Similarly, in 1963 the Convention urged "our Baptist people to take the full responsibilities of Christian citizenship, encouraging our men and women and to actively participate in governmental affairs in order that our government might reflect Christian principles and ideals."[78] The outlook was not unprecedented, but it was more widespread than in any previous period of Arkansas Baptist history.

The War in Vietnam

One issue of special interest during the 1960s was the Vietnam War. Resistance to this sustained conflict added to social tensions in several other areas and gradually pitched the whole American populace into a sea of discontent and confusion.

As one would expect, Arkansans reacted much less vociferously than citizens in many other states. Students on state university campuses voiced the strongest protest, and we may assume that Baptists joined them. At Ouachita, however, the President exulted in his 1970 report to the State Convention that, "when the national news media have had much to report that is discouraging on such topics as international warfare, racial tension, campus violence, economic uncertainties, and the growing acceptance of alcohol, narcotics, and sexual promiscuity as natural components of American college life," Ouachita had only "good news" to report.[79]

This is not to say that Arkansas Baptists had no concern. They tended rather to follow their customary route of supporting the government even when they wondered whether it was right. In 1966 the State Convention urged the churches "to pray God's leadership to be upon our governmental leaders at the local, state, and national levels, and . . .specifically for a near solution to the Viet Nam (sic) crisis."[80] Several years later, a resolution added encouragement to the efforts of President Nixon and his staff to bring the war "to a just and lasting peace."[81] The tone of both memoranda implied that war is the government's and not the churches' business.

After the war Arkansas Baptists participated in a resettlement program for Vietnamese refugees set up by the Home Mission Board of the Southern Baptist Convention. In 1975 they were helping to sponsor 53 "units" (an individual or a family).[82]

Church-State Relations

While Arkansas Baptists were assuming larger responsibility for their society, they were finding their own institutions wound up more and more tightly in one ball with the state. The interweaving of concerns which began with the depression of the 'thirties and continued through the Second World War went on apace during the period under discussion. The more problems mounted, the more the government turned to the churches for help in solving them. For their assistance it offered an even larger share in the public purse. The Jeffersonian "wall of separation," if it ever existed, was crumbling rapidly.

Arkansas Baptists, long time watchdogs regarding separation of church and state, reacted to this development with genuine alarm. They had repeatedly blown the trumpet on Roman Catholic efforts to knock down the wall of separation, and they continued to do so. But now they found themselves confronted with an either/or situation: either accept public monies of some kind to help support their institutions, or let the institutions go. Significative of the complexity of the issue—they went the former route with Ouachita, the latter with the Arkansas Baptist Medical Center. In both instances, as we saw in the preceding chapter, they were deeply involved with the government long before they made this decision.

Arkansas Baptists should not be faulted for either duplicity or inconsistency, though they probably held too naive a view of the relationship between church and state. They were quite consistent in opposing **obvious** and **blatant** infringements on separation of church and state, even their own. In 1951, for instance, they, along with other Southern Baptists, strongly protested the appointment of General Mark Clark as a diplomatic representative to the Vatican by

370

their fellow Southern Baptist Harry S. Truman. They asked all Arkansas congressmen to vote against the appointment.[83] A bit more on the fuzzy side but in their minds fairly clear since they did not have parochial schools any longer, in the early 'fifties they sounded warnings year by year against use of public funds for parochial schools—whether for payment of rent, salaries, or transportation.[84] In 1955 the State Convention authorized a committee to study and report on the use of tax money to aid parochial schools in Arkansas.[85] The Committee made a report the next year,[86] but whatever action it might have inspired was preempted by the recognition that Arkansas Baptists too were inextricably caught in the state's web.

One small sign of this came to their attention in 1959 in the form of tax exemptions for ordained ministers. At one time this matter posed few questions, for the ministry was more or less restricted to one form, the pastorate. In the post-war years, however, the ministry became pluriform. There were ministers of education, music, youth, social work, etc. Unless ordained, they could not receive tax exemptions. Although the State Convention authorized appointment of a committee to study this problem in 1959,[86] none was actually appointed until 1962, a year after the Southern Baptist Convention had decided to recognize others besides pastors "as commissioned ministers of the Gospel," thus qualifying for tax exemption also.[87] The Arkansas Convention approved this solution,[88] but it also adopted a much longer statement on ordination a year later.[89]

Far more serious problems arose in connection with the Arkansas Baptist Medical Center and the colleges. Advance warning of the Center's growing church-state dilemma turned up in 1953 and 1954, when the Executive Board, appealing for absolute adherence to separation of church and state, commended the Arkansas Baptist Hospital "for refusing to receive tax money from the Federal Government, and protests the policy of the Federal Government in this respect."[90] In 1963, however, the Hospital created a crisis by asking the Convention's approval to set up a mental health unit as a private corporation. With this arrangement the Hospital could receive federal funds under the Hill-Burton Act. The matter got Convention approval by the slim margin of 35 votes (297 to 262) and simmered for months. Many regarded the decision as a subterfuge to circumvent the church-state problem.[91] In 1966 the Hospital, which changed its name to the Arkansas Baptist Medical Center in 1965, asked for and received permission to become "a body corporate independent of the convention, solely under the control of its Board of Trustees and membership."[92] A year later, the Convention also voted to delete the word "Baptist" from

371

the title and to release the corporation and its Trustees "from any future obligations to select its members from Baptist personnel only; but instead, to be absolutely free to perpetuate itself regardless of race, color or creed."[93]

The hospital facility, as expected, was not released without opposition. The vote was 488 to 327. One person offered a substitute motion which would have allowed the Medical Center "to apply for and to receive public funds . . . for any of the purposes and objectives to which such funds lawfully and morally may be applied by its Board of Trustees." But this motion failed 601 to 436.[94] A motion to sell the Center also failed.[95] Finally, three pastors sought to block the transfer of title through a court suit, but the Arkansas Supreme court ruled in favor of the transaction.[96]

The Medical Center's problem, according to John A. Gilbreath, Administrator, was "intensified by the implementation of Medicare," as a result of which the hospital would lose $150,000 income per year. Medicare paid patient care in the hospital at a reduced rate. The government provided for other hospital needs—purchase of equipment, remodeling of existing buildings, payment of mortgages, and construction of new facilities—through a separate plan involving direct payments. Without taking those direct grants the Hospital could not maintain proper standards. After study of possible solutions the Trustees decided to ask the Convention to let the Hospital continue as a private non-profit corporation.[97]

A similar dilemma faced the Convention regarding Ouachita College. In 1965, noting the horns on which the institutions were impaled, the Resolutions Committee asked the Convention to "go on record as reaffirming our traditional Baptist position on the separation of church and state" and to "urge all of our Baptist institutions and programs to respect this principle." It also called for the appointment of a committee to study the problem and report to the Convention the next year.[98]

The report on federal aid to Baptist higher educational institutions in Arkansas observed that the federal government promoted over two hundred types of assistance programs in which Baptist colleges and universities could legally participate. It candidly listed the types of governmental assistance which the colleges had accepted in the past as well as types of aid not yet accepted. It went on to indicate immediate and long term needs. After dismissing possible objections that accepting help would entangle the colleges too much in government regulations, the Committee proceeded to build a strong case for the continued acceptance of certain kinds of assistance, without which the colleges would have a difficult time. Though urging continued refusal of direct grants of funds, they proposed continued acceptance of (1) aids to students (e.g. National Defense Loans, Equal Opportunity Act Jobs and scholarships, G.I. Training, scholarships for dependents of service men killed in service, and "similar programs"); (2) contractual agreements for performance of specific services for the government (e.g. R.O.T.C., training institutes, research grants, and "similar programs"); (3) building loans at rates of interest comparable to that charged other non-profit institutions; (4) acceptance and/or purchase of disposed surplus property; and (5) special scholarships and fellowships.[99]

Annual reports of both Ouachita and Southern, which became formally affiliated with the Convention in 1968, indicate that this report would not be the final word on church-state relations as far as the colleges were concerned. Both repeatedly spoke of "financial crisis" brought on by competition with much better funded public institutions. During the 'seventies, all denominational colleges had to come up with a stronger rationale for their existence and back up their claims with competitive educational quality, a difficult thing on limited resources. At the same time the colleges were getting a taste of the bad side of public assistance. In 1975 Daniel Grant, President of Ouachita, complained of "the growth of ridiculously minute Federal regulations on all colleges, public and private" and "bureaucratic quagmires threatening to eliminate some of the time-honored distinctive characteristics of the Christian college." He went on to say, "All Christian citizens need to work harder to see that all legislation, at whatever level, provides adequate guarantees for the religious liberty of religious institutions."[100]

Baptists and Education
Baptists have seldom recognized adequately the importance of institutions of higher learning and thus have never invested heavily in them. Usually, as in Arkansas, they have valued colleges for the immediate return they could make to the denomination in the training of ministers, in direct contributions to evangelism, or as citadels of "orthodoxy." The net result has been that the colleges have suffered as educational institutions which might make a significant impact on the culture of the country through the quality of graduates they turned out and through the effect they had on the culture itself.

In this period Arkansas Baptists, along with other Southern Baptists, took some important steps forward in financial support given to their two remaining educational institutions and in gaining a better grasp of their purposes. In both areas, however, the colleges still were hard put to keep pace with the educational revolution going on in America which clouded the future of church-related colleges.

373

Ouachita

Ouachita began this period on the down beat. It lost its accreditation. Its president, S.W. Eubanks, resigned. Its enrollment dropped to 475 as the flow of post-War beneficiaries of the G.I. bill halted and a new draft started for the Korean War. With substantially improved Convention support, however, its fortunes rapidly improved under the presidency of Ralph A. Phelps, Jr. (1951-1969) and later Daniel Grant (1970-   ). Thanks to the "baby boom" after World War II, enrollment escalated rapidly—from 475 in 1951 to 1,677 in 1977. Regaining accreditation in 1953, Ouachita improved its academic standing at a remarkable pace. The number of faculty with earned doctorates increased significantly (to 35 percent in 1973), enabling the school to begin offering Master's degree work in 1958 and to become a university in 1965. It gained special accreditation for its teachers' education program, being accepted as a member of the American Association of Colleges of Teacher Education in 1956, and for its Music Department, which was accredited by the National Association of Schools of Music in 1960. In 1968 the Gorman Report listed Ouachita second in the state in academic and administrative excellence, just behind the University of Arkansas.[101]

These startling developments notwithstanding, Ouachita still perched on the precipice it had long occupied. The huge sums federal and state governments poured into public colleges and universities put all private and especially church-related colleges at a decided disadvantage. Ouachita could not compete in facilities, faculty salaries, tuition costs to students, and other areas. In 1970, for instance, the Trustees openly pleaded for help in erecting new buildings, so badly needed, they argued, in a time "when literally millions of federal and state tax dollars are building beautiful buildings on state college campuses in Arkansas."[102] At the same time, noting that the University had retained its accreditation with the North Central Association, they candidly listed criticisms: (1) low faculty salaries, (2) too many one-man departments, (3) lack of adequate physical equipment, and (4) an operating deficit for the past two years.[103] Among Arkansas colleges Ouachita stood at the very bottom of the list on faculty salaries.

Ouachita sought to offset its disadvantages by accentuating its distinctive Christian purpose and by striving for academic excellence, despite limitations. Reports to the State Convention and college catalogues recited over and over the litany of special Christian contributions of Ouachita. Faculty and administration were "making a conscious effort to preserve those basic Christian values which have made the school distinctive in earlier days." The program at Ouachita was "qualitatively different from that found on tax-supported campuses."[104] Sometimes when financial needs grew great, these reports piped the tune they knew Arkansas Baptists most wanted to hear: "Every effort is made to win the lost to Christ and to deepen the spiritual lives of those who have already been born again," said one report.[105]

The effort to serve the denomination, of course, has sometimes caused Ouachita to become wired crossways in its own purposes. As an educational institution, it has to strive for academic excellence if it is to compete with comparable institutions. This necessitates freedom to use current methods of research in the physical sciences or other fields. On one or two occasions Arkansas Baptists have put serious stumblingblocks in the way of this purpose. During the 'twenties, as we saw earlier, they required an anti-evolution oath which resulted in the resignation of the president, C.E. Dicken, and several faculty. Along similar lines, during the Ralph Elliott controversy in the SBC, the school went on record as being "unashamedly conservative theologically" and, evidently against modern interpretation, affirmed the "historicity" of the Bible" as "a fact."[106]

Considering its severe financial and other limitations, Ouachita did a commendable job in combining academic excellence with Christian objectives. This achievement, of course, depended to a great degree on uncommon sacrifices by the faculty and administration. In the 'sixties, however, Christian education everywhere got a stout boost with a change in the national mood. Disillusionment with modern culture fell at the doorstep of public institutions of higher learning, which for so long had played gods with scientific and technological expertise. Many persons began to see that education of the head alone did not suffice. Genuine education, they contended, should involve the total person and take place within a context which might leave room for the spiritual. It should include cultivation of "the powers of transcendence" as well as the powers of observation and reason. The net result of this shift in outlook was a swing back toward church-supported schools.

Arkansas Baptist colleges benefited from this development not merely in increased enrollments but in financial support. In 1971 the State Convention undertook an "Advancement Campaign" to raise $3,000,000 for Ouachita and $1,000,000 for Southern Baptist.[107] Unlike many earlier fund drives, in a time of rapid inflation, this one clicked. Perhaps prematurely, in 1972 Ouachita Trustees celebrated the campaign as a "modern miracle," but they were not wrong to see an "unparalleled commitment of Arkansas Baptists to higher education."[108] The next year, the Committee for Christian Higher Education Development reported $5,644,441.65 in gifts and pledges, substantially more than the campaign called for.[109] Unfortunately the spectre of inflation constantly hovered over the American economy.

Southern Baptist College

Southern Baptist College was not officially adopted into the family of State Convention institutions until 1968, though it began receiving Cooperative Program funds in 1949. Initially emphasizing industrial arts and training for local ministers within a hundred mile radius, it evolved little by little into a real junior college.

Throughout this period, of course, Southern touted its "rural ministry training course" and the contributions its students and alumni made to the churches in northeastern Arkansas. In 1952 it revamped its Ministry Training Department to create "The Rural Theological Seminary of the South."[110] It was proud to "train the rural pastor for the rural church."[111]

Southern did not relinquish its strong emphasis on training rural ministers, but it was forced by circumstances to experiment with a variety of programs. Because of a swift decline in the number of persons training under the G.I. bill, in 1953 it eliminated most of its industrial education offerings.[112] Subsequently it emphasized education of ministers and teachers. As enrollment at Walnut Ridge fell, it started extension work at the Blytheville Air Force Base in 1966 and later at Senath, Missouri. Momentarily these programs inflated the enrollment during the late 'sixties and early 'seventies. In 1969-1970, the College's enrollment peaked at 1,341—736 at Walnut Ridge, 469 at Blytheville, 108 at Senath, and 28 at Hayti, Missouri. This prosperity, though, proved shortlived. A new community college opened in Blytheville in 1976 and forced termination of that extension. Meantime, Southern Baptist revised its curriculum offerings again. In 1974 it developed a new vocational program in connection with the Black River Vocational Technical School.[113] The next year it added programs in Business Management, Music, Church Recreation, and Secretarial Science.[114]

To compete with a growing number of colleges in the northeastern part of Arkansas, both public and private, Southern also had to improve its academic standing. Starting the process of applying for accreditation in the North Central Association of Colleges and Secondary Schools in 1965, it obtained full accreditation seven years later. In 1964 the president's report to the State Convention called attention to an increase in the number of honor students attending and cited with pride that the college was growing "in academic favor."[115] Like Ouachita, it sought to raise the number of faculty holding Ph.D.s.

Southern Baptist College also struggled financially. In its early

376

years its location helped to cut down on operating expenses. With innovative programs it managed to stay "in the black." At the same time, however, reports hinted at stringent budget measures which undercut the College's effectiveness. And the president and trustees pressed first for increase of Cooperative Program funds and then for admission into "the family of Arkansas Baptist institutions." In 1967 a special committee appointed to study the College's offer recommended the development of a policy on Christian education before acceptance. In 1968 it recommended full acceptance with the proviso that both Ouachita and Southern Baptist would come under a single board of trustees.[116] The Convention approved the recommendation of acceptance but, on motion of W.O. Vaught, Jr., pastor of Immanuel Baptist Church in Little Rock, rejected the merger of the boards. Vaught argued against a single board on several grounds: (1) the distance between the two institutions (200 miles), (2) their diverse types of administration, one being a senior and the other a junior college, and (3) that this would be unlike the pattern in other Southern Baptist colleges.[117]

Ministry to the Secular Campus

Although Baptist colleges benefited from the religious revival described above, the vast majority of Baptist students still attended public institutions of higher learning. This number rose rapidly. In 1946 3,383 Baptist students enrolled in state colleges. In 1950 this number had risen to 5,500; in 1960 to approximately 9,000; in 1968 to 16,800; and in 1978 to approximately 25,000.[118] Percentagewise, whereas in 1950 twenty percent of Baptist students attended church-related colleges, in 1978 only ten percent did so.

The difficulties of ministering to students in this setting are well known. The state university creates an environment for students which detaches them from their family and church setting. By design an **avant garde** institution, it challenges traditional values and thought and generates a critical attitude toward the current culture, including the religious one.

Under the guidance of Tom Logue, State BSU Director since 1955, Arkansas Baptists devised a number of programs to penetrate the campus more effectively. One consistent goal was to place campus ministers on every college campus in the state, both Baptist and non-Baptist. In 1955 Arkansas had only four local director positions funded by the State Convention: at the University of Arkansas, Arkansas State University, Arkansas Tech, and the University of Arkansas at Monticello. During the period under discussion, the number expanded to fifteen, the Convention funding thirteen and contributing to the salaries of directors at Ouachita College and Arkansas Medical Center: Southern Arkansas University in 1956, the University of Central Arkansas in 1956, city-wide BSU Director for Little Rock in 1958, Henderson State University in 1962, the University of Pine Bluff in 1963, a "roving director" position to minister to some of the smaller colleges in 1967, associate director at the University of Arkansas in 1972, associate director at Arkansas Tech University in 1974, and a separate position for the University of Arkansas at Little Rock in 1976.

During the same period, the number of student centers also multiplied. Whereas in 1955 Arkansas Baptists had only two permanent centers and two temporary ones, in 1978 they had thirteen, eleven of which were permanent. New permanent centers appeared year by year: at the University of Central Arkansas in 1956 (enlarged in 1977), the University of Arkansas at Fayetteville in 1957, Southern Arkansas University in 1959, the University of Arkansas Medical Center in 1960, the University of Arkansas at Pine Bluff in 1962, Henderson State University in 1967, Arkansas Tech in 1970 (replacing the original frame center built by the First Baptist Church of Russellville), and Arkansas State University in 1971. Temporary centers were located at the College of the Ozarks (in a house adjacent to the campus donated in 1965) and at Westark (in a house purchased by the BSU in 1969). Some older buildings also underwent renovation.

Baptist ministers to the campus had to compete with the ultra-conservative Campus Crusade for Christ in Arkansas as elsewhere. The Crusade's "hard sell" approach resulted in the closing of dormitories on some campuses, but the Baptist Student Union's approach did not suffer noticeably because it was more "cultivative." In the late 'sixties state BSUs reported a large number of conversions—85 in 1969, 97 in 1970, and 150 in 1972.

During the period being discussed, students took an increasingly active role in society. Among other things, they stated their views on pressing social issues, often ahead of their elders. In 1957, for instance, when the State Convention remained silent during the Little Rock crisis, the Baptist Student Convention, with only one dissenting vote, passed a resolution asserting their convictions on race relations.

We believe that the Christian position in the matter of race relations includes:
1. Upholding the teaching and example of Christ regarding the equal worth of all individuals regardless of race, color, or station in life.
2. Upholding the law of the land.
3. Abstaining from and discouraging violence in the settlement of any differences.[119]

The Baptist Student Union in Arkansas harnessed some of these student concerns and energies for service. The summer missions program, of course, continued, but innovative programs also appeared. At the University of Arkansas Medical Center, for instance, students operated "The Inn of the Fisherman," a Christian coffee house, between 1966 and 1968. The Inn's motto was: "The church needs to listen, as well as speak, to be a listening people who bare the marks of love."[120] It displayed Christian symbols, and those waiting on tables often stopped to discuss the physical, emotional, and spiritual needs of patrons.

In the summer of 1967 six students from Arkansas colleges formed the Meaning in Life Singers. Led by Jerry Blaylock, a medical student, they spent the summer touring churches and assemblies and presenting the gospel in song. Their itinerary included Student Week at Glorieta in 1967, the California International Retreat at Yosemite National Park in the winter of 1967, the bandshell at Daytona Beach, Florida during Easter of 1968, and Foreign Mission Week at Ridgecrest in 1968.

During the Easter recess of 1968, the Arkansas Student Department started a local ministry at Daytona Beach. Fifty students participated. This ministry, which was continued several years, was adopted by the Home Mission Board and expanded to include students from other states as well.

In the summer of 1968 twenty Arkansas students worked and lived among migrant workers in the sugar beet fields near Barley, Idaho. A few of the students took turns running a day care center for migrant children. At night they organized games and held Bible studies.

More than most programs, the Baptist Student Union has suffered from a lack of adequate support. In the mid-sixties a grass roots movement, led by Bob Langston, a Harrison physician, proposed the development of a separate board of trustees for the Baptist Student Union, analogous to the boards of Ouachita and Southern Baptist College. In January, 1968 the Executive Board asked a committee of five plus the Executive Secretary-Treasurer and the State BSU Director to "prepare necessary recommendations to the convention to implement the transfer of BSU from the Executive Board to a Board of Trustees."[121] At the request of James Sullivan, Executive Secretary of the Sunday School Board, SBC, the Arkansas Executive Board delayed its decision to await the outcome of an SBC study of the total BSU program. As a result, it authorized instead an eighteen-member State BSU Advisory Committee to offer active support to BSU. In 1976 this Committee presented to the State Convention a plan for a Third Century

Endowment Campaign, which would raise $1,000,000 from individuals and churches for support of the work of the Baptist Student Union. Income from this endowment, invested through the Arkansas Baptist Foundation, would earn approximately $70,000 to $80,000 annually.

Women in Arkansas Baptist Churches

After the Second World War, the women's equality movement, which had flagged somewhat during the depression of the 'thirties, gained new momentum. During the 'sixties, "women's liberation" joined the growing wave of liberation movements in full swing at the time. Women complained of oppression, male chauvinism, inequality in job opportunities and pay, lack of recognition, etc. They demanded the elimination of discrimination toward women as well as toward minority groups whose grievances American society was trying to redress. An accumulation of complaints led to the proposal of an Equal Rights Amendment in 1975 which had not been ratified at the time of writing.

The women's rights movement made an impact on Arkansas Baptists during this era, but, as one would expect, the impact was mixed. Women made some gains in representation on important committees in the State Convention. In 1969, for instance, the Constitution was amended so as to add women to the Executive Board on an official basis, one elected "from the bounds of each of the eight (8) districts in the state."[122] Previously the executive secretary of the state W.M.U. had held only an **ex officio** position. While this represented a slight advance for women, its limitations should also be recognized. As worded here, the Board will not have more than eight women. Given the total constituency, this means that women obtained only token representation.

As we noted earlier, women have always played important roles in Arkansas Baptist life. From the late nineteenth century on they did so chiefly through the Woman's Missionary Union. During the Second World War, however, they moved more and more into other slots, for instance, in campus ministry. The first full-time BSU director in Arkansas was a woman, Frances Barbour, and in 1945 all local directors were women—Mary Jane Redwine at the University of Arkansas, Marjory Toole at Central Baptist College, Elma Cobb at the Baptist State Hospital, and Ann Wollerman at Ouachita College.

At least one Arkansas church, the First Baptist Church of Arkadelphia, ordained women as deacons in 1975.[123] Although the church constitution called for the election of "six qualified men," the

Nominating Committee circulated a form asking for the names of "six qualified persons." After narrowing the list of 84 nominees to the fourteen mentioned most often the Committee found ten, including two women, willing to let their names be presented. A vote on these names led to the election of four men and two women. Subsequently the Church voted by more than the required two-thirds majority to alter their constitution to read "six qualified people." The two women, Mary King and Pat Chambliss, were ordained on March 28, 1976.

Although women served in a number of ministerial roles, there was strong resistance to the ordination of women for ministry. At the annual convention in 1977 a motion was made from the floor to send a letter of protest to the "Directors of the Home Mission Board" concerning employment of Suzanne Coyle, a woman ordained in Kentucky, in the South Jersey-Pennsylvania Convention. The letter would have opposed "the ordination of women as ministers or deacons" as "contrary to the Word of God" and "so fundamental and basic that any argument to the contrary would not be worthy of our attention." It went on to ask that the HMB "refrain from supporting or employing any more ordained women."[124] After referral the Resolutions Committee came back with a much more moderate resolution to be sent to the HMB. This resolution, which passed despite an effort to table it, asked the Convention to "go on record as looking with disfavor toward (financial support of ordained women)" not on biblical grounds but as "contradictory to the past practice of the Home Mission Board; . . ."[125]

Against this background it should scarcely occasion surprise to discover that the Arkansas Baptist State Convention went on record against the Equal Rights Amendment in 1978. The Amendment itself was poorly understood and, despite efforts to explain its purpose, raised many fears even among persons of moderate social views. Predictably the resolution stated its objections in terms of undermining biblical teaching concerning men and women and damaging the homes of America. It exhorted pastors "to warn the flock of the undermining effects that this amendment will have upon the homes and families of our nation" and church and people "to become involved in the fight against this amendment."[126]

White and Black

The most critical issue facing American citizens during the period under discussion was that of the civil rights of the black minority. The United States Supreme Court decision of 1954 brought to an end the doctrine of "separate but equal" which had in effect relegated blacks to the status of second-class citizens. In 1957 the federal government began the long and painful process of implementation. Meantime, blacks themselves, led by Martin Luther King, pressed for their rights through organized efforts. Tragically, in 1968, at a time when these efforts were beginning to make a showing, King fell to an assassin's bullet in Memphis. Simultaneously American cities were erupting with violent protest over dehumanizing living conditions, the War in Vietnam, the "military-industrial complex," the threat of nuclear holocaust, and ineffectiveness in government. The civil rights movement slowed, advancing by fits and starts.

Arkansas, along with the rest of the South, figured prominently in all of this. Like other southern states, it watched its black citizens make their way to the north to find jobs in cities like Chicago, Detroit, Pittsburgh, and New York. The black population of the state dropped steadily: from 426,639 in 1950 to 388,787 in 1960, to 352,495 in 1970. It took the center of the stage in implementation of the Supreme Court decision in 1957, Little Rock's Central High School being selected as the first southern school to undergo forced integration. It suffered painfully through months of racial tensions. Gradually Arkansas' citizens accepted the inevitable and began to work actively to achieve integration. By the late 'sixties the exodus to the north stopped and turned around. Blacks, along with other citizens, started returning.

Arkansas Baptists responded to the civil rights crisis, like most of their peers, in a variety of ways. As we have seen in earlier chapters, they had maintained at least token contact with black Baptists from the Civil War on. They offered assistance in education and mission work but hardly in a consistent way. During the depression, moreover, they let even these meager helps lapse.

In the present era the State Convention, prodded by the Home Mission Board, beefed up its assistance. At the outset the program was modest, as it always had been. In 1954, spurred on by the momentous happenings surrounding the Supreme Court decision, it picked up. The Missions Department of the Convention employed Clyde Hart as a full-time Secretary for Race Relations. In 1957 the Little Rock crisis injected a new urgency into the task and led to the creation of a separate Department of Race Relations headed by Hart. The program was expanded and got heavier financial backing, from 1960 on jointly sponsored by the State Convention and the Home Mission Board.

In 1968 a new phase of white and black relations opened. Responding to the American social crisis at its peak, the Southern Baptist Convention adopted a resolution specifically directing their Home Mission Board and other agencies to address themselves to the problem of racism. Arkansas Baptists followed suit. By 1970 their program was no longer aimed at doing something **for** black Baptists; it was doing something **with** them. First within their Missions Department and after 1974 as a separate department they engaged in "Cooperative Ministries with National Baptists." The old paternalism had begun to fade.

Brown versus Board of Education—1954

It will be interesting first to look more closely at Arkansas Baptist reactions to the Supreme Court decision in the case of **Brown versus Board of Education** which overturned **Plessy versus Ferguson,** the celebrated case in which the Supreme Court in 1896 upheld a Louisiana law requiring segregated railroad facilities. Although the decision did not put Arkansas Baptists on the spot in the way the integration of Little Rock schools did, it did affect their outlook.

As one would expect of a church organization emphasizing its democratic structure, the State Convention remained silent, even when parallel organizations in other denominations spoke. O.L. Bayless, pastor of First Baptist Church of Hot Springs and a member of the Home Mission Board and chairman of the State Mission Committee of the Executive Board of the State Convention, however, did speak. Writing in the **Arkansas Baptist** following the annual meeting of the Southern Baptist Convention, he expressed optimism that Arkansas Baptists would follow the Southern Baptist Convention in meeting the need. The SBC adopted a five-point statement, including an article approving the Supreme Court decision, but Bayless cited only the following:

That we urge our people and all Christians to conduct themselves in this period of adjustment in the spirit of Christ; that we pray that God may guide us in our thinking and in our attitudes that we may help and not hinder the progress of justice and brotherly love; that we may exercise patience and good will in the discussions that must take place, and give a good testimony to the meaning of Christian faith and discipleship.

That we urge Christian statesmen and leaders in our churches to use their leadership in positive thought and planning to the end that this crisis in our national history shall not be made the occasion for new and bitter prejudices, but a democracy that will commend freedom to all peoples.[127]

Bayless proceeded to urge establishment of a "joint-Director of Negro work in the Missions Department" and rapid upgrading of

383

assistance to blacks in promoting Sunday school, Training Union, W.M.U., men's work, evangelism, colleges, stewardship, and denominational leadership.[128]

In July the Missions Department hired Clyde Hart to work with black Baptists. His program called for supplementation of certain efforts then in existence and the development of new ones. In September, 1954 he outlined his main goals in terms of (1) promoting college and seminary extension schools; (2) conducting Bible institutes, stewardship conferences, and revivals; (3) organizing BSUs at Arkansas Baptist College, Philander Smith College, and Arkansas AM & N at Pine Bluff; (4) conducting vacation Bible schools and summer field work, using some black collegians; (5) supervising and directing the work of Gwendoline Luster in conducting youth camps and in helping to strengthen the work of black women's organizations in their churches; and (6) encouraging associational and church leaders to invite black leaders and workers to white vacation Bible school clinics and other training conferences "where they can receive instruction and training to carry back to their own churches."[129]

It is fairly obvious from the sketch given above that the work would proceed on the assumption of continuing segregation, which is probably as far as most persons would go at the time. White leaders worked vigorously to help Arkansas Baptist College keep its doors open.[130] They conducted separate camps for black youths, at first using a Methodist facility and later establishing "Hart of the Hills." They held separate institutes, schools, and conferences for training black leaders.

Still, even in 1954, the color line began giving way. Oak Grove Baptist Church in Green County Association, in northern Arkansas near Paragould, received ten blacks into membership on April 4. Unhappily the rationale given for this was not encouraging vis-a-vis desegregation. They were admitted, the report said, because there were "not more than fifty Negroes in the city" and because they had no church and had never had a service of their own. Moreover, the association was "planning to purchase a building and establish a permanent mission for the Negroes of Paragould."[131] A bit more promising, Arkansas Baptist Hospital granted temporary staff privileges to three black doctors in September and promised permanent positions if they were found qualified by the credentials' committee and approved by the trustees.[132]

On the whole, the tone of white Baptists still remained paternalistic. In 1955, for instance, the Executive Board of the State Convention withheld funds from Arkansas Baptist College, "pending a satisfactory adjustment of the situation," because it found a "proposed Administration of the College" "objectionable."[133] Blacks occasionally received invitations to make token appearances at white functions, but they did not assume leading roles. It is quite remarkable, in retrospect, that they accepted favors with grace and humor. But, being poorly educated and terribly deprived, they were not in a position to be choosers. They attended all the conferences and camps in substantial numbers. They heaped praise on whites for the assistance they gave. In September, 1957 the Board of Trustees of Arkansas Baptist College even voted to put eight whites on their Board.[134] Nevertheless, despite the good intentions of whites, blacks must have chafed with embarrassment.

Little Rock—1957

The Little Rock school crisis in 1957 and the decade of turmoil which followed began to turn things around and to quicken white sensitivities. The initial reaction of Baptists, however, was no more forthright and clear than that to the Supreme Court decision.

Neither the State Convention nor the local association— Pulaski County— issued any formal statement on the matter. The Pulaski County Association, however, did form an "Inter-Racial Commission." This Commission made much of a simultaneous revival in the Association participated in by 44 white and 15 black churches. The services were not integrated, but breakfast meetings were. They also promoted a $100,000 fund drive for Arkansas Baptist College.[135] When, a year later, the Association took note of the school crisis, it placed the burden on individuals. A resolution urged "the members of all the churches" of the Association "to pray earnestly and sincerely, both in private and in public assembly, for God's will to be done in the public school crisis now affecting the lives of so many of our people in this area."[136]

Some Baptists did speak out, as usual avowing that they spoke only for themselves. The conciliatory role of Congressman Brooks Hays was noted in the preceding chapter. Several Little Rock pastors—Dale Cowling, Second Baptist; W.O. Vaught, Immanuel Baptist; and Harold Hicks, Pulaski Heights Baptist—signed a statement protesting the action of Governor Orval E. Faubus. Only one pastor associated with the State Convention signed a statement of commendation, though several pastors affiliated with the Missionary Baptist Convention did so. The statement of censure said:

> *We, the undersigned ministers of Little Rock, strongly protest the action of Governor Orval E. Faubus in calling out the armed forces of the state to surround Central High School, thereby preventing integration in*

*compliance with the Supreme Court's decision of May
1954 and the order of the Federal Court of August 1957.*

*We deplore: (1) the overriding of the authority of the
local school administration; (2) the disregard of national
law; (3) the abuse of the autonomy of the local school
districts; (4) the policing of the great majority of law
abiding youth of the city; (5) the exciting of racial
tensions; (6) the reflections cast upon our local law
enforcement officers; (7) the destruction of the respect of
our citizens, young and old, for proper constitutional
authority.*

*We appeal to every citizen to unite with us in earnest
prayer to God that justice will be brought about and a
right example set for every child of our community.*[137]

Curiously, when the Convention met in November, it was W.O.
Vaught, Jr., one of the signers of this strong petition, who said, "I
trust this Convention will make no pronouncement of any kind on
current issues." He proceeded to explain to the messengers assembled in his own church that "We are not here to make
pronouncements that are to be handed down to the churches... Each
church will be guided in such things after prayer and meditation."[138]

Referral of touchy issues to private or corporate prayer is
typically Baptist and for many the only solution. The Acting
Executive Secretary of the Convention, Ralph Douglas, refused to
take a stand for or against integration. Instead, he touted the prayer
meetings in Little Rock as the key to solving the problem.[139] Other
leaders concluded, rightly as it turned out, that more progress would
be made by boosting their efforts to assist blacks and in that way to
alleviate racial tensions. Prophetically, in 1955, the State Missions
Committee of the State Convention wrote:

*Many other intricate problems will arise during the years
which lie ahead in regard to desegregation. We must,
therefore, keep a vital interest in Negro missions and try
to solve the problems facing them and us in a Christian
spirit and with Christian leadership.*[140]

Prior to the integration of the Little Rock schools, Erwin L.
McDonald, Editor of the **Arkansas Baptist,** argued that the
simultaneous revival crusade jointly planned and promoted by
whites and blacks in the Pulaski County Association "points in the
right direction."[141]

During the closing of schools in Little Rock by order of
Governor Faubus, Ouachita College operated an emergency Baptist

Academy for white students "regardless of religious affiliation, but with a preference for Baptists." Initiative for the school came from Baptists in Little Rock.[142] Although the action got "about unanimous" approval in the Pulaski Associaiton, it raised eyebrows elsewhere. Ralph Phelps, Jr., President of Ouachita, had to defend the measure as a "temporary" expedient "not intended as an involvement in the segregation-integregation controversy." He added that it was financed from tuition alone and not from Cooperative Program funds.[143] Taking note of severe criticisms for including white children only, he gave three reasons: (1) Arkansas Baptists had not yet desegregated their churches or authorized the college to do so; (2) "no facilities were made available for an integrated school"; and (3) the climate of Little Rock at the time would not allow it.[144]

Cooperative Ministries with National Baptists

We cannot take time to compile a detailed report on the Arkansas Baptist program of assistance during these years. For the most part the program followed the plan Clyde Hart devised in 1954. Like that of the Arkansas Baptist State Convention, it stressed training of leaders, stewardship education, and support for the colleges.

By the late 'sixties, as the American social crisis crested, Arkansas Baptists, like Southern Baptists elsewhere, had taken Paul Bunyan type steps in attitudes toward blacks. In 1968 they issued a "Resolution on Human Relations" which reflected their progress:

> *Whereas, Arkansas Baptists as evangelical Christians, have a major responsibility for the Christian witness both in the homeland and around the world, and*
> *Whereas, the progress made toward an easing of racial tensions and a Christian solution does not match the extreme urgency (sic) reflected in current crisis, and*
> *Whereas, Paul, in his letter to the Colossians (3:11) says, "There cannot be Greek and Jew, circumcision and uncircumcision, barbarians, Scythian, bondman, freeman; but Christ is all, and in all," therefore,*
> *Be it resolved by the messengers assembled in this 115th session of the Arkansas Baptist State Convention, that we:*
> *1. Rededicate ourselves in the spirit of Christ to a ministry of reconciliation among all men.*
> *2. Remind ourselves that all men stand as equals at the foot of the cross without distinction of color.*
> *3. Pledge ourselves to provide positive leadership in our communities, seeking through conciliation*

*and understanding to obtain peaceful com-
pliance with laws assuring equal rights for all.
We further pledge ourselves to go beyond these
laws in the practice of Christian love.*[145]

In 1969, following the resignation of Clyde Hart, the Race Relations Department reverted to the Missions Department. With the employment of Robert U. Ferguson in May of 1970 the title of the work shifted from "Race Relations" to "Work with National Baptists." In December of 1974 it became again a separate department, entitled "Cooperative Ministries with National Baptists."

The basic features of the program did not change completely with the name change. In 1975 the work still included extension centers and leadership training institutes, vacation Bible schools, summer youth camps, the BSU program at the University of Arkansas at Pine Bluff (formerly AM & N), scholarships for needy students, and student summer missions. Some new items, however, also appeared: an annual leadership conference for National and Southern Baptist leaders, state and associational joint committee work, promotion of Race Relations Day, and Women's Day of Prayer.[146] The accent lay on cooperation. In proposing the new department to the State Convention, the Executive Board remarked:

*The growing relationship between National and
Southern Baptists in Arkansas preview (sic) a stronger
Baptist influence in Arkansas affairs. In a day when
public officials are looking for answers to the complex
problems that face our pluralistic society, the Baptist
Churches of Arkansas need to be cooperating to the
fullest extent so that Christ and Christian values are
known to all people.*[147]

In addition to the joint leadership conference in February, 1975, National and Southern Baptists also held a joint prayer retreat at Camp Paron in February, 1976. Later, in connection with the nation's bicentennial, the Arkansas Baptist State Convention met in joint session with the Consolidated Baptist State Convention and the Regular Arkansas Missionary Baptist State Convention at Barton Coliseum in Little Rock. The meeting emphasized Christian education and the bicentennial theme of "Life and Liberty."[148] Approximately 3,000 messengers participated. In 1977 the three conventions sponsored an Annual Evangelistic Conference.

In 1978 the Joint Committee on Cooperative Ministries with National Baptists made proposals for (1) a state cooperative evangelism conference, (2) cooperative associational meetings or evangelistic crusade, (3) cooperative associational surveys to determine areas of specific church program needs, and (4) another combined convention session in Little Rock to emphasize "Our Baptist Family of Faith." It undergirded these with a confession of faith.

> *We believe that we have one Father who created all mankind from one blood, one Lord and Savior, Jesus Christ, one Holy Spirit, one commission to disciple all people, and one desire, which is to do the will of God; therefore, we will boldly declare our faith in 1979-80.*[149]

An Epilogue

These words sound a good note on which to bring this history to a close. We hear it, of course, knowing that realities seldom match ideals. Neither in their dealings with blacks nor in their relationships with one another during this period did Arkansas Baptists reach a pinnacle.

We have had to view what transpired during this period in terms of urbanization. Still predominantly rural when it began, Arkansas Baptists became predominantly urban. Urbanization meant changes in the outlook and behavior of Arkansans and, of necessity, of Arkansas Baptist churches. It brought affluence. It made it possible for the churches to improve physical facilities, develop programs, hire better trained staff people, and do other things they could not have done in the past.

But urbanization exacts a price for its favors. It produces radical changes in lifestyle that undermine established attitudes and customs. In this period it generated a crisis in American existence.

We have been able to identify some of the effects of the move to the city on Arkansas Baptist churches, institutions, and programs. Among obvious ones were declining participation in Sunday school, Church Training, W.M.U., Brotherhood, and other activities. There were also changed attitudes toward drinking alcoholic beverages, smoking, dancing, attending movies, gambling, and sabbath activities. Perhaps more crucial in the long run, people in the city were becoming more callous, less sensitive to the personal.

Still, not all changes of attitude were bad. Urbanization probably helped to improve relations between blacks and whites, if for no other reason than that the crisis it engendered forced Arkansas Baptists to seek solutions. It also assisted women in their struggle to achieve equality both within and outside the churches.

It would be wrong, however, to suggest that what has happened to Arkansas Baptists during this period of history resulted merely from urbanization. Arkansas Baptists have had a large hand in determining how they have advanced. It was not by accident that their constituency skyrocketed. While other groups marked time or slowed down, the Arkansas Baptist State Convention shot upwards at a remarkable rate.

The key to this, like the key to Southern Baptist progress elsewhere, lies, as we noted earlier, in singlemindedness of commitment to the Great Commission and in organized effort to discharge it. Viewed in this light, the decision made in 1901 to continue with the corporation model in affiliation with the SBC has to be regarded as the most crucial one in Arkansas Baptist history. Had the State Convention capitulated completely to the General Association, it would doubtless have advanced but at the much more modest rate of the Association and without a national and international dimension. Connection with the Southern Baptist Convention has proven increasingly important as time has passed.

NOTES

[1] Annual, ABSC, 1946, pp. 10-11.
[2] Annual, ABSC, 1958, pp. 51ff.
[3] Annual, ABSC, 1946, p. 68.
[4] Annual, ABSC, 1949, p. 88.
[5] Annual, ABSC, 1960, p. 40.
[6] Annual, ABSC, 1951, pp. 87-89.
[7] Annual, ABSC, 1969, pp. 67-69.
[8] Annual, ABSC, 1977, p. 82.
[9] Gaines S. Dobbins, Winning the Children (Nashville: Broadman Press, 1953), p. 1.
[10] Annual, ABSC, 1952, p. 49.
[11] Annual, ABSC, 1965, p. 78; 1977, pp. 162-3.
[12] Report of Anna Mary Wilson, secretary to the Director, Arkansas Church Music Department, Dec. 22, 1977.
[13] Annual, ABSC, 1967, p. 67.
[14] Annual, ABSC, 1972, pp. 74-75.
[15] Brooks Hays and John E. Steely, The Baptist Way of Life (Englewood Cliffs, N.J.: Prentice-Hall, Inc., 1963, p. 50.)
[16] Annual, ABSC, 1974, p. 45.
[17] Annual, ABSC, 1975, pp. 124-5.
[18] Annual, ABSC, 1973, pp. 39, 41.
[19] Annual, ABSC, 1951, p. 75.
[20] Annual, ABSC, 1953, p. 57.
[21] Annual, ABSC, 1968 p. 44.

[22] Annual, ABSC, 1959, p. 35.
[23] Arkansas Baptist, September 15, 1960, p. 3.
[24] Ibid., p. 16.
[25] Annual, ABSC, 1960, p. 37.
[26] Annual, ABSC, 1972, p. 46.
[27] Annual, ABSC, 1978, p. 49.
[28] Arkansas Baptist, December 2, 1965, pp. 6-7; bracketed words mine.
[29] Erwin L. McDonald, "Head-on Collision," Arkansas Baptist, October 21, 1965, pp. 3, 7.
[30] Annual, ABSC, 1965, pp. 31f.
[31] Annual, ABSC, 1965, p. 31.
[32] Annual, ABSC, 1968, pp. 28-29.
[33] Annual, ABSC, 1965, p. 33.
[34] Annual, ABSC, 1966, p. 27.
[35] Ibid., pp. 45-46.
[36] Annual, ABSC, 1968, p. 39.
[37] Annual, ABSC, 1971, p. 39.
[38] Annual, ABSC, 1973, p. 38.
[39] Annual, ABSC, 1973, p. 47.
[40] Annual, ABSC, 1974, p. 40.
[41] Ibid., p. 41.
[42] Annual, ABSC, 1967, p. 40; original motion by Carl Overton, p. 32.
[43] Annual, ABSC, 1969, p. 27.
[44] Annual, ABSC, 1970, pp. 61-62.
[45] Annual, ABSC, 1971, p. 33.
[46] Ibid., p. 34.
[47] Annual, ABSC, 1968, p. 30.
[48] Annual, ABSC, 1966, p.   .
[49] Annual, ABSC, 1953, p. 28.
[50] Arkansas Baptist, December 15, 1953, p. 4.
[51] American Baptist, February 1, 1954, pp. 5, 7.
[52] Annual, ABSC, 1954, pp. 36-7.
[53] Cited in Annual, ABSC, 1954, p. 97.
[54] See Annual, ABSC, 1951, pp. 48-49.
[55] Annual, ABSC, 1955, p. 28.
[56] Ibid., p. 27.
[57] Report to the ABSC in Annual, ABSC, 1963, p. 78.
[58] Annual, ABSC, 1962, pp. 26-27.
[59] Annual, ABSC, 1969, pp. 89-90; 1970, pp. 93-95.

[60] Annual, ABSC, 1952, p. 33; 1953, p. 30.

[61] Annual, ABSC, 1958, p. 34.

[62] Annual, ABSC, 1968, p. 43.

[63] Annual, ABSC, 1969, p. 40.

[63] Annual, ABSC, 1969, p. 40.

[64] Annual, ABSC, 1954, p. 32.

[65] Annual, ABSC, 1970, p. 39.

[66] Annual, ABSC, 1971, p. 43.

[67] Annual, ABSC, 1978, pp. 48-49.

[68] Annual, ABSC, 1953, p. 84.

[69] Annual, ABSC, 1970, p. 40.

[70] Annual, ABSC, 1971, p. 40.

[71] Annual, ABSC, 1978, p. 45.

[72] Annual, ABSC, 1971, p. 87; official name change, p. 35.

[73] Annual, ABSC, 1975, p. 37.

[74] Annual, ABSC, 1977, p. 43.

[75] Annual, ABSC, 1978, p. 46.

[76] Annual, ABSC, 1972, p. 48.

[77] Annual, ABSC, 1955, p. 78.

[78] Annual, ABSC, 1963, p. 39.

[79] Annual, ABSC, 1970, p. 87.

[80] Annual, ABSC, 1966, p. 64.

[81] Annual, ABSC, 1972, p. 46.

[820] Annual, ABSC, 1975, p. 73.

[83] Annual, ABSC, 1951, p. 79.

[84] Ibid., p. 83; Annual, ABSC, 1952, p. 33; 1953, p. 30; etc.

[85] Annual, ABSC, 1955, p. 27.

[86] Annual, ABSC, 1956, pp. 34-36.

[86a] Annual, ABSC, 1959, p. 28.

[87] Annual, ABSC, 1961, p. 154.

[88] Annual, ABSC, 1962, pp. 49-50.

[89] Annual, ABSC, 1963, pp. 30-33.

[90] Annual, ABSC, 1953, p. 63; 1954, p. 68.

[91] See Arkansas Baptist, November 14, 1963, pp. 3f.; December 12, 1963, p. 3.

[92] Annual, ABSC, 1966, p. 28.

[93] Annual, ABSC, 1967, p. 31.

[94] Annual, ABSC, 1966, pp. 28-29.

[95] Ibid., p. 29.

[96] Annual, ABSC, 1967, p. 55.

[97] Annual, ABSC, 1966, pp. 115-117.

[98] Annual, ABSC, 1965, p. 42.
[99] Annual, ABSC, 1966, pp. 35-44.
[100] Annual, ABSC, 1975, p. 90.
[101] Annual, ABSC, 1968, p. 101; also 1969, p. 91.
[102] Annual, ABSC, 1970, p. 91.
[103] Ibid., p. 88.
[104] Annual, ABSC, 1958, p. 74.
[105] Annual, ABSC, 1960, p. 80.
[106] Annual, ABSC, 1962, p. 84f.
[107] Annual, ABSC, 1971, p. 36.
[108] Annual, ABSC, 1972, p. 96.
[109] Annual, ABSC, 1973, p. 91.
[110] Annual, ABSC, 1952, p. 48.
[111] Annual, ABSC, 1956, p. 42.
[112] Annual, ABSC, 1953, pp. 34-36.
[113] Annual, ABSC, 1975, p. 92.
[114] Annual, ABSC, 1976, p. 108.
[115] Annual, ABSC, 1964, p. 80.
[116] Annual, ABSC, 1968, pp. 33f.
[117] Erwin L. McDonald, "Arkansas State Convention Accepts Southern College, Disciplines Churches," Arkansas Baptist, November 28, 1968, p. 11.
[118] Annual, ABSC, 1946, pp. 35-36; 1960, pp. 90-91; 1968, pp. 70-71.
[119] Minutes, BSU Convention, 1957, pp. 1-2.
[120] BSU State Scrapbook, 1966.
[121] Executive Board Minutes, January 22, 1968.
[122] Annual, ABSC, 1969, p. 35.
[123] Although the First Baptist Church of Benton installed six women as "deaconesses" in 1922, the one living member of this group remembers only that they served dinners, etc., to help raise money for the church. Information courtesy of Bernes K. Selph.
[124] Annual, ABSC, 1977, p. 39.
[125] Ibid., p. 44.
[126] Annual, ABSC, 1978, p. 50.
[127] Annual, ABSC, 1954, p. 56.
[128] Arkansas Baptist, June 24, 1954, p. 2.
[129] Arkansas Baptist, September 23, 1954, p. 11.
[130] See W.O. Vaught, Jr. "How We Can Help Save Our Negro Baptist College in Little Rock," Arkansas Baptist, January 17, 1957, pp. 1, 3.

[131] Arkansas Baptist, April 22, 1954, p. 5.

[132] Arkansas Baptist, September 23, 1954, p. 6.

[133] Annual, ABSC, 1955, p. 55.

[134] Arkansas Baptist, October 17, 1957, p. 9.

[135] Minutes, Pulaski County Baptist Association, 1957, pp. 48-49.

[136] Minutes, Pulaski County Baptist Association, 1958, p. 48.

[137] Arkansas Baptist, September 12, 1957, p. 3.

[138] Arkansas Baptist, November 28, 1957, p. 2.

[139] Arkansas Baptist, October 24, 1957, p. 16.

[140] Annual, ABSC, 1955, p. 80.

[141] Arkansas Baptist, May 2, 1957, p. 4.

[142] See Minutes, Pulaski County Baptist Association, 1958, p. 33.

[143] Annual, ABSC, 1958, pp. 73-74.

[144] Arkansas Baptist, October 30, 1958, p. 6.

[145] Annual, ABSC, 1968, pp. 43-43.

[146] Arkansas Baptist, January 17, 1974, p. 8.

[147] Annual, ABSC, 1974, p. 78.

[148] Annual, ABSC, 1976, pp. 39-40.

[149] Annual, ABSC, 1978, p. 46.

APPENDIX A-1
CONSTITUTION, 1848

Article 1. This body shall be styled the ARKANSAS BAPTIST STATE CONVENTION.

Art. 2. The convention shall be composed of delegates from Baptist Associations, churches, and individual contributors, who are members of the Baptist Church, in good standing.

Art. 3. Associations shall be entitled to five, and churches to three, delegates to the convention.

Art. 4. It is distinctly understood, that this convention shall have no ecclesiastical jurisdiction, nor even act as an advisory council, nor in any way interfere with the constitution of any Church or Association.

Art. 5. The primary objects of this convention shall be: to supply the destitute regions within its bounds, with the unadulterated Word of Life, and a living ministry, and to aid, by appropriate and scriptural means, all destitute and public churches, and also supply the community with such books as may be approved by this body, and as may be thought best calculated to communicate information as to the distinctive doctrines and ordinances of the Gospel of Christ, as received by our denomination. The convention may, whenever consistent with the condition of the treasury, adopt means for the advancement of education, and also for the cause of Foreign Missions.

Art. 6. The convention shall, at its annual meetings, elect a President and Recording Secretary, who shall perform the duties usually assigned to such officers, during its session.

Art. 7. The convention shall annually elect a President, two Vice Presidents, Corresponding Secretary, Treasurer, and ten or more Managers, who, together, shall compose the Executive Committee; five or whom shall constitute a quorum. The Executive Committee shall transact all business during the recess of the convention, and disburse the funds; shall fill all vacancies in its own body, and submit a report of their proceedings at each annual meeting. Each member of the convention shall be, ex-officio, a member of the convention.

Art. 8. The annual session of this convention shall commence on Thursday before the second Sabbath in October, of each year.

Art. 9. This constitution may be amended at any annual meeting of the convention, two-thirds of the members present concurring therein, except the fourth article, which shall for ever remain untouched.

The committee to whom was referred the subject of drafting a constitution for the convention, having examined and compared several of a similar character, having agreed upon the above; all of which is most respectfully submitted.

APPENDIX A-2
CONSTITUTION, 1902

ARTICLE I.—NAME AND OBJECT.

Section 1. The name of this body shall be: THE ARKANSAS BAPTIST STATE CONVENTION.

Section 2. The object of this Convention shall be to preach the gospel throughout our State and to evangelize the world; to aid by appropriate and Scriptural means our destitute and feeble churches; to supply the State with books and tracts best calculated to inculcate the doctrines and ordinances of Christ and to stimulate missionary effort; to encourage ministerial and Christian and general education; and to gather and preserve denominational statistics.

ARTICLE II.—MEMBERSHIP.

Section 1. The Convention shall be composed of messengers from regular Baptist churches which are in sympathy with the principles and purposes of this constitution, and which desire to co-operate with this Convention, and shall be entitled to seats upon presentation of their proper credentials, or satisfactory evidence of their appointment.

Section 2. Each church shall be entitled to three messengers, with one additional messenger for every fifty members, or major fraction thereof, above one hundred.

ARTICLE III.—AUTHORITY.

Section 1. This Convention shall never exercise any authority whatever over any church, nor shall it in any way interfere with the constitution of any church or with the exercise of its functions as the only ecclesiastical body, but will always cheerfully recognize and uphold the absolute independence of the churches.

ARTICLE IV.—OFFICERS.

Section 1. The officers of the Convention shall be a President, two Vice Presidents, two Recording Secretaries, a Treasurer, a Statistical Secretary and an Auditor, who shall be elected annually by ballot, *provided,* however, that any officer of the Convention may be elected by acclamation if no objection be made; and all officers shall hold their respective offices until their successors are elected.

Section 2. It shall be the duty of the President to preside over the deliberations of the Convention, and to discharge such other duties as are usually incumbent on the presiding officer of deliberative bodies. He shall appoint all committees, unless the Convention shall otherwise determine, and in his absence one of the Vice Presidents shall fill his place.

Section 3. It shall be the duty of the Recording Secretaries to keep a fair record of the proceedings of the Convention, and to file and keep in order all papers deemed important to be preserved.

Section 4. Officers shall be elected as soon as the names of messengers shall have been enrolled.

Section 5. All the officers of this Convention shall be elected by a majority of all the votes cast.

ARTICLE V.—BOARDS.

Section 1. The Convention shall elect the following Boards and parts of Boards.

(1.) The Executive Board of the Convention, which shall consist of fifteen brethren from the State at large, and one brother from the bounds of each Association in the State, who shall be elected annually, on account of their business ability, consecration and wisdom, seven of whom shall constitute a quorum; and the meetings of the Board shall be quarterly.

(2.) The Board of Trustees of Ouachita-Central System of Colleges and Academies, one-third of which shall be elected annually.

(3.) The Board of the Arkansas Baptist Orphan's Home, consisting of nine members, three of whom are to be elected annually.

(4.) A Sunday-school and Colportage Board, to consist of eleven members, which shall be elected annually.

(5.) A Board of Ministerial Education, to consist of seven members to be located at Arkadelphia, Ark., and to be elected annually.

(6.) A State Central Committee of nine women, whose duty it shall be to distribute literature, and to encourage women and children in systematic giving to missions.

Section 2. The Executive Board shall elect a Missionary Secretary to work under the direction of the Board, and they shall employ any other agencies, such as general missionaries and evangelists, office help, and any means, such as tracts, etc., which in their judgment may inure to the most speedy and rapid evangelization of our State and of the world. However, the Convention in session may elect the Missionary Secretary when it is deemed wise.

ARTICLE VI.—MEETINGS.

The Convention shall meet annually, "if God permit," on Friday before the third Sunday in November.

ARTICLE VII.—UNALTERABLE.

This constitution may be amended at any regular meeting of the Convention, two-thirds of the members voting concurring in the measure, except Article III., which shall forever remain unalterable.

APPENDIX A-3
CONSTITUTION, 1913

Article I.—Name and Object.

Section 1. The name of this body shall be "The Arkansas Baptist State Convention."

Sec. 2. The object of this Convention shall be to aid the churches in their divinely commissioned work of evangelization, education and beneficence.

Article II.—Membership.

Section 1. The Convention shall be composed of messengers from regular Baptist Churches which are in sympathy with the principles and purposes of this constitution, and which desire to co-operate with this Convention, and shall be entitled to seats upon presentation of their proper credentials, or satisfactory evidence of their appointment.

Sec. 2. Each church shall be entitled to three messengers with one additional messenger for every fifty members, or major fraction thereof, above one hundred.

Article III.—Authority.

Section 1. This Convention shall never exercise any authority whatever over any church, nor shall it in any way interfere with the constitution of any church or with the exercise of its functions as the only ecclesiastical body, but will always cheerfully recognize and uphold the absolute independence of the churches.

Article IV.—Officers.

Section 1. The officers of the Convention shall be a President, two Vice Presidents, a Secretary, a Treasurer, and an Auditor, who shall be elected annually by ballot, provided, however, that any officer of the Convention may be elected by acclamation if no objection is made; and all officers shall hold their respective offices until their successors are elected; and, provided further, that no one shall be elected to succeed himself to the office of President more than twice consecutively.

Sec. 2. It shall be the duty of the President to preside ever the deliberations of the Convention, and to discharge such other duties as are usually incumbent on the presiding officer of deliberative bodies. He shall appoint all committees, unless the Convention shall otherwise determine, and in his absence one of the Vice Presidents shall fill his place.

Sec. 3. It shall be the duty of the Secretary to keep a record of the proceedings of the Convention, and to file and keep in order all papers deemed important to be preserved.

Sec. 4. Officers shall be elected as soon as the names of messengers shall have been enrolled.

Sec. 5. All the officers of the Convention shall be elected by a majority of all the votes cast.

Article V.—Boards.

Section 1. This Convention shall elect an Executive Board which shall attend to the business and perform the duties of this Convention during the interim of its meetings.

(1.) This Board shall be composed of seventy-five (75) members, one from the bounds of each Association, the remainder from the State at large.

(2.) Upon the adoption of this constitution one-third of the members of this Board shall be elected to serve one year, one-third to serve two years, and one-third to serve three years; but hereafter each member shall be elected to serve three years, the Convention annually electing successors to all those whose terms expire and filling all vacancies otherwise occurring.

(3.) Fifteen members of this Board shall constitute a quorum, after due notice to all members at least five days before the time of meeting.

(4.) This Board shall co-operate with the churches in gathering and disbursing funds for evangelization, education, orphanage and hospital work, Sunday School, publication and B.Y.P.U. work and whatever other work this Convention may see fit to engage in not otherwise provided for; except that, without specific orders from the Convention, it shall not be the duty of this Board to raise endowments for educational institutions.

(5.) This Board shall report annually its work to this Convention.

(6.) This Board shall employ an adequate force of agents and workers to conduct its business.

(7.) This Board, upon the arising of an emergency, may change the time and place of the meeting of the Convention.

Sec. 2. The Convention shall also elect the following Boards, viz.:

(1.) A Board of Trustees of Ouachita Baptist College and a Board of Trustees of Central Baptist College, one-third of the members of whose boards shall be elected annually.

(2.) A Board of Trustees of the Arkansas Baptist Orphan's Home, consisting of nine members, three of whom shall be elected annually.

(3.) A Board of Ministerial Education, to consist of seven members, to be located at Arkadelphia, Ark., and to be elected annually.

(4.) A State Executive Committee, consisting of twelve women, whose duty it shall be to distribute literature and to encourage women and children in systematic beneficence toward all the objects fostered by this Convention.

Article VI.—Meetings.

The Convention shall meet annually, "if God Permit," on Thursday before the third Sunday in November.

Article VII—Unalterable.

This constitution may be amended at any regular meeting of the Convention, two-thirds of the members voting concurring in the measure, except Article III, which shall remain forever unalterable.

APPENDIX A-4
CONSTITUTION, 1921

Article I.—Name and Object.

Section 1. The name of this body shall be "The Arkansas Baptist State Convention."

Section 2. The object of this Convention shall be to aid the churches in their divinely commissioned work of evangelization, education and benevolence.

Article II.—Membership.

Section 1. The Convention shall be composed of messengers from regular Baptist Churches which are in sympathy with the principles and purposes of this Convention, and which desire to co-operate with this Convention, and shall be entitled to seats upon presentation of their proper credentials, or satisfactory evidence of their appointment.

Section 2. Each church shall be entitled to three messengers with one additional messenger for every fifty members, or major fraction thereof, above one hundred.

Article III.—Authority.

Section 1. This Convention shall never exercise any authority whatever over any church, nor shall it in any way interfere with the constitution of any church or with the exercise of its functions as the only ecclesiastical body, but will always cheerfully recognize and uphold the absolute independence of the churches.

Article IV.—Officers.

Section 1. The officers of the Convention shall be a President, two Vice Presidents, a Secretary, and a Treasurer, who shall be elected annually by ballot, provided, however, that any officer of the Convention may be elected by acclamation if no objection is made; and all officers shall hold their respective offices until their successors are elected; and, provided further, that no one shall be elected to succeed himself to the office of President more than twice consecutively.

Section 2. It shall be the duty of the President to preside over the deliberations of the Convention, and to discharge such other duties as are usually incumbent on the presiding officer of deliberative bodies. He shall appoint all committees, unless the Convention shall otherwise determine, and in his absence one of the Vice Presidents shall fill his place.

Section 3. It shall be the duty of the Secretary to keep a record of the proceedings of the Convention, and to file and keep in order all papers deemed important to be preserved.

Section 4. Officers shall be elected as soon as the names of messengers have been enrolled.

Section 5. All the officers of the Convention shall be elected by

401

a majority of all votes cast.

Article V. (As Amended)—Boards.

This Convention shall elect the following Boards, to serve three years, which shall be elected annually, except where charters forbid.

Section 1. An Executive Board composed of fifteen members chosen from the state at large, Pastors and Laymen, not more than three of them shall reside in any one city, town or community, and none of whom shall serve on any other Board or hold any other office under this Convention, ten of whom shall constitute a quorum. This Board shall be elected annually.

The duties of this Board shall be:

(1.) To promote and carry out the financial policies and program of this Convention, and their authority shall not extend beyond such instructions. Provided that they may change the time and place of the meeting of the Convention in the event of the arising of an emergency.

(2) To raise, collect, receive and disburse all funds of the Convention as they may be ordered by the Convention.

(3) To keep a full and complete record of their work and proceedings throughout the year and report the same faithfully to the Convention in annual session.

(4) To employ an adequate force of agents and workers to conduct the business committed to them.

(5) To represent the Convention in its relations with denominational bodies outside of the state.

(6) To direct the Convention's publications.

(7) This Board is not authorized to interfere with the internal policies or workings of any other Board.

Section 2. A State Mission Board composed of twenty-four members chosen from the state at large, not more than three of whom shall reside in any one city, town or community. This Board shall be elected annually.

The duties of this Board shall be:

(1) To function for the Convention in the entire field of the State Mission task, according to the instructions of the Convention.

(2) To employ an adequate force of agents and workers to execute the plans of the Convention in this respect.

(3) To make a full and complete report of its work annually to the Convention in session.

Section 3. A Hospital Commission composed of eighteen

members chosen from the state at large, to be elected annually.

The duties of this Commission shall be:

(1) To function for the Convention in the field of hospital work according to the instructions of the Convention.

(2) To employ an adequate force of agents and workers to execute the plans of the Convention in this respect.

(3) To make a full and complete report of their work to the Convention in annual session.

Section 4. Boards of Trustees for Ouachita College and Central College composed of members from the state at large, according to the provisions of their several charters.

The duties of these Boards shall be:

(1) To function for the denomination in their several departments of the field of education.

(2) To employ an adequate force of agents and workers to execute the plans of the Convention in this respect.

(3) To make faithful report of their work to the Convention in annual session.

Section 5. A Board of Trustees for the Arkansas Baptist Orphans' Home, consisting of nine members from the state at large, according to the provisions of the charter of the institution.

The duties of this Board shall be:

(1) To function for the denomination in respect to the work of caring for orphan children according to the instructions of the Convention.

(2) To employ an adequate force of agents and workers to carry out the plans of the Convention in this respect.

(3) To make faithful report of their work each year to the Convention in annual session.

Section 6. A Board of Ministerial Education to consist of seven members, and elected annually.

The duties of this Board shall be:

(1) To function for the denomination in the field of ministerial education according to the instructions of the Convention.

(2) To make full report of their work to the annual meetings of the Convention.

Section 7. A State Executive Committee consisting of twelve women from the state at large.

The duties of this Committee shall be:

(1) To distribute literature and encourage women and children in systematic beneficence toward all the objects fostered by the

Convention.

(2) To employ an adequate force of agents and workers to carry out the policy of the Convention in this respect.

(3) To make full report of this work annually to the Convention in session.

Article VI.—Meetings.

The Convention shall meet annually, "if God permit," on Wednesday after the first Sunday in December.

Article VII.—Unalterable

This Constitution may be amended at any regular meeting of the Convention, two-thirds of the members voting concurring in the measure, except Article III, which shall remain forever unalterable.

APPENDIX A-5
CONSTITUTION, 1926

Article I.—Name and Object

Sec. 1. The name of this body shall be "The Arkansas Baptist State Convention."

Sec. 2. The object of this Convention shall be to aid the churches in their divinely commissioned work of evangelism, education, and benevolence.

Article II.—Membership.

Sec. 1. The Convention shall be composed of messengers from regular Baptist churches which are in sympathy with the principles and purposes of this Convention, and which desire to co-operate with this Convention, and shall be entitled to seats upon presentation of their proper credentials, or satisfactory evidence of their appointment.

Sec. 2. Each church shall be entitled to three messengers, with one additional messenger for every fifty members or major fraction thereof, above one hundred.

Article III.—Authority

Sec. 1. This Convention shall never exercise any authority whatever over any church, nor shall it in any way interfere with the constitution of any church or with the exercise of its functions as the only ecclesiastical body, but will always cheerfully recognize and

404

uphold the absolute independence of the churches.

Article IV.—Officers.

Sec. 1. The officers of the Convention shall be a President, two Vice Presidents, a Secretary, and a Treasurer, who shall be elected annually by ballot: provided, however, that any officer of the Convention may be elected by acclamation if no objection is made and all officers shall hold their respective offices until their successors are elected; and provided, further, that no one shall be elected to succeed himself to the office of President more than once consecutively.

Sec. 2. It shall be the duty of the President to preside over the deliberations of the Convention and to discharge such other duties as are usually incumbent on the presiding officer of deliberative bodies. He shall appoint all committees, unless the Convention shall otherwise determine, and in his absence one of the Vice Presidents shall fill his place.

Sec. 3. It shall be the duty of the Secretary to keep a record of the proceedings of the Convention, and to file and keep in order all paper deemed important to be preserved.

Sec. 4. Officers shall be elected as soon as the names of messengers have been enrolled.

Sec. 5. All the officers of the Convention shall be elected by a majority of all votes cast.

Article V.—Executive Board.

The Executive Board of the Convention shall be composed of 15 members chosen from the State at large and one additional member from the bounds of each co-operating Association, and none of whom shall hold any remunerative office under the Convention or any of its institutions. One-third of this Board shall be elected annually and 15 shall constitute a quorum. The Executive Board is constituted and empowered by the Convention as its legal and business agent to administer all business committed to it by the Convention, and to employ such paid agents as it deems necessary in carrying out the missionary, educational and benevolent enterprises of the Convention. The Executive Board shall raise, collect, receive and disburse all the funds for the Baptist Co-operative Program, both state and South-wide. The office of the Executive Board is the clearing house for the business side of the Convention's work, and a headquarters for Baptist information. Its books, records and files shall at all times be open for the reference and inspection of anyone who may desire to examine them. The Executive Board shall render to the Convention annually a complete and detailed statement of all its business for the year.

Article VI.—Finance.

The Executive Board shall function for the Convention in the field of financial matters.

Article VII.—Trusteeships.

The Convention shall elect trustees to hold property, to manage and to operate its colleges, hospitals and orphanage as follows:

Sec. 1. Ouachita Colleges, 24; Central College, 24; Mountain Home College, 12; Baptist State Hospital, 18; Bottoms Baptist Orphanage, 12; Davis Hospital, 6.

Sec. 2. One third of each Board of Trustees shall be elected annually for a term of three years and not more than six (6) members of any Board shall reside in any one city, town or community.

Sec. 3. All trusteeships of the Convention shall be amenable to the Convention on all matters, through its Executive Board and no trusteeship shall be permitted to conduct extra movements to raise money outside of its regular producing sources of revenue and no trusteeship shall incur a deficit on running expenses or create debt, without the approval of the Executive Board, or the Convention in session.

Sec. 4. All trusteeships shall render to the Convention at each annual session complete and detailed statements of all their business and other activities for the year.

Article VIII.—Meetings.

The Convention shall meet annually, "if God permit," on a date to be fixed by the Convention, and the Executive Board is empowered in Emergencies, to call Special Sessions of the Convention and to change both the time and place of meetings as set by the Convention.

Article IX.—Unalterable.

This Constitution may be amended at any regular meeting of the Convention, two-thirds of the members voting concurring in the measure, except Article III, which shall remain forever unalterable.

APPENDIX A-6
DEBT AMENDMENT, JANUARY 1937 CONSTITUTION

Article IX

Sec. 1. Each Board, agency, and institution of this Convention shall submit to the Convention a detailed statement of its sources of income and a budget of proposed expenditures for the ensuing year. When received and adopted by the Convention, these budgets shall become the basis of operations for the ensuing year. Should any deficit occur in the operation of any board, institution, or agency, the same shall be included in the budget of the following year.

Sec. 2. Any proposal for indebtedness to be placed on this Convention, or any board, institution, or agency of the Convention shall be submitted to the Convention in annual session and approved by two successive annual sessions of the Convention before such indebtedness shall be incurred, except when three-fourths of the members of the Convention present and voting shall decide that an emergency exists which makes immediate authorization necessary.

Article X.—Unalterable.

This Constitution may be amended at any regular meeting of the Convention, two-thirds of the members voting concurring in the measure, except Article III, which shall remain forever unalterable.

Any proposed amendment shall be presented in writing to the Convention and shall lie on the table until the next annual session of the Convention.

APPENDIX A-7
CONSTITUTION AND BY-LAWS, 1946

CONSTITUTION

Article I.—The Name

The name of this body shall be "The Arkansas Baptist State Convention."

Article II.—The Purpose

The purpose of this Convention shall be to awaken and stimulate among the churches the greatest possible activity in evangelism, Christian education, and benevolent work throughout its bounds and to the ends of the earth; to cultivate closer co-operation among the churches and to promote concert of action in advancing all the interests of the Kingdom of God.

Article III.—Membership

Section 1. The Convention shall be composed of messengers from regular Baptist churches in Arkansas which are in sympathy with the principles and purposes of this Convention, and which desire to co-operate with the other churches through this Convention.

Section 2. Each co-operating church shall be entitled to three messengers, with one additional messenger for each additional one hundred members, or fraction thereof above one hundred.

Section 3. The Convention may appoint a committee on credentials at each session which shall make recommendations to the Convention with reference to seating messengers from any church not hitherto affiliated with the Convention.

Article IV.—Authority

Section 1. While independent and sovereign in its own sphere, this Convention shall never exercise any authority whatever over any church, nor shall it in any way interfere with the constitution of any church or with the exercise of its functions as the only ecclesiastical body, but will cheerfully recognize and uphold the absolute independence of the churches.

Article V.—Officers

Section 1. The officers of this Convention shall be: President, First Vice-President, Second Vice-President, Recording Secretary, and Treasurer. Each officer of the Convention shall be elected annually, and shall continue in office until his successor in office shall have been elected and qualified.

Section 2. It shall be the duty of the President to preside over the deliberations of the Convention and to discharge such other duties as may devolve upon the presiding officer of a deliberative body. He shall appoint all committees unless the Convention shall otherwise determine. In the absence of the President, one of the Vice-Presidents shall preside in his stead.

Section 3. It shall be the duty of the Secretary to keep a record of the proceedings of the Convention, to edit and arrange publication of a suitable number of the minutes for distribution among the churches, as the Convention may direct, as soon as reasonably possible after the close of the session. He shall file and keep in order all paper deemed important to the work of the Convention.

Article VI.—The Executive Board

Section 1. This Convention shall elect a Board of Trustees as provided for in the Convention's charter. This Board shall be known as "The Executive Board of the Arkansas Baptist State Convention." This Board shall be composed of fifteen (15) members chosen from the State at large, and one additional member from the bounds of each co-operating Association. No member of this Board shall hold any remunerative office under the Convention or any of its Institutions. One-third of this Board shall be elected annually to hold office for three years, and twenty (20) members shall constitute a quorum.

Section 2. The Executive Board shall be constituted and empowered by the Convention as its business and legal agent to administer all business committed to it by the Convention, and to employ such paid agents as it may deem necessary in carrying out the missionary, educational, benevolent and financial enterprises of the Convention. The Executive Board shall raise, collect, receive and disburse all the funds of the Baptist Co-operative Program, both State and Southwide. The Office of the Executive Board shall be a clearing house for administering the business affairs of the Convention, and a headquarters for Baptist information. Its books, records and files shall at all times be open for the reference and inspection of any co-operating church who may desire to examine them.

Section 3. The Executive Board shall render to the Convention annually a complete and detailed statement of all its business for the year.

Article VII.—Trusteeships

The Convention shall elect trustees to manage and to operate its Colleges, Hospitals, Orphanages and any other Institutions it may possess, as follows:

Section 1. Ouachita College, 24; Central College, 24; Baptist State Hospital, 18; Bottoms Baptist Orphanage, 12; Baptist Memorial Hospital, 9.

Section 2. One-third of the members of the Boards of Trustees shall be elected annually to serve for a term of three years.

Section 3. Each Board of Trustees shall elect from their membership a Chairman and a Recording Secretary and such other officers as seems advisable.

409

Section 4. All Trusteeships shall render to the Convention at each annual session complete and detailed reports of all transactions and business and any other activities for the year, and shall be subject to the direction of the Convention in all matters pertaining to the administering the affairs of the Institution with which their trusteeship is concerned.

Article VIII.—Operation of Agencies

Section 1. Each Board, Agency, and Institution of this Convention shall submit to the Executive Board at its annual Budget Planning Meeting, which is to be held prior to the annual meeting of the Convention, a detailed statement of its sources of income, and a budget of proposed expenditures for the ensuing year. When received and adopted by the Convention, these budgets shall become the basis for the operations for the ensuing year.

Article IX.—Meetings

Section 1. The Convention shall meet annually, "if God permit," on a date to be fixed by the Convention. The Executive Board is empowered in emergencies to call special sessions of the Convention and to change either the time or place of meeting or both should the occasion demand.

Article X.—Amendments

Section 1. This Constitution may be amended at any regular meeting of this Convention, two-thirds of the members voting concurring in the measure, except Article IV which shall remain forever unalterable in substance.

Section 2. Any proposed amendment to this Constitution shall be presented to the Convention in writing, for its consideration, upon the first day of the annual session, and may be voted on, on any subsequent day during the session, provided adequate publicity has been given in previous announcement.

BY-LAWS

In order to carry out the provisions of the Constitution, the following by-laws are enacted for the government of the Convention.

1. Enrollment of Messengers

The Secretary of the Convention shall enroll, upon arrival, messengers who present proper credentials from the churches. These messengers, together with others who may be enrolled upon presentation of approved credentials during the session, shall constitute the Convention. Any contention concerning seating messengers shall be presented to a Committee appointed by the President for recommendation to the Convention for its action.

2. Officers

The President, First Vice-President, Second Vice-President, Secretary, and Treasurer shall be elected on the morning of the second day of the Convention, their terms of office to begin with the final session of the Convention; and the President shall appoint and announce a Nominating Committee to report at the next session of the Convention.

The election of all officers shall be by ballot; provided, however, there is only one nomination for the office, then the Secretary, or any other present, may be directed to cast the ballot of the entire assembly for the single nominee.

Each officer of the Convention shall be elected by a majority of all votes cast.

In case of removal from office, by death or otherwise, of the President, the Vice-Presidents shall automatically succeed to the office of President in the order of their election. The President may not be elected for more than two consecutive terms.

The Treasurer of the Executive Board shall be also the Treasurer of the Convention.

All elected officers of this Convention shall be members of churches co-operating with this Convention. This must also apply to members of the Executive Board and the Institutional Boards of this Convention.

3. The Executive Board

The Executive Board, being the legal trustees of the Convention, shall be empowered by the Convention to administer all business committed to it by the Convention.

The Executive Board is empowered to act for the Convention between sessions of the Convention, provided that it shall never exercise any authority contrary to the expressed will of the Convention.

When any unforseen emergency occurs in any of the affairs of the Convention, or in any of the interests its controls, that in the judgment of the Executive Board requires action before the next session of the Convention, the Executive Board shall have full authority to take such action as may seem necessary, and all interests concerned shall be governed by such action, provided the Executive Board shall make full report of all matters pertaining thereunto to the next session of the Convention for its approval, and provided further, that nothing in this article shall be construed as giving the Executive Board authority to execute any matter already committed by the Convention to any of its Boards of Trustees of its Institutions unless such Board when so commissioned shall decline to act on the orders of the Convention.

All proposals requiring the expenditure of money by the Convention, or the Executive Board of the Convention, from the annual budget, shall be considered by the Executive Board, before being presented to the Convention.

This Board shall be charged with the responsibility to have the books and financial affairs of each and all of the Boards and Institutions of the Arkansas Baptist State Convention audited annually by an accredited firm of auditors, all audits to be accessible to the Executive Board at its budget planning session, and to be included in the Institutions Report to the Convention.

Members of the Executive Board, having served one term of three years shall not be eligible for re-election until as much as one year has elapsed.

4. Trusteeships

All Trusteeships of this Convention shall be amendable to the Convention on all matters, through its Executive Board. No Trusteeship shall conduct extra movements to raise money outside its regular revenue producing sources, nor shall a deficit in running expense or debt be incurred without the approval of the Convention in session or of the Executive Board in case of afore mentioned emergencies.

Members of Boards of Trustees having served one term of three years shall not be eligible for re-election until as much as one year has elapsed.

Not more than two (2) members of a Board of Trustees shall at the same time be members of the same church, nor shall more than six (6) members reside in any one Association.

A member of a Board of Trustees of one Institution of the Convention may not at the same time be a member of any other Board of Trustees of another Institution of the Convention.

Not more than four members of a Board of Trustees of any Institution of this Convention may at the same time be members of

412

the Executive Board of the Convention.

APPENDIX A-8
CONSTITUTION AND BY-LAWS, 1972

Article I. — The Name

The name of this body shall be "The Arkansas Baptist State Convention."

Article II. — The Purpose

The purpose of this Convention shall be to awaken and stimulate among the churches the greatest possible activity in evangelism, Christian education, and benevolent work throughout its bounds and to the ends of the earth; to cultivate closer cooperation among the churches and to promote concert of action in advancing all the interests of the Kingdom of God.

The Baptist Faith and Message as adopted by the Southern Baptist Convention on May 9, 1963, shall be the doctrinal guideline for this Convention.

Article III. — Membership

Section 1. The Convention shall be composed of messengers from regular Baptist churches which are in sympathy with the principles and purposes of this Convention, and which desire to co-operate with other churches through this Convention.

Regular Baptist churches are those Baptist churches which in doctrine and in practice adhere to the principles and the spirit of **The Baptist Faith and Message** as adopted by the 1963 session of the Southern Baptist Convention, and **The Baptist Faith and Message** shall not be interpreted as to permit open communion and/or alien immersion.

Section 2. Each co-operating church shall be entitled to three messengers, with one additional messenger for each additional one hundred members, or fraction thereof above one hundred, provided however, that no church shall be entitled to a total of more than ten messengers.

Section 3. The Convention may appoint a committee on credentials at each session which shall make recommendations to the Convention with reference to seating messengers from any church not hitherto affiliated with the Convention.

413

Article IV. — Authority

Section 1. While independent and sovereign in its own sphere, this Convention shall never exercise any authority whatever over any church, nor shall it in any way interfere with the constitution of any church, or with the exercise of its functions as the only ecclesiastical body, but will cheerfully recognize and uphold the absolute independence of the churches.

Article V. — Officers

Section 1. The officers of this Convention shall be: President, First Vice-President, Second Vice-President, Recording Secretary and Treasurer. Each officer of the Convention shall be elected annually, except the Recording Secretary and Treasurer who shall be the same as the Executive Secretary of the Executive Board, and shall continue in office until his successor in office shall have been elected and qualified.

Section 2. It shall be the duty of the President to preside over the deliberations of the Convention and to discharge such other duties as may devolve upon the presiding officer of a deliberative body. He shall appoint all committees unless the Convention shall otherwise determine. In the absence of the President, one of the Vice-Presidents shall preside in his stead.

Section 3. It shall be the duty of the Secretary to keep a record of the proceedings of the Convention, to edit and arrange publication of a suitable number of the minutes for distribution among the churches, as the Convention may direct, as soon as reasonably possible after the close of the session. He shall file and keep in order all papers deemed important to the work of the Convention.

Article VI. — The Executive Board

Section 1. This Convention shall elect a Board of Trustees as provided for in the Convention's charter. This Board shall be known as the "Executive Board of Arkansas Baptist State Convention." This Board shall be composed of one member from the bounds of each co-operating association with a membership up to 5,000, and one additional member for each additional 5,000 constituency, or major fraction thereof, provided however, that no association shall be entitled to more than five (5) members. In addition, the convention shall elect one lady from the bounds of each of the eight districts in the state to serve on the Executive Board. Upon the

414

removal of any Executive Board member from the bounds of his or her association, his or her membership on the Executive Board ceases therewith; his or her successor in office may be named by the Nominating Committee of the Executive Board to hold office until the next meeting of the Convention. No member of this board shall hold any remunerative office under the Convention or any of its institutions. One-third of this Board shall be elected annually to hold office for three years, and a majority of the board members shall constitute a quorum. Any member of the Executive Board who misses all the Executive Board meetings and the Executive Board committee meetings for one year shall be automatically dropped from membership on the Board.

Section 2. The Executive Board shall be constituted and empowered by the Convention as its business and legal agent to administer all business committed to it by the Convention, and to employ such paid agents as it may deem necessary in carrying out the missionary, educational, benevolent and financial enterprises of the Convention. The Executive Board shall raise, collect, receive and disburse all the funds of the Baptist Cooperative Program, both state and southwide. The office of the Executive Board shall be a clearing house for administering the business affairs of the Convention, and a headquarters for Baptist information. Its books, records and files shall at all times be open for the reference and inspection of any co-operating church who may desire to examine them.

Section 3. The Executive Board shall render to the Convention annually a complete and detailed statement of all its business for the year.

Article VII. — Trusteeships

The Convention shall elect trustees to manage and to operate institutions and agencies it may possess, as follows:

Section 1. Ouachita Baptist University, 24; Arkansas Baptist Family and Child Care Services, 18, Baptist Memorial Hospital (Memphis,) 9; Southern Baptist College, 24; Arkansas Baptist Foundation, 15.

Section 2. One-third of the members of the Boards of Trustees shall be elected annually to serve for a term of three years. Any member of any Board of Trustees who misses all the meetings of that Board for one year shall be automatically dropped from membership

415

on that Board.

Section 3. Each Board of Trustees shall elect from their membership a chairman and a recording secretary and such other officers as seems advisable.

Section 4. All trusteeships shall render to the Convention at each annual session complete and detailed reports of all transactions and business and any other activities for the year, and shall be subject to the direction of the Convention in all matters pertaining to administering the affairs of the institution with which their trusteeship is concerned.

Article VIII. — Operation of Agencies

Section 1. Each board, agency, and institution of this Convention shall submit to the Executive Board at its annual budget planning meeting, which is to be held prior to the annual meeting of the Convention, a detailed statement of its sources of income, and a budget of proposed expenditures for the ensuing year. When received and adopted by the Convention, these budgets shall become the basis for the operations for the ensuing year.

Article IX. — Meetings

Section 1. The Convention shall meet annually, "if God permit," on a date to be fixed by the Convention. The Executive Board is empowered in emergencies to call special sessions of the Convention and to change either the time or place of meeting or both should the occasion demand.

Article X. — Amendments

Section 1. This Constitution and By-Laws may be amended at any regular meeting of this Convention, two-thirds of the members voting concurring in the measure, except Article IV which shall remain forever unalterable in substance.

Section 2. Any proposed amendment to this Constitution shall be presented to the Convention in writing, for its consideration, upon the first day of the annual session, and may be voted on, on any subsequent day during the session, provided adequate publicity has been given in previous announcement.

Article XI. — Parliamentary Authority

Kerfoot's **Parliamentary Law** shall be the standard for deciding questions of parliamentary procedure.

Article XII. — Districts

The Convention shall establish such geographic districts as it may deem wise to facilitate its promotion, administration, and organization of its objectives, provided, it will never violate in any way the boundaries of any association within the area of the convention. The boundaries of such districts shall be drawn so as to provide equitable geographical and numerical voice and representation on all convention committees, commissions, boards, except the Executive Board, all trusteeships. Each tenth year hereafter, the whole matter of districts shall be readjusted to take in consideration the flow of membership in our Baptist churches.

BY-LAWS

In order to carry out the provisions of the Constitution, the following By-Laws are enacted for the government of the Convention.

1. Enrollment of Messengers

The Secretary of the Convention shall enroll, upon arrival, messengers who present proper credentials from the churches. These messengers, together with others who may be enrolled upon presentation of approved credentials during the session, shall constitute the Convention. Any contention concerning seating messengers shall be presented to a Committee appointed by the President for recommendation to the Convention for its action.

2. Officers

The President, First Vice-President, Second Vice-President, shall be elected on the second day of the Convention, their terms of office to begin with the final session of the Convention.

The election of all officers shall be by ballot; provided, however, there is only one nomination for the office, then the Secretary, or any other present, may be directed to cast the ballot of the entire assembly for the single nominee.

The first vice president shall be nominated and voted upon and elected after balloting for the president has been completed and the winner announced, and the second vice president shall be nominated and voted upon and elected after the balloting for the first vice president has been completed and the winner announced.

Each officer of the Convention shall be elected by a majority of all votes cast.

In case of removal from office, by death or otherwise, of the President, the Vice-Presidents shall automatically succeed to the office of President in the order of their election. The President may not be elected for more than two consecutive terms.

The Treasurer of the Executive Board shall be also the Treasurer of the Convention.

All elected officers of this Convention shall be members of churches co-operating with this Convention. This must also apply to members of the Executive Board and the institutional boards of this Convention.

3. The Executive Board

The Executive Board, being the legal trustee of the Convention, shall be empowered by the Convention to administer all business committed to it by the Convention.

The Executive Board is empowered to act for the Convention between sessions of the Convention, provided that it shall never exercise any authority contrary to the expressed will of the Convention.

When any unforseen emergency occurs in any of the affairs of the Convention, or in any of the interests it controls, that in the judgment of the Executive Board requires action before the next session of the Convention, the Executive Board shall have full authority to take such action as may seem necessary, and all interests concerned shall be governed by such action, provided the Executive Board shall make full report of all matters pertaining thereunto to the next session of the Convention for its approval, and provided further, that nothing in this article shall be construed as giving the Executive Board authority to execute any matter already committed by the Convention to any of its Boards of Trustees or its institutions unless such Board when so commissioned shall decline to act on the orders of the Convention.

All proposals requiring the expenditures of money by the

418

Convention, or the Executive Board of the Convention, from the annual budget, shall be considered by the Executive Board, before being presented to the Convention.

This Board shall be charged with the responsibility to have the books and financial affairs of each and all of the boards and institutions of the Arkansas Baptist State Convention audited annually by an accredited firm of auditors, all audits to be accessible to the Executive Board at its budget planning session, and to be included in the institution's report to the Convention.

Members of the Executive Board, having served two full terms of three years each shall not be eligible for re-election until as much as one year has elapsed.

The various associations of Arkansas whose churches are affiliated with this Convention, may submit to the committee on nominations names of those whom they believe should be considered for membership on the Executive Board as members from that association.

4. Trusteeships

All trusteeships of this Convention shall be amenable to the Convention on all matters, through its Executive Board. No trusteeship shall conduct extra movements to raise money outside its regular revenue producing sources, nor shall a deficit in running expense or debt be incurred without the approval of the Convention in session or of the Executive Board in case of aforementioned emergencies, except, as follows: when an emergency arises concerning the opportunity to purchase needed property for expansion, the president of the Convention, the president of the Executive Board and the Executive Secretary of the Executive Board (all three concurring) believing such an emergency exists and deeming it wise to incur indebtedness, may give the Trustees of an institution such permission, and make a full report to the Executive Board and to the next Convention in session.

Members of Boards of Trustees having served two full terms of three years each shall not be eligible for re-election until as much as one year has elapsed.

Not more than two (2) members of a Board of Trustees shall at the same time be members of the same local church, nor shall more than six (6) members reside in any one association.

A member of a Board of Trustees of one institution of the

Convention may not at the same time be a member of any other Board of Trustees of another institution of the Convention.

No member of a Board of Trustees of any institution of this Convention may at the same time be a member of the Executive Board of the Convention.

5. Committee Members

1. A nine-member rotating Nominating Committee, comprised of at least three laymen, will place in nomination at each annual convention names of persons to fill vacancies on all convention boards. At each annual convention, the president will appoint one-third of this committee to three-year terms to replace the one-third rotating off, plus filling any vacancies that may exist on the committee at that time. Nominations for all boards from this Nominating Committee must be as equitably divided as possible between the eight existing districts of our state convention. The president shall also name the chairman, who shall come from a one-year term member.

2. A member filling an unexpired term not having served the full term of years as provided by the Constitution, shall be, at the discretion of the Nominating Committee, eligible for election to a full term.

3. No member of a commission or committee delegated to study or make recommendations concerning our institutions shall be a member of any Board of Trustees of such institutions.

4. All associational missionaries or mission pastors receiving all or part compensation from the Convention through the Executive Board shall be considered employees of the Convention and shall not be members of any Convention or institutional board. The president of the Convention by virtue of his office shall be a member of the Executive Board for the duration of his term of office.

6. Constitution and By-Laws Committee

A standing Constitution and By-Laws Committee shall be composed of six (6) members to be nominated by the Nominating Committee. One-third of the membership (2) shall be elected annually to serve for a term of three (3) years. No member shall be eligible to serve more than two terms until one year has elapsed.

The president of the convention shall appoint the chairman of the Committee each year. The chairman must be one who has been a member of the Committee for at least one year and may succeed himself until his tenure of eligibility shall expire.

The Constitution and By-Laws Committee shall be charged with the responsibility of advising the presiding officer concerning constitutional matters during the annual session of the convention with reference to matters which may arise from the floor or from other committees. The committee will act ad interim in all matters concerning the Constitution and By-Laws referred to it by the boards and agencies of the convention. The committee will receive all proposed constitutional changes before the convention and will be responsible for presenting them in writing, for convention consideration, upon the first day of the annual session, after adequate publicity has been given. The duties of the committee in no way preclude amendments to the constitution by messengers to the convention.

APPENDIX B
CONVENTION CHARTER.

Section 1. Be it enacted by the General Assembly of the State of Arkansas, That T.B. Vanhorn, John H. Carlton, P.P. Siler, T.S.N. King, L.B. Fort, John Woods, Nat G. Smith, W.R. Trawick, M. Shelby Kennard, M.W. McCraw, J.J. Harris, E.M. Harris, A. Yates, D.C. Hall, James Woods and R.M. Thrasher, and their successors in office, shall be, and the same are hereby created a corporation, under the name and style of the Arkansas Baptist State Convention, and by that name and style shall have succession for 99 years, with power as a corporation, to sue and be sued, plead and be impleaded, acquire, hold and transfer, by deed or otherwise, real and personal property, contract and be contracted with for the use and benefit of the Arkansas Baptist State Convention, and shall have and use a common seal, and do other acts appertaining to a corporation, consistent with the constitution and laws of the State.

Section II. Be it further enacted, That the domicile of said corporation shall be Princeton, Ark., and all property, real and educational and charitable purposes, for the use and benefit and subject to the direction and control of said Arkansas Baptist State Convention.

Section III. Be it further enacted, That the trustees above named shall hold their office until the next annual meeting of said Convention, when their successors shall be elected; and the board of trustees shall be elected at every annual meeting of said Convention thereafter; and on failure of the Convention to hold any annual meetings the board of trustees shall hold over until the Convention does meet and elect their successors.

Section IV. Be it further enacted, That five of said trustees, shall constitute a quorum, for the transaction of all business; the board shall elect a president, secretary and treasurer, annually; the secretary shall make an annual report of the proceedings of the board to the said Convention. The treasurer shall give bond with good security, in a sum to be fixed by the board of trustees, conditioned for the faithful performance of his duties, and that he will account for and pay over upon the orders of the board, or to his successors in office, all moneys, chosen in action, and other assets that may come to his hands as treasurer of the corporation; and the treasurer shall also make an annual report to said Convention of the state of his accounts and financial transactions of the board of trustees.

Section V. Be it further enacted, That the board of trustees shall have power to make by-laws for their own government, subject to the direction and control of said Convention.

Approved February 12th, 1859.

APPENDIX C
HISTORICAL DIRECTORY

	Place	President	Secretary	Preacher
1848	Brownsville	Isaac Perkins	S. Stevenson	E. Haynes
	Dallas Co.			
1849	Mt. Zion	Jesse Hartwell	S. Stevenson	
	Hempstead Co.			
1850	Mt. Bethel	W. H. Bayliss	S. Stevenson	F. Courtney
	Clark Co.			
1851	Princeton	Jesse Hartwell	F. Courtney	E. Haynes
1852	El Dorado	E. Haynes	S. Stevenson	
1853	Camden	Jesse Hartwell	S. Stevenson	E. Haynes
1854	Tulip	Jesse Hartwell	S. Stevenson	S. Stevenson
1855	No Report			
1856	New Hope	Jesse Hartwell	R. J. Coleman	W. M. Lea
	Dallas Co.			
1857	Samaria	W. M. Lea	R. J. Coleman	
	Dallas Co.			
1858	Charleston	W. M. Lea	R. M. Thrasher	
1859	Little Rock	W. M. Lea	R. M. Thrasher	
1860	Pine Bluff	W. M. Lea	R. M. Thrasher	
1861	Fort Smith	W. M. Lea	R. M. Thrasher	
1862-1866 (inc.)	No Meetings — W. M. Lea, President			
1867	Little Rock	W. M. Lea	J. K. Brantley	S. Stevenson
1868	Little Rock	W. M. Lea	W. H. Roberts	W. D. Mayfield
1869	Helena	W. D. Mayfield	J. B. Searcy	J. R. Graves
1870	Arkadelphia	A. Yates	J. B. Searcy	W. D. Mayfield
1871	Monticello	M. Y. Moran	J. B. Searcy	Moses Green
1872	Austin	M. Y. Moran	J. B. Searcy	J. M. Hart
1873	Little Rock	M. Y. Moran	J. B. Searcy	R. M. Thrasher
1874	Dardanelle	W. W. Crawford	J. B. Searcy	J. R. G. W. N. Adams
1875	Arkadelphia	H. H. Coleman	J. B. Searcy	J. B. Searcy
1876	Searcy	H. H. Coleman	J. B. Searcy	
1877	Forrest City	H. H. Coleman	T. P. Boone	W. A. Forbes
1878	Monticello	J. M. Hart	W. F. Mack	M. D. Early
1879	Hope	J. M. Hart	J. R. G. W. N. Adams	R. J. Coleman
1880	Russellville	J. P. Eagle	J. R. G. W. N. Adams	J. D. Jameson
1881	Little Rock	J. P. Eagle	B. Thomas	J. B. Searcy
1882	Lonoke	J. P. Eagle	J. B. Searcy	W. E. Paxton
1883	Fayetteville	J. P. Eagle	J. B. Searcy	W. D. Mayfield
1884	Pine Bluff	J. P. Eagle	J. H. Holland	A. J. Kincaid

422

Year	Place			
1885	Hope	J. P. Eagle	J. H. Holland	A. J. Fawcett
1886	Forrest City	J. P. Eagle	J. H. Holland	A. B. Miller
1887	Morrilton	J. P. Eagle	J. H. Holland	A. S. Pettie
1888	Jonesboro	J. P. Eagle	Martin Ball	Enoch Winde
1889	Little Rock	W. E. Penn	J. G. B. Simms	J. R. Hughes
1890	Eureka Spgs.	J. P. Eagle	J. G. B. Simms	R. J. Coleman
1891	Arkadelphia	J. P. Eagle	J. G. B. Simms	W. T. Box
1892	Fort Smith	J. M. Hart	J. G. B. Simms	J. W. Lipsey
1893	Conway	W. P. Throgmorton	W. F. Blackwood	W. P. Throgmorton
1894	Lonoke	J. P. Eagle	W. F. Blackwood	J. H. Peay
1895	Monticello	J. P. Eagle	J. G. B. Simms	E. B. Miller
1896	Hot Springs	J. P. Eagle	J. G. B. Simms	A. H. Autry
1897	Pine Bluff	J. P. Eagle	J. G. B. Simms	O. L. Hailey
1898	Little Rock	J. P. Eagle	W. Theo Smith	W. H. Paslay
1899	Jonesboro	J. P. Eagle	W. Theo Smith	C. W. Daniel
1900	Hope	J. P. Eagle	W. Theo Smith	J. K. Pace
1901	Paragould	J. P. Eagle	W. Theo Smith	N. R. Pittman
1902	Conway	J. P. Eagle	Sam H. Campbell	O. J. Wade
1903	Little Rock	J. P. Eagle	Sam H. Campbell	A. J. Barton
1904	Pine Bluff	John Ayers	W. F. Dorris	W. A. Freeman
1905	Fort Smith	John Ayers	W. F. Dorris	Ben Cox
1906	Texarkana	W. E. Atkinson	Sam H. Campbell	F. F. Gibson
1907	Little Rock	W. E. Atkinson	John Jeter Hurt	H. L. Winburn
1908	Fayetteville	W. E. Atkinson	John Jeter Hurt	W. T. Amis
1909	Arkadelphia	H. T. Bradford	John Jeter Hurt	R. F. Treadway
1910	Fort Smith	H. T. Bradford	John Jeter Hurt	J. T. Christian
1911	Pine Bluff	H. T. Bradford	John Jeter Hurt	N. R. Townsend
1912	Hot Springs	P. C. Barton	E. P. J. Garrott	V. C. Neal
1913	Monticello	P. C. Barton	E. P. J. Garrott	N. M. Geren
1914	Little Rock	P. C. Barton	E. P. J. Garrott	A. H. Autry
1915	Conway	P. C. Barton	E. P. J. Garrott	W. J. E. Cox
1916	Malvern	J. W. Conger	E. P. J. Garrott	T. D. Brown
1917	Jonesboro	J. W. Conger	E. P. J. Garrott	B. B. Bailey
1918	Little Rock	L. E. Barton	D. S. Campbell	C. D. Wood
1919	Little Rock	L. E. Barton	D. S. Campbell	B. V. Ferguson
1920	Fort Smith	A. H. Autry	B. L. Bridges	Austin Crouch
1921	Pine Bluff	A. H. Autry	B. L. Bridges	Calvin B. Waller
1922	Little Rock	A. H. Autry	B. L. Bridges	E. P. J. Garrott
1923	Arkadelphia	G. W. Puryear	B. L. Bridges	J. W. Hulsey
1924	Little Rock	G. W. Puryear	B. L. Bridges	W. W. Kyzar
1925	Conway	G. W. Puryear	S. R. Doyle	O. J. Wade
1926	Little Rock	H. L. Winburn	S. R. Doyle	L. M. Sipes
1927	Jonesboro	H. L. Winburn	S. R. Doyle	T. H. Jordan
1928	Texarkana	H. L. Winburn	S. R. Doyle	Ben L. Bridges
1929	Hot Springs	Otto Whitington	J. B. Luck	Otto Whitington
1930	Fort Smith	Otto Whitington	J. B. Luck	Perry F. Webb
1931	Batesville	E. P. J. Garrott	J. B. Luck	A. S. Harwell
1932	Little Rock	E. P. J. Garrott	J. B. Luck	C. V. Hickerson
1933	No Meeting			
1934	El Dorado	O. J. Wade	J. B. Luck	L. M. Keeling
1935	Pine Bluff	O. J. Wade	J. B. Luck	J. G. Cothran
1936	Hot Springs	B. V. Ferguson	J. B. Luck	T. L. Harris
1937	Paragould (January)	B. V. Ferguson	J. B. Luck	C. W. Daniel
1937	Fort Smith (November)	L. M. Sipes	J. B. Luck	Thomas W. Croxton
1938	Arkadelphia	L. M. Sipes	J. B. Luck	Elmer J. Kirkbride
1939	Camden	Calvin B. Waller	J. B. Luck	A. M. Herrington
1940	Monticello	Calvin B. Waller	J. B. Luck	O. L. Powers
1941	Jonesboro	J. S. Rogers	Taylor Stanfill	C. C. Warren
1942	Little Rock	J. S. Rogers	Taylor Stanfill	W. J. Hinsley
1943	Little Rock	T. L. Harris	Taylor Stanfill	W. R. Vestal
1944	Little Rock	T. L. Harris	Taylor Stanfill	J. F. Queen
1945	Little Rock	W. J. Hinsley	Taylor Stanfill	V. H. Coffman
1946	Texarkana	W. J. Hinsley	Taylor Stanfill	M. Ray McKay
1947	Little Rock	W. J. Hinsley	Taylor Stanfill	B. H. Duncan
1948	Little Rock	E. C. Brown	Taylor Stanfill	B. V. Ferguson
1949	Little Rock	E. C. Brown	W. Dawson King	J. A. Overton
1950	Little Rock	T. H. Jordan	W. Dawson King	H. A. Elledge
1951	Little Rock	T. H. Jordan	W. Dawson King	Lloyd A. Sparkman
1952	Little Rock	Lloyd A. Sparkman	W. Dawson King	W. M. Pratt
1953	Hot Springs	Lloyd A. Sparkman	W. Dawson King	W. O. Vaught
1954	Little Rock	W. O. Vaught	W. Dawson King	T. K. Rucker
1955	Little Rock	W. O. Vaught	W. Dawson King	C. Z. Holland
1956	Little Rock	Rel Gray	W. Dawson King	S. A. Whitlow
1957	Little Rock	Rel Gray	W. Dawson King	Hugh Cantrell
1958	Little Rock	T. K. Rucker	W. Dawson King	W. Harold Hicks
1959	Little Rock	T. K. Rucker	S. A. Whitlow	Don Hook
1960	Fayetteville	Bernes K. Selph	S. A. Whitlow	S. W. Eubanks
1961	Little Rock	Bernes K. Selph	S. A. Whitlow	Robert L. Smith
1962	Little Rock	C. Z. Holland	S. A. Whitlow	Minor E. Cole
1963	Little Rock	C. Z. Holland	S. A. Whitlow	Lloyd L. Hunnicutt
1964	El Dorado	Walter L. Yeldell	S. A. Whitlow	E. E. Griever

Year	City		President		Secretary		Preacher
1965	Little Rock		Walter L. Yeldell		S. A. Whitlow		Lehman F. Webb
1966	Little Rock		Don Hook		S. A. Whitlow		Dale Cowling
1967	Little Rock		Don Hook		S. A. Whitlow		Thomas A. Hinson
1968	Hot Springs		Thomas A. Hinson		S. A. Whitlow		Andrew Hall
1969	Fort Smith		Thomas A. Hinson		Charles H. Ashcraft		Herbert Hodges
1970	Little Rock		Tal Bonham		Charles H. Ashcraft		William L. Bennett
1971	Little Rock		Tal Bonham		Charles H. Ashcraft		Wilbur Herring
1972	Hot Springs		Rheubin L. South		Charles H. Ashcraft		Bernes K. Selph
1973	Little Rock		Rheubin L. South		Charles H. Ashcraft		George T. Blackmon
1974	Little Rock		Don Moore		Charles H. Ashcraft		C.W. Caldwell
1975	Fort Smith		Don Moore		Charles H. Ashcraft		John McClanahan
1976	No. Little Rock		R. Wilbur Herring		Charles H. Ashcraft		Loyd Hunnicutt
1977	Little Rock		R. Wilbur Herring		Charles H. Ashcraft		Johnny Jackson, Sr.
1978	Little Rock		Johnny Jackson, Sr.		Charles H. Ashcraft		Kendell Black

APPENDIX D
STATISTICAL SUMMARY

	Assoc.	Churches	Church Mbrshp.	Bapt.	S.S. Enroll.	V.B.S. Enroll.	T.U. Enroll.	W.M.U. Enroll.	Bro'd. Enroll.	Missions Gifts	Music	Total Gifts	Valued Ch. Prop.
1828	1	16	124	11									
1831	2	27	189										
1840	3	25	372	2									
1841	6	43	798	105									
1842	6	46	860	8									
1843	7	56	1,782	44									
1844	5	51	1,621	227									
1845	6	58	1,771	150									
1846	6	67	2,015	75									
1847	5	58	1,600	75									
1848	6	73	2,355	307								77.55	
1849	6	78	2,509	310								752.00*	
1850	6	78	2,509	310								650.00*	
1851	9	120	3,752	443						770.68		491.00*	
1852	...No Figures Given in the Baptist Almanac ...											99.00*	
1853	9	129	4,483	537								622.00*	
1854	12	144	5,155	644								660.00*	
1855	15	166	5,859	888									
1856	15	179	6,479	945									
1857	16	213	7,158	972									
1858	16	255	8,704	971									
1859	16	269	9,491	838									
1860	16	301	10,924	1,204						65.55			
1861	16	321	11,341	1,272						32.50			
1867					60					7.00 to SBC Domestic Board			
1868					210					140.00 to SBC Boards			
1869										79.40 to SBC Boards			
1870	28	547	30,297	1,030	5,000					5,335.46			
1871										130.40 to SBC Boards			
1872			10,057	1,031	3,000					1,586.00			
1873										71.28 to SBC Boards			
1874	32		26,055	3,084						475.75			
1875										217.10 to SBC Boards			
1876										467.40 to SBC Boards			
1877	36	993	44,619	3,000						291.62 to SBC Boards			
1878	42	1,101	48,005	2,304						1,152.31 to SBC Boards			
1879										282.58 to SBC Boards			
1880	38	820	35,997	1,662	5,500			21		6,612.32		6,612.32	
1881										6,201.22		7,685.42	
1882	35	830	37,116	265						561.30 from 4 Asso.			
1883	36	863	39,151	2,028									
+1884	40	937	43,500	2,335									
	11	344	22,413	434						3,841			
1885	40	927	40,486	2,446								4,365.72	
	12	417	28,191	628								674.25	
1886	41	976	45,338	3,399								13,667.99	
	14	450	30,829	349								801.21	
1887	39	1,028	47,604	4,308								22,629.19	
	19	403	29,597	459								4,701.70	
1888	41	1,053	49,793	4,248								48,407.73	151,900.00
	25	450	32,699	684								5,918.25	
1889	43	1,092	52,402	5,349								45,710.81	217,689.00
	5	466	32,493	358								1,895.86	
1890	42	1,125	55,497	4,725	9,154			47				59,936.73	246,625.00
		468	32,493										
1891	47	1,176	59,345	5,375								59,443.70	239,150.00
		437	30,793	570								10,315.50	
1892	48	1,255	64,912	4,859								64,679.34	293,430.00
		558	37,405	965						4,397.14		1,610.75	
1893	49	1,240	63,758	4,859								87,304.39	385,136.00
1894	50	1,302	67,895	6,986								78,032.31	391,614.00
1895	50	1,345	71,171	5,145						800.30		62,319.72	383,661.00
1896	49	1,372	72,560	6,534	19,190					10,025.54		69,302.02	426,832.00
1897	48	1,396	74,360	5,262	20,136					9,743.30		66,836.63	447,635.00
1898	47	1,354	71,223	2,599	19,127					13,957.02		69,091.94	447,750.00
1899	48	1,341	70,955	3,896	17,398					17,515.64		74,757.75	469,146.00
1900	47	1,321	71,419	4,241	18,943	3	40			18,236.62		101,001.64	488,708.00
1901	47	1,331	74,117	5,994	21,612					20,633.34		102,982.79	511,840.00
1902	47	1,243	75,977	4,588	22,686					21,179.62		113,970.01	557,280.00
1903	47	1,327	77,590	5,117	25,480					28,973.20		114,123.51	585,099.00
1904	49	1,355	80,705	5,547	23,569					36,642.47		132,471.41	612,855.00
1905	49	1,368	84,642	5,809	24,213			74		38,650.74		157,086.45	718,257.00
1906	49	1,389	88,262	7,372	27,702					49,110.58		189,242.42	800,597.00
1907	49	1,449	92,821	7,157	30,014					60,597.77		225,048.19	926,783.00

424

APPENDIX D
STATISTICAL SUMMARY

Year	Assoc.	Churches	Church Mbrshp.	Bapt.	S.S. Enroll.	V.B.S. Enroll.	T.U. Enroll.	W.M.U. Enroll.	Bro'd. Enroll.	Missions Gifts	Music	Total Gifts	Valued Ch. Prop.
1908	49	1,490	99,872	7,265	38,122							225,360.89	1,137,771.00
1909	50	1,536	105,455	6,337	36,897					90,749.64			
1910	51	1,534	106,628	7,243	41,047		3,200	3,972				395,534.64	1,496,835.00
1911	50	1,527	108,248	5,996	41,418					85,400.25			
1912	50	1,531	109,629	4,596	42,815					70,118.04		332,988.18	1,692,495.00
1913	50	1,528	111,991	4,296	45,519					85,331.25		342,931.01	1,741,010.00
1914	50	1,514	111,185	6,362	51,519					95,469.87		371,222.86	2,017,821.00
1915	52	1,483	114,713	7,278	57,865		6,916	7,302		105,490.58		371,751.83	1,957,951.00
1916	54	1,488	118,930	7,397	59,243					122,018.67		411,475.91	2,031,770.00
1917	54	1,547	112,635	6,419	61,359					174,685.35		443,811.04	2,147,504.00
1918	56	1,489	121,484	4,435	65,965					171,891.59		537,442.15	2,046,477.00
1919	51	1,529	128,115	3,992	59,189					369,768.26		525,442.15	2,150,052.00
1920	51	1,428	124,024	6,833	55,975		7,250	701		223,816.98		1,028,024.97	2,794,717.23
1921	48	1,135	98,376	7,912	56,582		6,248			275,713.23		824,164.11	3,015,275.00
1922	49	1,174	106,409	8,910	67,110		8,172			265,607.93		1,100,538.67	3,455,702.00
1923	42	998	100,302	7,132	69,518		10,659			307,769.68		1,102,837.20	3,715,463.00
1924	41	920	101,589	7,674	74,370		16,320			324,647.87		1,294,222.78	3,019,110.00
1925	41	953	106,374	7,988	87,206		13,279	961		338,609.31		1,216,374.80	4,223,025.00
1926	45	1,030	112,231	7,165	79,440		14,743					1,288,882.49	4,564,977.00
1927	45	961	108,961	6,936	88,686		14,775			184,407.09		1,215,464.82	5,307,511.82
1928	44	917	106,804	6,427	85,875		16,013			192,336.00		1,205,423.28	5,721,291.82
1929	45	854	108,137	6,123	81,682	575	15,825			236,047.43		1,241,608.93	6,343,111.00
1930	45	827	108,860	6,648	84,399	3,830	15,747	14,675	30	248,095.20		1,218,693.82	6,317,430.00
1931	45	820	110,962	7,691	86,247	10 sch	18,780	15,010		146,884.86		943,673.17	6,170,833.00
1932	43	803	112,815	8,668	87,995	965	20,474	16,937		116,132.12		778,897.49	5,597,929.10
1933	43	824	119,876	9,432	89,993	1,640	22,054	10,860		87,295.99		685,017.10	5,248,740.00
1934	42	822	125,827	8,414	90,985	2,330	23,087	18,800		113,177.31		746,220.28	5,384,298.00
1935	42	853	129,903	7,458	96,566	4,020	25,130	21,815		122,062.25		783,863.23	5,374,264.00
1936	40	877	132,870	7,462	99,102	5,129	24,430	21,813		129,049.33		878,647.57	5,413,316.00
1937	40	864	135,854	6,965	99,831	9,047	33,337	22,000		291,741.47		1,059,688.11	5,484,690.00
1938	40	892	145,386	10,501	108,089	13,648	35,013	25,312		166,608.79		1,032,898.35	5,578,990.00
1939	40	929	152,773	11,854	118,055	12,496	45,100	26,490		174,976.23		1,143,720.85	5,714,722.00
1940	40	903	154,635	11,636	122,864	151	41,464	27,775		194,869.85		1,383,944.83	5,657,782.00
1941	40	904	158,443	8,923	117,126	18,372	39,953	28,154		279,816.00		1,641,011.34	5,870,712.00
1942	40	973	170,017	8,046	118,526	160	36,090	26,396	667	290,186.61		1,709,571.54	6,453,803.91
1943	40	920	169,171	7,577	106,680	161	26,712	15,574	503	391,702.76		2,233,040.77	6,837,585.00
1944	40	887	176,292	8,183	105,501	170	28,024	16,619	390	471,637.51		2,712,729.62	7,410,421.00
1945	40	892	181,060	9,539	113,356	185	33,278	28,248	677	601,070.00		3,314,104.00	8,307,796.00
1946	42	920	189,930	9,930	123,974	296	39,507	22,702	2,377	873,417.00		1,058,590.00	9,603,314.00
1947	42	1,034	200,572	11,476	135,543	31,254	43,296	23,021	2,240	922,470.00		5,629,260.00	11,372,893.00
1948	42	961	211,728	13,947	148,400	36,375	51,015	25,896	4,427	976,480.00		5,663,111.00	14,858,787.00
1949	42	992	218,514	14,560	160,305	39,285	61,462	28,502	4,910	1,192,800.41		6,955,931.20	16,617,943.00
1950	43	1,033	235,306	16,367	172,254	43,706	67,546	31,315	6,433	2,069,697.77		8,617,799.81	20,351,274.27
1951	44	1,003	242,156	14,023	181,406	47,850	73,319	31,843	6,441	1,154,840.00		7,463,317.00	23,429,692.00
1952	45	1,043	252,930	14,948	169,187	56,660	75,555	30,242	8,322	1,505,495.00		8,389,662.00	28,874,978.00
1953	45	1,093	261,277	13,418	186,520	64,724	81,416	35,492	8,347	1,638,267.00		8,997,833.00	33,641,717.00
1954	45	1,137	273,323	14,693	201,005	49,480	90,458	39,380	8,850	1,721,929.00		10,001,492.00	36,731,384.00
1955	45	1,146	283,820	15,037	206,455	75,543	94,452	36,574	11,942	1,872,565.00		10,696,915.00	41,438,545.00
1956	45	1,169	285,402	13,452	209,864	75,896	94,406	36,420	12,105	2,074,569.00		11,848,952.00	46,103,573.00
1957	44	1,143	289,981	12,232	204,840	78,201	92,093	36,263	12,061	2,166,705.00		11,585,421.00	48,452,202.00
1958	44	1,152	294,056	12,919	207,526	81,669	91,337	37,069	10,522	2,227,910.00		11,663,200.00	53,726,171.00
1959	44	1,155	296,945	12,681	208,411	77,556	93,656	37,250	11,561	2,322,344.00		13,034,828.00	57,887,934.00
1960	44	1,158	301,435	11,838	210,733	82,725	93,911	36,583	11,285	2,420,481.00		13,702,776.00	61,056,837.00
1961	44	1,164	309,931	12,771	215,158	82,539	96,711	36,697	11,998	2,505,362.00	19,549	14,210,331.00	64,909,872.00
1962	43	1,177	313,806	11,248	215,507	84,103	95,319	36,177	9,923	2,854,565.00	21,396	15,568,888.00	70,517,141.00
1963	43	1,178	318,378	10,226	215,501	85,289	95,845	36,017	9,436	2,854,565.00	21,509	16,086,432.00	76,778,640.00
1964	43	1,184	321,664	10,413	215,969	86,464	93,605	34,373	8,586	3,024,896.00	22,909	16,917,823.00	81,309,653.00
1965	43	1,188	326,354	10,401	215,049	84,145	94,032	35,534	9,259	3,128,603.00	23,472	17,889,465.00	84,024,094.00
1966	43	1,190	332,198	10,411	213,261	82,580	91,781	33,971	8,741	3,401,770.00	25,530	18,906,315.00	92,180,559.00
1967	43	1,191	338,471	11,598	212,961	86,088	92,459	34,555	9,263	3,594,676.00	28,483	20,602,971.00	97,933,807.00
1968	44	1,189	343,336	11,386	213,496	85,978	100,476	34,957	9,049	3,901,368.00	29,021	23,111,680.00	101,418,714.00
1969	44	1,183	344,990	10,733	208,620	80,936	95,103	31,373	8,584	4,027,653.00	28,819	24,120,608.00	109,713,000.00
1970	44	1,187	349,661	11,197	207,144	81,321	91,911	28,764	7,819	4,180,310.00	28,714	25,166,317.00	113,762,000.00
1971	44	1,188	356,703	12,335	205,853	79,241	84,326	27,431	9,001	4,883,232.00	29,429	27,587,756.00	119,949,000.00
1972	44	1,193	367,620	14,551	212,555	90,369	84,772	27,089	9,324	6,048,663.00	31,183	31,672,637.00	126,829,000.00
1973	44	1,198	378,117	13,918	215,928	90,286	84,010	26,028	8,643	6,451,591.00	35,381	35,279,313.00	137,574,000.00
1974	44	1,198	390,333	14,606	222,559	95,668	83,327	26,171	8,491	7,714,637.00	37,863	40,884,034.00	154,654,000.00
1975	42	1,205	398,116	14,086	226,387	100,266	83,514	26,231	8,940	8,371,852.00	38,351	45,507,398.00	170,104,000.00
1976	42	1,213	406,878	13,237	233,211	98,245	83,173	26,298	9,016	9,180,311.00	38,740	51,804,371.00	189,917,000.00
1977	42	1,229	416,338	11,492	232,694	95,812	80,321	26,958	9,664	10,862,849.00	40,935	56,936,860.00	214,685,000.00

*Amounts received by State Convention as per the 1854 State Convention Annual
+Double figures indicate White and Colored
Statistical information for earlier years, see ENCYCLOPEDIA OF SOUTHERN BAPTISTS.
Vol. I, page 80 - 1828-1954
Vol. III, page 1579 - 1955-1968

APPENDIX E-1
ASSOCIATIONS IN THE ABSC

Currently Active	Association	Began	Ended	Comments
	Arkansas	1841	?	
	Arkansas Co.	1920	1933	
★	Arkansas Valley	1920		
★	Ashley Co.	1950		
	Baptist	1884	1887	
★	Bartholomew	1850		
★	Benton Co.	1885		
	Benton Co. #1	1885		In 1903 two Benton Cos. began to be listed. Benton Co. #1 became Landmark in 1920.
	Benton Co.#2	1903		This association continued in the ABSC.
★	Big Creek	1874		
	Big Ford	1886	1897	
★	Black River	1914		
	Blue Mountain	1874		Blue Mountain became Landmark in 1920, but was still listed in ABSC in 1921-22.
	Boone	1951	1962	Boone was formed by division of Boone-Carroll in 1951; in 1962 it united with Newton Co. to form Boone-Newton.
	Boone-Carroll	1938	1951	Boone-Carroll was formed by union of Crooked Creek and Carroll Co.; in 1951 it divided into Boone and Carroll.
	Boone-Newton	1962	1974	Boone-Newton was formed by union of Boone and Newton in 1962; in 1974 its name was changed to North Arkansas.
★	Buckner	1878		The SBC **Annual** for 1892 identified this as South Concord.
★	Buckville	1889		
★	Caddo River	1853		
	Caddo River, South	1910	1912	This was listed in SBC **Annual** in 1911-13, but, since only one report was received, it may have closed in 1911.
	Caddo Valley	1913	1923	
★	Calvary	1962		
★	Carey	1915		
★	Caroline	1885		
	Carroll Co.	1870	1938	In 1938 Carroll united with Crooked
		1951	1974	Creek to form Boone-Carroll; it divided in 1951 again.
★	Centennial	1946		
★	Central	1884	1891	Central consolidate with Velvet Ridge in 1891 to form Steven's Creek; in 1920 it was again listed in ABSC.
★	Clear Creek	1872		
	Columbia	1852		Columbia became Landmark in 1920.
★	Concord	1870		

	Concord West	1886	1889	
★	Conway-Perry	1948		
	Crooked Creek	1867	1938	Crooked Creek united with Carroll Co. to form Boone-Carroll in 1938.
	Current River	1880	1975	Current River united with Gainsville to form Current-Gains in 1975. A Landmark Current River also began in 1923.
★	Current-Gains	1975		
	Dardanelle	1854	1932	Dardanelle united with Russellville in 1932.
★	Dardanelle-Russell-ville	1932		
★	Delta	1929		
	Elberta	1927	1931	Prior to 1927 Elberta was the Howard Co. Assoc.; in 1931 it consolidated with Little River.
★	Faulkner Co.	1928		Faulkner Co. was formerly Greenbrier.
	Fayetteville	1870		Fayetteville became Landmark in 1920.
	Fellowship	1927	1929	
	Fourche Valley	1881	1941	
	Friendship	1872		Friendship became Landmark in 1921.
	Gainsville	1869	1975	Gainsville united with Current River in 1975 to form Current-Gains.
	Grand Prairie	1874		Grand Prairie became Landmark in 1923.
★	Greene Co.	1925		
	Greenbrier	1883	1928	Greenbrier became Faulkner Co. in 1928. A Greenbrier Missionary Assoc. also began in 1920 (LM).
★	Harmony	1918		A Landmark Harmony Assoc. formed in 1920, but one also continued in ABSC.
	Hope	1908	1976	
	Howard Co.	1893	1927	A Landmark Howard Co. began in 1920; in 1927 the ABSC Howard Co. became Elberts Assoc.
★	Independence	1850		
	Jonesboro	1899		Jonesboro became Landmark in 1920.
	Judson	1854		Judson became Landmark in 1920.
★	Liberty	1845		
★	Little Red River	1872		
★	Little River	1915		Consolidated with Elberta in 1931, Little River continued as Little River.
	Little Rock	1824	1832	
	Macedonia	1885	1896	A Landmark Macedonia began in 1920.
	Madison Co.	1888	1932	The **Annual** of ABSC began listing a Washington-Madison Assoc. in 1941.
	Miller Co.	1904	1908	Miller Co. disbanded and joined Hope.
★	Mississippi Co.	1925		
	Monroe	1931	1938	Monroe merged with Arkansas Valley and Tri-County.
	Motor Cities	1952	1957	

427

	Mount Vernon	1867	Mount Vernon became Landmark in 1920.
★	Mount Zion	1852	
	New Salem	1848	1852
	Newton Co.	1945	1962 Newton Co. consolidated with Boone to form Boone-Newton.
★	North Arkansas	1974	North Arkansas was named Boone-Newton prior to 1974.
★	North Pulaski	1962	
	Osceola	1872	1900
★	Ouachita	1870	
	Pee Dee	1883	1924 Pee Dee was last listed in the State Convention **Annual** in 1924.
	Perry Co.	1943	1948 A Landmark Perry Co. began in 1920. In 1943 the ABSC began to list a Perry Co; in 1948 it became Conway-Perry.
	Pike Co.	1909	1923 Pike Co. became Landmark in 1923 and united with Clarke Co.
	Pine Bluff	1862	Pine Bluff became Landmark in 1920.
	Pleasant Plains	1884	1886
★	Pulaski Co.	1916	
★	Red River	1848	
★	Rocky Bayou	1840	A Rocky Bayou Landmark Assoc began in 1921, but this one continued in the ABSC.
	Russellville	1880	1932 Russellville united with Dardanelle in 1932 to form Dardanelle-Russellville.
	Salem in N.W. Ark.	1840	?
	Salem near Bates-ville	1847	1848
	Saline	1836	Saline became Landmark in 1920.
	St. Francis Co.	1831	1850
		1924	1925 A St. Francis was listed in the SBC **Annual** again in 1925.
	Searcy Co.	1923	1944 Searcy Co. was apparently inactive
		1971	1978 from 1935 to 1944. In 1944 it united with Stone Van Buren. This union divided in 1971. Searcy disbanded in 1978.
	Sebastian Co.	1920	1922
★	Southwest Arkansas	1976	
	Southwestern	1880	Southwestern became Landmark in 1920.
	Spring River	1829	1840
		1868	Spring River became Landmark in 1923.
	Springtown	1883	1885 Springtown consolidated with Benton-ville in 1885 to form Benton Co.
	Spring Valley	1891	1893
	State Corner	1885	1836
	State Line	1874	1924 State Line was absorbed by Current River.

428

Stevens Creek	1891		Stevens Creek was formed by consolidation of Central and Velvet Ridge. It became Landmark in 1920. It was also listed in the variant spelling of Stephens Creek.
Stone Co.	1919	1932	Stone Co. consolidated with Van Buren in 1932.
Stone-Van Buren	1933	1944	Stone-Van Buren was a consolidation of these two assocs.
Stone-Van Buren-Searcy	1944	1971	After division in 1971 Van Buren and Searcy continued separately.
Texarkana	1873	1896	
Trace Ridge	1891		Trace Ridge became Landmark in 1923.
★ Tri-County	1925		
★ Trinity	1938		
Union	1871		A Union #1 was listed as Landmark in 1920, in ABSC in 1921, and as Landmark from 1922 on. A Union #2 was also listed as Landmark in 1920, in ABSC in 1921, but not listed after 1921.
Union #1	1871		
Union #2	1877	1921?	
United	1874		United became Landmark in 1923.
Van Buren Co.	1923	1932	Van Buren Co. consolidated with Stone Co. and later with Searcy Co.
★ Van Buren Co.	1971		In 1971 it separated again.
Velvet Ridge	1889	1891	Velvet Ridge consolidated with Central to form Stevens Creek.
Washington Co.	1919	1941	Washington Co. merged with Madison Co. in 1941.
★ Washington-Madison	1941		
West Arkansas	1884	1887	
White Co.	1926	1961	
★ White River	1840		
White River Valley	1872	1910	
Woodruff	1928	1961	

429

APPENDIX E-2
LANDMARK ASSOCIATIONS

Association	Began	Became Landmark	Comments
Benton Co.	1885	1920	Benton Co. was listed first as Benton Co. #1.
Bethlehem	1922	1922	
Blue Mountain	1874	1920	Blue Mountain was listed as Landmark in 1920, ABSC in 1921, 1922, and Landmark thereafter.
Caglesville	1923	1923	
Centerpoint	1920		
Clarke Co.	1920		
Clarke-Pike	1923	1923	Clarke-Pike was formed by a union of Clarke Co., which was Landmark from the beginning with Pike Co., which became Landmark in 1923.
Columbia	1852	1920	
Current River	1880	1923	Current River was probably rooted in the ABSC assoc. of the same name.
Fayetteville	1870	1920	
Friendship	1872	1921	
Grand Prairie	1874	1923	
Greenbrier Missionary	1920	1920	G.M. was probably rooted in the Greenbrier Assoc.
Harmony	1920	1920	Harmony probably grew out of the ABSC Harmony Assoc.
Howard Co.	1893	1920	A Howard Co. became Elberta Assoc. in ABSC in 1927. It is uncertain whether this is the same assoc.
Jonesboro	1899	1920	
Judson	1854	1920	
Lonoke	1921	1921	
Macedonia	1920	1920	A Macedonia Assoc. was connected with the ABSC between 1885 and 1896.
Mount Hope	1920	1920	
Mount Vernon	1867	1920	
Mo.-Ark.	1922	1922	
New Prospect	1920	1920	
Perry Co.	1920	1920	A Perry Co. was listed in the 1943 ABSC Annual; it joined Conway in 1947. It is not known if a Landmark assoc. continued.
Pike Co.	1909	1923	This assoc. ceased separate existence when it became Landmark, joining Clarke Co. in 1923.
Pine Bluff	1862	1920	
Rocky Bayou	1840	1921	Rocky Bayou was probably rooted in the ABSC assoc. of the same name.
Saline	1836	1920	
Southwestern	1880	1920	
Spring River	1868	1923	
Stevens Creek	1890	1920	
Trace Ridge	1889	1923	

Union	1920	1920	Union apparently grew out of Union #1, which became Landmark in 1920, and Union #2 which was listed as Landmark in 1921 but not referred to thereafter.
United	1874	1923	

APPENDIX F
ARKANSAS BAPTIST CHURCHES
AND THEIR FOUNDING DATES
LISTED BY ASSOCIATION

Arkansas Valley

Barton	1921	Lambrock	1955
Brickeys Community	1945	Lexa	1932
Brinkley, First	1883	Marianna	1858
Calvary	1974	Marvell, First	1877
Chatfield	1920	Monroe	1937
Clarendon, First	1895	Moro	1918
Elaine	1908	Northside	1954
Friendship	1938	Pettys Chapel	1933
Helena, First	1851	Snow Lake	1953
Holly Grove	1978	Turner	1920
Hughes	1922	West Helena, First	1911
Immanuel	1976	West Helena, Second	1954
Lakeland			

Ashley County

Calvary	1955	Magnolia	1911
Corinth	1906	Martinville	1950
Crossett, First	1906	Merician	1866
Crossett, Second	1950	Mount Pleasant	1876
Eden	1910	Mt. Olive, Crossett	1906
Fellowship	1864	North Crossett, First	1944
Fountain Hill, First	1845	Sardis	1875
Gardner	1964	Shiloh	1894
Hamburg, First	1859	Temple	1953
Jarvis Chapel	1915		

Bartholomew

Antioch	1848	Monticello, First	1860
Cominto	1938	Monticello, Second	1922
Corinth	1923	Northside	1944
Eagle Lk Cr Rds	1922	Old Union	1944
Ebenezer	1854	Pleasant Grove	1941
Enon	1885	Prairie Grove	1869
Florence	1895	Saline	1910
Hermitage	1847	Selma	1934
Immanuel	1940	Union Hill	1856
Ladelle	1913	Warren, First	1868
Macedonia	1901	West Side	1965
Marsden	1909	Wilmar	1899

Benton Association

Bella Vista	1973	Mason Valley	1879
Bentonville, First	1884	Mount NE	1946
Centerion, First	1919	Open Door	1973
Central Avenue	1953	Park Street	1971
Decator, First	1869	Pea Ridge, First	1872
Faith	1973	Pleasant Hill	1852
Garfield, First	1889	Ro Lynn Hills	1976
Gentry, First	1895	Rogers, First	1889
Gravette, First	1896	Siloam Springs, First	1868
Gum Springs	1889	Sugar Creek	1897
Harvard Avenue	1954	Sulphur Springs, First	1896
Highfill, First	1910	Sunnyside	1954
Immanuel	1941	Trinity	1961
Lake View	1954	Twelve Corners	1846
Lowell	1868		

Big Creek Association

Cherokee Vlg., First	1973	Mammoth Springs	1894
County Line	1900	Mount Zion	1866
Eliazbeth	1953	Saddle	1951
Enterprise	1884	Spring River	1891
Flora	1904	Viola	1893
Gum Springs	1919		

Black River Association

Alicia	1897	New Hope No. 1	1844
Amagon	1963	New Hope, Hardy	1875
Banks	1946	Newport, First	1892
Black Rock, First	1888	Old Walnut Ridge	1882
Campbell Station	1956	Pitts	1953
Clear Spring	1885	Pleasant Ridge	1955
College City	1948	Ravenden, First	1942
Diaz	1940	Sedgwick	1907
Grubbs, First	1898	Smithville	1866
Horseshoe	1912	Southside Newport	1976
Hoxie, First	1906	Spring Lake	1965
Imboden, First	1893	Swifton	1906
Immanuel	1948	Tuckerman, First	1894
Jacksonport	1945	Walnut Ridge, First	1889
Murphy's Corner	1972	White Oak	1933

Buckner Association

Abbott	1939	Ione	1873
Abbott Pleasant Grv	1884	James Fork	1874
Bates	1914	Long Ridge	1863
Calvary	1952	Mansfield, First	1904
Cauthron	1915	Midland, First	1904
Cedar Creek	1904	New Providence	1889
Clarks Chapel	1947	Parks	1893
Dayton	1874	Pleasant Grove Waldr	1871

Denton	1909	Rock Creek	1927
Evening Shade	1960	Shiloh	1872
Fellowship	1888	Temple	1962
Friendship	1912	Union Hope	1878
Hartford, First	1901	Unity	1892
Haw Creek	1911	Waldron, First	1882
Hon	1880	West Hartford	1885
Huntington, First	1890	Winfield	1868

Buckville Association

Cedar Glades	1877	Mount Tabor	1871
Concord	1907	Rock Springs	1866

Caddo River Association

Amity	1891	Mount Ida, First	1914
Black Springs	1880	Murphy	1948
Caddo Gap	1905	Norman	1908
Glenwood	1910	Oak Grove	1888
Hillside	1958	Oden	1916
Lake Ouachita	1975	Pencil Bluff	1958
Liberty	1850	Pine Ridge	1939
Little Hope	1904	Refuge	1885
Mount Gilead	1838	Sulphur Springs	1906

Calvary Association

Antioch	1875	Midway	1950
Augusta, First	1873	Morrow	1944
Beebe, First	1889	Morton	1936
Bethany	1908	Mount Hebron	1876
Central	1898	Pangburn, First	1912
Cotton Plant, First	1910	Patterson, First	1950
Crosby	1921	Pleasant Grove	1860
Denmark	1967	Pleasant Valley	1909
Denmark, First	1977	Raynor Grove	1926
El Paso	1848	Rocky Point	1942
Good Hope	1889	Rose Bud	1878
Grace	1965	Royal Hill	1976
Gregory	1947	Searcy, First	1870
Griffithville, First	1891	Searcy, Second	1953
Higginson	1880	Temple	1962
Hunter, First	1914	Trinity	1962
Judsonia, First	1872	Tupelo, First	1867
Kensett, First	1886	Union Valley	1927
Liberty	1890	Valley	1977
McCrory, First	1905	West Point	1854
McRae, First	1918		

Carey Association

Bearden, First	1895	New Hope	1843
Bethesda	1847	Ouachita	1887
Calvary, Camden	1952	Prosperity	1904
Dalark	1896	Shady Grove	1919

433

Eagle Mills	1953	Southside	1955
Faith	1966	Sparkman, First	1914
Fordyce, First	1850	Thornton, First	1889
Hampton, First	1906	Tinsman	1907
Harmony	1919	Tulip	1963
Holly Springs	1845	Willow	1957
Manning	1915		

Caroline Association

Austin Station	1901	Hazen, First	1882
Baugh Chapel	1880	Hummoke	1954
Biscoe, First	1926	Immanuel	1966
Brownsville	1934	Keo	1896
Cabot, First	1876	Lonoke	1869
Cabot, Second	1965	Mount Carmel	1948
Calvary	1977	Mountain Springs	1974
Caney Creek	1896	New Hope	1850
Carlisle, First	1877	Oak Grove	1891
Chambers	1940	Old Austin	1835
Coclebur	1960	Pleasant Hill	1855
Coy	1921	Steel Bridge	1911
Cross Roads	1880	Toltec	1937
De Valls, First	1902	Ward, First	1925
Des Ark, First	1859	Wattensaw	1856
England, First	1876		

Centennial Association

Aberdeen, First	1970	North Maple	1956
Almyra, First	1896	Reydell	1931
Dewitt, First	1858	Southside	1962
Eastside	1948	St. Charles	1952
Gillett	1950	Stuttgart, First	1976
Gillett, First	1965	Tichnor	1977
Hagler	1850		

Central

Antioch	1891	Leonard St.	1972
Benton, First	1836	Lonsdale	1900
Benton, Trinity	1960	Malvern, Third	1914
Bryant, First	1965	Malvern, Trinity	1965
Buie	1953	Memorial	1947
Calvary	1949	Millcreek	1948
Central	1924	Mount Vernon	1936
Emmanuel	1949	Mountain Pine	1936
Fairdale	1957	Mountain Valley	1935
Faith	1955	Old Union	1830
Gilead	1950	Owensville	1926
Grand Avenue	1949	Park Place	1902
Gravel Hill	1895	Pearcy	1951
Harvey's Chapel	1888	Perla	1873
Highland Heights	1960	Piney	1940
Hilldale	1975	Pleasant Hill	1906
Hot Springs, First	1836	Rector Heights	1962
Hot Springs, Second	1903	Ridgcrest	1954
Hurricane Lake	1975	Riverside	1956

Indian Springs	1975	Salem	1968
Jessieville	1936	Sheridan, First	1955
Lake Hamilton	1932	Shorewood Hills	1944
Lakeshore Heights	1964	Vista Height	1969
Lakeside	1965	Walnut Valley	1939
Lee Chapel	1948		

Clear Creek Association

Alma, First	1873	Clarksville, First	1885
Altus, First	1929	Clarksville, Second	1954
Batson	1970	Coal Hill, First	1884
Cass	1952	Concord	1872
Cedarville	1934	Dyer	1872
East Mount Zion Trinity	1909	Shady Grove	1900
Hagarville	1920	Shilbey	1925
Hartman	1950	Spadra	1905
Kibler	1898	Trinity	1946
Lamar	1954	Union Grove	1874
Mountainburg, First	1954	Uniontown	1927
Mulberry, First	1880	Van Buren, First	1887
Oak Grove	1883	Van Buren, Second	1958
Ozark, First	1866	Vine Prairie	1974
Ozone	1920	Webb City	1929
Ruby	1907	Woodland	1950

Concord Association

Barling	1907	Magazine	1880
Bethel	1964	Mixon	1896
Bloomer	1888	Mount Harmony	1912
Bluff Avenue	1868	New Hope	1974
Branch, First	1869	North Side, Fort Smith	1914
Burnsville	1885	Northside, Charleston	1952
Calvary	1909	Oak Cliff	1960
Charleston, First	1846	Palestine	1879
Delaware, First	1976	Paris	1874
East Side	1953	Phoenix Village	1939
Enterprise	1964	Pine Log	1871
Excelsior	1907	Ratcliff	1908
Fort Smith, First	1857	Roseville	1898
Glendale	1872	Rye Hill	1934
Grand Avenue	1934	Scranton, First	1968
Grayson	1963	South Side	1948
Greenwood	1870	Southside, Booneville	1963
Hackett, First	1905	Spradling	1951
Hackett, Memorial	1960	Temple	1916
Haven Heights	1964	Trinity	1922
Highway 96	1955	Union Hall	1927
Immanuel	1906	Vesta	1888
Jenny Lind	1949	Westside	1977
Lavaca	1860	Windsor Park	1955

Conway-Perry Association

Bigelow	1890	Nimrod	1946
Casa	1898	Oppelo, First	1976
Harmony	1873	Perry	1928
Houston	1900	Perryville	1900
Morrilton	1860	Pleasant Grove	1916

| Plumerville | 1891 | Stony | 1958 |
| Solgohachia | 1950 | Union Valley | 1948 |

Current-Gains Association

Antioch	1976	Nimmons	1939
Biggers	1904	Oak Grove	1867
Brown's Chapel	1904	Peach Orchard	1922
Calvary	1960	Piggott, First	1887
Columbia	1937	Pocahontas, First	1899
Corning, First	1887	Ravenden Springs	1910
Emmanuel	1961	Rector, First	1887
Greenway, First	1888	Reyno, First	1878
Harmony	1927	Shannon	1951
Holly Island	1951	Shiloh Clay	1866
Hopewell	1908	St. Francis	1909
Knobel	1953	Success, First	1903
Moark	1883	Tipperary	1948
Mount Pleasant	1886	Witts Chapel	1884
New Hope	1846		

Dardanelle-Russellville Association

Atkins, First	1876	John Grace Memorial	1891
Baker Creek	1944	Kelley Heights	1957
Bluffton	1906	Knoxville	1859
Centerville	1886	London	1880
Danville, First	1900	Moreland, First	1925
Dardanelle, First	1859	New Hope	1867
Dover	1842	Ola	1901
East Point	1872	Pittsburg	1898
Fair Park	1961	Pleasant View	1954
Havana	1902	Pottsville, First	1962
Hector, First	1969	Plainview	1909
Hopewell	1875	Rover	1888
Immanuel	1973	Russellville, Second	1956

Delta Association

Arkansas City	1910	Chickasaw	1952
Aulds	1935	Collins	1889
Bayou Mason	1948	Daniel Chapel	1939
Bellaire	1918	Dermott	1904
Boydell	1800	Eudora	1902
Gaines	1911	Omega	
Halley	1978	Parkdale	1908
Jennie	1934	Parkway	1969
Jerome	1950	Portland	1969
Kelso	1940	Richland	1945
Lake Village, First	1861	Shiloh	1964
McArthur		South McGehee	1966
McGehee, First	1909	Temple	1957
Montrose	1905	Tillar, First	1912
New Hope	1939	Watson	1943
Northside	1974	Wilmot	1908

Faulkner Association

| Beryl | 1889 | Holland | 1869 |
| Bono | 1917 | Mayflower | 1915 |

Brumley Chapel	1946	Mount Vernon	1849
Cadron Ridge	1892	Naylor	1947
Conway, First	1871	New Bethel	1925
Conway, Second	1921	Oak Bowery	1972
Emmanuel, Conway	1934	Pickles Gap	1878
Enola	1883	Pleasant Grove	1894
Friendship	1917	Saltillo Heights	1977
Gold Creek	1977	Southside	1912
Happy Hollow	1907	Union Hill	1883
Harlan Park	1966	Wooster	1916
Harmony	1966		

Green Association

Alexander	1921	Light	1895
Beech Grove	1910	Marmaduke, First	1888
Bethel	1911	New Friendship	1886
Big Creek	1907	New Liberty	1907
Brighton	1932	Nutts Chapel	1901
Browns Chapel	1959	Oak Grove	1952
Calvary	1959	Paragould, First	1885
Center Hill	1883	Pleasant Valley	1942
Clarks Chapel	1908	Robbs Chapel	1916
Delaplaine	1922	Rosewood	1973
East Side	1912	Stanford	1910
Fairview	1857	Stonewall	1912
Finch	1872	Third Avenue	1951
Fontaine	1950	Unity	1879
Immanuel	1955	Vines Chapel	1940
Lafe	1922	Walcott	1891
Lake Street	1955	West View	1960

Harmony Association

Altheimer, First	1943	Kingsland, First	1885
Anderson Chapel	1927	Lee Memorial	1924
Bethel	1964	Linwood	1951
Centennial	1956	Matthews Memorial	1939
Central	1947	Northside	1964
Dollarway	1960	Oak Grove	1937
Douglas	1956	Oakland	1941
Dumas, First	1954	Pine Bluff, First	1853
East Side	1969	Pine Bluff, Second	1904
Evergreen	1944	Plum Bayou	1938
Forrest Park	1950	Rankin Chapel	1940
Gould, First	1922	Rison	1886
Grady, First	1954	Shannon Road	1962
Green Meadows	1975	South Side	1917
Greenlee Memorial	1936	Star City, First	1873
Hardin	1931	Tucker Baptist Ch.	1978
Hickory Grove	1872	Wabbaseka	1925
Humphrey	1908	Watson Chapel	1961
Immanuel	1914	White Sulphur Springs	1898
		Yorktown	1925

Independence Association

Arbana	1966	Mountain View, First	1890
Batesville	1847	Northside	1975
Calvary	1939	Pilgrim Rest	1854
Calvary Timbe	1967	Pleasant Plains	1879
Cord	1906	Rehobeth	1826
Cushman	1952	Rosie	1907
Desha, First	1936	Ruddell Hill	1940
Eastside Southern	1961	Salado	1946
Emmanuel	1968	Sulphur Rock	1887
Floral	1889	West Batesville	1909
Marcella	1901	White River	1939
Mount Zion	1873		

Liberty Association

Caledonia	1849	Camden, First	1842
Calion, First	1903	Camden, Second	1952
Chidester	1865	Marrable Hill	1952
Cross Roads	1960	Midway	1851
Cullendale, First	1929	New London	1844
East Main	1956	Norphlet, First	1895
Ebenezer	1879	Parkview	1943
El Dorado, Second	1923	Philadelphia	1892
El Dorado, First	1845	Salem	1848
Elliott	1890	Smackover, First	1924
Fairview Road	1960	South Side	1950
Felsenthal	1906	Stephens, First	1876
Galilee	1912	Strong	1903
Grace	1956	Sylvan Hills	1961
Harmony	1954	Temple Camden	1955
Hillside	1954	Temple El Dorado	1952
Hutteg, First	1909	Three Creeks	1890
Immanuel	1942	Trinity	1845
Joyce City	1934	Union	1845
Junction City, First	1894	Urbana, First	1916
Knowles	1906	Victory	1961
La Pile	1911	Village	1887
Lawson	1912	Wesson	1894
Liberty	1932	West Side	1924
Louann	1925	White City	1954
Maple Avenue	1955	Wildwood	1969

Little Red River Association

Brownsville	(records burned)	Palestine	1861
Center Ridge	1962	Pines	1971
Concord	1938	Pleasant Ridge	1904
Harris Chapel	1939	Pleasant Valley	1941
Heber Springs, First	1885	Post Oak	1922
Lifeline	1970	Quitman	1880
Lone Star	1933	South Side	1950
Mount Olive	1864	Westside, First	1856
Mount Zion	1920	Woodrow	1967
New Bethel	1911		

Little River Association

Ashdown, First	1894	Lone Oak	1942
Ben Lomond, First	1902	Mount Moriah	1945
Bingen, First	1847	Murfreesboro, First	1910
Brownstown	1879	Nashville, First	1836
Central	1924	New Home	1909
Chapel Hill	1955	Oak Grove	1948
Columbus	1893	Ogden	1914
Dierks, First	1917	Ozan	dropped from Association
Foreman, First	1902	Ridgeway	1968
Hicks, First	1965	Rock Hill	1946
Horatio, First	1902	State Line	1939
Kern Heights	1960	Washington	1836
Liberty	1876	Wilton	1890
Locksburg, First	1892	Winthrop	1945

Mississippi Association

Armorel	1930	Luxora	1895
Bethany	1967	Manila, First	1901
Blackwater	1922	Mary's Chapel	1894
Blytheville, First	1889	Memorial	1971
Brinkley's Chapel	1939	New Harmony	1947
Brown's	1932	New Liberty	1933
Calvary, Osceola	1953	New Providence	1933
Calvary, Blytheville	1908	Nodena	1939
Central Dyess	1937	Number Nine	1941
Clear Lake	1896	Osceola, First	1850
Cole Ridge	1938	Ridgecrest	1957
Crossroads	1938	Rosa	1948
Dell	1920	Tomato	1950
East Side	1969	Trinity	1951
Emmanuel	1935	Wardell	1940
Etowah	1956	Westside	1957
Gosnell	1886	Whitton	1925
Joiner	1944	Wilson	1925
Keiser, First	1918	Woodland Corner	1942
Leachville	1915	Yarbro	1949
Leachville, Second	1922		

Mount Zion Association

Alsup	1956	Monette, First	1898
Bay	1888	Mount Pisgah	1900
Bethabara	1887	Mount Zion	1840
Black Oak, First	1914	Needham	1957
Bono, First	1951	Nettleton	1906
Bowman	1952	New Antioch	1906
Brookland	1897	New Hope, Black Oak	1924
Buffalo	1947	New Hope, Jonesboro	1866
Caraway, First	1920	North Main	1957
Cash	1913	Philadelphia	1860
Central	1933	Providence	1940
Childress	1924	Rowes Chapel	1943

Dixie	1923	Southside	1976
Egypt	1909	Straw Floor	1951
Fischer Street	1927	University	1963
Friendly Hope	1932	Walnut Street	1913
Jonesboro, First	1852	Westvale	1968
Lake City	1923	Wood Spring	1961
Lunsford	1914		

North Arkansas Association

Alphena	1901	Hopewell	1886
Batavia	1947	Jasper	1916
Bear Creek Springs	1919	Lead Hill, First	1883
Bellefonte	1860	Marble Falls, First	1976
Berryville, First	1891	Marshall, First	1870
Blue Eye, First	1883	New Hope	1942
Buxley	1934	Northvale	1949
Burlington	1911	Omaha	1883
Cassville	1949	Oregon Flat	1907
Deer	1940	Osage	1966
Eagle Heights	1949	Parthenon	1917
Elmwood	1953	Rock Springs	1853
Emmanuel	1960	Rudd	1968
Everton, First	1952	Saint Joe, First	1951
Freeman Heights	1958	Southside, Lead Hill	1950
Gaither	1931	Trinity	1975
Grandview	1886	Union	1906
Green Forest	1868	Valley Springs	1904
Grubb Spring	1911	Woodland Heights	1958
Harrison, First	1890		

North Pulaski Association

Amboy	1951	Jacksonville, First	1872
Baring Cross	1903	Jacksonville, Second	1970
Bayou Meto	1958	Levy	1906
Berea	1955	Marshall Road	1961
Bethany	1947	Maumelle, First	1977
Calvary	1949	Morrison Chapel	1965
Cedar Heights	1950	N. Little Rock, First	1889
Central	1910	Oakwood	1939
Chapel Hill	1963	Park Hill	1947
Crystal Valley	1945	Pike Avenue	1944
Forty-seventh Street	1948	Remount	1954
Grace	1943	Runyan, First	1968
Gravel Ridge, First	1949	Sherwood, First	1950
Graves Memorial	1934	Sixteenth Street	1949
Highway	1949	Stanfill	1942
Hill Top	1945	Sylvan Hills, First	1939
Indian Hills	1967	Zion Hill	1859

Ouachita Association

Acron	1932	Hatfield	1901
Board Camp	1861	Hatton	1942
Calvary-Mena	1966	Lower Big Fork	1952
Cherry Hill	1934	Mena, First	1897
Concord	1885	New Hope	1880
Cove	1912	Salem	1906
Dallas Avenue	1949	Two Mile	1914
Dequeen, First	1897	Vandervoort	1896
Gillham	1912	Wickes	1910
Grannis	1892	Yocana	1870

Pulaski Association

Alexander	1951	Markham Street	1951
Archview	1957	Martindale	1940
Baptist Tabernacle	1908	Nalls Memorial	1933
Barnett Memorial	1959	Natural Steps	1913
Bingham Road	1975	North Point	1936
Brookwood, First	1945	Olivet	1946
Calvary	1937	Pine Grove	1869
Chicot Road	1973	Plainview	1916
Crossroad	1971	Pleasant Grove	1852
Crystal Hill	1933	Pulaski Heights	1913
Douglassville	1942	Reynolds Memorial	1914
East End	1936	Roland	1919
Forest Highlands	1958	Rosedale	1947
Forest Tower	1966	Shady Grove	1941
Garden Homes	1954	Shannon Hills, First	1967
Geyer Springs	1926	Sheidan, First	1858
Hebron	1925	South Highland	1916
Holly Springs	1926	Sunset Lane	1941
Immanuel	1892	Tyler Street	1948
Ironton	1893	Vimy Ridge Immanuel	1917
Lakeshore Drive	1970	Wakefield, First	1967
Life Line	1914	West Side	1947
Little Rock, First	1858	Woodlawn	1926
Little Rock, Second	1884	Woodson	1938

Red River Association

Anchor	1851	Hollywood	1881
Antoine	1939	Lakeview	1904
Arkadelphia, First	1851	Marlbrook	1956
Arkadelphia, Second	1905	Mt. Bethel	1836
Beech Street	1915	Mt. Olive	1887
Beirne	1907	Mt. Zion	1894
Bethel	1946	Okolona	1869
Bethlehem	1851	Parkhill	1953
Boughton	1893	Prescott, First	1896
Caddo Valley	1900	Reader, First	1924
Cedar Grove	1957	Richwood	1877
Center Point	1953	Shady Grove	1936
Curtis	1927	Shiloh	1883
De Gray	1853	South Fork	1856
East Whelen	1953	Sycamore Grove	1885
Emmet	1873	Third Street	1951

441

| Fairview | 1941 | Unity | 1857 |
| Harmony Hill | 1848 | Whelen Springs | 1914 |

Rocky Bayou Association

Ash Flat	1933	Melbourne	1851
Baptist Chapel, Horseshoe Bend	1851	Mount Pleasant	1950
Belview	1851	Myron	1960
Boswell	1850	Oxford	1937
Calico Rock	1903	Sage	1923
Dolph	1959	Salem, First	1887
Evening Shade	1946	Sidney	1904
Finley Creek	1868	Sylamore, First	
Franklin	1895	Wiseman	1949
Guion, First	1935	Zion Hill	1877
Hardy, First	1898		

Searcy Association

Leslie, First	1903	New Hopewell	1948
Morning Star	1968	Snowball	1952

Southwest Arkansas Association

Anderson	1945	Immanuel, Magnolia	1950
Arabella Heights	1946	Lewisville, First	1890
Beech Street, First	1904	Macedonia, Bloomburg	1856
Bradley	1902	Macedonia, Fouke	1890
Bronway Heights	1953	Mandeville	1933
Calvary, Texarkana	1947	Memorial	1952
Calvary, Hope	1959	Mitchell Street	1970
Canfield, First	1944	Mount Zion	1859
Central	1907	North East	1974
Faith	1976	Piney Grove	1889
Fouke, First	1896	Pisgah	1850
Fulton	1948	Red River	1918
Garland	1925	Rocky Mound	1924
Genoa	1931	Shiloh Memorial	1906
Guernsey	1946	South Texarkana	1916
Haley Lake	1939	Springhill	1917
Harmony Grove	1901	Stamps, First	1897
Hickory Street	1952	Sylverino	1858
Highland Hills	1946	Tennessee	1884
Hope, First	1868	Trinity, Texarkana	1937
Immanuel, Texarkana	1903	Westside	1959

Tri-County

Antioch	1944	Jericho	1940
Barton Chapel	1930	Makison	1937
Beckspur	1941	Marion	1925
Burnt Cane	1955	Midway	1964
Calvary	1954	Palestine	1938
Cherry Valley	1891	Parkin	1913
Colt	1889	Pine Tree	1942
Crawfordsville	1906	Shell Lake	1944
Earle	1902	Temple	1975
Emmanuel	1958	Tilton	1949
Fair Oaks	1944	Togo	1924

Faith	1969	Turrell	1949
Fitzgerald	1945	Union Avenue	1960
Forrest City, First	1869	Vanderbilt Avenue	1954
Forrest City, Second	1952	Vanndale	1907
Fortune	1952	West Memphis, First	1924
Gladden	1925	West Memphis, Second	1954
Goodwin	1926	Wheatley	1908
Harris Chapel	1926	Widener	1956
Hydrick	1854	Wynne	1889
Ingram Boulevard	1948		

Trinity Association

Anderson Tully	1942	Neals Chapel	1955
Bethel	1860	Neiswander	1939
Black Oak	1953	Pleasant Grove	1863
Calvary	1959	Pleasant Hill	1907
Calvary, Lepanto	1976	Pleasant Valley	1941
Corners Chapel	1941	Providence	1964
Eastside	1953	Red Oak	1943
Faith	1953	Rivervale	1953
Fisher	1936	Shiloh	1976
Freer	1941	Trinity, Marked Tree	1970
Greenfield	1939	Truman	1908
Harrisburg	1885	Tyronza	1914
Lebanon	1925	Valley View	1945
Lepanto	1908	Waldenburg	1976
Maple Grove	1929	Weiner	1923
Marked Tree	1909	West Ridge	1938
McCormick	1961		

Van Buren Association

Angora	1977	Plant	1935
Bee Branch	1926	Pleasant Valley	1905
Botkinburg	1959	Rupert	1960
Corinth	1873	Scotland	1873
Formosa	1922	Shady Grove	1896
Friendship	1965	Shirley	1876
Immanuel	1977	Standley	1967
Lexington	1886	Zion	1935
Pee Dee	1881		

Washington-Madison Association

Berry Street	1951	Kingston, First	1965
Black Oak	1946	Liberty	1883
Brush Creek Church	1877	Lincoln, First	1921
Calvary	1963	New Hope	1897
Caddle Avenue	1950	Oak Grove	1965
Combs	1960	Prairie Grove, First	1871
Elkins	1947	Providence	1891
Elkins, First	1970	Ridgeview	1961
Elmdale	1961	Rolling Hills	1972
Farmington, First	1948	Silent Grove	1963
Fayetteville, First	1858	Sonora	1929

Fayetteville, Second	1945	Southside	1955
Friendship	1847	Spring Valley	1848
Greenland	1971	Springdale, First	1870
Hindsville	1907	Sulphur City	1866
Hunsville, First	1891	University	1953
Immanuel, Fayetteville	1950	West Fork	1942
Johnson	1944	Winslow	1947

White River Association

Antioch	1891	Mountain Home, First	1868
Arlana	1975	New Hope	1881
Bruno	1871	Norfork, First	1913
Bull Shoals, First	1975	Oak Grove	1884
Cutter, First	1904	Peel, First	1908
Eastside	1960	Pilgrim Rest	1872
Flippin, First	1945	Pyatt	1961
Gassville	1868	Rea Valley	1959
Henderson, First	1971	Summit	1964
Hilltop	1977	Tomahawk	1962
Hopewell	1874	Whiteville	1892
Lone Rock	1931	Yellville	1913
Midway	1967		

Misc. Associations

Bethany	1976	Half Moon	1953
Clear Creek S. Bap. Ch.	1978	Malvern, First	1878
Clinton, First	1935	Russellville, First	1873
Eureka Springs, First	1912		

APPENDIX G-1
ACADEMIES, HIGH SCHOOLS, MOUNTAIN SCHOOLS

Schools	Founded	Closed	Comments
Arkadelphia Female Institute	1851	1860	Closed by the Civil War
Arkadelphia Male Institute	1851	1860	
Arkadelphia Baptist High School	1876	1886	Forerunner of Ouachita College.
Bentonville Academy	1901	1911	A part of Ouachita-Central System.
Caledonia Academy	1920	1926	
Camden Female Institute	1851	1860	Closed by the Civil War.
Centennial Institute	1875	1882	
Forrest City Baptist High School	1876	1881	
Friendship High School	1899	1911	
Hagarville Academy	1919	1927	A Mountain School. Merged with public schools between 1923 and 1925.
Judson Academy	1902	1908	A part of Ouachita-Central System.
Judson High School	1894	1902	In 1902 the High School became Judson Academy.
Magazine Academy	1901	1911	A part of Ouachita-Central System.
Maynard Academy	1900	1927	Closed in 1913-14. In 1916 Maynard became a Mountain School. A part of Ouachita-Central System until 1912.

444

Mine Creek Male and Female School	1851	1860	Closed by the Civil War.
Montview Institute	1918	1930	Located in Blue Eye, Mo., Montview became Carroll Co. Institute, Mo-Ark Academy and Armo Academy. It was also a Mountain School.
Mount Ida Academy	1920	1929	A Mountain School. Mt. Ida also operated with public funds for a time. In 1923 it came under control of the Executive Board of the ABSC.
Mount Vernon High School	1900	1909	Also called Trenton Baptist High School, Brinkley Baptist High School, and Collegiate Institute.
Newton County Academy	1920	1929	A Mountain School.
Red River Baptist Academy	1876	?	
Shiloh Baptist Institute	1872	1875	
Union High School	1896	1911	
Woodland Baptist College	1902	1912	Although using the name college, Woodland was actually an academy.

According to Frank Norfleet, "A History of Arkansas Baptists to 1900," (Louisville: Southern Baptist Theological Seminary, 1950), pp. 132-3, 83 private schools having some form of Baptist affiliation had charters in the state from 1836 to 1861.

II. COLLEGES

Buckner College	1882	1897	Buckner was under Episcopal control between 1887 and 1900. In 1904 the land was deeded to the Arkansas Baptist General Assoc.
Central College	1892	1950	A women's college. Reorganized as a junior college in 1922. In 1947-1948 it moved from Conway to Little Rock.
Eureka Springs Baptist College	1883?		Mentioned in State Convention **Proceedings** in 1883 as being newly chartered.
Jonesboro College	1924	1935	An outgrowth of Woodland. Controlled by the Home Mission Board, SBC.
Judson Baptist University	1871	1883	Began as a high school. It reached college standing but was forced to close.
Mountain Home College	1893	1933	
Ouachita College	1886		
Southern Baptist College	1941		

APPENDIX G-2
OUACHITA-CENTRAL SYSTEM

A PLAN FOR THE AFFILIATION OF ALL BAPTIST SCHOOLS IN ARKANSAS UNDER THE AUSPICES OF THE ARKANSAS BAPTIST STATE CONVENTION.

It is hereby declared to be the object and purpose of this act of affiliation to promote and foster the best interests, and to increase the patronage, and to reduce the expense of operating, and to increase the amount of money to be raised for, and to destroy friction between, and to preserve the integrity of all the schools entering the system.

1. The system is to be known as "The Ouachita-Central System of Colleges and Academies."

2. All the schools of the system shall be under the direction of one board of trustees, composed of fifteen members to be nominated by the present boards of Ouachita and Central colleges, and to be elected by the Convention at its present session; and one-third of that number shall be nominated annually by the board, subject to the election by the Convention.

3. An Executive or Advisory Committee for each school, consisting of three or more discreet persons suitably located, and who may be others than members of said board, may be appointed by the board of trustees who shall have supervision over their respective schools. There shall be only two schools with power to issue diplomas; namely, Ouachita, for both men and women, and Central, for women only.

4. It shall be the duty of the board of control to see that the two colleges and all the academies are well equipped with such apparatus, fixtures, improvements and additions to grounds and building as will best fit them for the work mapped out for each; and in apportioning funds for this purpose the schools shall be kept as nearly abreast as possible, no intentional discrimination being made in schools of the same class.

5. All property, moneys, incomes, rights, credits, and effects belonging to the several schools entering this system shall belong to and be controlled by the board of control as trustees for the respective schools, and said board shall assume the debts of both the colleges.

APPENDIX H-1
RELIGIOUS BODIES IN ARKANSAS

Name	1906 Chs.	1906 Mbship.	1916 Chs.	1916 Mbship.	1926 Chs.	1926 Mbship.	1936 Chs.	1936 Mbship.	1971 Chs.	1971 Full Mbship.	1971 Consts.
Adventist:											
Advent Chr.	3	120	3	84	19	706	13	1,002			
S-D Adventist	22	544	20	601	3	155	15	584	38	2,931	4,026*
Chs. of God in Christ			10	499							
Assemblies of God, Gen. C.			12	923	72	3,641			370	48,716	59,024*
Baptist:											
ABA (MBA)					560	41,281	379	37,424			
Clrd. Freewill	20	840	2	67							
Clrd. Primit.	8	337	31	519	25	1,441	25	491			
Free (clrd.)	10	371	62	2,926							
Freewill	54	2,035	36	1,227	103	5,270	71	4,014	211	18,500	22,555*
General					35	1,898	30	1,528	47	3,277	3,995*
Negro	1,115	93,364	1,473	174,157	1,375	134,720	1,155	150,664			
Primit.	109	2,591	97	2,247	91	1,979	54	1,745			
S-D	4	254	3	184	3	122	3	155			
SBC	1,419	91,631	1,410	113,192	860	103,346	479	78,825	1,187	356,739	435,183*
Two-Seed-in the Spirit	10	175	4	32							
United	35	1,646									
Brethren:											
Ch. of Breth. (Dunkers)	9	172	8	149	5	162	3	38	1	52	66*
Breth. Ch. (Prog. Dks.)	1	27									
Plym. Breth.									2	7	11*
Christadelph.	3	74	5	127	6	182	5	139			
Chr. Union	5	157	5	96	6	149	4	117			
Ch. of Christ (Holiness)					7	287	5	251			
Ch. of Christ (Scientist)	3	82			15	506	15	623			
Chs. of God:											
Ch. of God (An)					31	631	12	491	31	1,435	3,032*
Ch. of God (Cl)							20	384	77	3,234	4,000*
(Orig.) Ch.					4	98	16	525			

447

Ch. of God (Salem, W. Va.)											
Ch. of God	190	11,006	514	26,239	626	823	3	54	5	205	247*
Ch. of God in Christ	156	10,269	155	13,275	153	2,305	22	716	109	8,357	14,563*
Ch. of Naz.	23	737	14	564	15	2,024	31	879			
Chr. Chs.:							69	3,931			
Chr. Chs. and Chs. of C.						39,678	270	16,557	47	4,401	4,956*
Disciples						17,198	101	14,120	81	10,843	13,145*
Chs. of God in N. Am.			34	1,857	23	607	7	260			
Chs. of Liv. God:											
Ch. of L.G. for Fellowship	11	765									
Ch. of L.G. (Apost.)	8	338									
Ch. of Christ in God	1	15									
Chs. of New Jerus.	2	54				1,683	12	277			
Episcopal	67	4,315	54	4,431	37	4,823	67	5,872	51	12,293	15,762*
Federated Chs.					4	469	4	342			
Free Chr. Zion Ch. of Christ	14	1,635	20	4,150	5	187	4	847			
Friends, U.S.A.									3	40	49*
Ger. Ev. Synod of N. Am.	3	250	6	309							
Independent	38	1,629	9	519							
Jewish Cgrs.	11	673	12	1,451	14	4,949	12	4,224			
L-D Saints:											
Ch. of J.C.	1	248	3	454			3	179			
Reorg. Ch.			6	547	5	387	6	706			4,538*
Lutheran:											
Am. Luth. Ch.											
Ev. Luth. Syn. Conf. of Am.	22	1,886	17	2,516					2	293	399*
Ev. Luth. Syn. of Iowa, etc.	4	194	2	186							
Luth. Ch. Am.									6	852	969*
Luth. Ch.-Mo.					24	3,550	24	4,343	46	7,723	10,184*
Mennonite:											
Amish	1	45									
Menn. Ch.								6	104	130	
Methodist:											
A.M.E. Ch.	485	26,903	435	30,457	404	25,249	266	29,483			
A.M.E. Zion	65	2,404	125	7,668	89	14,344	100	11,105			
Clrd. M.E.	211	11,506	216	15,269	220	10,887	266	18,265			
Cgr. Meth. E.	26	684	7	50	7	287	3	127			
Free Meth.	8	146									
Meth. E.	252	12,569	213	12,419	170	10,452	68	4,249	2	35	37*
M.E. South	1,110	81,699	1,216	110,993	1,004	123,676	753	114,924			
M. Prot.	166	6,658	77	4,087	92	5,439	48	2,884			

Denomination	1906 Ch.	1906 Mem.	1916 Ch.	1916 Mem.	1926 Ch.	1926 Mem.	1936 Ch.	1936 Mem.	1971 Ch.	1971 Mem.	1971 Mem. (est.)
U.M.C.									777	171,702	182,725*
Wesleyan									8	305	376*
Nonsectarian Chs.											
Nonsectarian Chs. of Bible Faith											
Pent. Holiness	21	640							10	403	590*
Presbyterian:											
As. Ref. Pr.	13	854	8	888	7	938	7	800	8	800	976*
Cumb. Pr.	260	11,990	142	5,400	105	4,106	60	2,655	72	4,632	5,574*
Pr. U.S.	89	7,357	116	10,762	111	14,499	106	14,720	160	19,681	24,926*
Pr. U.S.A.	23	809	127	7,451	111	7,223	75	5,846	68	6,398	7,776*
Un. Pr.	3	146	3	107							
Ref. Ch. U.S.	1	60	2	107							
Rom. Cath.	77	32,307	205	21,120	146	20,415	144	24,743	118	0	55,025*
Calv. Army	5	159	4	224	5	505	7	711	9	314	2,084*
Unitar.-Univ.	3	85	4	164					4	238	399*
UCC:											
Congr.	4	344	3	740	3	619	3	611			
Ev. and Ref.							3	241			
Un. Ch. of Chr.											
United Breth.							5	106			
All Others	7	162	7	162	17	1,112	24	1,530	4	295	367*

Figures for 1906, 1916, 1926, 1936 from U.S. Department of Commerce. Bureau of the Census. Religious Bodies, 1906, I. 160-162; 1916, I. 152-3; 1926, I. 146-9; 1936, I. 174-7; for 1971 from Douglas W. Johnson, Paul R. Picard and Bernard Quinn, Churches and Church Membership in the United States (Washington, D.C.: Glenmary Research Center, 1974).

*Estimated

APPENDIX H-2
CHURCHES AND CHURCH MEMBERSHIP BY COUNTY AND DENOMINATION: 1971*

County and Denomination	Number of Churches	Communicant, confirmed full members	Total adherents		
			Number	Percent of total population	Percent of total adherents
THE STATE	3,568	686,386	880,433*	45.8	100.0
ARKANSAS	44	9,591	12,012*	51.4	100.0
029 Amer. Luth. Ch.	1	204	254	1.1	2.1
059 Bapt. Miss. Assn.	8	417	512*	2.2	4.3
081 Catholic	2	0	560	2.4	4.7
093 Cr. Ch. (Disc.)	1	296	364*	1.6	3.0
097 Cr. C. and C. Cr.	2	335	412*	1.8	3.4
165 Ch. of Nazarene	2	68	87	0.4	0.7
193 Episcopal	1	114	130	0.6	1.1
226 Friends-USA	1	25	31*	0.1	0.3
283 Luth.—MO Synod	3	903	1,177	5.0	9.8
357 Presb. Ch. US	1	176	216*	0.9	1.8
419 So. Bapt. Conv.	11	3,852	4,732*	20.3	39.4
449 Un. Methodist	11	3,201	3,537	15.1	29.4
ASHLEY	42	9,362	11,806*	47.3	100.0
059 Bapt. Miss. Assn.	2	287	362*	1.4	3.1
081 Catholic	1	0	165	0.7	1.4
123 Ch. God (Ander.)	1	55	173	0.7	1.5
193 Episcopal	1	153	184	0.7	1.6
283 Luth.—MO Synod	1	25	33	0.1	0.3
357 Presb. Ch. US	2	171	215*	0.9	1.8
419 So. Bapt. Conv.	26	7,287	9,179*	36.8	77.7
449 Un. Methodist	8	1,384	1,495	6.0	12.7
BAXTER	33	5,296	6,711*	43.8	100.0
059 Bapt. Miss. Assn.	2	52	60*	0.4	0.9
081 Catholic	1	0	604	3.9	9.0
093 Cr. Ch. (Disc.)	1	195	225*	1.5	3.4
097 Cr. C. and C. Cr.	1	198	228*	1.5	3.4
127 Ch. God (Cleve.)	2	61	70*	0.5	1.0
165 Ch. of Nazarene	2	70	124	0.8	1.8
185 Cumber. Presb.	1	107	123*	0.8	1.8
193 Episcopal	1	70	142	0.9	2.1
283 Luth.—MO Synod	1	505	595	3.9	8.9
285 Mennonite Ch.	1	11	13*	0.1	0.2
357 Presb. Ch. US	3	395	455*	3.0	6.8
413 S-D Adventists	1	43	50*	0.3	0.7
419 So. Bapt. Conv.	12	2,467	2,842*	18.6	42.3
449 Un. Methodist	4	1,122	1,180	7.7	17.6
BENTON	101	17,688	22,420*	44.4	100.0
059 Bapt. Miss. Assn.	14	1,029	1,238*	2.5	5.5
081 Catholic	2	0	1,120	2.2	5.0

—Represents a percent less than 0.1   Percentages may not total due to rounding.

*Data used by permission from Douglas W. Johnson, Paul R. Picard and Bernard Quinn, **Churches and Church Membership in the United States**(Washington, D.C.: Glenmary Research Center, 1974). Please consult the introduction to this volume for a discussion of the limitations of the data.

450

Churches and Church Membership by County and Denomination: 1971

County and Denomination	Number of churches	Communicant, confirmed full members	Total adherents		
			Number	Percent of total population	Percent of total adherents
093 Cr. Ch. (Disc.)	4	668	804*	1.6	3.6
097 Cr. C. and C. Cr.	5	445	535*	1.1	2.4
127 Ch. God (Cleve.)	1	17	20*	—	0.1
165 Ch. of Nazarene	6	518	1,038	2.1	4.6
193 Episcopal	1	225	325	0.6	1.5
221 Free Meth. C. Na.	1	20	22	—	0.1
281 Luth Ch. Amer.	1	127	167	0.3	0.7
283 Luth.—MO Synod	2	233	309	0.6	1.4
349 Pent. Holiness	4	138	166*	0.3	0.7
357 Presb. Ch. US	6	521	627*	1.2	2.8
413 S-D Adventists	6	707	851*	1.7	3.8
419 So Bapt. Conv.	26	8,557	10,297*	20.4	45.9
Un. Methodist	16	3,950	4,259	8.4	19.0
453 Un. Pres. Ch. USA	6	533	641*	1.3	2.9
BOONE	**49**	**7,157**	**8,956***	**47.0**	**100.0**
081 Catholic	1	0	375	2.0	4.2
093 Cr. Ch. (Disc.)	3	439	523*	2.7	5.8
123 Ch. God (Ander.)	2	88	258	1.4	2.9
127 Ch. God (Cleve.)	1	35	42*	0.2	0.5
165 Ch. of Nazarene	1	60	114	0.6	1.3
185 Cumber. Presb.	1	33	39*	0.2	0.4
193 Episcopal	1	172	234	1.2	2.6
283 Luth.—MO Synod	1	75	101	0.5	1.1
353 Ply. Brethren	1	5	6	—	0.1
357 Presb. Ch. US	2	271	323*	1.7	3.6
413 S-D Adventists	1	111	132*	0.7	1.5
419 So. Bapt. Conv.	24	4,350	5,178*	27.1	57.8
449 Un. Methodist	8	1,236	1,295	6.8	14.5
453 Un. Pres. Ch. USA	2	282	336*	1.8	3.8
BRADLEY	**33**	**5,603**	**6,661***	**52.1**	**100.0**
055 As. Ref. Pres. Ch.	1	48	58*	0.5	0.9
059 Bapt. Miss. Assn.	7	881	1,058*	8.3	15.9
081 Catholic	1	0	120	0.9	1.8
127 Ch. God. (Cleve.)	2	84	101*	0.8	1.5
357 Presb. Ch. US	3	391	470*	3.7	7.1
419 So. Bapt. Conv.	13	3,258	3,913*	30.6	58.7
449 Un. Methodist	6	941	941	7.4	14.1
CALHOUN	**18**	**1,906**	**2,189***	**39.3**	**100.0**
059 Bapt. Miss. Assn.	8	482	573*	10.3	26.2
185 Cumber. Presb.	1	248	295*	5.3	13.5
419 So. Bapt. Conv.	5	768	913*	16.4	41.7
449 Un. Methodist	4	408	408	7.3	18.6
CARROLL	**27**	**3,545**	**4,395***	**35.7**	**100.0**
059 Bapt. Miss. Assn.	1	25	29*	0.2	0.7
081 Catholic	2	0	309	2.5	7.0
093 Cr. Ch (Disc.)	1	126	148*	1.2	3.4

—Represents a percent less than 0.1   Percentages may not total due to rounding.

*Total adherents estimated from known number of communicant, confirmed, full members.

451

Churches and Church Membership by
County and Denomination: 1971

County and Denomination	Number of churches	Communicant, confirmed full members	Total adherents		
			Number	Percent of total population	Percent of total adherents
097 Cr. C. and C. Cr.	2	60	70*	0.6	1.6
165 Ch. of Nazarene	2	34	129	1.0	2.9
193 Episcopal	1	105	119	1.0	2.7
353 Ply. Brethren	1	2	5	—	0.1
357 Presb. Ch. US	2	79	93*	0.8	2.1
419 So. Bapt. Conv.	8	2,024	2,376*	19.3	54.1
449 Un. Methodist	5	1,035	1,052	8.6	23.9
453 Un. Presb. Ch. USA	2	55	65*	0.5	1.5
CHICOT	**25**	**4,839**	**6,620***	**36.4**	**100.0**
059 Bapt. Miss. Assn.	2	208	262*	1.4	4.0
081 Catholic	2	0	680	3.7	10.3
127 Ch. God (Cleve.)	1	32	40*	0.2	0.6
193 Episcopal	1	72	86	0.5	1.3
357 Presb. Ch. US	3	216	272*	1.5	4.1
419 So. Bapt. Conv.	12	3,584	4,520*	24.9	68.3
449 Un. Methodist	4	727	760	4.2	11.5
CLARK	**59**	**9,697**	**11,384***	**52.9**	**100.0**
059 Bapt. Miss. Assn.	5	712	831*	3.9	7.3
081 Catholic	1	0	103	0.5	0.9
093 Cr. Ch. (Disc.)	3	179	209*	1.0	1.8
123 Ch. God. (Ander.)	2	50	130	0.6	1.1
165 Ch. of Nazarene	2	76	196	0.9	1.7
193 Episcopal	1	52	63	0.3	0.6
283 Luth.—MO Synod	1	19	19	0.1	0.2
357 Presb. Ch. US	4	448	523*	2.4	4.6
419 So. Bapt. Conv.	28	5,890	6,877*	31.9	60.4
449 Un. Methodist	11	2,255	2,414	11.2	21.2
453 Un. Pres. Ch. USA	1	16	19*	0.1	0.2
CLAY	**49**	**6,735**	**8,118***	**43.2**	**100.0**
059 Bapt. Miss. Assn.	5	291	346*	1.8	4.3
081 Catholic	3	0	293	1.6	3.6
097 Cr. C. and C. Cr.	2	285	339*	1.8	4.2
123 Ch. God (Ander.)	1	65	174	0.9	2.1
165 Ch. of Nazarene	1	14	40	0.2	0.5
283 Luth.—MO Synod	1	64	92	0.5	1.1
419 So. Bapt. Conv.	20	3,770	4,480*	23.9	55.2
449 Un. Methodist	16	2,246	2,354	12.5	
CLEBURNE	**35**	**4,336**	**5,100***	**49.3**	**100.0**
059 Bapt. Miss. Assn.	6	465	543*	5.2	10.6
081 Catholic	1	0	102	1.0	2.0
123 Ch. God (Ander.)	1	18	70	0.7	1.4
127 Ch. God (Cleve.)	2	52	61*	0.6	1.2
165 Ch. of Nazarene	2	43	70	0.7	1.4
357 Presb. Ch. US	1	114	133*	1.3	2.6
419 So. Bapt. Conv.	15	2,543	2,970*	28.7	58.2
449 Un. Methodist	7	1,101	1,151	11.1	22.6

—Represents a percent less than 0.1

Percentages may not total due to rounding.

*Total adherents estimated from known number of communicant, confirmed, full members.

452

Churches and Church Membership by
County and Denomination: 1971

County and Denomination	Number of churches	Communicant, confirmed full members	Total adherents		
			Number	Percent of total population	Percent of total adherents
CLEVELAND	22	2,206	2,569*	38.9	100.0
055 As. Ref. Pres. Ch.	1	19	23*	0.3	0.9
059 Bapt. Miss. Assn.	8	779	944*	14.3	36.7
123 Ch. God (Ander.)	1	32	84	1.3	3.3
127 Ch. God (Cleve.)	1	20	24*	0.4	0.9
357 Presb. Ch. US	1	14	17*	0.3	0.7
419 So. Bapt. Conv.	2	575	697*	10.6	27.1
449 Un. Methodist	8	767	780	11.8	30.4
COLUMBIA	57	10,773	12,609*	48.6	100.0
059 Bapt. Miss. Assn.	23	4,069	4,898*	18.9	38.8
081 Catholic	1	0	151	0.6	1.2
093 Cr. Ch. (Disc.)	1	5	6*	—	—
123 Ch. God (Ander.)	1	23	46	0.2	0.4
165 Ch. of Nazarene	1	36	69	0.3	0.5
185 Cumber. Presb.	2	106	128*	0.5	1.0
193 Episcopal	1	44	50	0.2	0.4
283 Luth.—MO Synod	1	49	71	0.3	0.6
357 Presb. Ch. US	1	245	295*	1.1	2.3
419 So. Bapt. Conv.	6	2,684	3,231*	12.4	25.6
449 Un. Methodist	19	3,512	3,664	14.1	29.1
CONWAY	33	3,954	5,844*	34.8	100.0
059 Bapt. Miss. Assn.	8	942	1,149*	6.8	19.7
081 Catholic	4	0	1,275	7.6	21.8
165 Ch. of Nazarene	1	77	122	0.7	2.1
185 Cumber. Presb.	2	137	167*	1.0	2.9
283 Luth.—MO Synod	1	12	12	0.1	0.2
357 Presb. Ch. US	2	131	160*	1.0	2.7
419 So. Bapt. Conv.	3	1,020	1,244*	7.4	21.3
449 Un. Methodist	10	1,503	1,554	9.2	26.6
453 Un. Pres. Ch. USA	2	132	161*	1.0	2.8
CRAIGHEAD	98	24,058	29,980*	57.6	100.0
059 Bapt. Miss. Assn.	23	3,477	4,170*	8.0	13.9
081 Catholic	2	0	1,345	2.6	4.5
093 Cr. Ch. (Disc.)		390	468*	0.9	1.6
097 Cr. C. and C. Cr.	242	290*	0.6	1.0	
127 Ch. God (Cleve.)	3	105	126*	0.2	0.4
165 Ch. of Nazarene	3	309	558	1.1	1.9
193 Episcopal	1	246	344	0.7	1.1
283 Luth.—MO Synod	1	93	125	0.2	0.4
357 Presb. Ch. US	2	460	552*	1.1	1.8
403 Salvation Army	1	64	222	0.4	0.7
413 S-D Adventists	1	77	92*	0.2	0.3
419 So. Bapt. Conv.	34	12,937	15,517*	29.8	51.8
435 Unitarian-Univ.	1	13	13	—	—
449 Un. Methodist	21	5,645	6,158	11.8	20.5
CRAWFORD	45	7,666	9,312*	36.3	100.0
081 Catholic	1	0	202	0.8	2.2

—Represents a percent less than 0.1   Percentages may not total due to rounding.

*Total adherents estimated from known number of communicant, confirmed, full members.

453

Churches and Church Membership by
County and Denomination: 1971

County and Denomination	Number of churches	Communicant, confirmed full members	Total adherents		
			Number	Percent of total population	Percent of total adherents
093 Cr. Ch. (Disc.)	3	203	248*	1.0	2.7
097 Cr. C. and C. Cr.	1	36	44*	0.2	0.5
127 Ch. God (Cleve.)	1	19	23*	0.1	0.2
165 Ch. of Nazarene	2	168	315	1.2	3.4
185 Cumber. Presb.	1	13	16*	0.1	0.2
193 Episcopal	1	128	135	0.5	1.4
357 Presb. Ch. US	3	190	232*	0.9	2.5
413 S-D Adventists	2	165	202*	0.8	2.2
419 So. Bapt. Conv.	15	4,679	5,715*	22.3	61.4
449 Un. Methodist	12	1,865	1,936	7.5	20.8
453 Un. Presb. Ch. USA	3	200	244*	1.0	2.6
CRITTENDEN	**33**	**10,055**	**13,982***	**29.1**	**100.0**
059 Bapt. Miss. Assn.	3	199	261*	0.5	1.9
081 Catholic	3	0	1,021	2.1	7.3
093 Cr. Ch. (Disc.)	1	35	46*	0.1	0.3
127 Ch. God (Cleve.)	2	122	160*	0.3	1.1
165 Ch. of Nazarene	2	159	455	0.9	3.3
193 Episcopal	1	159	191	0.4	1.4
283 Luth.—MO Synod	1	55	75	0.2	0.5
357 Presb. Ch. US	3	627	821*	1.7	5.9
413 S-D Adventists	1	45	59*	0.1	0.4
419 So. Bapt. Conv.	10	6,363	8,334*	17.3	59.6
449 Un. Methodist	6	2,291	2,559	5.3	18.3
CROSS	**38**	**7,000**	**8,697***	**44.0**	**100.0**
059 Bapt. Miss. Assn.	4	415	526*	2.7	6.0
081 Catholic	1	0	300	1.5	3.4
093 Cr. Ch. (Disc.)	1	25	32*	0.2	0.4
127 Ch. God (Cleve)	5	179	227*	1.1	2.6
157 Ch. of Brethren	1	52	66*	0.3	0.8
193 Episcopal	1	16	23	0.1	0.3
357 Presb. Ch. US	2	280	355*	1.8	4.1
419 So. Bapt. Conv.	13	3,849	4,883*	24.7	56.1
449 Un. Methodist	10	2,184	2,285	11.6	26.3
DALLAS	**37**	**4,072**	**4,714***	**47.0**	**100.0**
059 Bapt. Miss. Assn.	6	661	792*	7.9	16.8
165 Ch. of Nazarene	1	23	53	0.5	1.1
357 Presb. Ch. US	3	143	171*	1.7	3.6
419 So. Bapt. Conv.	12	2,030	2,433*	24.3	51.6
449 Un. Methodist	15	1,215	1,265	12.6	26.8
DESHA	**27**	**6,418**	**7,984***	**42.6**	**100.0**
059 Bapt. Miss. Assn.	3	378	477*	2.5	6.0
081 Catholic	2	0	164	0.9	2.1
097 Cr. C. and C. Cr.	1	135	170*	0.9	2.1
165 Ch. of Nazarene	1	38	62	0.3	0.8
193 Episcopal	2	23	30	0.2	0.4
357 Presb. Ch. US	1	179	226*	1.2	2.8
419 So. Bapt. Conv.	12	4,124	5,208*	27.8	65.2

—Represents a percent less than 0.1   Percentages may not total due to rounding.

*Total adherents estimated from known number of communicant, confirmed, full members.

Churches and Church Membership by
County and Denomination: 1971

County and Denomination	Number of churches	Communicant, confirmed full members	Total adherents		
			Number	Percent of total population	Percent of total adherents
449 Un. Methodist	5	1,541	1,647	8.8	20.6
DREW	32	5,397	6,371*	43.0	100.0
055 As. Ref. Pres. Ch.	1	104	126*	0.8	2.0
059 Bapt. Miss. Assn.	1	186	226*	1.5	3.5
185 Cumber. Presb.	1	114	138*	0.9	2.2
193 Episcopal	1	43	52	0.3	0.8
357 Presb. Ch. US	3	273	331*	2.2	5.2
413 S-D Adventists	1	25	30*	0.2	0.5
419 So. Bapt. Conv.	14	3,573	4,334*	28.6	68.0
449 Un. Methodist	9	1,046	1,096	7.2	17.2
453 Un. Presb. Ch. USA	1	33	40*	0.3	0.6
FAULKNER	69	11,623	15,980*	50.6	100.0
059 Bapt. Miss. Assn.	20	3,086	3,660*	11.6	22.9
081 Catholic	1	0	2,225	7.0	13.9
093 Cr. Ch. (Disc.)	1	39	46*	0.1	0.3
121 Ch. God (Abr.)	1	75	89*	0.3	0.6
165 Ch. of Nazarene	7	593	897	2.8	5.6
193 Episcopal	1	111	126	0.4	0.8
283 Luth.—MO Synod	1	92	127	0.4	0.8
357 Presb. Ch. US	2	107	127*	0.4	0.8
419 So. Bapt. Conv.	21	5,019	5,952*	18.9	37.2
449 Un. Methodist	12	2,390	2,599	8.2	16.3
453 Un. Presb. Ch. USA	2	111	132*	0.4	0.8
FRANKLIN	31	4,028	5,602*	49.6	100.0
081 Catholic	2	0	970	8.6	17.3
093 Cr. Ch. (Disc.)	1	112	134*	1.2	2.4
163 Ch. of Nazarene	2	48	124	1.1	2.2
185 Cumber. Presb.	1	48	57*	0.5	1.0
221 Free Meth. C. Na.	1	15	15	0.1	0.3
357 Presb. Ch. US	1	67	80*	0.7	1.4
419 So. Bapt. Conv.	8	2,017	2,608*	21.3	43.0
449 Un. Methodist	11	1,571	1,635	14.5	29.2
453 Un. Pres. Ch. USA	4	150	179*	1.6	3.2
FULTON	22	2,044	2,295*	29.8	100.0
059 Bapt. Miss. Assn.	1	32	37*	0.5	1.6
093 Cr. Ch. (Disc.)	1	58	67*	0.9	2.9
127 Ch. God (Cleve.)	2	30	35*	0.5	1.5
163 Cumber. Presb.	1	39	45*	0.6	2.0
357 Presb. Ch. US	1	43	50*	0.6	2.2
413 S-D Adventists	1	32	37*	0.5	1.6
419 So. Bapt. Conv.	11	1,236	1,433*	18.6	62.4
449 Un. Methodist	4	574	591	7.7	25.8
GARLAND	59	19,627	25,615*	47.3	100.0
081 Catholic	2	0	2,505	4.6	9.8
093 Cr. Ch. (Disc.)	2	767	927*	1.7	3.6
121 Ch. God (Abr.)	1	45	53*	0.1	0.2

—Represents a percent less than 0.1   Percentages may not total due to rounding.

*Total adherents estimated from known number of communicant, confirmed, full members.

455

Churches and Church Membership by County and Denomination: 1971

County and Denomination	Number of churches	Communicant, confirmed full members	Total adherents		
			Number	Percent of total population	Percent of total adherents
127 Ch. God (Cleve.)	1	39	46*	0.1	0.2
165 Ch. of Nazarene	3	432	683	1.3	2.7
193 Episcopal	1	521	631	1.2	2.5
281 Luth. Ch. Amer	1	179	217	0.4	0.8
283 Luth.—MO Synod	1	248	297	0.5	1.2
357 Presb. Ch. US	4	1,178	1,387*	2.6	5.4
403 Salvation Army	1	74	303	0.6	1.2
413 S-D Adventists	2	232	273*	0.5	1.1
419 So. Bapt. Conv.	29	11,486	13,525*	25.0	52.8
435 Unitarian-Univ.	1	20	20	—	0.1
449 Un. Methodist	10	4,386	4,748	8.8	18.5
GRANT	16	2,194	2,547*	26.2	100.0
059 Bapt. Miss. Assn.	1	122	147*	1.5	5.8
081 Catholic	1	0	70	0.7	2.7
093 Cr. Ch. (Disc.)	2	93	112*	1.2	4.4
127 Ch. God (Cleve.)	1	30	36*	0.4	1.4
419 So. Bapt. Conv.	4	895	1,080*	11.1	42.4
449 Un. Methodist	7	1,054	1,102	11.3	43.3
GREENE	64	11,019	13,381*	54.0	100.0
059 Bapt. Miss. Assn.	2	184	220*	0.9	1.6
081 Catholic	1	0	505	2.0	3.8
093 Cr. Ch. (Disc.)	1	18	22*	0.1	0.2
097 Cr. C. and C. Cr.	1	50	60*	0.2	0.4
123 Ch. God (Ander.)	1	78	168	0.7	1.3
127 Ch. God (Cleve.)	1	43	51*	0.2	0.4
165 Ch. of Nazarene	2	86	160	0.6	1.2
193 Episcopal	1	66	105	0.4	0.8
283 Luth.—MO Synod	2	179	221	0.9	1.7
357 Presb. Ch. US	1	85	102*	0.4	0.8
419 So. Bapt. Conv.	38	7,427	8,885*	35.9	66.4
449 Un. Methodist	13	2,803	2,882	11.6	21.5
HEMPSTEAD	50	7,609	9,106*	47.2	100.0
059 Bapt. Miss. Assn.	15	2,593	3,120*	16.2	34.3
081 Catholic	1	0	117	0.6	1.3
093 Cr. Ch. (Disc.)	1	81	97*	0.5	1.1
123 Ch. God (Ander.)	2	46	105	0.5	1.2
193 Episcopal	1	51	67	0.3	0.7
357 Presb. Ch. US	2	231	278*	1.4	3.1
419 So. Bapt. Conv.	12	2,522	3,034*	15.7	33.3
449 Un. Methodist	13	1,963	2,053	10.6	22.5
HOT SPRING	28	4,005	5,093*	23.2	100.0
059 Bapt. Miss. Assn.	2	125	149*	0.7	2.9
081 Catholic	1	0	94	0.4	1.8
123 Ch. God (Ander.)	5	346	786	3.6	15.4
127 Ch. God (Cleve.)	1	77	92*	0.4	1.8
165 Ch. of Nazarene	1	23	86	0.4	1.7
283 Luth.—MO Synod	1	49	79	0.4	1.6

—Represents a percent less than 0.1   Percentages may not total due to rounding.

*Total adherents estimated from known number of communicant, confirmed, full members.

456

Churches and Church Membership by County and Denomination: 1971

County and Denomination	Number of churches	Communicant, confirmed full members	Total adherents		
			Number	Percent of total population	Percent of total adherents
357 Presb. Ch. US	1	161	192*	0.9	3.8
413 S-D Adventists	1	91	109*	0.5	2.1
419 So. Bapt. Conv.	6	1,372	1,637*	7.5	32.1
449 Un. Methodist	9	1,761	1,869	8.5	36.7
HOWARD	**36**	**4,657**	**5,478***	**48.0**	**100.0**
059 Bapt. Miss. Assn.	15	1,689	2,026*	17.8	37.0
081 Catholic	1	0	75	0.7	1.4
093 Cr. Ch. (Disc.)	2	97	116*	1.0	2.1
097 Cr. C. and C. Cr.	2	64	77*	0.7	1.4
123 Ch. God (Ander.)	1	40	90	0.8	1.6
419 So. Bapt. Conv.	5	1,575	1,889*	16.6	34.5
449 Un. Methodist	10	1,192	1,205	10.6	22.0
INDEPENDENCE	**63**	**9,447**	**11,343***	**49.9**	**100.0**
059 Bapt. Miss. Assn.	6	862	1,023*	4.5	9.0
081 Catholic	1	0	505	2.2	4.5
123 Ch. God (Ander.)	1	14	37	0.2	0.3
127 Ch. God (Cleve.)	1	22	26*	0.1	0.2
165 Ch. of Nazarene	1	128	197	0.9	1.7
185 Cumber. Presb.	3	107	127*	0.6	1.1
193 Episcopal	1	152	225	1.0	2.0
357 Presb. Ch. US	2	267	317*	1.4	2.8
413 S-D Adventists	1	69	82*	0.4	0.7
419 So. Bapt. Conv.	18	4,305	5,109*	22.5	45.0
449 Un. Methodist	28	3,521	3,695	16.3	32.6
IZARD	**34**	**3,178**	**3,696***	**50.1**	**100.0**
059 Bapt. Miss. Assn.	1	89	103*	1.4	2.8
081 Catholic	1	0	130	1.8	3.5
185 Cumber. Presb.	5	269	312*	4.2	8.4
285 Mennonite Ch.	3	54	63*	0.9	1.7
357 Presb. Ch. US	1	49	57*	0.8	1.5
419 So. Bapt. Conv.	15	1,824	2,114*	28.6	57.2
449 Un. Methodist	8	893	917	12.4	24.8
JACKSON	**29**	**5,197**	**6,249***	**30.6**	**100.0**
059 Bapt. Miss. Assn.	3	317	384*	1.9	6.1
081 Catholic	1	0	75	0.4	1.2
093 Cr. Ch. (Disc.)	1	124	150*	0.7	2.4
123 Ch. God (Ander.)	1	8	26	0.1	0.4
127 Ch. God (Cleve.)	1	6	7*	—	0.1
165 Ch. of Nazarene	1	79	81	0.4	1.3
193 Episcopal	1	233	354	1.7	5.7
357 Presb. Ch. US	1	105	127*	0.6	2.0
413 S-D Adventists	1	39	47*	0.2	0.8
419 So. Bapt. Conv.	11	2,934	3,555*	17.4	56.9
449 Un. Methodist	7	1,352	1,443	7.1	23.1
JEFFERSON	**73**	**24,746**	**32,808***	**38.4**	**100.0**

—Represents a percent less than 0.1   Percentages may not total due to rounding.

*Total adherents estimated from known number of communicant, confirmed, full members.

457

Churches and Church Membership by
County and Denomination: 1971

County and Denomination	Number of churches	Communicant, confirmed full members	Total adherents		
			Number	Percent of total population	Percent of total adherents
029 Amer. Luth. Ch.	1	94	145	0.2	0.4
059 Bapt. Miss. Assn.	8	894	1,117*	1.3	3.4
081 Catholic	3	0	2,090	2.4	6.4
093 Cr. Ch. (Disc.)	2	501	626*	0.7	1.9
097 Cr. C. and C. Cr.	1	80	100*	0.1	0.3
123 Ch. God (Ander.)	3	41	101	0.1	0.3
127 Ch. God (Cleve.)	2	100	125*	0.1	0.4
165 Ch. of Nazarene	2	197	359	0.4	1.1
185 Cumber. Presb.	2	265	331*	0.4	1.0
193 Episcopal	2	524	983	1.2	3.0
283 Luth.—MO Synod	1	252	340	0.4	1.0
357 Presb. Ch. US	5	1,663	2,079*	2.4	6.3
403 Salvation Army	1	34	132	0.2	0.4
413 S-D Adventists	1	43	54*	0.1	0.2
419 So. Bapt. Conv.	25	14,081	17,600*	20.6	53.6
449 Un. Methodist	14	5,977	6,626	7.8	20.2
JOHNSON	33	4,320	5,434*	39.9	100.0
059 Bapt. Miss. Assn.	1	52	61*	0.4	1.1
081 Catholic	2	0	453	3.3	8.3
097 Cr. C and C. Cr.	1	15	18*	0.1	0.3
165 Ch. of Nazarene	1	41	171	1.3	3.1
185 Cumber. Presb.	1	4	5*	—	0.1
283 Luth.—MO Synod	1	45	54	0.4	1.0
357 Presb. Ch. US	4	292	344*	2.5	6.3
419 So. Bapt. Conv.	13	2,080	2,448*	18.0	45.0
449 Un. Methodist	5	1,512	1,552	11.4	28.6
453 Un. Presb. Ch. USA	4	279	328*	2.4	6.0
LAFAYETTE	26	4,019	4,725*	47.2	100.0
059 Bapt. Miss. Assn.	9	1,010	1,245*	12.4	26.3
093 Cr. Ch. (Disc.)	1	12	15*	0.1	0.3
357 Presb. Ch. US	2	37	46*	0.5	1.0
419 So. Bapt. Conv.	6	1,830	2,257*	22.5	47.8
449 Un. Methodist	8	1,130	1,162	11.6	24.6
LAWRENCE	30	4,270	5,248*	32.0	100.0
059 Bapt. Miss. Assn.	2	224	264*	1.6	5.0
081 Catholic	1	0	274	1.7	5.2
165 Ch. of Nazarene	1	40	120	0.7	2.3
185 Cumber. Presb.	1	30	35*	0.2	0.7
357 Presb. Ch. US	1	72	85*	0.5	1.6
419 So. Bapt. Conv.	13	2,889	3,408*	20.9	64.9
449 Un. Methodist	11	1,015	1,062	6.5	20.2
LEE	18	3,371	4,284*	22.7	100.0
059 Bapt. Miss. Assn.	2	250	321*	1.7	7.5
081 Catholic	1	0	120	0.6	2.8
093 Cr. Ch. (Disc.)	1	146	187*	1.0	4.4
097 Cr. C. and C. Cr.	1	150	193*	1.0	4.5

—Represents a percent less than 0.1   Percentages may not total due to rounding.

*Total adherents estimated from known number of communicant, confirmed, full members.

Churches and Church Membership by
County and Denomination: 1971

County and Denomination	Number of churches	Communicant, confirmed full members	Total adherents		
			Number	Percent of total population	Percent of total adherents
127 Ch. God (Cleve.)	1	18	23*	0.1	0.5
193 Episcopal	1	90	134	0.7	3.1
357 Presb. Ch. US	1	132	170*	0.9	4.0
413 S-D Adventists	1	2	3*	—	0.1
419 So. Bapt. Conv.	5	1,862	2,391*	12.7	55.8
449 Un. Methodist	4	721	742	3.9	17.3
LINCOLN	22	3,352	4,032*	31.2	100.0
081 Catholic	1		0	60	0.5
093 Cr. Ch. (Disc.)	1	70	86*	0.7	2.1
127 Ch. God (Cleve.)	1	20	25*	0.2	0.6
185 Cumber. Presb.	1	41	51*	0.4	1.3
357 Presb. Ch. US	2	243	299*	2.3	7.4
419 So. Bapt. Conv.	10	2,301	2,834*	21.9	70.3
449 Un. Methodist	6	677	677	5.2	16.8
LITTLE RIVER	27	3,555	4,372*	39.1	100.0
059 Bapt. Miss. Assn.	3	475	595*	5.3	13.6
081 Catholic	1	0	50	0.4	1.1
097 Cr. C. and C. Cr.	1	45	56*	0.5	1.3
165 Ch. of Nazarene	1	28	93	0.8	2.1
185 Cumber. Presb.	3	97	122*	1.1	2.8
193 Episcopal	1	69	87	0.8	2.0
357 Presb. Ch. US	1	90	113*	1.0	2.6
419 So. Bapt. Conv.	8	1,876	2,351*	21.0	53.8
449 Un. Methodist	8	875	905	8.1	20.7
LOGAN	46	6,029	9,174*	54.6	100.0
059 Bapt. Miss. Assn.	1	39	47*	0.3	0.5
081 Catholic	7	0	2,277	13.6	24.8
093 Cr. Ch. (Disc.)	1	116	139*	0.8	1.5
127 Ch. God (Cleve.)	1	13	16*	0.1	0.2
185 Cumber. Presb.	7	345	413*	2.5	4.5
357 Presb. Ch. US	1	26	31*	0.2	0.3
413 S-D Adventists	1	19	23*	0.1	0.3
419 So. Bapt. Conv.	14	3,366	4,025*	24.0	43.9
449 Un. Methodist	12	2,079	2,172	12.9	23.7
453 Un. Pres. Ch. USA	1	26	31*	0.2	0.3
LONOKE	65	10,467	12,816*	48.8	100.0
059 Bapt. Miss. Assn.	9	1,346	1,665*	6.3	13.0
081 Catholic	1	0	247	0.9	1.9
093 Cr. Ch. (Disc.)	4	65	80*	0.3	0.6
165 Ch. of Nazarene	4	122	283	1.1	2.2
185 Cumber. Presb.	1	38	47*	0.2	0.4
357 Presb. Ch. US	3	261	323*	1.2	2.5
419 So. Bapt. Conv.	23	5,794	7,167*	27.3	55.9
449 Un. Methodist	20	2,841	3,004	11.4	23.4
MADISON	15	1,012	1,284*	13.6	100.0

—Represents a percent less than 0.1   Percentages may not total due to rounding.

*Total adherents estimated from known number of communicant, confirmed, full members.

459

Churches and Church Membership by
County and Denomination: 1971

County and Denomination	Number of churches	Communicant, confirmed full members	Total adherents		
			Number	Percent of total population	Percent of total adherents
059 Bapt. Miss. Assn.	1	128	152*	1.6	11.8
081 Catholic		0	125	1.3	9.7
357 Presb. Ch. US	2	33	39*	0.4	3.0
413 S-D Adventists	1	51	61*	0.6	4.8
419 So. Bapt. Conv.	5	526	626*	6.6	48.8
449 Un. Methodist	3	245	247	2.6	19.2
453 Un. Presb. Ch. USA	2	29	34*	0.4	2.6
MARION	**19**	**2,359**	**2,701***	**38.6**	**100.0**
093 Cr. Ch. (Disc.)	1	80	93*	1.3	3.4
097 Cr. C. and C. Cr.	2	205	239*	3.4	8.8
127 Ch. God (Cleve.)	1	32	37*	0.5	1.4
357 Presb. Ch. US	2	191	222*	3.2	8.2
419 So. Bapt. Conv.	8	1,418	1,651*	23.6	61.1
449 Un. Methodist	4	390	409	5.8	15.1
453 Un. Pres. Ch. USA	1	43	50*	0.7	1.9
MILLER	**52**	**11,755**	**15,278***	**45.8**	**100.0**
059 Bapt. Miss. Assn.	2	158	194*	0.6	1.3
081 Catholic	1	0	1,065	3.2	7.0
093 Cr. Ch. (Disc.)	1	540	665*	2.0	4.4
165 Ch. of Nazarene	1	136	263	0.8	1.7
357 Presb. Ch. US	2	402	495*	1.5	3.2
413 S-D Adventists	1	120	148*	0.4	1.0
419 So. Bapt. Conv.	28	8,066	9,929*	29.7	65.0
443 Un. C. of Christ	1	30	37*	0.1	0.2
449 Un. Methodist	14	2,288	2,464	7.4	16.1
453 Un. Presb. Ch. USA	1	15	18*	0.1	0.1
MISSISSIPPI	**87**	**23,164**	**29,196***	**47.0**	**100.0**
059 Bapt. Miss. Assn.	8	1,201	1,511*	2.4	5.2
081 Catholic	2	0	750	1.2	2.6
093 Cr. Ch. (Disc.)	2	337	424*	0.7	1.5
127 Ch. God (Cleve.)	8	362	455*	0.7	1.6
165 Ch. of Nazarene	2	200	319	0.5	1.1
193 Episcopal	2	235	269	0.4	0.9
283 Luth.—MO Synod	1	124	187	0.3	0.6
349 Pent. Holiness	1	46	58*	0.1	0.2
357 Presb. Ch. US	3	631	794*	1.3	2.7
419 So. Bapt. Conv.	44	15,428	19,405*	31.3	66.5
449 Un. Methodist	14	4,600	5,024	8.1	17.2
MONROE	**19**	**3,612**	**4,469***	**28.5**	**100.0**
059 Bapt. Miss. Assn.	4	274	343*	2.2	7.7
081 Catholic	1	0	180	1.1	4.0
283 Luth.—MO Synod	1	100	133	0.8	3.0
357 Presb. Ch. US	3	301	377*	2.4	8.4
419 So. Bapt. Conv.	4	1,798	2,249*	14.4	50.3
449 Un. Methodist	6	1,139	1,187	7.6	26.6

—Represents a percent less than 0.1   Percentages may not total due to rounding.

*Total adherents estimated from known number of communicant, confirmed, full members.

460

Churches and Church Membership by
County and Denomination: 1971

County and Denomination	Number of churches	Communicant, confirmed full members	Total adherents		
			Number	Percent of total population	Percent of total adherents
MONTGOMERY	23	1,922	2,253*	38.7	100.0
081 Catholic	1	0	33	0.6	1.5
185 Cumber. Presb.	1	47	55*	0.9	2.4
357 Presb. Ch. US	3	138	163*	2.8	7.2
419 So. Bapt. Conv.	14	1,428	1,682*	28.9	74.7
449 Un. Methodist	4	309	320	5.5	14.2
NEVADA	32	4,080	4,746*	46.9	100.0
059 Bapt. Miss. Assn.	17	2,080	2,464*	24.4	51.9
093 Cr. Ch. (Disc.)	1	58	69*	0.7	1.5
123 Ch. God (Ander.)	1	20	55	0.5	1.2
165 Ch. of Nazarene	2	129	189	1.9	4.0
185 Cumber. Presb.	2	18	21*	0.2	0.4
357 Presb. Ch. US	1	131	155*	1.5	3.3
419 So. Bapt. Conv.	3	800	948*	9.4	20.0
449 Un. Methodist	5	844	845	8.4	17.8
NEWTON	9	753	893*	15.3	100.0
093 Cr. Ch. (Disc.)	1	80	96*	1.6	10.8
097 Cr. C. and C. Cr.	1	150	180*	3.1	20.2
127 Ch God (Cleve.)	1	37	44*	0.8	4.9
419 So. Bapt. Conv.	5	347	417*	7.1	46.7
449 Un. Methodist	1	139	156	2.7	17.5
OUACHITA	62	11,959	14,091*	45.6	100.0
059 Bapt. Miss. Assn.	6	950	1,140*	3.7	8.1
081 Catholic	1	0	262	0.8	1.9
093 Cr. Ch. (Disc.)	1	93	112*	0.4	0.8
123 Ch. God (Ander.)	1	20	36	0.1	0.3
165 Ch. of Nazarene	1	49	88	0.3	0.6
185 Cumber. Presb.	5	306	367*	1.2	2.6
193 Episcopal	1	137	182	0.6	1.3
283 Luth.—MO Synod	1	10	24	0.1	0.2
357 Presb. Ch. US	4	439	527*	1.7	3.7
413 S-D Adventists	1	32	38*	0.1	0.3
419 So. Bapt. Conv.	19	5,879	7,052*	22.8	50.0
449 Un. Methodist	19	4,015	4,228	13.7	30.0
453 Un. Presb. Ch. USA	2	29	35*	0.1	0.2
PERRY	22	1,775	2,361*	41.9	100.0
081 Catholic	1	0	245	4.3	10.4
349 Pent. Holiness	2	87	106*	1.9	4.5
413 S-D Adventists	1	26	32*	0.6	1.4
419 So. Bapt. Conv.	12	1,318	1,607*	28.5	68.1
449 Un. Methodist	6	344	371	6.6	15.7
PHILLIPS	37	10,283	13,676*	34.2	100.0
059 Bapt. Miss. Assn.	6	840	1,077*	2.7	7.9
081 Catholic	2	0	813	2.0	5.9

—Represents a percent less than 0.1　　　　　Percentages may not total due to rounding.

*Total adherents estimated from known number of communicant, confirmed, full members.

Churches and Church Membership by
County and Denomination: 1971

County and Denomination	Number of churches	Communicant, confirmed full members	Total adherents		
			Number	Percent of total population	Percent of total adherents
097 Cr. C. and C. Cr.	1	52	67*	0.2	0.5
127 Ch. God (Cleve.)	2	98	126*	0.3	0.9
165 Ch. of Nazarene	1	99	175	0.4	1.3
193 Episcopal	1	308	397	1.0	2.9
283 Luth.—MO Synod	1	35	51	0.1	0.4
357 Presb. Ch. US	3	510	654*	1.6	4.8
413 S-D Adventists	1	28	36*	0.1	0.3
419 So. Bapt. Conv.	11	5,920	7,590*	19.0	55.5
443 Un. C. of Christ	1	72	92*	0.2	0.7
449 Un. Methodist	7	2,321	2,598	6.5	19.0
PIKE	**19**	**1,989**	**2,261***	**26.0**	**100.0**
059 Bapt. Miss. Assn.	1	54	64*	0.7	2.8
093 Cr. Ch. (Disc.)	2	43	51*	0.6	2.3
097 Cr. C. and C. Cr.	3	330	392*	4.5	17.3
413 S-D Adventists	1	90	107*	1.2	4.7
419 So. Bapt. Conv.	5	784	932*	10.7	41.2
449 Un. Methodist	7	688	715	8.2	31.6
POINSETT	**57**	**10,442**	**12,746***	**47.5**	**100.0**
059 Bapt. Miss. Assn.	3	358	443*	1.7	3.5
081 Catholic	2	0	220	0.8	1.7
093 Cr. Ch. (Disc.)	3	145	179*	0.7	1.4
097 Cr. C. and C. Cr.	1	75	93*	0.3	0.7
127 Ch. God (Cleve.)	4	262	324*	1.2	2.5
283 Luth.—MO Synod	1	149	200	0.7	1.6
357 Presb. Ch. US	1	36	45*	0.2	0.4
419 So. Bapt. Conv.	31	7,088	8,765*	32.7	68.8
449 Un. Methodist	11	2,329	2,477	9.2	19.4
POLK	**46**	**5,951**	**7,146***	**53.7**	**100.0**
059 Bapt. Miss. Assn.	1	50	59*	0.4	0.8
081 Catholic	1	0	220	1.7	3.1
097 Cr. C. and C. Cr.	3	575	684*	5.1	9.6
127 Ch. God (Cleve.)	2	52	62*	0.5	0.9
165 Ch. of Nazaren.	3	102	174	1.3	2.4
193 Episcopal	1	48	60	0.5	0.8
283 Luth.—MO Synod	1	48	64	0.5	0.9
357 Presb. Ch. US	3	212	252*	1.9	3.5
419 So. Bapt. Conv.	19	3,615	4,297*	32.3	60.1
449 Un. Methodist	10	1,224	1,224	9.4	17.4
453 Un. Presb. Ch. USA	2	25	30*	0.2	0.4
POPE	**50**	**7,761**	**10,018***	**35.0**	**100.0**
055 As. Ref. Pres. Ch.	2	169	204*	0.7	2.0
059 Bapt. Miss. Assn.	1	74	89*	0.3	0.9
081 Catholic	2	0	754	2.6	7.5
093 Cr. Ch. (Disc.)	2	191	230*	0.8	2.3
127 Ch. God (Cleve.)	1	19	23*	0.1	0.2
165 Ch. of Nazarene	1	46	62	0.2	0.6

—Represents a percent less than 0.1

Percentages may not total due to rounding.

*Total adherents estimated from known number of communicant, confirmed, full members.

Churches and Church Membership by
County and Denomination: 1971

County and Denomination	Number of churches	Communicant, confirmed full members	Total adherents		
			Number	Percent of total population	Percent of total adherents
185 Cumber. Presb.	8	875	1,055*	3.7	10.5
193 Episcopal	1	123	178	0.6	1.8
283 Luth.—MO Synod	2	332	432	1.5	4.3
357 Presb. Ch. US	3	314	379*	1.3	3.8
413 S-D Adventists	1	31	37*	0.1	0.6
419 So. Bapt. Conv.	15	3,489	4,208*	14.7	42.0
449 Un. Methodist	9	1,832	2,046	7.2	20.4
453 Un. Presb. Ch. USA	2	266	321*	1.1	3.2
PRAIRIE	**21**	**2,915**	**3,843***	**37.5**	**100.0**
059 Bapt. Miss. Assn.	1	68	84*	0.8	2.2
081 Catholic	2	0	357	3.5	9.3
093 Cr. Ch. (Disc.)	1	24	30*	0.3	0.8
193 Episcopal	1	151	246	2.4	6.4
283 Luth.—MO Synod	1	221	308	3.0	8.0
357 Presb. Ch. US	1	36	44*	0.4	1.1
413 S-D Adventists	1	14	17*	0.2	0.4
419 So. Bapt. Conv.	5	1,287	1,582*	15.4	41.2
449 Un. Methodist	8	1,114	1,175	11.5	30.6
PULASKI	**236**	**102,454**	**139,195***	**48.5**	**100.0**
055 As. Ref. Pres. Ch.	2	405	499*	0.2	0.4
059 Bapt. Miss. Assn.	19	4,360	5,367*	1.9	3.9
081 Catholic	14	0	14,888	5.2	10.7
093 Cr. Ch. (Disc.)	10	2,426	2,988*	1.0	2.1
097 Cr. C. and C. Cr.	3	179	220*	0.1	0.2
121 Ch. God (Abr.)	3	85	105*	—	0.1
123 Ch. God (Ander.)	2	197	424	0.1	0.3
127 Ch. God (Cleve.)	5	188	231*	0.1	0.2
165 Ch. of Nazarene	15	2,347	3,953	1.4	2.8
185 Cumber. Presb.	3	292	359*	0.1	0.3
193 Episcopal	7	4,819	6,026	2.1	4.3
226 Friends-USA	1	13	16*	-	—
281 Luth. Ch. Amer.	2	226	335	0.1	0.2
283 Luth.—MO Synod	6	1,883	2,453	0.9	1.8
357 Presb. Ch. US	12	2,528	3,112*	1.1	2.2
403 Salvation Army	2	126	640	0.2	0.5
413 S-D Adventists	2	315	388*	0.1	0.3
419 So. Bapt. Conv.	75	50,415	62,062*	21.6	44.6
435 Unitarian-Univ.	1	153	284	0.1	0.2
443 Un. C. of Christ	2	193	238*	0.1	0.2
449 Un. Methodist	39	28,851	31,589	11.0	22.7
453 Un. Presb. Ch. USA	11	2,453	3,020*	1.1	2.2
RANDOLPH	**23**	**3,084**	**4,784***	**37.8**	**100.0**
059 Bapt. Miss. Assn.	1	162	193*	1.5	4.0
081 Catholic	2	0	1,220	9.6	25.5
357 Presb. Ch. US	1	21	25*	0.2	0.5
413 S-D Adventists	1	30	36*	0.3	0.8
419 So. Bapt. Conv.	11	2,123	2,535*	20.0	53.0
449 Un. Methodist	7	748	775	6.1	16.2

—Represents a percent less than 0.1   Percentages may not total due to rounding.

*Total adherents estimated from known number of communicant, confirmed, full members.

463

Churches and Church Membership by
County and Denomination: 1971

County and Denomination	Number of churches	Communicant, confirmed full members	Total adherents		
			Number	Percent of total population	Percent of total adherents
ST. FRANCIS	46	9,520	12,151*	39.5	100.0
059 Bapt. Miss. Assn.	3	527	677*	2.2	5.6
081 Catholic	1	0	366	1.2	3.0
093 Cr. Ch. (Disc.)	1	63	81*	0.3	0.7
127 Ch. God (Cleve.)	3	202	260*	0.8	2.1
165 Ch. of Nazarene	1	55	97	0.3	0.8
185 Cumber. Presb.	1	125	161*	0.5	1.3
193 Episcopal	2	211	243	0.8	2.0
283 Luth.—MO Synod	1	40	68	0.2	0.6
357 Presb. Ch. US	4	447	575*	1.9	4.7
419 So. Bapt. Conv.	17	5,468	7,028*	22.8	57.8
449 Un. Methodist	12	2,382	2,595	8.4	21.4
SALINE	42	9,330	11,687*	32.4	100.0
059 Bapt. Miss. Assn.	2	230	281*	0.8	2.4
081 Catholic	1	0	404	1.1	3.5
093 Cr. Ch. (Disc.)	1	56	68*	0.2	0.6
123 Ch. God (Ander.)	2	87	231	0.6	2.0
127 Ch. God (Cleve.)	4	247	302*	0.8	2.6
165 Ch. of Nazarene	1	68	161	0.4	1.4
193 Episcopal	1	73	98	0.3	0.8
283 Luth.—MO Synod	2	224	318	0.9	2.7
357 Presb. Ch. US	1	86	105*	0.3	0.9
413 S-D Adventists	1	51	62*	0.2	0.5
419 So. Bapt. Conv.	16	5,416	6,622*	18.3	56.7
449 Un. Methodist	9	2,710	2,935	8.1	25.1
453 Un. Presb. Ch. USA	1	82	100*	0.3	0.9
SCOTT	32	3,486	4,311*	52.5	100.0
081 Catholic	1	0	50	0.6	1.2
165 Ch. of Nazarene	2	170	350	4.3	8.1
185 Cumber. Presb.	2	135	152*	2.0	3.8
419 So. Bapt. Conv.	21	2,673	3,212*	39.1	74.5
449 Un. Methodist	6	508	537	6.5	12.5
SEARCY	12	1,518	1,746*	22.6	100.0
127 Ch. God (Cleve.)	1	23	27*	0.3	1.5
413 S-D Adventists	1	42	50*	0.6	2.9
419 So. Bapt. Conv.	7	1,101	1,304*	16.9	74.7
449 Un. Methodist	3	352	365	4.7	20.9
SEBASTIAN	102	36,319	50,226*	63.4	100.0
059 Bapt. Miss. Assn.	2	230	282*	0.4	0.6
081 Catholic	6	0	6,215	7.8	12.4
093 Cr. Ch. (Disc.)	1	651	798*	1.0	1.6
097 Cr. C. and C. Cr.	3	445	546*	0.7	1.1
123 Ch. God (Ander.)	1	145	320	0.4	0.6
127 Ch. God (Cleve.)	1	39	48*	0.1	0.1
165 Ch. of Nazarene	4	324	542	0.7	1.1
185 Cumber. Presb.	1	175	215*	0.3	0.4

—Represents a percent less than 0.1   Percentages may not total due to rounding.

*Total adherents estimated from known number of communicant, confirmed, full members.

Churches and Church Membership by
County and Denomination: 1971

County and Denomination	Number of churches	Communicant, confirmed full members	Total adherents		
			Number	Percent of total population	Percent of total adherents
193 Episcopal	3	1,085	1,359	1.7	2.7
281 Luth. Ch. Amer.	1	209	286	0.4	0.6
283 Luth.—MO Synod	3	911	1,239	1.6	2.5
349 Pent. Holiness	1	40	49*	0.1	0.1
357 Presb. Ch. US	6	619	759*	1.0	1.5
403 Salvation Army	1	136	430	0.5	0.9
419 So. Bapt. Conv.	40	20,936	25,678*	32.4	51.1
449 Un. Methodist	22	9,507	10,397	13.1	20.7
453 Un. Presb. Ch. USA	6	867	1,063*	1.3	2.1
SEVIER	35	4,536	5,560*	49.3	100.0
059 Bapt. Miss. Assn.	2	349	423*	3.8	7.6
081 Catholic	1	0	214	1.9	3.8
093 Cr. Ch. (Disc.)	1	72	87*	0.8	1.8
165 Ch. of Nazarene	2	57	108	1.0	1.9
185 Cumber. Presb.	6	223	270*	2.4	4.9
357 Presb. Ch. US	1	105	127*	1.1	2.3
413 S-D Adventists	1	176	213*	1.9	3.8
419 So. Bapt. Conv.	10	2,430	2,947*	26.1	53.0
449 Un. Methodist	11	1,124	1,171	10.4	21.1
SHARP	32	2,768	3,269*	40.0	100.0
059 Bapt. Miss. Assn.	4	244	284*	3.4	8.6
081 Catholic	1	0	182	2.2	5.5
093 Cr. Ch. (Disc.)	1	7	8*	0.1	0.2
127 Ch. God (Cleve.)	1	25	29*	0.4	0.9
165 Ch. of Nazarene	1	11	16	0.2	0.5
185 Cumber. Presb.	1	31	36*	0.4	1.1
193 Episcopal	1	56	89	1.1	2.7
283 Luth.—MO Synod	1	146	177	2.1	5.4
357 Presb. Ch. US	1	144	167*	2.0	5.1
419 So. Bapt. Conv.	10	1,154	1,341*	16.3	40.7
449 Un. Methodist	10	950	967	11.7	29.3
STONE	13	1,197	1,443*	21.1	100.0
081 Catholic	1	0	60	0.9	4.2
097 Cr. C. and C. Cr.	1	60	71*	1.0	4.9
285 Mennonite Ch.	2	26	31*	0.5	2.1
419 So. Bapt. Conv.	7	849	1,010*	14.8	70.0
449 Un. Methodist	2	262	271	4.0	18.8
UNION	82	23,106	27,920*	61.5	100.0

—Represents a percent less than 0.1   Percentages may not total due to rounding.

*Total adherents estimated from known number of communicant, confirmed, full members.

Churches and Church Membership by
County and Denomination: 1971

County and Denomination	Number of churches	Communicant, confirmed full members	Total adherents		
			Number	Percent of total population	Percent of total adherents
059 Bapt. Miss. Assn.	10	1,574	1,899*	4.2	6.8
081 Catholic	1	0	550	1.2	2.0
093 Cr. Ch. (Disc.)	1	248	299*	0.7	1.1
123 Ch. God. (Ander.)	1	58	150	0.3	0.5
165 Ch. of Nazarene	2	136	197	0.4	0.7
185 Cumber. Presb.	1	113	136*	0.3	0.5
193 Episcopal	1	512	619	1.4	2.2
283 Luth.—MO Synod	1	102	133	0.3	0.5
285 Mennonite Ch.	1	20	24*	0.1	0.1
357 Presb. Ch. US	5	1,023	1,234*	2.7	4.4
403 Salvation Army	1	48	207	0.5	0.7
413 S-D Adventists	1	49	59*	0.1	0.2
419 So. Bapt. Conv.	35	13,388	16,155*	35.6	57.9
449 Un. Methodist	21	5,835	6,258	13.8	22.4
VAN BUREN	23	2,856	3,376*	40.8	100.0
059 Bapt. Miss. Assn.	2	80	94*	1.1	2.8
081 Catholic	2	0	135	1.6	4.0
165 Ch. of Nazarene	1	25	37	0.4	1.1
419 So. Bapt. Conv.	17	2,003	2,355*	28.5	69.8
449 Un. Methodist	1	748	755	9.1	22.4
WASHINGTON	119	24,097	32,264*	41.7	100.0
059 Bapt. Miss. Assn.	14	2,418	2,899*	3.7	9.0
081 Catholic	5	0	3,514	4.5	10.9
093 Cr. Ch. (Disc.)	5	799	958*	1.2	3.0
097 Cr. C. and C. Cr.	5	395	474*	0.6	1.5
123 Ch. God (Ander.)	1	4	11	—	—
127 Ch. God (Cleve.)	4	99	119*	0.2	0.4
165 Ch. of Nazarene	5	365	787	1.0	2.4
185 Cumber. Presb.	1	61	73*	0.1	0.2
193 Episcopal	2	1,033	1,085	1.4	3.4
226 Friends-USA	1	2	2*	—	—
281 Luth. Ch. Amer.	1	111	181	0.2	0.6
283 Luth.—MO Synod	2	500	670	0.9	2.1
349 Pent. Holiness	2	53	64*	0.1	0.2
357 Presb. Ch. US	10	691	828*	1.1	2.6
403 Salvation Army	2	32	150	0.2	0.5
413 S-D Adventists	3	176	211*	0.3	0.7
419 So. Bapt. Conv.	29	10,380	12,444*	16.1	35.6
435 Unitarian-Univ.	1	52	82	0.1	0.3
449 Un. Methodist	16	6,223	6,669	8.9	21.3

—Represents a percent less than 0.1   Percentages may not total due to rounding.

*Total adherents estimated from known number of communicant, confirmed, full members.

466

Churches and Church Membership by
County and Denomination: 1971

County and Denomination	Number of churches	Communicant, confirmed full members	Total adherents		
			Number	Percent of total population	Percent of total adherents
453 Un. Presb. Ch. USA	10	703	843*	1.1	2.6
WHITE	89	13,096	15,576*	39.7	100.0
059 Bapt. Miss. Assn.	15	2,371	2,838*	7.2	18.2
081 Catholic	3	0	297	0.8	1.9
093 Cr. Ch. (Disc.)	3	200	239*	0.6	1.5
127 Ch. God (Cleve.)	3	217	260*	0.7	1.7
165 Ch. of Nazarene	4	311	493	1.3	3.2
185 Cumber. Presb.	4	192	230*	0.6	1.5
193 Episcopal	1	63	90	0.2	0.6
349 Pent. Holiness	1	39	47*	0.1	0.3
357 Presb. Ch. US	2	152	182*	0.5	1.2
419 So. Bapt. Conv.	27	5,949	7,121*	18.1	45.7
449 Un. Methodist	26	3,602	3,779	9.6	24.3
WOODRUFF	28	4,711	5,663*	49.0	100.0
059 Bapt. Miss. Assn.	3	488	602*	5.2	10.6
081 Catholic	1	0	75	0.6	1.3
127 Ch. God (Cleve.)	1	190	234*	2.0	4.1
165 Ch. of Nazarene	1	83	160	1.4	2.8
357 Presb. Ch. US	2	58	72*	0.6	1.3
419 So. Bapt. Conv.	11	2,322	2,863*	24.8	50.6
449 Un. Methodist	8	1,549	1,631	14.1	28.8
453 Un. Presb. Ch. USA	1	21	26*	0.2	0.5
YELL	39	4,364	5,074*	35.7	100.0
055 As. Ref. Pres. Ch.	1	55	66*	0.5	1.3
059 Bapt. Miss. Assn.	2	104	124*	0.9	2.4
081 Catholic	1	0	100	0.7	2.0
127 Ch. God (Cleve.)	1	36	43*	0.3	0.8
165 Ch. of Nazarene	1	12	45	0.3	0.9
185 Cumber. Presb.	1	125	150*	1.1	3.0
419 So. Bapt. Conv.	10	2,166	2,591*	18.2	51.1
449 Un. Methodist	21	1,816	1,895	13.3	37.3
453 Un. Presb. Ch. USA	1	50	60*	0.4	1.2
CO DATA NOT AVAIL	267	22,101	31,487*	N/A	N/A
151 L-D Saints	0	0	4,538	N/A	N/A
223 Free Will Bapt.	211	18,500	22,555*	N/A	N/A
231 General Bapt.	47	3,277	3,995*	N/A	N/A
285 Mennonite Ch.	1	19	23*	N/A	N/A
487 Wesleyan	8	305	376	N/A	N/A

467

APPENDIX J
PRESIDENTS OF ARKANSAS WOMAN'S WORK

(1)   Presidents of Central Committee

1883-1893   Mrs. J.P. Eagle., Little Rock
1893-1894   Mrs. A.L. Crudup, Ozark
1894-1902   Mrs. J.P. Eagle, Little Rock
1902-1908   Mrs. E. Longley, Little Rock
(In 1908 the name of the "Central Committee" was officially changed to "WMU Executive Board".)

(2)   Presidents of Executive Boards

1908-1910   Mrs. E. Longley, Little Rock
1910-1912   Mrs. H.C. Fox, Pine Bluff
1912-1914   Mrs. M.G. Thompson, Hot Springs
1914-1916   Mrs. W.T. McCurry, El Dorado and Little Rock
1916-1919   Mrs. C.M. Roberts, Hot Springs
1919-1922   Mrs. J.H. Crawford, Arkadelphia
1922-1923   Mrs. O.O. Florence, Conway
1923-1929   Mrs. W.D. Pye, Little Rock
1929-1932   Mrs. J.M. Flenniken, Little Rock
1932-1938   Mrs. C.H. Ray, Little Rock
1938-1941   Mrs. L.M. Sipes, Little Rock
1941-1948   Mrs. J.L. Short, Pine Bluff
1948-1952   Mrs. F.E. Goodbar, Danville
1952-1957   Mrs. J.R. Grant, Little Rock
1957-1964   Miss Elma Cobb, Little Rock
1964-1969   Mrs. Roy E. Snider, Camden
1969-1974   Mrs. J.A. Hogan
1974-1976   Mrs. George Tharel, Fayetteville
1976-   Mrs. James Sawyer, Benton

VICE-PRESIDENTS FROM ARKANSAS
WOMAN'S MISSIONARY UNION
SOUTHERN BAPTIST CONVENTION

1888-1889	Mrs. M.D. Early
1889-1890	Mrs. W.A. Forbes
1890-1899	Mrs. E. Longley
1899-1903	Mrs. J.P. Eagle
1903-1908	Mrs. E. Longley
1908-1910	Mrs. W.T. Amis
1910-1912	Mrs. C.E. Witt
1912-1913	Mrs. E. Longley
1913-1915	Mrs. J.G. Jackson
1915-1926	Mrs. John L. Hawkins
1926-1929	Mrs. W.D. Pye
1929-1932	Mrs. J.M. Flenniken
1932-1938	Mrs. C.H. Ray
1938-1941	Mrs. L.M. Sipes
1941-1948	Mrs. J.L. Short
1948-1952	Mrs. F.E. Goodbar
1952-1957	Mrs. J.R. Grant
1957-1964	Miss Elma Cobb
1964-1969	Mrs. Roy E. Snider
1969-1974	Mrs. J.A. Hogan
1974-1976	Mrs. George Tharel
1976-	Mrs. James Sawyer

APPENDIX K
CONTRIBUTORS OF RESEARCH ARTICLES

Arrington, Michael, and Daniel R. Grant. "History of Higher Education Among Arkansas Baptists."

Ashcraft, Charles. "History of Relations With Other Denominations."

Biggs, Johnny C. "Arkansas Baptist Orphans' Home."

Bjorkman, Nadine B. "History of State Organization."

Bridges, Winfred P. "Ordination."

Bridges, Winfred P. "The Pastor's Pay."

Bridges, Winfred P. "The Role of Women as Leaders in the Local Churches."

Coppenger, Agnes. "Arkansas Baptist Missionary Camping."

Davis, Ralph W. "History of Educational Organizations in Arkansas Baptist Churches."

Ferguson, Robert U. "History of Racial Tensions and Attempts at Integration in Arkansas."

Hatfield, Lawson. "The History of the Arkansas Baptist Assembly."

Hook, J. Don. "Fundamentalism in Arkansas."

Johnson, C.A. "History of Worship in Arkansas."

Lewis, Roy F. "The History of Stewardship in Arkansas."

Logue, Tom J. "The History of Campus Ministry."

McClanahan, John H. "The Impact and/or Influence of the 'Charismatic Movement' on Southern Baptist Churches in Arkansas in the Last Twenty-Five Years: 1952-1977."

McDonald, Erwin L. "The Issue of Alien Immersion and Close Communion in the Arkansas Baptist State Convention."

Miley, Burton A. "Independent Churches in Arkansas to 1977."

Reed, Jesse S. "History of Arkansas Baptist Evangelism."

Rucker, T.K. "The History of State Missions in Arkansas."

Savage, E. Fred. "A History of the Campbellite Influence."

Selph, Bernes. "How Baptists Got Started in Arkansas (up to 1845)."

Smith, Melvin, Mrs. "Some Baptists of Northwestern Arkansas, Up to 1850."

Sneed, Everett. "Baptist Papers in Arkansas."

Snider, Ruby. "History of Women in the Life of the Churches."

Taylor, Orville W. "Baptists and Slavery in Arkansas."

Trantham, William E. "History of Music in Arkansas Baptist Churches."

Trulove, Harry D. "History of the Arkansas Baptist Foundation."

Williams, H.E. "Anti-Missionism and Anti-Organizationism."

INDEX OF PERSONS

472

Bridges, Ben L. - 257, 258, 260, 265, 281, 318
Briggs, F.E. - 245
Brooks, Joseph - 105
Brough, Ann Wade Roark - 217, 247
Brough, Charles H. - 173, 216-17, 200, 243, 247
Brown, T.D. - 238
Browning, J.O. - 80
Brundridge, J.M. - 83
Bryan, William Jennings - 199

Caldwell, C.W. - 262, 329
Campbell, Alexander - 14, 15, 16, 33, 36, 43, 44-45, 46, 82, 112,
    142
Carter, D.M. - 203
Chadoin, W.N. - 84
Chambliss, Pat - 381
Chenault, E.N. - 50, 71
Christian, John T. - 190
Clarke, Benjamin - 1, 4, 6, 27
Clark, John - 1
Clark, W.A. - 84, 98, 118, 129, 175, 176, 178, 197
Clarke, James P. - 146
Clayton, Powell - 105, 148
Clements, Tom - 57
Cobb, Elma - 380
Coffman, V.H. - 286
Coggs, P.W. - 309
Cole, Mrs. E.L. - 286
Coleman, H.H. - 80
Coleman, L.H. - 360
Coleman, L.W. - 90
Coleman, R.J. - 70, 71-72, 82
Compere, E.L. - 68, 71, 82, 86, 89, 97, 207, 286
Compere, J.S. - 199, 207-208, 247, 281-282
Compere, Pen Lile - 207-209, 247
Compere, W.L. - 197, 246
Conger, J.W. - 140, 146, 152, 155
Cossey, J.I. - 206-207
Cowling, Dale - 385
Cox, Benjamin - 166, 190, 198, 242
Cox, J.E. - 270

Craig, J.T. - 83
Crockett, Davy - 27
Crowder, W.J. - 89
Cunningham, O.H.L. - 206

Davidson, Mrs. C.B. - 104
Danner, N.C. - 182
Davis, Jeff - 113, 149, 172, 215-216
Davis, Jefferson - 66
Davis, John - 20
Davis, Wayne B. - 362
Dehoney, Wayne - 363
DeLaughter, David - 80
Dew, James F. - 196
DeWoody, Ruth - 258
Dicken, C.E. - 235, 375
Digby, Tom - 355
Dobbins, Gaines S. - 334
Dodd, David - 25
Douglas, Ralph - 386
Doyle, J.G. - 137, 146
Duncan, B.H. - 364
Duren, W.M. - 12
Durrett, C.L. - 306

Eagle, James P. - 67, 112, 113, 127, 128, 132, 135, 148, 156, 160,
    170, 174, 175, 176, 186, 216, 264, 290
Eagle, Mary K. - 112, 135, 156, 157, 158, 159, 160-61, 238
Early, D.A. (Mrs. M.D.) - 156, 158, 159
Early, M.D. - 84, 156
Edmunds, J.P. - 277
Edwards, James Phillip - 4, 7
Eisenhower, Dwight D. - 292
Elledge, A.W. - 38
Elliott, E.J. - 286
Ellis, E.C. - 245
Espy, T.B. - 85, 109
Estes, W.K. - 12
Eubanks, S.W. - 374

Faubus, Orval - 292, 366, 385, 386

Faulkner, J.D.J. - 93
Featherstonbough, George W. - 17
Ferguson, Barbour Vaugh - 212, 213, 221, 247, 282
Ferguson, Robert U. - 388
Finley, Mollie - 59
Fitzgerald, James - 204, 273, 275, 276
Forbes, W.A. - 67, 98
Forey, R.M. - 96
Freeman, W.A. - 245
Frost, J. - 11
Fulton, William S. - 18

Gambrell, J.B. - 222
Gardiner, Mayme - 160
Gardner, Hannah Hyatt - 151
Gardner, W.W. - 151
Garrott, E.P.J. - 306, 364
Gerstaecker, Friedrich - 18, 23
Gibson, Finley F. - 212
Gilkey, James Hilton - 48
Gill, George - 2, 5, 27, 31
Gold, Mary Logan - 206
Goodbar, Mrs. F.E. - 286
Graham, John B. - 6
Grant, Daniel - 373, 374
Grant, J.R. - 298
Grant, Ulysses S. - 71, 93, 105
Graves, J.R. - 16, 33, 40, 41, 43-44, 45, 47, 50, 82, 83, 112, 140, 145, 358
Green, Moses - 82

Hailey, O.L. - 128, 146, 175
Hale, John C. - 100-101
Hale, Sarah Gardner - 100
Hall, A.S. - 129
Hall, Benjamin - 15
Hall, J.N. - 140
Halliburton, Samuel - 68
Hamilton, H.V. - 200
Harbuck, Don - 359
Hardwick, Nancy - 56

Harmon, B.W. - 126
Harris, T.L. - 364
Hart, Clyde - 332, 384, 387, 388
Hart, J.M. - 84
Hartwell, Miss M.H. - 103
Hartwell, Jesse B. - 48, 71, 103
Hawkins, Benjamin - 5, 6, 27
Hays, Brooks - 251, 252, 267, 280, 289-92, 311, 312, 316, 353, 385, 390
Hempstead, H.E. - 84
Hickerson, Clyde V. - 283
Hicks, Bessie - 236
Hicks, Harold - 385
Hinsley, W.J. - 226
Hinson, Thomas A. - 363
Hobbs, A.N. - 156
Hollis, A.N. - 230
Holmes, Oliver Wendell - 244
Holmes, Willis A. - 107
Hook, Don - 359
Hooton, J.F. - 50
Houston, Sam - 27
Howell, J.F. - 141
Howell, R.B.C. - 43, 50
Hunt, John Jeter - 198
Hyatt, Hannah - 150

Inlow, R.M. - 190
Izard, Mark W. - 11-12, 17

Jackson, Andrew - 17
Jackson, D.N. - 364
Jackson, L.B. - 267
Jackson, W.A. - 303
James, Frank and Jesse - 93
James, Jesse - 1, 4
Jefferson, Thomas - 1, 17
Jester, J.B. - 45
Johnson, Andrew - 104
Johnson, John - 67-68
Johnson, Lyndon Baines - 47

Johnston, J.O. - 221
Jowdon, B.A. - 101
Jumper, John - 89

Karr, W.B. - 6, 27
Kellett, William - 6, 27
Kelly, Samuel - 94-95
Kennard, George W. - 38
Kennard, M.S. - 97, 141
Kennedy, John F. - 356
Kime, W.P. - 139-40
King, Jacob - 71
King, Martin Luther - 382
King, Mary - 381
King, T.J.D. - 71
Kitchens, J.H. - 177

Langson, Bob - 379
Larkin, Frank - 59
Lea, William M. - 59, 82, 83, 86
Leavell, Clarence S. - 200
Lewis, Roy - 320
Lincoln, Abraham - 66
Lindsey, Caleb - 2, 19
Lindsey, John Young - 2, 100
Littell, Philander - 12
Locke, M.F. - 122
Longley, Laura - 119
Logue, Tom - 377
Love, J.F. - 198
Lovelace, J.P. - 12
Lucas, O.M. - 86, 117, 136
Luster, Gwendoline - 309, 329

McCarthy, John - 6, 27
McClanahan, John - 360, 362
McCoy, Isaac - 20
McDonald, Ed. F. - 320
McDonald, Erwin L. - 386, 391, 393
McElmurry, Henry - 6, 27, 36, 38, 42
McKinney, E.J.A. - XIII, 22, 197, 198, 218, 219

Scofield, A.P. - 199
Scott, Allen M. - 48
Searcy, J.B. - XIII, 1, 22, 50, 62, 71, 82, 83, 84, 85, 86, 89, 90, 91, 97, 101, 109, 110, 198
Settle, William W. - 6, 27
Shackleford, Joseph - 97, 98
Shaw, Helen - 267
Shipman, Paul - 270
Siler, Peter - 70
Simms, J.G.B. - 166
Sledge, W.H. - 245
Smith, Al - 217, 282, 356
Smith, J. Harold - 213
Smith, Nathaniel G. - 101
Snead, James M. - 38
South, Reubin L. - 355
Southwick, Miss H.M.R. - 103
Squyres, P.A. - 267
Staryan, James - 57
Steely, John E. - 353, 390
Stevenson, Samuel - 48, 49, 54, 82, 84
Stockdon, Purl - 273
Stranburg, W.L.A. - 203, 247
Street, William - 4, 11
Strother, E.N. - 236, 259, 300
Sturgham, Corney S. - 25
Sullivan, James - 379
Sumerlin, Claude - 60
Summers, L.D. - 306

Taft, William H. - 219
Taylor, I.E. - 303
Taylor, John - 14, 16, 75, 112
Taylor, W.O. - XV, 61, 63, 64, 203
Tedford, L.C. - 364
Terral, Governor - 245
Thomas, B.F. - 83
Thomas, J.S. - 115, 122
Thomas, M.L. - 197
Thomasson, H.G. - 267
Thompson, Charles B. - 358

480

INDEX OF SUBJECTS

Baptist Missionary Association - 326, 328
Baptist National Education Convention - 163
Baptist Student Union - 236, 273, 277, 300-301, 333, 377-80
Baptist World Alliance - 284
Baptist Young People's Union - 128, 136, 138, 188, 192, 193, 194, 197, 199, 200, 210-11, 255, 264, 265, 276, 277
Bentonville Academy - 229
Blacks - 34, 35, 51-61, 67, 73, 75, 104-108, 141-42, 143, 148, 162-66, 201, 213, 226, 239-44, 251-52, 294-95, 307-309, 316, 329, 381-89
Brinkley Baptist High School - 230
Brooks-Baxter War - 93, 105
Buckner College - 89, 97, 99, 151, 153, 183

Caddoe Indians - 19
Camden Female Institute - 48, 102
Camp Meetings - 30
Campaign, 75-Million - 184, 186, 188, 192, 193, 194-95, 196, 198, 202, 211, 225, 233, 234, 235, 245, 253, 264
Campbellism - 14-16, 33, 34, 38, 42-47, 75, 82, 140, 142, 145
Caroline Female Institute - 96
Centennial Baptist Institute - 89, 97, 98, 151
Central Female College - 153, 162, 194, 207, 217, 229-31, 232, 236, 252, 255
Cherokee Indians - 17, 23, 68
Children's missionary societies - 119
Choctaw Indians - 19, 89
Christian Church, the - 15, 142
Christian Civic Foundation - 366, 367, 368
Church buildings, description of - 9, 39, 70, 91, 92, 212
Church discipline - 41, 93-95, 133-35, 205, 216, 217, 276
Church of Christ - 95, 201
Civil rights - 105, 308, 382
Civil War - 24, 36, 42, 45, 48, 50, 51, 61, 65, 66-70, 71, 72, 73, 74, 75, 90, 94, 96, 101, 102, 103, 104, 105, 107, 108, 120, 131, 135, 137, 149, 151, 154, 161, 164
Collegiate Institute - 230
Cooperative Program - 196, 253-5, 260, 264-65, 293, 343
Creek Indians - 20, 55, 82, 88
Cumberland Presbyterians - 30, 142, 143

484

Magazine Academy - 229
Maynard Academy - 229, 231, 232
Methodists - 30, 46, 52, 105, 130, 138, 142, 143, 145, 198, 201, 202, 212, 213, 227, 281, 324, 326
Mexican War - 27-28
Millerism - 27
Mine Creek Male and Female School - 48
Ministerial Education, Board of, Arkansas Baptist State Convention - 86, 95-96, 228
Missions - 3, 4-8, 13, 14, 16, 20, 25, 26-27, 31, 33, 34, 35, 38, 42, 47, 50, 54-55, 65, 69, 70, 71, 75, 80, 81, 82, 83-85, 88, 89, 100, 101, 103, 106, 109, 115-18, 122, 123-29, 139-40, 145, 156-57, 158, 161, 182, 186, 188, 189, 194, 195, 211, 226, 236, 237, 238, 241, 242, 252, 259-63, 329-30, 379
Missionary Baptist Association - 363-64
Missouri Mount Ida Academy - 232
Montview Institute - 232
Mt. Lebanon University - 49
Mount Vernon High School - 230
Mountain Home College - 140-41, 153, 229, 231, 232, 233, 235, 236, 252, 255, 295
Mountain Schools - 140-41, 153, 194, 228, 229, 232-33, 252

National Baptist Convention of America - 164, 239, 240
New County Academy - 232, 233

Osage Indians - 1, 19
Ouachita College - 48, 80, 96, 97, 99, 116, 140, 141, 152, 153, 154, 155, 160, 162, 190, 191, 194, 199, 207, 208, 212, 228, 229-31, 232, 235, 252, 254, 257, 275, 289, 295, 296, 297-99, 352, 353, 370, 372-73, 374-76, 377

Pentecostals - 227
Presbyterians - 138, 142, 143, 145, 201, 213, 281, 324
Prohibition - 214, 217-19

Quapaw Indians - 19

Regular Missionary Baptist State Convention - 106
Revivals - 13, 16, 27, 30-31, 40, 130-31, 203, 213
Roman Catholicism - 46, 143-44, 145, 201, 214, 225, 226, 281,

282-83, 291, 324, 356-57, 370, 371